LIBRA
St. Michael's College Prep...
19292 El Toro Rd., Silverado, CA 92676

8965

P9-EDF-046

59 *American Literary Critics and Scholars, 1800-1850,* edited by John W. Rathbun and Monica M. Grecu (1987)

60 *Canadian Writers Since 1960,* Second Series, edited by W. H. New (1987)

61 *American Writers for Children Since 1960: Poets, Illustrators, and Nonfiction Authors,* edited by Glenn E. Estes (1987)

62 *Elizabethan Dramatists,* edited by Fredson Bowers (1987)

63 *Modern American Critics, 1920-1955,* edited by Gregory S. Jay (1988)

64 *American Literary Critics and Scholars, 1850-1880,* edited by John W. Rathbun and Monica M. Grecu (1988)

65 *French Novelists, 1900-1930,* edited by Catharine Savage Brosman (1988)

66 *German Fiction Writers, 1885-1913,* 2 parts, edited by James Hardin (1988)

67 *Modern American Critics Since 1955,* edited by Gregory S. Jay (1988)

68 *Canadian Writers, 1920-1959,* First Series, edited by W. H. New (1988)

69 *Contemporary German Fiction Writers,* First Series, edited by Wolfgang D. Elfe and James Hardin (1988)

70 *British Mystery Writers, 1860-1919,* edited by Bernard Benstock and Thomas F. Staley (1988)

71 *American Literary Critics and Scholars, 1880-1900,* edited by John W. Rathbun and Monica M. Grecu (1988)

72 *French Novelists, 1930-1960,* edited by Catharine Savage Brosman (1988)

73 *American Magazine Journalists, 1741-1850,* edited by Sam G. Riley (1988)

74 *American Short-Story Writers Before 1880,* edited by Bobby Ellen Kimbel, with the assistance of William E. Grant (1988)

75 *Contemporary German Fiction Writers,* Second Series, edited by Wolfgang D. Elfe and James Hardin (1988)

76 *Afro-American Writers, 1940-1955,* edited by Trudier Harris (1988)

77 *British Mystery Writers, 1920-1939,* edited by Bernard Benstock and Thomas F. Staley (1988)

78 *American Short-Story Writers, 1880-1910,* edited by Bobby Ellen Kimbel, with the assistance of William E. Grant (1988)

79 *American Magazine Journalists, 1850-1900,* edited by Sam G. Riley (1988)

80 *Restoration and Eighteenth-Century Dramatists,* First Series, edited by Paula R. Backscheider (1989)

81 *Austrian Fiction Writers, 1875-1913,* edited by James Hardin and Donald G. Daviau (1989)

82 *Chicano Writers,* First Series, edited by Francisco A. Lomelí and Carl R. Shirley (1989)

83 *French Novelists Since 1960,* edited by Catharine Savage Brosman (1989)

84 *Restoration and Eighteenth-Century Dramatists,* Second Series, edited by Paula R. Backscheider (1989)

85 *Austrian Fiction Writers After 1914,* edited by James Hardin and Donald G. Daviau (1989)

86 *American Short-Story Writers, 1910-1945,* First Series, edited by Bobby Ellen Kimbel (1989)

87 *British Mystery and Thriller Writers Since 1940,* First Series, edited by Bernard Benstock and Thomas F. Staley (1989)

88 *Canadian Writers, 1920-1959,* Second Series, edited by W. H. New (1989)

89 *Restoration and Eighteenth-Century Dramatists,* Third Series, edited by Paula R. Backscheider (1989)

90 *German Writers in the Age of Goethe, 1789-1832,* edited by James Hardin and Christoph E. Schweitzer (1989)

91 *American Magazine Journalists, 1900-1960,* First Series, edited by Sam G. Riley (1990)

92 *Canadian Writers, 1890-1920,* edited by W. H. New (1990)

93 *British Romantic Poets, 1789-1832,* First Series, edited by John R. Greenfield (1990)

94 *German Writers in the Age of Goethe: Sturm und Drang to Classicism,* edited by James Hardin and Christoph E. Schweitzer (1990)

95 *Eighteenth-Century British Poets,* First Series, edited by John Sitter (1990)

96 *British Romantic Poets, 1789-1832,* Second Series, edited by John R. Greenfield (1990)

97 *German Writers from the Enlightenment to Sturm und Drang, 1720-1764,* edited by James Hardin and Christoph E. Schweitzer (1990)

98 *Modern British Essayists,* First Series, edited by Robert Beum (1990)

99 *Canadian Writers Before 1890,* edited by W. H. New (1990)

100 *Modern British Essayists,* Second Series, edited by Robert Beum (1990)

101 *British Prose Writers, 1660-1800,* First Series, edited by Donald T. Siebert (1991)

102 *American Short-Story Writers, 1910-1945,* Second Series, edited by Bobby Ellen Kimbel (1991)

103 *American Literary Biographers,* First Series, edited by Steven Serafin (1991)

104 *British Prose Writers, 1660-1800,* Second Series, edited by Donald T. Siebert (1991)

105 *American Poets Since World War II,* Second Series, edited by R. S. Gwynn (1991)

106 *British Literary Publishing Houses, 1820-1880,* edited by Patricia J. Anderson and Jonathan Rose (1991)

107 *British Romantic Prose Writers, 1789-1832,* First Series, edited by John R. Greenfield (1991)

108 *Twentieth-Century Spanish Poets,* First Series, edited by Michael L. Perna (1991)

109 *Eighteenth-Century British Poets,* Second Series, edited by John Sitter (1991)

110 *British Romantic Prose Writers, 1789-1832,* Second Series, edited by John R. Greenfield (1991)

111 *American Literary Biographers,* Second Series, edited by Steven Serafin (1991)

112 *British Literary Publishing Houses, 1881-1965,* edited by Jonathan Rose and Patricia J. Anderson (1991)

113 *Modern Latin-American Fiction Writers,* First Series, edited by William Luis (1992)

114 *Twentieth-Century Italian Poets,* First Series, edited by Giovanna Wedel De Stasio, Glauco Cambon, and Antonio Illiano (1992)

115 *Medieval Philosophers,* edited by Jeremiah Hackett (1992)

116 *British Romantic Novelists, 1789-1832,* edited by Bradford K. Mudge (1992)

117 *Twentieth-Century Caribbean and Black African Writers,* First Series, edited by Bernth Lindfors and Reinhard Sander (1992)

118 *Twentieth-Century German Dramatists, 1889-1918,* edited by Wolfgang D. Elfe and James Hardin (1992)

119 *Nineteenth-Century French Fiction Writers: Romanticism and Realism, 1800-*

Dictionary of Literary Biography®
Yearbook: 1992

Dictionary of Literary Biography®
Yearbook: 1992

Edited by
James W. Hipp

George Garrett, Consulting Editor

8965

A Bruccoli Clark Layman Book
Gale Research Inc.
Detroit, London

Advisory Board for
DICTIONARY OF LITERARY BIOGRAPHY

John Baker
William Cagle
Jane Christensen
Patrick O'Connor
Peter S. Prescott

Matthew J. Bruccoli and Richard Layman, Editorial Directors
C. E. Frazer Clark, Jr., Managing Editor
Karen L. Rood, Senior Editor

Printed in the United States of America

Published simultaneously in the United Kingdom
by Gale Research International Limited
(An affiliated company of Gale Research Inc.)

The paper used in this publication meets the minimum requirements
of American National Standard for Information Sciences–Permanence
Paper for Printed Library Materials, ANSI Z39.48-1984. ∞ ™

This publication is a creative work fully protected by all applicable copyright laws, as well as by misappropriation, trade secret,
unfair competition, and other applicable laws. The authors and
editors of this work have added value to the underlying factual
material herein through one or more of the following: unique
and original selection, coordination, expression, arrangement,
and classification of the information.

All rights to this publication will be vigorously defended.

Copyright © 1993 by Gale Research Inc.
835 Penobscot Building
Detroit, MI 48226

All rights reserved including the right of reproduction in
whole or in part in any form

Library of Congress Catalog Card Number 82-645187
ISBN 0-8103-5543-4

"Nobel Banquet Statement" and "Nobel Lecture 1992" by Derek Walcott
Copyright © 1992 by the Nobel Foundation

10 9 8 7 6 5 4 3 2 1

I(T)P™

The trademark ITP is used under license.

Contents

Obituaries

Plan of the Series

. . . Almost the most prodigious asset of a country, and perhaps its most precious possession, is its native literary product – when that product is fine and noble and enduring.

Mark Twain*

The advisory board, the editors, and the publisher of the *Dictionary of Literary Biography* are joined in endorsing Mark Twain's declaration. The literature of a nation provides an inexhaustible resource of permanent worth. We intend to make literature and its creators better understood and more accessible to students and the reading public, while satisfying the standards of teachers and scholars.

To meet these requirements, *literary biography* has been construed in terms of the author's achievement. The most important thing about a writer is his writing. Accordingly, the entries in *DLB* are career biographies, tracing the development of the author's canon and the evolution of his reputation.

The purpose of *DLB* is not only to provide reliable information in a convenient format but also to place the figures in the larger perspective of literary history and to offer appraisals of their accomplishments by qualified scholars.

The publication plan for *DLB* resulted from two years of preparation. The project was proposed to Bruccoli Clark by Frederick C. Ruffner, president of the Gale Research Company, in November 1975. After specimen entries were prepared and typeset, an advisory board was formed to refine the entry format and develop the series rationale. In meetings held during 1976, the publisher, series editors, and advisory board approved the scheme for a comprehensive biographical dictionary of persons who contributed to North American literature. Editorial work on the first volume began in January 1977, and it was published in 1978. In order to make *DLB* more than a reference tool and to com-

pile volumes that individually have claim to status as literary history, it was decided to organize volumes by topic, period, or genre. Each of these free-standing volumes provides a biographical-bibliographical guide and overview for a particular area of literature. We are convinced that this organization – as opposed to a single alphabet method – constitutes a valuable innovation in the presentation of reference material. The volume plan necessarily requires many decisions for the placement and treatment of authors who might properly be included in two or three volumes. In some instances a major figure will be included in separate volumes, but with different entries emphasizing the aspect of his career appropriate to each volume. Ernest Hemingway, for example, is represented in *American Writers in Paris, 1920–1939* by an entry focusing on his expatriate apprenticeship; he is also in *American Novelists, 1910–1945* with an entry surveying his entire career. Each volume includes a cumulative index of the subject authors and articles. Comprehensive indexes to the entire series are planned.

With volume ten in 1982 it was decided to enlarge the scope of *DLB*. By the end of 1986 twenty-one volumes treating British literature had been published, and volumes for Commonwealth and Modern European literature were in progress. The series has been further augmented by the *DLB Yearbooks* (since 1981) which update published entries and add new entries to keep the *DLB* current with contemporary activity. There have also been *DLB Documentary Series* volumes which provide biographical and critical source materials for figures whose work is judged to have particular interest for students. One of these companion volumes is entirely devoted to Tennessee Williams.

We define literature as the *intellectual commerce of a nation:* not merely as belles lettres but as that ample and complex process by which ideas are generated, shaped, and transmitted. *DLB* entries are not limited to "creative writers" but extend to other figures who in their time and in their way influenced the mind of a people. Thus the series encompasses historians, journalists, publishers, and screenwriters. By this means readers of *DLB* may be aided

---

*From an unpublished section of Mark Twain's autobiography, copyright by the Mark Twain Company

to perceive literature not as cult scripture in the keeping of intellectual high priests but firmly positioned at the center of a nation's life.

DLB includes the major writers appropriate to each volume and those standing in the ranks immediately behind them. Scholarly and critical counsel has been sought in deciding which minor figures to include and how full their entries should be. Wherever possible, useful references are made to figures who do not warrant separate entries.

Each *DLB* volume has a volume editor responsible for planning the volume, selecting the figures for inclusion, and assigning the entries. Volume editors are also responsible for preparing, where appropriate, appendices surveying the major periodicals and literary and intellectual movements for their volumes, as well as lists of further readings. Work on the series as a whole is coordinated at the Bruccoli Clark Layman editorial center in Columbia, South Carolina, where the editorial staff is responsible for accuracy of the published volumes.

One feature that distinguishes *DLB* is the illustration policy – its concern with the iconography of literature. Just as an author is influenced by his surroundings, so is the reader's understanding of the author enhanced by a knowledge of his environment. Therefore *DLB* volumes include not only drawings, paintings, and photographs of authors, often depicting them at various stages in their careers, but also illustrations of their families and places where they lived. Title pages are regularly reproduced in facsimile along with dust jackets for modern authors. The dust jackets are a special feature of *DLB* because they often document better than anything else the way in which an author's work was perceived in its own time. Specimens of the writers' manuscripts are included when feasible.

Samuel Johnson rightly decreed that "The chief glory of every people arises from its authors." The purpose of the *Dictionary of Literary Biography* is to compile literary history in the surest way available to us – by accurate and comprehensive treatment of the lives and work of those who contributed to it.

The *DLB* Advisory Board

Foreword

The *Dictionary of Literary Biography Yearbook* is guided by the same principles that have provided the basic rationale for the entire *DLB* series: 1) the literature of a nation represents an inexhaustible resource of permanent worth; 2) the surest way to trace the outlines of literary history is by a comprehensive treatment of the lives and works of those who contributed to it; and 3) the greatest service the series can provide is to make literary achievement better understood and more accessible to students and the literate public, while serving the needs of scholars. In keeping with those principles, the *Yearbook* has been planned to augment *DLB* by reflecting the vitality of contemporary literature and summarizing current literary activity. The librarian, scholar, or student attempting to stay informed of literary developments is faced with an endless task. The purpose of *DLB Yearbook* is to serve those readers while at the same time enlarging the scope of *DLB*.

The *Yearbook* is divided into two sections: articles about the past year's literary events or topics; and obituaries and tributes. The updates and new author entries previously included as supplements to published *DLB* volumes have been omitted. (These essays will appear in future *DLB* volumes.) Included in the articles section are an overview of the literary collections at the Huntington Library, the first reprinting in the United States of three newspaper stories by Ernest Hemingway, interviews with John Caldwell Guilds and James Hardin, and extended discussions of the year's work in fiction, poetry, drama, literary theory, and literary biography. The *Yearbook* continues two surveys begun in 1987, an overview of new literary journals, and an in-depth examination of the practice of book reviewing in America. In addition, the *Yearbook* features an article on the recipient of the 1992 Nobel Prize in literature, Derek Walcott, including Walcott's Nobel lectures.

The death of a literary figure prompts an assessment of his achievements and reputation. The obituaries section marks the passing of Isaac Asimov and Richard Yates.

Each *Yearbook* includes a list of literary prizes and awards, a necrology, and a checklist of books about literary history and biography published during the year.

This *Yearbook* introduces a new feature, the *Dictionary of Literary Biography Yearbook* Awards for novel, first novel, volume of short stories, volume of poetry, and literary biography.

From the outset, the *DLB* series has undertaken to compile literary history as it is revealed in the lives and works of authors. The *Yearbook* supports that commitment, providing a useful and necessary current record.

Acknowledgments

This book was produced by Bruccoli Clark Layman, Inc. Karen L. Rood is senior editor for the *Dictionary of Literary Biography* series.

Photography editors are Edward Scott and Timothy C. Lundy. Layout and graphics supervisor is Penney L. Haughton. Copyediting supervisor is Bill Adams. Typesetting supervisor is Kathleen M. Flanagan. Samuel Bruce is editorial associate. Systems manager is George F. Dodge. The production staff includes Rowena Betts, Steve Borsanyi, Barbara Brannon, Patricia Coate, Rebecca Crawford, Margaret McGinty Cureton, Denise Edwards, Sarah A. Estes, Joyce Fowler, Robert Fowler, Brenda A. Gillie, Bonita Graham, Jolyon M. Helterman, Ellen McCracken, Kathy Lawler Merlette, John Myrick, Pamela D. Norton, Thomas J. Pickett, Patricia Salisbury, Maxine K. Smalls, Deborah P. Stokes, and Wilma Weant.

Walter W. Ross and Suzanne Burry did library research. They were assisted by the following librarians at the Thomas Cooper Library of the University of South Carolina: Linda Holderfield and the interlibrary-loan staff; reference librarians Gwen Baxter, Daniel Boice, Faye Chadwell, Cathy Eckman, Rhonda Felder, Gary Geer, Qun "Gerry" Jiao, Jackie Kinder, Laurie Preston, Jean Rhyne, Carol Tobin, Carolyn Tyler, Virginia Weathers, Elizabeth Whiznant, and Connie Widney; circulation-department head Thomas Marcil; and acquisitions-searching supervisor David Haggard.

Dictionary of Literary Biography®
Yearbook: 1992

Dictionary of Literary Biography Yearbook Awards

When you look at the lists at the back of this book, you might conclude that there are too many literary prizes. And you might be right. Besides which, everybody knows and even agrees (whether or not they openly admit it) that the very idea of prizes for works of art is not a good one. You can take any given literary prize or award and easily come up with your own list of equally good, even superior competitors in the same category, judged by the same criteria. We like prizes of all kinds because they are fun (for everybody but the losers), not because they really mean anything or do much good. They can, of course, help a given and gifted writer gain some needed and probably deserved recognition; and one of the arguments in favor of prizes, allowing that prizes are unfair and often undeserved, is that the whole form – fiction, poetry, biography, and so forth – is really being recognized and honored by means of the award made to one (or more) among many artists.

So, if all of the above is true, what are we doing here creating yet another group of literary prizes? Who needs the *DLB Yearbook* prizes in novel, first novel, short story, poetry, and literary biography? The answer is: we think *we* do. And we like to think that, all things considered, you will agree with us. We think our prizes are, by design and definitions, a little different from all the others. For one thing, our prizes (each one) are a matter of personal choice. No committees, no juries, no panels. One absolute judge, in this case the single critic who wrote the individual essay-report on the year's work in a particular field. What we did, then, was ask each of ourselves, among all the works you read, following the field you studied for the year, what was your favorite? Presumably any one of us could easily enough have dodged the question and the issue by simply saying that there was none or that there were too many. But that didn't happen. What happened was that every one of us had a special favorite to put forward. (And never mind *why;* we don't have to argue; we don't have to sell; we are just announcing our results.) No other considerations other than excellence and pleasure, instruction and delight, within the context of a year's work.

It's about honor then, not money or ribbons or medals. Just an honest appraisal and judgment by one person who kept up with a form (novel, first novel, poetry, short story, literary biography) over the past year. In that sense we can argue that our prizes are as important as any others. But that is, finally, irrelevant. What matters is that some critics here and now took a stand and seek to honor outstanding work. We intend to do so next year and in years ahead. Meantime we are pleased and proud to celebrate some first-rate writers and their work.

– *George Garrett*

The 1992 Nobel Prize in Literature
Derek Walcott

(23 January 1930 –   )

Edward Halsey Foster
Stevens Institute of Technology

See also the Walcott entries in *DLB Yearbook: 1981* and *DLB 117: Twentieth-Century Caribbean and Black African Writers, First Series.*

BOOKS: *25 Poems* (Port of Spain: Guardian, 1948);
Epitaph for the Young (Bridgetown, Barbados: Advocate, 1949);
Henri Christophe: A Chronicle in Seven Scenes (Bridgetown, Barbados: Advocate, 1950);
Poems (Kingston, Jamaica: City Printery, 1951);
Harry Dernier (Bridgetown, Barbados: Advocate, 1952);
The Sea at Dauphin (Mona, Jamaica: Extra-Mural Department, University College of the West Indies, 1954);
Ione: A Play with Music (Mona, Jamaica: Extra-Mural Department, University College of the West Indies, 1957);
Ti-Jean: A Play in One Act (Kingston, Jamaica: Extra-Mural Department, University College of the West Indies, 1958);
In a Green Night: Poems, 1948–1960 (London: Cape, 1962);
Selected Poems (New York: Farrar, Straus, 1964);
The Castaway and Other Poems (London: Cape, 1965);
Malcauchon; or, The Six in the Rain (Port of Spain: Extra-Mural Department, University College of the West Indies, 1966);
The Charlatan (Mona, Jamaica: Extra-Mural Department, University College of the West Indies, 1967);
The Gulf, and Other Poems (London: Cape, 1969); republished as *The Gulf: Poems* (New York: Farrar, Straus & Giroux, 1970);
Dream on Monkey Mountain and Other Plays (New York: Farrar, Straus & Giroux, 1970; London: Cape, 1972);
Another Life (New York: Farrar, Straus & Giroux, 1973; London: Cape, 1973);

Derek Walcott (photograph © The Nobel Foundation)

Sea Grapes (London: Cape, 1976; New York: Farrar, Straus & Giroux, 1976);
The Joker of Seville & O Babylon! (New York: Farrar, Straus & Giroux, 1978; London: Cape, 1979);
The Star-Apple Kingdom (New York: Farrar, Straus & Giroux, 1979; London: Cape, 1980);
Remembrance and Pantomime (New York: Farrar, Straus & Giroux, 1980);
The Fortunate Traveller (New York: Farrar, Straus & Giroux, 1981; London: Faber & Faber, 1982);

Selected Poetry, selected by Wayne Brown (London & Kingston, Jamaica: Heinemann, 1981);

The Caribbean Poetry of Derek Walcott, and the Art of Romare Bearden (New York: Limited Editions Club, 1983);

Midsummer (New York: Farrar, Straus & Giroux, 1984; London & Boston: Faber & Faber, 1984);

Three Plays: The Last Carnival; Beef, No Chicken; and A Branch of the Blue Nile (New York: Farrar, Straus & Giroux, 1986);

Collected Poems, 1948–1984 (New York: Farrar, Straus & Giroux, 1986; London: Faber & Faber, 1986);

The Arkansas Testament (New York: Farrar, Straus & Giroux, 1987; London: Faber & Faber, 1988);

The Poet in the Theatre (London: Poetry Book Society, 1990);

Omeros (New York: Farrar, Straus & Giroux, 1990; London: Faber & Faber, 1990).

PLAY PRODUCTIONS: *Henri Christophe,* Castries, Saint Lucia, Saint Joseph's Convent, 9 September 1950; London, 1951;

Paolo and Francesca, Castries, Saint Lucia, Saint Joseph's Convent, 1951;

Wine of the Country, Mona, Jamaica, Whitehall Players Theatre, 1953;

The Sea at Dauphin, Port of Spain, Whitehall Players Theatre, 13 August 1954; London, 1960;

Ione, Kingston, Jamaica, Ward Theatre, 16 March 1957;

Ti-Jean and His Brothers, Castries, Saint Lucia, R. C. Boys Infant School, 16 December 1957; New York, Delacorte Theatre, 20 July 1972;

Drums and Colours, Kingston, Jamaica, Royal Botanical Gardens, 25 April 1958;

Malcauchon; or, Six in the Rain, Castries, Saint Lucia, Castries Town Hall, 12 March 1959; produced again as *Six in the Rain,* London, 1960; produced again as *Malcochon,* in *An Evening of One Acts,* New York, 25 March 1969;

Dream on Monkey Mountain, Toronto, Central Library Theatre, 12 August 1967; New York: Saint Mark's Playhouse, 9 March 1971;

In a Fine Castle, Port of Spain, Little Carib Theatre, 1971; revised as *The Last Carnival,* Port of Spain, Government Training Center, 1 July 1982;

Franklin, Port of Spain, Bishop's Auditorium, 14 April 1973;

The Charlatan, with music by Galt MacDermot, Los Angeles, Mark Taper Forum, June 1974;

The Joker of Seville, with music by MacDermot, Port of Spain, Little Carib Theatre, 28 November 1974;

O Babylon!, with music by MacDermot, Port of Spain, Little Carib Theatre, 19 March 1976;

Remembrance, Saint Croix, U.S. Virgin Islands, Dorsch Centre, 22 April 1977; New York, Shakespeare Festival, 24 April 1979;

Pantomime, Port of Spain, Little Carib Theatre, 12 April 1978; London, BBC, 25 January 1979;

Beef, No Chicken, Port of Spain, Little Carib Theatre, 30 April 1981;

A Branch of the Blue Nile, Bridgetown, Barbados, Stage One, 25 November 1983;

Steel, Cambridge, Mass., American Repertory Theatre, 3 April 1991.

OTHER: "The Muse of History," in *Is Massa Day Dead?,* edited by Orde Coombs (Garden City, N.Y.: Doubleday, 1974), pp. 1–28.

SELECTED PERIODICAL PUBLICATIONS – UNCOLLECTED: *Drums and Colours,* Caribbean Quarterly, special issue, 7 (March–June 1961);

"Young Trinidadian Poets," *Trinidad Sunday Guardian,* 19 June 1966, p. 5;

"What the Lower House Demands," *Trinidad Guardian,* 6 July 1966, p. 5;

"Meanings," *Savacou,* 2 (1970): 45–51;

"The Caribbean: Culture or Mimicry?," *Journal of Interamerican Studies and World Affairs,* 16 (February 1974): 3–13;

"Soul Brother to 'The Joker of Seville,'" *Trinidad Guardian,* 6 November 1974, p. 4;

"On Robert Lowell," *New York Review of Books,* 31 (1 March 1984): 25–31;

"Cafe Martinique," *House and Garden,* 157 (March 1985): 140, 222–228.

No matter where [Derek Walcott] finds himself – be it Rome, Argentina, or Van Gogh's orchards – he carries his island inside. – Rita Dove

Ezra Pound traced the beginnings of modernism in English poetry to that moment when, in works like his own, "the pentameter" was broken – the moment, that is, when poetry ceased to depend on conventional meter and adopted what he called "the sequence of the musical phrase." Pound's observation led some critics and literary historians to see modernist poetry as essentially a formalist break with the past. At the same time, they felt justified to label as reactionary or conservative those who continue to utilize established measures.

The tradition in which Pound worked and for which he was largely responsible was, of course, never the only version of modernism in practice. Other modernists – T. S. Eliot and W. H. Auden among them – generally worked within metrical conventions, and it is their work that one finds behind the poetry and plays of Derek Walcott, winner of the 1992 Nobel Prize in literature.

In an interview with Robert D. Hamner, Walcott claimed that "all English verse makes an agonized effort to return to the pentameter" – a statement which puts the Pound tradition on the defensive and sets it off as the exception, as indeed an eccentricity, in the history of literature in English. Walcott suggests a very different version of modernism from the one to which we are accustomed, but in any representative gathering of poets, his position might well find as much opposition as agreement.

Who then is right? Is the writer whose work reasserts the pentameter essentially repeating or defending gestures of the past? Does Walcott's preference for traditional English prosody make him essentially conservative? Or is there room both for his position and Pound's as well?

In fact, in Walcott's work there is no unthinking admiration for the past. An attentive reading reveals instead a rupture from British origins as profound as one finds in nineteenth-century Americans such as Emily Dickinson. Whatever Walcott owes to the English literary tradition, he does not evoke its conventions nostalgically: whatever he borrows is transformed. He defines his own course, and it is one which is ultimately as distinctive from everything which has preceded it as it is from Pound's.

Like Dickinson, Walcott, working in a culture that had freed itself from Britain politically, faced a literary tradition that had to be thoroughly reshaped if it were to express the writer's own historical situation and perspective. Hostile critics may see him as imprisoned in a literary past, but his works propose a radical new course for the literature of the postcolonial, English-speaking world. Walcott has made it very clear in interviews that it is not his intention to write himself into the history of British literature. When asked by the poet Edward Hirsch where he saw himself in the English poetic tradition, he said that he did not; he was a Caribbean writer, and if he belonged to any tradition, it was one that was just beginning.

The assumption on the part of modernists like Eliot and Pound that literature should defend the Western cultural tradition has made them problematic for writers from postcolonial cultures. After all, the belief in the presumed authority of that tradition had been used to justify the intellectual as well as the

economic colonization of the Caribbean. It comes as no surprise that, as Simon Gikandi notes in *Writing in Limbo: Modernism and Caribbean Literature* (1992), modernists who gave greater emphasis to aesthetic innovation than social and political change have often been ignored or condemned by recent Caribbean writers.

Some postcolonial writers adopted local dialects and folk cultures in their work, but Walcott chose the more subversive route, transforming the tradition from within. In his work a tradition that, in the view of humanist critics and scholars, served as a repository of monolithic truths becomes an agent for social and cultural disruption and reform.

Walcott began his work in "the house of literature," as he said in his long autobiographical poem *Another Life* (1973), "as a houseboy," but he was never a docile, submissive imitator. In "Prelude," written when he was eighteen, he was already beginning to draw a line between his own poetic ambitions and those of his "masters." Listing images that might be found in a poem by Eliot (that is, "[t]he turned doorhandle"), he says that it is too soon for him to use them. First he must learn "to suffer / In accurate iambics."

That statement is ironic. "Prelude" is not the modest or self-effacing statement of an apprentice that some critics have assumed; Walcott says that it is not time yet to speak openly, but that, of course, is exactly what he is doing. The poem is in fact a criticism of such early Eliot poems as "The Love Song of J. Alfred Prufrock" – poems, that is, built from the kind of uncertainties and indecisions that Walcott's poetry abjures.

"The Love Song of J. Alfred Prufrock" opens with an image of passivity and submission – the evening sky as "a patient etherised upon a table" – but "Prelude" begins with an image of constrained power: "variegated fists of clouds" above the "uncouth features" of a Caribbean landscape. Both poems were written when their respective authors were young, but an essential difference in the way the two poets view themselves may be suggested by the fact that while the speaker in Eliot's poem is an older man who finds he can no longer communicate his feelings to the women he loves, Walcott's speaker chooses a young man who is just beginning to learn how.

Walcott took what he needed technically from a literary past that, in Eliot, had become a literature of hesitation and doubt, and then began writing works that take their authority from the immediacy of intense experience and feeling. "I require nothing // from poetry," he writes in "Winding Up," "but true feeling."

One of Walcott's more significant achievements has been to give the West Indies a voice, and he has done so precisely by centering on its emotional life. In, for example, *Omeros* (1990), the most widely admired of his works, he rewrote the Homeric epics in terms of the life of Saint Lucia, the island in the West Indies where he spent his childhood. His Achilles (or "Achille," as he is called in *Omeros*) is not a warrior but a fisherman, and Helen is a waitress rather than a queen. They insist on their independence, however, and take no authority beyond their emotions and convictions. The result, as in all of Walcott's major work, is an emotional geography as distinctive and complex as Robert Frost's New England or William Faulkner's Mississippi.

Walcott was born on 23 January 1930 in Castries on Saint Lucia. When he was a child, Saint Lucia was known to the rest of the world primarily as a tourist resort, but behind the glitter lay a grim history of British colonial rule by men like "B," the character in *Another Life* who selects from workers in his cane fields "nubile coolie girls" for his personal pleasure.

Both of Walcott's grandmothers were of African descent, and both grandfathers were white Europeans. His grandfather on his father's side was British; on his mother's side, Dutch. Walcott's father, Warwick, was the clerk of the First District Court, and his mother, Alix, was a teacher. Occupying a middle ground between the white aristocracy and the underclass of black laborers and fishermen, the Walcotts lived a comfortable middle-class life, relatively free of the worst abuses of colonial life.

When Walcott was slightly more than a year old, his father died. Warwick Walcott had been an amateur poet and artist, and his ambitions clearly had their influence on his son. (Derek Walcott is not only a writer but a very accomplished painter.) When Walcott was eighteen, he completed his first book, *25 Poems* (1948), which he published himself, borrowing two hundred dollars from his mother to pay the printer and soon selling enough copies to pay her back.

That same year Walcott graduated from a private high school on Saint Lucia and entered the University College of the West Indies in Jamaica. Both schools had strong British curricula – a fact of enormous consequence to his future work. It was an education he would never regret, although he would certainly turn it to his own purposes. In "Meanings," an essay published nearly twenty years

after he was graduated from college, he said that British education "must have ranked with the finest in the world." Both high school and college gave particular emphasis to literature, and so it is not surprising that when Walcott began his work as a writer, as he said in "What the Twilight Said," he thought of himself as working in the tradition of Christopher Marlowe and John Milton. At the same time, however, he was not uncritical of that tradition, dismissing, in *Another Life*, poems like John Keats's "Ode to a Nightingale" as "romantic taxidermy."

British culture, in any case, reached very deeply into the young writer, and in his interview with Charles H. Rowell, he said that when he was a student in the late 1940s he saw no split between his British and Caribbean heritages. Nonetheless, when his ambitions as a writer led him to look for local writers who might serve as models, he could find none. The consequence was a long process searching for a regional voice that would not altogether abandon what he had gained from his British education.

Although Walcott is perhaps most celebrated as a poet, he is also very widely admired as the writer of deeply poetic, lyrical plays, and in his career as a playwright one sees very plainly his progress from conventional literary influences toward characteristically West Indian kinds of expression. His first play, *Henri Christophe* (1950), was, as he admitted in "What the Twilight Says," the product of "a mind drenched in Elizabethan literature." It dealt, however, with an episode in Caribbean history, and in the play's fundamental concern – "one race's quarrel with another's God" – one finds again that gulf that informs "Prelude," the gulf between the poet and colonial authority.

During the 1950s Walcott wrote several plays, including *The Sea at Dauphin* (1954), which he based on John Millington Synge's *Riders to the Sea* (1904). *The Sea at Dauphin*, which deals with the fishermen of Saint Lucia rather than the kind of grand heroes one finds in *Henri Christophe*, represented a major step forward and set the course for Walcott's major plays, which would center on ordinary West Indian figures and would utilize local dialects.

Walcott immersed himself in a study of contemporary theater during visits to New York in 1957 and, supported by a Rockefeller fellowship, returned the following year to study under José Quintero and Stuart Vaughan. He also studied Kabuki, Bertolt Brecht, modern dance, and films by Akira Kurosawa, especially *Rashomon* (1951), which argues against the idea of authority by suggesting

Stamps issued by Sweden in honor of Walcott in recognition of his Nobel Prize (courtesy of Reinhard Sander)

that the "real" is contingent on one's point of view. In 1959 he was back in the West Indies, where he established the Trinidad Theatre Workshop, which remained a central focus in his career until he resigned in 1976.

During his first stay in New York, he wrote *Ti-Jean and His Brothers* (1957), which he called his "first real experience . . . of writing a stylized West Indian play" and which utilizes folk materials as well as dialect and West Indian characters. In 1959 he began work on what would prove to be his principal contribution to West Indian drama, and the play for which he is still best known, *Dream on Monkey Mountain.* Originally produced by the Trinidad Theatre Workshop in 1967, it was revised several times before it reached its published version in 1970. The New York production, which opened in 1971, was awarded an Obie that year as the season's best foreign play.

Divided into a series of scenes structured as dreams that poetically express the minds of the characters, *Dream on Monkey Mountain* concerns a struggle for identity in the postcolonial world. The principal character is Marak, a charcoal burner from Saint Lucia, who, searching for his black identity, returns to Africa under the promptings of a white goddess. But Africa does not satisfy his needs; his identity, he realizes, belongs to Saint Lucia, and it is there that he finally decides to stay — a choice which may reflect Walcott's own decision to create a West Indian art ultimately subordinate to no outside tradition, European or African. At the end of the play, Marak says that he is "going back

home" with the desire that someday people will say, "Marak lives where he has always lived, in the dream of his people."

Dream on Monkey Mountain utilizes West Indian dialect, which Walcott as a rule reserves for characters in plays and poems rather than when speaking in his own voice. Walcott, as he told Hirsch, has three languages: conventional English and local French and English dialects. Since his education was "academically privileged," he could not, however, write as if he usually spoke like "the St. Lucia peasant or fisherman." And, of course, it was always possible that, had he chosen to use dialect generally for his own voice, it could have seemed false, even patronizing. Patois, he told Hamner, was his "real language, and tonally [his] basic language," but it is also the language of a class to which, socially and educationally, he never belonged.

On the other hand, as Walcott told Hirsch, he was guided in his work by the desire "to find a voice that was not inflected by influences." In "What the Twilight Said," he wrote that he wanted "an electric fusion of the old and new" in his language. "Deliverance from servitude," he said, lay in "the forging of a language that went beyond mimicry, a dialect which had the force of revelation as it invented names for things, one which finally settled on its own mode of inflection."

An exceptionally fine instance of this is found in "The Schooner *Flight,*" which takes its cadences from West Indian speech (for example, "All you see me talking to the wind, so you think I mad"). But as Walcott says in his essay "On Robert Lowell," his style "had been, perhaps still is, that of a magpie," and in the series of deeply meditative poems collected in *Midsummer* (1984), the cadences may owe less to the Caribbean than to recent meditative poetry among Walcott's contemporaries and near contemporaries – John Berryman, Elizabeth Bishop, Lowell, and others. There is, in any case, a great versatility in Walcott, but at all times, at his best he avoids doings things simply as they have been done before. One of the more obvious and satisfying aspects of *Omeros,* for example, is its resistance to an epic tone. Walcott has no desire to make his Achille and Odysseus heroic in the Homeric mode, and in keeping with the poem's focus on the ordinary, the tone approaches the prosaic: "'This is how, one sunrise, we cut down them canoes,'" the poem begins. The speaker, we learn, is Philoctete, a fisherman, speaking to tourists. There is no invocation to the muse and no attempt to satisfy simply with high rhetoric. Writing in this way, *Omeros* steers clear of "romantic taxidermy" and consequent dishonesty.

V. S. Naipaul claims in *The Middle Passage: The Caribbean Revisited* (1962) that "[h]istory was built around achievement and creation" and that "nothing was created in the West Indies." This implies history as Ralph Waldo Emerson defined it – "the lengthened shadow of a man" – an elitist view, of course, and one in which an oppressed culture must always seem inadequate and weak. History as a pattern of "achievement and creation" may also imply the cultural and political domination of one person or group by another. Walcott's poems and plays search the underside of this view of history, suggesting that what it presents as progress may from another angle be exploitation and oppression.

Given Walcott's position, the people who are most admirable may be those who are least influential, and it is these who are generally the subjects of his work. At the same time he is never a sentimentalist. He knows that the oppressed are in no essential way better than their oppressors, and that the roles can easily be reversed. As he points out in "Ruins of a Great House," one of his earliest poems, the British themselves had been colonized long before they became the colonists.

Behind Walcott's view of history lie his personal experiences with racial and ethnic hatreds. "Blues," in *The Gulf, and Other Poems* (1969), for example, concerns a time in Greenwich Village when a gang of young men beat him for no apparent reason except that he was black, leaving him to "[crawl] four flights upstairs." "The Arkansas Testament," the title poem in a volume published in 1987, is set in Fayetteville, Arkansas. The poet is

staying in a motel, and much of the work is spent characterizing the seemingly bland, unthreatening landscape of diners and motels such as one finds in the periphery of most American cities. But even here the reality of racial hatred cannot be escaped, and when he goes for coffee early in the morning, he must, as a black, make the delicate decision as to where he can sit so as to attract the least hostility. No matter how impersonal the world may seem, the evils of racism persist, and there is no reason to think it will ever disappear: "What we know of evil / is that it will never end."

"The Fortunate Traveller," the title poem in a volume published in 1981, argues that "the heart of darkness" is not in Joseph Conrad's Africa but in the Holocaust. Walcott suggests that the history of slavery and indentured labor, the oppressions of colonization, and the cringing servility which oppressed people need to survive reached their extreme, at least for our time, in Dachau. The Holocaust has become for him the supreme instance of the racial hatreds of our time. "This century's pastorals," he wrote in *Midsummer,* were created "by the chimneys of Dachau, of Auschwitz, of Sachsenhausen."

The answer to the horrors of these hatreds is not, Walcott believes, separatism. As produced in New York, *Dream on Monkey Mountain* was made to seem a manifesto for black power, but as he told Seldon Rodman, he himself had intended the play to be an expression of spiritual crisis. "Most black writers," he said, "cripple themselves by their separatism. *You can't be a poet and believe in the division of man.*"

In "A Far Cry from Africa," one of Walcott's earliest and most reprinted poems, he asks how he can "choose / Between this Africa and the English tongue I love?" The tension cannot be resolved through nostalgic longing for an African homeland. His play *O Babylon!* (1976), for example, suggests that the Rastafarians – Caribbean people of African descent who prepare themselves for a return to Africa – are devising a new myth that sees history as progressive. Identification with African culture, Walcott told Hirsch, could be seductive, but it could become "even a slave longing, for another master."

In Walcott's moral universe, paradise is simply not within reach. The drive for power, particularly power over others, remains, and as a result history is pervaded by evil. In "Ruins of a Great House," he points out that although the colonialists have left the West Indies, "[t]he rot remains with

Dust jacket for Walcott's epic without epic heroes

us." It is one thing to overcome one's enemy, but how does one overcome the evil in oneself ?

Walcott's investigations of language, poetics, and history converge in *Omeros,* his epic without epic heroes. Like Pound's *Cantos* (1919–1959), Walcott's book pays homage to Dante and Homer. Walcott, for example, employs Dante's terza rima (although the *aba* rhyme scheme is only irregularly maintained), while Pound takes Dante's canto as his poetic unit and originally planned to divide his work, like *The Divine Comedy,* into three parts – a hell, a purgatory, and a paradise. *Omeros* borrows Homeric figures such as Achilles, Helen, and Odysseus, recasting them, as noted earlier, as residents of modern Saint Lucia; the *Cantos* begins with Pound's version of a passage from book 11 of the *Odyssey,* rewritten to place the author in the role of Odysseus.

In matters of form and technique, Pound's work is, of course, by far the more radical, but his attempt to write an epic poem – which he defined as a poem "containing history" – leads to celebrations of tradition, authority, and, ultimately, Benito Mussolini's fascism. What is one to make

of Pound's admiration for Sigismondo Malatesta, the Renaissance condottiere, who did indeed support scholarship and the arts, but whose barbarism earned him recognition as one of the monsters of history? And how can one respond to Pound's anti-Semitism with anything less than disgust?

On the surface, *Omeros* seems the more conservative text, but in political and moral contexts it is the more radical. It is too suspicious of history to celebrate "achievement and creation." Its heroes are not Mussolini or Malatesta but the fishermen of Saint Lucia. There are aristocrats and warriors in *Omeros,* but they are not the poem's true heroes. These, John Figueroa points out, "are not nobles" but rather "noble people."

For certain critics, Walcott's reputation remains haunted by the accusation that his work, borrowing heavily from the past, is itself colonized and still under the literary and linguistic control of British and Continental traditions. But the accusation will not stand. "To change your language," Walcott writes in "Codicil," "you must change your life." That change was made for him in part by the end of colonialism. Pound's overriding precept for the writer was to "make it new," and responding to the historical crisis of his time, that is exactly what Walcott did. There is no unthinking subservience here. In what he has done, one finds, rather, one of the great morally transformative acts in literature.

References:

Edward Baugh, *Memory as Vision: Derek Walcott: Another Life* (London: Longman, 1978);

Stewart Brown, ed., *The Art of Derek Walcott* (Chester Springs, Pa.: Dufour Editions, 1991);

Rita Dove, "Either I'm Nobody or I'm a Nation," *Parnassus: Poetry in Review,* 14, no. 1 (1987): 49–76;

John Figueroa, "*Omeros,*" in Brown, *The Art of Derek Walcott;*

Simon Gikandi, *Writing in Limbo: Modernism and Caribbean Literature* (Ithaca, N.Y.: Cornell University Press, 1992);

Robert D. Hamner, "Conversation with Derek Walcott," *World Literature Written in English,* 16, no. 2 (1977): 409–420;

Hamner, *Derek Walcott* (Boston: Twayne, 1981);

Edward Hirsch, "An Interview with Derek Walcott," *Contemporary Literature,* 20 no. 3 (1980): 279–292;

V. S. Naipaul, *The Middle Passage: The Caribbean Revisited* (London: Deutsch, 1962);

Charles H. Rowell, "An Interview with Derek Walcott," *Callaloo,* 34 (Winter 1988): 80–89;

Rei Terada, *Derek Walcott's Poetry: American Mimicry* (Boston: Northeastern University Press, 1992).

NOBEL BANQUET STATEMENT
Derek Walcott

Your Royal Highnesses,
Distinguished Representatives of the Nobel Foundation, Honourable Members of the Academies, the Caroline Institute and Election Committees, Students, Ladies and Gentlemen

The honour that you pay me is accepted in the one name that comprises all of the supposedly broken languages of the Caribbean. They cohere in this moment, a moment that recognises their endeavour and one which I receive with pride and humility on their behalf. Pride in the continuing struggle of Antillean writers, humility in the glare of representing them by my own evanescent image.

NOBEL LECTURE 1992
Derek Walcott

THE ANTILLES: FRAGMENTS OF EPIC MEMORY

Felicity is a village in Trinidad on the edge of the Caroni plain, the wide central plain that still grows sugar and to which indentured cane cutters were brought after emancipation, so the small population of Felicity is East Indian, and on the afternoon that I visited it with friends from America, all the faces along its road were Indian, which, as I hope to show, was a moving, beautiful thing, because this Saturday afternoon *Ramleela,* the epic dramatization of the Hindu epic the *Ramayana,* was going to be performed, and the costumed actors from the village were assembling on a field strung with different-coloured flags, like a new gas station, and beautiful Indian boys in red and black were aiming arrows haphazardly into the afternoon light. Low blue mountains on the horizon, bright grass, clouds that would gather colour before the light went. Felicity! What a gentle Anglo-Saxon name for an epical memory.

Under an open shed on the edge of the field, there were two huge armatures of bamboo that looked like immense cages. They were parts of the body of a god, his calves or thighs, which, fitted and reared, would make a gigantic effigy. This effigy would be burnt as a conclusion to the epic. The cane structures flashed a predictable parallel: Shelley's sonnet on the fallen statue of Ozymandias and his empire, that "colossal wreck" in its empty desert.

Drummers had lit a fire in the shed and they eased the skins of their tablas nearer the flames to tighten them. The saffron flames, the bright grass, and the hand-woven armatures of the fragmented god who would be burnt were not in any desert where imperial power had finally toppled but were part of a ritual, evergreen season that, like the cane-burning harvest, is annually repeated, the point of such sacrifice being its repetition, the point of the destruction being renewed through fire.

Deities were entering the field. What we generally call "Indian music" was blaring from the open platformed shed from which the epic would be narrated. Costumed actors were arriving. Princes and gods, I supposed. What an unfortunate confession! "Gods, I suppose" is the shrug that embodies our African and Asian diasporas. I had often thought of but never seen *Ramleela,* and had never seen this theatre, an open field, with village children as warriors, princes, and gods. I had no idea what the epic story was, who its hero was, what enemies he fought, yet I had recently adapted the *Odyssey* for a theatre in England, presuming that the audience knew the trials of Odysseus, hero of another Asia Minor epic, while nobody in Trinidad knew any more than I did about Rama, Kali, Shiva, Vishnu, apart from the Indians, a phrase I use pervertedly because that is the kind of remark you can still hear in Trinidad: "apart from the Indians."

It was as if, on the edge of the Central Plain, there was another plateau, a raft on which the *Ramayana* would be poorly performed in this ocean of cane, but that was my writer's view of things, and it is wrong. I was seeing the *Ramleela* at Felicity as theatre when it was faith.

Multiply that moment of self-conviction when an actor, made-up and costumed, nods to his mirror before stopping onstage in the belief that he is a reality entering an illusion and you would have what I presumed was happening to the actors of this epic. But they were not actors. They had been chosen; or they themselves had chosen their roles in this sacred story that would go on for nine afternoons over a two-hour period till the sun set. They were not amateurs but believers. There was no theatrical term to define them. They did not have to psych themselves up to play their roles. Their acting would probably be as buoyant and as natural as those bamboo arrows crisscrossing the afternoon pasture. They believed in what they were playing, in the sacredness of the text, the validity of India, while I, out of the writer's habit, searched for some sense of elegy, of loss, even of degenerative mimicry in the happy faces of the boy-warriors or the heraldic profiles of the village princes. I was polluting the afternoon with doubt and with the patronage of admiration. I misread the event through a visual echo of History — the cane fields, indenture, the evocation of vanished armies, temples, and trumpeting elephants — when all around me there was quite the opposite: elation, delight in the boys' screams, in the sweets-stalls, in more and more costumed characters appearing; a delight of conviction, not loss. The name Felicity made sense.

Consider the scale of Asia reduced to these fragments: the small white exclamations of minarets or the stone balls of temples in the cane fields, and one can understand the self-mockery and embarrassment of those who see these rites as parodic, even degenerate. These purists look on such ceremonies as grammarians look at a dialect, as cities look on provinces and empires on their colonies. Memory that yearns to join the centre, a limb re-

membering the body from which it has been severed, like those bamboo thighs of the god. In other words, the way that the Caribbean is still looked at, illegitimate, rootless, mongrelized. "No people there," to quote Froude, "in the true sense of the word." No people. Fragments and echoes of real people, unoriginal and broken.

The performance was like a dialect, a branch of its original language, an abridgement of it, but not a distortion or even a reduction of its epic scale. Here in Trinidad I had discovered that one of the greatest epics of the world was seasonally performed, not with that desperate resignation of preserving a culture, but with an openness of belief that was as steady as the wind bending the cane lances of the Caroni plain. We had to leave before the play began to go through the creeks of the Caroni Swamp, to catch the scarlet ibises coming home at dusk. In a performance as natural as those of the actors of the *Ramleela,* we watched the flocks come in as bright as the scarlet of the boy archers, as the red flags, and cover an islet until it turned into a flowering tree, an anchored immortelle. The sigh of History meant nothing here. These two visions, the *Ramleela* and the arrowing flocks of scarlet ibises, blent into a single gasp of gratitude. Visual surprise is natural in the Caribbean; it comes with the landscape, and faced with its beauty, the sigh of History dissolves.

We make too much of that long groan which underlines the past. I felt privileged to discover the ibises as well as the scarlet archers of Felicity.

The sigh of History rises over ruins, not over landscapes, and in the Antilles there are few ruins to sigh over, apart from the ruins of sugar estates and abandoned forts. Looking around slowly, as a camera would, taking in the low blue hills over Port of Spain, the village road and houses, the warrior-archers, the god-actors and their handlers, and music already on the sound track, I wanted to make a film that would be a long-drawn sigh over Felicity. I was filtering the afternoon with evocations of a lost India, but why "evocations?" Why not "celebrations of a real presence?" Why should India be "lost" when none of these villagers ever really knew it, and why not "continuing," why not the perpetuation of joy in Felicity and in all the other nouns of the Central Plain: Couva, Chaguanas, Charley Village? Why was I not letting my pleasure open its windows wide? I was entitled like any Trinidadian to the ecstasies of their claim, because ecstasy was the pitch of the sinuous drumming in the loudspeakers. I was entitled to the feast of Husein, to the mirrors and crêpe-paper temples of the Muslim epic, to the Chinese Dragon Dance, to the rites of that Sephardic Jewish synagogue that was once on Something Street. I am only one-eighth the writer I might have been had I contained all the fragmented languages of Trinidad.

Break a vase, and the love that reassembles the fragments is stronger than that love which took its symmetry for granted when it was whole. The glue that fits the pieces is the sealing of its original shape. It is such a love that reassembles our African and Asiatic fragments, the cracked heirlooms whose restoration shows its white scars. This gathering of broken pieces is the care and pain of the Antilles, and if the pieces are disparate, ill-fitting, they contain more pain than their original sculpture, those icons and sacred vessels taken for granted in their ancestral places. Antillean art is this restoration of our shattered histories, our shards of vocabulary, our archipelago becoming a synonym for pieces broken off from the original continent.

And this is the exact process of the making of poetry, or what should be called not its "making" but its remaking, the fragmented memory, the armature that frames the god, even the rite that surrenders it to a funeral pyre; the god assembled cane by cane, reed by weaving reed, line by plaited line, as the artisans of Felicity would erect his holy echo.

Poetry, which is perfection's sweat but which must seem as fresh as the raindrops on a statue's brow, combines the natural and the marmoreal; it conjugates both tenses simultaneously: the past and the present, if the past is the sculpture and the present the beads of dew or rain on the forehead of the past. There is the buried language and there is the individual vocabulary, and the process of poetry is one of excavation and of self-discovery. Tonally the individual voice is a dialect; it shapes its own accent, its own vocabulary and melody in defiance of an imperial concept of language, the language of Ozymandias, libraries and dictionaries, law courts and critics, and churches, universities, political dogma, the diction of institutions. Poetry is an island that breaks away from the main. The dialects of my archipelago seem as fresh to me as those raindrops on the statue's forehead, not the sweat made from the classic exertion of frowning marble, but the condensations of a refreshing element, rain and salt.

Deprived of their original language, the captured and indentured tribes create their own, accreting and secreting fragments of an old, an epic vocabulary, from Asia and from Africa, but to an ancestral, an ecstatic rhythm in the blood that cannot be subdued by slavery or indenture, while nouns are renamed and the given names of places accepted like Felicity village or Choiseul. The original language dissolves from the exhaustion of distance like fog trying to cross an ocean, but this process of renaming, of finding new metaphors, is the same process that the poet faces every morning of his working day, making his own tools like Crusoe, assembling nouns from necessity, from Felicity, even renaming himself. The stripped man is driven back to that self-astonishing, elemental force, his mind. That is the basis of the Antillean experience, this shipwreck of fragments, these echoes, these shards of a huge tribal vocabulary, these partially remembered customs, and they are not decayed but strong. They survived the Middle Passage and the *Fatel Rozack,* the ship that carried the first indentured Indians from the port of Madras to the cane fields of Felicity, that carried the chained Cromwellian convict and the Sephardic Jew, the Chinese grocer and the Lebanese merchant selling cloth samples on his bicycle.

And here they are, all in a single Caribbean city, Port of Spain, the sum of history, Froude's "non-people." A downtown babel of shop signs and streets, mongrelized, polyglot, a ferment without a history, like heaven. Because that is what such a city is, in the New World, a writer's heaven.

A culture, we all know, is made by its cities.

Another first morning home, impatient for the sunrise – a broken sleep. Darkness at five, and the drapes not worth opening; then, in the sudden light, a cream-walled, brown-roofed police station bordered with short royal palms, in the colonial style, back of it frothing trees and taller palms, a pigeon fluttering into the cover of an eave, a rain-stained block of once-modern apartments, the morning side road into the station without traffic. All part of a surprising peace. This quiet happens with every visit to a city that has deepened itself in me. The flowers and the hills are easy, affection for them predictable; it is the architecture that, for the first morning, disorients. A return from American seductions used to make the traveller feel that something was missing, something was trying to complete itself, like the stained concrete apartments. Pan left along the window and the excrescences rear – a city trying to soar, trying to be brutal, like an American city in silhouette, stamped from the same mould as Columbus or Des Moines. An assertion of power, its decor bland, its air conditioning pitched to the point where its secretarial and executive staff sport competing cardigans; the colder the offices the more important, an imitation of another climate. A longing, even an envy of feeling cold.

In serious cities, in grey, militant winter with its short afternoons, the days seem to pass by in buttoned overcoats, every building appears as a barracks with lights on in its windows, and when snow comes, one has the illusion of living in a Russian novel, in the nineteenth century, because of the literature of winter. So visitors to the Caribbean must feel that they are inhabiting a succession of postcards. Both climates are shaped by what we have read of them. For tourists, the sunshine cannot be serious. Winter adds depth and darkness to life as well as to literature, and in the unending summer of the tropics not even poverty or poetry (in the Antilles poverty is poetry with a V, *une vie,* a condition of life as well as of imagination) seems capable of being profound because the nature around it is so exultant, so resolutely ecstatic, like its music. A culture based on joy is bound to be shallow. Sadly, to sell itself, the Caribbean encourages the delights of mindlessness, of brilliant vacuity, as a place to flee not only winter but that seriousness that comes only out of culture with four seasons. So how can there be a people there, in the true sense of the word?

They know nothing about seasons in which leaves let go of the year, in which spires fade in blizzards and streets whiten, of the erasures of whole cities by fog, of reflection in fireplaces; instead, they inhabit a geography whose rhythm, like their music, is limited to two stresses, hot and wet, sun and rain, light and shadow, day and night, the limitations of an incomplete metre, and are therefore a people incapable of the subtleties of contradiction, of imaginative complexity. So be it. We cannot change contempt.

Ours are not cities in the accepted sense, but no one wants them to be. They dictate their own proportions, their own definitions in particular places and in a prose equal to that of their detractors, so that now it is not just St. James but the streets and yards that Naipaul commemorates, its lanes as short and brilliant as his sentences; not just the noise and jostle of Tunapuna but the origins of C. L. R. James's *Beyond a Boundary,* not just Felicity village on the Caroni plain, but Selvon Country, and that is the way it goes up the islands now: the old Dominica of Jean Rhys still very much the way she wrote of it; and the Martinique of the early Césaire; Perse's Guadeloupe, even without the pith helmets and the mules; and what delight and privilege there was in watching a literature – one literature in several imperial languages, French, English, Spanish – bud and open island after island in the

early morning of a culture, not timid, not derivative, any more than the hard white petals of the frangipani are derivative and timid. This is not a belligerent boast but a simple celebration of inevitability: that this flowering had to come.

On a heat-stoned afternoon in Port of Spain, some alley white with glare, with love vine spilling over a fence, palms and a hazed mountain appear around a corner to the evocation of Vaughn or Herbert's "that shady city of palm-trees," or to the memory of a Hammond organ from a wooden chapel in Castries, where the congregation sang "Jerusalem, the Golden." It is hard for me to see such emptiness as desolation. It is the patience that is the width of Antillean life, and the secret is not to ask the wrong thing of it, not to demand of it an ambition it has no interest in. The traveller reads this as lethargy, as torpor.

Here there are not enough books, one says, no theatres, no museums, simply not enough to do. Yet, deprived of books, a man must fall back on thought, and out of thought, if he can learn to order it, will come the urge to record, and in extremity, if he has no means of recording, recitation, the ordering of memory which leads to metre, to commemoration. There can be virtues in deprivation, and certainly one virtue is salvation from a cascade of high mediocrity, since books are now not so much created as remade. Cities create a culture, and all we have are these magnified market towns, so what are the proportions of the ideal Caribbean city? A surrounding, accessible countryside with leafy suburbs, and if the city is lucky, behind it, spacious plains. Behind it, fine mountains; before it, an indigo sea. Spires would pin its centre and around them would be leafy, shadowy parks. Pigeons would cross its sky in alphabetic patterns, carrying with them memories of a belief in augury, and at the heart of the city there would be horses, yes, horses, those animals last seen at the end of the nineteenth century drawing broughams and carriages with top-hatted citizens, horses that live in the present tense without elegiac echoes from their hooves, emerging from paddocks at the Queen's Park Savannah at sunrise, when mist is unthreading from the cool mountains above the roofs, and at the centre of the city seasonally there would be races, so that citizens could roar at the speed and grace of these nineteenth-century animals. Its docks, not obscured by smoke or deafened by too much machinery, and above all, it would be so racially various that the cultures of the world – the Asiatic, the Mediterranean, the European, the African – would be represented in it, its humane variety more exciting than Joyce's Dublin. Its citizens would intermarry as they chose, from instinct, not tradition, until their children find it increasingly futile to trace their genealogy. It would not have too many avenues difficult or dangerous for pedestrians, its mercantile area would be a cacophony of accents, fragments of the old language that would be silenced immediately at five o'clock, its docks resolutely vacant on Sundays.

This is Port of Spain to me, a city ideal in its commercial and human proportions, where a citizen is a walker and not a pedestrian, and this is how Athens may have been before it became a cultural echo.

The finest silhouettes of Port of Spain are idealizations of the craftsman's handiwork, not of concrete and glass, but of baroque woodwork, each fantasy looking more like an involved drawing of itself than the actual building. Behind the city is the Caroni plain, with its villages, Indian prayer flags, and fruit vendors' stalls along the highway over which ibises come like floating flags. Photogenic poverty! Postcard sadnesses! I am not re-creating Eden; I mean, by "the Antilles," the reality of light, of work, of survival. I mean a house on the side of a country road, I mean the Caribbean Sea, whose smell is the smell of refreshing possibility as well as survival. Survival is the triumph of stubbornness, a sublime stupidity, is what makes the occupation of poetry endure, when there are so many things that should make it futile. Those things added together can go under one collective noun: "the world."

This is the visible poetry of the Antilles, then. Survival.

If you wish to understand that consoling pity with which the islands were regarded, look at the tinted engravings of Antillean forests, with their proper palm trees, ferns and waterfalls. They have a civilizing decency, like Botanical Gardens, as if the sky were a glass ceiling under which a colonized vegetation is arranged for quiet walks and carriage rides. Those views are incised with a pathos that guides the engraver's tool and the topographer's pencil, and it is this pathos which, tenderly ironic, gave villages names like Felicity. A century looked at a landscape furious with vegetation in the wrong light and with the wrong eye. It is such pictures that are saddening rather than the tropics itself. These delicate engravings of sugar mills and harbours, of native women in costume, are seen as part of History, that History which looked over the shoulder of the engraver and, later, the photographer. History can alter the eye and the moving hand to con-

form a view of itself; it can rename places for the nostalgia in an echo; it can temper the glare of tropical light to elegiac monotony in prose, the tone of judgement in Conrad, in the travel journals of Trollope.

These travellers carried with them the infection of their own malaise, and their prose reduced even the landscape to melancholia and self-contempt. Every endeavor is belittled as imitation, from architecture to music. There was this conviction in Froude that since History is based on achievement, and since the history of the Antilles was so genetically corrupt, so depressing in its cycles of massacres, slavery, and indenture, a culture was inconceivable and nothing could ever be created in those ramshackle ports, those monotonously feudal sugar estates. Not only the light and salt of Antillean mountains defied this, but the demotic vigour and variety of their inhabitants. Stand close to a waterfall and you will stop hearing its roar. To be still in the nineteenth century, like horses, as Brodsky has written, may not be such a bad deal, and much of our life in the Antilles still seems to be in the rhythm of the last century, like the West Indian novel.

By writers even as refreshing as Graham Greene, the Caribbean is looked at with elegiac pathos, a prolonged sadness to which Lévi-Strauss has supplied an epigraph: *Tristes Tropiques*. Their *tristesse* derives from an attitude to the Caribbean dusk, to rain, to uncontrollable vegetation, to the provincial ambition of Caribbean cities where brutal replicas of modern architecture dwarf the small houses and streets. The mood is understandable, the melancholy as contagious as the fever of the sunset, like the gold fronds of diseased coconut palms, but there is something alien and ultimately wrong in the way such a sadness, even a morbidity, is described by English, French, or some of our exiled writers. It relates to a misunderstanding of the light and the people on whom the light falls.

These writers describe the ambitions of our unfinished cities, their unrealized, homiletic conclusion, but the Caribbean city may conclude just at the point where it is satisfied with its own scale, just as Caribbean culture is not evolving but already shaped. Its proportions are not to be measured by the traveller or the exile, but by its own citizenry and architecture. To be told you are not yet a city or a culture requires this response. I am not your city or your culture. There might be less of *Tristes Tropiques* after that.

Here, on the raft of this dais, there is the sound of the applauding surf: our landscape, our history recognized, "at last." *At Last* is one of the first Caribbean books. It was written by the Victorian traveller Charles Kingsley. It is one of the early books to admit the Antillean landscape and its features into English literature. I have never read it but gather that its tone is benign. The Antillean archipelago was there to be written about, not to write itself, by Trollope, by Patrick Leigh-Fermor, in the very tone in which I almost wrote about the village spectacle at Felicity, as a compassionate and beguiled outsider, distancing myself from Felicity village even while I was enjoying it. What is hidden cannot be loved. The traveller cannot love, since love is stasis and travel is motion. If he returns to what he loved in a landscape and stays there, he is no longer a traveller but in stasis and concentration, the lover of that particular part of earth, a native. So many people say they "love the Caribbean," meaning that someday they plan to return for a visit but could never live there, the usual benign insult of the traveller, the tourist. These travellers, at their kindest, were devoted to the same patronage, the islands passing in profile, their vegetal luxury, their backwardness and poverty. Victorian prose dignified them. They passed by in beautiful profiles and were forgotten, like a vacation.

Alexis Saint-Léger Léger, whose writer's name is Saint-John Perse, was the first Antillean to win this prize for poetry. He was born in Guadeloupe and wrote in French, but before him, there was nothing as fresh and clear in feeling as those poems of his childhood, that of a privileged white child on an Antillean plantation, *"Pour Fêter une Enfance," "Éloges,"* and later *"Images à Crusoe."* At last, the first breeze on the page, salt-edged and self-renewing as the trade winds, the sound of pages and palm trees turning as "the odour of coffee ascents the stairs."

Caribbean genius is condemned to contradict itself. To celebrate Perse, we might be told, is to celebrate the old plantation system, to celebrate the *bequé,* or plantation rider, verandahs and mulatto servants, a white French language in a white pith helmet, to celebrate a rhetoric of patronage and hauteur; and even if Perse denied his origins, great writers often have this folly of trying to smother their source, we cannot deny him any more than we can the African Aimé Césaire. This is not accommodation, this is the ironic republic that is poetry, since, when I see cabbage palms moving their fronds at sunrise, I think they are reciting Perse.

The fragrant and privileged poetry that Perse composed to celebrate his white childhood and the recorded Indian music behind the brown young archers of Felicity, with the same cabbage palms against the same Antillean sky, pierce me equally. I feel the same poignancy of pride in the poems as in the faces. Why, given the history of the Antilles, should this be remarkable? The history of the world, by which of course we mean Europe, is a record of intertribal lacerations, of ethnic cleansings. At last, islands not written about but writing themselves! The palms and the Muslim minarets are Antillean exclamations. At last! the royal palms of Guadeloupe recite "*Éloges*" by heart.

Later, in "*Anabase,*" Perse assembled fragments of an imaginary epic, with the clicking teeth of frontier gates, barren wadis with the froth of poisonous lakes, horsemen burnoosed in sandstorms, the opposite of cool Caribbean mornings, yet not necessarily a contrast any more than some young brown archer at Felicity, hearing the sacred text blared across the flagged field, with its battles and elephants and monkey-gods, in a contrast to the white child in Guadeloupe assembling fragments of his own epic from the lances of the cane fields, the estate carts and oxens, and the calligraphy of bamboo leaves from the ancient languages, Hindi, Chinese, and Arabic, on the Antillean sky. From the *Ramayana* to Anabasis, from Guadeloupe to Trinidad, all that archaeology of fragments lying around, from the broken African kingdoms, from the crevasses of Canton, from Syria and Lebanon, vibrating not under the earth but in our raucous, demotic streets.

A boy with weak eyes skims a flat stone across the flat water of an Aegean inlet, and that ordinary action with the scything elbow contains the skipping lines of the *Iliad* and the *Odyssey,* and another child aims a bamboo arrow at a village festival, another hears the rustling march of cabbage palms in a Caribbean sunrise, and from that sound, with its fragments of tribal myth, the compact expedition of Perse's epic is launched, centuries and archipelagoes apart. For every poet it is always morning in the world. History a forgotten, insomniac night; History and elemental awe are always our early beginning, because the fate of poetry is to fall in love with the world, in spite of History.

There is a force of exultation, a celebration of luck, when a writer finds himself a witness to the early morning of a culture that is defining itself, branch by branch, leaf by leaf, in that self-defining dawn, which is why, especially at the edge of the sea, it is good to make a ritual of the sunrise. Then the noun, the "Antilles" ripples like brightening water, and the sounds of leaves, palm fronds, and birds are the sounds of a fresh dialect, the native tongue. The personal vocabulary, the individual melody whose metre is one's biography, joins in that sound, with any luck, and the body moves like a walking, a waking island.

This is the benediction that is celebrated, a fresh language and a fresh people, and this is the frightening duty owed.

I stand here in their name, if not their image — but also in the name of the dialect they exchange like the leaves of the trees whose names are suppler, greener, more morning-stirred than English — *laurier canelles, bois-flot, bois-canot* — or the valleys the trees mention — *Fond St. Jacques, Mabonya, Forestièr, Roseau, Mahaut* — or the empty beaches — *L'Anse Ivrogne, Case en Bas, Paradis* — all songs and histories in themselves, pronounced not in French — but in patois.

One rose hearing two languages, one of the trees, one of schoolchildren reciting in English:

I am monarch of all I survey,
My right there is none to dispute;
From the centre all round to the sea
I am lord of the fowl and the brute.
Oh, solitude! where are the charms
That sages have seen in thy face?
Better dwell in the midst of alarms,
Than reign in this horrible place . . .

While in the country to the same metre, but to organic instruments, hand-made violin, chac-chac, and goatskin drum, a girl named Sensenne singing:

Si mwen di 'ous' ça fait mwen la peine
'Ous kai dire ça vrai.
(If I told you that caused me pain
You'll say, "It's true.")
Si mwen di 'ous ça pentetrait mwen
'Ous peut dire ça vrai
(If I told you you pierced my heart
You'd say, "It's true.")
Ces mamailles actuellement
Pas ka faire l'amour z'autres pour un rien.
(Children nowadays
Don't make love for nothing.)

It is not that History is obliterated by this sunrise. It is there in Antillean geography, in the vegetation itself. The sea sighs with the drowned from the Middle Passage, the butchery of its aborigines, Carib and Aruac and Taino, bleeds in the scarlet of the immortelle, and even the actions of surf on sand cannot erase the African memory, or the lances of cane as a green prison where indentured Asians, the ancestors of Felicity, are still serving time.

That is what I have read around me from boyhood, from the beginnings of poetry, the grace of ef-

fort. In the hard mahogany of woodcutters: faces, resinous men, charcoal burners; in a man with a cutlass cradled across his forearm, who stands on the verge with the usual anonymous khaki dog; in the extra clothes he put on this morning, when it was cold when he rose in the thinning dark to go and make his garden in the heights, — the heights, the garden, being miles away from his house, but that is where he has his land — not to mention the fishermen, the footmen on trucks, groaning up mornes, all fragments of Africa originally but shaped and hardened and rooted now in the island's life, illiterate in the way leaves are illiterate; they do not read, they are there to be read, and if they are properly read, they create their own literature.

But in our tourist brochures the Caribbean is a blue pool into which the republic dangles the extended foot of Florida as inflated rubber islands bob and drinks with umbrellas float towards her on a raft. This is how the islands from the shame of necessity sell themselves; this is the seasonal erosion of their identity, that high-pitched repetition of the same images of service that cannot distinguish one island from another, with a future of polluted marinas, land deals negotiated by ministers, and all of this conducted to the music of Happy Hour and the rictus of a smile. What is the earthly paradise for our visitors? Two weeks without rain and a mahogany tan, and, at sunset, local troubadours in straw hats and floral shirts beating "Yellow Bird" and "Banana Boat Song" to death. There is a territory wider than this — wider than the limits made by the map of an island — which is the illimitable sea and what it remembers.

All of the Antilles, every island, is an effort of memory; every mind, every racial biography culminating in amnesia and fog. Pieces of sunlight through the fog and sudden rainbows, *arcs-enciel*. That is the effort, the labour of the Antillean imagination, rebuilding its gods from bamboo frames, phrase by phrase.

Decimation from the Aruac downwards is the blasted root of Antillean history, and the benign blight that is tourism can infect all of those island nations, not gradually, but with imperceptible speed, until each rock is whitened by the guano of white-winged hotels, the arc and descent of progress.

Before it is all gone, before only a few valleys are left, pockets of an older life, before development turns every artist into an anthropologist or folklorist, there are still cherishable places, little valleys that do not echo with ideas, a simplicity of rebeginnings, not yet corrupted by the dangers of change. Not nostalgic sites but occluded sanctities as common and simple as their sunlight. Places as threatened by this prose as a headland is by the bulldozer or a sea almond grove by the surveyor's string, or from blight, the mountain laurel.

One last epiphany: A basic stone church in a thick valley outside Soufrière, the hills almost shoving the houses around into a brown river, a sunlight that looks oily on the leaves, a backward place, unimportant, and one now being corrupted into significance by this prose. The idea is not to hallow or invest the place with anything, not even memory. African children in Sunday frocks come down the ordinary concrete steps into the church, banana leaves hang and glisten, a truck is parked in a yard, and old women totter towards the entrance. Here is where a real fresco should be painted, one without importance, but one with real faith, mapless, Historyless.

How quickly it could all disappear! And how it is beginning to drive us further into where we hope are impenetrable places, green secrets at the end of bad roads, headlands where the next view is not of a hotel but of some long beach without a figure and the hanging question of some fisherman's smoke at its far end. The Caribbean is not an idyll; not to its natives. They draw their working strength from it organically, like trees, like the sea almond or the spice laurel of the heights. Its peasantry and its fishermen are not there to be loved or even photographed; they are trees who sweat, and whose bark is filmed with salt, but every day on some island, rootless trees in suits are signing favourable tax breaks with entrepreneurs, poisoning the sea almond and the spice laurel of the mountains to their roots. A morning could come in which governments might ask what happened not merely to the forests and the bays but to a whole people.

They are here again, they recur, the faces, corruptible angels, smooth black skins and white eyes huge with an alarming joy, like those of the Asian children of Felicity at *Ramleela*; two different religions, two different continents, both filling the heart with the pain that is joy.

But what is joy without fear? The fear of selfishness that, here on this podium with the world paying attention not to them but to me, I should like to keep these simple joys inviolate, not because they are innocent, but because they are true. They are as true as when, in the grace of this gift, Perse heard the fragments of his own epic of Asia Minor in the rustling of cabbage palms, that inner Asia of the soul through which imagination wanders, if there is such a thing as imagination as opposed to the collective memory of our entire race, as true as the delight of that warrior-child who flew a bamboo arrow over the flags in the field at Felicity; and now as grateful a joy and a blessed fear as when a boy opened an exercise book and, within the discipline of its margins, framed stanzas that might contain the light of the hills on an island blest by obscurity, cherishing our insignificance.

The Year in the Novel

George Garrett
University of Virginia

Being declared a good writer is an obscure honor, like being elected to the Lacrosse Hall of Fame, which I believe is in Baltimore.

— Kurt Vonnegut, speaking at a memorial service for Richard Yates; quoted in the *Washington Post,* 27 December

The numbers are not yet available at this writing; so we are left for now with anecdotal evidence as to what kind of year 1992 was for the "literary" novel. Since the economy was slow in recovery and perceived to be weaker than it was until late in the year, since it was an election year at home and a year of crises and troubles abroad, it was generally taken by the publishing industry to be at least a slow year, maybe a bad one for most of its bumpy course. The novel was a low-priority item in the publishing scene. Some evidence of this is found in the book pages of the major newspapers, which devote roughly two-thirds of their coverage to nonfiction. (See "Book Reviewing in America VI.") But the perception of people in the business may have been more influenced by outside events and consensual moods than facts. Certainly it was a busy and interesting year for the novel. For the most part, with brief exciting exceptions when literary works appeared and disappeared like kids peeping over the top of a wall, the best-seller lists belonged to blockbusters and the makers thereof (a few new faces, but mostly the tried-and-true performers). Stephen King led the list twice, with two novels declared to be more "mainstream" than genre products – *Gerald's Game* (Viking) and, later in the year, *Dolores Claiborne* (Viking). Other best-selling performers included Judith Krantz (*Scruples Two,* Crown), Danielle Steel (*Jewels* and *Mixed Blessings,* Delacorte), James Michener (*Mexico,* Random House), Dick Francis (*Driving Force,* Putnam's), Sidney Sheldon (*The Stars Shine Down,* Morrow), pop singer Jimmy Buffett (*Where Is Joe Merchant?,* Harcourt Brace Jovanovich), lawyer John Grisham (*The Pelican Brief,* Doubleday), Anne Rice's latest vampire chronicle (*The Tale of the Body Thief,* Knopf) and

so forth and so on. Not many surprises, true, but there were a few. Robert James Waller found himself on the lists for a quiet love story, *The Bridges of Madison County* (Warner), raised to public interest chiefly by the enthusiasm of booksellers – or so the story goes. Nick Bantock's highly imaginative presentation of epistolary romance put two "novels" on all the lists: *Griffin & Sabine* and *Sabine's Notebook* (Chronicle). Several serious novels by African-American writers also found, for a time, places on the best-seller lists, most prominently Terry McMillan's *Waiting to Exhale* (Viking) and Toni Morrison's *Jazz* (Knopf), but also Alice Walker's forbidding and unpleasant *Possessing the Secret of Joy* (Harcourt Brace Jovanovich).

Another kind of book, written by someone with public visibility and presumably from some standpoint of inside knowledge, is the "Beltway Potboiler," at worst a quick buck earned and no harm done, by people such as Richard Perle (*Hard Line,* Random House), Jack Valenti (*Protect and Defend,* Doubleday), Tom Wicker (*Donovan's Wife,* Morrow), Marilyn T. Quayle and her sister Nancy T. Northcott (*Embrace the Serpent,* Crown), Jim Lehrer (*Short List,* Putnam's), and Robert MacNeil (*Burden of Desire,* Doubleday) – of the MacNeil-Lehrer News Hour – and others of the kind, most written, at best, in the easygoing style of Tom Wicker. A media consultant says of Wicker's congressman protagonist, "He may be dishwater in person but, believe me – on the tube Victor T. Donovan knocks your socks off." Other people playing the novel game in 1992 include actor Kirk Douglas with a story about Portuguese bullfighting (*The Gift,* Warner), publisher Michael Korda's novel about the affairs of the late John and Robert Kennedy with the late Marilyn Monroe (*The Immortals,* Poseidon), and former best-selling author Erich Segal's *Acts of Faith* (Bantam).

But the separation of literary fiction from the world of blockbusters was seldom challenged and rarely crossed. New York City may not be the heart of the land of the free and the home of the brave, but it remains the center of publishing and can produce a crowd of writers on reasonably short notice to talk on a variety of subjects. On the night of Thursday, 24 September, eight novelists – Harold Brodkey, Norman Mailer, Oscar Hijuelos, Norman Rush, Mona Simpson, Paule Marshall, Michael Cunningham, and Barbara Probst Solomon – appeared at Town Hall to sound off on "The Death of the Novel, the Life of the Novel." These dignitaries arrived at no significant conclusions. Earlier *Esquire,* in its annual June "literary" issue, presented the American literary world as a garden ("It's No Bed of Roses"), featuring blossoming writing programs and teacher\writers from coast to coast.

And the making and marketing of literary fiction busily continued. The introduction of new talent went bravely ahead, even though many literary agents asserted that it was a bad time for placing first novels. No first novel since, maybe, *Gone With the Wind* has received the attention that was lavished on Donna Tartt's *The Secret History* (Knopf). The book was reviewed and the author was interviewed everywhere. This attention generated extraordinary sales (no *Gone With the Wind, History* nevertheless sold more than two hundred thousand copies in hard cover) and made the author (together with Pongo, her dog) a public figure. Reviews were mixed. Madison Smartt Bell called it "a surprisingly good book" in the *Baltimore Sun* (27 September). And the *New Yorker* called the novel "the genuine article." Richard Eder of the *Los Angeles Times* (13 September) was less charitable: "Often it is hard to believe that Tartt is not, in fact, writing a far-fetched spoof." In the *New York Times Book Review* (13 September), Andrew Rosenheim noted some echoes of William Harrison's novel *In a Wild Sanctuary.* Lee Lascaze of the *Wall Street Journal* ("Groves of Academe Shed Gold and Yawns," 9 September) hurled a critical stun grenade: "*The Secret History* is the story of six loathesome students at a small, elite New England college (Ms. Tartt went to Bennington) who pursue a drunken, drug-using childish course through an exotic curriculum of Greek and Latin taught by a strange and cultic professor. Along the way they become murderers." "I've been interested in murder ever since I was a girl," Tartt told *Esquire* (September) for a story featuring her $450,000 advance – "Tartt's Sweet Deal." For "Tartt Language," she added the observation, to Paul Gediman of *Mirabella* (September): "All the great characters in novels, the ones we really love, are really evil. Becky Sharp, Captain Ahab, Mr. Kurtz." *The Secret History* is a pretty good novel by a gifted young writer, and the world-class hustle,

Dust jacket for Dorothy Allison's novel about growing up in a ' poor and troubled family in Greenville, South Carolina

from the promotion to the object itself – a book as pretty and chic in its design as any this year – was great fun while it lasted. No harm done. Unless you factor in the case of a somewhat similar story line (four college friends at Yale University kill a street person named Friar Pete, and that leads to more trouble) in *Falling Leaves of Ivy* (Longmeadow), the first novel of African-American Yolanda Joe.

There were first novel writers who had earlier established themselves in other genres. Among those are several that merit significant attention. Dorothy Allison had already published *Trash* (1989), an award-winning collection of stories, before she brought out her extraordinary and powerful novel, *Bastard Out of Carolina* (Dutton), the story of Ruth Anne, called "Bone," growing up in a large, poor, troubled, and lively family in and around Greenville, South Carolina. Told in a steady and perfectly controlled first-person narrative, in a style that can curse or caress at will, Allison's story offers up unflinching and unsentimental details of pov-

Rita Dove, author of Through the Ivory Gate *(photograph by Fred Viebahn)*

erty. In a rare moment of self-consciousness, Bone reflects (accurately) on her future:

> Stupid or smart, there wasn't much choice about what was going to happen to me, or to Grey and Garvey, or to any of us. Growing up was like falling into a hole. The boys would quit school and sooner or later go to jail for something silly . . . What was I going to do in five years? Work in the textile mill? Join Mama at the diner? It all looked bleak to me. No wonder people got crazy as they grew up.

There is no conventional happy ending, but the superbly dimensional Bone endures everything and is powerfully alive – "I would be thirteen in a few weeks. I was already who I was going to be." This novel has been nominated for several of the year's prizes.

Robin Hemley is another topflight story writer (*All You Can Eat*, 1988) who made the leap to the novel form. His story of a small, troubled family in South Bend, Indiana (where the last Studebaker plant closed down, bringing disaster to them), in

The Last Studebaker (Graywolf) has not yet received the attention it deserves. *Through the Ivory Gate* (Pantheon) by poet Rita Dove (a Pulitzer Prize winner in 1987) is best described in the author's own words (*Charlottesville* (Virginia) *Daily Progress,* 20 December): "In *Through the Ivory Gate* my main character is a black woman (Virginia King) – a puppeteer in her mid 20's. The novel takes place in the mid-1970s, right after the Watergate era. You see Watergate and how it touches her, but it's from a distance. You get a sense of the mood of the time." Since the book deals with the African-American experience, some readers were surprised at the absence of the conventional tropes of rage and self-pity. Novelist and poet Kelly Cherry, reviewing the novel for the *Los Angeles Times* (22 November), called it "almost shocking in its sweet optimism, its willingness to forgive. Here is narrative prose whose first impulse is to describe the world precisely, without preconception." Another established story writer, Susan Straight, who is not black but writes about African-Americans, told the story of twenty-five years in the life of Marietta Cook, a Gullah-speaking woman in the South Carolina Low Country in *I Been in Sorrow's Kitchen and Licked Out All the Pots* (Hyperion). Meanwhile, some African-American first novelists presented different angles on "the black experience." In *Company Man* (Algonquin) Brent Wade tells the story of a black corporate executive who has come close to losing his ethnic heritage, what his sharp-tongued grandmother calls his "niggerishness." Dennis A. Williams, a former journalist now teaching at Cornell, writes of the conflicts of a young black man in an Ivy League college arising between his goals and his aspirations and his growing sense of his black identity. His novel, *Crossover* (Summit), is set in the late 1960s and early 1970s. In *Your Blues Ain't Like Mine* (Putnam's), loosely based on the murder of Emmett Till (the victim, Armstrong Todd, is murdered for speaking French to a white woman), Bebe Moore Campbell covers the history of her times from the 1950s through the 1980s. Author of two previous works of nonfiction, Campbell was praised by reviewers for her empathetic ability to create white characters as well as black. Another murder is crucial to the plot of *1959* (Grove Weidenfeld) by Thulani Davis, who has published poetry and been active in film and theater (she wrote the libretto for the opera *X: The Life and Times of Malcolm X*). Her central character, Willie Tarrant, tells what happened in her twelfth year ("Billie Holiday died and I turned twelve on the same hot July day"), just as the civil rights movement was stumbling into being in the town of

Turner, Virginia. This, too, is a story of the black middle class; Willie's father is a college professor. Best known and most widely and favorably reviewed among these first novels by African-American writers is Darryl Pinckney's *High Cotton* (Farrar, Straus and Giroux), which won Pinckney the 1992 Art Seidenbaum Award for First Fiction given by the *Los Angeles Times*. (The short list of finalists included *1959*.) Pinckney, who lives in Berlin, has written a richly ironic account of growing up black and well-to-do in America and Europe, together with a generational history seen from the point of view of the unnamed first person narrator. This young man is witty, intelligent, clear-eyed, and open-minded. ("I had not been South since my childhood and still believed in the hurry-sundown Dixie of movieland. The New South was a surprise.") Educated at Columbia University, Pinckney had already received most of the major grants and awards before this book was published.

Three first novels by white women deal directly with interracial love affairs. In Sandie Frazier's *I Married Vietnam* (Braziller), the narrator, Samantha, tells the story of her black husband, Jeremy Freeman, a Vietnam veteran who met and married her after the war. *Doin' the Box-Step* (Random House), by Suzanne Falter-Barns, is a social satire set in Chestnut Hill ("Beechwood"), in which the rich young heroine's fiancé is an African-American, Bennett Edwards, whose "blackness" is scarcely noticed by anyone else in the story. The best of these novels by far is Nanci Kincaid's *Crossing Blood* (Putnam's). This tells the fully realized and complex story of two families who live close together on California Street in Tallahassee and whose lives are much engaged during the early 1960s. The central character is the white girl, Lucy Conyers, who comes to love Skippy, the son of the Conyers's maid:

> I closed my eyes and listened to his heart make fists, his red blood pumping. I began to cry. I put my arms around his neck and held to him as tightly as I could, wanting this to be a skinless hug, where our blood would join and run together like crazy.

Kincaid has published short stories which have been widely praised and selected for anthologies.

Todd Gitlin, who has written six books of television criticism and social commentary, created *The Murder of Albert Einstein* (Farrar, Straus and Giroux) featuring Margo Ross, "a connoisseur of disappointment" and TV reporter for the show "In Depth" and her friend, "cult novelist and connoisseur of

conspiracy," Harry Kramer. They follow a lead, trying to determine after forty years if Einstein was murdered. It turns into a thriller and may lead to another novel with the character Margo Ross. Another figure involved in American popular culture, screenwriter and producer Harold Nebenzal, crafted the novel *Cafe Berlin* (Overlook), a story actually authored in diary form from November 1943 to 30 April 1945 by Daniel Saporta, a Jew in hiding. Much of his story concerns the final days of the Weimar Republic and the first years of the Third Reich, during which he ran a successful cabaret – Klub Kaukasus. The story is a fine-tuned mixture of fact and fiction, though Nebenzal insists on the factual framework for it all: "The political and military events described herein are historically sound and in no way fictitious." Spalding Gray, who has earned a national reputation as an autobiographical monologuist on stage and television, does much the same thing on the printed page with *Impossible Vacation* (Knopf) using "Brewster North" to tell a personal story.

Of all the writers who have standing reputations for mastery in other forms, no first novelist coming on the scene has the accumulated honor and interest earned by Annie Dillard. With a book of poems and six works of nonfiction, which have earned her awards and a cult status among readers, her first book-length work of fiction aroused great interest and received widespread attention. Dillard's *The Living* (HarperCollins) is a large-scale story set in the Washington Territory in the town of Whatcom on Bellingham Bay, from the middle to the end of the nineteenth century. Roughly, it is bracketed by the Fraser River gold rush of 1858 and the Klondike rush of 1897. It is organized in seven "Books" and seventy-five chapters, concerning a host of characters and families, native Americans as well as settlers, but chiefly built around the lives of three men: Clare Fishburn, John Ireland Sharp, and Beal Obenchain. The picture of the life of the settlers is a harsh one, and death is constant and commonplace: "Men died from trafficking in superior forces, like rivers and horses, bulls, steam saws, mill gears, quarried rock, or falling trees and rolling logs. Women died in the rivers, too, and under trees and rockslides, and men took fevers, too, and fevers took men." *The Living* earned mixed reviews. In the *Wall Street Journal* ("Death Comes to the Northwest Coast") Merle Rubin describes it as "this shapeless, depressing, endless-seeming novel." The *New York Times Book Review* took a much more positive position, selecting *The Living* for its "Notable Books of the Year" (6 December), describing it as a novel "in

THE ENGLISH PATIENT

Michael Ondaatje

Dust jacket for the novel that was the co-winner of the 1992 Booker Prize

a genuine epic mode, [that] concerns what befell nearly everyone in the 19th-century Washington Territory."

Several first novels were written by authors with famous family names. Esther Freud, a twenty-nine-year-old actress and the great-granddaughter of Sigmund Freud, published an autobiographical novel, *Hideous Kinky* (Harcourt Brace Jovanovich), about young children traveling with their mother in Morocco. Lorian Hemingway, granddaughter of Ernest Hemingway, writes of madness and murder as she relates the life of Eva, daughter of psychopathic parents, in *Walking Into the River* (Simon and Schuster). Benjamin Cheever, son of the late John Cheever and editor of *The Letters of John Cheever,* tells a version of his own life in *The Plagiarist* (Atheneum), a comic accounting of the life and hard times of one

Arthur Prentice, son of Icarus Prentice, "an aging, acerbic, alcoholic, and much-acclaimed American writer."

Two first novels use Columbia University and its graduate school as their settings. Alisa Kwitney's *'Till the Fat Lady Sings* (HarperCollins) is concerned with Manya Mitelman and her friend, the punk queen Ophelia. Manya studies Victorian feminist literature under the celebrated Emilia Larsdaiter. But it is the style, not the substance, which identifies this novel. Writing for the *New York Times Book Review* (6 September), Maxine Chernoff does her level best to describe the singularity of the novel: "If Milan Kundera, Tama Janowitz and Dr. Joyce Brothers had collaborated on a book, they might have replicated Alisa Kwitney's imaginative and quirky first novel, "'Till the Fat Lady Sings." Kwitney is an editor for *DC Comics.* Iris Vegan ("I was the daughter of a linguistics professor and a Norwegian mother, born and bred in a small town, Webster, Minnesota. I had first come to New York for graduate school at Columbia University in literature") is the heroine of Siri Hustvedt's *The Blindfold* (Poseidon). She studies and has an affair with Professor Michael Rose who teaches "Hegel, Marx and the Nineteenth Century Novel." And, innocently at the outset, she studies in the school of hard and strange experience in the city, strongly affected, in separate episodes, by four strong, complicated characters, the most important of which is Paris, "the small, unattractive, but not uninteresting art critic." In the end she must flee from him (and herself) when he articulates the truth about her: "I think you are interested in dirt, in a hint of cruelty. It excites you. Life is a circus, my dear. Why fight it?" Hustvedt's novel received considerable attention from reviewers, in part because of its subject matter, in part because she is the wife of novelist Paul Auster, to whom the book is dedicated, and partly, perhaps, because of strong dust-jacket endorsements by Don DeLillo, Russell Banks, and Peter Straus. Another first novel involving graduate school in New York in the 1970s is Jean McGarry's *The Courage of Girls* (Rutgers University Press). And originating from Columbia University Press is the first novel by critic/scholar Julia Kristeva, *The Samurai.* This is an autobiographical roman à clef involving most of the prominent postwar French intellectuals, some by name and some with pseudonyms. (American Philip Roth makes an appearance as Jerry Saltzman.) Perhaps a summation for all these academic novels is the casual remark of one character in *The Samurai* – "Do these people have any idea how strange they seem?"

Not regional, but deeply rooted in region and place, are several of the year's best first novels. The territory explored by Carolyn Chute in *The Beans of Egypt, Maine* (1985), the grinding poverty of rural upper New England, is examined artfully in *Cold Times* (Summit) by Elizabeth Jordan Moore and *Postcards* (Scribners) by E. Annie Proulx. Proulx had previously published a collection of short stories, *Heart Songs* (1988), but this is a large novel, a saga of fifty years, beginning in the 1940s. Proulx follows her protagonist, Loyal Blood, as he flees across the country, finding no escape from the weight of poverty and loss. Meanwhile his family at home suffers a destructive sequence of terrible losses. Moore's *Cold Times* involves two troubled and suffering and connected families, the Rudges and the Pembrokes, and is set in and around Portland, Maine. Madison Smartt Bell is accurate in calling attention (in a jacket endorsement) to "her extraordinarily graceful and expressive writing," adding: "There are precious few contemporary writers who could rival the careful nuance of her prose – or approach the power of its carefully refined ferocity." Poet, editor, and storywriter Robley Wilson brought out a novel also set in Maine. *The Victim's Daughter* (Simon and Schuster) concerns a violent murder and the search for the killer in Scoggin, Maine. *Little Altars Everywhere* (Broken Moon), by Rebecca Wells, was the winner of the Western States Book Award for 1992. Wells is a resident of Seattle but writes in this novel about her native region and people – the Walker family clan of Thornton, Louisiana. The story is told by several narrators and covers roughly thirty years up to the present. Among the novel's voices, none has attracted more attention than Miss Siddalee Walker ("a force of nature and a tool of fate"). South Carolina in the late 1960s is the setting for M. A. Harper's *For the Love of Robert E. Lee,* in which Garnet Laney, a sixteen-year-old with a deformed leg, is obsessed with the image and reality of Robert E. Lee. Another Southern story is *Begin to Exit Here* (Algonquin) by John Welter. Welter, a writer of a humor column in the *Chapel Hill* (N.C.) *Herald,* writes about Kurt Clausen, a journalist and recovering alcoholic. Upper East Side Manhattan is the world for a group of first wives who join together to bring grief and woe to their former husbands in *The First Wives Club* (Poseidon) by Olivia Goldsmith. Atlanta is the setting for two novels: Marilyn Dorn Staats's *Looking For Atlanta* (Georgia), the story of one Margaret Hunter Bridges in suburban Atlanta in 1981; and an outstanding work by Liza Wieland, *The Names of the Lost* (Southern Methodist University Press). This story, told in mysterious and lyri-

cal language by a series of narrators, is mainly set during the summer of 1980, when black children were being kidnapped and murdered in Atlanta. Wieland is a master of character; all of her speakers, and the others around them – young and old, black and white – ring deeply true. This novel introduces a major new talent, and Southern Methodist University Press, which is rapidly earning a name for "cutting edge" publishing, deserves congratulations and gratitude for bringing *The Names of the Lost* to life.

The American West and Midwest serve as more than theatrical background for several of the year's new novelists. Curtis White's *Idea of Home* (Sun and Moon) is an autobiographical story of growing up in the 1950s and 1960s in a persistently counterculture milieu in San Lorenzo, California. Robin Cody's *Ricochet River* (Knopf) – set in the Oregon logging town of Calamus in the summer of 1960 and told by Wade, a high school senior – concerns the impact on the community of Jesse Howl, a Kalamath Indian. Robert James Waller's *Bridges of Madison County* (Warner) is set in Iowa, telling the story of a brief affair between a photographer and a farmwife. Thanks to the interest and enthusiasm of booksellers, it sold more than one hundred thousand copies in hard cover. Seeking to explain why it pleased sellers and readers, David Streitfeld writes (*Washington Post Book World,* 30 August): "This is a novel for all those who hope that someone incredibly wonderful is waiting for them elsewhere, but who meanwhile want to reassure themselves they've made the right choice by staying exactly where they are. It's a contradictory message, but apparently pleasing to many." Houston, Texas, is the setting of *The Lord's Motel* (Persea), the story of Colleen Sweeney and her "service-to-the-Unserved" library program. Thanks to her no-good boyfriend, Web Disiderio, she gets into serious trouble with the law and needs the down-home services of Chisholm Jim, a Texas-style lawyer. Idaho is the setting for *Her Monster* (Soho) by Jeff Collignon. A version of "Beauty and the Beast," it tells the story of Eddie Talbot, hunchbacked and hairy and the author of an apocalyptic sci-fi novel, and the beautiful Katherine. Plain in style, it won praise from Scott Bradfield in the *New York Times Book Review* (21 June):

> There is something roughly hewn about it, much like Eddie. It is wildly improbable, preposterously melodramatic and cornball, and often rather crudely written – yet on every page it communicates a powerful sense of loneliness, self-estrangement and loss.

Bradfield calls *Her Monster* "a moving and unforgettable first novel." Walter Kirn, previously an editor for *Vanity Fair* and *Spy* (even now he writes pieces for magazines such as *Mirabella* and *GQ*) and a former Mormon farmboy, writes his first novel, *She Needed Me* (Pocket), about born-again Weaver Walquist and Kim Lindgren, who meet in front of an abortion clinic in Saint Paul, Minnesota. They make a pilgrimage together to the Walquist family farm in North Dakota. And love conquers all. *She Needed Me* received widespread national notice. John Blades, formerly book editor for the *Chicago Tribune,* writes in *Small Game* (Holt) about Scott Ryan, who buys an old house in the suburbs and tries to restore it. Kodiak Island, Alaska, is where Jack Dempsey Cliff goes in search of news and truth about his dead father in David Cates's *Hunger in America* (Simon and Schuster).

Many of 1992's first novels have foreign settings or are written by foreign writers. South Dakota lawyer and politician Vincent S. Green creates a classy legal thriller with depth and resonance in *The Price of Victory* (Walker), a story of dope dealing and murder in the U.S. Army in Germany. Francisco Goldman, a New Yorker and a contributing editor of *Harper's,* writes with such authenticity about Guatemala and is so at ease with the techniques of Latin American writing that his fiction has been mistaken for translation. Goldman has Guatemalan roots, and he writes about them in the heavily promoted *Long Night of the White Chickens* (Atlantic Monthly Press). It is the story of Roger Graetz, his father, a Jew from Boston, and his mother, a Guatemalan aristocrat. Set mainly in Guatemala in the 1980s it tells, in the ways of "magic realism," the story of Roger and his best friend, the journalist Luis Moya, and their search for the answer to the murder of Flor de Mayo, once the Graetz's family maid (they send her through Wellesley College), "more than a sister, less than a lover: she is an obsession." Technically, it is adventurous, shifting from first to third person and back, sometimes with the narrator's and Roger's points of view merging then splitting apart; and it moves freely fore and aft in time. Daniel Richler (son of Mordecai Richler) sets *Kicking Tomorrow* (Random House) in Montreal in the 1970s. It tells the tale of Robbie Bookbinder, eighteen-year-old punk rocker in the band "Hell's Yells." The book is described in the *New York Times Book Review* as "a sex, drugs and rock-and-roll extravaganza." Jean Rouaud's *Fields of Glory* (Arcade) won France's Prix Goncourt. A nostalgic account of life on the lower Loire in the 1950s, it is a best-seller in France. Brazilian poet and actress Ana Miranda writes of seventeenth-century Bahia in *The Bay of All Saints and Every Conceivable Sin* (Viking). At the center of her story, built around the assassination of Bahia's military commander, are two historical figures – the Jesuit padre António Vieira and the poet Gregório de Matos Guerra. Another novel set in the past, making use of historical figures, is Brian O'Doherty's *The Strange Case of Mademoiselle P.* (Pantheon). Set in eighteenth-century Vienna, it depicts the treatment of a blind patient, Marie Therese Paradies, by the celebrated doctor – and the original hypnotist – Franz Anton Mesmer. Somewhat more complex in the blending of fact and fiction in the context of historical fiction are Allen Kurzwell's *A Case of Curiosities* (Harcourt Brace Jovanovich) and Lawrence Norfolk's *Lempriere's Dictionary* (Harmony). Kurzwell tells a complex and fascinating story of Claude Page, an eighteenth-century creator whose masterpiece, the Talking Turk, was able to say "Vive le roi," alas just in time for the French Revolution. The mechanical Turk was subsequently guillotined for his impudence. Norfolk's *Dictionary* is about as intricate and complicated as a novel can get and still be more or less accessible. Several discreet events – the founding of the East India Company and the siege of La Rochelle, both in the seventeenth century, and the creation of John Lempriere's celebrated dictionary of classical myth (out of Ovid and elsewhere) – are shown, in the world of the novel at least, to be closely related and dependent. The main, if somewhat hazy, line of action begins on the island of Jersey in 1780, but time is relative here. With high hopes the publisher invokes Umberto Eco and *The Name of the Rose* in the first sentence of the jacket copy. But this brilliant book, widely reviewed with enthusiasm and courage, is sui generis: "at once a quest, a tragedy, a political thriller, and a cultural meditation," the *London Times* put it. Reviewing it for the *Chicago Tribune,* Paul West called it "a wonderful epitome of the mind's inwardness." Not a lot easier and an equal challenge to the powers of book reviewers are *When Nietzsche Wept* (Basic), by Irvin K. Yalom, a psychiatrist and professor of psychiatry at Stanford University, and Massachusetts Institute of Technology physicist Alan Lightman's *Einstein's Dreams* (Pantheon). Yalom's book, the second novel published in the forty-year history of Basic Books, is set in October 1882 in Vienna and brings together "real" characters (Sigmund Freud, Friedrich Nietzsche, the fabulous Lou Andreas-Salomé, and Dr. Josef Breuer) with fictional ones – Yalom, for example, gives Josef Breuer a brother, Max the urologist. Lightman's book deals with thirty imaginary dreams of Albert Einstein in Bern, Switzerland, during April, May, and June of 1905, just as he was putting together his theory of relativity. As Richard Eder describes the thirty dreams (*Los Angeles Times,* 10 January 1993), they are "fables that imagine the sub-conscious seed bed from which the thinker's theory of time – part of his work on relativity – emerges." Time is different in each of the dreams that compose the subtle larger fable. "Time weeps and laughs in the perplexed inhabitants of his fables," Eder writes, "and it glitters in the radiant mountaintops and painted sky that suddenly overshadow their humanity in a story about time ending."

The intricate fusion of fact and fiction, almost a convention of this year's literature, is tested in *Alma* (Houghton Mifflin) by British journalist and nonfiction writer Gordon Burn. It was perceived as a work serious enough to merit an essay review by Hilary Mantel in the *New York Review of Books* (24 September). The historical Alma Coogan, a pop singer famous for novelty numbers such as "Never Do A Tango With An Eskimo," died in 1966. But in this novel she lives on into the present. More surprisingly (and a subject of some serious critical argument in England), this is a first-person narration, told by Alma in her own voice. The voice has great freedom and is not seriously imitative of or limited to her presumed "real" style. Defending Burn's liberties, Mantel wrote: "The impersonation of the voices of the dead is an interesting enterprise, no doubt, but some would feel it is outmoded and essentially dishonest." The story manages to recapitulate the terrible events involving a pair of British serial killers, Myra Hindley and Ian Brady – a story, then, of the madness close to the heart of popular culture. American writer Michael Herr calls it "a dark meditation on fame" and "a ruthless antidote to nostalgia." Also from Britain came a first novel by an author of ten works of nonfiction. Peter Conrad, who teaches literature at Oxford, produced a kind of fantasy novel in *Underworld* (Poseidon), the principal irony of which is that the present reality is so dangerously close to the dystopia he imagines. Almost in the form of a timeless parable, *Underworld* tells of a shining city and its next-door neighbor, the Valley, full of huts and peopled by criminals, the homeless, crazies, and outcasts. The conflict of classes leads to terrible things.

From Ireland came *The Run of the Country* (St. Martin's Press), written by Shane Connaughton, author of the screenplay of the film *My Left Foot*. The novel covers a year in the life of a seventeen-year-old boy in a border community. *The Killing Frost* (St.

Martin's Press) is an Irish historical novel leading up to the events of the 1916 Easter Rebellion. The author, Thomas Hayden, died before the book appeared. From Scotland arrived *O Caledonia* (Harcourt Brace Jovanovich) by Elspeth Barker, widow of British poet George Barker, which is centered on the story of the disturbed eldest daughter of a Scottish family who lives in a crumbling castle. Under the pseudonym of Sonia Rami came the Egyptian novel *Antiquity Street* (Farrar, Straus and Giroux). A huge best-seller in Mexico since it first appeared in 1990, Laura Esquivel's *Like Water For Chocolate* (Doubleday) is a contemporary narrative with its story built around the recipe collection of great-aunt Tita. The novel is presented in the form of monthly installments, including recipes, romances, and home remedies. Probably no first novel of foreign origin received more attention and praise than Sunetra Gupta's story of an Indian woman from Calcutta living in London in *Memories of Rain* (Grove Weidenfeld). Fellow countryman Shashi Tharoor, an under secretary at the United Nations and himself a distinguished novelist, wrote in the *Washington Post Book Review* (29 March): "Not since Anita Desai has an Indian woman written like this or written so well." Other first novels of 1992 which deserve honorable mention include: *Worry Beads* (Louisiana State University Press) by Kay Sloan; *The Day the Televisions Stopped* (Harcourt Brace Jovanovich) by S. B. Sutton; *A Matter of Life and Sex* (Dutton) by Oscar Moore; *She's Come Undone* (Pocket) by Wally Lamb; *Salaryman* (Viking) by Meg Pei; *The Sharpest Sight* (University of Oklahoma Press) by Louis Owens; and an autobiographical novel, *Dreams of Long Lasting* (Warner), by Mark Medoff, author of the play and film *Children of a Lesser God*.

The year was a busy one for new and old editions of novels out of print, as well as new translations of classic works. J. S. Sanders of Nashville, under the series editorship of M. E. Bradford, continued to add to its Southern Classics Series reprintings of Southern literature in uniform trade paperback editions, each with an introduction by a contemporary critic or novelist. These editions range from works by Augustus Baldwin Longstreet and Thomas Nelson Page to those by Robert Penn Warren (*Night Rider*) and Andrew Lytle (*A Wake for the Living*). Meanwhile the Library of America Editions continued to bring out editions of classic American authors – notably in 1992, Sinclair Lewis. Beginning in the fall of 1991 Knopf "relaunched" the Everyman Library and by the end of 1992 had brought out 110 titles, each with a new introduction. Random House likewise resurrected the Mod-

Ian McEwan, author of Black Dogs *(photograph by Jane Bown)*

ern Library list, sometimes using different editions of the same titles. Some observers were baffled that two imprints within the same corporation would be in competition with each other. But the alternative was to allow a competitive corporation to develop one of these series. As it is, for the time being at least, they are both "under the same umbrella," Advance Publications. Howard Fast, who had once been blacklisted and forced to publish his work under pen names, brought forward a new edition of the novel *Sylvia* (Brich Lane), his name replacing "E. V. Cunningham." Richard Pevear and Larissa Volokhonsky produced a new translation of Fyodor Dostoyevski's *Crime and Punishment* (Knopf). Anchor Books brought back the work of an African-American writer of the 1920s with *An Intimation of Things Distant: The Collected Fiction of Nella Larsen.* Working closer to our own time, Southern Methodist University Press published trade paperback editions of John Yount's *Hardcastle,* a story of Kentucky coal mining in the 1930s; R. G. Vliet's *Rockspring,* the tale of the abduction of a fourteen-year-old girl by Mexican outlaws, set in Texas in the 1830s; and Alan Cheuse's *The Tennessee Waltz.* H. D.'s previously unpublished novel *Asphodel* was published

by Duke University Press. Harcourt Brace Jovanovich published a fiftieth anniversary edition of Eudora Welty's *A Curtain of Green.* Another book resurrected after more than sixty years (originally published in German in 1928) was Austrian writer Leo Perutz's story of the obsessive, vengeful search of Georg Vittorin for Selyukov, the commandant of a czarist Russian prison camp – *Little Apple* (Little, Brown). Robert DeMaria's black comedy, *The Satyr,* of twenty years ago was brought out by Second Chance. Carroll and Graf published *Anthony Trollope: The Complete Shorter Fiction,* and Cambridge University Press produced the "unexpurgated" version of D. H. Lawrence's *Sons and Lovers,* based on the original manuscript. Milan Kundera's *The Joke* (1969) was republished by HarperCollins in a revised and newly translated edition. Soho published a new edition of Nora Wain's *The House of Exile,* a best-seller in 1933. Sholom Aleichem's *The Bloody Hoax,* a story of Jews in czarist Russia, reappeared, courtesy of Indiana University Press. Ann Petry's story of Harlem in the 1940s, *The Street,* was republished by Houghton Mifflin. McPherson brought out G. V. Desani's picaresque novel written in an inventive dialect of "Rigamarole English," *All About H. Hatterr* (1948). This Indian novel has been admired by T. S. Eliot, Saul Bellow, Anthony Burgess, and others. *The Dangerous Age,* a Danish novel by Karin Michaelis, first published in 1910 and dealing with the mid-life crisis of Elsie Lindtner, once sold a million copies in twelve languages and has been the basis of three movies. The newest edition is from Northwestern University Press.

The huge success of Alexander Ripley's *Scarlet* (1991) led publishers to look for other highly commercial sequels. After a good deal of press coverage in England, British writer Susan Hill signed on to write a sequel to Daphne du Maurier's *Rebecca.* On the other hand, plans to develop a sequel to Boris Pasternak's *Dr. Zhivago* collapsed when his estate unconditionally rejected the idea. The saddest sequel of the year was surely *Leaving Cold Sassy: The Unfinished Sequel to "Cold Sassy Tree"* (Ticknor and Fields) by the late Olive Ann Burns, who died in 1990. The fragmentary sequel sends the novel's Will Tweedy to college, graduation, and his marriage to a schoolteacher. The book includes an appreciation of Burns by its editor Katrina Kenison.

Many diverse ways of building on an earlier success were tried by other serious writers. Marguerite Duras, for example, put together a narrative much like a screen treatment of her earlier novel, *The Lover,* in *The North China Lover* (New Press). Evidently Duras, whose own screenplay had been rejected, was not pleased with the film version of *The Lover.* Another novel by Duras, *Summer Rain* (Scribners) is also based on a film of her own, *Les Enfants* (1984). Robert Roper, in *The Trespassers* (Ticknor and Fields), uses the plot of D. H. Lawrence's *Lady Chatterly's Lover,* calling it "a retelling." This version, Roper's third novel, is set in California and involves Catherine and Rick Mansure and Henry Bascombe, a part-time musician who "gardens" marijuana. Michiko Kakutani complains in the *New York Times* (24 November) of "embarrassingly mawkish passages that make the reader cringe." In *H: The Story of Heathcliff's Journey Back to Wuthering Heights* (Pocket), Lin Hare-Sargeant produces at once a sequel, a critique, and a revision of *Wuthering Heights* (1847). On a train to Leeds, Charlotte Brontë, principal narrator of this story, meets and talks with characters from *Wuthering Heights.* Emily Brontë tells Charlotte: "Some stories can never be told. The heart of some stories can never be known. They can only be felt." Geoff Ryman's fourth novel, *Was* (Knopf), depends on *The Wizard of Oz,* as a book and film. In what Kakutani of the *New York Times* calls (9 June) "an inventive improvisation on Frank Baum's classic story," Ryman handles three distinct, related narrative threads. One involves the "real" Dorothy and her sad story in nineteenth-century Kansas. L. Frank Baum is her teacher for a time. Dorothy grows up to be a prostitute and is finally committed to an institution called "Home." This story is intercut with stories involving Judy Garland in Hollywood and a narrative of Jonathan, a contemporary actor in Los Angeles dying of AIDS, whose favorite book is *The Wizard of Oz.* In a note Ryman tells readers that he is "a fantasy writer who fell in love with realism."

Yet another sort of sequel involves expanding, revising, and rearranging one's own fiction. For example, Leonard Michaels in *Sylvia,* a paperback original published by Mercury House, returns in a "fictional memoir" to material he earlier treated in both fiction and nonfiction, mainly the story of his own marriage, which ended with the suicide of his wife Sylvia. Here the story is revised, seen from different angles, and modified. To be sure, an autobiographical novelist, one working in the form of the fictional memoir, is revising events and creating sequels out of subsequent ones. Clancy Sigal's *Secret Defector* (HarperCollins) is a case in point. Sigal, who once had an affair with novelist Doris Lessing — one publicly acknowledged on both sides — appears as the character Saul Green in Lessing's celebrated novel *The Golden Notebook.* Here, in his

version of the affair, he is Gus Black, and Lessing is Rose O'Malley. Just in case anybody should fail to understand the underpinnings of this fiction, he wrote a factual account of it for the *New York Times Book Review* (12 April): "'You Can't Do It!' I Shouted. 'Oh, Can't I?' She Shouted Back." Sigal's story is sincere and, intentionally or otherwise, sincerely funny: "How had I, a future hero of Socialist Writing, a once or future Jack London or John Reed, become a kept man?" Sigal might well and wisely have listened to Hungarian writer George Konrad in *his* autobiographical novel *A Feast in the Garden* (Harcourt Brace): "Reality is indescribable, and publicizing your private life is boring and improper."

Ever more imaginative and adventurous, contemporary British fiction is more and more familiar to American readers. Part of the transatlantic impetus comes from the fact that British companies own large chunks of several American publishing conglomerates. The work and literary habits of British writers are well enough known that John Banville (literary editor of the *Irish Times*) could have some fun at their expense in a 14 May review in the *New York Review of Books:*

> Alternatives have occurred, accommodations have been reached; Julian Barnes has adapted French theory for English tastes, Martin Amis has learned to bellow with the best of the Americans. David Lodge and Malcolm Bradbury have taken the campus novel and turned it into a barometer of social change, even magic realism has been absorbed, especially in the work of women writers such as Jeanette Winterton and the late Angela Carter.

Another sign of the security of British writers on the American scene in 1992 is the unique gesture of the *Washington Post Book World* in commissioning David Lodge to write a series of brief essays on aspects of the art and craft of the novelist.

In a note an author writes: "Fact and fiction are so interwoven in this book that it may help the reader to know what is historical and what is not." The writer is Pat Barker and her novel, *Regeneration* (Dutton), was on every list of the best books of 1992. It is the factually correct story of (real) Dr. William Rivers of Craiglockhart War Hospital, where he treats the poets Wilfred Owen and Siegfried Sassoon, healing them so that they can return to the Great War. Robert Graves is also involved, and H. G. Wells and Bertrand Russell play cameo roles. The *New York Times* (6 December) calls it "a magnificent antiwar novel." It is put more concretely by Sassoon to Owen in the novel: "A hundred years from now they'll still be ploughing up skulls." Another novel – set in the time of another war, World War II – which also ended up on all lists of the "best" is *The English Patient* (Knopf) by Michael Ondaatje. Born in Sri Lanka, Ondaatje is, in fact, a Canadian, and his poetry has won two Governor General's Awards; but this book comes to us from Britain where it was a cowinner of the Booker Prize. Set in the Villa San Girolamo in Italy during the final days of World War II, the novel involves four central characters. Selecting *Patient* as number one on its list – *the* best work of fiction in 1992 – *Time* writes: "Ondaatje's characters – a dying burn victim, a young nurse, a morphine thief and a Sikh defuser of unexploded Luftwaffe bombs – are spun of dreams and verbal magic." A cowinner of the Booker Prize was Barry Unsworth, whose *Sacred Hunger* (Doubleday) is the complex story of the *Liverpool Merchant,* a slave ship in 1752. Fatal disease on board leads to revolt and mutiny. The survivors join together, sail the vessel to Florida, and for a time achieve a Utopian community before the world finds them out. The winner of the 1991 Booker Prize arrived on these shores also – Ben Okri's *The Famished Road* (Doubleday). Its narrator, drawn from Yoruban mythology (Okri is from the Urhobo people), is Azaro, a mystical figure who describes himself as "a spirit child rebelling against the spirits" and, in another place, as "an unwilling adventurer into chaos and sunlight, into the dreams of the living and the dead."

(Prizes and awards can matter enormously to the literary writer. See Sally Emerson, "Glittering Prizes and Sour Grapes," *Washington Post Book World,* 1 November. But when a prizewinner does something radically different from all expectation, trouble can follow like a slap in the face. Larry Heinemann, an American novelist who has won the National Book Award for fiction, elected to try a comedy – *Cooler By the Lake* [Farrar, Straus and Giroux] – arousing this response from Jonathan Yardley of the *Washington Post:* "By contrast, with the humor of *Cooler By the Lake,* that of the Three Stooges is sophisticated and witty; you'll find more laughs in a film by Oliver Stone or Ingmar Bergman.")

Caryl Phillips, a West Indian who was raised and schooled in England, presents his fourth novel, *Cambridge* (Knopf), in the form of two journals – one by Emily Cartwright, a thirty-year-old Englishwoman, the other by a black slave, Cambridge. Set in the early nineteenth century in Great Britain and the West Indies, this wise and tragic book received the highest praise in America. Another view of colonial days in the West Indies is Marina

Warner's *Indigo* (Simon and Schuster). From London in 1948 we move to the imaginary island of Liamuiga (now called Enfant-Beate) in 1600, in a story that parallels William Shakespeare's *The Tempest,* though it focuses more on the female characters Sycorax and Miranda than on Prospero and Caliban.

In the final volume of a trilogy, *The Gates of Ivory* (Viking), Margaret Drabble is mainly concerned with psychiatrist Liz Headleand and her efforts to find out what happened to writer Stephen Cox, who has vanished in Cambodia. A little whiff of metafiction allows Drabble to enter the fiction from time to time, as in this sense of the limits of fiction with its focus on representative individuals: "A queasiness, a moral scruple overcomes the writer at the prospect of selecting individuals from the mass of history, the human soup." Stoyo Petkanov, former leader of an unnamed Iron Curtain country (clearly Bulgaria), feels a little bit the same way about "the human soup" as he defends himself against a conniving and duplicitous democratic prosecutor in *The Porcupine* (Knopf) by Julian Barnes: "They want stability and hope. We gave them that. Things might not have been perfect, but with Socialism people could dream that one day they might be. You – you have only given them instability and hopelessness. A crime wave. The black market. Pornography. Prostitution. You are proud of these swift achievements." Various interviews with Barnes indicate that he takes the arguments of his former Communist dictator seriously and does not view the breakdown of the Berlin Wall as an unmitigated triumph. Paul Levy of the *Wall Street Journal* ("British Author, French Flare," 11 December) quotes Barnes on the subject:

> I dislike the triumphal reaction of the Western countries to the downfall of communist regimes.... That's why I have Petkanov reminding the officials of the court at his trial that they were all born in hospitals and educated in schools built under socialism, and fed and clothed by socialist economic policies.

It appears that, with the exception of certain academic diehards, readers and reviewers are interested in the subject but not much in Barnes's views. D. M. Thomas, who tends to push his luck to the limits, took on the idea of the assassination of John F. Kennedy in *Flying in to Love* (Scribners), his ninth novel. Very postmodern, the book offers alternate stories of the event and some shocking and unrealistic versions of "real" people. Most American reviewers found the book offensive and annoying. Most readers must have agreed with the quotation

Dust jacket for Darcey Steinke's novel about sex and obsession in contemporary San Francisco

on the jacket from the *Sunday Telegraph:* "It succeeds brilliantly in illuminating the no man's land of pain between sleeping and waking." Modern history is at the heart of two novels, which weave together stories set in World War II and its aftermath with the cracking of the Iron Curtain in 1989. Ian McEwan, in *Black Dogs* (Doubleday), swiftly and efficiently, from several angles, tells the story of Bernard Tremaine, former Communist and now a political commentator, and his estranged wife, June, whose terrifying experience with the dogs of the title (dogs which had belonged to the Gestapo) in France shortly after the war, changed the world for her and charged her with a spiritual life. The story is told by their son-in-law. Dead, they continue to hold fast to irreconcilable positions. In 1987 the dying June tells the son-in-law: "Jeremy, that morning I came face to face with evil . . . It's something in our hearts." Jeremy can imagine Bernard's reply: "As for the inner life, try having one of those on an empty stomach." Irish writer Hugo Hamilton's second novel, *The Last Shot* (Farrar, Straus and Giroux), is beautifully constructed of two story lines, one in May 1945 during the final and confused days of World War

II, related to the other, a first-person story, told by a young American in Germany in November 1989 as the Berlin Wall comes down. The earlier story tells of Franz Kern, German officer, and Bertha Sommer, a civilian worker, who flee for home together from Laun, near Prague. Franz, as it happens, fires what may have been the last shot of the war in order to save Bertha's life. The young American in 1989 links the stories together; for he is Bertha's son and has been searching for some years to find Franz, who alone can tell him his mother's story and who may possibly be his father. The stories tie together with an impeccable logic to form a powerful fable for the last half of the century. The prolific Peter Ackroyd (at forty-three he has already published three books of poems, six novels, and three biographies) tells the story of Clement Harcombe and his son Tim and their Chemical Theater in *English Music* (Knopf). Every other chapter is of Tim in a dream state as he enters into books and paintings – all the art of England that he calls its "music." There are nine "dreams" and 150 pastiches, as Tim is, for example, cast ashore with Robinson Crusoe or guided around London in person by William Hogarth. Malcolm Bradbury's sixth novel, *Doctor Criminale* (Viking), sends its journalist/narrator off to seek out Bazlo Criminale, ostensibly a sage of our time, more accurately described by book editor Carlin Romano of the *Philadelphia Inquirer* (8 November) as "a kind of punk belletrist."

"Here is the realm of the unbrave and the unbold, who seem incapable of having fun," writes Lucinda Fleeson (the *Philadelphia Inquirer,* 3 May) about the world of Anita Brookner's *A Closed Eye* (Random House), a subtle novel of lost chances. Brookner describes her protagonist as something less than a bundle of joy: "Nothing was expected of her except that she be reasonable and decorative. She had no trouble being either." Somewhat more predictably passionate and troubled is Nell, trying to raise two sons Tristan and Paddy (who drowns in an accident) in Edna O'Brien's *Time and Tide* (Farrar, Straus and Giroux). The novel is set in London where O'Brien has made her home for many years.

Among other British fictions which received notice in America were Fay Weldon's *Life Force* (Viking), which links a wide range of characters and events to the story of one Leslie Beck, a man endowed with a huge penis; A. N. Wilson's *Daughters of Albion* (Viking), covering the time from World War II to the present, is about radio actor Julian Ramsay (who has appeared in earlier novels) trying to write a biography of writer Albion Pugh; David Lodge's latest, *Paradise News* (Viking), a clashing of British and American culture, sends an English priest, Bernard Walsh, to Hawaii and into culture shock; *Day of Atonement* (Random House), third novel by A. Alvarez, is set in London's Camden Town and is described by Michael Heyward (the *Washington Post Book World,* 23 August) as "a credible portrait of a happy marriage suddenly exposed to the stress of adultery and mistrust." Susan Howatch continues her series of novels about the Church of England with *Mystical Paths* (Knopf), whose hero is Nicholas Darrow, a priest with psychic powers. In *Clairvoyant* (Hyperion) Alison Leslie undertakes to imagine the life of James Joyce's schizophrenic daughter, Lucia. "Life, I have come to see," says Brian Jessell, a middle-aged bureaucrat in Michael Frayn's *A Landing on the Sun* (Viking), "is nothing more nor less than another way of writing *file*." Investigating, through a document search, the death of S. Summerchild in 1974, he learns things that cannot be captured in official papers. "These are, I should warn you, the words of a dead man," begins Bill Unwin, who is editing the notebook of an ancestor and telling of his own life for forty years, in *Ever*

After (Knopf) by Graham Swift. There is a double narrative here, but reviewers tended to take the position expressed by Hilary Mantel (the *New York Review of Books,* 11 June): "His characters are afloat, barely, in a pale sea of abstraction." Ursula K. Le Guin did not like it very much either (the *Washington Post Book World,* 22 March): "A tale of lovers, desertions, and suicides finally lacks emotion, because the narrating voice so meticulously protects itself from any possible charge of 'cheapness' or sentimentality."

To be sure, first-class examples of traditional social comedy continue to find American readers. Among these in 1992 were Shena Mackay's sixth novel (though her first to appear in the United States), *A Bowl of Cherries* (Moyer Bell); Angela Huth's *Invitation to the Married Life* (Grove Weidenfeld), the second of her five novels to be published in America; and *A Dubious Legacy* (Viking), the eighth novel by the prolific Mary Wesley, who published her first novel at the age of seventy-one.

David Lodge and Malcolm Bradbury may have patents on the contemporary academic novel, but that has not discouraged Americans from producing their own variations on the subject. Robert Grudin's *Book: A Novel* (Random House), the satirical story of one Adam Snell of the English department, University of Washington, is described by the *New York Times* in "Notable Books of the Year" (6 December): "A light comic tale about a disappearing professor, prankishly rendered as a satire on post-modern, post-structuralist literary theories." Herbert Burkholz's tenth novel, *Writer in Residence* (Permanent), the first volume of a projected trilogy, sends Max Levi-Morris, a New Yorker who has lived for years on Ibiza, to teach at Chadwick College, North Carolina. In *The Divine Comedy of John Venner* (Poseidon), the second novel by Gregory Blake, a thirty-five-year-old professor of eighteenth-century studies falls in love with Sister Sabbathday, a Shakeress. His wife Sally, not amused, models herself on Medusa and takes on that name. Another academic satire is Edward Allen's *Mustang Sally* (Norton), whose protagonist is Packard Schmidt, an associate professor at Amherst University of Indiana. Poor Schmidt, a liberal Republican, finds himself trapped in a department which features "a gender-focused, multicultural, third-world-intensive curriculum." Possibly the most ambitious and at times the most amusing academic novel of the year is Jay Parini's *Bay of Arrows* (Holt), which combines and intercuts the satirical story of poet, professor, and desultory family man, forty-two-year-old Christopher Genovese, with the story of Christopher Columbus and the discovery of the New World. Many P.C. attitudes and highjinks (nice to know those folks can laugh at *something*) and a good deal of belated Columbus bashing do not detract from a lively and imaginative telling of a few familiar tales. John Updike's *Memories of the Ford Administration* (Knopf) was not taken or described as being "an academic novel." But, of course, it is precisely that. Taking the form of an extended memo from Alfred B. ("Alf") Clayton, a history teacher at Wayward College, to the Northern New England Association of American Historians, it alternates at will between Alf's observations of the Gerald R. Ford years, admissions and confessions about his life, and parts of Alf's unpublished biography of President James Buchanan. The novel received the most widespread and simultaneous reviews of any book mentioned in this essay, but the reviews, even when favorable, seemed profoundly uncomprehending. The principals are transformed – Buchanan as a nearly tragic figure who *almost* saved the Union from its bloody fate, Alf as wiser than he acts or seems: "Are things now any different? AIDS, famine, boat people, ghetto hopelessness, children by the millions born to misery. If a man had half a heart, he'd drown." A wise and compassionate book without a whiff of the simplicities of P.C.

Dennis Feeney, writing in the *Wall Street Journal* (16 September), has this challenging comment for American writers: "If American novelists are the world's best story tellers, as arguably they are, it is because they have the world's best story to tell. Their story is an existential nation, creating itself anew every day." True or false, the range and variety of the novel in America continue to surprise. This year saw many stars in the American literary firmament publishing new work. Cult figure Ken Kesey of Pleasant Hill, Oregon, brought out his first novel in twenty-eight years – *Sailor Song* (Viking), a bold version of life in the near future, centered in the Alaskan fishing village of Kuinak and focused on some memorably eccentric characters like Alice the Angry Aleut and Ike Sallas "the Backatcha Bandit." *Sailor Song* has magic realism and everything else you can think of or ask for. This writer found it a wonderful, rollicking tale for our times. Not all reviewers agreed. In "Sometimes a Great Commotion" (the *Washington Post,* 9 September) David Streitfeld notes that the novel received "the most contradictory set of reviews in recent history." Chip Brown, writing in *Esquire* ("Ken Kesey Kisses No Ass," September), observed that the literati were surprised when Kesey wrote a new novel: "Many people in literary circles considered Kesey a magician only in the sense that he'd pulled off one of the great vanishing acts of American literature." Gore Vidal brought out the slender and blasphemous (with much to offend anyone and everyone, even secular humanists) *Live From Golgotha* (Random House) with, thanks to the wonders of television and time travel, Jesus Christ and Shirley MacLaine on camera together. Madeleine L'Engle uses the Bible more positively, playing off the story of King David against a modern counterpart, eighty-seven-year-old actor David Wheaton who wants to play King David, in *Certain Women* (Farrar, Straus and Giroux). William T. Vollman brought out (in 990 close pages, including notes, glossaries, chronology, maps, and more) *Fathers and Crows* (Viking), the second volume of a projected seven-volume series, this one told as seven "Dreams," with running commentary by the author who calls himself "William the Blind." The novel is about the sixteenth-century clash between the Indians and the Jesuits. Vollman also brought out a somewhat more conventional novel in 1992, *Whores for Gloria* (Pantheon).

Equally odd is *Vox* (Random House) by Nicholson Baker. This brief novel, which is about sex-by-phone and involves only the disembodied voices and very erotic imaginations of Jim and Abby, earned a great deal of attention and was thought to be Baker's "breakthrough" book. It is every bit as brilliant and daring as his earlier work, but it did not do so well either with the critics or at the marketplace. It may be that his singular touch, which allows him to be satiric and yet engaged and sympathetic at the same time – where one of his greatest gifts is a consistent authorial ambivalence – will not work to best advantage with a sensitive subject like sex in the age of AIDS. Some reviewers, however, liked *Vox* a lot; they were best exemplified by James Kaplan of *Vanity Fair* ("Hot Vox," January), who argued: "Not since *Portnoy's Complaint* has this kind of imagination (and writing gift) turned to sex." Another novel of uninhibited sex was Darcey Steinke's *Suicide Blonde* (Atlantic Monthly Press), spinning out its story, in a well-realized, evocative San Francisco setting, of nightmarish, grubby sex and degradation. The central character is a twenty-nine-year-old woman, beautiful, but desperately and dangerously in love with a bisexual man, described by prizewinning novelist John Casey as "a whirling dervish of a novel character – one-half frenzied flesh, one-half spirit of a cursed poet." Another kind of frenzy and poetry are to be found in Jay McInerney's *Brightness Falls* (Knopf), a story of the

Richard Price, author of Clockers *(photograph by Ralph Gibson)*

1980s. It is mostly the story of young and upwardly mobile Russell and Corinne Calloway – he formerly a poet and now a book editor, she a stock analyst; Jeff Pierce, author and vaguely parodic shadow of author McInerney; and Victor Propp, a pompous author, rumored to have a resemblance to the real Harold Brodkey ("The trouble with art is the kind of company it attracts," says Jeff). Together with black editor Washington Lee and entrepreneur Bernard Melman, Russell tries to engineer a hostile takeover of his publishing company. It is a sort of brat-pack version of *Bonfire of the Vanities* and seems to have thrived in spite of mixed notices. There is a good deal of "inside" information about the workings of the publishing world, bad news that one can only hope is fantasy. There is a good deal of fantasy and fun and no pretense at any inside information about anything in brat-packer Tama Janowitz's latest, *The Male Cross-Dresser Support Group*. It is an entertaining airhead version of the reality of her narrator and protagonist Pamela Trowel who finds herself attached to a clever nine-year-old named Abdhul. Michael Upchurch is exactly right

in his *Washington Post Book World* review (30 August): "There is a lot of deft humor in it, but you have to wade through a lot of dreck to get there."

Although it is set across the river in New Jersey, Richard Price's *Clockers* (Houghton Mifflin) is still part of the megacity in and around New York. And a very different city it is in this story of dope dealing in the housing projects, murder, and a homicide investigation. Price, a highly regarded novelist and screenwriter, generated much interest not so much from his story line as from his writing (a perfect ear for street talk) and, above all, for his capacity to create credible and sympathetic characters, especially the cocaine dealer, the young black man named Ronald Dunham and called Strike, and the wonderfully realized white detective, Rocco Klein. *Clockers* is a large novel – 599 pages of high energy. So, in a different way, is Larry McMurtry's sequel to *Terms of Endearment – The Evening Star* (Simon and Schuster, 637 pages). Aurora Greenway is now in her seventies and her official boyfriend, General Hector Scott, is eighty-six. Of the three grandchildren she was left to raise at the end of *Terms,* Tommy is in prison, Teddy has been in and out of mental hospitals, and Melanie is pregnant. Of her own diminishing sex life the indefatigable Aurora says, "I guess it's not as easy to be a lewd old woman as I'd always hoped it would be." This is a highly inventive, bittersweet comedy about the sad business of growing old, but full of fun and even allotted a happy ending. Many reviewers did not like it much. They were wrong.

Janet Burroway's *Cutting Stone* (Houghton Mifflin) is set in Bowie, Arizona, at the time of World War I and, centering on the lives of Laurel Poindexter and his wife, Eleanor, is built around the occasion of the visit of Pancho Villa to their town. A deeper and closer look at Pancho Villa and other historical figures of the Mexican revolution of 1914 is offered in *The Prison Notebooks of Ricardo Flores Magon* (Harcourt Brace Jovanovich) by Douglas Day. Day – a National Book Award winner for his biography of Malcolm Lowry and recipient of the Rosenthal Award from the American Academy of Arts and Letters for his first novel, *Journey of the Wolf* (1978) – lets the historical Flores Magon tell his story in journal form while he was a prisoner in America in 1922. Close to the hero Emiliano Zapata, Flores Magon knew all the leaders on both sides, and they are powerfully depicted here. Joyce Carol Oates handles fact and fiction in *Black Water* (Dutton). Based on the story of Chappaquiddick, though here set on Grayling Island in Maine and in the present, it is told from the point of view of the drowning young woman, Kelly Kelleher, trapped in a submerged, rented Toyota of the "Senator," whose carelessness put her there and whose cowardice left her there to die. Her version depends a good deal on the original event for its impact. Reviewing it for the *New York Times Book Review* (10 May) Richard Bausch concluded: "Taut, powerfully imagined and beautifully written, *Black Water* ranks with the best of Joyce Carol Oates' already long list of distinguished achievements."

Elie Wiesel depends also on the knowledge of fact and historical reality for his story of Elbhanan Rosenbaum, Holocaust survivor and psychotherapist, in *The Forgotten* (Summit). Here the elderly Rosenbaum is losing his deepest possession, memory, because of Alzheimer's disease. His son, Malkiel, who writes obituaries for the *New York Times,* goes to the Hungarian village of Feherfalu (much like Sighet, where Wiesel grew up) to seek out traces of his father's life. Memory and history, but not factual reality, are at the heart of William Kennedy's latest volume in the Albany Cycle – *Very Old Bones* (Viking). Here the story of the Phelan clan is set, loosely, around a family gathering in 1958. The book is Orson Purcell's memoir, though much of it deals with his father (who does not acknowledge his parenthood), the gifted painter Peter Phelan. It is by Phelan's art, the *Malachi Suite,* that Orson and others learn a terrible secret from 1887 at the heart of Phelan's story. Art and reality are the subject of *Very Old Bones.* As Orson writes of his crazy ancestor Malachi: "When you cross the border out of the real world, as he did, the way back, if you can find it, is perilous at best; and not only for yourself." Peter Phelan puts it a little differently. "We try to embrace the universe," he says, "but we end up throwing our arms around the local dunghill."

John L'Heureux's *The Shrine At Altamira* (Viking) tells the story of a horrible domestic crime and of its consequences. Russell Whitaker sets his young son, John, on fire, and the boy lives on to suffer a lifetime. All of the characters – Maria Alvarez, the mother, Whitaker, John, and Dr. Clark, who looks after the boy – are credible and well realized. But it is given to an old priest (L'Heureux is a former Jesuit) to state the theme: "What makes life so horrible is that even our salvation never comes in the form we would have chosen." Another story of an injured child is Chaim Potok's *I Am the Clay* (Knopf). Until now Potok has written about Jews, but here he writes a parable about an elderly Korean couple fleeing for their lives during the Korean War who find a badly wounded boy by the road

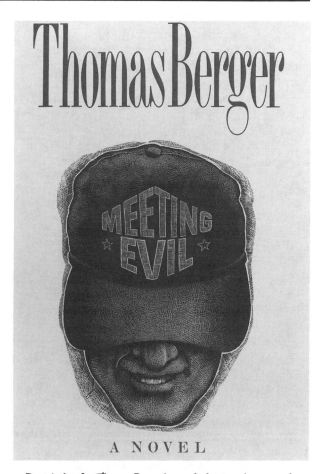

Dust jacket for Thomas Berger's novel about a nice man who accidentally falls in with a vicious sociopath

and take him as the son they never had and heal him. Potok, who served more than a year in Korea as a chaplain during the war, knows the people, the landscape, the weather. His poetic story is completely credible.

"I wanted to write a book no one could call comic," said Thomas Berger to a reporter of the *New York Times* (12 July) of his eighteenth novel, *Meeting Evil* (Little, Brown). He must have said it with a wink, for the story of John Felton – nice guy who falls in, by accident, with the vicious sociopath, Richie, and finds himself more like him than he could have imagined – is fundamentally a comic idea. Even Berger's haughty dismissal of Richie in the same interview ("He's like a piece of filth that sticks to the bottom of your shoe") is funny. Craig Nova's *Trombone* (Grove Weidenfeld) has some aspects of evil and the banality of it. It is the story of Roy Gollancz, his mother Marge, and his father Dean, who is a printer by trade and an arsonist by profession. Dean plays the trombone. It is a novel with many eccentric characters, gangsters, and religious nuts, and, in the words of George Stade (the *New York Times Book Review,* 12 July), it has "a prophetic and apocalyptic allure." Rosellen Brown's eighth book, *Before and After* (Farrar, Straus and Giroux), is also concerned with crime. Her story, set in a small New England town, concerns the damage to a fine family, Ben and Carolyn Reiser and their children Jacob and Judith, when a young local girl, Martha, is murdered and Jacob is seriously implicated. Carolyn is a pediatrician and highly rational; Ben, a sculptor, is strongly intuitive. They are all tested to the quick.

Other prominent American women writers published novels deserving serious notice. Maureen Howard's *Natural History* (Norton) was promptly, widely, and extensively reviewed. Telling a complex story, it covers forty years in Howard's favorite setting of Bridgeport, Connecticut. It mainly concerns the family of Billy (chief detective of the county) and Nell Gray and their two children, James, a film actor married to a radio star, and his sister Catherine. But a large cast of characters and certain technical devices — double columns, separate narratives, documenting histories, and collages — give it a public story larger than the central domestic one. Richard Eder of the *Los Angeles Times* (25 October) called *Natural History* "immensely elaborate." Reviewing *Natural History* for the *Washington Post Book World* (22 November) Noel Perrin called it "almost unreadable." Susan Minot, who has earned a high-ranking reputation for her fiction, also told a story covering many years (in Boston) in her second novel – *Folly* (Houghton Mifflin). It is a cool and slightly distant story of Lilian Eliot of Beacon Hill and the two great loves in her life – Walter Vail and Gilbert Finch. Details of society in Boston from before World War I are authentic and interesting. Francine Prose is a writer earning more and more attention from readers and reviewers. Her eighth novel, *Primitive People* (Farrar, Straus and Giroux), is a dark satire set in Hudson Landing, New York, and built around the impact and influence of a woman, Simone from Haiti, and the family she works for. Carol Anshaw's *Aquamarine* (Houghton Mifflin) starts with Jesse Austin, winner of a silver medal in the 1968 Olympics and develops, in a mildly experimental manner, three alternative future lives for her. Susan Shreve, an outstanding novelist who has not (yet) earned her due, dealt with five generations of American women over a period of a hundred years in *Daughters of the New World* (Doubleday). In her third novel, *At Weddings and Wakes* (Farrar, Straus and Giroux), Alice McDermott tells a three-generation story of the Irish-American Towne family: Mary ("Momma"), son John, four middle-aged stepdaughters, one of whom, Lucy, has three children from whose point of view much of the tale is seen. It is set in Brooklyn and Long Island. It has been specially praised for its evocation of the past. Mona Simpson's second novel, *The Lost Father* (Knopf), turns out to be a sequel with a few new twists to her first – *Anywhere But Here.* The new one deals with the obsessive and self-destructive search for her long-gone Egyptian father by the same Ann Stevenson, now twenty-eight years old and calling herself Mayan Amneh Stevenson. Cynthia Kadohata's *In the Heart of the Valley of Love* (Viking) is set in Los Angeles in 2052. Which future, according to Francie, the nineteen-year-old Japanese-American narrator, is not much different from the present as we know it, only worse in many details. Alice Hoffman is a highly regarded novelist whose latest, *Turtle Moon* (Putnam's), aroused interest among literary journalists. Partly a domestic story and part murder mystery set in Verity, Florida, and Great Neck, Long Island, the novel is about a twelve-year-old boy, Keith Rosen, his mother Lucy, and a local cop – Julian Cash. Kit Reed called it "a quality thriller" in her 10 May review in the *Philadelphia Inquirer.*

It was a fruitful and significant year for several outstanding African-American writers. Toni Morrison's *Jazz* (Knopf), told by a nameless narrator, is about love and desire in 1920s Harlem, spotlighting the story of Joe Trace, a middle-aged salesman; Dorcas, a seventeen-year-old girl; and Joe's wife, Violet, who becomes obsessed with the life and murder of Dorcas. "What's the world for if you can't make it up the way you want it?" asks Violet. In *Bailey's Cafe* (Harcourt Brace Jovanovich), Gloria Naylor's characters, regulars at Bailey's, tell all kinds of stories, realistic and fantastic, about their lives and times. Featured are Bailey, his wife Nadine, and Eve, who runs a nearby boarding house that doubles as a convent and a whorehouse. Alice Walker's dedication to *Possessing the Secret of Joy* (Harcourt Brace Jovanovich) – "This book is dedicated with tenderness and respect to the blameless vulva" – generated almost as much discussion as the novel itself. The story consists of a series of first-person episodes told by eight central characters and focused on Tashi, a young African woman of the "Olinka" people (in a highly imaginary country), later to be known as Mrs. Evelyn Johnson in America. The subject, endured by disastrous choice by Tashi, is female circumcision. Thus, in a larger sense, the subject is the brutal male oppression and misogyny in much of the developing world. Marita

Golden's *And Do Remember Me* (Doubleday) follows the lives of two women – Jesse, a poor child from Columbus, Mississippi, who grows up to be an actress on stage and television; and Macon, a sociologist from the black middle class. The story begins in Mississippi in the Freedom Summer of 1964 and runs to the present. Novelist Ellen Douglas honored its good heart and serious intentions (*Washington Post Book World,* 21 June), adding: "But seriousness is not enough to make a good novel or to give it staying power." Terry McMillan's third novel, *Waiting to Exhale* (Viking), earned as much attention for its amazing paperback sale, $2.64 million, as for its style and substance; but nevertheless this story of four single women (two have been married) in their thirties – Robin, Gloria, Bernadine, and Savannah – who, in a context of comedy, trash the male animal, was widely reviewed. Writing in *The World & I* (October), Charles R. Larson called it a "deliciously funny" novel and cited the approval of filmmaker Spike Lee. One of the most ambitious and interesting novels by an African-American is Leon Forrest's *Divine Days* (Another Chicago Press). This fourth novel by Forrest, formerly managing editor of *Muhammad Speaks,* is a huge (1,138 pages divided into fifteen sections) Joycean account of one week beginning 16 February 1966 in the life of black playwright Joubert Jones of Chicago. Much of the action takes place in the Night Light Lounge. Although the author has been championed by critics like Nathan A. Scott, Jr., and the book was favorably featured by *Chicago Tribune* book critic Joseph Coates ("A Vast Swirl of Voices," 2 August), national attention was limited. Perhaps it was too long for journalist-reviewers; or, perhaps, publication by a small press limited its short-term review possibilities. Time will tell. Forrest is chairman of African-American studies at Northwestern University.

Another very large and long novel is native American Leslie Marmon Silko's *Almanac of the Dead* (Simon and Schuster), an epic of unrelieved victimization, rich with rage, full of sound and fury. Signifying? Paul West put it nicely in the *Los Angeles Times Book Review* (2 February) – "The problem with this book is that Silko deals more graphically with myth than with folks." Among other novels treating the native American experience are Lawrence Thornton's *Ghost Woman* (Ticknor and Fields), set in California in the 1800s and concerned with the plight of the Humash Indians and a woman among them named Soledad. In Gerald Vizenor's *Dead Voices* (Oklahoma), the setting is Oakland, California, as an old Indian woman, Bagese, tells a Berkeley professor her animal stories. In *Sweet Med-*

icine (Crown) by David Seals we meet a self-reflexive Indian "Storyteller" who professes, from time to time, to be an antagonist of the author – "You're just encouraging him if you keep reading."

Another example of American ethnicity and cultural diversity is Cristina Garcia's *Dreaming in Cuban* (Knopf) selected by *Time* (4 January 1993) as one of the five best works of fiction in 1992: "This first novel by a Cuban American tells the poignant, often funny story of three generations of Cuban women and their varying responses to Fidel's revolution." The action takes place in Havana and New York City. *Cantora* (University of New Mexico Press), by Sylvia Lopez Medina, is a five-part novel, beginning in 1978 but covering four generations of Mexican and Mexican-American women. Arte Publico published *Eldorado in East Harlem* by Victor Rodriguez, the story of a Puerto Rican family in Harlem in the 1960s. In *The Devil in Texas* (Anchor), praised by Alan Cheuse in "*Tribune* Books," 7 June, Hispanic-American Aristeo Brito has an unnamed narrator telling stories of Presidio, Texas, in 1883, 1942, and 1970.

As our world has expanded, more and more Americans are writing about other societies in what might be defined as the international novel. Richard Wiley's *Indigo* (Dutton) is a case in point. Wiley, a former winner of the coveted PEN/Faulkner Award for *Soldiers in Hiding* (1986), sets his story in Nigeria at the time of the 1984 coup. Its protagonist is Jerry Neal, a fifty-seven-year-old widower and American headmaster of a school in Lagos. Innocently, he finds himself deeply involved with a revolutionary group and its leader – Benny Abubakar. The story is divided, like a triptych, in three "panels," about which form a character, a Nigerian artist, allows: "I tried to pound dese my panels wit de truth, but when you look at 'em de truth will move around a bit, depending on who is looking. Get it? Dat is the way wit art." Bernard Packer invents a realistic story taking place in the imaginary South American nation of Santa Cruz in *Flags of Convenience* (Ticknor and Fields). In *Brazil-Maru* (Coffee House), Japanese-American Karen Tei Yamashita tells of a colony of Japanese Christians who went to Brazil in 1925 to found a Utopian community called Hope (*Speranca*). Michael Doane's fourth novel, *City of Light* (Knopf) is the story of Thomas Zane who covers Africa for ABRI, an international human rights organization based in Paris. Set in 1988, it is a new kind of thriller; and some of it takes place in Mali as Zane tries to find out what has happened to his friend Harry Street. James Michener has been writing a popular version of the international novel, more

W. P. Kinsella, author of Box Socials *(photograph by Scott Norris)*

docudrama than fiction, for a long time. His latest, *Mexico* (Random House), theoretically set in 1961 and involving Norman Clay, American newsman and narrator, in a story about bullfighting, is a guided tour to fifteen hundred years of Mexican history. Michener also published *My Lost Mexico* (State House), telling how he traveled to Mexico in the 1930s, how he began to write *Mexico* in 1959, lost the manuscript in 1961, and how it was found years later in a closet by his cousin Virginia Turnbull.

Fact and fiction are often inextricably intertwined in American fiction, sometimes in the form of giving fictional character and voice to real figures. For example, Sam Toperoff (a sports reporter) has written a novel of Marilyn Monroe – *Queen of Desire* (HarperCollins). Samuel Charters imagines a lengthy monologue from a hotel room in 1957 in *Elvis Presley Calls His Mother After the Ed Sullivan Show* (Coffee House). (In Laura Kalpakian's fourth novel, *Graced Land,* published by Grove Weidenfeld, Elvis appears not in person, but in an elaborate front porch Elvis shrine created by Joyce Jackson.). In *A Good Man To Know,* Barry Gifford (Clark City Press) mingles fact and fiction about himself, depending, he says, on the Japanese concept of

Shosetau, an embroidered memory. Historical fiction of various kinds almost always involves at least the appearance of some real historical characters. An interesting example from 1992 is Judith Chernaik's *Love's Children* (Knopf), set in Geneva in 1816 and 1817 and told in a mixture of fictional and actual documents, narrating the story of Percy Bysshe Shelley from the views of the four most important women in his life.

In "Dreams That Money Can Buy" (*New York Review of Books,* 5 November), scientist Stephen Jay Gould, arguing that baseball is for Americans an "all purpose symbol," wrote a roundup review of some of the year's baseball books, including the novels *The Dreyfus Affair* (Random House) by Peter Lefcourt, *Box Socials* (Ballantine) by W. P. Kinsella, and Luke Salisbury's *The Cleveland Indian: The Legend of King Saturday* (The Smith). Salisbury's story is closely modeled on the true story of Louis Sockalexis, a Penobscot Indian who played for the old Cleveland Spiders. Kinsella, who has written stories and two novels involving baseball, most notably *Shoeless Joe,* which became the movie *Field of Dreams,* sets this one in rural Alberta, Canada, during the 1930s and 1940s. Baseball is only part of the story, but a vital part when local star Truckbox Al McClintock goes down in three pitches by Bob Feller. *The Dreyfus Affair* gets about as postmodern and P.C. as you can get (it is set ahead in the late 1990s) when Los Angeles shortstop Randy Dreyfus falls in love with the second baseman D. J. Picket. Lefcourt is a television writer and wrote the satirical Hollywood novel *The Deal.* Another book more widely and seriously reviewed than any of the above is not really much about baseball, though the game touches the lives of the characters. Set in Camas, Washington, mainly in the 1960s and the early 1970s, *The Brothers K* (Doubleday), by David James Duncan, is the story of Hugh ("Papa Toe") Chance, his wife Laura, and their four sons and twin daughters, all of whom take different directions from each other and, as a family, live intensely amid those troubled times.

Major novels tend to fall outside of categories. Any number of novelists produced work that may last well beyond this year. Widely praised, winner of the National Book Award, and nominated (at this writing) for just about everything else is *All the Pretty Horses* (Knopf) by Cormac McCarthy. Picked by *Time* as one of the five best works of fiction of the year, *Horses* is the first volume of a projected trilogy. This is the story, set in 1949, of John Grady Cole, sixteen years old, and his friend Lacey Rawlins, who ride out of Texas into Mexico to find work they love and to hold onto a way of life that is vanishing in their own country. They find life and love and great grief in this beautifully written book. Robert Stone is one of our most honored writers, and his fifth and latest novel, *Outerbridge Reach* (Ticknor and Fields) has been on every list of the year's best books, including "Editors' Choice" of the *New York Times Book Review* (6 December). *Outerbridge Reach* sends a man in his early forties, Owen Browne, on an attempted solo sail around the world. The other central characters, left ashore, are his conflicted wife, Anne, and a filmmaker, Ron Strickland. The consequences for all three are worked out in painful, engrossing detail.

Ray Bradbury, longtime imaginative professional, tells, in lightly veiled form, of the 1953 trip to Ireland he made to work with John Huston on the film version of *Moby Dick,* in *Green Shadows, White Whale* (Knopf), an echo of another title about Huston – Clint Eastwood's film *White Hunter, Black Heart.* Bradbury mixes the quasi-documentary account of his relationship with Huston with a wild fantasia of Irish characters and caricatures. Most critics faulted the book for its Irish blarney. In *Indian Affairs* (Atheneum), Larry Woiwode returns to Chris and Ellen, central characters of his earliest published fiction, and places them in northern Michigan where Chris has to come to terms with that part of him which is descended from the Blackfoot Indian tribe. Novelist and poet Richard Elman, for twenty-five years a genuine presence in American literature, hits a home run with *Tar Beach* (Sun and Moon Press), about growing up Jewish in Brooklyn right after World War II. Peter Pintobasco, an eight-year-old, who wants to live in Uganda and speaks a mixture of Yiddish and Swahili that he and his father call Swidish, is a memorable creation.

Except for a side trip to Alaska, Thomas McGuane's latest, *Nothing But Blue Skies* (Houghton Mifflin) takes place in and around his established turf of Deadrock, Montana. It is the story of good-old-boy Frank Copenhaver whose wife, Gracie, leaves him, his business falls apart, and his love life leaves a lot to be desired. There is some marvelous fly-fishing that restores his soul and the reader's. Popular gay writer Armistead Maupin weighed in with *Maybe the Moon* (HarperCollins), his first novel since he finished his Tales of the City series. This one is about Cadence ("Cady") Roth, a dwarf actress who wants to be a movie star and cheerfully describes herself as "the biggest fag hag this side of Susan Sarandon." In *Carmichael's Dog* (Norton) R. M. Koster spins an odd little yarn whereby a best-sell-

ing author is possessed by a legion of powerful, painful, and real demons, but finally is set free thanks to a new puppy dog named Furfante.

Writing about Paul West's *Love's Mansion* (Random House) in the *Chicago Tribune* (18 October) Joseph Coates said: "In *Love's Mansion* West takes on the supreme challenge of inhabiting those historic, even mythic, personages most important to each of us, our parents, whom we never quite outlive or outgrow or really comprehend." In a quiet display of imaginative daring, West gives us the lives of Hilly and Harry Moxon, she the daughter of a butcher and a gifted pianist, he a battered veteran of World War I while still a child (he was in combat at fifteen). The story is filtered through the point of view of their son Clive, a novelist. Of his mother and his art Clive thinks: "Language was a woman, his mother was his muse, and language never turned its back on you provided you obeyed its rules."

Two of the most highly regarded of the middle generation of American novelists are Paul Auster and Richard Bausch, both represented by outstanding books this year. Auster's *Leviathan* (Viking), dedicated to fellow postmodernist Don DeLillo, is an urgent first-person account by Peter Aaron, a writer and a version of Auster, of the life and death of his friend Benjamin Sachs who moved from writing novels to making bombs and engaging in acts of social terrorism. *Violence* (Houghton Mifflin), Bausch's fifth novel, is at once a more straightforward, accessible, and complex experience. A master of the subtle joys and strains of contemporary family life, Bausch tells the powerful story of the impact of a single act of violence upon the lives of decent and well-meaning Charles and Carol Conally and their family. But it is not a study of violence as such. Rather this book is, in words Bausch used in an interview (*Washington Post,* 2 March), "about love and the obdurate force of love. That's what everything I write is about. I don't write my opinions. I tell stories."

Other worthwhile American novels include Malcolm Bosse's version of the dark side of eighteenth-century London (which gives a cameo role to Henry Fielding), *The Vast Memory of Love* (Ticknor and Fields); *Franklin's Crossing* (Dutton), third novel by Clay Reynolds, which takes a wagon train, led by the heroic black man Moses Franklin, through hell and high water; and *The Venerable Bead* (St. Martin's Press), twenty-fifth novel by Richard Condon and the satirical story of Leila Aluja, an Iraqi immigrant who owns the largest fast-food chain in the world.

The South may be "the Old Country" in Darryl Pinckney's *High Cotton* (Farrar, Straus and Giroux), but it remains a seedbed for fiction and has continued to produce a variety of novels, major and minor, based firmly on its own literary tradition. The productive Clyde Edgerton's latest, *The Memory of Junior* (Algonquin), is a series of precisely realized and very funny first-person narrations, dealing with the problems of a family (the Bales) estate. The *New Yorker* (30 November) described it as "benign and bemused smalltown comedy from a North Carolina novelist whose sensibility is as sharp as it is gentle." Also from Algonquin came Robert Love Taylor's *Lady of Spain,* a story of smalltown living in the 1950s. Amanda Heller of the *Boston Globe* had high praise for Taylor (22 November). "His characterizations are rich and sensitive, his narrative is lyrical, and his evocation of the era is thoroughly persuasive without resorting to any of the pop-culture cliches that so often constitute images of that decade." A major Southern novel by a productive and imaginative writer who has already earned the highest praise is Lee Smith's *The Devil's Dream* (Putnam's). Using multiple narrators she tells the story of four generations of the Bailey family from 1884 (Grassy Branch, Virginia) to the 1970s (Opryland Hotel) and, through them, a history of country music in America. Writing about Smith in the *Southern Review* (Autumn 1992) Fred Chappell states: "She is the only contemporary author I know of whose books get unfalteringly better each after each." Southern Gothic seems to be in good shape, judging by the latest novel, *Scar Lover* (Poseidon) by its self-proclaimed master, Harry Crews. This, his twelfth novel, deals with country people living in and around Jacksonville after the Korean War, and centers around Pete Butcher who finally arrives at some honest self-esteem – "Being Pete Butcher was more than all right, it was pretty damn fine." Richard Marius, in his third novel, *After the War* (Knopf), which received widespread, serious review attention, tells the complex story, set in Bourbonville, Tennessee, during the decade from 1917 to 1927, of a Greek named Kephalopolus, now calling himself Paul Alexander. He came there from the horrors of the western front of World War I where his two best and closest friends were killed. Here he begins a new life, finds his first love, works for the remarkable Moreland J. Pinkerton and, for a time, befriends a black man – Moreland Pinkerton Brown. There are bits and pieces of magic realism in this story of the South in the century's early years; for example, Paul often talks to his two dead friends and they reply.

Reynolds Price, in his ninth novel *Blue Calhoun* (Atheneum), elects to let sixty-five-year-old Bluford Calhoun tell the story of his own life from the 1950s to the present in the form of a letter to his granddaughter, asking for mercy for the ways he has walked in ever since he met, on 28 April 1956, a sixteen-year-old girl named Luna and fell instantly and obsessively in love. ("It tore the ground from under my feet, and everything around me shook the way a mad dog shakes a howling child.") *Blue Calhoun* earned mostly mixed reviews. It may be that many critics were not able to handle the flinty integrity of Calhoun's first-person confession. Typically, Robert Long (*Philadelphia Inquirer,* 5 July) said of Calhoun: "He is perhaps the most unintentionally unsympathetic character I've encountered in contemporary fiction."

"I had this vision of a world full of happy women and it depressed the hell out of me," says emergency room physician Monroe Hopkins in North Carolina novelist Lawrence Naumoff's *Taller Women: A Cautionary Tale* (Harcourt Brace). Some of the women around him are Katy, Lydia, and Ronnie Cutler, just eighteen years old. His earlier novel, *Rootie Kazootie,* and his hip and sometimes hard-edged style ("She had hung around for years, as if she could not take a hint.") established Naumoff as a member-in-good-standing of the Southern school of Barry Hannah and Richard Ford.

An important new Southern writer is Denise Giardina whose third novel, *The Unquiet Earth* (Norton), won her the 1992 Lillian Smith Award for Southern fiction. Set in the hardscrabble, coal-mining county of Justice and a sequel to *Storming Heaven* (1987), the story covers six decades of our times, from the early 1930s to the early 1990s. At the center of the story are two cousins, Rachel Honaker and Dillon Freeman, and Rachel's daughter, Jackie, who becomes a journalist. Told by multiple narrators, it is the powerful, poetic, and tragic story of the proud, but losing battles of "little people" fighting against rapacious coal companies.

Slow Poison (Knopf), Sheila Bosworth's second novel, starts and ends in New Orleans where "the men are too passionate, the food is too rich, the women are too beautiful," and tells the story of Rory Cade, a screenwriter in her early forties, and her family. *The Wisdom of Serpents* (Scribners) by Ronald Levitsky is about Nate Rosen, a Jewish lawyer who is involved in the defense of a snake-handling religious cult. Rosemary Daniel's latest venture into fiction, *The Hurricane Season* (Morrow), following the life of one Easter O'Brien, a woman in her forties, is described in the *Boston Globe* (22 November) as "a progress through the second half of the century from Southern Gothic to suburban Gothic." Ellen Gilchrist's *Net of Jewels* (Little, Brown) continues the story of Rhoda Manning of Dunleith, Alabama, who has appeared in other Gilchrist fiction. In a postmodern technical device the author allows Rhoda to write a preface to the novel, describing the story in terms which it does not, in fact, follow or deliver. Cruce Stark's *Chasing Uncle Charley* (Southern Methodist University Press) follows the wild and woolly, picaresque adventures of Mirabeau ("Bo") Lamar Johnson in the post–Civil War Southwest. Sallie Bingham, of the prominent newspaper family, who has published fiction, poetry and nonfiction, writes about two sisters living in North Carolina in the 1950s – *Small Victories* (Zoland). *B-Four* (St. Martin's Press) by Sam Hodges is all about young Beauregard Forrest, who works for a Birmingham newspaper. The title refers to his nickname and the closest (page B–4) he can get to a front-page story. Out of the past where he was something of a literary star and successful screenwriter (credits include *Barbarella, Easy Rider, Dr. Strangelove, The Loved One*) and here supported by lively blurbs from Norman Mailer, Gore Vidal, Kurt Vonnegut, Joseph Heller, and others, comes Terry Southern with a new novel – *Texas Summer* (Arcade). Starting from an earlier short story, "Red Dirt Marijuana," the novel tells the story of Harold Stevens, age twelve, growing up fast, mostly under the tutelage of C. K., the black hired hand on his father's farm. Something went wrong with the distribution and the promotion of this book. It and its author deserve much more attention than they received. Memories in publishing are short, but they should not be so hazy as to forget Terry Southern. Louisiana State University Press published Albert Belisle Davis's second novel, *Marquis At Bay,* a large novel built in multiple, sometimes documentary, narration in linked fragments and mainly concerning the life and times of James Peter Marquis, an outcast lawyer from New Orleans. Another writer with a New Orleans background, Nancy LeMann, has placed her narrator and central character, journalist Storey Culliver from New Orleans, among a group of exiled and refugee Southerners, but in the settings of New York and Orient Point, Long Island.

Genre fiction, though steadily popular and marketable, has long been relegated to a kind of second-class status. In bookstores it is usually to be found separated from mainstream literary fiction. The book pages of the newspapers regularly review genre fiction, but usually in brief and in segregated

Cormac McCarthy, author of All the Pretty Horses, *which won the Pulitzer Prize, the National Book Award, and the National Book Critics Circle Award (photograph © Marion Ettlinger)*

sections. But lately, and noticeably in 1992, genre authors have moved into the literary mainstream. Among the various masters of the thrillers, Elmore Leonard has become as respectable as he has been productive. *Rum Punch* (Delacorte) is his thirtieth novel and deals boldly with middle-aged heroes and villains in a story of south Florida low life and big-time gunrunning and gun dealing. Speaking of the change in his status (*Washington Post,* 8 September), he told an interviewer that he now has the luxury of auditioning his fictional characters: "They have to be able to talk. I audition them, and if they don't hold up, either they get a less important role, or they're out." This year Lawrence Block's latest Matthew Scudder mystery – *A Walk Among the Tombstones* (Morrow) – received full-scale literary treatment by many reviewers. Martin Cruz Smith, whose third novel in the popular series featuring Arkady Renko, chief police investigator in Moscow, *Red Square* (Random House), earned wide literary attention, has been thought of as an overnight literary phenomenon since *Gorky Park* (1981). But the truth is that he wrote many books, some of them hackwork novelizations of movies, under some thirty pen names before he crossed over with *Gorky Park*. Anthony Olcott was reviewed as a creator of "upscale thrillers" for *Rough Beast* (Colgate), his third Ivan Duvakin novel. James Ellroy had a literary hit with *White Jazz* (Knopf) a story set in Los Angeles between October 1948 and January 1949, starring a ruthless policeman, able to hold his own in a "beebop *noir*" world which includes real figures Mickey Cohen and Howard Hughes. Reviewing the book (*Washington Post,* 14 September) Bruce Cook celebrated Ellroy's writing most, saying that his style reads "like Celine on speed." Also writing thrillers set in Los Angeles in the 1940s and 1950s is African-American writer Walter Mosley, whose *White Butterfly* (Norton) once again stars the black private eye, Easy Rawlins. Mosley himself is featured in a profile ("The Tribes of Walter Mosley," by Christopher Hitchens) in *Vanity Fair* (February 1993), where he is identified as "Bill Clinton's favorite thriller novelist." Another writer gaining a literary reputation is Daniel Woodrell. His new book, *The Ones You Do* (Holt), concerns John X. Shade who, owing the bad guys big bucks, takes his daughter and runs from Mobile, ending in Saint Bruno, Louisiana, which has been featured in several other Woodrell novels. Louisiana is the setting for James Lee Burke's David Robicheaux novels, of which *A Stained White Radiance* (Hyperion) is the fifth. Dave now works out of the Iberia Parish Sheriff's Department and joins forces with his long-time buddy Cletus Purcel. Solid professional Joseph Wambaugh wrote about Breda Burrows, a former police officer in *Fugitive Nights* (Morrow). George V. Higgins knows what he is doing (he teaches creative writing at Boston University) and what he does is splendidly his own. His new novel, his thirteenth, *Defending Billy Ryan* (Holt) is his third Jerry Kennedy novel. Kennedy is in deep this time defending the longtime commissioner of public works. Fellow writer Evan Hunter is simply correct in his jacket praise for Higgins: "George V. Higgins has created a genre of his own, in which the people are so real that it doesn't matter what they're doing or how they go about doing it; just being in their company is pleasure enough." Other genre writers who have acquired space for themselves on mainstream shelves include hardboiled *Miami Herald* journalist Edna Buchanan whose *Contents Under Pressure* (Hyperion) stars the investigative reporter Britt Montero; and David Lindsey whose detective, in *Body of Truth* (Doubleday), goes to Guatemala in search of a missing woman, young and rich. It is not easy – "In Guatemala, maintaining a sensitivity to madness was no small accomplishment." Another writer who has moved from genre to mainstream, Boston's Robert Parker, published his latest, *Double Deuce* (Putnam's), with the benefit of full-scale advertising and promotion.

Sometimes it works the other way around with literary writers also successfully creating genre fiction. Joyce Carol Oates writes thrillers as Rosamond Smith, the latest of which is *Snake Eyes* (Dutton). Novelist and story writer Kit Reed used the pseudonym Kit Craig to write *Gone* (Little, Brown), a highly successful (soon to be a film) account of a family's desperate battle for survival from the terror of a pathological murderer. *Fatherland* (Random House) by Robert Harris was taken from the start as a literary novel, but it is also a thriller in the form of a "what if." The premise is that it is 1964 in the Greater Reich. Germany won the war. Adolf Hitler is seventy-five. Old Joseph P. Kennedy is president of the United States. Harris's detective hero is Xavier March, former U-boat captain and now a homicide investigator. Together with American journalist Charlotte Maguire, he uncovers Germany's deepest national secret – the Holocaust.

In spite of many examples of first-rate work in our time, the historical novel remains the poor cousin of contemporary fiction. Susan Sontag, America's intellectual-in-residence, produced her first novel in twenty-five years – *The Volcano Lover* (Farrar, Straus and Giroux), subtitled a "Romance" and dealing in original ways with a familiar story – the love affair of Admiral Horatio Nelson with the Lady Emma Hamilton, wife of the British ambassador to the Kingdom of the Two Sicilies (Naples). The trappings for a historical romance, together with a record of fictional treatment of this true story, were all in place. But Sontag, by a variety of postmodern technical devices and in interviews, distanced herself from the conventions of the historical novel. She was quoted by Richard Jenkyns in the *New Republic* (7–14 September): "The point is I don't want to write only a historical novel, but I do want it to be historical." Widely and prominently reviewed, *The Volcano Lover* earned mixed notices ("As one might expect of Ms. Sontag, the writing is stylized, digressive, earnest and learned." – *Baltimore Sun;* "It's People or even the National Inquirer, but with legitimate historical celebrities." – *Chicago Tribune*) but did well in the bookstores. Other more traditional historical fictions of the year include Margaret George's latest – *Mary Queen of Scotland and the Isles* (St. Martin's Press); Patricia Finney's story of spying and assassination plots in the reign of Elizabeth I – *Firedrake's Eye* (St. Martin's Press); Michael Ennis has two celebrated heroines, the cousins Isabella of Aragon and Beatrice d'Este in his version of fifteenth-century Italy, *Duchess of Milan* (Viking); and Guy Gavriel Kay's *A Song for Arbonne* (Crown) is *imaginary* history, closely based on the landscape and reality of medieval Provence.

One of the most unusual publishing stories of the last few years involves the "discovery" of British novelist Patrick O'Brian by Starling Lawrence of Norton. O'Brian had written novels, biographies, and had translated from the French (he now lives in the south of France) for many years; but until recent years the series of novels about the Royal Navy in the eighteenth century, featuring seagoing Lucky Jack Aubrey and surgeon Stephen Maturin (the Aubrey/Maturin novels), though well known in Britain, were mostly unknown and unpublished in America. Now, with the publication of the latest installment, *The Truelove* (Norton), there are fifteen of these in print and all the signs that a genuine Aubrey/Maturin cult has formed. (See Ken Ringle, "Is This the Best Writer You Never Heard Of?," *Washington Post,* 2 August.) Praising O'Brian's work, American novelist Stephen Becker writes: "It accomplishes nobly the three grand purposes of art: to entertain, to edify and to awe."

Finally, if the past is often the source of popular genre fiction, so is the mysterious future, as witness Michael Crichton's latest blockbuster, *Rising Sun* (Knopf) which has Japan taking over the American economy.

In a world where mainstream novelists matter-of-factly use all the latest postmodern metafictional techniques, and writers feel free to try almost anything that works, it is becoming more difficult to define the "experimental." Nevertheless, like pornography, the reader can know the experimental when he or she sees it. Nobody has yet called Kathy Acker anything else. She has said: "I am a poet and what I do is sacred. The people who keep me from the few lousy instruments I need to disseminate this crap are evil." This "crap" has moved more or less mainstream with the publication of her *Portrait of an Eye: Three Novels* (Pantheon), the experience of which, according to Kate Braverman (*Los Angeles Times,* 22 March), is "like a broken movie projector or a kind of psychic stutter." An old-timer on the American avant-garde scene is Gilbert Sorrentino whose *Under the Shadow* (Dalkey Archive) is a complex loop of fifty-nine vignettes. If there were an honor roll for American experimental writing, Thomas McGonigle would have a high place on it. His first novel, *The Corpse Dream of N. Petkov* (Dalkey

Archive, 1987), is one of the most powerful indictments of the "powers that were" behind the Iron Curtain. In *Going To Patchogue* (Dalkey Archive) McGonigle traces the journey of a depressed and suicidal narrator (named Tom McGonigle) from New York City to his hometown on Long Island, Patchogue, and back. It is a book about memory and trying to remember and forget. *Publishers Weekly* accepted him into the fold: "While many will find this literate and haunting novel difficult, others will treasure it as an exploration of those recesses of the mind where we can be most honestly ourselves." And the *New York Times* (Thomas Clavin, "On Reaching Patchogue In the Mind and Spirit," 10 May) treated him as a local author with a full-scale and respectful interview. A few years ago Mark Leyner's *Et, Tu, Babe* (Harmony), at once satirical and surreal, a novel all about a thirty-six-year-old writer named Mark Leyner, would have qualified as experimental. But now, after the success of his first two "novels," *I Smell Esther Williams* and *My Cousin, the Gastroenterologist,* he is something of a literary cult figure who is expected to do what he does. Describing the experience positively, Jonathan Yardley wrote in the *Washington Post Book World:* "Reading his books is like watching a blend of *Saturday Night Live* and *Monty Python;* they have the energy and insouciance of high-risk, off-the-wall performance."

Though it seemed to be a slower year than usual for foreign fiction in English, still the world came to American readers from many places; and some of the work was important and influential.

From Japan came *Taiko* (Kodansha) by Eiji Yoshikawa, based on the story of Toyotom Hideyoshi (1536–1598), a peasant who rose to be a powerful warlord, from sandal bearer to generalissimo. From the Rock Spring Collection of Japanese Literature (Stone Bridge Press) came two recent Japanese novels – *Death March on Mount Hakkuda* by Jiro Nitta, and *Wind and Stone* by Masaaki Tachihara.

Nobel Prize-winner José Camilo Cela published a large novel, *Mazurka For Two Dead Men* (New Directions), set in the author's native Galicia during the first four decades of this century, and told by multiple narrators, one of whom is a novelist who may be writing this novel. Cela is also the author of *San Camilo, 1936* (Duke University Press), which takes place during ten days of July 1936, and is done in the form of a prose collage. Cuban writer G. Cabrera Infante, who now lives in London and calls himself "the only English writer who writes in Spanish," wrote a self-reflexive kind of metafiction, *A Twentieth Century Job* (Faber), which is the semi-autobiographical story of G. Cain, a Cuban film

Dust jacket for Terry Southern's novel about coming of age
in Texas

critic who, like Infante, reviews movies from 1954 to 1960. Edoardo Mendoza develops a story of murder and intrigue in Barcelona during the period from 1917 to 1919 in *The Truth About the Savolta Case* (Pantheon). Argentine writer Luisa Valenzuela presents the highly self-reflexive narrative of a trip through the underground and underworld of New York City in search of the reason why a young actress was murdered in *Black Novel (With Argentines)* (Simon and Schuster). Colombian novelist Alvaro Mutis, who lives in Mexico, has linked three novellas with the same central character, a picaresque hustler, the eponymous *Magroll* (Viking) in each one. He is described by the *New York Times Book Review* (6 December) as "a rootless, philosophical polyglot," and his story is full of mystery, enigma, dreams and visions. There is also surprising good fun – like the brothel where all of the prostitutes wear the uniforms of airline stewardesses. *Daimon* (Atheneum), second book in a trilogy by the Argentine diplomat and novelist Abel Posse, tells the

story of the brutal Spanish adventurer of the sixteenth century – Lope de Aguirre. Here, in chapters whose titles are taken from the tarot deck, Aguirre and his soldiers are resurrected to live a kind of hazy and timeless half-life. *Some Clouds* (Viking), by Paco Ignacio Jaibo III, is a brief murder story. To solve the case it is necessary to bring in a detective-novelist named Paco Ignacio. Nelida Pinon's *Caetana's Sweet Song* (Knopf) is the story of Caetana, an actress who can lip-synch to recordings of Maria Callas, returning home to try to recapture her lost life and love (Polidoro, a cattle rancher). She says: "The thing I want to hear is my own story." One of the finest and most admired of Spanish-language writers, Chilean novelist José Donoso, who has been mentioned more than once as a potential Nobel laureate, published *The Garden Next Door* (Grove) about a Chilean writer, Julio, down on his luck and living in exile in Madrid, and his wife Gloria. In a subtle and funny satire of the writer's way of life, Donoso makes the world turn upside down for Julio, right side up for Gloria.

Nobel Prize-winning author Naguib Mahfouz had two books in English during the year, both from Doubleday. *Sugar Street* (1957) is the final volume of Mahfouz's *Cairo Trilogy* and brings the family of Sayyid Ahmad Abl al-Jawad up into the middle years of the twentieth century. Very different is the brief evocative fable, *The Journey of Ibn Fattouma* (1983), a kind of Arabic *Candide* concerning a life-long quest – Ibn visits and lives in five different countries, each with a different kind of society and a different form of government – seeking to arrive at the mysterious land of Gebel.

Bapsi Sidhwa of Pakistan brought out her third novel since 1983 – *The Crow Eaters* (Milkweed), the chronicle of a family's rise to prosperity in the early years of this century. It is about Faredoon Junglewalla, a Parsi called Freddy, his wife, Putli, and their seven children. They move from a village to Lahore and later manage to visit London.

Shashi Tharoor found enough free time as an under secretary of the United Nations to complete and bring out his second novel, *Show Business* (Arcade), a story set in Bombay, the world's biggest and busiest film center. The story, told in a mix of scenarios and monologues by various characters, covers the ups and downs of a film star, Ashok Banhara, in film and politics.

Nuruddin Farah, novelist from Somalia, is author of *Variations on the Theme of an African Dictatorship* (Graywolf), which consists of three stories about his native land – "Sweet and Sour Milk," "Sardines," and "Close Sesame." In *Yoruba Girl Dancing* (Viking), Simi Bradford tells the story of an upperclass Nigerian girl who is sent off to England at age six. Guyanese novelist Roy Heath writes in *The Murderer* (Persea) of the unhappy Galton Flood, who flees from the coast of Guyana to the interior and has adventures and misadventures, concluding at last that "Life is one long hell." Two other novels from Africa made a mark in 1992. G. F. Michelsen's *To Sleep With Ghosts* (Bantam) is about Samuel Kimbu, once a seaman, now a customs inspector in East Africa, caught between the worlds of old Africa and new Africa. Nigerian writer T. Obinkaram Echewa's *I Saw the Sky Catch Fire* (Dutton) is a book about storytelling, as a way of life and a source for memory, and about *Ndom,* "the universal community of women." It covers several generations in Nigeria.

From the Yiddish of 1967, as first published in the *Jewish Daily Forward,* Nobel laureate Isaac Bashevis Singer's autobiographical story of Warsaw in the 1920s, *The Certificate* (Farrar, Straus and Giroux), was at last published in English. Originally in Hebrew, Israeli writer Aharon Appelfeld's *Katerina* (Random House) tells the story, through the recollections of an eighty-year-old woman after World War II, of her life as a peasant girl who became a servant in a number of Jewish households. For the most part it was very well received with the exception of the review by Louis Begley in the *Boston Globe* (27 September), who wrote: "I dislike this book almost as much as I respect its author." A. B. Yehoshua's *Mr. Mani* (Doubleday) is a series of dramatic monologues and conversations concerning several generations of the Mani, a Sephardic family deeply rooted in the past of Palestine/Israel. These conversations take place in Israel in 1982, Crete in 1944, Jerusalem in 1918, and Poland in 1891 and 1848. Ida Fink, an Israeli of Polish extraction, tells, in *The Journey* (Farrar, Straus and Giroux), of Sarah Crewe and her sister in Poland in 1942 and how they survive, constantly changing their names and identities.

Czech writer Ivan Klima's *Love and Garbage* (Knopf) tells the story of the writer as street cleaner, who celebrates an epiphany about his art form: "I realized the amazing power of literature and of the human imagination generally: to make the dead live and to stop the living from dying." *Truck Stop Rainbows* (Farrar, Straus and Giroux) by Iva Pekarkova tells of heroine Fialka who hitchhikes back and forth in Czechoslovakia and goes into prostitution for a good cause. *October, Eight O'Clock* (Grove Weidenfeld), by Romanian Norman

Marea, is a series of nightmarish tales linked by the same central character. Hungarian writer Tamas Aczel, who writes in English, sets the story of *The Hunt* (Little, Brown) at a country estate in the 1950s. Three prominent figures – the Defense Minister, the Chief Justice, and the Roman Catholic prelate, all involved in the execution of one Ladislas Jarek – are brought together to face the consequences of their earlier action. Following the success of *Children of the Arbat* by Anatoli Rybakov, Little, Brown has brought out *Fear,* chiefly concerned with Joseph Stalin at the outset of the show trials of 1936 and 1937. Some of the characters of the earlier novel are carried over in this narrative rich with details of life in the Soviet Union in the 1930s.

The most controversial novel in Europe this year was Günter Grass's *The Toad* (Harcourt Brace Jovanovich). Beginning in Gdansk, Poland, only days before the Berlin Wall came down, and taking place through May 1991 (though told seven years later), it is the story of a couple who meet while buying asters for graves, fall in love, and form the German-Polish Cemetery Association, dedicated to bringing corpses home across national boundaries: "The Poles as well as the Germans must recognize the right of the dead to repatriation. It is a human right that knows no frontiers." The novel is decorated with the author's drawings of toads. Toads, still abundant in Poland, are scarce in industrial Germany. The call of a toad in German folklore is a warning of doom. Part of the doom that Grass envisions is exemplified by a Mr. Chaterjee from Bengal whose bicycle rickshas become a huge success in the cities of Europe.

An example of the new international novel is *Infanta* (Viking) by Bodo Kirchoff, the story of a love affair between Lukas, a German male model, and a beautiful young cook, Mayla, played out in the Philippines during the downfall of Ferdinand Marcos. *On the Mountain* (Marlboro), by the late Thomas Bernhard, was begun thirty years ago by the Austrian novelist, and is a highly experimental multivoiced narrative. In the form of memories of two old women, *The Bride Price* (Godine) by Grete Weil (born 1906), is a fusion of fact and fiction, alternating first-person stories – one by Michal, the biblical wife of King David, the other an autobiographical story by the author. From the Italian, *Inshallah* (Doubleday) is a mixture of fact and fiction concerning the 1983 Multinational Force in Beirut, with special emphasis on the Italian contingent, by Orianna Fallaci. *A Man's Place* (Four Walls Eight Windows) by Annie Ernaux, which won the Prix Renaudot in 1984, is a short (ninety-nine pages) di-

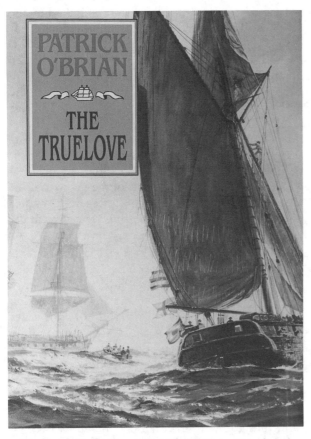

Dust jacket for the latest in Patrick O'Brian's series of novels dealing with the eighteenth-century Royal Navy

rect tale about the real death of the author's father in his native Normandy. "No lyrical reminiscences," she writes, "no triumphant displays of irony." *Hortense in Exile* (Dalkey Archive), by Jacques Roubaud, a leader in the celebrated Oulipo experimental group, is the third volume of the Hortense series and was praised by Colin Walters (*Washington Times,* 26 July) as "an amalgam of love story, detective thriller and dramatic tragicomedy, plus anything else I may be forgetting to mention."

In a technical sense this next is a North African novel written in French. *The Honor of the Tribe* (Morrow) by Rachid Mimouni concerns four generations of the El Mabrouks in the town of Zitovna. An elder of the Moslem tribe is telling the story into a tape recorder. Another French writer far from metropolitan France, Maryse Conde II of Guadeloupe, who teaches French at the University of Virginia, published two novels in translation this year: *Tree of Life* (Ballantine), a chronicle history of the Louis family of Guadeloupe; an *I, Tituba, Black Witch of Salem* (Virginia), which is based upon a historical figure from Barbados who was tried as a

witch in Salem. Winner of France's Grand Prix Literaire de la Femme (1986), the novel takes Tituba to Salem in 1692 (where she meets Hester Prynne in jail), then home again where she is hanged for revolutionary activities.

Several novels from Down Under present a picture of working-class life in Australia. Peter Carey's *The Tax Inspector* (Knopf), his fourth novel, takes up four days in the life of the Catchprice family, who have been compared with the Bean family of *The Beans of Egypt, Maine.* Someone accurately dubbed this novel "Australian Gothic." In *The Last Magician* (Holt), Janette Turner Hospital writes about (in the words of Carol Anshaw in the *Washington Post*) "four children, now grown to adults, all haunted by a shared piece of the past." Tim Winton's sixth novel, *Cloudstreet* (Graywolf), covers the years from the 1940s to the 1960s and concerns two working-class Australian families in Cloudstreet (Perth) — the Pickles and the Lambs. New Zealand's Maurice Shadbolt's *Monday's Warriors* (Godine) is set in the nineteenth-century wars between the Maoris and the British and involves many characters, chief among whom is the Maori leader Titokowaru, called Titoko, and Kimball Bent, an American-born British deserter.

The future has already arrived in publishing in protean shapes and forms. The new CD-ROM electronic books are reported to offer text, sound, music, animation, and video footage. They are capable of obeying an order ("Read to me") and to read text aloud. Another command can make the story interactive. Through a search feature the reader can access the story from the point of view of each separate character. One of the publishing novelties of the year was *Agrippa: Book of the Dead* (Kevin Begos), written by William Gibson (a leader in cyberpunk fiction) and illustrated with etchings by Dennis Ashbaugh. The package comes in a metal box containing a partly burned and leatherbound volume in which there is to be found a computer disk containing the text of the autobiographical novel by Gibson. The Ashbaugh etchings are printed in an ink that mutates when exposed to light. The text of the novel (a memory) is programmed and coded to self-destruct after it has been read one time. A total of 455 copies were made, in three limited editions ranging in price from $450 to $7,500 per package.

Is this the shape of the book in the future?

Other novels of 1992, good and bad and indifferent, inevitably escaped the notice of this reviewer. It happens that way. It is a happy thing, however, to conclude with mention of two odd and original books which reached a lot of readers all year long without, at first, many of the usual trappings of publicity and promotion, thus defying what David Streitfeld (*Washington Post,* 19 January) called "The Law of Media Attention, which says the greater the attention the more copies sold." It is difficult to describe the two astonishing best-sellers, written and created by Nick Bantock and published by Chronicle Books of San Francisco – *Griffin & Sabine* (1991) and its sequel *Sabine's Notebook* – because, taking full advantage of all the latest methods of bookmaking and printing (already explored in the making of outstanding children's books), the artist-author and the publisher have created a colorful mass-market product which gives the *appearance* of being unique. Since the form is epistolary, there are "real" letters, which can be opened and removed and read, "real" stamps, postcards, photographs, sketches – all the fun of a children's book built around "a possibly supernatural love affair." (See *Los Angeles Times Book Review,* 20 December, "An Extraordinary Romance.") The story is the correspondence of Griffin Moss, London postcard artist, and Sabine Stroheim, stamp designer and natural historian. In the beginning ten thousand copies were ordered by the publisher: "Two hundred thousand copies later, Bantock has emerged as a full-fledged cult figure with a passionate following." The story has already turned into a trilogy. *The Golden Mean* is scheduled for 1993 publication. Perhaps all three will find simultaneous places on the best-seller lists.

There is one other cause for hope. (See Esther B. Fein, "Publishers' Best Seller: The Backlist," *New York Times,* 8 June.) The point of the piece is that publishers are arriving at the (obvious?) conclusion that in a chancy business such as theirs, backlist books can be a source of security and profit. "Backlist isn't sexy," said Carl Lennertz, director of backlist marketing for the Random House adult trade division, "but it pays the bills." With some of the finest novels of the century silently out of print, this "discovery" by publishers may bode well for readers.

Dictionary of Literary Biography Yearbook Award for Distinguished Novels Published in 1992

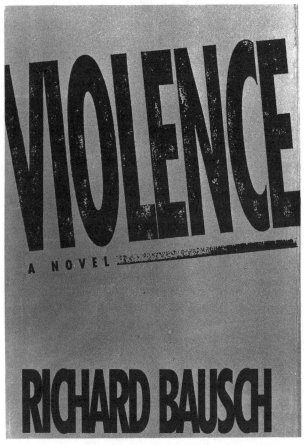
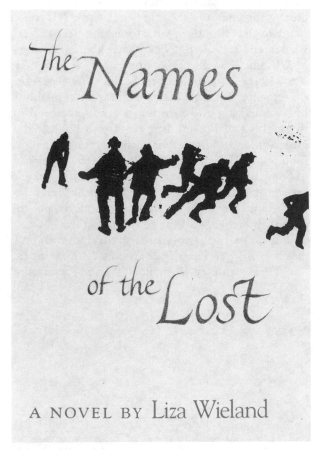

Dust jackets for (left) Richard Bausch's novel about the impact of a single act of violence on a family, and (right) Liza Wieland's novel set during the Atlanta child murders of the early 1980s

NOVEL

Richard Bausch has published four novels and two collections of short stories since 1980. Everything he has done is first-rate and this year's *Violence* (Houghton Mifflin/Seymour Lawrence) is his finest work to date. Nobody else can quite do what he does — which is (mainly) to demonstrate and celebrate the viability of human virtues, without sentimentality or illusions, against terrible challenges and temptations. A poet of the core of magic at the heart of ordinary things, Bausch proves in *Violence* (in the words of one of his characters) "that there can be more sheer bravery in just simply pausing to pet a cat, or in changing a baby's diaper, than in all the wars and car chases and foiling the bank robbery."

Violence is a wonderful novel, a model of excellence.
— *George Garrett*

FIRST NOVEL

As in other years, there were many excellent first novels published during 1992, but none that I know of that is so daring and resonant as *The Names of the Lost* (Southern Methodist University Press) by Liza Wieland. Both author and publisher are honored; for it required real courage for Liza Wieland to stick to her artistic choice of fractioning her complex story into the widely various voices of multiple narrators and yet to create a story which is at once accessible and deeply moving. Southern Methodist University Press is her partner here, showing a courage and commitment which matches the author's.
— *George Garrett*

The Year in the Short Story

David R. Slavitt
University of Pennsylvania

It is a dismaying prospect. This pile of books on my table offers . . . utter incoherence. Or say that it defies categorization. Books of short stories happen, it seems, in absolutely random ways, the heavy-hitting conglomerate publishers putting forth their candidates (often with acknowledgments of appearances in the *New Yorker*). But the university presses and small presses also bring out their short-story collections, some of them winners of formal competitions (publication being the prize, of course), and others just the work of writers they — or their outside readers – have found engaging and meritorious. One would think the short story was an endangered species, like poetry, with only three or four trade houses in New York still dabbling occasionally either out of principle or merely for snobbishness. But while, in their high-minded if low-budget way, the university and small presses are operating soup kitchens for poor and needy genres, it seems absolutely impossible to account for the differences in fate between those books of short stories that come out from Farrar, Straus and Giroux, Knopf, or Harcourt Brace Jovanovich and those that appear from the University of Missouri Press or Coffee House or Story Line, or any of those whose books are difficult to find on the shelves of the bookstore chain outlets.

But an underlying irrationality is, perhaps, appropriate. The shiftiness of the short story is such that it doesn't like to be categorized. Poems are taught in schools – not because students or teachers particularly like them, but because they are short and there is an elaborate critical vocabulary for their analysis and discussion. The short story, without the benefit of such deathly patronage as critics and instructors can bring to it, plods on as if it were a lively art, as if people wrote stories for other people to read for fun. And, in a weird way, the short story is exactly that. I remember an older woman of intimidating cultivation telling me that she never read novels, but, now that she was getting on in years, had time only for poetry and the theater. Which was very aristocratic of her, I thought. The short story is also aristocratic, or can be. It can strike a pose, make a gesture, ingratiate or annoy with a tone of voice, perform some mysterious trope or turn, and then vanish, leaving its resonance behind in the negative space in which we mostly live but which we now find transformed by this sudden confrontation with fiction in its purest state.

Poems have all that linguistic orchestration to them (or they do if the poets know how to use it). Stories just stand there and talk, murmur, cajole, inveigle, or mumble in prose that does not particularly call attention to itself. Several smart and shrewd people I know confess that short stories are the only prose works they ever actually finish reading. But what has gone on? What has been the nature of the transaction? Robert Penn Warren used to tell his students that a short story was "a moment of re-vision." The paradigmatic story opens up by saying that this is how things are, then turns, and revises, or reenvisions, so that we get – not this, but that. And the seeing-through to that second, more profound truth is what gives us, often, the feeling of stasis, resolution, cloture, or whatever it is that we come away with.

That's true, I think, more often than not, but so general as to be of little help in the discussion of actual stories. And such discussion is difficult at best, because with some of the best short stories, we are not even sure how it is that the trick has been managed. What is that satisfactory representation of a small incident or event and how does it resonate and implicate the rest of the world? For the story confesses its ignorance as much as it asserts its wisdom, and we tend to accept the wisdom all the more agreeably because of the innate modesty of the form.

We may as well begin with the two biggest books of stories of 1992 – monster tomes, really. One of these is John O'Hara's *Gibbsville, Pa* (Carroll and Graff), which gives us fifty-three tales. O'Hara's fiction turns the Schuylkill County region into a mythical place, a kind of generic middle America but with an industrial grittiness and a

Dust jacket for the English edition of the Irish writer's collection of stories

Pennsylvania Dutch particularity. John Updike has continued O'Hara's chronicle in a way that cannot be accidental – and that I have always assumed to be an act of homage.

O'Hara is an uneven writer, not very intelligent, often socially irksome – he never got one of those honorary degrees he always yearned for because he kept asking for them – and, in the prose where it matters, awkward sometimes and annoying. In that dogged professionalism of which he was so proud, he could turn out hackwork, but it was seldom unredeemed hacking. There are, in the shufflings and dealings of his tired deck of verismo face cards, unpredictable moments of dexterity in which he can pull off some gesture of breathtaking finesse. How to deal with such a writer? One tries to be grateful for the good pieces and paragraphs and not too captious about the quantity of dross through which it is necessary to sift. O'Hara is a kind of American Anthony Trollope, with many of the same virtues and defects. And in these stories, we see him at his best, his worst, and his most average – in other words, truly.

At his worst, there is a sniggering adolescent who tells us about the respectable X family, and then, in the socko ending, reveals their dirty little secret (the moment of re-vision). And there are several such tiresome exercises that seem, fifty years later, particularly dated. But the reverse gesture – the revelation of decency and virtue in the evidently sordid – as in "Imagine Kissing Pete," is a fine performance, one of the great American short stories. I find it particularly engaging because its heroine, Bobbie McCrae, was one of the women with whom Julian English danced on that awful night at the Gibbsville Country Club (English, of course, is the protagonist of *Appointment in Samarra*). But beyond such private winks and waves, there is the unimpeachable authority of which O'Hara is capable, the magisterial telling of stories, of his time, his place, his people. He can sometimes bring off that civilized Horatian clubbiness that one wouldn't dare question:

> With the friends of later life you may exchange boyhood stories that seem worth telling, but boyhood is not all stories. It is mostly not stories, but day-to-day, unepisodic living. And most of us are too polite to burden our later life friends with unexciting anecdotes about people they will never meet. (Likewise we hope they will not burden us.) But it is easy to bring old friends up to day in your mental dossiers by the addition of a few vital facts.

How suave, grand, off-hand, and . . . efficient! For O'Hara has turned the reader into one of Bobbie McCrae's old friends, earning our assent and our trust, and setting us up to care what happens to this rather bedraggled heroine. There is an even more suave efficiency in *The Collected Stories of William Trevor* (Viking), a 1,261-page doorstop of a volume that gives us another large view of a career. The two long stories of *Two Lives,* "Reading Turgenev" and "My House in Umbria," were published separately last year, but even without those pieces this is longer than V. S. Pritchett's collected stories of last year, and more than twice as long as, say, John Cheever's or Isaac Bashevis Singer's or Irwin Shaw's. And clearly, Trevor is in that league. He is less well known, I think, because he is one of those careful, meticulous craftsmen. His approach to the short story is deliberately unflashy, and he writes mostly in transparent sentences that do not call attention to themselves. Even when he is funny – and he can be quite comical – his humor is wry and reserved. The pieces convince us not by their rhetoric but by their careful observations of setting and their precise considerations of character. The tone is always matter-of-fact, and one can find, over and over, recitations of the almost defiantly dreary donnée, the humdrum details that he promises to bring alive for us: "Mr. Mockler was a tailor. He carried on his business in a house that after twenty-five years of mortgage arrangements had finally become his: 22 Juniper Street, SW 17." Or, "They met in the most casual way, in the upstairs office of Chaharbagh Tours Inc. In the downstairs office a boy asked Normanton to go upstairs and wait: the tour would start a little later because they were having trouble with the engine of the minibus." Typical and not at all astonishing – yet, after only a handful of these stories, I cannot think that many readers will find that Graham Greene was indulging in hyperbole or puffery when he said, of one of Trevor's collections, that it was "Surely one of the best collections, if not the best collection, since [James] Joyce's *Dubliners.*"

　　Only a notch or two below this giddy level of impressive accomplishment, there are several collections of stories from established writers who are working at the top of their form. Some of these are taking interesting chances and making efforts deliberately to push the boundaries of the form to see what it can yield. One such adventurer is George Garrett, whose new and selected stories, *An Evening Performance,* came out in 1985 – a volume of some five-hundred-odd pages. Now, he has a new and quite different kind of book, *Whistling in the Dark* (Harcourt Brace Jovanovich), for which he provides a helpful subtitle, "True Stories and Other Fables." That these narratives may have some basis in fact and that the first person narrator of these tales may bear some resemblance to Garrett are not denied but are beside the point. These are not conventional confessional pieces. On the contrary, what Garrett seems to be interested in is how a narrative becomes a story, or even a "fable," with the suggestiveness and the shimmer that such terms imply. To take pieces of actual happenings, however selected and filtered by memory and *amour propre,* and use them as tesserae, making them into an artifact that behaves like any other made thing . . . is a piece of magic! (One of his earlier novellas is called, not entirely facetiously, *The Magic Striptease.*) The title piece of the new book begins with an account of a couple of soldiers getting into uniform for a tour of MP duty that they have drawn. The little overture depends for its effectiveness on such trivial secrets of military dressing as that the ammo pouches, for instance, are "worn up front, just to the right – two eyelets over, I seem to recall – of the belt buckle." They walk out into a clear bright day, the first

Dust jacket for Garrett's collection of stories explaining the nature of narrative and fable

bright day since they have arrived here near Linz, and, for the first time, they see mountains all around:

> It has been so gray and close, wet and foggy since they got here that they never knew there were mountains within sight until this minute. They don't say anything. What is there to say? They are old-timers, short timers in the U.S. Army now. It is not that they are not surprised. It is that they are continually astonished by everything. They don't speak, but they stop in midstride. They stand there and just look around. The young corporal allows himself to whistle softly between his teeth. "Let's go," the sergeant says then. "We're fixing to be late." They move off side by side, in step. I can't remember the corporal's name for the life of me. The sergeant, of course, is myself.

　　The opening up of the sky and by-the-bye mention of that "feeling of continual astonishment" are what give the piece its character, what make the last revelation – that the sergeant is our narrator – its charge. And it is by such subtle rhetorical contrivances that Garrett works, first turning the account of another odd discovery (that, as a boy, Adolf Hitler exhibited a talent for whistling) into a poem, and then turning that poem, by juxtaposition, into the story we are reading. It is a dizzying piece of literary legerdemain, the kind of thing that – like the bumblebee – ought not to be able to fly, except that it does.

Lazy and ungrateful reviewers complain that Joyce Carol Oates is an overproducer, which seems to me absurd. What they are really complaining about is not just that she writes a great many books, but that the books continue to be interesting, demanding our attention and offering new pleasures and rewards. She continues, in other words, to be worth reviewing. Her new book of stories, *Where Is Here?* (Ecco) is only 193 pages long, but there are thirty-five stories, which means that many of them are quite short. On the other hand, no one would call them minimalist, for they are furnished, even crammed, with extravagance. Prose poems, then? Not really, or better say that these prose pieces are informed by Oates's fiction in much the way that her narrative poetry (which she does extraordinarily well) is enabled and enriched by her experience as a novelist and short-story writer. In the long run, it doesn't matter what one calls these things; they are *writing* in the same way that Garrett's "True Stories and Other Fables" are *writing*. She is clearly thinking of fables, from Aesop or Oscar Wilde, and of children's stories and even of parables, as in "The Maker of Parables," in which she tells us:

> M., the maker of parables, a small dwarfish delicately built man with shining dark eyes, lived inside a large slovenly bearlike man of late middle age. Each morning the two clambered up out of sleep, the one trembling with anticipation to set down, in the crystalline prose for which, while yet living, he had become immortal, the beautiful and terrifying wisdom yielded him by night; the other trembling with anticipation to eat – to eat, and eat, and eat. For there was a ravenous hole in his belly.

There are three more paragraphs, a couple of flourishes really, and she's done. It's strange and nifty, a little bit reminiscent of Halo Calvino, or perhaps Elias Canetti, but also characteristically her own series of very serious games. And the pleasures of her generous talent are evident in abundance.

Rather different in timbre, but with the same interest in brevity, John Taylor has an extraordinary book in *The Presence of Things Past* (Story Line Press) in which the work of two tiny volumes that were first published in France – *Tower Park* and *The View from the Upper Window* – is presented for Ameri-

cans. Taylor lives in France, but these are stories about the American Midwest, nostalgic takes and glimpses, deft and suggestive as some of those simple drawings by which Pablo Picasso could suggest a bird or a woman's backside, or whatever. . . . Taylor is an impressively accomplished writer, as this paragraph, which is just over half of the entire story, so indisputably demonstrates:

> Every now and then I catch myself thinking of what to buy my mother for a present. The lights strung across the street, the frost, the exhaust; I stop in front of a shopwindow and contemplate that red porcelain cup– Royal Albert "Lady Hamilton" – or on my way across town to meet Françoise remember that coffee pot I sent to my mother from Greece. It was a tin *briki*. Then I remember – the wind swirls, the buses roar by – that my mother has been dead for years.

The book, or these books, make up a kind of poetic novel, for the first person persists and we get an amplitude of experience and vision that is paradoxically enabled by the abruptness of the individual piece. There are, in fact, several books of related stories, which is an odd form, not really a novel but perhaps more like the suite that has become so important in twentieth century poetry. Dabney Stuart's *Sweet Lucy Wine* (Louisiana State University Press) is one of these, a loosely, or maybe not so loosely, connected set of tales about Mark Random, a young boy growing up in a southern town. The trick here is the point of view, that steady, spooky gaze of latency on the curious antics of those who are either older or younger. These are deft, humane, and sometimes very funny pieces about the consonance and dissonance of "head truth" and another, deeper kind.

It strikes me that Garrett, Oates, and Stuart are all poets, but none of their stories is what one might expect of poets taking a flier in – or condescending to – prose. The most one can say is that their sentences are a bit more lithe and lively, their rhythms a little more supple and subtle. . . . And this is also the case with Robert Morgan, an estimable poet, whose book of related stories, *The Mountains Won't Remember Us* (Peachtree Publishers), appeared this year. Morgan's stories are about a family in western North Carolina, up in the hills, and they work much in the way that Fred Chappell's remarkable stories do, playing off the Theocritan and Virgilian pastoral tradition and allowing apparently simple country folk to exhibit enough ornery complexity to keep us city slickers just a little off balance. The pastoral figure is, in a typical story, first asserted, then complicated or denied, but then finally reasserted so that the rocky truths we might have dismissed as too easy now seem rich and precious. Morgan seems a bit more rueful than Chappell – a bit less fanciful perhaps, but the terrain is the same, and the skill is up in Chappell's stratospheric range. It is no mere coincidence that many of these old codgers in bib overalls are named Homer and Virgil. Those authors are alive for these people. The educated squirearchy Edmund Wilson used to imagine was not altogether a figment.

There are a couple of other praiseworthy volumes of connected stories, particularly Tom Chiarella's *Foley's Luck* (Knopf) and Linda Svendsen's *Marine Life* (Farrar, Straus and Giroux). What is especially pleasing to report is that both of these are debut volumes and that both Chiarella and Svendsen are impressively gifted, not only promising but already richly accomplished. Chiarella has been publishing some of these stories in prestigious magazines where the name of the continuing character is Berard; in the volume, "Berard's Luck," "Berard's Life Story," "Berard's Rapture," and such are now "Foley's Luck," "Foley's Life Story," "Foley's Rapture," and so on. But whatever the character's name, he is a kind of suburban everyman whose trivial welter of mishaps nudges up against the metaphysical and cosmological. Chiarella is a little like Thomas Berger sometimes, which is altogether fine.

Svendsen, meanwhile, promises to be a bit like Alice Munro (who supplies a most generous but accurate blurb for *Marine Life,* by the way). Her family is working-class, shifting as well as they can, some of them shiftier than others, and some quite shiftless . . . The women throw in their lots with men about whom they do not know enough or know too much, and everyone hurts. "White Shoulders," the concluding piece in this volume, is about child abuse and its victim's suicide and is probably the most powerful single story I have read all year.

Or is it Kit Reed's "In the *Squalus,*" the first piece in her collection, *Thief of Lives* (University of Missouri Press)? It would be a difficult question to answer, a hard call indeed. "In the *Squalus* " is about a survivor of a submarine disaster in which some of the crew are killed. His life thereafter is as much changed as are those of holocaust survivors, ruined by the vision of the awful truth that he can never forget or escape, except by drinking too much. This could have been a melodramatic and impossible subject, but Reed's innate tact and talent are such that there is never a false note anywhere. The power of huge things to affect and infect the smaller

Dennis Cooper, author of the collection Wrong *(photograph by Michel Delson)*

ones is what she uses like levers for their mechanical advantage. The negligible domestic detail and the ordinary exchanges of conversations can resonate with cosmic significance . . . and she makes this happen.

At this point, my train of thought collapses, and we are left with a handful of books that are good, worth at least mentioning, but not amenable to even the most latitudinarian categorization. For lack of anything better, and in candor, then, I give the rest of them, an even dozen, in alphabetical order (by authors' last names):

Dennis Cooper's *Wrong* (Grove Weidenfeld) is an unabashedly repellent book, in the tradition of Edgar Allan Poe, Louis-Ferdinand Céline, Jean Genet, and Henry Bataille, full of violence and perversity, and one can either stand it or not. But even a cursory glance is enough to make one aware that there is more to these stories than sordidness and shock. When a character muses, "But that's the beauty of dead kids . . . Everything they ever did seems incredibly moving in retrospect," we are forced to admit that from these horrors a kind of truth arises.

Dust jacket for Kenan's collection of stories about the black experience in America

Alfred DePew is one of the winners of the Flannery O'Connor Award for Short Fiction, which amounts to publication by the University of Georgia Press. DePew's collection, *The Melancholy of Departure,* is slightly cockeyed, just a bit askew, so that one can never be quite sure where any given story is going. But then, when DePew gets to the place where he performs his turn, there can be an astonishing making-good of what seemed the most long-odds set-up. A white-faced clown with whom one of the narrators falls in love turns, for just a moment (but a moment can be enough!), into "a sort of Ba'al Shem Tov with laughing children on his shoulders, a man whom God had put on this earth to show us the study of Talmud was not the only path." These may be improbable moves that DePew attempts, but his success with most of them is all the more remarkable. It is a fine collection.

Deborah Eisenberg's *Under the 82nd Airborne* (Farrar, Straus and Giroux) is a second collection (Eisenberg's earlier book was *Transactions in a Foreign Currency*). Several of these appeared in the *New York-*er and, for those who do not bother reading the acknowledgments (I generally look at them first) there is an extra hint in the dedication: "For and because of William Shawn." Well, OK, and they are good solid pieces, admirable mostly, if a little mannered here and there. Seven carefully wrought stories in which surfaces collapse, or nets that are established catch more than one first expected. My favorite piece is "Holy Week," which first appeared in the *Western Humanities Review* (which probably means that the *New Yorker* rejected it), but I am being crabby perhaps.

Gloria Frym's *How I Learned* (Coffee House Press) is mostly about the underbelly of San Francisco — tough gritty stories about the despised and rejected in prisons or out on the streets in the tenderloin, where they are waiting, many of them, to get caught. What keeps these stories from being programmatic and tiresome is that Frym is tough and funny, as much committed to the art of fiction as to the demands of political correctness. It also helps that she is a poet and can make sentences snap and crackle.

Dennis Hathaway is the other Flannery O'Connor Award winner this year, with *Consequences of Desire* (University of Georgia Press). Hathaway lives in Venice, California, and he writes about that Golden State, where what most of us think of as day-to-day reality is visible only when the weather is weird. Literary culture there, I expect, is a curiosity like any other, and perhaps for that reason Hathaway is able to do some extraordinary things. One of his stories grabs us by the lapels with this opening, "Annie, once Ann, named Anna after the tragic heroine of what her father called the greatest novel ever written, wishes that she had been named Emma after the Madame whose equally unhappy demise seemed in its Frenchness somehow more sublime." He is a fancy-Dan, a strutter, and performer, and he is as much a pleasure to read as he will be a delight to follow.

G. W. Hawkes — there is no way to tell what the initials stand for, but there is a dust-jacket picture showing a bearded young man — is a lively writer whose *Spies in the Blue Smoke* (Missouri) is, at the very least, engaging. Hawkes can do voices, and the reason I checked for the name and the gender was that the women are particularly convincing and plausible. After I had read "The Guy Downstairs Blows Sax," with its depiction of a woman's giving assent to a man and a life, I had to look. In this and other pieces, some brief fragments and others rather more fully developed, there is a wonderfully persuasive sense of lived lives, which is one of the things we read for.

Randall Kenan's extraordinary *Let the Dead Bury Their Dead* (Harcourt Brace Jovanovich) has the historical sweep of David Bradley, a vision of what the black experience in America has been that is rooted as much in reading as in living, and in this fine volume of stories each of those sources of knowledge enriches and refines the other. "Cornsilk" is a series of numbered takes in which a young black man reveals the terrible secret of his incestuous relationship with his half-sister . . . and what could have been sordid or melodramatic is, in Kenan's capable and lively prose, moving, funny, and altogether persuasive. The title piece describes itself as the "Annotated Oral History of the Former Maroon Society called Snatchit and then Tearshirt and later the Town of Tims Creek, North Carolina [circa 1854–1895]" and is a brilliant riff in which text, footnotes, and subtext jostle one another, turning into a series of voices that ring in several heads at once – not least important in ours.

Jane McCafferty's *Director of the World & Other Stories* is the winner of the Drue Heinz Literature Prize, which does not include a pickle but which carries with it publication by the University of Pittsburgh Press. A panel of judges selected a few finalists from the 279 entries – almost certainly all of them deserving publication – and from these a judge (this year it was John Edgar Wideman) chose the one he liked. One can see why McCafferty's work was appealing. These are lively stories about dissonance and displacement, and the writing is full of verve and sassy charm. "A seven-inch Virgin Mary was glued to the white dashboard of the '67 aqua Nova and usually surrounded by crumpled sheets of lipsticked Kleenex. She stood in all her blue plastic glory throughout the days of my childhood, cheap, constant, and watching the road – unlike the driver, my mother." That is the start of the first story, and McCafferty maintains this pitch fairly consistently. "The people who have mattered to me have revealed themselves in autumn. This is no coincidence, but rather reflects the fact that in autumn I feel at my strongest, more at home in the world, almost (though never entirely) willing to accept yearning itself as a partner." No question but that we shall be hearing more from this writer.

Jill McCorkle's *Crash Diet* (Algonquin Books of Chapel Hill) is bright and sassy, verging nearly on sitcom, but then turning out to be OK. McCorkle is a little like Lee Smith, having the same fun with those tacky queens of the K-Mart with whom the New South abounds. Thus "Comparison Shopping" starts out, "The big news in my neighborhood is that Tom and Sue are going to be on 'The Newly-

wed Game' or rather, 'The *New* Newlywed Game,' as Sue has corrected me over the past four months." But do not be too quick to mock, for this piece appeared in the *Southern Review,* which is classier than *Cosmo* (although *Cosmopolitan* pays better – and McCorkle has published there, too).

Reginald McKnight's *The Kind of Light that Shines on Texas* (Little, Brown) is a series of monologues about African-American life, its stresses and contradictions and its satisfactions and joys. The title story was in the *Kenyon Review* and *Prize Stories 1990: The O. Henry Awards* and is a moving account of the experience of a black kid in a Texas schoolroom with a bigot for a teacher and bullies in the class. That the protagonist is saved by Marvin – the one other black male in the class, a huge, ugly fellow who sleeps a lot and who smells bad – is agonizing for the kinds of questions it raises about who he is, what he can expect, and where his loyalties lie. This impressive performance is no fluke, either, as the other pieces in the book so clearly demonstrate.

Helen Norris's *The Burning Glass* (Louisiana State University Press) is a book of large ambitions, unafraid of intimidating subjects – Vietnamese jungles, Polish concentration camps, orphans, mafiosi, spies. Nothing seems to daunt this writer. And if she sometimes overreaches a bit with her plotting, there are many smaller and more secure achievements of an acute observer and a most generous spirit. Norris is the author of four novels and two previous collections of stories, and she may well be deliberately courting the difficult and dangerous, at which she is mostly successful. Her intensity can be an almost unbearable series of hammer blows, with each carefully wrought sentence taking its toll:

> While she was standing there talking to him, she could see herself five minutes from then already down in the street below, taking a cab, riding away in the winter dusk and into the years that would make her forget she was telling her father, "You're scum to me," and watching the shock spread over his face. The shock in his face spread over her own. It gave her pleasure to feel his shock, to know she had found the words for it. Like the right key that would throw the lock.

C. E. Poverman's *Skin* (Ontario Review Press) is his second collection of stories – he has also written three novels, including *My Father in Dreams*. He flirts with the psychopathological, the violent, and the bizarre, but he manages mostly to put these excesses to good use, intensifying reality rather than abandoning it. My own favorite among these is one of the relatively more cautious pieces, "Beautiful," about a woman who does maquillage in one of those cosmetic departments in a large store. And the *inventio* is so elegant and so brilliantly simple: "There's something about the way they give themselves to you which makes you feel responsible, care," the beautician remarks about these strangers with whom she works in such great intimacy as she reinvents their faces.

So, that is the dozen. But how to end this? Where can we go to give the piece a sense of stasis and conclusion, as if it were, say, some kind of story? I am all but ready to shrug and give up, when the doorbell rings and the UPS (United Parcel Service) man appears with one more package – my enthusiasm for these has begun to wane in recent weeks, I must admit. Another book of stories? At this late date? From the University of Tennessee Press . . . I cannot recall asking them for anything, but I must have done so. I open the package and it is Rachel Maddux's *The Way Things Are,* a 270-page collection of all the stories of hers that Nancy A. Walker, the book's editor, could find. Rachel Maddux lived from 1913 to 1983, published only eight stories during her lifetime (the latest of these appeared in 1959), and is, the editor tells us, "known primarily for her novels – *The Green Kingdom* (1957), *Abel's Daughter* (1960), and *A Walk in the Spring Rain* (1966) – and her nonfiction work *The Orchard Children* (1977)." Known by others, perhaps, but not me.

All right, though. I figure I may as well take a look, and I do, and I find that these are fine stories, accomplished, lively, slightly pushing at the limits of what we think of as real, wonderfully located in time and place, particularly the Midwest. She is very, very good! Different from, say, William Trevor, but . . . in her way, every bit as estimable. Serious and even philosophical stories, they resonate with authority and linger in the mind. And she's dead, and, as a short-story writer at least, virtually unknown.

Because she is a woman, though, there was a political advantage she had: her obscurity could be considered not merely as a matter of bad luck but as a shared grievance; there is a feminist point to be made in Professor Walker's resurrection of her work. Professor Walker, a member of the English department at Vanderbilt University, is director of the Women's Studies program there. She is also the editor of several other Rachel Maddux books the University of Tennessee has republished. Some other poor, forgotten, excellent writer who had the poor judgment to have been born male might have been excluded from the benefit of these fortuitous wrinkles in the moment's intellectual linen. And that troubles me. Nevertheless, these are wonderful stories, truly remarkable, and one must be more churlish than I not to feel grateful for any series of quirks that retrieved them from oblivion. It makes no sense, but then that's what I started out saying, didn't I?

Dictionary of Literary Biography Yearbook Award for a Distinguished Volume of Short Stories Published in 1992

The Way Things Are

The Stories of Rachel Maddux • Edited, with an introduction, by Nancy A. Walker

Dust jacket for Rachel Maddux's collection of short stories about the "effort to locate the fragile, yet crucial, quality of true human connectedness"

Rachel Maddux's *The Way Things Are,* is a 270-page collection of twenty-eight stories, all that Nancy A. Walker, the book's editor, was able to find. Rachel Maddux lived from 1913 to 1983, published only eight stories during her lifetime (the latest appeared in 1959), and is, Professor Walker tells us, "known primarily for her novels – *The Green Kingdom* (1957), *Abel's Daughter* (1960), and *A Walk in the Spring Rain* (1966) – and her nonfiction work, *The Orchard Children* (1977).

These are fine pieces, accomplished, lively, slightly but firmly pushing at the limits of what we think of as real, wonderfully located in time and place, particularly the midwest. Serious and even philosophical stories, they resonate with authority and linger in the mind. And she's dead, and, as a short story writer at least, virtually unknown. That her stories are often about chance meetings and missed opportunities – suggestions of what sculptors would think of as negative space – turns out to be dismally appropriate. But thanks to the dedication of Nancy Walker and the courage of the University of Tennessee Press, this fine work is now available and deserves what it never got in its author's lifetime – attention!

– *David R. Slavitt*

The Year in Poetry

Robert McPhillips
Iona College

The year 1992 saw a change of guard in Washington that, among other things, seems to bode well for the state of the arts in America, particularly for poetry. President-elect Bill Clinton, a friend of Miller Williams, the poet and director of the University of Arkansas Press, was the first president since John F. Kennedy to commission a poem to be read at his inauguration. Clinton's selection was Arkansas-bred poet Maya Angelou. Angelou, an actress and speaker with a richly musical voice, who is technically a better prose writer – of such autobiographical volumes as *I Know Why the Caged Bird Sings* (1969) – than a poet, came through with a spirited reading at Clinton's 20 January 1993 inauguration of "On the Pulse of Morning," a Whitmanesque catalogue of America's diversity and a statement of equally Whitmanesque beliefs both in the potential spiritual strength to be derived from democratic diversity and in the role that poetry can play in helping the country to fulfill its democratic potential. Angelou's rhythmic, free-verse plea for a new beginning for the United States ended with this peroration:

The horizon leans forward,
Offering you space to place new steps of change.
Here, on the pulse of this fine day
You may have the courage
To look up and out and upon me, the
Rock, the River, the Tree, your country.
No less to Midas than the mendicant.
No less to you now than the mastodon then.

Here, on the pulse of this new day
You may have the grace to look up and out
And into your sister's eyes, and into
Your brother's face, your country
And say simply
Very simply
With hope –
Good morning.

In choosing Angelou, Clinton implicitly answered in the affirmative the question Dana Gioia asked in his 1991 *Atlantic* essay that my predeces-

sor, R. S. Gwynn, discussed in his roundup discussion of the poetry of 1991 for last year's *Yearbook*. Gioia's essay ("Can Poetry Matter?") seems to have brought about a general cultural awareness of the role poetry can play in all our lives. For the last five years Sam Gwynn has set a very tough standard to live up to in his own discerning discussion of what is good and bad about contemporary poetry, about what matters and what does not and why. And while I anticipate as awkward a transition into his shoes as Clinton has shown in his early days adjusting to life in Washington, it is more because of the immensity of the job, which one cannot quite anticipate before assuming it, and not because of any aesthetic differences between myself and Gwynn. Like him, I recognize the necessity to see past the ethnic, ideological, and aesthetic allegiances so endemic to contemporary American poetry, reading as a practical critic concerned first and foremost with individual poets writing in distinctive voices that communicate powerfully to the common reader. Unlike Gwynn, I am not primarily a poet, and I do not teach creative writing. I am therefore a bit less concerned with the goings-on among the members of the Associated Writing Programs, though I am aware how crucial a role that organization plays in what poetry gets published where and with which blurbs, and hence of the necessity of the critic to block out to whatever extent possible the ephemera of a book's publication and focus on the poems at hand. And how hard that is to do. To whatever extent possible, however, I hope to maintain Gwynn's independent standards as a critic.

Still, objectivity is not such an easy matter when confronting contemporary American poetry if only because its very diversity has produced a climate of rivaling aesthetics among groups of poets who see their goals as mutually exclusive. To simplify matters, I would say that this situation arises from three phenomena: the modernist revolt against rhyme and meter as valid tools for post-Victorian poets – a movement magisterially documented in Hugh Kenner's *The Pound Era* and soberly critiqued in Timothy Steele's *Missing Measures* – that has resulted in a poetics of relativity; the civil rights movements of the 1960s which placed primary emphasis on ethnicity, gender, and sexual orientation in the evaluation of literature; and the academization of American poetry since World War II, both in the areas of literary criticism, from the New Critics to the Deconstructionists to the New Historicists, and in the rise of the poetry workshop, which tended to influence the form and content of poetry in their varying ways. Amid such an atmosphere it is easier to take sides than to attempt objectivity. Nevertheless, it seems to me a sign for optimism that three books of practical criticism on contemporary poetry by poet-critics largely removed from considerations of political or poetic correctness, but rather with sober and enthusiastic engagement in the life of poetry, were published in 1992 – David Lehman's *The Line Forms Here* (University of Michigan Press), Dana Gioia's *Can Poetry Matter? Essays on Poetry and American Culture* (Graywolf), and Henry Taylor's *Compulsory Figures: Essays on Recent American Poets* (Louisiana State University Press). (Another notable, albeit quite different sort of critical book published this year is a compellingly contemporary reading of a classical Roman poet, *Catullus* [Yale], by the gifted poet Charles Martin. Notable too is Donald Hall's *Their Ancient Glittering Eyes: Remembering Poets and Other Poets* [Ticknor and Fields], a reprint of *Remembering Poets* [1978], his memoirs of Robert Frost, T. S. Eliot, Ezra Pound, and Dylan Thomas, now expanded to include essays on Marianne Moore, Archibald MacLeish, and Yvor Winters).

Taylor won the Pulitzer Prize for his most recent collection of poetry, *The Flying Change* (1985). *Compulsory Figures* consists of individual essays on seventeen contemporary poets. These essays, the majority of which originally appeared in the *Hollins Critic,* one of the few extant journals devoted to such essays, demonstrate Taylor's eclectic taste. To be sure, Taylor, who grew up on a Virginia farm where he trained show horses and whose own poetry arises from the southern agrarian tradition, has insightful things to say about poets with whom he shares both regional and poetic affinities such as George Garrett, William Jay Smith, and Fred Chappell. But it extends far beyond that to appreciations of poets as diverse as Gwendolyn Brooks and John Hall Wheelock, and J. V. Cunningham and Jackson MacLow, as well as such others as Anthony Hecht, May Sarton, Louis Simpson, James Wright, William Stafford, David Slavitt, and William Meredith. He also focuses on such lesser-known figures as

Henry Taylor, author of Compulsory Figures: Essays on Recent American Poets *(photograph by Hilary Schwab)*

Brewster Ghiselin and John Woods. Taylor's readings are close and sympathetic and refreshingly independent.

As a companion volume to this first collection of Taylor's criticism, Louisiana State University Press has brought together his first two books of poetry, *The Horse Show at Midnight* and *An Afternoon of Pocket Billiards. Horse Show* is a youthful volume that announces his rural subject matter and that implicitly compares the art of poetry with that of controlling a show horse. It also contains a memorable narrative poem, "Things Not Solved Though Tomorrow Came," as well as highly amusing parodies of contemporary poets, among them James Dickey, Robert Creeley and Denise Levertov, and James Wright and Robert Bly. *Pocket Billiards* contains some of the strongest of Taylor's poems. "Divorce" is a powerful epigram:

He travels fastest who travels alone,
And he kills two birds with one rolling stone.

Dust jacket for Dana Gioia's book of essays on poets and poetry and their role in contemporary culture

By contrast, the longer, intricately crafted "An Afternoon of Pocket Billiards" juxtaposes a description of playing billiards with the breakup of the poet's first marriage even as it anticipates erotic renewal:

> . . . I rise to air,
> to dust and vacant noise and old despair.
> Error still holds me here,
>
> but I'll be right someday:
>
>
> though one song of old love has died away,
> an older song is falling into place.
> From now on I will play to make it speak,
> to see the form its words give to this game.
> I see, as I move into another rack,
> that all days in this cavern are the same:
> endless struggles to know
> how cold skill and a force like love can flow
> together in my veins, and be at peace.

At his quiet best Taylor shows how powerfully poetry speaks when psychological nuance and philosophical wisdom are seamlessly embodied in a poem's form.

Lehman, the series editor of the annual *Best American Poetry* anthology since its inception in 1988 and the author of two volumes of poetry, has, among other things, taught literature at Hamilton College and film at Ithaca College, done a stint as a staff book critic at *Newsweek* (where he was actually able to review a variety of volumes of poetry in its pages, which is virtually unheard of in our mass-market magazines), and written a brilliant book-length piece of investigative journalism of the highest sort, *Signs of the Times: Deconstruction and the Fall of Paul de Man* (1991), a persuasive attack on the reign of literary theory within the academy. *The Line Forms Here* includes twenty pieces ranging from the journalistic ("Tales of Oulipo" and "Under the Influence of Harold Bloom," both written for *Newsweek*) to the more scholarly ("Elemental Bravery: The Unity of James Merrill's Poetry," from *James Merrill: Essays in Criticism,* a collection coedited by Lehman and Charles Berger for Cornell University Press in 1983). In addition to his piece on Merrill, Lehman has written insightful essays in practical criticism on nine other poets, among them Elizabeth Bishop, John Hollander, and John Ashbery, in a very accessible piece titled "The Pleasures of John Ashbery's Poetry." The collection is rounded out with essays on poetic form in a section titled "Lines and Form"; nine essays on the contemporary literary scene, collected under the rubric "The Life of Words"; and an interview with the author. Perhaps the most provocative essay in the collection is "Criticism in Crisis," which, like his book on Paul de Man, laments the dominance of literary theory within the country's literary departments and concludes – in contrast to Gioia's attack on poetry workshops in "Can Poetry Matter?" – with this thought worth pondering:

> Not very long ago the idea of teaching creative writing was regarded askance by English department traditionalists. What an irony that it is now in creative writing seminars that the traditional values of literary study stand their best chance of being transmitted.

I came to a similar conclusion when asked to respond to Gioia's *Atlantic* essay, for the *Poetry Society of America Newsletter,* the quarterly publication of the Poetry Society of America. One wonders how Gioia feels about this proposition, now that he has left behind the business world – Lehman discusses Gioia's dual role as businessman-poet in "Poets Who Work for a Living" in his *The Line Forms Here* – to edit textbooks and teach part-time in writing programs at Johns Hopkins University, Wesleyan University, and Sarah Lawrence College. In any case, that essay is now the title piece to Gioia's first collection of criticism, *Can Poetry Matter? Essays on Poetry and American Culture,* named a Notable Book of the Year by *Publishers Weekly* and nominated for this year's National Book Critics Circle Award for Criticism. As much attention as the title essay has garnished, I hope that it does not obscure what I consider Gioia's greatest strength as a critic, which is his staunch independence in writing about marginal poets whose work he considers insufficiently appreciated – most notably Weldon Kees, but also Robinson Jeffers, Donald Justice, Howard Moss, Ted Kooser, Thomas M. Disch, Jared Carter, and Radcliffe Squires – while occasionally deflating the reputations of those he considers overrated – Robert Bly, John Ashbery, James Dickey, and Margaret Atwood. When he writes favorably about established poets, he does so from a unique perspective. In pieces on Wallace Stevens and T. S. Eliot he is less interested in explicating their already minutely dissected poetic oeuvres than he is in discussing how they managed to write some of the very best poems in our literature while balancing full-time careers as an insurance lawyer and a banker, respectively. Similarly, in his essay "The Example of Elizabeth Bishop," he eschews close readings of the poetry of Bishop – with whom he studied while a graduate student at Harvard – focusing instead on the model of reticence about her personal life and of the integrity of the craft of poetry she presented to his generation of poets, who came of age during the exhibitionist era of the Beat and Confessional poets:

> She implied that while style might not in itself be character, it was certainly the product of character, and that excellence came from imaginative integrity rather than any method. In a confusing time she affirmed poetry's freedom to move in delight and discovery. Her presence was gentle and reassuring, but her lessons were difficult. If today one finds it hard to identify her students by any obvious family resemblance, then she proves a most successful teacher.

In addition to the title essay, *Can Poetry Matter?* contains two very important theoretical essays on the emergence of the New Formalism and the New

Narrative among younger American poets from the late 1970s through the present, "Notes on the New Formalism" and "The Poet in an Age of Prose." In "Notes," Gioia does not reject free verse as an option for the contemporary poet, even if he ingeniously demonstrates that one of the most famous free-verse poems, William Carlos Williams's "The Red Wheel Barrow," is free verse derived from "two rather undistinguished lines of blank verse," leading him to the conclusion: "That Williams wrote blank verse while thinking he was pioneering new trails in prosody doesn't necessarily invalidate his theories (though it may lead one to examine them with a certain skepticism)." Instead, he is primarily concerned with the contemporary poet's being free to exploit any poetic technique available to write good poems. "Working in free verse," he argues in the essay's central statement,

> helped keep the language of my formal poems varied and contemporary, just as writing in form helped keep my free verse more focused and precise. I find it puzzling therefore that so many poets see these modes as opposing aesthetics rather than as complementary techniques. Why shouldn't a poet explore the full resources the English language offers?

In "The Poet in an Age of Prose," Gioia discusses the difficulty contemporary poets face reaching a common reader. Unlike the "postmodernist" poets such as Ashbery and Creeley who are interested in continuing the modernist revolution in art and are content to limit their audience to an elite, usually academic, coterie (whose critical high priestess is Marjorie Perloff), the spirit of the New Formalists is contrary, reacting against the postmodernist norm, drawing upon

> a new imaginative road that took the materials of popular art – the accessible genres, the genuinely emotional subject matter, the irreverent humor, the narrative vitality, and the linguistic authenticity – and combined it with the precision, compression, and ambition of high art. They remained committed to the standards of excellence embodied in high culture but recognized that the serious arts had grown remote and inbred.

In short, "the New Formalists undertook the reclamation of contemporary poetry by mixing democratic and elitist models into a new synthesis."

In an interview I conducted with Gioia which was published in the Summer 1992 issue of *Verse,* he took his views on the relationship of modernism to contemporary poetry even further. "Modernism is dead," he asserted:

Its historical moment has passed. Although it still influences what any serious American poet hopes to do, it is no longer a viable tradition. Of course, there is a group of poets and critics who pretend Modernism is still the vital mainstream. They desperately try to perpetuate the theory that the avant-garde remains a living force. To me, being avant-garde in the 1990's is a kind of antiquarianism. The central task for poets in my generation is the perennial challenge of reinventing poetry for the present moment. We must find a way to reconcile the achievements of Modernism with the necessity of creating a more inclusive and accessible kind of poetry.

Here Gioia not only proposes a challenge to the poets of his generation to revitalize poetry; he also explains the dilemma faced by the contemporary critic of poetry who wishes to be more than an advocate of one type of poetry: how to judge what is most vital and significant among contemporary poets seemingly in a state of aesthetic transition. What aspects of modernism in any given poet's work is "antiquarian," what viably "for the present moment"? It is a challenge I felt most strongly this year in trying to assess the quality of the most recent collections of John Ashbery – which I will get to – who was once considered generally to be the best living American poet, after the success of *Self-Portrait in a Convex Mirror* (1975) and the deaths of Robert Lowell and Elizabeth Bishop, and who continues to win major awards such as the 1992 Ruth Lilly Poetry Prize from *Poetry* magazine, but whose critical reputation seems far more tentative today.

To a lesser extent, the legacy of modernism as utilized by the 1992 Nobel Prize–winner Derek Walcott, the West Indian poet from Saint Lucia who spends much of his time in the United States where he teaches at Boston University, becomes crucial in assessing how successful some of his most ambitious poems – especially his recent book-length Caribbean epic, *Omeros* (1991) – actually are. That Walcott is a major poet is indisputable; he is, among other things, a master of a variety of traditional English metrical and stanzaic forms. He shows himself to be particularly adept with rhymed quatrains in many of his poems in *The Arkansas Testament* (1987), as in these stanzas from "A Latin Primer," a poem that deals with Walcott's major theme, the conflict between his Caribbean homeland and the classical British education he received in Saint Lucia:

I had nothing against which
to notch the growth of my work
but the horizon, no language

but the shallows in my long walk

home, so I shook all the help
my young right hand could use
from the sand-crusted kelp
of distant literatures.

Walcott has written splendidly from the beginning of his career on the theme of his mixed ethnic and cultural heritage, as in "A Far Cry from Africa" from *In a Green Night* (1962):

Again brutish necessity wipes its hands
Upon the napkin of a dirty cause, again
A waste of compassion, as with Spain,
The gorilla wrestles with the superman.
I who am poisoned with the blood of both,
Where shall I turn, divided to the vein?
I who have cursed
The drunken officer of British rule, how choose
Between this Africa and the English tongue I love?
Betray them both, or give back what they give?
How can I face such slaughter and be cool?
How can I turn from Africa and live?

From the beginning, too, Walcott has insisted upon the necessity of poetry imposed on him by his cultural situation, as in his early, Eliotic "Prelude," (which also echoes Frost's famous "choice") also from *In a Green Night:*

Time creeps over the patient who are too long patient,
So I, who have made one choice,
Discover that my boyhood has gone over.

And my life, too early of course for the profound
        cigarette,
The turned doorhandle, the knife turning
In the bowels of the hours, must not be made public
Until I have learnt to suffer
In accurate iambics.

This sentiment still lies behind a much later poem from *The Star-Apple Kingdom* (1979), "Forest of Europe," dedicated to that other exiled Nobel laureate, Joseph Brodsky:

The tourist archipelagoes of my South
are prisons too, corruptible, and though
there is no harder prison than writing verse,
what's poetry, if it is worth its salt,
but a phrase men can pass from hand to mouth?

Walcott not only has written one of the most impressive book-length autobiographical narratives in English in this century, in *Another Life* (1973), he also has written impressive narrative poems of medium length dealing with Caribbean life, such as

"The Schooner *Flight*," also contained in *The Star-Apple Kingdom*. And he writes as well about life in the United States as in the Caribbean in such lyrics as "Bleeker Street, Summer," from *In a Green Night* and "God Rest Ye Merry, Gentleman," from *The Castaway and Other Poems* (1965), which provides this image of Greenwich Village in the winter:

> Splitting from Jack Delaney's, Sheridan Square,
> that winter night, stewed, seasoned in bourbon,
> my body kindled by the whistling air
> snowing the Village that Christ was reborn,
> I lurched like any lush by his own glow
> across towards Sixth, and froze before the tracks
> of footprints bleeding on the virgin snow.

Here Walcott presents a memorable portrait not only of New York City but of the poet in exile who traces these bloody footprints during the Christmas season to discover "one / man's pulped and beaten face," leading him to wish for his native island, "for darkness, evil that was warm."

By contrast, "God Rest Ye Merry, Gentleman: Part II," published in the more recent *The Arkansas Testament,* presents a similar image of urban blight on Christmas Eve in Newark, but here Walcott's horror seems less personal than it does political and contrived, as if Walcott's public recognition as a world-class poet by this time entitled him to make lofty moral judgments, comparing the "police patrol cars" of Newark to "the cattle train / from Warsaw" of the Holocaust. And indeed the long title poem of that volume about the racism he apparently experienced while teaching at the University of Arkansas in the 1980s rings a bit hollow and self-pitying for a man who has found such success in this country, where he counts among his friends other "foreign" poets who spend at least part of the year in the Boston area, such as Joseph Brodsky and Seamus Heaney. In fact, with the exception of such lyrics in *The Arkansas Testament* as "Eulogy to W. H. Auden" and "French Colonial: 'Vers de Societe,'" – both of which demonstrate the positive influence that Auden has been for him – much of Walcott's more recent work seems less impressive than his earlier work, work which unquestionably justifies his Nobel Prize. *Midsummer* (1984), for instance, a book-length autobiographical sequence of numbered poems all of approximately the same length, seems both derivative of and as loosely crafted and unmemorable as Robert Lowell's unrhymed sonnets in *History* (1973).

But for me the major disappointment among Walcott's work, and the one that makes the reader question the techniques of modernist and post-modernist poetry, particularly with regard to "epic" poems, is *Omeros,* which was published to universal acclaim two years ago. I have no problem with the poem's premise, to write a postmodern Homeric epic on postcolonial Saint Lucia, creating parallels between characters from the *Iliad* and the *Odyssey* among the native and colonial inhabitants of the island. What I find disappointing in Walcott's execution of this plan is how difficult it is to follow the work's plot and how difficult it is to distinguish among its native characters who seem more poorly imagined than the British colonials. Given the narrative skills and the clarity he has demonstrated in his earlier work, one wonders why he has chosen, in his longest poem – it runs to three hundred and twenty-five pages – to tell his tale so indirectly and to self-consciously interrupt his already slow-moving narrative with such asides as the following:

> This wound I have stitched into Plunkett's character.
> He has to be wounded, affliction is one theme
> of this work, this fiction, since every "I" is a
>
> fiction, finally.

By now this type of interruption is a postmodern cliché, and it takes the skill of a Vladimir Nabokov, an Italo Calvino, an Umberto Eco, or, most recently, an A. S. Byatt, to pull off. Indeed, the success of Jane Smiley's 1991 novel *A Thousand Acres,* which used the plot and characters of *King Lear* to relate a contemporary tragedy on an Iowa farm without any self-conscious asides or indirect narrative techniques to "modernize" her powerful tale, suggests the level of achievement Walcott could have accomplished had he had faith in his more traditional strengths. Ironically, *Omeros* is at its clearest when Walcott enters the poem himself in scenes set in Boston. Happily, he has already made Saint Lucia into an indelible literary landscape in his extraordinary earlier work.

James Merrill, an American poet good enough to deserve a Nobel Prize, though his family wealth and the often hedonistically aristocratic subject matter will no doubt prevent him from doing so, did not win any major awards in 1992. However, Knopf did bring out, in *Selected Poems: 1946–1985,* a revised edition of his earlier selected volume, *From the First Nine,* as well as reprint his problematically ambitious epic poem, *The Changing Light at Sandover,* originally published in its entirety in one volume in 1982 – books which present a similar aesthetic dilemma as Walcott's. Merrill writes in a more elevated, and often more elegant, style than Walcott, a style that seems appropriate to his more aristocratically cosmopolitan background – his father, Charles Edward Merrill, was the founder of Merrill Lynch, the investment banking firm – and one that prompted Harold Bloom to declare him "a verse artist comparable to Milton, Tennyson and Pope" who "will be remembered as the Mozart of American poetry, classical rather than mannerist or baroque, master of the changing light of perfection that consoles." Despite the difference in their social backgrounds, both Merrill and Walcott have drawn, in their own ways, upon classical English metrical and stanzaic forms to craft some of the most memorable lyrics written in English in the second half of the twentieth century.

Merrill's *Selected Poems,* then, is a most welcome volume containing, one could convincingly argue, more strong lyrics than any other volume published in 1992. These range from the title poem of Merrill's second 1959 trade volume, "The Country of a Thousand Years of Peace," the early elegy to Merrill's Swiss friend, Hans Lodeizen, who died in his mid twenties in 1950, to such later poems as "Lost in Translation," from *Divine Comedies* (1976) and "Bronze," from *Late Settings* (1985), the first of Merrill's post-*Sandover* collections of lyrics. While splitting his adult life up among residences in Stonington, Connecticut, Athens and the Greek Islands, and Key West, with significant forays into Japan – landscapes all reflected in his poetry – Merrill's strongest lyrics remain for me his Proustian reminiscences of his privileged but unhappy childhood in New York City, including "Days of 1935" and "18 West 11th Street" from *Braving the Elements* (1992), and "Days of 1941 and '44," from *Late Settings*. Both "Days of 1935" and "Days of 1941 and '44" are from an ongoing series of similarly titled and dated poems derived from the Greek Alexandrian poet C. P. Cavafy. In the latter, Merrill reminisces on such embarrassing adolescent experiences in prep school as this:

The nightmare shower room. My tormentor leers
In mock lust – surely? – at my crotch.
The towel I reach for held just out of reach,
I gaze back petrified, past speech, past tears.

In "Days of 1935," Merrill recalls his envy of the kidnapped (and subsequently murdered) Lindbergh baby, imagining himself being abducted by a couple named Jean and Floyd, sharing an adventure more exciting than his life among the hired help in Manhattan. In this imagined scenario the young poet is disappointed at the prospect of being released:

What was happening? Had my parents
Paid? pulled strings? Or maybe I
Had failed in manners, or appearance?
Must this be goodbye?

I'd hoped I was worth more than crime
Itself, which never paid, could pay.
Worth more than my own father's time
Or mother's negligée

Undone where dim ends barely met,
This being a Depression year . . .
I'd hoped, I guess, that they would let
Floyd and Jean keep me here.

In "18 West 11th Street," Merrill is reminded of the first five years of his life, spent in this Greenwich Village brownstone, when it explodes in 1970, having been a bomb factory for the 1960s radical group the Weathermen. The source of Merrill's childhood unhappiness is succinctly summarized in three quatrains from "The Broken Home" in *Nights and Days* (1966), a thumbnail sketch of his father:

My father, who had flown in World War I,
Might have continued to invest his life
In cloud banks well above Wall Street and wife.
But the race was run below, and the point was to win.

Too late now, I make out his blue gaze
(Through the smoked glass of being thirty-six)
The soul eclipsed by twin black pupils, sex
And business; time was money in those days.

Each thirteenth year he married. When he died
There were already several chilled wives
In sable orbit – rings, cars, permanent waves,
We'd felt him warming up for a green bride.

In his lyrics on his adult life – "Days of 1964," also from *Nights and Days;* "The Friend of the Fourth Decade," "Mornings in a New House," and "The Summer People," from *The Fire Screen* (1969); "After the Fire" and "Days of 1971," from *Braving the Elements;* and "Clearing the Title," from *Late Settings,* among the best of them – Merrill writes of his shared life with David Jackson and of the family of friends, American and Greek, artists, a beloved servant, which have compensated for his early years of domestic disappointment.

The best and most accessible episodes of his 560-page Ouija-board–inspired epic, *The Changing Light at Sandover,* deal with similar autobiographical details. Had Merrill been content to limit his scope to the autobiographical intermixed with supernatural conversations with such old dead friends as

W. H. Auden, Maya Deren, Maria Mitsotáki, with guest appearances ranging from David Jackson's mother to Wallace Stevens, he unquestionably would have written at least a minor masterpiece. But if Walcott's Homeric ambitions combined with his use of postmodernist technique considerably diminish the accomplishment of *Omeros,* so too does Merrill's Dantean ambition to create a cosmological poem drawing upon modern physics render it a lesser work, albeit one whose "difficulty" is likely to insure Merrill the kind of academic critics that his superior lyrics can certainly support but hardly require.

Whatever its ultimate success, *Sandover,* because it is replete with campy wit and engaging dialogue – particularly that involving Auden – rewards wading through its increasingly murky philosophic-scientific rhetoric. One welcomes Knopf's returning *Sandover* to print as well as the revised volume of Merrill's selected shorter work, but with some pointed reservations. Since leaving Atheneum to become poetry editor at Knopf a few years back, Harry Ford has devoted most of his budget, it would seem, to reprinting work earlier available from Atheneum. Because the poets involved are important, this is a valuable service. But one would think that it would have been more of a service to readers if *Sandover* had been published simultaneously in paperback –which, in its entirety, it never has been – and that he had included poems from Merrill's most recent new Knopf volume, *The Inner Room* (1988), to make the new *Selected Poems* (shorter, incidentally, than *From the First Nine,* despite inclusion of work from *Last Settings*) representative of the entirety of Merrill's lyric output. No new work, then, is included in these volumes; but for younger readers who are not acquainted with Merrill's extraordinary body of work, these are the most important volumes of American poetry published this year. And for those readers who just cannot get enough Merrill, the Spring 1992 issue of the *Paris Review* contains a lengthy Ouija-board–conducted "interview," "The Plato Club," among Merrill and Jackson and such dead luminaries as Alice B. Toklas, Gertrude Stein, Henry James, Colette, Pablo Picasso, Wallace Stevens, Elizabeth Bowen, William Carlos Williams, and Jean Genet. Much of the discussion focuses on the sexuality – usually gay – of the artists admitted to the heaven to which Merrill and Jackson have supernatural access, with Williams left as the rather boorish defender of heterosexuality, or, perhaps more precisely, the denunciator of what he calls "homosex," com-

plaining "I have long felt that American literature has given too much attention to homo-poets. Reason? Publishers & public seeking perverse thrills." Jackson denounces him as a "homophobe."

Two other living American poets whose lifetime accomplishments might be considered by many to rival those of either Walcott or Merrill and who have published definitive works recently are John Ashbery and James Dickey, two decidedly distinct talents. Dickey merits discussion here on the basis of the 1992 publication of *The Whole Motion: Collected Poems 1945–1992* (Wesleyan), while Ashbery qualifies on the back-to-back publications of the book-length meditation on – as far as I can discern – the poetic imagination, *Flow Chart* (Knopf, 1991), and a long new collection of lyrics, *Hotel Lautréamont* (Knopf, 1992).

Sam Gwynn thanked Ashbery's publisher for failing to send him a copy of *Flow Chart* last year, relieving him of the burden of discussing it. (For the record, after numerous letters and phone calls to Knopf publicity, I was supplied with the 1992 paperback reprint of *Flow Chart* and a variety of their other new titles, though *Hotel Lautréamont* and the two Merrill titles were not among them.) Ashbery is a poet who usually evokes strong feelings one way or another: either one considers him a master of the sublime and the finest of our living poets or else as tediously pretentious and virtually unreadable. I have mixed feelings about Ashbery, having studied him in graduate school and having won a prize for, and subsequently publishing, a modest but admiring essay on his poem "As One Put Drunk in the Packet-Boat." To read Ashbery successfully, I think one needs to immerse oneself completely in his work, reading it and rereading it until one feels on Ashbery's frequency, not an easy thing to do. (David Kalstone, Helen Vendler, and Laurence Lieberman – in addition to David Lehman, as cited above – have all written clear and sympathetic essays on Ashbery, whereas James Fenton and Robert McDowell have both played effective devil's advocates.) I was determined, then, to approach *Flow Chart* – which Thomas Disch declared nothing less than fun to read in the *Washington Post Book World!* – with an open mind, but I'm afraid, though not really surprised, that Sam Gwynn's misapprehensions were well founded. *Flow Chart* was predictably praised by Marjorie Perloff in the *New York Times Book Review,* comparing it to William Wordsworth's *Prelude* while proclaiming that, while Ashbery "has produced a remarkable series of longer poems. . . . perhaps none is quite so various, so beautiful and so new as *Flow Chart.*"

But I suspect that Helen Vendler's carefully worded praise in the *New Yorker* comes closer to the truth. Knopf publishes the following blurb on the dust jacket of Ashbery's new book:

> *Flow Chart* is like one huge party line, with everyone in the English-speaking world, past and present, from Chaucer to Ann Landers, interrupting each other. . . . [Ashbery's] very effect – that one is gazing down through a stream of transparent words into pure consciousness – depends on the reader's noting, at least subconsciously, the whole orchestral potential of the English language.

It should be mentioned, in unpacking this piece of critical prose, that in the past Vendler has placed Ashbery in the elite company of Emily Dickinson and Wallace Stevens as the most sublime of American poets, so she is determined to find a masterpiece in *Flow Chart* if one is to be found. Instead of a masterpiece, we have a "party line" – a curious form for a major poem – with everyone from Geoffrey Chaucer to Ann Landers present. But this is a rowdy bunch of voices, constantly interrupting each other. Rather than a carefully crafted work of art, Vendler tells us we are dealing instead with "pure consciousness." Finally, if the reader intends to make any sense out of this piece of "pure consciousness," he had best come with his homework done as he will need, "at least subconsciously," to be prepared to encounter "the whole orchestral potential of the English language" in *Flow Chart*. I think it is worth calling special attention to Vendler's use of the word *potential* here, for it suggests to me that while everything needed to produce a major poem is somewhere to be found in *Flow Chart,* the reader, curiously, should be expected to create it for himself, for Ashbery, content to let these various voices flow passively through him, makes little effort to organize them in a coherent fashion, but, rather, allows them to interrupt themselves at will.

Vendler goes on to say that she herself most enjoyed the work when she could plug into its wavelength – which was infrequently. She found a passage, for example, which she identified as an autobiographical meditation on growing up homosexual; but she was able to do so only because she came to the text equipped with such biographical information. For, unlike Merrill, Ashbery virtually never makes direct autobiographical statements; he seems afraid to – and that seems the key to his indirect style and to the multiple voices to be found in his poetry. This seeming lack of confidence is both the source of his strengths and his weaknesses as a poet. I can only report that though *Flow Chart* is di-

vided into six numbered sections, I never felt sure if any of these sections had a definable subject or if the work itself were advancing any kind of chronologically ordered statement about the growth or the constitution of the poetic mind. At one point late in the poem Ashbery writes:

> . . . That is the archetypal kind of development
> we're interested in here at the window girls move past
>   continually. Something
> must be happening beyond the point where they turn
> and become mere fragments. But to find out what that is,
> we should be forced to relinquish this vantage point, so
> deeply fought for, hardly won.

Ashbery seems to be defending the "deeply fought for" though "hardly won" aesthetic right not to make sense of the fragments that fill his consciousness. That apparently is his reader's task, should he be masochistic enough to attempt to do so. Whatever else you can say about Ashbery, he is our most adamant disciple of the deconstructed self.

It is not as easy to dismiss *Hotel Lautréamont,* which runs to 157 pages and contains no fewer than eighty-two poems, making it the longest of Ashbery's collections of lyrics. Harold Bloom – who would seem to be on Knopf's payroll – declares that with this collection "Ashbery seems to be to the second half of our century what Stevens and Yeats were to the first," here achieving "fresh greatness as a poet." While most of these poems are as vague, abstract, and as flat as the majority of Ashbery's poems, even his best ones such as "Self-Portrait in a Convex Mirror," there is also the same kind of elegiac poignancy of tone which it is easier to recognize in Ashbery's poems than to describe. His typical lyric voice seems disembodied, as if floating above both language and the real world rather than being an engaged participant in either. One could almost quote at random from any of Ashbery's volumes to demonstrate his psychic fluidity. Here is a passage from "Irresolutions on a Theme of La Rochefoucauld," where the poet's tentative sense of self is reflected in the poem's title:

> So each day the predicament
> emerges different, yet the same – you want
> to have birds at your shoulders and wrists, to connive
> with nature in her song, but something always
> leaves you. Suddenly there are no more disappointments to be had
> and the laziest are crowned and anointed for their efforts:
> somewhere we see in something which is shyly wrong,

some corner of the heart, bird-
haunted, by birdsong haunted, as though we two
were far away, and these others strangely near –
a paradise, if we had the facts to open it.

Still, amid the vagueness of "each day" being both
"different" and "the same," the repeated "something" and "somewhere," there is a sense of Romantic melancholy in the "birdsong haunted" speaker
who senses the closeness of "a paradise" juxtaposed
with its inaccessibility. Ashbery is a poet suspicious
of the possibilities of epiphanies as if, because of
their evanescence, it is better to avoid them altogether rather than to be disappointed in their aftermath. And indeed, while there are playful poems
here such as "From Palookaville" and "The Youth's
Magic Horn," as well as an unexpectedly simple
lyric in rhymed quatrains, "Seasonal," and a coyly
titled "Villanelle" which is not a villanelle, many of
the poems here are unexpectedly dark as Ashbery,
now sixty-five, confronts the indignities of the onslaught of old age. Not a few of these poems –
"Baked Alaska," "Withered Compliments," "Love's
Old Sweet Song," "Central Air," "Elephant Visitors," "The Old Complex" – seem set partially in
old-age complexes. And the volume's final poem,
the unpunctuated "How to Continue," seems to be
about how AIDS has transformed an "island" like
Fire Island, "this unsafe quarter" where once

> the parties went on from house to house
> There were friends and lovers galore
> all around the shore
> There was moonshine in winter
> and starshine in summer
> and everybody was happy to have discovered
> what they discovered[,]

into a landscape where "the wind whispered it to
the stars / the people all go up to go / and looked
back on love." I am not at all sure, despite his
vaunted reputation as a virtuoso of American dialect, if Ashbery's language has sufficient vigor,
beauty, or musicality even to discuss him on a plane
with William Butler Yeats or Stevens, or, for that
matter, with Eliot, Frost, or Stephen Crane; still,
despite the ubiquitous frustration that Ashbery's
obliqueness engenders in readers, there is a somber beauty to much of this volume as difficult to
describe as it is to deny.

If Ashbery is the wallflower of contemporary poetry then James Dickey is its good old boy,
a role he etched indelibly for himself in his portrayal of a southern police officer in the movie
version of his novel *Deliverance*. Arguably, by the

*Dust jacket for James Dickey's 1992 book, which includes
twenty-five previously unpublished early poems*

time Dickey courted this image, his best poetry may
well have been behind him. Nevertheless, at his
best, Dickey is an original who gave renewed vigor
to American poetry in the 1960s, a scene dominated
by the neurasthenic confessionalism of Sylvia Plath,
Anne Sexton (who wooed Dickey's affections after
he wrote one of the most brutal reviews of her early
poetry), Lowell, and John Berryman and the Beat
Zen-pranksterism of Allen Ginsberg, Gary Snyder,
and company. By contrast, Dickey distinguished
himself as a master of the dramatic monologue,
whose speakers include a lifeguard, a World War II
firebomber, a stewardess falling from an airplane,
and, giving a new spin to the tradition of southern
Gothic, the offspring of a sheep and a teenage boy.
In these poems Dickey expanded the subject matter
of American poetry, extending the tradition of the
sensational narrative poem developed earlier in the
century by the Californian Robinson Jeffers, beyond the more genteel Yankee and midwestern
realms of Frost, Edwin Arlington Robinson, and
Edgar Lee Masters, while serving as a model for

such younger narrative poets as Robert McDowell, Mark Jarman, David Mason, and Paul Lake.

The Whole Motion collects almost all of Dickey's poetry, 235 poems in all from his early collections *Drowning with Others* (1962) and *Buckdancer's Choice* (1965), which won the National Book Award, through his most recent volume, *The Eagle's Mile* (1990), as well as a selection of twenty-five previously unpublished early poems, here gathered under the title *Summons.* Among his more controversial sequences from his middle and late periods, *The Zodiac* (1976) is included in its entirety, while his sequence of love lyrics, *Puella* (1982), harshly criticized by Gioia in *Can Poetry Matter?,* is represented by only six of its original eighteen poems. Dickey's strength is in narrative, and his later attempts, as in *Puella* and *The Eagle's Mile,* to write extravagantly expansive lyrics are largely unsuccessful. But Dickey's empathy with nature – human and otherwise – is fully realized in such poems as various as "The Lifeguard," "The Heaven of Animals," and "The Owl King," from *Drowning with Others;* "Cherrylog Road" and "Drinking from a Helmet," from *Helmets* (1964); "The Firebombing" and "Slave Quarters," from *Buckdancer's Choice;* "Falling" and "The Sheep Child," from *Falling, May Day Sermon, and Other Poems,* included in *Poems 1957–1967* (1967); and the title poem from *The Strength of Fields* (1979).

All of these narratives, from the troubling "The Firebombing," which presents the prideful bombing of Japan from the perspective of an ordinary American soldier (Dickey was a navigator in World War II), to "Slave Quarters," about sexual relations on a plantation between the plantation owner and a slave woman, present unflinching portraits both of the war and of life in the South. But Dickey can also be a moving lyric poet at times and for me his strongest lyric, "The String," an early poem from *Into the Stone* (1960), about the death of the poet's older brother and the consequent guilt he felt throughout the rest of his life, provides the key to the tenderness, grief, guilt, and anger that underlie most of his best poems. Here is one of the most moving stanzas of "The String":

> I believe in my father and mother
> Finding no hope in these lines.
> Out of grief, I was myself
> Conceived, and brought to life
> To replace the incredible child
> Who built in this string in a fever
> *Dead before I was born.*

Such lines reverberate in these lines from "The Lifeguard":

> Stepping outward from earth onto water
> In quest of the miracle
>
> This village of children believed
> That I could perform as I dived
> For one who had sunk from my sight.
> I saw his cropped haircut go under.
> I leapt, and my steep body flashed
> Once, in the sun.
>
> Dark drew all the light from my eyes.
> Like a man who explores his death
> By the pull of his slow-moving shoulders,
> I hung head down in the cold,
> Wide-eyed, contained, and alone
> Among the weeds,
>
> And my fingertips turned into stone
> From clutching immovable blackness.
> Time after time I leapt upward
> Exploding in breath, and fell back
> From the change in the children's faces
> At my defeat.

They underlie, as well, the emotion of the successful bomber of "The Firebombing," as well as that of the father listening to his sons sleep in the moving lyric, "To His Children in Darkness." At his best Dickey is a superb poet and, as *The Whole Motion* attests, one of much wider range of feeling and subject matter than is generally recognized.

Mona Van Duyn is a poet who, in her early seventies, is coming back into vogue. After winning the Pulitzer Prize in 1991 for *Near Changes* (Knopf, 1990), she was the first woman named poet laureate of the United States, in 1992; and Knopf will be publishing both a volume of collected poems dating prior to *Near Changes, If It Not Be I: Collected Poems 1959–1982,* as well as a collection of new lyrics, *Firefall,* early in 1993. One's first thought on hearing of Van Duyn's selection as poet laureate was to wonder if politics had prevented the more radical Adrienne Rich from receiving this honor. I suspect that may be the case, but it would be a disservice to hold this against Van Duyn, for both she and Rich are arguably both better poets than a few of the men who have already been named to this relatively new position. Reading through Van Duyn's poems in their entirety proved to be a great pleasure for, while she might arguably be placed within the tradition of American woman poets with quirky "feminine" sensibilities – Marianne Moore, Elizabeth Bishop, May Swenson, and Amy Clampitt among them – likely to focus their poetic attention upon natural objects, ordinary and exotic (for Van Duyn, whose second collection is entitled *A Time of Bees,* is fond of nature, particularly her garden), the simple fact that she has been married, to Jarvis Thurston, for many decades has made her focus more directly on domestic and social relationships as well as on bodily functions. If she has a fault, it is prolixity; but this is usually neutralized by the numerous local verbal effects one finds in most of her poems, because of her abiding trust that poetic meter and form are integral parts of even the most discursive poems. Indeed, in an engaging *ars poetica,* "Since You Asked Me. . . . ," from *Merciful Disguises: Published and Unpublished Poems* (1973), Van Duyn delightfully answers two questions: "Why rhyme?" and "why use measure?" To the former she responds:

> To say I love you to language, especially now
> that its only viable components seem to be
> "like," "y'know?" and "Wow!",
> to tickle the ear of those with musical savvy,
> to break down the distinction between light verse and
>   heavy,
> to say that human ingenuity
> can walk hand in hand with responsibility.
> It's a challenge to chaos *hurled.*
> Why use it? Why, simply
> to save the world.

Her defense of measure is a critique of the free-verse lyric that anticipates her sonnets to "minimalists" in *Near Change*:

> But don't write those little tiny
> poems like "THE", centered on a blank page.
> Even Henny-Penny,
> when she thought the sky was falling,
> considered it a more important outrage
> than might be expressed in a poem like "Feeling/
> tired by midnight
>   of
>   it
>   all/I
> went to bed."
> Surely, given mind and senses, there's more to be said.

Van Duyn is a poet of "mind and senses" who, in the work of more than three decades, has registered what it has been like to be alive – as a poet, a daughter, a wife, a friend – to reading, to loving, to music, to travel, to gardening; as well as to be aware of suffering, both in public forms as in the Vietnam War, and in the private realm, observing her parents die, and now her and her husband's own aging and ailments – alive both in language and in the day-to-day world we all inhabit.

Perhaps it was poetic justice that Adrienne Rich should have been awarded the Lenore Marshall/*Nation* Poetry Prize for 1992 for *An Atlas of the*

Difficult World (Norton), judged by Edward Hirsch, Thomas Lux, and Van Duyn, the last of whom wrote up the citation for *The Nation,* stating:

> I do not wish to condescend to the poetry with the all-too-common critical psychologizing I feel is unworthy of it, but obviously some kind of healing has taken place, a freeing of the self that enables her to aim her anger, her war against loneliness and suffering, her love and tenderness at a greater target: the human condition on this astonishing, fragile and beautiful planet.

Though I do not, in fact, consider *Atlas* to be among Rich's strongest books – I think her best work is to be found in *Diving into the Wreck* (1973), *The Dream of a Common Language* (1978), and *A Wild Patience Has Taken Me This Far* (1981) – her award for it was perhaps the least surprising of the major awards given out for poetry in 1992.

Last year Sam Gwynn complained about the most-recent winners of the Pulitzer Prize, rationalizing that both Van Duyn and Charles Simic were clearly given the award for the entirety of their work and not for the individual volume upon which it was bestowed. What can explain, then, the Pulitzer committee's decision to bestow its 1992 poetry prize on James Tate's *Selected Poems* (Wesleyan University Press/University Press of New England). As Gwynn commented last year (certainly never anticipating that Tate would win the Pulitzer), Tate won the Yale Younger Poet's Award for *The Lost Pilot* (1967), which contains one genuinely moving poem, the title poem, which tells of Tate's father's death in World War II while the poet was an infant. Other than that, Tate's early poems were either minimalist free-verse exercises or short prose poems that had some of the exuberance as well as much of the antiestablishment puerility characteristic of the young poets whose first volumes appeared during the hippie-oriented "Age of Aquarius," the late 1960s. Though he has continued to publish prolifically, and his subject has changed somewhat to incorporate suburbia, Tate's vision has hardly matured any more than has his craft. He had, it seemed, ceased to matter as a poet, though I guess it helps to have John Ashbery and apparently Jorie Graham on your side, as the former provides a blurb for *Selected Poems,* declaring Tate "one of the finest voices of his generation," while Graham provided the author's dust-jacket photo. Still, reading through a volume which contains such poems as "Fuck the Astronauts," which, among numerous inanities, contains the phrase "his clitoris" (an example of Tate's adolescent wit and vision) and another, "Lewis and Clark Overheard in Conversation," which consists of one line – "then we'll get us some wine and spare ribs" – repeated twenty-three times, the mind boggles to consider what judges comprised the committee responsible for this decidedly irresponsible award.

As a voting member of the National Book Critics Circle, I was surprised that Albert Goldbarth's *Heaven and Earth: A Cosmology* (University of Georgia Press) was nominated for the NBCC Award for Poetry and astonished when it won. I should point out to the readers of the *DLB Yearbook,* however, that these awards are not as democratically determined as Sam Gwynn suggested last year. In fact, each of the group's nearly six hundred members can cast ballots listing up to five books in each of five major categories – fiction, general nonfiction, biography and autobiography, poetry, and criticism. However, for a book to be automatically nominated by the membership at large, it must be listed on at least 20 percent of the ballots received; and a maximum of three such titles can be directly nominated in any of the five categories, leaving the twenty-four members of the board of directors to vote on filling the remaining slots. Usually this means that several popular novels are automatically nominated, while few books of poetry are. Last year the trend was ironically different when only Jane Smiley (the eventual winner) received enough votes for *A Thousand Acres* to be nominated automatically for the fiction prize, while two books of poetry, Rich's and Philip Levine's *What Work Is* were directly nominated by the members at large. (By contrast, this year no book of poetry received the requisite thirty-two votes to be nominated automatically, hence, all five titles were chosen by the board.) Three poets – Goldbarth, Allen Grossman, and Diane Ackerman – were recommended by the head of last year's poetry subcommittee, Herbert Leibowitz, the editor of *Parnassus,* who, in his speech presenting the award to Goldbarth, said *Heaven and Earth* was the best book of poetry *he* had read in the past few years. He was apparently able to convince the rest of the board that this was the case by arguing for the book's "verbal exuberance" as he passed his copy around the conference table; according to another member of the board, many of the members on this deciding panel had not received copies of Goldbarth's book to read before voting. When, in accepting the award, Goldbarth said how much it meant to him because it was bestowed upon him by a group that actually *read* poetry, my initial cynical response was that he had won the award because no one much cares about poetry and because Herb

Leibowitz liked his book. This, then, was not a populist award.

These circumstances, combined with the fact that Goldbarth was the first person I ever saw give a poetry reading when I was a freshman at Colgate University, and the most memorable thing Goldbarth did was to sing Frost's "Stopping by Woods on a Snowy Evening" to the tune of the cancan, made me a skeptical reader, then, of *Heaven and Earth.* Having read the book, though I still think the award should have gone to Dana Gioia's completely overlooked *Gods of Winter* (Graywolf), I *was* impressed by Goldbarth's verbal exuberance. Goldbarth still is a smart ass and his book, despite such sections bearing the titles "Love" and "Physics" and Goldbarth's breadth of reading, hardly justifies its subtitle; it is a thoroughly energetic meditation on subjects ranging from love (and sex) and mortality (and sex) to chaos theory to comic books and back again to sex. Goldbarth is the best poet I have read in quite awhile who demonstrates the potential vitality of the free-verse lyric as long as it is in the hands of someone as intellectually and linguistically precocious as Goldbarth has clearly become.

The 1992 National Book Award for Poetry went to Mary Oliver for her *New and Selected Poems* (Beacon). Oliver, whose *American Primitive* (1983) won the Pulitzer Prize, can hardly be considered a surprise winner, and her modern-day-Thoreau-like devotion to nature has won her an appreciative audience, making her something akin to contemporary poetry's Annie Dillard. What is surprising is how relatively little Oliver has evolved as a poet in twenty-five years and how lightweight her accomplishment seems in the context of this comprehensive volume. It is easy to see her appeal to readers: she has a vivid eye and a nice ear for internal rhyme which makes her free-verse lyrics go down easy. Her critical appeal is harder to fathom, however, because Oliver's view of nature is so benign as to seem sappy. Some may find the relative absence of Oliver's human presence – she is nothing if not a "transparent eyeball" – refreshing at first, but I find it hard, finally, to care much about a body of work where the poet seems content to do little more than passively reflect the "beauty" of the natural world (though one might envy her apparent serenity). Oliver's true weakness as a poet can best be seen when she attempts to take on a significant human subject – and what could be a more serious topic for a contemporary poet than the Holocaust, which Oliver addresses in "1945–1985: Poem for the Anniversary" from *Dream Work* (1986). The poem's perspective shifts from the speaker's present in 1985, where she is walking her dog in the woods, to the Germany of 1945 and the garden of Joseph Mengele. It is hard to believe that a poem about the Holocaust could open with this stanza:

Sometimes,
walking for hours through the woods,
I don't know what I'm looking for,
maybe for something
shy and beautiful to come
frisking out of the undergrowth.

or that it could continue of in such a fashion:

The way I'd like to go on living in this world
wouldn't hurt anything, I'd just go on
walking uphill and downhill, looking around,
and so what if half the time I don't know what for –

so what if it doesn't come
to a hill of beans –

so what if I vote liberal

and am Jewish,
or Lutheran –

or a game warden –

or a bingo addict –

and smoke a pipe?

While Oliver is so nonchalantly sauntering through the wood, something "shy and beautiful" *does* come "frisking out" her way, to wit, a fawn who is frightened by the poet's dog while its equally relaxed mother "was probably / down in Round Pond, swizzling up / the sweet marsh grass and dreaming / that everything was fine" – only to realize that the fawn might be in danger. But not to worry, the poet's is a "gentle dog" that gets along fetchingly with the fawn who, at the poem's conclusion, is reunited with the doe who "nuzzled her child wildly." Oliver unbelievably includes two stanzas related to the Holocaust with this sentimental nature tale, one seeming to equate the plight of the Holocaust victims in "lush, green, musical Germany" with that of the fawn, the other presenting the paradox that a man as evil as Mengele could inhabit a serene garden and be otherwise cultured. Talk about metaphysical conceits. Are we meant to be consoled by Oliver's benign conclusion, as if Nature somehow transcended human nature and the existence of evil? Or is Oliver trying to present a stoic vision of a universe oblivious to human nature and evil?

Whatever her poetic virtues, Oliver is not a poet who has the language to adequately address serious moral problems. This is inspirational verse almost on the level of Rod McKuen or of Hallmark greeting cards; what it is doing winning Pulitzer Prizes, National Book Awards, and rave reviews in places such as the *Village Voice* (not to mention the *New York Times Book Review*) is beyond me.

The runners-up to Oliver for the National Book Award were Hayden Carruth for *Collected Shorter Poems 1946–1991* (Copper Canyon); Louise Glück for *The Wild Iris* (Ecco Press); Susan Mitchell for *Rapture* (HarperCollins); and Gary Snyder for *No Nature: New and Selected Poems* (Pantheon). Glück, whose *Ararat* (Ecco, 1991), with Mark Strand's *The Continuous Life* (Knopf, 1990), was the corecipient of the 1992 Rebekah Johnson Bobbitt National Prize for Poetry, a ten-thousand-dollar prize for "the most distinguished book of poetry written by an American and published in the preceding two years," has to my mind long been one of the most overrated of contemporary poets. (Indeed, *Ararat*, which certainly had the most pretentious jacket copy in recent memory, arrogantly suggesting that if Sigmund Freud and Carl Jung had only worked out their differences, Glück would not have needed to write it [as if she were a major figure in psychoanalysis], ranks in my mind as one of the worst books of poetry by a name poet I can recall reading). Like Oliver, Glück draws heavily upon nature for her imagery, though she is also extremely concerned with myth, depth psychology, and family relationships, and her vision is far darker than Oliver's. To say that *The Wild Iris,* Glück's sixth collection, is a better book than *Ararat* is to say very little. It was written, the dust jacket informs us, "during a ten-week period in the summer of 1991," as if this assures us of the volume's vatic intensity rather than raising questions about how well crafted a book so quickly written (and rushed into print by Ecco in June 1992) might be. In fact, the book needs to be read as a rather minor poetic sequence of a religious nature, as Glück charts the year against the changes in her garden and alternates poems named after seasons and flowers with ones named after prayers (seven are entitled "Matins," ten, "Vespers"). Glück has always been a poet more in thrall with her subject matter than with the medium of poetry itself, and hence it is easier for the reader to care – or fail to care – for the author's psyche than for her poems. *The Wild Iris* contains no individual poems that stand apart from the others, a situation common to Glück's books, and one that I believe will ultimately render this much-awarded

*Cover for Hayden Carruth's 1992 book, which includes
thirty-one previously uncollected poems written between
1986 and 1991*

sistence of the old growth forests of the far west; to the snowy peaks of the Pacific crest, and to some great teachers.

One could probably imagine from this piece of late-century Beat poetics what the inaugural poem would have sounded like had Jerry Brown been elected president. Reading the fifteen brief new poems included in this volume in juxtaposition with a hundred or so pages from Snyder's earliest work contained here reminds us how little he has changed. At his best, as in "The Bath," Snyder combines his love of nature and his mysticism with his eroticism to create some memorable poems. For lovers of Snyder, this will prove an indispensable collection, but, for the rest of us, it seems overkill. Snyder will be remembered as the best West Coast Beat poet, just as Allen Ginsberg will be remembered as the best East Coast Beat, with his long poems "Howl" and "Kaddish" giving him the edge for the dubious title of the best of both coasts. But both poets will be remembered for their bohemian legacy to American culture more than for their poetry, for the best of which we can rely on the anthologies rather than their collected oeuvres.

In addition to being nominated for the National Book Award, Susan Mitchell was one of five poets to receive 1992 Lannan Literary Fellowships, each worth forty thousand dollars; Thomas Centolella, Killarney Clary, Suzanne Gardiner, and Luis J. Rodriguez were the other recipients of fellowships, while the 1992 Lannan Literary Award for Poetry, worth the same amount, went to A. R. Ammons. Like all the other nominees for the NBA, Mitchell is much concerned with nature and landscape, in her case often that of the Caribbean and the Florida coast, imaginative landscapes usually connected with Wallace Stevens's early work. Her range, however, is notably wider than that of Oliver, Glück, or Snyder, and *Rapture,* Mitchell's second volume of poetry, is one of the most notable single volumes of the year. Mitchell's poetry is verbally lush and discursive, sensual and earthy, erudite and literate, yet also slangy and colloquial. In a poem such as "Wave," set on the Florida coast (Mitchell currently lives in Boca Raton), Mitchell, eyes always focused on the landscape, playfully expands upon all of the possible meanings that the poem's title might suggest ("I don't mean this as a command, though / if you want to wave to someone / there's no reason why you shouldn't."); "Night Music" begins as a meditation on the Chaucerian phrase "about the birds that *slepen al the nyght / with open ye*" that leads her to free-associate about pas-

and frequently anthologized poet a far more minor figure than her current reputation would make her seem.

Gary Snyder is another poet with an intense interest in nature, though, like Glück, he is more concerned with the erotic than Oliver, but where Glück is interested in myth and psychoanalysis, Snyder, a West Coast poet, is drawn to the mysticism of Zen Buddhism. Better yet, let Snyder describe his own poetry as he does in his preface to *No Nature*:

These poems belong to the west coast tongue, Anglofranco American Indo-European, and to the emergent Pacific culture. Some of them owe much to my readings of Chinese and Japanese short poems, some are instructed by ethnopoetics, and most are in the debt of the mid-twentieth-century masters. [One wonders about Snyder's short list.] I also make my bows to Native American song, story, and subsistence; to the per-

sages in the works of Anton Chekhov and Samuel Taylor Coleridge and then on to the language of the troubadours to the spoken language of Chicago – and on still. In the third section of the poem "From the Book of Prophets," "Boca Raton, 1990," Mitchell writes one of two quirkily metered and rhymed sonnets contained in its three parts that gives a good sense of her use of imagery and diction:

Say the night was a cliff, a huge expectancy
the car climbed at right angles to a sky
floating its jets and fountains, its flimsy
chiffons of spray. I'm a sucker for beauty.
Besides, the seekers after comfort had gone
to the bar for daiquiris and drinks that foam.
Sometimes I dare myself to swim alone
where wind sells the imagination
black and something big as an ocean
takes a long drag, then heaves itself back.
When it happens, I don't want to come back.
Maybe I don't want to be believed.
Whatever it hisses into my ear, for me
only – unshared, undiluted, unsheathed.

This is an impressive collection creating high expectations for Mitchell's future work.

Good as Mitchell is, if I were limited to the books nominated, I would have given the NBA to Hayden Carruth's *Collected Shorter Poems,* which, in addition to selections from thirteen earlier volumes ranging from *The Crow and the Heart* (1959) to *Sonnets* (1989) and *Tell Me Again How the White Heron Rises and Flies Across the Nacreous River at Twilight Toward the Distant Lands* (1989), includes an impressive group of thirty-one previously uncollected poems written between 1986 and 1991. To be sure, Carruth is an uneven poet, as one would expect of one so prolific; this densely printed 420-page volume "comprises," according to the poet, "perhaps one-fifth or less of all the poems I've written." Of the selection presented here, Carruth has mixed feelings: "At times I think this collection is everything I wish to save. At other times I think it is simply all I dare to offer. It doesn't matter. It is enough." Or perhaps a bit much. Certainly his selection of fifty-five haiku from *The Clay Hill Anthology* (1970) could have been painlessly excised. Why would one want to "collect" so banal an exercise as this:

Over and over
and over and over and
over and over.

or one that a critic could easily use to criticize these haiku and many other a poem in this volume:

Today my poems seem
only the spells I muttered
while waiting for the poems.[?]

But such complaints can be leveled at virtually any volume of collected poems and, given the number of genuinely moving poems contained here – from formal sonnets to dramatic monologues to Williams-inspired free verse; from eclogues to elegies to political poems to extremely erotic love lyrics – to complain would seem churlish. In some ways Carruth can be seen as a Northeast regional poet. Originally a New Englander who has lived in rural Connecticut and Vermont as well as suburban Syracuse, where he taught at Syracuse University for many years, Carruth celebrates both the landscapes and the inhabitants of these regions. His earliest poems from *The Crow and the Heart* and *The Norfolk Poems of Hayden Carruth* (1962) show Carruth working in traditional rhyme and meter as was typical of most poets who began writing in the 1950s, just before the Beat and Confessional poets, as well as the disciples of William Carlos Williams and Charles Olson and the Black Mountain poets, radically changed the face of American poetry in the early 1960s. These poems are often marred by their use of archaic and florid diction, but several of these early poems, such as "The Fact of the Matter," which effectively explores the difference between reality and myth, focusing on the metaphor of the phoenix, and "On a Certain Engagement South of Seoul," about the role war plays in the contemporary imagination, show Carruth's genuine potential. And, though the powerful influence of Williams was both positive and negative on Carruth, he has never abandoned the fixed forms which serve him well in his more mature poetry, including the extremely erotic and moving *Sonnets,* celebrating the revival of love late in life.

There are moving love poems to his wife in Carruth's *Nothing for Tigers* (1965), including "Essay on Marriage," which successfully combines his meditation on his recent marriage with one on Williams's "variable foot" which concludes both modestly and movingly in lines that both describe Carruth's poetic work and embody it at close to its best:

Poems will come inevitably like the seasons
Imperfect and beautiful like the deathly woods,
    Expanse of labor and expanse of time,
        Like seasons and woods,

Like mechanisms, parts of the universe which means
Nothing, I guess, but simply moves, on and on,

Imperfect and beautiful as only things
    May be that have no minds.

The meaning is all in my Rose Marie's tears.
    We are grateful for their evanescence, creating
        Her the infinite wife, perfect and true,
            And me the infinite husband.

While his 1973 volume, *From Snow and Rock, From Chaos,* contains such good poems about love, farming, and war as "Tabula Rasa," "Concerning Necessity," and "The Birds of Vietnam," his 1974 collection *Dark World* seems weakened by the curious influence of Allen Ginsberg, while his next, *The Bloomingdale Papers* (originally written in 1953 while he was a psychiatric patient at the New York Hospital of the Bloomingdale estate in White Plains, New York), is most concerned, at least in the sections excerpted here, in "Words for My Daughter from the Asylum," with whom he "addresses . . . only in my mind":

Distance that leaves me powerless to know you
Preserves you from my love, my hurt. Your fate
Far from this room is hidden in the cold north;
Nothing of me goes forth
To father you, lost daughter, but a prayer.

That some small wisdom always may endure
Amidst your weariness; that lovers may
Be kind to you; that beauty may arouse
You; that the crazy house
May never, never be your home: I pray.

Carruth falters a bit in *Brothers, I Loved You All* (1978), especially in dramatic monologues written in a stilted Yankee dialect; on the contrary, those monologues spoken in the voice of central New Yorkers in *Asphalt Georgics* (1985) are far more successful; indeed no poet, to my mind, has written so successfully on the area, except perhaps the British poet Charles Tomlinson. But for decades Carruth has been writing dozens of lyric poems of varying lengths – on the landscape, on erotic love and parental love, and on politics and mortality – which should have placed him in the forefront of contemporary poets. But, as Ted Solotaroff lamented in his review of this book, given the nature of literary politics today, Carruth's strengths have not received the critical or popular acclaim they deserve.

This lack of public recognition has, happily, not affected the quality of Carruth's poetry as evidenced in such late poems as "Sex," a poem about sexual desire in old age when the mind is willing but the body cannot obey; "Living Alone," an elegy to John Cheever; "Essay on Death"; "Songs About What Comes Down: The Complete Works of Mr. Septic Tanck," a series of comic dramatic monologues; and the love poem "Renaissance," all from "New Poems: 1986–1991." But perhaps the quality of this late work is best represented in "Ray," his elegy to his friend and colleague at Syracuse University, Raymond Carver:

. . . What crazies we writers are,
our heads full of language like buckets of minnows
    standing in the moonlight of a dock. Ray
was a good writer, a wonderful writer, and his
    poems are good, most of them, and they made me
cry, there at my kitchen table with my head down,
    me, a sixty-seven-year-old galoot, an old fool
because all men are old fools, they have to be,
    shovelling big, jagged chunks of that ordinary pie
into my mouth, and the water falling from my eyes
    onto the pie, the plate, my hand, little speckles
shining in the light, brightening the colors, and I
    ate the goddamn pie, and it tasted good to me.

However flawed or uneven his work, Carruth at his best is deeply moving; his poems, even his nature poems, are concerned with what is most human – what makes us suffer, feel, love, grieve, rage – and one hopes that his *Collected Shorter Poems* will earn him the acclaim and readership he so richly deserves and rewards.

Carruth's is the only book nominated for the National Book Award to have been nominated for the 1993 National Book Critics Circle (NBCC) Award for Poetry. (In fact, as the galley proofs for this piece arrived, Carruth had just been named the well-deserved winner of that prize.) Curiously, one of the four other nominees is David Ferry for his translation of *Gilgamesh* (Farrar, Straus and Giroux), a highly unusual move for a group who does not, on principle, nominate volumes of collected or selected poems unless they contain a considerable amount of new work. How a translation qualified as a considerably original new poem is puzzling to say the least. No doubt Richard Poirier's blurb – which does Ferry no service by so blatantly overstating the quality of his version of *Gilgamesh* – provided all the justification needed; he claims "Ferry's *Gilgamesh* is entirely of his own making, and his great poem is no more indebted to earlier versions of its story than is anything of Shakespeare's to North's *Plutarch*." This is certainly a highly readable rendering of the *Gilgamesh* saga, with its tale of heroic friendship and the sorrow felt by Gilgamesh after the death of his friend Enkidu and subsequent account of the flood that parallels the biblical tale of Noah and reads like a fragmentary excerpt from a full-length epic by Homer and Virgil. Such notable modern translators of these authors as Robert Fitzgerald, Richard Lattimore, and Robert Fagles, to name but a few, have won awards as translators, not as poets, even though their feats were far more prodigious than Ferry's. To suggest that this book, running a mere ninety-two pages, excluding notes but including the fragment "Gilgamesh, Enkidu, and the Nether World," is in any way comparable to a William Shakespeare play is absurd. That the poetry subcommittee did not even recommend such superior works of contemporary poetry published in 1992 as X. J. Kennedy's *Dark Horses: New Poems* (Johns Hopkins University Press) or Gjertrud Schnackenberg's *A Gilded Lapse of Time* (Farrar, Straus and Giroux) for members to consider when voting in this category has dealt contemporary poets a critical blow with this undeserved nomination.

The three other legitimate nominees for the NBCC award for books of poetry published in 1992 are Maxine Kumin's *Looking for Luck* (Norton), Sharon Olds's *The Father* (Knopf), and C. K. Williams's *A Dream of Mind* (Farrar, Straus and Giroux). To my mind, neither Olds nor Williams, both of whom have won this award before, she in 1985 for *The Living and the Dead* (which also won the 1993 Lamont Poetry Prize), he in 1988 for *Flesh and Blood,* deserve nominations this time around. Olds has gained a loyal following for her poetry, largely among women, because, like Alicia Ostriker, she is a poet carrying on the feminist tradition of poetry that developed in the 1960s and 1970s in emulation of the Confessional mode of Plath and Sexton that made no subject having to do with female experience and the female body taboo; indeed, Roland Flint has asked rhetorically, "What is Sharon Olds but the gifted and startling poet of the body?" In *The Father,* however, she is not only the poet of her own body (though of course she remains that), but also that of her father's body, which, in this book-length sequence of fifty-one poems obsessed with it, is dying of cancer. Some readers might admire what they might consider the brutal honesty of poems with such titles as "The Exact Moment of His Death," "His Smell," and "The Dead Body" (all of the poems in this volume have such prosaic titles). From my perspective, Olds uses her father's death as an occasion to remind us of his weaknesses – particularly his alcoholism – even as he is dying, a process which Olds finds obscenely compelling. This is not a book mourning her father's passing; it is one celebrating a daughter's apparent sensitivity. "The Glass," a poem devoted entirely to the description of her dying father, his throat blocked by a tumor,

expectorating into a glass, getting "the heavy sputum out, / full of bubbles and moving around like yeast – ," which becomes, finally, the symbol of "his death, bright glass of / spit on the table, these last mouthfuls." The egotism on display in most of these poems is even more obscene. In "I Wanted to Be There When My Father Died," Olds explains that her reasons are

> because I wanted to see him die –
> and not just to know him, down to
> the ground, the dirt of his unmaking, and not
> just to give him a last chance
> to give me something, or take his loathing
> back. All summer he had gagged, as if trying
> to cough his whole esophagus out,
> surely his pain and depression had appeased me,
> and yet I wanted to see him die
> not just to see no soul come out,
> free of his body, no mucal genie of
> spirit jump
> forth from his mouth,
> proving the body on earth is all we have got,
> I wanted to watch my father die
> because I hated him. Oh, I loved him. . . .

After such a statement – she does not "just" want to see her father die because she wants to give him a last chance to make amends for all the wrongs he inflicted on her, but because she also wants to be sure that there is no salvation for him after his death, and because she hates him – the reader really is not interested to hear, in the rest of the poem, the qualified way in which, despite all his faults, she "loved" him as well. And it is almost incredible to read in "What Shocked Me When My Father Died" that "what shocked" her had nothing to do with her father's death but rather with her *husband's* actions while making love after her father's death in response to her weeping:

> . . . I
> sobbed and he quieted me – the children just
> outside the door and my father's wife
> through a thin wall – when he shushed my sobbing
> by gently laying his palm over my
> mouth almost as if thinking my sobbing
> could sound as if I were coming, *that* shocked me.

Such self-centeredness shocks me too. But Olds cannot be stifled, and at least now the kids and the "father's wife" know what was what. For Olds, any emotion seems only as important as the poem she can crank out from it. For her, poetry is more important than life, but for all the wrong reasons.

C. K. Williams also has a penchant for prosaic and often ugly subject matter in his poetry, though he is perhaps most noted for his use of extremely long poetic lines. *A Dream of Mind* is divided between poems that dramatize psychological states and extreme behavior and the title sequence of poems that attempts to explore the operation of consciousness itself. In dealing with abstractions, Williams is out of his depth. His strengths are rooted to his use of concrete details. Williams is a more energetic poet than Olds, sometimes coming on (like Albert Goldbarth at his worst) like a hyperactive kid. But usually his energy combines with a musicality, absent from such poets as Philip Levine, whose poetry Williams's work bears some affinity with, to fill out his lines effectively and keep his poems flowing. Perhaps Williams is at his most effective here in the book's final poem, "Helen," another poem on death, this told from the perspective of a man making love to his dying wife and in the process coming to understand fully his love for her:

> But still, he gave himself to her, without moving moved
>   to her: she was still his place of peace.
> He listened for her breath: was she still here with him,
>   did he have her that way, too?
> He heard only the flow of the silent darkness, but he
>   knew now that in it they'd become it,
> their shells of flesh and form, the old delusion of
>   their separateness and incompletion, gone.

Williams, for me, is at his least appealing in a lyric such as "Harm," in which the speaker describes a scene of horrific ugliness – a homeless man in Manhattan who, in the middle of the road:

> undid his pants, and, not even bothering to squat,
>   sputtered out a noxious, almost liquid stream.
>
> There was that, and that his bony shanks and buttocks
>   were already stained beyond redemption,
> that his scarlet testicles were blown up bigger than a
>   bull's with some sorrowful disease....

The speaker witnesses this in the presence of a beautiful adolescent girl whom he realizes also sees this scene. His first reaction is to assure her that this is not really reality, but his final thought is "but she was gone, so I could think, But isn't it like this, isn't this just what it is?" Having witnessed a similar scene outside of a grocery store in an Upper East Side residential neighborhood in Manhattan – a scene that went virtually ignored by the many people strolling the late afternoon streets on Labor Day – I have to acknowledge that, on a very basic level, this is a truth. But is it a compelling aesthetic? I think that poets should seek a higher form of truth and beauty, or, in this case, to at least try to human-

ize the obscene vision presented. What is most irksome about this poem is the glib delight – touched no doubt with a sexual thrill in connection with the "slender adolescent girl" – in sticking the reader's nose in it and insisting upon it as a kind of ultimate truth. Indeed, it is the Williams persona that most detracts from his poetry. Nowhere is he as annoyingly self-righteous as in another long poem, "She, Though," where the speaker reminisces about his early days as a poet when he posed nude as an artist's model for a female acquaintance whose subsequent sexual advances he rebuffs:

> Finally she just said, "Let's do it," but I turned her
>   down, in a way which at the time
> I thought was very bright but which may certainly
>   have had to do with how badly things turned out.
> I told her that I liked her but that I could only sleep
>   with girls I loved, really loved.
> She accepted my refusal in the spirit I'd hoped she
>   would, as an example of my inner seriousness,
> and as having to do – though I don't recall what track
>   – with my dedication as an artist.

Williams goes on and on in this manner, preening about how sexually desirable he is, yet virtuous and a serious artist to boot. Such narcissism almost reads as a parody of the sensitive artist.

Given the unpleasant egotism of both Olds and Williams, it is refreshing to come across a talent as modest and appealing as Maxine Kumin. Though she has served as poetry consultant to the Library of Congress (a position that currently bears the title poet laureate) and won the Pulitzer Prize for Poetry in 1973 for *Up Country*, it is sometimes easy to overlook this poet who spends most of her time on her farm in New Hampshire. Perhaps it was Diane Middlebrook's justifiably sympathetic portrayal (in last year's *Anne Sexton: A Biography*) of Kumin, even under the most trying circumstances, as the close friend and poetic adviser to Anne Sexton, Kumin's former neighbor in Newton, Massachusetts – Kumin had lunch with Sexton on the day of the latter's suicide – that has helped bring her own poetry back into the spotlight. *Looking for Luck,* like most of Kumin's poetry, confines itself primarily to the landscape of her farm, though there are various forays to Bangkok, Southern California, the Milledgeville, Georgia, farm of the late Flannery O'Connor, and elsewhere. "A Brief History of Passion" deftly juxtaposes the details of the documented lives and loves of the likes of Katherine Mansfield and John Middleton Murray, Frieda and D. H. Lawrence, Leonard and Virginia Woolf, and Rainer Maria Rilke and his

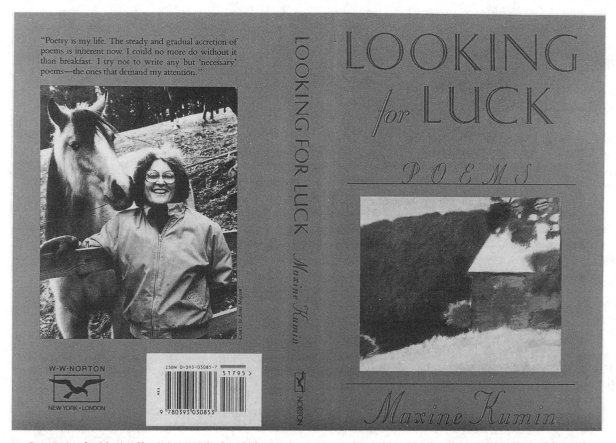

Dust jacket for Maxine Kumin's 1992 book, which comprises poems concentrating on landscapes and the routines of farm life

Muse, with the marriage of her parents. But the routines of farm life remain central to Kumin, and, like Oliver, she has come to have faith in her ability to live a rich life in sync with nature. But Kumin's interaction with both landscape and animals, from horses to bears, seems more active than Oliver's, somehow more human. This characteristic is perhaps best on display in "A Morning on the Hill," in which a seemingly drunken man is recklessly driving a farm vehicle and "gouging the green sweetness" of the hill, an action which provokes the speaker initially to wish for the man's death, only to lead her to recall another morning when a death did occur:

Waking, I remember the way a friend's
husband died beside her in his sleep.
Her voice on the phone was calm but taut as rope
that morning: *Joe is dead. Do me a favor?*
Call 911 for me. I've forgotten the number.

Of course I'll call them. I'll come too.
Nobody dead up here this morning, though
the fat man tried. Now a relentless sun
licks the far hill alight. Its red balloon

lifts over lush pastures as if nothing new
has happened. Indeed enough comes true.

How unlike her friend Sexton, that poet of suicide and despair and self-dramatization whose death came true, is Kumin, whose gift for solace and trust in the nature of things has brought her the luck of a genuine poet and a survivor.

Charles Simic has not eased up since his controversial win of the Pulitzer Prize for Poetry in 1990 for his book of prose poems, *The World Doesn't End*. In 1992 he has followed up last year's book of lyrics, *The Book of Gods and Devils*, with another, *Hotel Insomnia* (Harcourt Brace Jovanovich). In addition, he edited *The Best American Poetry: 1992* (Scribners) and wrote a short book on art, *Dime-Store Alchemy: The Art of Joseph Cornell* (Ecco Press), a series of brief, prose-poem-like essays on Cornell's American brand of surrealism, which Simic tries to emulate in his poems. Of his own two books, the Cornell study is the far more successful, its brief sections unified by Simic's fascination with Cornell's life, the artistic technique behind his boxes and collages, and the influences of Edgar

Allan Poe, Walt Whitman, Emily Dickinson, and the French surrealists and dadaists on his work. Simic successfully portrays Cornell as a Poe-like loner, traveling daily to Manhattan on the subway from his house in Bayside, Queens. Cornell lived most of his life until his death in 1972 with his mother and his invalid brother and wandered the city where he amassed the objects which "chance" would eventually assemble in his quietly dazzling boxes. Describing Cornell's aesthetic, Simic defines his own:

> His is a practice of divination. Dada and surrealism gave him a precedent and a freedom. I have in mind especially their astonishing discovery that lyric poetry can come out of chance operations. Cornell believed in the same magic, and he was right! All art is a magic operation, or, if you prefer, a prayer for a new image.

The collage technique serves Simic well here; magic strikes, producing a real gem. It is a Cornellian-box of a book, as much a book about poetry as about art, and more poetic, in fact, than many of Simic's own volumes of poetry, including *Hotel Insomnia,* whose most impressive image is the cover photo – seemingly a montage reminiscent of Cornell's work – "Bless the Home and Eagle," by Jerry Uelsmann. Simic's problem is the same of so many contemporary poets influenced by modern art, whether cubism, abstract expressionism, or the collage, "that act of reassembling images in such a way as to form a new image," that Simic considers "the most important innovation in the art of this century." Language, quite simply, is not visual – though poets such as Wallace Stevens can make it seem so – and seems to depend more on linearity for its effect on the reader than do the spatial visual arts. Simic has written some effectively visual poems such as "Tapestry," but, in general, his language is so flat, so unpoetic and drab, that his poems tend to be inert. There are a few exceptions here, such as "Makers of Labyrinths," which largely echo the stronger meditations on form to be found in *Dime-Store Alchemy.*

As an anthologist, Simic produces one of the best volumes so far of the generally lackluster *Best American Poetry* series since its initiation in 1988. The real treat in the book is "Dear, My Compass . . . ," a newly found poem by Elizabeth Bishop which originally appeared in the *New Yorker.* In addition to Hayden Carruth's "Sex," other strong poems in the volume are those by Ashbery, Marilyn Hacker, Donald Hall, Lawrence Joseph, Carolyn Kizer, Kumin, Li-Young Lee, Adrienne Rich, and Stephen Yenser, poems which outweigh such clunkers as those by Jorie Graham, Charles Bernstein, and

Glück (who amazingly admits, in the volume's "Contributor's Notes and Comments" – an otherwise tedious collection of comments best to be avoided – to not liking her poem included here), as well as two rather embarrassing poems on sexuality, the very long "My Mother's Nipples," by Robert Hass, and the thankfully brief but unbearably titled "The Night the Lightning Bugs Lit Last in the Field Then Went Their Way," by Liam Rector. The best poem in the volume, on the other hand, is the melodic and surprisingly direct "Days of Autumn," by John Hollander – not quite a hat trick, then, but a good year, all told, for Simic.

Among the other anthologies published in 1992, the most notable would have to be *The Top 500 Poems* (Columbia University Press), edited by William Harmon, a volume containing the five hundred most-anthologized poems in the English language, according to *The Columbia Granger's Index to Poetry,* with some brief, judicious notes on the poems by Harmon. The contents range from the anonymous medieval lyric "Cuckoo Song" and Geoffrey Chaucer's "General Prologue" to *The Canterbury Tales* through Allen Ginsberg's "A Supermarket in California" and Sylvia Plath's "Daddy." The only living poets included are Richard Eberhardt, Stephen Spender, Gwendolyn Brooks, Richard Wilbur, and Ginsberg. One could quibble about the "objectivity" involved in the inclusion of these and other twentieth-century poets and the exclusion of others, but why bother. I cannot think of a better introduction to the best poetry in our language or a better present, for that matter. Though one wonders, in our multimedia era, how many people would be grateful to receive it – a rather saddening thought.

A revised and enlarged edition of Edward Field's 1979 anthology, *A Geography of Poets, A New Geography of Poets* (University of Arkansas Press), has been edited by Field and coeditors Gerald Locklin and Charles Stetler. It is a generally good collection of American poetry organized by geographical region with welcome new poems by, among others, Molly Peacock, Elizabeth Alexander, George Garrett, R. S. Gwynn, Miller Williams, and Timothy Steele; among the notable absent poets I will mention only Dana Gioia, who has written as well about California, northern and southern, New York City, and the Northeast as any of the poets here included, and Gjertrud Schnackenberg, who has written impeccable lyrics on both the Northwest and New England. Field, it should be mentioned, has also published a somewhat prosaic but largely witty and entertaining book of his own poems, *Counting Myself Lucky:*

Selected Poems 1963–1992 (Black Sparrow Press). If his inspiration is Cavafy, the poems here read like the kind of "I do this, I do that poems" that Frank O'Hara would write if he were Jewish and living in New York today in the age of AIDS, albeit there is an occasionally misogynistic streak which might reasonably be considered to give some offense.

An anthology of far more limited interest, and of much lower quality, is *A Gathering of Poets* (Kent State University Press), edited by Maggie Anderson and Alex Gilden, with Raymond Craig the associate editor. The occasion for this book was a massive poetry reading by more than three hundred poets conducted on the campus of Kent State in 1990 to commemorate the four students shot there by the National Guard during an anti–Vietnam War demonstration on 4 May 1970. Nothing here is as memorable, I am sad to say, as the Crosby, Stills, Nash, and Young song, "Ohio," inspired by the same incident. Anderson, meanwhile, has published her third, generally lackluster, collection of poems, *A Space Filled with Moving* (University of Pittsburgh Press), the best poem of which is, perhaps, the nonpolitical "Anything You Want, You Got It," a poem which declares "Twenty years is everything – / your whole life, each leaf and fallen branch, / every random pile of stones," and celebrates a friendship with someone twenty years her junior. Keeping the spirit of multiculturalism alive is *After Aztlan: Latino Poets of the Nineties* (Godine), edited by Ray González, including poems by Latino men and women, most notably Jimmy Santiago Baca, Martín Espada, Victor Hernández Cruz, Alberto Ríos, Gary Soto, and Alma Luz Villanueva. Most notable by her absence is Sandra Cisneros, whose short stories have made her a darling of anthologists over the past three years (indeed, four of her very brief tales appear in the 1992 *Oxford Book of American Short Stories,* edited by Joyce Carol Oates) and whose second collection of poems, *My Wicked Wicked Ways,* originally published in paperback by the small Third Woman Press, was reprinted in its first hardcover edition in 1992 by Turtle Bay Books.

The men's movement, perhaps most amusingly, has also made its mark among the year's poetry anthologies, most prominently in the massive *Rag and Bone Shop of the Heart: Poems for Men* (HarperCollins), edited by those three wild men, Robert Bly, James Hillman, and Michael Meade. The poems collected here are those "which moved men the most, spoken in gatherings over the last ten years. The uttered or sounded poem that speaks to men in a rhetoric calculated to penetrate the bone," and are divided into sixteen sec-

tions bearing such titles as "I Know the Earth, And I Am Sad," "The Naive Male," "Zaniness," "The Second Layer: Anger, Hatred, Outrage," and my favorite, "Making a Hole in Denial." "Iron John" Bly has also published a collection of most of his prose poems, *What Have I Ever Lost By Dying?* (HarperCollins), and a selection, with inspirational commentary, from the writings of Thoreau, *The Winged Life: The Poetic Voice on Henry David Thoreau* (HarperCollins). Rounding out the year in anthologies is *Men of Our Time: An Anthology of Male Poetry in Contemporary America* (University of Georgia Press), edited by Fred Moramarco and Al Zolynas, also thematically organized, though minus running commentary. Bly and company at least admitted women into their anthology, from Emily Dickinson and Marianne Moore through Sharon Olds and Katha Pollitt. Moramarco and Zolynas's is an exclusively male club with "275 poems from more than 170 poets." I guess you have got to ride a trend when it is hot.

A variety of books of historical interest appeared in 1992. Christopher MacGowan has completed the scholarly work he began with A. Walton Litz by bringing the third and final volume of the annotated edition of William Carlos Williams's collected poems into print with the revised edition of the modernist epic, *Paterson* (New Directions). Perhaps of even more interest, *First Awakenings: The Early Poems of Laura Riding* (Persea Press), edited and with an introduction by Elizabeth Friedmann, Alan J. Clark, and Robert Nye, with a preface by Laura (Riding) Jackson written shortly before her death, presents four newly discovered sequences written before Riding left the United States for England in 1925, as well as a fifth sequence of poems from the same period published in periodicals but never collected by the author. These poems, some of them difficult, some of them stunning in their lyric beauty and simplicity, show (Riding) Jackson's debt to and argument with the tradition of the Romantic poets (as in her "Address to Shelley," contained in an appendix) and will allow critics finally to attempt a full assessment of this enigmatic poet who spent most of her later years trying to keep her poems out of print and arguing with virtually every critical assessment made of them.

Robert Phillips has continued his campaign, as Delmore Schwartz's literary executor, to see all of Schwartz's work in print by editing *Shenandoah and Other Verse Plays* (BOA Editions), bringing together for the first time in one volume all five of Schwartz's plays. While lacking the intensity of Schwartz's best poetry, they provide an interesting psychological portrait of this troubled poet, with emphasis on his problematic relationship with his parents. Perhaps most interesting is the previously unpublished *Venus in the Back Room,* written in 1937 and dealing with Schwartz's notorious anxiety about homosexuality.

Two volumes of selected poems attempt to revive the reputation of two late-mid-century women poets, one with considerably more success than the other. In an embarrassingly overstated preface marred by feminist jargon, Kate Daniels attempts to establish Muriel Rukeyser's reputation as equal to Walt Whitman's, arguing that "Together, they are the most uncanonical and fiercely individual poets in the history of American Poetry." Nothing in the densely printed, "pared down, more apprehensible, version of the collected poems," *Out of Silence: Selected Poems* (TriQuarterly Books), comes close to justifying such an outrageous comparison. If anything, the leaden work here proves how quickly a poet who takes her themes primarily from politics — sexual and otherwise — becomes outmoded. I do not doubt the sincerity of Rukeyser, or her generosity; I can simply report that "The Book of the Dead," a thirty-page sequence on the rate of silicosis among a community of West Virginia miners during the late 1930s tells us nothing more than a journalistic account would — indeed, probably less — and has no intrinsic aesthetic value.

While Daniels eschews what she refers to as the "nightingale tradition" of American women poets, including Sara Teasdale, Marianne Moore, and Elizabeth Bishop, to praise the fact that "Rukeyser's poetic imperative resided elsewhere" than "in the abstract idea of received forms," J. D. McClatchy invokes the tradition of Moore and Bishop to praise Jean Garrigue's more lyrical verse in his introduction to her *Selected Poems* (University of Illinois Press). I do not think that Garrigue is in the league of either Moore or Bishop, though she clearly aspired to be; nor do I agree with McClatchy that Garrigue's best work is to be found in her final, posthumous volume, *Studies for an Actress and Other Poems* (1973), much of which was written after she had been diagnosed with Hodgkin's disease, from which she would die at age sixty in 1972. I prefer such longer lyrical meditations written in the late 1950s and early 1960s as "For the Fountains and Fountaineers of Villa d'Este" and "Pays Perdu," or her more concise lyrics such as "A Note to Fontaine," celebrating — as it was in her romantic nature to do — the grasshopper at the expense of the ant:

Survival is *not* the test, and is long life the best?
Fie on righteous dullards

So proud of their sweltering summer labor
That allows them to live without honor through winter.
The grasshoppers have more grace
Than to make out for themselves, in any case.
With that knowledge that they'll die
Spitting into the bleak eye
Of those who never had such song
To make life seem dancing to be warm.

Perhaps it should also be mentioned here that, shortly before her death in late 1992 from cancer — a disease about which she wrote so bravely — Audre Lorde prepared a revised version of her 1982 *Undersong: Chosen Poems Old and New* (Norton). Lorde, more in the tradition of Rukeyser and Rich than Moore and Garrigue, in addition to her writing on cancer, is best known for her groundbreaking poems on black lesbian subjects.

Julia Randall, who won the first Poet's Prize for her 1987 volume, *Moving in Memory,* has also published a welcome volume of recent and earlier work, *The Path to Fairview: New and Selected Poems,* bringing back into print the best poems from such strong but long-out-of-print volumes as *The Puritan Carpenter* (1965), *Adam's Dream* (1969), and *The Farewells* (1981). Randall's aesthetic — hardly one to earn her the reputation she deserved in the political climate of the 1960s when some of her strongest work was written — is best ascertained among the new poems in this volume in "A Book." While dusting a shelf "containing / Gawain to Vaughan," the persona comes upon an extra copy of book 1 of *The Faerie Queene,* a volume that had been handed down since 1885 from one Randall generation to another. The discovery leads the poet both to read the accumulated marginal notes and to reflect on the exercises she once wrote in Spenserian stanzas and on the fact that, childless herself, "No one will add / to this family saga." Yet, rather than throw the volume away, she decides to keep it:

I need the shelf-room. I could abandon
this relic, but I put it down
dusted, behind the Malory. To K. and J.
Randall, I (Fidelia?) might say:
"Arthur is coming. Pass it on."

Domesticity and high literature share the same plane in Randall's imagination. She is a distinctly regional poet, her landscapes sometimes urban (she was born in Baltimore) but mostly rural Maryland; Roanoke, Virginia, where Randall has taught at Hollins College, Henry Taylor being among her students; and North Bennington, Vermont, where she currently lives. Quite unselfconsciously, Randall writes in the tradition of the great English Romantic poets, most notably William Wordsworth with his nature-derived "philosophic mind," but Samuel Taylor Coleridge as well, with whom she shares an abiding passion for the Arthurian romances of Edmund Spenser and Sir Thomas Malory. In "Derivative," from *Adam's Dream,* Randall demonstrates a lack of the anxiety of influence in an homage to another poetic avatar, Emily Dickinson:

> Yet I've seen you send a poem you've cut
> like pansies from the stock
> the careful Pilgrims brought – so here's my packet
> to press in the memory-book. I know a few things by
> heart:
> carpel from corn, how crocus grow, how blue is shut
> in the jay's egg, how my separate songs
> are yours also.

Randall might well be speaking to contemporary readers and poetry readers of the future as she is to Dickinson here, for *The Path to Fairview* is her "packet" of "separate songs," songs written with a grace and assurance that places them within the timeless frame of the purest of poems, ones that will weather the storms of fashion far better than poets who have achieved more fame than Randall in her lifetime. In the shorter run, however, I would hope that the poetic climate is now more appropriate for appreciating the genuine accomplishment of this still-living poet than it is for the considerably less significant Rukeyser.

The achievement of Donald Justice, a poet who, despite the 1980 Pulitzer Prize for his *Selected Poems,* has never received the level of recognition that his deceptively modest but deeply resonant poetry deserves, is honored by a special feature on him in the Winter/Spring issue of *Verse,* edited by Dana Gioia and William Logan and containing memoirs, poems, critical essays, and even a collage, by former and current colleagues, students, and friends, as well as his wife, Jean Ross. Among the distinguished contributors to this feature, in addition to Gioia and Logan, are W. D. Snodgrass, Mark Strand, Charles Wright, Debora Gregor, the late Henri Coulette, Bruce Bawer, Tom Disch, Jorie Graham, and Marvin Bell. Michael Peich provides a checklist of Justice's fine-press books useful to prospective Justice scholars. This feature in *Verse* felicitously coincides with the publication *A Donald Justice Reader: Selected Poetry and Prose* (Middlebury College Press/University Press of New England), a volume in the new Bread Loaf Contemporary series which provides as ideal an introduction to Justice's work as one could possibly hope for. Justice's main

subjects are music and memory, both most plangently connected with his childhood in Miami and other southern locales. In twenty-five consecutive pages here – which include the poems "The Piano Teachers: A Memoir of the Thirties," "Mrs. Snow," "The Pupil," "On a Woman of Spirit Who Taught Both Piano and Dance," "Dance Lessons of the Thirties," "After-school Practice: A Short Story," and "The Sunset Maker," and the memoir "Piano Lessons: Notes on a Provincial Culture" – one has nothing less than a concise and moving autobiography of Justice's childhood. In addition, the volume contains two excellent short stories, "Little Elegy for Cello and Piano," a brief piece memorializing a friend and a work of art kept alive in the narrator's mind, and "The Artificial Moonlight," a brilliant evocation of the early years of marriage of several couples, and three essays on prosody, all of which make one wish that Justice had written more prose. It also contains dozens of other first-rate poems, including "First Death," "Childhood," "Tremayne," "In Memory of the Unknown Poet, Robert Boardman Vaughn," "On the Death of Friends in Childhood," "Bus Stop," and "Men at Forty," which closes on a typically elegiac note from Justice:

> And deep in mirrors
> They rediscover
> The face of the boy as he practices tying
> His father's tie there in secret
>
> And the face of that father,
> Still warm with the mystery of lather.
> They are more fathers than sons themselves now.
> Something is filling them, something
>
> That is like the twilight sound
> of the crickets, immense,
> Filling the woods at the foot of the slope
> Behind the mortgaged houses.

A Donald Justice Reader is barely 170 pages long, but it is hard to think of a volume that contains as much consistently good writing as this slender treasure.

Three other poets of Justice's generation – X. J. Kennedy, Thom Gunn, and Miller Williams – each published new volumes of distinction in 1992. In *Dark Horses: New Poems* (Johns Hopkins University Press), Kennedy writes in the same, distinctive, formal style that he had already mastered in his first book, *Nude Descending a Staircase* (1961), for which he received the Lamont Poetry Prize, a volume at once playful, reverent (and irreverent), and erotic. Sober clarity is what most characterizes Kennedy's poems here, whether they are addressed to a young man dying of AIDS, like "For Jed," which concludes with the stoic wisdom tinged with genuine sorrow, "No one, nobody human / Stays immune forever," or to an old poet friend already dead, as in the fittingly "Terse Elegy for J. V. Cunningham":

> May one day eyes unborn wake to esteem
> His steady, baleful, solitary gleam.
> Poets may come whose work more quickly strikes
> Love, and yet – ah, who'll live to see his likes.

Kennedy is as adept at epigram as he is at elegy, as witnessed in his sequence of nine rhymed couplets, "City Churchyard," including the ribald "Lecher": "I who could once erect a throbbing bone / Salute you now with rigid, skinned-back stone." And he can move from the comic verse of "Emily Dickinson Leaves a Message to the World, Now That Her Homestead in Amherst Has an Answering Machine" (imitating Dickinson's eccentric use of rhyme and punctuation) to poems with serious human subjects including a violent homeless man ("On the Square") and a cancer patient ("Rat"). But perhaps my favorite poem here is one that recalls the seemingly surreal, though quite realistic, memory of childhood drives through Connecticut en route to or from Hartford, "The Waterbury Cross," which stands upon a hill in that blighted industrial city:

> Did even Wallace Stevens at the last,
> Having sown all his philosophe's wild oats,
> Gape for the sacred wafer and clutch fast
> To Mother Church's swaddling petticoats?
>
> Connecticut's conversions stun. Is there
> Still a pale Christ who clings to hope for me,
> Who bides time in a cloud? Choking, my car
> Walks over water, across to Danbury.

British-born Gunn, who has lived in San Francisco since 1954, when he was in his mid twenties, shares with Kennedy an affinity for the metrically regular quatrains championed not only by J. V. Cunningham on the East Coast, but also by Yvor Winters, the California poet who taught at Stanford until his death in 1968 and of whom Gunn was a friend and colleague. Originally paired with that other rebel British poet who came on the scene in the mid 1950s, Ted Hughes, with whom he shared a fascination for violence, Gunn's poetry, since his move to the Bay Area, has been an unusual blend of traditional metrics with the extreme subject matter of the San Francisco Beat culture, in particular that associated with the gay S and M scene of leather bars we associate with the pre-AIDS decade of the 1970s. Gunn's latest collection is *The Man with Night*

Sweats (Farrar, Straus and Giroux), the final section of which is an extended elegiac sequence to a generation of the poet's friends dead or dying of AIDS. Earlier in the book, Gunn is not averse to writing about the persistence of erotic desire in late middle age, as in his poems "Bone" – celebrating male beauty – and "Lines for My 55th Birthday," reminiscent of Carruth's "Sex," as its opening couplet attests: "The love of old men is not worth a lot, / Desperate and dry even when it is hot." Gunn's ease with couplets is also in evidence in his congenial tour of his city, "An Invitation," which bears the subheading "from San Francisco to my brother," and which alternates lines of iambic pentameter with ones of iambic tetrameter. Like Kennedy, Gunn is drawn to the epigram, as in "Barren Leaves" or the perceptive "Jamesian" ("Their relationship consisted / In discussing if it existed"); and, like Kennedy, he has written his own, even terser elegy to Cunningham, "JVC." His AIDS poems are reminiscent of Vikram Seth's "Soon," from last year's *All You Who Sleep Tonight* (Knopf), a poem dismissed here last year by Sam Gwynn but which I consider to be among the most powerful on the subject. The similarity is most noticeable in "Memory Unsettled," which includes this quatrain (like Seth's poem reversing the traditional logic of the Western love lyric where the confident poet tells a skeptical mistress that his poetry can grant her eternity):

> When near your death a friend
> Asked you what he could do,
> "Remember me," you said.
> We will remember you.

Here, the poet is responding to a friend's request, not boasting. Many of Gunn's best AIDS poems, however, are those addressed to students, younger men whose untimely deaths speak powerfully to the older poet. These poems include "To a Dead Graduate Student" and "The J Car," which concludes:

> Of course. It tears me still that he should die
> As only an apprentice to his trade,
> The ultimate engagements not yet made.
> His gifts had been withdrawing one by one
> Even before their usefulness was done:
> This optic nerve would never be relit;
> The other flickered, soon to be with it.
> Unready, disappointed, unachieved,
> He knew he would not write the much-conceived
> Much-hoped-for work now, nor yet help create
> A love he might in full reciprocate.

Newsweek devoted a recent cover story, in light of the death of Rudolf Nureyev, to the generation of artists being lost to AIDS; this could be that generation's epitaph.

Miller Williams is, like Louis Simpson, a poet of middle-class life, its manners and its idiom. Unlike Simpson, however, Williams shares an affection for his characters; and, unlike Simpson's later work, Williams, while staying true to the cadences of ordinary speech, writes unobtrusively rhymed and metered poetry. It is rather astonishing to realize how much ground Williams covers in his most recent, deceptively slender, collection, *Adjusting to the Light* (University of Missouri Press), from an appreciation of Auguste Rodin to a playful debunking of deconstruction; from an elegy to Chet Baker to a dramatic monologue spoken by God; from a sonnet to a (shrinking) sestina. And the volume has a kind of running joke, or at least a running motif, of poems focused on a "Young Preacher" with a wandering mind. "To a Friend, An Unhappy Poet," may or may not be a response to Gioia's "Can Poetry Matter?" with these consoling words:

> You fret how few now read what's hard to write.
> There barely are any
> but this is not something we can fix.
> There never were many.
>
> About the same percentage of people always
> could love a noun.
> What mother in London's slums opened her Blake
> or Milton after the children were yelled down?

Miller, like Kennedy and Gunn, devotes some of his energy to the epigram, here collected as a series of twelve "Rubrics." But perhaps the most memorable poems in this most readable collection are two dramatic monologues, "The Art Photographer Puts His Model at Ease" and "The Stripper." The latter is spoken by an older stripper who, with seeming good nature, passes on her experience, the tricks of the trade, to a newcomer to the profession, only in its final stanza revealing its full pathos of the aging woman being replaced by youth:

> There's this little place where I like to go.
> They have good boiled shrimp and a nice bar.
> We've done enough for now. I'd like to know
> where you stood in your graduating class,
> what magazines you read, if you like to sew,
> and who in a hundred hells you think you are.

How skillfully Williams captures American speech in rhymed iambic pentameter lines; how effortlessly his narrative runs its surprisingly inevitable course.

The two most impressive individual volumes published in 1992 by established younger poets are Alfred Corn's *Autobiographies* (Viking) and Gjertrud Schnackenberg's long-awaited third book, *A Gilded Lapse of Time* (Farrar, Straus and Giroux). Corn's previous book, *The West Door* (1988), was an extremely disappointing collection of uninspired lyrics and a rather bad shorter narrative poem, "An Xmas Murder." With his latest volume, Corn seems back on the path he set for himself in his earlier collections of lyrics, especially *The Various Light* (1980) and his book-length autobiographical narrative, *Notes from a Child of Paradise* (1984). *Autobiographies* contains a baker's dozen of lyrics and dramatic monologues that rank among his best, followed by a long autobiographical narrative, "1992," which picks up where *Notes* left off. "My Neighbor, The Distinguished Count" is an interesting dramatic monologue updating the Dracula legend (a popular trend these days), while "La Madeleine" is an eight-part meditation on Mary Magdalene and Marcel Proust's *Remembrance of Things Past*. "Resolutions" seems obliquely to deal with life as it is lived in Manhattan since the onslaught of AIDS:

> for Sunday lunch, three friends, staunch, kind,
> gifted at what (and not) to say. Safeguards....
> Still, when that unknown tenant, shopping
> bag in hand, steps into the elevator,
> glances a split second, then looks down –
>
> *Oh, if being guarded meant the same as being safe.*

But the main draw here is the immensely readable and sympathetic "1992," which juxtaposes, in twenty numbered and dated sections, ranging, in nonchronological order, from 1949 to 1992, episodes from the poet's life with imagined episodes from the lives of fictional characters occupying the same city as the poet finds himself in at the time. In this way Corn gives us his own panoramic vision of America since mid century, as the poem finds him traveling from his native Georgia to Manhattan, where he currently lives, to various places – Cincinnati, Minneapolis–Saint Paul, Berkeley, Los Angeles – he visits on teaching stints, reading tours, and vacations. While *Notes* was concerned largely with the amicable breakup of his marriage (recalled here in section 3, "1987") and his coming to terms with his homosexuality, the autobiographical half of "1992," while it chronicles numerous relationships and such events as Robert Lowell's funeral in 1977 and a more recent trip to the campus of the University of Minnesota to observe the Washington Avenue Bridge from which John Berryman leapt to his death in 1972, focuses mainly on the breakup of his relationship with poet and critic J. D. McClatchy (referred to as Sandy), and the at first nervous but increasingly more steady relationship with a younger man and his simultaneous reembracement of Christianity. The fictional characters range from a black lesbian nurse in Atlanta to a young, gay Chinese-American man in San Francisco, to a young boy in Ohio just given his first gun for his birthday, to a woman in Los Angeles working with AIDS patients. Some might fault Corn for his perhaps heavy-handed attempt to create as politically correct a multicultural quilt as he can, but few could argue that the entire poem is not compulsively readable and that Corn's ability to create characters distinct from his lyric or narrative "I" is far more certain here than it was in "An Xmas Murder." My main reservation about "1992" is that Corn's language and meter are so relaxed here, rendering the piece perhaps a bit too prosaic.

Gjertrud Schnackenberg's aesthetic dilemma in *A Gilded Lapse of Time* is the opposite of Corn's in this ambitious triptych of poems about religion, history, art, and the significance of poetry: she risks writing on such a refined plane as potentially to render her poetry too intellectually abstract, though ultimately she succeeds in avoiding this fate because she writes so well and with such spiritual passion. In her first two books, *Portraits and Elegies* (1982) and *The Lamplit Answer* (1985), Schnackenberg established herself as one of the very finest poets of her generation, writing some nearly flawless lyrics meditating upon the death of her father in the "Laughing with One Eye" sequence in her first book and in the exquisitely rhymed tercets of "Supernatural Love" in her second. From the beginning, though, Schnackenberg's interests have extended beyond the personal in poems such as "Darwin in 1881" (included in both of her first two books) and "Kremlin in Smoke," a sequence on Frédéric Chopin, and "Heavenly Feast," on the life and death of Simone Weil. Sometimes, as in her Weil poem, the results were stunning; other times, as in her Chopin poem, or her re-creation of Sleeping Beauty, "Imaginary Prisons" in *The Lamplit Answer,* the results were merely ponderous. While she is a master of language, meter, and the image, she is less successful in creating narrative tension in her longer poems, and this weakness, clearly to be found in *A Gilded Lapse of Time,* might render the volume inaccessible to some readers, as it did to me on a quick first reading. Had I not respected her earlier work so much, I might not have returned to this volume to read it more carefully and with dif-

ferent expectations, as I have done more than once since it appeared in November.

Such effort has largely proved worthwhile, for it takes time to begin to understand the ambition underlying this volume and the degree of its achievement, both of which are considerable. Though her second book concluded on a triumphant note with the vision of resurrection embodied in "Supernatural Love," where Schnackenberg seems to be miraculously united with both Christ and her dead father through the mediation of poetry, the penultimate section of *The Lamplit Answer* was comprised of a series of troubled love poems that seems to end in despair. The "gilded lapse of time" referred to in the title of her latest book – derived from John Keats's sonnet "How Many Bards Gild the Lapses of Time," where the poet says of a "few of them," "I could brood / Over their beauties, earthly, or sublime," those few bards who "Make pleasing music, and not wild uproar" (Schnackenberg does not identify this, and other allusions to Keats, in her extensive notes on the poem) – in part refers to the seven-year lapse between Schnackenberg's second and third books, a silence apparently derived from a time "When I thought poetry was love, and I had / Sickened of poetry."

"A Gilded Lapse of Time," then, is about Schnackenberg's spiritual journey to Ravenna, the city of Dante's exile from his native Florence and the site of his tomb, in order to regain her poetic voice, a quest that is, for Schnackenberg, connected to her attempt to accept Christ as her personal redeemer. (One of the two essays Schnackenberg published during her poetic silence was a scholarly yet personal interpretation of Paul's Epistle to the Colossians which appeared in *Incarnation* [Viking, 1990], edited by Alfred Corn.) Dante, then, is the "bard" upon whose life and works Schnackenberg has considered it most relevant to "brood." The poem is structured as a prayer, a twenty-part spiritual meditation, with Schnackenberg frequently playing upon the linguistic similarity between the words "lapse" and "apse," suggesting that her poetic silence will end only through religious devotion. The poem in fact shows Schnackenberg in full command of the language in numerous long passages of exquisitely beautiful poetry, such as this one, playing on the linguistic connection between three other words, "guilt," "gilt," and "gold" (elsewhere she will use "gold" in a passage echoing Keats's description of George Chapman's *Homer* as comprising "realms of gold"):

Lord, we cannot discern
The guilt of our callings –

Let me turn away, at fault, and overawed;
Let me say, *You are still my Lord and my God,*
Let me say I am unable to ascertain
The guilt of poetry, and leave a prayer scribbled
In the gold room where the written word
Presses us back –
You are the God
Of a word we have not learned,
And the *verbum visibilum* really does
Flicker in the gilt of the apse
Where it once burned.

The sequence concludes with an ambivalent dream
the persona has after returning to her hotel room in
Ravenna, the door to Dante's tomb "shut" behind
her, in which both Dante and the angel Gabriel
appear, one or the other bearing the gift of a honey-
laden honeycomb which she identifies as a symbol
for poetry which Saul had forbidden the Israelites to
eat in 1 Samuel, but which his son Jonathan nonetheless does, with the result that "his eyes were
enlightened." In Schnackenberg's dream:

I had left the honeycomb dripping on the ground
In the woods hear, a profanity
Of waste, and the bees whirled into my ears

Their endless sequences, their burning rhymes
I groped among for what I meant to say.
Angels were there, and one of them turned

And struck me when I spoke, and I lifted my hand
And touched blood on my mouth, and then I saw
They were holding an impression from your face –

Or rather a heavy honeycomb, and your words
Were a stream of bees floating toward me in sunlight.
When I opened your book I thought you spoke,

Or else it was Gabriel lifting to my lips
A tablespoon of golden, boiling smoke
So wounding to my mouth I turned my back

On the source of poetry, and then I woke.

Yet how can one help but read this poem as written
by one who has turned herself back *toward* "the
source of poetry"?

The volume's second sequence, "Crux of Radiance," presents a series of meditations on paintings of Christ's Passion, while the third, "A moment
in Utopia," is concerned with the life and death
under Joseph Stalin of Osip Mandelstam, clearly for
Schnackenberg a twentieth-century Christ figure
even as Stalin is a twentieth-century Herod. But
here, while Schnackenberg still is concerned with the
painful cost – both psychological and historical – at
which poetry is written, she also imagines an

ahistorical Utopia where the imagination is freed
from suffering and history, a landscape comprised of
roses

Flowering past our multitudes
Of local eras, our eschatologies,
Our beginnings and ends,
Our indictions, our "destinies of kingdoms,"
Our fifteen-year cycles, our holy days
And warring calendars,
Our Era of Martyrs,

Flowering past the fence
Above our death dates hidden even
From the angels –
Transitory monuments
Pouring out their whorls,
Piling up their treasure heedlessly
In the vaults of air.

In addition to the essay on Saint Paul, Schnackenberg also wrote an essay on T. S. Eliot between
publishing *The Lamplit Answer* and *A Gilded Lapse of
Time;* if, like Eliot, Schnackenberg perceives much
of human existence as occurring in a spiritual waste-
land, she also, like Eliot, yearns eloquently to transcend history, to achieve transcendence, to reside in
a timeless paradise. Difficult as *A Gilded Lapse of
Time* can be, with Schnackenberg's sentences sometimes taking several stanzas to fully unwind, I suspect that it will be recognized, with *Four Quartets,* to
be one of the great poems on the interconnection of
poetry and religion written in the twentieth century.

Frederick Turner is perhaps best known both
as the author of two unusually ambitious and readable epic poems, *The New World* (1985) and *Genesis*
(1988), and as one of the major proponents of "Expansive Poetry," a literary movement devoted to
the revival of both metrical and rhymed poetry and
of narrative poetry, the goal being to "expand"
poetry's audience. In 1992 Turner published a pair
of books meant to be read in tandem, *April Wind and
Other Poems* (University Press of Virginia), a collection of his lyrics written over the past decade, and
Beauty: The Value of Morals (University Press of Virginia), a collection of nine essays outlining his aesthetic and corresponding to the nine sections of lyrics in *April Wind.* In addition, in collaboration with
Zsuzsanna Ozváth, Turner selected and translated,
in *Foamy Sky: The Major Poems of Miklós Radnóti*
(Princeton University Press), the works of a
Hungarian poet killed by the Nazis. (Indeed, tying
all three volumes together, *April Wind* contains a
lyric entitled "On Sitting Down with Zsuzsanna
Ozváth to Translate Radnóti," while he discusses
Radnóti's sequence "Calendar" in "The Experience

of Beauty," the first essay in his critical book.) In an earlier essay, "The Neural Lyre: Poetic Meter, The Brain, and Time," Turner argued, with Ernst Pöppel, from a scientific perspective, that the human brain has been programmed to respond to poetic meter, hence metrical poetry will always, "objectively," be aesthetically superior to nonmetrical free verse. In *Beauty,* Turner draws upon a variety of areas, including neurobiology, chaos theory, and fractal physics, to argue that "beauty" is an objective value system that has evolved with other human characteristics. Turner, in an age of deconstruction, then, is an essentialist. (Those interested in reading a more orthodox defense of the deconstructionist poetics of the L=A=N=-G=U=A=G=E poets should consult Charles Bernstein's *Poetics* [Harvard University Press], an amalgam of poetry and prose where Bernstein argues that:

> What I hear, then, in the poetries of this New American fin de siècle is an implicit refusal of unity that is the result of our prodigious and magnanimous outpouring of words. In saying this, I register my own particular passion – everywhere reflected in this book – for poetry that insists of running its own course, finding its own measures, charting worlds otherwise hidden or denied or, perhaps best of all, never before existing.)

While Turner's organization of *April Wind* is so rational and rigid as outlined in his "Preface" as well as in *Beauty,* making it seem as if his lyrics were written to prove a theory depriving them of the sense of originality and spontaneity we value in even the most formal of poems, there are superb lyrics here – "The Blackness of the Grackle," "Against Aporia," "Last Evening in California," "Amaryllis," "Maine Summer, with Friends," "For Mei Lin on Our Twenty-Second Wedding Anniversary," and "Pheromones," to name just some – which firmly establish Turner as a lyric poet of genuine stature, enhancing the reputation he has already established for himself as a narrative poet of the first rank. The Radnóti translations (which are rhymed and metered) demonstrate Radnóti to be, like Turner, both a fine nature poet and a beautiful love poet. Turner is a man of prodigious learning and energy whose views are original and provocative. Both his poems and his aesthetic essays deserve wide audiences. They have the ability to change the way one looks at the world.

Another poet associated with what has been called the New Narrative is Mark Jarman, whose *Iris* (Story Line Press) is his first book-length poem that is both influenced by and to some extent a med-

itation on the poet Robinson Jeffers, whose book-length narratives Jarman and his publisher, Robert McDowell, have both championed in essays in their now-defunct journal, the *Reaper.* This is far from a metapoetic text, however. Instead, it is a powerful look at the violent life of a working-class woman who became interested in Jeffers in college through an English professor with whom she had an ill-fated affair. It is a saga that begins in Kentucky, moves abruptly to southern California after Iris and her daughter survive a mass murder at her mother's mobile home, and ends, decades later, in Jeffers's country, Carmel, California. The poem is divided into three sections, of which the first, set in Kentucky, is the strongest. The poem loses focus after that, with Iris's long sojourn in southern California in the second section seeming arbitrary, whereas the third, in which Iris picks up a hitchhiker with her own weird past (one is reminded in this section of a protracted *Thelma and Louise*), ends without the kind of catharsis one would expect; it is anticlimactic.

I was more impressed by Ian McDonald's *Essequibo* (Story Line Press/Peterloo Poets), a book-length sequence of poems set along the Essequibo River in the South American Caribbean nation of Guyana, reminiscent at once of the poetry of Derek Walcott (McDonald, the author's note tells us, "is Antiguan and St. Kittian by ancestry, Trinidadian by birth, Guyanese by adoption and describes himself as West Indian by conviction"; he was also Cambridge-educated) and the magic-realistic fiction of Gabriel García Márquez. The book's first poem, "Amerindian," establishes the volume's mythic time frame, and its colorful lyrics describe both the river's exotic landscape and culture. Perhaps the strongest of its poems is "'Hangman' Cory," a ballad, employing local patois, about a man who thinks he deserves to die for killing his unfaithful wife and her lover, only, years later, to become a godlike hero, saving the lives of many during a violent jungle storm. McDonald is a well-known fiction writer in the Caribbean; his poetic debut in the United States (the book was copublished in England) with this, his second volume of poems, is most welcome. Another narrative poem of interest is Brendan Galvin's *Saints in Their Ox-hide Boat* (Louisiana State University Press), a mini-epic on the fifth-century voyages of Saint Brendan, based partially upon an anonymous ninth-century Latin work, *Voyage of St. Brendan,* though Galvin has created many new characters. His work here seems more imaginative than that of David Ferry in his version of *Gilgamesh,* and his poetic accomplishment comparable.

Emily Grosholz and Rachel Hadas, poets who have been identified as New Formalists, each published new volumes of lyrics in 1992. In addition to their affinity to writing formal poetry (Hadas more than Grosholz), both are college professors and mothers, and books and domestic life form the subject of a good deal of their verse. *Eden* (Johns Hopkins University Press), Grosholz's third book of poetry but the first since the birth of her son, is divided into four sections: on travel and her marriage; on her adolescence in suburban Philadelphia; a series of letters, including the prose "Letter from Toronto" addressed to the *Hudson Review*; and about her new son. The book's strongest poems include "A Poem for Polly," about a friend from high school with whom the poet's path diverged; "Elegy," in memory of another poet's son who died in infancy; and "Thirty-six Weeks," a wonderful poem about pregnancy.

Hadas's *Mirrors of Astonishment* (Rutgers University Press) is comprised of three sequences of lyrics – at which the poet excels – carrying off the themes established in such earlier volumes as *Pass It On* (1989) and *Living In Time* (1990) about passing life and learning, through the body and the mind, to her son and to her students, as her parents, including her father, classics scholar from Columbia University, Moses Hadas, had to her. (The volume is dedicated to Hadas's mother, a Latin teacher, who died in 1992.) The volume's middle section, including the poems "The Mirror," "116th Street," and "Genealogies," is the strongest. "Genealogies," which begins with the line "The Muses are the daughters of Memory," addresses the role her father played in her life, concluding: "Father, I age / and turn to you as I would turn a page. / The Muses are the daughters of Memory." Earlier in the year, Hadas published another volume of poems and prose growing out of an AIDS poetry workshop she teaches at the Gay Men's Health Crisis, *Unending Dialogue: Voices from an AIDS Poetry Workshop* (Faber and Faber). This volume includes poems both by Hadas and by many of her students.

Of the four books chosen for the National Poetry Series published in 1992, Judith Hall's *To Put the Mouth To* (William Morrow/Quill), chosen by Richard Howard, is the strongest. The volume is concerned with female desire, as in its opening sequence, "Fragments of an Eve: Scraps from Her Album." Lynn Emanuel's *The Dig* (University of Illinois Press), chosen by Gerald Stern, has some evocative if prosy poems about growing up in Ely, Nevada, in the 1950s under the unnatural light of nuclear bomb tests. James Richardson's *As If* (Per-

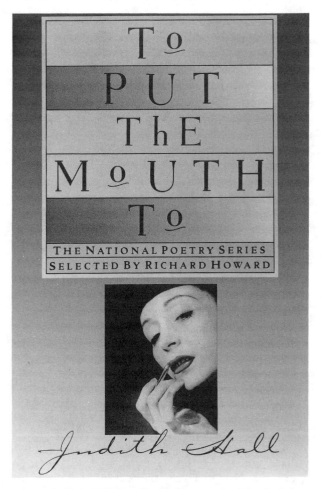

Cover for Judith Hall's collection of poems about female desire

sea Press), chosen by Amy Clampitt, has a few interesting poems in the final of its three sections, especially "Out of School" and "Song for Kate," ruminating upon the different consciousnesses of adults and adolescent girls in the former, and a father and his infant daughter in the latter; but, for the most part, the book seems a rather dull attempt to emulate John Ashbery and Jorie Graham. David Romtvedt, on the other hand, is concerned primarily with world politics, ecology, and the landscape of the western United States in *A Flower Whose Name I Do Not Know* (Copper Canyon Press), chosen by John Haines.

The 1992 Lamont Poetry Selection of the Academy of American Poets for the best second volume of poetry, judged by Lucille Clifton, Jorie Graham, and Robert Morgan, went to Kathryn Stripling Byer for *Wildwood Flower* (Louisiana State University Press), a collection of interrelated lyrics that tell of the life of a woman living in the Blue Ridge Mountains earlier in the century. It is best at its evocation of the sudden onslaught as well as the evanescence of romance and the difficulties of a woman surviving alone in this landscape during the winter. The AAP's Walt Whitman Award for the best first book of poems, judged by Charles Wright, went to Greg Glazner's *From the Iron Chair* (Norton), which contains powerful lyrics on the western landscapes of New Mexico and Montana. Nicholas Samaras was named the Yale Younger Poet by James Dickey for *Hands of the Saddlemaker* (Yale University Press). The son of a Greek Orthodox priest, Samaras, in his most moving poems, addresses concern the quest for the spiritual in the modern world, as in "In the Shell of a Modern Cathedral," and his love for a young woman who died in her teens, the subject of the book's strongest poem, "Easter in the Cancer Ward." Amy Uyematsu won the 1992 Nicholas Roerich Prize for *30 Miles from J-town* (Story Line Press), which contains poems about the social displacement the poet felt growing up a sansei – a third-generation Japanese-American – in a predominantly white neighborhood in suburban Los Angeles, far from the desirably "hip" Japan town in downtown Los Angeles.

Certainly no more striking or outrageous first volume was published in 1992 than novelist Alexander Theroux's *The Lollipop Trollops* (Dalkey Archive Press), a book of stinging satirical verse written with the formality of a neoclassicist. Among Theroux's numerous targets (and no individual or group is safe from Theroux) seems to be the controversial author of *Sexual Personae* and academic media-darling-of-the-moment, Camille Paglia, in "Passacaglia for an Italian Witch." (A handsome limited edition of some of these poems was published as *History Is Made At Night* by Aralia Press.) By contrast, Jan Schreiber's *Wily Apparitions* (Cummington Press) is a mature and quietly moving collection of traditional lyrics combined with some clever epigrams.

My favorite first book by a poet who grew up in the rock and roll era is Tony Hoagland's *Sweet Ruin* (University of Wisconsin Press), awarded the Brittingham Prize in Poetry by Donald Justice. The title "All Along the Watchtower" is derived from Bob Dylan, while Cole Porter inspires "You're the Top," about Hoagland's grandmother's appreciation for the "bright and beautiful and useless." Hoagland is best at conveying awkward states of contemporary sexual dilemmas as in "Poem for Men Only," "My Country," "One Season," and "Carnal Knowledge." Almost as impressive is Eva Salzman's *The English Earthquake* (Bloodaxe Books/Dufour Editions) by a young American poet living in Brighton, England. Salzman writes equally

well on both England ("Station Waiting") and the United States ("Rain in New York"), as well as about the universal condition of love ("Coming to Bed"). Elizabeth Macklin's first volume, *A Woman Kneeling in the Big City,* is distinguished, if nothing else, by the fact that thirty-two of its forty-eight poems originally appeared in the *New Yorker;* it reads like a poet's careful, quirky field guide to life in Manhattan. Edward Hirsch perhaps most aptly describes Macklin as "part Frank O'Hara, part Emily Dickinson." Among her most engaging poems are "Field Guide to Lesser Desires," "Now the Heroine Weakens and Speaks," and "Surface Tension," describing "Desire tak[ing] a long, cool bath / indistinct at first in the blue water."

Two unusually striking first books by gay poets appeared in 1992: one, *Vox Angelica* (Alice James Books), by Timothy Liu, a Chinese-American poet raised as a Mormon, the other, *In the Blood* (Northeastern University Press), by Carl Phillips, an African-American graduate student in classical philology at Harvard and the winner of the 1992 Morse Poetry Prize judged by Rachel Hadas. Liu effectively writes about graphic sexual encounters ("SFO/HIV/JFK"), about AIDS ("Volunteers at the AIDS Foundation" and "The Quilt"), and about spirituality ("Vox Angelica" and "His Body Like Christ Passed In And Out Of My Life"). Phillips also combines the religious with the erotic in "Passion" and weaves both classical and African culture smoothly into such poems as "Africa Says," "Sappho and the Camera," and "Leda, After the Swan." Nancy Boutilier, on the other hand, writes ebulliently about lesbian experience in *According to Her Contours* (Black Sparrow Press); Boutilier has the humor to use a picture of herself on her women's basketball team as the author's photo.

Both Richard Foerster in *Sudden Harbor* (Orchises Press) and Maureen Seaton in *The Sea Among the Cupboards* (New Rivers Press) write well about the tensions, sexual and otherwise, of growing up in New York City and suburban Westchester County, both escaping bad marriages to find more serenity in early middle age. Seaton and Foerster both have a formal bent, but she is feisty while he is at once more solemn and a more assured craftsman. Julia Kasdorf's *Sleeping Preacher* (University of Pittsburgh Press) contains poems about life in New York City and in the Mennonite community in Pennsylvania where she grew up. In "At the Acme Bar and Grill," her "memory of calico / bonnets to keep the gray air and stench / of chicken off your hair" from her childhood is evoked while eating Buffalo chicken wings in a hip Manhattan watering hole. Enid

Shomer's *This Close to Earth* (University of Arkansas Press) is highlighted by the sequence "Pope Joan" and by two sonnets, "Into the Motion of Other Things" and "Refusing the Call."

Richard Cecil's *Alcatraz* (Purdue University Press) and Elton Glazer's *Color Photographs of the Ruins* (University of Pittsburgh Press) are both concerned, to varying degrees, with pop culture, though both poets are also academics with poems on the 1987 MLA Convention in San Francisco. Glazer is the more cerebral and engaging, especially in "*Film Noir*" and "Confluences at San Francisco – MLA, 1987." Glazer is effective in "Ballad of Dead Actresses." Deborah Pope's *Fanatic Heart* (Louisiana State University Press) contains two good poems about paintings ("Frank Benson, *Portrait of My Daughters,* 1907" and "Klimt, *The Fulfillment*"), while Julie Suk's *The Angel of Obsession* (University of Arkansas Press) contains extremely fine love poems, most impressively "Floating Tethered." Both Susan Prospere, in *Sub Rosa,* and Cathy Smith Bowers, in *The Love That Ended Yesterday in Texas,* write evocatively about growing up female in the South. Margaret D. Smith's *The Holy Struggle: Unspoken Thoughts of Hopkins* (Harold Shaw Publishers) is an engaging sonnet sequence that imagines Gerard Manley Hopkins's love for a young nun, though Robert Bernard Martin's recent revelations about Hopkins's suppressed erotic inclinations might call the credibility of Smith's speculations into doubt. Frances McCue won the 1991 Barnard New Women Poets Prize for *The Stenographer's Notebook* (Beacon Press), while Steve Kronen's *Empirical Evidence* (University of Georgia Press) and Dean Young's *Beloved Infidel* (Wesleyan University Press) are both notable first volumes.

Among more established poets, Gerald Barrax is one of our most distinguished African-American poets, who has written, in his collection *Leaning Against the Sun* (University of Arkansas Press), a memorable meditation on music, love, an artist's maturation, and Whitman, which ranges from unpunctuated free verse to a tempered villanelle which begins:

Before we know how much we can presume
Upon the perfect pitch of compatibility,
We play to make time stand still in the room.
In our adagio ease, slow duets bloom
In afternoons that beggar hyperbole
Until we learn how little we can presume.

A nocturne together, a prize rare as a black plume:
Naked bodies tuned on the balcony over a moonlit sea
We play to make time stand still in the room.

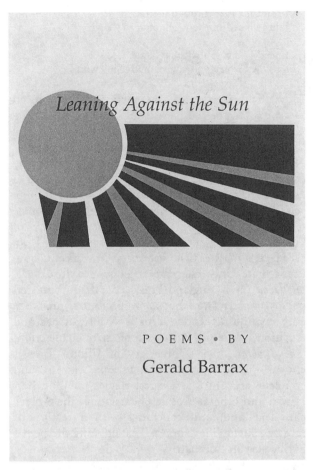

Dust jacket for Gerald Barrax's collection of poems about music, love, and Walt Whitman

In *My Father's Geography,* another, younger, black poet, Michael S. Weaver, writes rhetorically resonant lyrics such as "Thanksgiving 1968" and "My Father's Geography," as well as a sequence of historical narratives set in colonial times in "New England." Essex Hemphill's *Ceremonies* (Plume) is a polemical collection of poems and essays on black, gay identity, while Nancy Glancy's *Claiming Breath* (University of Nebraska Press) presents Native American experience in the form of a yearlong journal in both poetry and prose.

I particularly enjoyed the "fuchsia" poetry of Greg Delanty's *Southward* (Louisiana State University Press) where the Irish-born poet's florid grasp of language, memory, elegy, and mythmaking produces a steady flow of delightfully personal and musical utterances. "The Worrier" is a fine example of Delanty's youthful stance as poetic loner:

But tonight making my way on my own
the birds of worry have eaten my crumb trail.

I can't make it through the fog alone
& am locked in the witch of worry's jail.

I need you to outwit that hag & free me
for now I worry that you've tired of my worry.

Lloyd Schwartz writes congenial, prosy poems in *Goodnight, Gracie* (University of Chicago Press), including the humorous "Reports of My Death" and "House Hunting." Less successful is a sequence, "Fourteen People," based on a series of paintings by Ralph Hamilton of such denizens of the Boston area as Robert Pinsky, Frank Bidart, and Schwartz himself. "For Ephraim," "Above a Trappist Monastery," and even the jarring "The First Day of Christmas" are standouts of harsh emotion in Robert Hazel's *Clock of Clay: New and Selected Poems* (Louisiana State University Press). James Hayford's *Uphill Home* (New England Press) contains a hundred poems, mostly short but all well crafted, unabashedly continuing Robert Frost's American pastoral tradition, while Jim Barnes, in his strong collection, *The Sawdust War* (University of Illinois Press), churns out accomplished quatrains, tercets, and couplets, erecting war elegies, elegies for John Berryman and others, prosaic poems about the American heartland, and concludes with a section of mostly sixteen-line "sonnets" cataloguing the poet's idyllic stay in Lombardy.

Finally, other notable volumes published by established poets in 1992 include William Matthews's *Selected Poems and Translations 1967–1991* (Houghton Mifflin); Stephen Berg's *New and Collected Poems* (Copper Canyon Press); Tom Clark's *Sleepwalker's Fate: New and Selected Poems 1965–1992* (Black Sparrow Press); Robert Peters's *Poems: Selected and New 1967–1991* (Asylum Arts); Denise Levertov's *Evening Train* (New Directions); Tess Gallagher's *Moon Crossing Bridge* (Graywolf) and *Portable Kisses: Love Poems* (Capra Press); Nicholas Christopher's *In the Year of the Comet* (Viking Penguin); Jeffery Skinner's *The Company of Heaven* (University of Pittsburgh Press); Jonathan Holden's *American Gothic* (University of Georgia Press); Carl Dennis's *Meeting With Time* (Viking Penguin); Gerald Stern's *Bread Without Sugar* (Norton); Robert Francis's *Late Fire Late Snow: New and Uncollected Poems* (University of Massachusetts Press); Jean Valentine's *The River at Wolf* (Alice James Books); Ellen Bryant Voigt's *Two Trees*; Stephen Sandy's *Thanksgiving Over the Water* (Knopf); W. S. DePiero's *The Restorers* (University of Chicago Press); Mark Halliday's *Tasker Street* (University of Massachusetts Press); Bruce Weigl's *What Saves Us* (TriQuarterly Books); and John Yau's *Edificio Sayonara* (Black Sparrow Press).

Dust jacket for Gjertrud Schnackenberg's volume of poems about the interconnection of religion and poetry

Gjertrud Schnackenberg's *A Gilded Lapse of Time* (Farrar, Straus and Giroux), this extraordinarily gifted poet's third volume of poetry, marks a brave and successful advance over her first two highly praised and elegantly crafted books, *Portraits and Elegies* (1982) and *The Lamplit Answer* (1985). While these earlier books focused on the death of the poet's father, a history professor, while she was still a teenager, and the love of history, language, and high culture that was his legacy to her, Schnackenberg's third volume eschews addressing the autobiographical underpinnings of the gestation of her poetic imagination and instead examines her difficult yet triumphant rebirth into poetry after seven years of poetic silence.

A Gilded Lapse of Time is composed of three extended sequences that, taken together, comprise a spiritual autobiography reminiscent of T. S. Eliot's *Four Quartets* (1943). All three sections are in the form of extended meditations: the first, "A Gilded Lapse of Time," on Dante's tomb in Ravenna; the second, "Crux of Radiance," on paintings of Christ's Passion; the third on the life and writings of Osip Mandelstam. Such heady material might sink a less gifted poet, but Schnackenberg's spiritual intensity combines here with a use of language that frequently is nothing less than sublime. In an era when lyric poetry seems all too often to be tethered prosaically to the more banal or grotesque elements of the mundane real world, Gjertrud Schnackenberg's poems move from despair to salvation through the medium of her miraculously angelic language that places her well into the upper echelons of contemporary English-language poets.

– *Robert McPhillips*

91

The Year in Drama

Howard Kissel
New York Daily News

Probably the most unusual theater event of 1992 in New York was the importation from France of Arianne Mnouchkine's *Les Atrides,* an adaptation of Aeschylus's *Oresteia* with Euripides' *Iphigenia in Aulis* tacked on as a sort of "curtain raiser." Probably no plays in the classical repertoire are harder to present today than the Greek tragedies, and it must be said at once that Mnouchkine did not really make them work – she only made them *fashionable.*

Mnouchkine's *Les Atrides* seems a useful way to begin a survey of the year in theater precisely because it demonstrated what theatrical fashions are. It also made clear that the avant-garde is as depleted of new ideas as the commercial theater, still drawing on concepts and devices that seemed promising decades ago but that have never really developed. Perhaps it is naive to be surprised at this turn of events, since, as Mnouchkine's compatriot Paul Valéry observed many years ago, "Everything changes except the avant-garde."

Les Atrides was presented by the Brooklyn Academy of Music (BAM), whose "Next Wave" series has been the bellwether of the avant-garde for some time. Many of the "Next Wave" presentations have taken place in the BAM Majestic, a restored theater that made its debut with Peter Brook's *Mahabharata* in 1987. The Majestic was a deserted old movie palace whose interior was "distressed" to Brook's specifications so that it seemed like the ruin of some ancient amphitheater, which might have made it an ideal venue for Mnouchkine's traversal of Greek tragedy.

Perhaps because the stage was not large enough for Mnouchkine's conception (or because the seating capacity was not large enough for BAM's always deficit-ridden budget), *Les Atrides* was presented instead in an armory near Prospect Park in Brooklyn. Its cavernous space was able to house a gigantic stage, gigantic bleachers, and an area behind the bleachers with wooden tabernacles in which audience members could watch the actors put on their costumes and makeup.

Yet another reason for the change of venue might have been that the backless benches in the Majestic, though uncomfortable, were not uncomfortable enough for Mnouchkine. They were, after all, padded, which Mnouchkine's narrow card-table chairs were not. At least since Jerzy Grotowski, the trailblazer of the 1960s, it has been a hallmark of the avant-garde that the theatergoer must not be distracted from the demanding work to which he is being exposed by any form of bourgeois comfort. This may have been one of the areas in which Mnouchkine's efforts were an advance over her aesthetic forebears'; if part of the avant-garde experience is indeed mortification of the posterior flesh, her choice of chairs was pioneering.

As for the stage, it was quite enormous. Its structure was that of a bullfight ring, and it seemed sizable enough to serve the bullfighting needs of some medium-sized Spanish city. The notion of Greek tragedy taking place in an arena designed for confrontations between man and primeval force is, of course, tantalizing. Mnouchkine made surprisingly little use of her theoretically potent image.

To the right of this huge space was an elevated area, certainly no smaller than the orchestra pit of the Metropolitan Opera, which housed the musical instruments that served as background throughout the performances. This mammoth space was filled largely by percussion instruments, and part of the drama was watching the three musicians race from one drum to another as the play progressed.

The music began well before the play, with the ominous murmur of drums accompanying the audience's entry into the theater. In the avant-garde tradition, of course, the audience is not permitted to enter "the space" in any conventional manner. A long line formed outside the armory as patrons were allowed in a few at a time. (In this preperformance ritual none of his successors has matched the expertise of Grotowski, who had the audience lounge about outside "the space" for half an hour after the stated curtain time; then suddenly the staff rushed the audience onto backless benches – unpadded, thus more uncomfortable than Brook's, but less uncomfortable than Mnouchkine's only because Grotowski's "pieces" were shorter than hers.)

The one fulfilling aspect of this tradition is that the audience enters a darkened, somewhat bewildering space that, for a few moments at least, does suggest a place of mystery rather than a place of entertainment. This potentially entrancing mood is invariably broken by the actual logistics of finding a place to sit, since only Brook accepts the bourgeois notion of reserved seats.

The sense of "event" is heightened by the opening moments of the plays. Mnouchkine's minions, in their imposing costumes, can be seen making an end run from the wooden tabernacles behind the bleachers around the orchestra and onto the stage. The moment resembles that in which teams run heroically onto the field before an athletic event. All well and good. But the actual staging of these difficult plays – which chart an extraordinary journey from human sacrifice to bloody vengeance to the birth of modern ideas of justice – was seldom more involving than conventional attempts to bring them to life.

Tactically it was probably a mistake to start the series with Euripides' *Iphigenia in Aulis*. To begin with, Euripides is a more sophisticated, more *theatrical* playwright than Aeschylus. His recounting of the story of how Agamemnon sacrificed his daughter Iphigenia to placate the gods so that the Greek fleet could sail to Troy is full of subtleties and surprises. It is far more effective as theater than any of the plays in the Aeschylus trilogy, which seem, by contrast, a form of patriotic oratory. (To a certain extent, after all, they were.)

More important, Euripides ends his play with the revelation that at the last moment Iphigenia was not sacrificed on the priestly altar. Like the biblical Isaac, whose life was spared from his father's raised knife by the sudden appearance of a ram in the thicket, Iphigenia's life was saved by the appearance of a doe on the altar. She herself was transported to the realm of the gods.

This knowledge undercuts the force of Aeschylus's plays, which hinge on the wrath of Clytemnestra. If we begin where Aeschylus begins, we do not know that Iphigenia has been saved by a deus ex machina. We can then sympathize with Clytemnestra's anguished desire for vengeance. But if we know that Iphigenia has not been sacrificed – if we see that even Clytemnestra knows of the last minute substitution – her subsequent rage for revenge seems far less justified.

The ideas that animated Mnouchkine's staging generally fell within the categories of the politically fashionable. In the first play, for example, Iphigenia's suitor, Achilles, was played as a somewhat effeminate, thoroughly ineffectual young man. This seems a serious misreading of Greek notions of homosexuality. The attachment of men to one another was not a sign of effeminacy. (Even the attachment of the handsome young soldier Alcibiades to the elderly Socrates was a far more complex form of love, at least as Plato describes it in *The Symposium,* than anything that might appear in the literature of, say, ACT-UP.) To reduce the greatest of Greek warriors to a caricature does not seem truly in the spirit of these plays.

Throughout the cycle the chorus, rather than standing staidly on the sidelines commenting on the action, dances out its responses in a choreography that veers between European folk dances and the sensuous movements of Indian sacred dancing, with occasional jerky movements to connote violence. The mere mention of the word dance was invariably a pretext to do one. At first the idea seems fresh, but the steps quickly grow monotonous. Ultimately the dances distract from rather than intensify the action.

For all Mnouchkine's efforts at innovation, her staging was, for the most part, very conventional, very French – the leading characters, in time-honored French tradition, stood stage center and declaimed. The major difference was that, unlike classical French actors, who pride themselves on their rich, sonorous voices, Mnouchkine's multinational cast, with a few exceptions, had voices ranging from ordinary to shrill.

Only in *The Libation Bearers* did Mnouchkine make use of the bullfight imagery inherent in the huge set. Orestes, who has come to revenge his father's death, points his sword at his mother in a way that seems very much like a matador setting on his prey. Since, however, like everything else, the action was highly stylized, the moment seemed mechanical rather than genuinely dramatic.

Perhaps the most effective image of *The Libation Bearers* was that in which the bodies of the murdered Clytemnestra and her lover Egisthus lie on a platform. A pair of attendants, as in Japanese theater, attempt to move the platform offstage. It is too heavy. Only the assistance of members of the chorus – that is to say, a communal effort – can expunge this bloody deed.

This makes an effective prologue to the final play, *The Eumenides,* in which the cycle of retribution is broken when Athena brings the idea of justice to the city named for her. In this play the members of the androgynous chorus doff the skirts they have worn in the previous three plays and the silly beards they wore in *Agamemnon* to become the Furies and their attendant hounds. Theoretically we are to be terrified by them, but Mnouchkine's Furies are merely a bunch of squawky hoboes. Their hounds were costumed as something between wild dogs and baboons, making them seem too fanciful, too cute, to be frightening.

Even the novelties in the staging – the use of Kabuki-like moving platforms, for example, on which characters suddenly arrive on stage, transported from under the audience bleachers – though they created momentary frissons, also came to seem mechanical. For that matter the eclecticism of Mnouchkine's vision, the elements borrowed from India and Japan, far from making it exotic, made *Les Atrides* seem rather academic. The audience's recognition of these borrowings encourage a feeling of self-congratulation rather than participation in a harrowing tragedy. Even the music, which borrowed heavily from foreign traditions, became stereotyped, especially in the thunderous accompaniments to violent action. All too often, however, it sounded like the innocuous background music you hear in Indian or Japanese restaurants.

Interestingly, the audience, apart from trendies and celebrities, seemed very academic. It was, after all, a spectacle that lent itself to scholarly discussion and annotation. Catching its allusions to other cultural traditions afforded an excitement roughly akin to skimming through a chapter to consult the footnotes at the end. To borrow again from the wisdom of Paul Valéry, "Everything winds up at the Sorbonne," and it seemed a bit sad that this much heralded event was ultimately a bloodless account of Greek tragedy. It had far less visceral impact than Richard Schechner's interpretation of an admittedly juicier play, Euripides' *The Bacchae,* retitled *Dionysus in '69.* Mnouchkine's version could be of interest only to an audience eager to find allusions, cultural parallels, and the "statements" about gender that seem to excite contemporary academics. At least the cycle had its grand pretensions. Most of the year's theater offerings seemed utterly without pretension or intellectual content.

Among the more interesting plays was David Mamet's *Oleanna.* The title, by the way, conveys some sense of Mamet's quirkiness. Its meaning is entirely personal. It is a town in Wisconsin near which the Chicago-born Mamet attended camp as a boy. The name has always sounded to him like that of some peaceful community or utopia. The use of

the name for a play about the perils of academic politics is, of course, deeply ironic, but the irony is clear only if you happen to know the playwright's early history (or happen to have read an interview in which he explains the title.)

While you are in the theater, *Oleanna* irritates because the mannerisms of the playwright (who also directed the production) are so blatant as to verge on self-parody. At one time the halting speech of Mamet's characters, with its repetitiveness and rigidly controlled rhythms, seemed an attempt to mirror the hesitancies of everyday speech. Now it seems merely the author's self-conscious signature. Where once this signature evoked the portentous style of Mamet's sometime mentor Harold Pinter, now it suggests the dizzy repetitiveness of Gertrude Stein.

In the first act of *Oleanna,* a female student has come to her professor because she has frankly understood nothing in his course, which she has failed. The professor is preoccupied with whether or not he will secure a mortgage for his new home. Getting the mortgage depends on whether he will get tenure, which seems fairly certain. He tries to help the young woman but he is rather cynical about education in general. He refers to it as "a virtual warehousing of the young." She is clearly bewildered by his urbanity. At one point, trying to comfort her, he puts his arm on her shoulder.

When the second act begins this gesture of paternal solicitude has jeopardized his career and, of course, his mortgage. He has been accused of sexual harassment. The young woman, who seemed, frankly, quite dumb in the first act, now has a mastery of political jargon that makes her thoroughly intimidating. Her transformation into an American equivalent of the Red Guard is as startling as it is unexpected. She makes references to her "group," which suggests that her plea for help in the first act was a setup, a feminist effort to entrap this politically rearguard professor.

Ultimately the play is dissatisfying because we cannot help feeling that the ambiguities Mamet has created do not stem from deeply rounded characters but rather from his desire to toy with us, to manipulate – almost cruelly – our emotional responses. By the end of the play the professor is so enraged by the student's rhetoric and emotional impassivity that he lunges at her, obviously eager to inflict physical harm. His transformation from a worldly cynic to a hapless victim of his own worst impulses is troubling, but also annoying because it seems so schematic.

Mamet's own sympathies are clearly on the side of the professor, and, perhaps to redress the balance of the play, in which nothing about the student is appealing or sympathetic, Mamet directed his longtime colleague W. H. Macy to play the teacher in such a way that even when he was being aloof, witty and charming, he seemed somehow neurotic and disturbed, thus almost as unengaging as his student (who was played with admirable abrasiveness by Mamet's wife, the English actress Rebecca Pidgeon.) If the play is disturbing despite its irritations, it is because it reflects the brutal struggle for power behind what seem to be merely battles of ideas and perceptions.

Another supposed play of ideas was Ariel Dorfman's *Death and the Maiden*. Dorfman, a native of Chile and a supporter of Salvador Allende Gossens, went into exile when Allende was driven from power in 1973. With the restoration of at least the semblance of democracy, Dorfman, who had lived in the United States and Great Britain, returned to Chile. He wanted to write a play about how democracy can function in a country that has lived through a nightmare, a country in which those who instigated the nightmare are still among the citizenry, often in positions of power.

Dorfman's attempt to confront this genuinely troubling situation is *Death and the Maiden*. The play has three characters: a woman who underwent torture at the hands of the former regime; her husband, who has just been appointed to a commission to investigate the human rights violations of that regime, and a stranger who gives the husband a ride to the couple's beach house when his car breaks down. The woman is convinced that the stranger was her torturer many years before.

During the night she ties the Good Samaritan to a chair, and for the rest of the play taunts him, even threatening to kill him, trying to determine if he is indeed the man who degraded her. Her husband remains oddly detached, as if what is going on in his living room is already the tribunal on which he must sit and weigh evidence dispassionately.

Late in the play, when the two men are alone, we sense that he is more sympathetic to this stranger than to his distraught, vengeful wife. It is not the only time during the play when Dorfman settles for an obvious, politically fashionable point – in this case, the power of male solidarity to override even questions of human justice – to buttress a play that is full of rhetoric and theatrical manipulativeness.

The title refers to the Franz Schubert string quartet, to which the woman's torturers listened while they were at work. The play ends some time later, when the three characters are by chance at a concert. The husband speaks glibly of the commission's now completed efforts, and, as the music begins, his wife makes eye contact with her supposed tormentor in another box. Nothing has been resolved, but the characters suppress their private feelings in an evening of high culture.

The play was done with great success in London with relatively unknown actors. The Broadway production featured three Hollywood stars – Glenn Close as the woman, Richard Dreyfuss as her husband and Gene Hackman as the putative torturer. Their broad American accents had a dislocating effect on the play. So did Tony Walton's rather glamorous rendition of the beach house (in London the design was apparently a simple shack), which made the whole thing seem like an evening of improvisations in Malibu.

Another play that toyed with political ideas was Frank McGuinness's *Someone Who'll Watch Over Me*, which was about three hostages chained to a basement wall somewhere in the Middle East. The three are an African American, an Irishman, and an Englishman, and most of the character development hinges on national stereotypes. The American is open, optimistic, a bit naive. The Irishman is gregarious, chatty; the Englishman a bit effete and somewhat reserved. The latter two engage in expressions of national rivalry. All three play games of imagination to bolster their spirits.

Although the play succeeds when it shows the men rising above their situation, it seldom conveys the starkness of that situation. Especially in the second act, when the American has been removed, the improvisations get a little silly – the two remaining prisoners mimic a sequence from *Chitty Chitty Bang Bang* – and the play loses its bearings.

The latest installment in August Wilson's continuing decade-by-decade survey of African-American life was *Two Trains Running*, set in a little neighborhood restaurant in Pittsburgh in 1969. Little about the play suggests the turbulence of the 1960s, but perhaps it is Wilson's point that there is a bedrock of African-American life that subsists regardless of the surface change.

The action of the play is almost nonexistent. We hear reports on the lying-in-state of a popular minister in the funeral parlor across the street. A lovable half-wit, the victim of white injustice, arrives from time to time demanding a ham that has been stolen from him. The owner of the restaurant has a running battle with someone who uses his public phone for numbers running. An ex-convict whose fingers are still a little sticky flirts with a tight-lipped waitress, who, in obedience to some dark personal god, has carved ridges into her calves.

At times the exchanges between these characters verge on the mechanical, but what always keeps the play engaging is Wilson's gift for capturing the rhythms and charm of African-American speech. His plays have a musical quality that gives them interest beyond the circumstances of character or plot.

One of the most literate of the plays that reached New York in 1992 was Richard Nelson's *Two Shakespearean Actors,* which is about the Astor Place Riots of 1849, in which thirty-five people lost their lives over the seemingly not very burning issue of whether an English actor should perform *Macbeth* on the same night an American was scheduled to do so. The Englishman was William Charles Macready, the American, Edwin Forrest. Most historians agree that the riots had less to do with the public's concern about the niceties of Shakespeare interpretation than with the congenital hatred of the English by the New York Irish, whose numbers had recently been swollen by victims of the potato famine that had ravaged Ireland the previous few years.

What gave Nelson's play its distinction was that it eschewed any conventional depiction of these historical events, focusing instead on the chitchat, the gossip, malicious or trivial, of the supporting actors in the two rival companies. We learn everything in bars and restaurants, where actors drink and gossip after the shows. It was history viewed – with considerable wit – through the wrong end of the telescope. The petty jealousies, humiliations, and idiocies that make up an actor's life filled the foreground; the deaths of thirty-five people were merely "noises off."

Ultimately the play never came into focus despite its many insights. At the end of the evening Nelson had the two actors meet (which, in history, they did not). Among other things, they discuss their differing approaches to their profession. In preparing to play Hamlet, Forrest, the American, says he has been visiting insane asylums. His English counterpart retorts drily, "You study asylums. I study the play."

This exchange suggests that the American and English styles of acting – one oriented toward naturalism, the other toward technique – were already crystallized, but Nelson is not interested in acting theory. As in his earlier *Some Americans Abroad,* he is fascinated by the power plays executed in "polite"

society. There the players were tatty academics. Here they are actors, who lack the intellectual jargon and gambits to mask their political moves or their snobbism. Their pettiness is at once more transparent and more comic.

The play was splendidly acted, especially by Brian Bedford as the stunningly pompous Macready. (In some sense this was an unfair characterization on Nelson's part, since the historical Macready was a great friend of Charles Dickens's, who, one suspects, would not have tolerated intimacy with so obvious a compendium of pretensions.) Because much of the dialogue is about the theater, *Two Shakespearean Actors* at times seems like an extended in-joke about the foibles of the profession and its poignant, pathetic practitioners. But its strength is its powerful sense of how little the preoccupations of the people in the wings reflect the anxieties and crises enacted in the historical spotlight. In this quirky understanding *Two Shakespearean Actors* is an original, witty, and affecting piece of writing.

Neil Simon's offering this year was *Jake's Women,* a frankly autobiographical work about a writer's relationship with the women in his life – his first wife, who died when quite young, his second, an actress he met while working on one of his plays (and to whom the play can easily be read as an invitation, nay a plea, to return to him) as well as his catty sister and his female shrink. The play was short on structure. The multilevel set was an image of Jake's mind, through which the various women flitted as he interacted with and analyzed them.

At one point, the writer, watching his characters, declares, "If I can *create* that kind of intimacy, why can't I experience it in real life?" The problem was that Simon never really created any feeling of intimacy with his characters. Nor could Alan Alda, who played Jake, convince us that the writer really craved self-knowledge. Constantly flashing his "aw, shucks" modest smile, Alda projected a self-satisfaction too complacent for Jake's overwrought self-obsession. (Woody Allen used this subtextual smugness well in his film *Crimes and Misdemeanors.* Here it was almost too intense for the play.)

Jake's Women was originally to have reached Broadway in the spring of 1990, but, for the first time in Simon's career, he agreed to close the show on the road. He then went on to write *Lost in Yonkers,* the first of his plays to win the Pulitzer Prize and only the second to win a Tony for Best Play. The most instructive thing about these events is that the purely imaginary *Yonkers* was a much more deeply felt, provocative play than *Jake's Women.* It, too, had a character who keeps even those closest to her at a great distance, the icy Grandma Kurnitz. Simon was able to create more genuine emotions and sympathy for her than for his autobiographical hero in *Jake's Women*.

The greatest weakness of the latter play is its earnestness, which is probably more appropriate to the therapist's couch than the theater. ("There's pain here, and we're not going to be able to do anything until we get in touch with our emotions," one of the characters pontificates.) There is something fascinating about the unsatisfying play Simon has fashioned and his obvious need to make a statement about his relationships with women. Plays are invariably fueled by some personal need, but it seems symptomatic of our time that even for so a formidable craftsman as Simon the personal statement has taken precedence over the needs of the theater.

Much the reverse was true of Wendy Wasserstein in *The Sisters Rosensweig*. At the heart of the play is the theme of returning to one's roots, in this case not Moscow but Brooklyn. These three sisters are Jewish girls from Brooklyn, each of whom has achieved success in her chosen field.

The most celebrated of the three is the oldest, Sara Goode, whose fifty-fourth birthday in London is the occasion for their reunion. Sara is a banker, and, from the elegance of her London townhouse, you might never imagine her origins were in prosaic Brooklyn. The most interesting action of the play is that Sara looks behind the mask of worldliness and sophistication she has assumed to see if there is something worth recovering in the world she has left behind.

The reason for this inward journey is twofold. The urbane, powerful, wealthy London politician she imagines is interested in her gives her an unusually impersonal birthday present, a teakettle, almost as a way of reinforcing the fact that he does not regard her as someone special. On the positive side she is courted by a New York furrier (reformed – he now does only synthetics), who reminds her of the charm, the warmth, and humor of the Jewish world she has left behind.

It might be argued that the impetus to self-examination ought to be weightier than a night with a furrier, but it seems characteristic of *The Sisters Rosensweig* that it never veers too far from the frivolous, as if Wasserstein were afraid to abandon the humor on which she has built her career even when she has legitimately serious issues to ponder.

If Sara's self-examination seems the center ring of the play, it would be easy to ignore it for all that goes on in the sideshows. Sara's middle sister,

Program cover for the production at the Ethel Barrymore Theatre of Wendy Wasserstein's comedy about three Jewish sisters

Gorgeous Teitelbaum, is someone who, though she has moved several hundred miles from Brooklyn, has not forsaken her ethnic origins. The doyenne of Newton, Massachusetts, she leads the annual pilgrimages of her temple sisterhood and has scheduled this year's journey to London to coincide with Sara's birthday. Gorgeous, who is also the star of a cable television show in Newton, experiences her own epiphany while she is in London. Through the generosity of her fellow parishioners, Gorgeous, a lifelong connoisseur of knockoffs, is able to buy her first genuine Chanel.

If the character of Gorgeous is pure farce, the third sister, Pfeni, is the least defined. Once a writer for radical publications, a voice for the oppressed, Pfeni is now a travel writer. By contrast to the other sisters she seems colorless, and her decision to return to politically activist writing hardly seems remarkable. She serves the plot by having a boyfriend – a bisexual theater director – who introduces the furrier to Sara. The furrier might as easily have been an acquaintance of Gorgeous's, and Pfeni's sexual relationship with the director raises certain questions in 1992 that Wasserstein deals with only cursorily. The director is yet another source of humor, another sideshow, although an admittedly entertaining one.

Without all the comical distractions, *The Sisters Rosensweig* might have seemed pallid. And yet there is a very touching scene in which Sara recounts a visit to the very town in Poland from which her forebears fled. She has returned as a kind of economic savior and savors the reverses of fate that have created her triumph. The writing here suggests Wasserstein's imagination can function very potently on serious matters.

In any event, the play was perfectly cast, with Jane Alexander extremely affecting as Sara, Madeline Kahn hilarious as Gorgeous, and Frances McNormand strong in the unrewarding role of Pfeni. There was also expert work by the comedian Robert Klein as the furrier and John Vickery as the bisexual director.

Another play focusing on the foibles of Jewish family life was Herb Gardner's *Conversations With My Father,* a portrait of a tough, garrulous Jewish bartender and his son, both struggling with questions of ethnic and religious identity. Although the play is full of the eloquent and funny tirades that have characterized many of Gardner's works, it seems without focus. Much of its energy is dissipated in minor characters who frequent the bar, whose links to the play's concerns are tangential at best.

A more challenging examination of intergenerational relationships came in Alan Brody's *Inventions for Fathers and Sons,* presented by the American Jewish Theater. The premise of Brody's play was that at some point in every lifetime a son and his father meet not in the problematic ongoing relationship that defines them but simply as two men. This theme was developed in ways that often seemed unequal to its potential provocativeness and poetry, but there were scenes of genuine dramatic power throughout.

Many of the plays that were done by the Off- and Off-Off Broadway companies were so marginal they do not bear discussing. An exception was the Manhattan Theater Club's presentation of Donald Margulies' *Sight Unseen,* a provocative play about a New York artist coming to grips with his success and his past. In some of his earlier work, particularly the droll *The Loman Family Picnic,* Margulies has attempted to leap beyond the walls of middle-class

Jewish living rooms, in which his characters dwell with increasing discomfort.

In this play he has made the leap. His protagonist, a Jewish artist who has scored great success with "political" paintings, is an international star. But ultimately we learn too little about him and wonder if in fact we might not have spent a little more time in the middle-class Jewish living room where he grew up.

As it is, the best part of the play is its pungent wit about the contemporary art scene, particularly a series of encounters with a sharp but humorless German woman who is interviewing him for television. When her line of thought becomes too blunt for him, he uses the Holocaust as a device to deflect her questions.

Whatever its weaknesses, *Sight Unseen* marked a new maturity for Margulies, whose intelligence and wit are a welcome addition to a New York theater scene in which neither plays a major role.

Another worthwhile Off-Broadway offering was Circle Rep's coproduction of Larry Kramer's *The Destiny of Me.* Even before his 1985 *The Normal Heart,* Kramer, an early activist in the movement to make the public aware of the AIDS menace, had become a public figure. Writing about his plays seemed less an act of theater criticism than one of commentary on the public utterance of a politician. In his latest, Kramer tells the story of his early childhood and growing awareness that he is homosexual alongside an account of his stay in a hospital where he is a guinea pig for a doctor's experimental drug to cure AIDS.

The scenes of family life – the suffocating mother, the ineffectual but belligerent father – resemble those in numerous middle-class Jewish coming-of-age plays and novels over the last forty years. The scenes in the hospital have a crazily bellicose quality – the Kramer character constantly taunts his would-be benefactor about his politics and motives – that probably reflect Kramer's own vexatious personality but do not add coherence or strength to the play.

Circle Rep also presented Paula Vogel's *The Baltimore Waltz,* which is worth noting only because it is the sort of play that wins awards and grants. (It was presented with the aid of a grant from AT&T.) Such plays are invariably noteworthy more for their politically correct ideas than their dramaturgical persuasiveness. *Baltimore Waltz* is a kind of fairy-tale play in which a brother and sister go in search of a magical elixir.

The sister is an elementary school teacher who has the dreaded ATD, Acquired Toilet Disease, a fatal illness you pick up from unsanitary toilet seats. It hits only single teachers. Those with children of their own develop immunities. Immunities is, of course, the operative word that presumably lifts *Baltimore Waltz* out of the province of a skit into Important Theater.

When the young woman is diagnosed as having ATD she asks if it can be transmitted sexually. Assured that it cannot, she does what I suppose anyone would do – takes off for Europe, where she has sex with as many strangers as possible. Her traveling companion is her brother, who always wears pajamas, sometimes covered by a trench coat or a blazer. Hidden under his coat is his teddy bear. Many of the men he meets in Europe also have teddy bears hidden under their raincoats. While his sister is coupling with bellhops, and others, he is caressing other men's teddy bears. At play's end we learn that the sister's sexual romp through Europe has been a fantasy. Nor is she the sick one. Her brother lies dead in a hospital in Baltimore.

The sister's journey is a conscious parody of Oliver Reed's great film *The Third Man.* But the parody is entirely adolescent, as is the ultimate resolution. The cure for her disease, which she discovers in the office of a grotesque Viennese physician, is her own urine, a specimen of which the doctor guzzles down with grotesque ferocity. In the final scene she dances with her brother's dead body, already stiff with rigor mortis. Then he appears to her in an elegant Viennese military uniform, and the play ends with a tender waltz.

The play's greatest virtue is its overt theatricality. The fact that it is a play about AIDS is apparently significant enough to make us overlook the fact that its content is smart-alecky and childish.

A "growth area" in New York theater seems to be the monologue, which these days falls under the heading of "performance art." Whatever it is called, its new popularity stems doubtless from its economic attractiveness. It is also an opportunity for a performer to display virtuoso abilities, as John Leguizamo did in *Spic-O-Rama,* in which he played members of a dysfunctional Puerto Rican family. In some ways his characterizations reinforce ethnic stereotypes, but at his best he has a sharp sense of humor and satire, particularly playing a siren of the Laundromat and a young actor who imagines he is the illegitimate son of Laurence Olivier.

The most consistently entertaining of these pieces was Josh Kornbluth's *Red Diaper Baby,* a reminiscence about growing up as the son of ardent Upper West Side Communists. The young Kornbluth was shunted back and forth between his

divorced parents, living mainly with his father, who awakened him every morning singing the Internationale. Unaware of its revolutionary implications, the boy interpreted its opening line, "Arise, ye prisoners of starvation," as a highfalutin way of saying, "Wake up. It's time for breakfast."

His parents and their friends invested even the most trivial moments of their lives with religious fervor. When, for example, they played Monopoly, he recalled, "No one wants to pass Go. No one wants to collect $200. Everybody wants to go to jail to stage a hunger strike." Though the monologue occasionally verges on stand-up comedy, it never has the professional comic's swagger, his desperate need to make the audience laugh. The humor is never forced. It has instead a sympathetic understanding of the depth of human folly. Kornbluth's closing vignette, a description of his father's burial amidst the alien corn of rural Michigan, is genuinely moving, drawing on the emotional resources that enrich Kornbluth's memories but which he wisely restrains for most of the evening.

One of the most interesting of these one-person shows was *Fires in the Mirror,* in which Anna Deavere Smith examined the events that inflamed the Crown Heights section of Brooklyn in August of 1991. This area of Brooklyn is inhabited by poor African Americans and Hispanics and a growing community of ultraorthodox Hasidic Jews. Over the years there has been great friction between the two communities, which was exacerbated when a car in a procession of Hasidim veered out of control and killed a nine-year-old boy standing on a street corner. The accident touched off several days of rioting in which a rabbinical student from Australia was murdered by a group of blacks yelling anti-Semitic slogans.

Smith creates a collage about these events. She interviewed eyewitnesses and quotes from texts relating to questions of Jewish and African-American identity. She plays both her interviewees and the authors of the texts (like Angela Davis and Ntozake Shange.) In some ways she is a stronger journalist than she is an actress. Her characterizations of her subjects has less vibrancy than the remarks she drew from them as an interviewer. Nevertheless she builds an affecting evening out of these prickly materials.

Among the less successful of these monologues was *and,* which was written by the former *Time* magazine essayist Roger Rosenblatt and performed by Ron Silver. The evening, for all Silver's manic energy, left one with a new appreciation for Gertrude Stein's admonishment to Ernest Hemingway: "Remarks are not literature." In this case, opinions, however provocative, did not constitute theater.

An odd but promising pair of plays was presented by the American Jewish Theater. Charlie Schulman's one-act *Angel of Death* is about Josef Mengele – the man who stood at the gates of Auschwitz assigning, with a nod of his head, some to a living hell as camp workers, others to immediate death in the gas chambers. Mengele was long assumed to be hiding out in South America, and Schulman imagines him as a nightclub performer in Asunción, Paraguay.

Wearing a frowsy straw hat, a loose-fitting powder blue sport jacket, a jazzy shirt and pants whose wrinkles would horrify an SS officer, he sings, with a giddy little smile, "I like a Wagner tune – how about you?" This is outrageous humor, reminiscent of the "Springtime for Hitler" production number in Mel Brooks's film *The Producers,* but it has a wild originality, and, until halfway through, when Schulman begins making topical political jokes, it demonstrates a raw, quirky, upsetting talent.

Also on the bill was Brian Goluboff's *Big Al,* which is about two young men fantasizing about writing a screenplay for Al Pacino. One is a rabid Pacino fan with a special attachment to his sickest film, *Scarface.* Here too the humor is wild, but Goluboff is better able to sustain a savage tone. The feral, manic quality that underscores Goluboff's humor reflects an uncannily perceptive understanding of the energy Pacino radiates on the screen.

Pacino himself made one of his infrequent stage appearances doing two plays in repertory, Oscar Wilde's *Salome,* in which he gave an account of Herod that made him seem like a typical Pacino street-crazy, and a new play of no consequence, *Chinese Coffee,* by Charles Cioffe.

The largely foolish, aimless production of *Salome* was typical of the kind of classical theater New York sees with distressing regularity. The New York Shakespeare Festival, which built a solid reputation for undermining its namesake has, since the death of its founder, Joseph Papp, branched out in an effort to discredit other writers as well. This year Papp's successor, JoAnne Akalaitis, bungled two major plays, John Ford's *'Tis Pity She's a Whore,* which gained nothing by being set in Fascist Italy, and Georg Buchner's *Woyzeck,* generally considered

the first modern play, which she drained of all its wrenching emotional energy and its proto-Expressionistic power.

Possibly the most interesting of the Shakespeare Festival's failures was a production of Federico García Lorca's 1932 *Blood Wedding* in a translation/adaptation by Langston Hughes, directed by Melia Bensussen. Hughes's version, made a few years after the play was written, has never been produced before. Perhaps if it had been done during the Depression with an all-black cast, it might have had its own integrity. But in 1992, with a barely competent multiracial cast, the ineptly directed production only pointed up the disparities between García Lorca's intensely Spanish vision and Hughes's black, but ultimately very American, sensibility.

Although there are some analogies between the African-American experience and the Spanish poet's dark vision, the two worlds never jelled in this production. This was sensed at once, when the rigid, staccato rhythms of flamenco with which the play opened gave way to the laid-black blues of Michele Navazio's original background score. Both musical forms have their roots in human suffering, but they are quite different. The blues grow out of a sense of human cruelty. Flamenco, which dates from Moorish times, stems from a profound sense of the harshness of the cosmos.

Throughout the evening the two traditions were at war. Some of the actors were Hispanic (though their accents suggested San Juan rather than Andalusia.) Some were black. Most of the costumes were traditionally, severely Spanish. Suddenly, toward the end, the actors wore garb more appropriate to sharecroppers in the American South. For most of the evening the set had a dignified Spanish austerity. Toward the end the colors suddenly became garish, as if García Lorca had written an early piece of South American "magic realism."

This jumbling of styles is what passes in the theater for "multicultural" or "postmodern." At one time it would simply have been considered "incoherent." Coherence, of course, emotional or intellectual, is now of only marginal concern. As in *Les Atrides,* we are in a theater where cultural allusions, nontraditional casting, gender issues, and other instances of intellectual fashion all matter more than the writer's vision.

The Year in London Theatre

Blanche Marvin
London Theatre Reviews

The big news is the *Evening Standard* Award which leads us gently into the summary of the year:

Best Actress.........................DIANA RIGG (*Medea*)
Best Actor.... NIGEL HAWTHORNE (*George III*)
Best Director....................... STEPHEN DALDRY
          (*An Inspector Calls*)
Best Play...........................*ANGELS IN AMERICA*
          (by Tony Kushner)
Best Musical......*KISS OF THE SPIDER WOMAN*
Best Comedy........ *RISE AND FALL OF LITTLE*
   VOICE (by Jim Cartwright)
Most Promising Playwright ....Philip Ridley
   for *FASTEST CLOCK IN THE UNIVERSE*

All the awards were justly given, but the last two will not suit American tastes. However, to look into this year and come up with important promising writers requires a backward glance into the Irish writers: putting aside the established Brian Friel (*Dancing at Lughnasa* and *Philadelphia Here I Come*), there are Billy Roche (*Wexford Trilogy*), Frank McGuiness (*Someone Who'll Watch Over Me*), and Tom Murphy (*Gigli Concert*). Then there are Chris Hannan, the Scottish writer (*Pretenders, Gamblers,* and *Evil Doers*), and English writers such as Doug Lucie (*Fashion, Hard Feelings*), Michael Wall (*Women Laughing*), Chay Yew (*Porcelain*), and Rod McGregor (*Phoenix*). There are the new works of established writers such as David Hare, Keith Waterhouse, Howard Barker, James Saunders, and Alan Ayckbourn. But the overall impact of the season, or year, was brilliant adaptations of European classics not seen before in England. As a general rule the productions along with directorial and scenic concepts were the revolutionary leaps made in the theater, rather than momentous occasions through the text. No new writers have the stature of the 1960s batch.

However, it is quite different when it comes to actors. The new stars are Juliet Stevenson, Alan Rickman, Harriet Walter, Daniel Day Lewis, Frances Barber, Ralph Fiennes, Corin Redgrave, Emelda Staunton, Kate O'Mara, Jonathan Hyde, Brent Carver – and stars-in-the-making Dawn Hope (*Josephine*) and Jules Melvin (*The Rape of Tamar*). Judi Dench, Maggie Smith, Paul Scofield, Vanessa Redgrave, Felicity Kendall, Julia McKenzie, Albert Finney, Stephen Rea, Diana Rigg, Kenneth Branagh, Ian McKellen, Michael Gambon, Helen Mirren, Nigel Hawthorne, Brian Cox, and Fiona Shaw are just a few of the many remaining stars of the establishment making their mark in the theater in 1992. The only two working actors of the old school are John Gielgud and Wendy Hiller.

Ian McKellen's Uncle Vanya; Nigel Hawthorne's George III; Ann Mitchell's Hecuba, Brent Carver's Molina, the gay window dresser in *Kiss Of The Spider Woman;* Henry Goodman's Charles Guiteau in the *Assassins;* Frances Barber's Eliza in *Pygmalion;* Albert Finney's performance in *Reflected Glory* as he sang and danced with a humor rarely seen in his previous work; Judi Dench's Bessy in *Plough and the Stars;* Moira Buffini as actress-author in *Jordan;* and Marsha Raven, blues singer extraordinaire in *Blues Angels,* would be my choices for the most memorable London acting performances in 1992.

In the West End the new musicals created this year, *Kiss Of The Spider Woman, Assassins,* and *Radio Times,* dominate the scene. The American musical has redeemed itself in its revivals (*Annie Get Your Gun* and *Carousel*), and it is the newly advanced productions such as *Carousel* that are shaking and making the audiences and that have recouped the international position of the musical as an American art form. *Travels With My Aunt, Philadelphia Here I Come, Our Song, Lost in Yonkers, Don't Dress For Dinner, It Runs In The Family, Death and the Maiden, Six Degrees of Separation,* and *Dancing at Lughnasa* are the new plays most remembered in the West End – along with the revivals of *Ideal Husband, Becket, A Woman of No Importance,* and *Heartbreak House.* The two news events were Albert Finney's comic performance in *Reflected Glory* and the disappointment in John

Malkovich's writing in and performance of *Slip of the Tongue.*

It is the National Theatre that takes the prize this season for all the great theater presented on the South Bank shores, such as Alan Bennett's *The Madness of George III,* Bernard Shaw's *Pygmalion,* Tony Kushner's *Angels in America,* Anton Chekhov's *Uncle Vanya,* Jim Cartwright's *Rise and Fall of Little Voice,* J. B. Priestley's *An Inspector Calls* as directed by Stephen Daldry, Robert LePage's *Needles and Opium,* Theatre Complicite's *Street of Crocodiles,* Declan Donellan's production of Lope de Vega's *Fuente Ovejune,* Hare's *Murmuring Judges,* and Ian McKellan's *Richard III.*

The emerging overall picture is of the National Theatre at its apex in production style, which no other exceeds except for the American Hal Prince with his visual genius. The Almeida begins to tower in competition with the National, without the same resources, but its mark is as significant in mixing classics with the contemporary play, in addition to its experimentation in opera. The Royal Shakespeare Company (RSC) shines with Terry Hand's production of Christopher Marlowe's *Tamburlaine the Great,* starring Tony Sher, Trevor Nunn's *The Blue Angel* and *Measure for Measure,* Kate Mitchell's production of *The Dybbuk,* Robert Stephen's performance as Falstaff in *Henry IV,* and Ostrovsky's *Artists and Admirers.* The new play by Peter Shaffer, *The Gift of the Gorgon,* is ringing all the bells of anticipation.

But, in choosing the greatest theatrical event of the year, one has to say Ariane Mnouchkine's *Les Atrides* first, then Peter Brook's *Tempest.* The sheer genius of the total Mnouchkine enterprise, which included a cycle of four Greek classics assembled to make a story of continuity in the tragedy of the house of Atreus, or *Les Atrides,* is of striking magnitude. The stark simplicity in which Brook told the story of the *Tempest,* allowing even the metaphors and symbolic props to remain a woven part of the tapestry, is at the other end of the pole from *Les Atrides.* The latter used elaborate makeup and costumes in an epic-sized production, cast with a huge chorus which danced to magical rhythms and "music of the spheres," played on 290 ancient musical instruments. A review of *Les Atrides* is reproduced below.

The Edinburgh Festival is always a major event, but its impact was not great this year, and the festival had little influence in the theater of London. A recap of the festival is printed below in order to discuss some of the plays which later reached London, thus making them relevant in gaining a total picture of the year's theater.

The arrival and anticipated arrival on the scene of two major Hamlets, those of Alan Rickman and Kenneth Branagh, is theater history. Rickman gave a performance of intense introspection which never left a doubt as to Hamlet's sanity. But, sadly, the crew and remaining cast did not do justice to his performance of Hamlet, instead undermining what might have been an overall effective production. Branagh's performance is yet to come.

The important new companies which must be mentioned are the Start Here Company for its *Don Carlos* (Friedrich Schiller), Theatre Manoeuvres for Schiller's *Cabal and Love* and Molina's *The Rape of Tamar,* and Trampoline Company in *A Woman is a Weathercock.* The Bush Pub Theatre in Roche's *Wexford Trilogy* – which won the Empty Space Peter Brook Award – the Tricycle Theatre in Nikolay Gogol's *The Gamblers,* the Kings Head Pub Theatre for Friel's *Philadelphia Here I Come,* and the Royal Court for Chay Yew's *Porcelain,* Wall's *Women Laughing,* Byrne's *Colquhoun and MacBryde,* and John Guare's *Six Degrees of Separation* are the most outstanding to be remembered as theater companies on an upward move.

The productions of *Ubu Roi* and *Ajax* by avant-garde French companies, introducing the plays of Roman Valle-Inclan and Ken Campbell's hilarious *Pigspurt,* all performed at the Riverside Studios, were highlights of 1992. Mikhail Bulgakov's *Master and Margarita* at the Lyric Theatre Hammersmith's Studio, along with Harley Granville-Barker's *Madras House;* the Gate's productions of contemporary non-English plays such as Judith Thompson's *Crackwalker* and Snoo Wilson's adaptation of Erofeyev's *Walpurgis Night,* then classics such as Euripides' *Hecuba* and Federico García Lorca's *House of Bernarda Alba* and their Spanish Golden Era Classics Season; James Saunders's *Making It Better* at Hampstead; the work of the Orange Tree Theatre with Shiela Yeger's *Self Portrait, Cerceau,* and Friel's *The Faith Healer;* the Almeida Theatre with Euripedes' *Medea,* Tom Murphy's *Gigli Concert,* Luigi Pirandello's *Rules of the Game,* and Howard Barker's opera *Terrible Mouth; Dead Soil,* German environmental expressionism, at the Studio Theatre Leicester; and *BAC* for Maureen Chadwick's *Josephine,* David Glass's *Gormenghast,* and McFerran's *Obsession* are just indications of the exciting burst of new plays, new adaptations of classics and foreign plays, plus new companies with new concepts of production that startle the imagination.

The old fringe moves with the times in the development of new plays, along with new directors and scenic concepts, which are a definite part of the establishment as new fringe theaters pop up all over London, developing their local clientele. There is an energy that is amazing as castles are built out of air at a time when the recession has fallen into depression and "... *things* fall apart as the centre of *art* holds. . . ." The West End produces some of its own but is fed mostly by the fringe and subsidized theaters, as no West End theater remains dark. It even has two new additions, the renovated Donmar warehouse and the Criterion, which are both jewels in the crown of the West End.

Future first nights in London are as follows: *The Witches*, 2 December at the Duke of York's; Robert Lindsay in John Wells's version of Edmond Rostand's *Cyrano De Bergerac*, 14 December at the Haymarket; Keith Waterhouse and Willis Hall's *Billy Liar*, 15 December at the Cottesloe National Theatre; Peter Hall directing Judi Dench with Michael Pennington as a writer who has an explosive marriage in Peter Shaffer's new play, *The Gift of the Gorgon*, 16 December at the Pit, RSC; *Barnum* from Theatre Royal Plymouth, 17 December, at the Dominion; Stephen King's *Misery*, a new play, written and directed by Simon Moore, 17 December at the Criterion; Branagh's *Hamlet* along with RSC members – the delicious Richard Bonneville and David Bradley, Jane Lapotaire, John Shrapnel, and Joanne Pearce – 18 December at the RSC; *The Comedy of Errors* from Stratford, 23 December at the RSC; Neil Bartlett's adaptation of Marivaux's *The Game of Love and Chance*, directed by Mike Alfred and Neil Bartlett, starring Maggie Steed, 12 January at the Cottesloe National Theatre; *King Baby*, a new play written by James Robson, directed by Simon Usher, 19 January at the Pit, RSC; *King Lear*, 21 January at the Royal Court directed by Max Stafford-Clark; *Weldon Rising*, a brutal and funny new play by Phyllis Nagy set in the meat-packing section of New York City, 7 December at the Royal Court; Barrie Rutter's acclaimed Yorkshire dialect version of *Richard III*, 9 December at Riverside Studios; Japanese Ninagawa's *Tempest*, from the 1988 Edinburgh Festival, 4 December at the RSC; John Whiting's comedy of English eccentrics, *Penny for a Song*, directed by Sam Walters, 7 December at the Orange Tree; Sheffield's Compass Theatre Company's envigorating *Hamlet* and *King Lear*, 7 December at the Lilian Baylis Theatre; David Farr's tragicomedy, *Neville Southall's Washbag*, performed by gifted Talking Tongues, 5 December at Finborough Pub Theatre. And that should give you a picture of the exciting year 1992 in London and the United Kingdom.

EDINBURGH FESTIVAL

The Edinburgh Festival, held every year for a three-week period in late August and early September, has a new administrator. The range of performed works in all the arts (music, ballet, opera, painting) grows each year by leaps and bounds, searching for and filling all available space and making the job for any administrator of setting theme or policy all but impossible.

Brian McMaster, the new festival administrator, unlike the flamboyant Frank Dunlop, has quality taste which he hopes to make popular rather than the popular taste that Dunlop wanted to make accessible. McMaster is nervy compared to Dunlop's affability. McMaster has proved very successful with programming in his blending of musical talent but less so in the theatrical vein. He was ingenious in bringing together Peter Stein with Pierre Boulez in *Pelleas and Melisande* in Cardiff. He's still exploring for Edinburgh.

The main line for the theatrical side of the Festival had C. P. Taylor and Harley Granville Barker as its theme. Seven plays of Barker and Taylor were spread over the entire festival period and in various venues. I might add that the National Theatre of Bucharest did perform Andrei Serban's *Ancient Trilogy* at the Corn Exchange, an old amalgamation of Greek tragedies from several authors in promenade style which he had produced at La Mama in New York 18 years ago. It's still considered au fait for today.

Barker (1877–1946) is the resurrected hero of British Theatre, as a leading actor, as the initial producer of Shaw's plays, as a revolutionary director of Shakespeare ... all at the Royal Court ... as well as a prophetic playwright with a grasp of the economic and financial world of trade markets and its people which is prophetic ... But why the resurrection in Edinburgh?

Taylor (1929–1981) is known more for his name than his plays. He was discovered in Edinburgh at the Traverse Theatre with *Happy Days Are Here Again*, a Marxist farce. After that he ran the gamut of every genre of theatre, from children's plays to political dramas like *Good*. He founded Iron Press to publish new writers and continued with an outpouring of his own works. He should be celebrated in Scotland, being a Scotsman, and so well loved with a prolific output of plays but of what quality of talent?

Barker's *His Majesty* (St. Bride's) and *Madras House* (Lyceum) were co-produced by London theatres and are now playing in London.

Barker's *The Voysey Inheritance* (Lyceum) as directed by William Gaskill received acceptable notices but not strong enough for London. The production didn't excel Richard Eyre's brilliant one at the National Theatre in 1989. It will tour and hopefully the ensemble acting will improve with time. Peter Lindford playing the son Edward, who tries to salvage his father's fraud with integrity, holds the play together by his strong performance of a priggish young man who matures from lecturing on morality to a pragmatist dealing with greedy creditors. I previously recommended *The Voysey Inheritance* for the USA because the play deals with insider trading and concerns a lawyer who used his clients' capital to increase his own fortune while providing his clients with their usual monthly interest-income. It's about the morality of money influenced by the glamour of outrageous crime rather than the dullness of abiding the law. A very relevant subject.

The Barker play readings at the Lyceum were *Rococo*, a one-act comedy, less than gripping, centred on a row over the inheritance of a hideous rococo vase and *Farewell To The Theatre*, another fluffy one act in which an actress-manager quits the theatre to retire to an abbey leaving her lawyer to remain a grass-widowed lover. *The Secret Life,* his last full length play, regarding the political and personal passions of a retired prime minister who refuses to answer the call of his country for help, starring a sharp-edged but politically weary Alan Howard, was given an impressive rehearsed reading.

Barker's *Voysey Inheritance, Madras House, Waste,* and *The Secret Life* are his best works and will always be rediscovered.

As far as C. P. Taylor is concerned, all of the productions are not worth full reviews but rather summary listings as most of the work does not hold up nor does the author remain with any great stature outside of the play *Good*, written in 1981 and not performed at the festival, but brilliantly revived at the Tron Theatre, Glasgow, by Michael Boyd with more skill than all seven Taylor productions combined in Edinburgh. *Good* shows the growth of the mentality that created an Auschwitz guard and Goethe expert, Halder, who treads a dangerous line of balance between accommodating to the times for survival and living with the philosophical rationale he has studied.

The same production of Taylor's adaptation of *Schippel, The Plumber*, which was first performed at Greenwich, was brilliantly repeated at the Edinburgh Festival.

Taylor's *Walter* at St. Bride's Centre, a rambling piece about an old Glaswegian Jewish music hall star, Walter Jackson, whose dilemmas are unappealing.

Taylor's *The Ballachulish Beat* at the Corn Exchange, a previously unperformed play about a socialist rock group who give up principles for principal.

Taylor's *Operation Elvis*, a bad children's play at the Corn Exchange about a ten-year-old who's besotted by Presley but eventually finds his own identity.

Taylor's *The Black and White Minstrels* at Church Hill, a dated play poorly performed coming to the King's Head in London, about a record salesman turned author trying to make sense of his life while a Nigerian lady who lodges in the flat is besieged by a house full of sexual free-wheeling liberal males, some of whom attempt to sexually attack her and others who attempt to evict her. Immature politics sublimated into sexual dances symbolise the impotency of politics when privately used as a cure for neuroses.

– adapted from *London Theatre Reviews*
(August 1992)

FRINGE REVIEWS OF THE EDINBURGH FESTIVAL

Simon Donald's *The Life of Stuff* is the best new play seen anywhere in the UK. Performed at the Traverse Theatre, it's set in an urban jungle like Blackhill in Glasgow where life is easy come and easier to go forever; where drugs take you anywhere if you can afford the price and gangland, clubland, publand, discoland, council estate land, slumland are the journeys on drugs, on booze, on the make, on contracts to kill, or on the run. The writing is brutal but accurate, its acid humour filled with compassion, its jagged edges cut without shattering. The drama unfolds, the characters hold. The discovery of an important playwright and actor who understands the structure of playwriting, the performance of language with a content that is so highly charged in an immediate environment that invades the subculture of Glasgow.

Edwin Morgan's *Cyrano de Bergerac* was performed at the Traverse Theatre by the distinctive company of Communicado who've vigorously adapted the play to Glasgow, with a swashbuckling performance of fun and lyricism from Tom Mannion as the lead.

Patricia Burke Brogan's *Eclipsed* at the Demarco Gallery is realism from Ireland in understated tones. The plight of unmarried mothers in the 60's who were shamefully forced to work in convent laundries cruelly separated from their loved children while the men are left unpunished. Powerful ensemble acting.

David Ian Neville's *Exile* at the Chaplaincy Centre offers bleak scorching monologues about an Irish terrorist's wife and father plus the victim's wife as they render their life stories after the bomb blast.

Nada Company's *Ubu* is the funniest retelling of Ma and Pa Ubu with characters portrayed by vegetables.

Robert Butler's *Drop of Fred* at Theatre Zoo follows the story of an Astaire fan who's all thumbs with his feet until he magically learns to twinkle his toes. Gary Lyon's *Frankie and Tommy* at the Assembly Rooms is the discovery by the Hull Truck Company of the war time period of Tommy Cooper's career when he entertained the troops in Egypt with Frankie Lyons, both being famed English comics. Gary is the son of Frankie Lyons. Jeremy Weller's *Mad* which is the end of the trilogy of *Glad, Bad, and Mad*, at St. Mary's Land, is the final work of 11 women who relate their experiences of mental illness to the audience as they act out their psychosis.

Please note that the best performances at the festival have played in London before the festival or will play in London afterwards. The shows *Like Me Myself Us* at the Assembly Rooms and *Desdemona, If Only You Had Spoken* as acted by Eleanor Bron at the Pleasance are not reviewed as they remain acting vehicles for the performer.

— adapted from *London Theatre Reviews*
(August 1992)

ARIANE MNOUCHKINE'S LE THÉÂTRE DU SOLEIL'S *LES ATRIDES*

Presented by BRADFORD THEATRES and THE NATIONAL THEATRE under producership of THELMA HOLT and DUNCAN WHELDON as part of the EUROPEAN ARTS FESTIVAL
Music by JEAN-JACQUES LEMETRE
Set by GUY-CLAUDE FRANÇOIS
Costumes by NATHALIE THOMAS and MARIE-HÉLÈNE BOUVET
Make-up design by CATHERINE SCHAUB
Choreography by CATHERINE SCHAUB, SIMON ABKARIAN and NIRUPAMA NITYANADAN
Adaptors JEAN and MAYOTTE BOLLACK for *IPHÉGENIE A AULIS*, HÉLÈNE CIXOUS for *LES*

EUMENIDES, ARIANE MNOUCHKINE for *AGAMEMNON* and *LES CHOEPHORES*
Directed by ARIANE MNOUCHKINE
At THE ROBIN MILLS WAREHOUSE, BRADFORD

This is not just a review of the cycle of the four plays, *The House of Atreus,* but also of the implications of the event itself and the effect of the European Community, the European Arts Festival and the force of the arts in reawakening the whole city of Bradford in order to prepare for *Les Atrides*. The huge warehouse at Robin Mills (manufacturers of hand woollen knitwear) was chosen after being viewed by Théâtre du Soleil's designer, Guy-Claude François, and approved by Mnouchkine as the building most suitable due to unencumbered space (no pillars and sound-isolated) of enormous dimensions which allowed Mnouchkine to reproduce her theatre outside of Paris (the munitions factory, La Cartoucherie) to its exactness in Bradford. It is on the second floor accessible by scaffolded staircases built on the outside. The first floor with the same huge dimensions is sectioned off into open areas for the information and ticket desk, the book stalls, the lobby with chairs and tables and the restaurant set up as self service. The decor by Paul Hughes (senior lecturer in interior design at Bradford and Ilkley Community College) is brilliantly conceived and executed using natural Yorkshire materials. White calico banners formed a ballooned ceiling with wooden rods at either end of each banner giving the effect of large scrolls. It covered the entire ceiling of this vast open space. Counters were made of heavy Yorkshire wood and stone whilst the columns, chairs and tables were wrapped in the white calico cloth tied with rope just as Cristo had done to the bridges in Paris. The theatre was inundated with offers of help from every kind of organisation, large and small, in order to facilitate the conversion of this building into a theatre within three weeks. The whole city of Bradford rallied to a theatrical Olympics. The Royal Engineers worked alongside interior design students, portacabin suppliers supported *cordon bleu* chefs, mill owners and stone wallers devised and created along with the high-tech lighting experts and designers. The Bradford Theatre's technicians with volunteer carpenters built the wooden stage floor and the heavy solid wooden set whose walls with ramways on top formed a square, round the stage with entrance ways on four sides like the bull rings of Spain, a moving ramp that shot out from under the front of the stage to allow entrances and exits that were magical yet uncluttered and clean, palace gates behind the walls, blue curtaining round the stage with black curtaining surrounding the auditorium, raked scaffolded seats (approximately 750) and staircases under which the actors' dressing rooms sprawled permitting the audience to wander through before the show in order to see the make-up and costumes.

London, Glasgow, and Edinburgh made strong bids for this classical Greek cycle of ten hours of drama spread over three days and nights or to be seen nightly over two weeks. But Bradford won. It all happened because the Bradford Council in 1968 commissioned the refurbishment of the Alhambra Theatre with the help of EC money which in turn made possible the appearance of Jacques Delors at the opening ceremony, declaring the theatre as "a little part of Europe." Six years later, the Council's casting of bread upon its waters was rewarded with the major event of the Festival, *Les Atrides*.

In order to describe the productions one must first begin with the music which completely scores all the shows, brings a continuity to the stories, heightens the drama, makes possible the dances, exhilarates and colours the Grecian sounds sustained by 290 instruments occupying an open elevated stage area in which one watches the composer play and coordinate with three other assistants a complete score of the cycle taking cues from the actors for exact timing and punctuation. One watched the feat of the master composer-player as one watched the plays. The most extraordinary music, with ancient instruments of strings like lutes and harps, woodwinds and reeds like flutes, percussions, gongs, bells of all shapes and sizes, kept audience feet tapping with such fantastic melodic rhythms.

The costumes must be described next as the elaborate designs of costume and make-up so flamboyantly stand out against a severely stark set and have a strong Javanese influence added to the Grecian foundation. The chorus, in particular (outside of the last play, *Les Eumenides*, where they are apes with blackened faces) blazons the stage with gorgeous robes of gold and black to start, then into reds with headdresses, beards and moustaches resembling Egyptian pharaohs, or change to women slaves with black and gold headdresses and skirts that twirl like whirling dervishes. The make-up, always being extreme in white faced, eastern, medieval, mask-like effects, separates the chorus from the individuals. The gods are in white Grecian robes, Cassandra in white priest-like robes,

Clytemnestra, Orestes, Agamemnon and Elektra are in elaborately layered and colourful Grecian designs with a touch of the orient or Egypt. In *Iphegenia* the dominant colour is gold and black. When Agamemnon returns in the play *Agamemnon* he is dressed in the gold and black of his departure in *Iphegenia* and then changes into the outlandish red robes with an amazing wig of Egyptian manifestation. The white face and black hair are constant in all the characters but unmask-like enough to allow the strong individual expressions and animation. Only in the last play is the costuming confusing and disappointing with the three Furies dressed as peasant bag ladies throwing their placement in time and their representation of the old laws out of kilter along with the black-faced ape chorus that is meant to be primitive man. The black faces leave no possibility of animation and ape-like movement limits any dance choreography, both of which are more needed in this static play than in any of the other three.

The cycle is the combination of Aeschylus's *Oresteia* and Euripedes's *Iphegenia a Aulis*. It sets the mood and myth on a highly emotional plane by introducing Euripedes, who wrote cynically as he watched the increasing horrors of the Peloponnesian War believing in the destructive anarchy of human beings as compared to Aeschylus who lived in the golden Athenian age and believed in the harmony of reason ruling man. But one follows the events and the characters throughout. Clytemnestra is portrayed as more of the avenging mother whose child is unconscionably murdered rather than sacrificed by the father. Clytemnestra's murder of Agamemnon is vindicated by the unquenchable rage and pain at the death of her well-loved daughter, who, instead of sailing to her wedding, is slaughtered by her father as a sacrifice making possible the sailing of his ships to Troy for a war over a woman considered a whore. Clytemnestra, the malicious adulteress, no longer murders to sustain her ambition to rule after Agamemnon's ten years of absence which was Aeschylus's original concept. Keeping that in mind, the story continues with an Agamemnon who has taken on Cassandra as a loving mistress making even greater sympathy for Clytemnestra to kill this conquering hero when he returns as adulterer as well as dictator. His arrogant entrance on a white and red moving platform-cum-throne later sensually stroking Cassandra contrasts with the image of their blood soaked bodies after their murder when they are dragged onto stage. In turn, Clytemnestra's frenzied attempts at escaping Orestes's grasp in order to prevent her own death along with her terror-stricken face at being caught, in addition to Orestes's agony at having to spill her blood, make a horrendous picture as they disappear on the moving ramp. The family vendetta continues, jeopardising the house of Atreus, as the Furies seek vengeance for the mother's murder. The death of Clytemnestra was encouraged by the younger God, Apollo, whose new morality introduces the new concept of motive to murder, which the Furies reject. *Agamemnon* ends with the powerful image of the dead body of Aegisthus spread over the blood-stained Clytemnestra slit at the throat. Neither Electra nor Orestes can remove the bodies from on stage . . . they will not, can not budge . . . murder of his mother will not, can not be removed. Only with the help of the Furies and part of the chorus are the bodies carried to their burial. Again the stricken horror on the faces of Electra and Orestes are unforgettable. The old law states death is the punishment for matricide. Clytemnestra in killing her husband did not kill one of her own blood. The Furies want the blood of Orestes. Apollo calls for Athena the Goddess of justice and reason to intervene and pass judgment. Both sides debate their cause as Orestes seeks Apollo's protection. Apollo points out that Orestes's mother not only killed his father but also stole his crown. The new society now has hereditary laws of lineage for the crown. The Furies demand the old laws remain or family could then be destroyed. The decision is in Orestes's favour. Athena convinces the Furies that shedding blood no longer is justice but reasoned debate in court will provide the answer from the outside which society must abide to keep law and order with justice for all in their new civilisation.

Simon Abkarian, who plays Agamemnon, the leader of the male Chorus and Orestes, is phenomenal. He leaps and dives like an animal in constant flight with an emotional range of striking depth. His humorous rendition of the nurse is the only comic moment in the cycle. Shahrokh Meshkin Ghalam as Apollo gives life to a God as he flies over ledges and leaps over walls with a command of his surround that leaves no doubt of his god-like potency. The choruses dance and move with a precision of oneness. Nirupama Nityanadan as Iphegenia has moving innocence but as Electra does not bear enough strength. Juliana Canciro da Cunha as Clytemnestra and Athena moves and dances exquisitely, projects pain and fury, but never the power of a mature and sexy woman capable of dealing in a man's world without fear. Having Catherine Schaub as a leader in the female dance chorus and one of the Furies is mesmerising. She gives them patterns and formations with dance movements that make rhythms contagious.

The size and stature of the event outstrips whatever criticisms one may have and there are several as far as some of the acting and casting are concerned. The genius of Mnouchkine cannot be denied nor can the impact of this historical production which will be written about and discussed for generations to come. This visionary avant garde pioneer in intepreting the classics is France's most famous director who happens to be a woman. She has reinvented theatre on its most theatrical terms.

— adapted from *London Theatre Reviews*
(June/July 1992)

The Year in Children's Books

Caroline Hunt
College of Charleston

Juvenile books made news throughout 1992. On the first Sunday in January, Dr. Seuss's (Theodor Seuss Geisel) last book, *Oh, the Places You'll Go!* (Random House), still clung to its number fifteen place on the *New York Times* best-seller list after ninety-two weeks. Three other juvenile titles were on the same week's list: Chris Van Allsburg's *Polar Express* (Houghton Mifflin) at number seven (thirty-three weeks), the Ahlbergs' *Jolly Christmas Postman* (Little, Brown) at number eight (three weeks), and *Disney's Beauty and the Beast* (Gallery) at number eleven (two weeks). Christmas shopping alone does not account for these rankings or for the frequent appearance on this and other, adult lists of Susan Jeffers's picture book *Brother Eagle, Sister Sky* (Dial), adapted from a speech by Chief Seattle. At year's end children's books made news in a very different way when Joseph Fernandez, chancellor of New York City's schools, suspended an entire district school board in a dispute over a multicultural curriculum which included books on gay and lesbian families.

The year 1992 was also the year of books about Columbus, his voyages, and his times. (The many Columbus books which came out during 1990 and 1991 will not be considered here.) In the continuing focus on "multiculturalism," reviewers looked at attitudes toward slavery and exploitation more than any other single feature. Of the 1992 titles the two poles were occupied by Jean Fritz's *The Great Adventures of Christopher Columbus: A Pop-Up Book* (Putnam's), and, ironically, the same author's collaboration with Katherine Paterson, Frederick and Patricia McKissack, Margaret Mahy, and Jamake Highwater, *The World in 1492* (Holt). The pop-up book, illustrated by Tomie de Paola, was thought to trivialize its subject despite de Paola's skills. Reviewers objected to the portrayal of indigenous groups in this book (as well as most of the 1990 and 1991 Columbus books). Less simplistic, *The World in 1492* consists of a series of presentations by specialists, each writing about one geographical area: Highwater's section covers the New

Dust jacket for the book that won the 1992 Newbery Medal for best children's book

World in the age of Columbus, Paterson discusses the Orient, and so on. The book focuses on a much broader subject area than simply the voyages, thus de-emphasizing the controversy over how Columbus the man should be presented to young readers. Piero Ventura's *1492: The Year of the New World* (Putnam's) also documents the social climate of the time, not with expository essays but through vignettes of fictitious characters. Some Columbus books relegate the explorer to the periphery of the story, showing the "discovery" primarily from the viewpoint of indigenous groups. Michael Dorris, a member of the Modoc tribe who trained as an anthropologist, describes the lives of a twelve-year-old Taino Indian girl and her brother in *Morning Girl* (Hyperion), a wistful picture of a primitive culture. Although readers sense that the Europeans signal the end of a peaceful way of life, Dorris emphasizes the Taino people more than he does the foreigners. Jane Yolen's picture book *Encounter,* illustrated by David Shannon, tells the same story in a different key; here the Europeans, shown with leering faces and conspicuous teeth, are clearly villains. The young narrator, selected to be taken to Spain, escapes and spends the rest of his life trying to warn the people of other islands about the coming danger; he never gets back to his own island, nor does anyone listen to him.

The most notorious juvenile titles of the year, more controversial by far than any Columbus book, came from a series "for and about kids with lesbian and gay parents" put out by Alyson Press. The only titles in this overview which do not have U.S. publication dates in 1992, these books went virtually unnoticed at first and began attracting attention in May 1991, when the Boston *Globe* reviewed them; they are, as newspaper readers all over the country subsequently learned, Lesléa Newman's *Heather Has Two Mommies* (1989) and Michael Willhoite's *Daddy's Roommate* (1990). The inclusion of these two titles in elementary school curricula drew protests from parents and church groups; their addition to school and public library collections caused community power struggles in many states. Public library trustees voted on *Daddy's Roommate* in Roswell, New Mexico; in Goldsboro, North Carolina, the local newspaper supported efforts to remove the book from the Wayne County Library. *Time* magazine cited this particular attack in its coverage of the presidential campaign. In the same state a Fayetteville citizens' group attempted first to have both books removed, then, when that failed, to defeat a library bond issue in apparent retaliation. The publisher appeared on *Larry King Live* to debate two conservative opponents. The "flap" over *Daddy's Roommate* was a cover story of the December *American Libraries,* the journal of the American Library Association (ALA); at that point, according to a full-page special report by Mary Jo Godwin, nearly twenty major challenges to one or both of the books had been recorded by the ALA's Office for Intellectual Freedom within a six-month period. Later that month, District 24's entire school board in Queens was suspended by the chancellor of the New York City schools for refusing to consider a multicultural curriculum which included, among other titles, *Daddy's Roommate* and *Heather Has Two Mommies.* The

Board of Education reinstated the district board, making Chancellor Fernandez (whose contract had six months left to run) potentially the highest-ranking casualty of the *Daddy* and *Heather* wars.

Though equally didactic, the two books differ considerably in message and in tone. *Daddy's Roommate* presents a small boy whose parents have recently divorced and whose father now lives with a male lover, Frank. When the boy visits his father, he observes that the two "Work together, Eat together, Sleep together, And sometimes even fight together, But they always make up." His mother "says Daddy and Frank are gay," which means nothing to the boy. "So she explained it. Being gay is just one more kind of love." Willhoite, a cartoonist, illustrates these ideas with rounded outlines and cheerful colors. It is, and is intended to be, a soothing book for children confronting something unfamiliar and threatening. *Heather Has Two Mommies,* on the other hand, is less reassuring. Diana Souza's pictures are full of action; spiky lines and angles predominate, and clothing is covered with busy patterns. Newman's text relates how Heather's mommies, Mama Jane and Mama Kate, "realized that they were very much in love with each other." In more detail than some might consider suitable, young readers learn of Heather's conception ("the doctor . . . put some sperm into Jane's vagina. The sperm swam up into Jane's womb") and birth. Heather's play group has children with two daddies, children with stepparents, and children who are adopted; they draw pictures of their families and are told, "Each family is special. The most important thing about a family is that all the people in it love each other."

More-recent titles from Alyson Press have not received the attention accorded *Daddy's Roommate* and *Heather Has Two Mommies. Gloria Goes to Gay Pride,* also by Newman, describes a gay rights parade; a coloring book by Willhoite, *Families,* shows the diversity of family patterns. Newman and Willhoite collaborated on *Belinda's Bouquet,* which deals with body image. These three titles, however, are not readily available except by mail.

Alyson Press was not the only newcomer to public notice; in spring 1992 Candlewick Press began publishing American editions of children's books from Walker, the British firm. Its outstanding offering for 1992 was a reissue of Peter and Iona Opie's 1947 collection of children's rhymes, *I Saw Esau: The Schoolchild's Pocket Book* (known in 1947 as *I Saw Esau: Traditional Rhymes of Youth*). Originally printed under grim postwar publishing conditions and before the Opies became well known, *I Saw*

Esau was the couple's first major collaborative effort; this gem of a collection has not had its due until now. The handsome small volume features new illustrations by Maurice Sendak, surely among the first pictures to reflect accurately the psychological implications of some of the rhymes (especially those about food). The rhymes include game rhymes, insults, nonsense verses, counting-out rhymes, and much more. Particularly choice are some inspired by teachers, such as this one on Benjamin Jowett, the master of Balliol College, Oxford:

> First come I; my name is Jowett,
> There is no knowledge but I know it.
> I am master of this college:
> What I don't know isn't knowledge.

Candlewick also published some contemporary British picture books, notably two by Martin Waddell: a "second U.S. edition" of the classic *Can't You Sleep, Little Bear?*, a bedtime story published in Britain in 1988 to rave reviews; and one of the year's outstanding picture books, *Farmer Duck*, a tale of animals taking revenge on a lazy farmer who makes a hapless duck do all his work. The gross, unkempt farmer sprawls over a double-page spread at the beginning of the story; standing to one side, the duck carries an immaculately appointed breakfast tray. The farmer utters a single line, "How goes the work?" on every page, sometimes several times, as the patient duck is seen ironing, sawing wood, and performing various barnyard chores. Finally the animals rescue their friend by driving the farmer out. Helen Oxenbury's softly colored illustrations make this seem like a tale of simple justice rather than a rewrite of *Animal Farm*.

Controversies come and go, and new presses too, but the main business of producing and reviewing books for children goes on much the same from year to year; 1992 was no exception. The year's offerings will, in this first annual survey, be considered under the headings of picture books, middle grade titles, and young adult books; all (with the exception of the Alyson Press books) bear a U.S. publication date of 1992. A final section mentions some children's writers who died during the year.

The year traditionally begins with the two most prestigious U.S. awards for juvenile books, announced in January by the ALA. The Newbery Award for best children's book went to Phyllis Reynolds Naylor for *Shiloh* (Atheneum), and the Caldecott, for best children's picture book, to David Wiesner for *Tuesday* (Clarion). Although *Shiloh*, a feel-good story about a boy who saves a mistreated beagle, may not be her strongest book, the popular and prolific Naylor was overdue for the Newbery. There was widespread enthusiasm for the ingenious picture book *Tuesday*, with its pictures of imperturbable flying frogs on lily pads. Both authors also produced books in 1992, which are discussed below.

Books for the youngest readers, and picture books generally, were of high quality in 1992. Of the most notable, three came from recent award winners. David Wiesner followed last year's Caldecott award book with *June 29, 1999* (Clarion), a hilarious story of a science experiment gone wrong; giant vegetables rain from the sky, and an alliterative text contributes to the zany logic of the story. Ed Young, Caldecott winner in 1990 for *Lon Po Po: A Red Riding Hood Story from China* (Philomel, 1989), was represented by the stunning *Seven Blind Mice* (Putnam's), a retelling of an Indian tale, with full-page pictures and few words. After a series of adaptations of stories from and about his native China, the setting and bolder style of *Seven Blind Mice* marked a significant development for Young. A success with adults and children alike was Jan Scieszka's irreverent *The Stinky Cheese Man and Other Fairly Stupid Tales,* illustrated by Lane Smith (Viking), in which traditional stories take an original turn. No one chases after the Cheese Man because, unlike the Gingerbread Man on whom he is modeled, he smells so terrible that he is not worth catching. A little-red-hen figure and the narrator, Jack, intrude constantly. Even the endpapers and the International Standard Book Number are worked into the parody. Scieszka capitalizes here on his 1989 hit *The True Story of the Three Little Pigs*, told from the wolf's point of view.

Picture books for the youngest included, in addition to the usual board books, alphabets, and counting books, some excellent bedtime stories. Denys Cazet's *I'm Not Sleepy* (Orchard), illustrated by the author, is a story-within-a-story about a boy who goes for a bedtime walk in a "boily, boily jungle" and is chased by a large "thingamajig" up a "giant pooa-pooa tree" to the moon; rescued by a shooting star, he returns to his bed and falls asleep. Jeanne Titherington's illustrations for the traditional rhyme *Baby's Boat* (Greenwillow) are irresistible. And Mirra Ginsburg's *Asleep, Asleep* (Greenwillow), with pictures by Nancy Tafuri, shows animal babies sleeping to the reiterated words, "asleep, asleep." Colored borders in muted colors reinforce the quiet, safe tone of the book. Also reassuring to the very youngest, though not a traditional bedtime tale, the best-selling *Carl's Masquerade* (Farrar, Straus and Giroux), by Alexandra Day, takes the benevolent Rottweiler and his young charge to a masquerade party; at story's end the little girl safely falls asleep in her crib while her parents, returning from the masquerade too, compliment Carl on an uneventful evening.

Stories of everyday life in families, in a variety of ethnic and geographic settings, abounded for the read-aloud years as well as for those just beginning to read for themselves. Nancy White Carlstrom's *Baby-O* (Little, Brown), with bright pictures by Suçie Stevenson, follows a family in the West Indies as it travels by jitney to the market; a distinctive sound is associated with each member of the family, forming a cheerful song. Cynthia Rylant's *Henry and Mudge and the Long Weekend* (Bradbury), also illustrated by Stevenson, shows the appeal of everyday family activities as Henry, his father, and the huge mastifflike Mudge build a castle from an old refrigerator box; this is the eleventh in the Henry and Mudge series for beginning readers. Patricia Polacco's *Chicken Sunday* (Philomel), illustrated by the author, is an autobiographical story in which the author and two black friends win over a hostile storekeeper to obtain an Easter hat for the black children's grandmother. Every detail of this story works: the grandmother's glorious singing in church and her eccentric dying wish, the Ukrainian Easter eggs the children make, even the suspicious storekeeper's change of heart. Another excellent picture book on the family theme is *My Great-Aunt Arizona* (HarperCollins), by Gloria Houston, with pictures by Susan Condie Lamb, which takes place in Appalachia (and, like Polacco's book, is based on the author's own life). Gloria Jean Pinkney's first picture book, *Back Home* (Dial), with wonderful pictures by Jerry Pinkney, describes a brief vacation trip to Lumberton, North Carolina, by a young African-American girl. Sherley Anne Williams's first book for children, *Working Cotton* (Harcourt Brace Jovanovich), combines a poetic text with splendid acrylic paintings by Carole Bayard to describe a day in the life of a migrant family. And, in one of the few holiday books worth mentioning, Nina Jaffe weaves a tale of wealth, poverty, and the irresistible smell of *latkes* in *In the Month of Kislev* (Viking). The stylized illustrations, rich in purple and indigo and burgundy, are by Louise August.

Four excellent picture books were set in Africa. In *Somewhere in Africa* (Dutton), by Ingrid Mennen and Nikki Daly , a small South African boy named Ashraf is fascinated by wild animals — which he reads about in books from his neighborhood library — because he is an urban child. This book, with striking primitive-style illustrations by Nikolaas Maaritz, helps to dispel a common stereotype about African culture. For slightly older children Virginia Kroll's *Masai and I* (Four Winds), with pictures by Nancy Carpenter, depicts an African-American girl who imagines what life would be like among the Masai, with whom she has begun to identify after studying East Africa in school. In *Why the Sky Is Far Away* (Joy Street / Little, Brown), Mary-Joan Gerson retells a Nigerian folktale with ecological overtones; Carla Golembe provides flat, simple, and altogether suitable pictures. And, in a departure from his usual fantasy settings, Lloyd Alexander locates the trickster plot of *The Fortune-tellers* (Dutton) in Cameroon. The colorful and warmly humorous illustrations are by Trina Schart Hyman and the book is dedicated to her grandson Michou, whose father comes from Cameroon.

The music of one of America's jazz greats is the basis for Christopher Raschka's picture book, *Charlie Parker Played Be Bop* (Orchard), a promising entry by an author-illustrator who has done only one previous book for children. Raschka epitomizes the energy and verve of Parker's music in this plotless, imaginative picture book, with watercolor and charcoal pencil illustrations of the musician himself and of what the sounds of a saxophone might look like. Another original concept was the rhymed picture book *Old Black Fly* (Holt), by Jim Aylesworth, with pictures by Stephen Gammell, in which a particularly unpleasant looking red-eyed fly lands in twenty-six alphabetically arranged unsuitable places until he is finally obliterated. Trails of flung paint link the incidents together and complement the gloriously messy household terrorized by the fly.

New to the juvenile publishing scene were two celebrities, Amy Tan and Whoopi Goldberg. Tan's picture book *The Moon Lady* (Macmillan) is a chapter from her 1989 best-seller, *The Joy Luck Club*. Despite its excellent writing and the attractive illustrations by Gretchen Schields, *The Moon Lady* seems more likely to appeal to adults than to children. The same is true of Goldberg's *Alice* (Bantam), a loose adaptation of the Alice story to a modern urban setting; bold and highly original drawings by John Rocco complement Goldberg's ironic text.

Two popular picture books are based on fact. Jane Yolen's *Letting Swift River Go* (Little, Brown), with pictures by Barbara Cooney, tells of the disappearance of a group of small towns in Massachusetts to make way for a reservoir. The balance between nostalgia and "progress" strikes just the right note in this fictionalized account, which might easily have been either strident or sentimental. *The Magic School Bus on the Ocean Floor* (Scholastic), by Barbara Brown, continues the best-selling informative Magic School Bus series with an exploration of marine life. The colorful pictures are again by Bruce Degen.

Picture books for all ages included some fine retellings of traditional European tales. Naomi Lewis translated Hans Christian Andersen's *The Steadfast Tin Soldier* (Harcourt Brace Jovanovich) without losing the tragic quality of the tale; illustrations are by P. J. Lynch. Older readers would enjoy retellings of Greek tales by two author-illustrators: Warwick Hutton's version of *The Trojan Horse* (Margaret McElderry), with watercolor pictures, and Charles Mikolaycak's *Orpheus* (Harcourt Brace Jovanovich), the latter recommended for young adults because its characters are shown nude. (Either by Micolaycak's design or by editorial fiat, a long strip of white fabric is suspended artfully in front of the hero's torso in a few pictures.) One of the best books in this category was Nancy Willard's adaptation of *Beauty and the Beast* (Harcourt Brace Jovanovich), illustrated by Barry Moser; the setting is turn-of-the-century New York City, and Moser's illustrations are, appropriately, black-and-white wood engravings. And, in a genuinely international book, Claire Martin retold *Boots & the Glass Mountain* (Dial) with elaborately detailed and richly colored paintings by the Russian artist Gennady Spirin. Boots's oafish brothers seem to have strayed from a Brueghel painting, and Spirin's fantasy horses, pavilions, and court costumes are everything that fairytale illustrations should be.

Three folk-style books are actually original stories. The first two are by Ursula K. Le Guin. *A Ride on the Red Mare's Back* (Orchard), with paintings by Julie Downing, tells of a Swedish girl's rescue of her brother with the aid of a carved wooden horse that comes to life. *Fish Soup* (Atheneum), in which the Thinking Man of Moha and his friend the Writing Woman of Maho imagine two children who actually materialize, contrasts the man's orderly existence with the woman's houseful of cats, clutter, furballs, and flying mice (all neatly set forth in Patrick Wynne's drawings). From a collaboration between Katherine Paterson and the Russian artist Vladimir Vagin comes the revisionist story *The King's Equal* (HarperCollins), in which a poor country girl reforms her country's prince. Although the orientation of all three of these tales owes a great deal to feminist criticism, the messages do not obtrude unduly.

Among the year's best picture books is a handful from some acknowledged masters of the form. Van Allsburg's Halloween book, *The Widow's Broom* (Houghton Mifflin), marks a return to the striking treatment of illusion in his finest early work. In Jane Yolen's *Eeny, Meeny, Miney Mole* (Harcourt Brace Jovanovich), illustrated by Kathryn Brown, a mole ventures up from underground to compare real life up above to what she has heard from a worm, a centipede, and a snake; her two sisters, myopic in every way, scoff at her yearnings. The softly colored illustrations are reminiscent of *The Wind in the Willows*. And William Joyce's *Bently & egg* (HarperCollins) develops the idea of responsibility with a plot akin to Seuss's classic *Horton Hatches the Egg*, but with less slapstick humor and greater lyricism. The resourcefulness of Bently, a shy young frog, will win over readers of all ages. A bouncy text and bright colors illuminate an import, the New Zealand writer Margaret Mahy's *The Horrendous Hullaballoo* (Viking), in which a pirate named Peregrine seriously misjudges his aunt and misses a wonderful party of dozens of parrots: "They were speckled, they were freckled; they were streaked and striped like rollicking rags of rainbow." The aunt and parrots eventually take over Peregrine's ship, leaving him to put on the "pirate pinafore" and clean up. Patricia McCarthy's pictures match the text perfectly, including the pinafore covered with a neat skull-and-crossbones pattern. Mahy's other important picture book for 1992 was the better-known collaboration with Helen Oxenbury, *The Dragon of an Ordinary Family* (Dial). Stung by his wife's criticism ("Don't be a FUDDY-DUDDY, dear!"), Mr. Belsaki purchases a very small, cheap dragon . . . which grows and grows until it is banished by the mayor. After a sojourn in the Isles of Magic, the Belsakis return to their ordinary life.

Also among the year's best pictures books were some titles by less well known author-illustrators. Emily Arnold McCully's *Mirette on the High Wire* (Putnam's) evokes the theatrical world of nineteenth-century Paris, not a very common setting for picture books. More than just an imaginative evocation of its mileau, this is one of the most effective treatments of overcoming fear to appear in many years. *The Return of Freddy Legrand* (Farrar, Straus and Giroux), by Jon Agee, is an old-fashioned adventure story about an early aviator and a French farming couple, Sophie and Albert, who help him and become addicted to flying. And, on a more comic note, *Martha Speaks* (Houghton Mifflin), by Susan Meddaugh, tells what happens when a dog eats alphabet soup and gains the power of speech.

Dust jacket for the book that won the 1992 Caldecott award for the best children's picture book

All four made the *New York Times Book Review* list of the year's ten best-illustrated books.

Poetry collections bridged the gap between the youngest readers and middle graders. Three especially distinguished collections for a range of ages were Myra Cohn Livingston's *I Never Told and Other Poems* (Margaret McElderry), Barbara Esbensen's charming *Who Shrank My Grandmother's House?* (HarperCollins), and an anthology of children's folk rhymes edited by Alvin Schwartz, *And the Green Grass Grew All Around: Folk Poems from Everyone* (HarperCollins), with drawings by Sue Truesdell. This is rather like an American version of *I Saw Esau* and includes both old favorites such as "Do your ears hang low" and some less familiar rhymes such as this one to be sung to the tune of "John Brown's Body":

Mary had a little lamb,
A little pork, a little ham
A little egg, a little toast,
A lobster and some prunes,
A glass of milk, some macaroons.
It made the waiters grin
To see her order so,

And when they carried Mary out
Her face was white as snow.

Reissues of old favorites included Jane Taylor's *Twinkle, Twinkle, Little Star* (Scholastic) for the youngest, with updated pictures by Julia Noonan; the classic nursery collection *Ring o'Roses,* with the grand old illustrations by L. Leslie Brooke (Clarion), and a matching edition from the same publisher of Brooke's *The Golden Goose Book;* Edward Lear's illustrated alphabet, *A Was Once an Apple Pie* (Candlewick); and Hilaire Belloc's *Matilda, Who Told Such Dreadful Lies and Was Burned to Death* (Knopf/Random House), a rather gruesome excerpt from his *Cautionary Tales* of 1941.

The great array of "middle" readers – those at a stage between easy picture books and young adult new realism – were well served by nonfiction in 1992. While professionals continued to lament the unappealing nature of the label "nonfiction" and authors continued to complain that fiction received most of the attention, some exceptional books were being produced in this category. Many of them concerned ecology, either directly or indirectly, and nearly every professional reviewing source carried an essay on ecology books at some point in 1992; Janet Maslin performed the same service for a more general audience in the *New York Times Book Review* on 30 August.

Although some ecology books tended to be very alarmist (as most of the reviewers, whatever their political leanings, pointed out), others were both well informed and well written. Two concerned salmon: *The Atlantic Salmon* (Dutton), by Bianca Lavies, a straightforward nature book, and the Sierra Club's *Come Back, Salmon,* by Molly Cone, a more propagandistic but still compelling tale of how a fifth-grade class in rural Washington State rescued a polluted creek and restocked it with salmon raised in their classroom. Gloria Rand told a similar true story in *Prince William* (Holt) about Prince William Sound. Jim Arnosky's whimsically illustrated *Crinkleroot's Guide to Knowing the Trees* (Bradbury) was widely reviewed and read; less well known was Brenda Z. Guiberson's picture book for slightly older children, *Spoonbill Swamp* (Holt), with lyrical pictures by Megan Lloyd. Jean Craighead George offered a fictionalized swamp story, *The Missing 'Gator of Gumbo Limbo* (HarperCollins). Finally, Paul Fleischman, in a departure from his award-winning poetry, produced the lucid and graceful account of a little-known bird, *Townsend's Warbler* (HarperCollins).

Many books treated distant or little-known places and cultures. Two of the best for middle readers were photo essays: Russ Kendall's *Eskimo Boy: Life in an Inuipaq Eskimo Village* (Scholastic), with photographs by the author, follows a pattern laid down in recent years by several books about children in native American cultures but portrays its subjects, and their bleak land, exceptionally well. Brent Ashabranner's *Land of Yesterday, Land of Tomorrow* (Cobblehill Books), with photographs by Paul, David, and Peter Conklin, shows life in remote Xinjiang province during the 1980s, when the province was (briefly) open to foreigners. Not merely an essay in the picturesque, this fine book traces the old Silk Road across the centuries.

Biography and reference were also strong in 1992. In addition to the various Columbus books, there were some distinguished biographies and autobiographies for children. Betsy Byars recalled her development as a writer in *The Moon and I* (Simon and Schuster), a personal memoir ingeniously structured around the sight of a black snake. Another moonstruck children's writer was remembered in a fine biography for adult readers, Leonard Marcus's *Margaret Wise Brown: Awakened*

by the Moon (Beacon). Diana Et and Peter Vennema produced *Bard of Avon: The Story of William Shakespeare* (Morrow), a well-written and elegantly illustrated account. James Haskins continued his work in African-American biography with the workmanlike *Thurgood Marshall: A Life for Justice* (Holt) as well as two other civil-rights-era books. Several publishing houses brought out important encyclopedias. Foremost among these was the revised *Oxford Children's Encyclopedia,* an extensively rewritten edition which came out in Britain in late 1991 and in the United States in April 1992. Though some criticized its uncompromisingly British stance, this encyclopedia sets a standard that will be hard to match. The *Kingfisher Children's Encyclopedia* and *Kingfisher Illustrated Encyclopedia of the Animals* were less extensive reference volumes; the former is actually a reissue of the 1990 *Doubleday Children's Encyclopedia.*

One of the most engaging nonfiction books of the year was on an unpromising topic: the potato. Milton Meltzer offers *The Amazing Potato: A Story in Which the Inca, Conquistadors, Marie Antoinette, Thomas Jefferson, Wars, Famines, Immigrants, and French Fries All Play a Part* (HarperCollins). Every bit as engaging as its title, the book includes a wonderful bibliography. Another unexpected pleasure was the uncompromisingly titled *Feathers* (Cobblehill), by Dorothy Hinshaw Patent, with photographs by William Muñoz. Patent explains types of feathers, the physics of feathers, the development of feathers, and everything imaginable about feathers, in this lucid presentation.

In the area of fiction for the middle grades, marketing and selection issues predominated. Encompassing readers from about age nine to age twelve or thirteen, this is the category in which most juvenile "classics" fall (and from which the Newbery winners, as well as other state and professional winners, usually come). It is also the category in which certain problems arise that are virtually unknown with picture books. Parents of middle-grade students objected, during 1991, to books which included (among other things) visualization, dragons, witches — and, more predictably, "bad" language. Librarians, particularly in schools, experienced more pressure on these counts in 1991 and 1992 than previously. At the other extreme, middle-grade readers themselves pressured stores and libraries to stock series books in preference to more demanding single titles.

Although censorship pressure, the targets of which in 1992 included contemporary award winners such as Katherine Paterson as well as the more usual targets, increased somewhat in volume during the year, few if any of the titles in question were actually new books. In terms of influencing the production of high-quality fiction for these readers, the pressure from series may well be even more significant. Easily in first place by any measure, the Baby-Sitters Club series (Gray Castle Press) took up yards of space in every bookstore in the country. Libraries, reluctant to spend their shrinking funds on series books, put out signs asking for donations of used Baby-Sitters books to meet demand. In a lengthy article in the *New York Times Magazine,* the author defended her formulaic stories with the predictable (but sound) argument that they encourage children to read. Other series focused on ballet, camp, horseback riding, and sleuthing. Meanwhile, professional reviewing sources began to cover series books, sometimes in a separate section; in a full-page article in the *New York Times Book Review* (8 November), Ilene Cooper of *Booklist* presented a well-informed and reasonable account of the appeal of series, "Sweet Are the Uses of Predictability."

Looking beyond the series offerings, readers could find new titles by Phyllis Reynolds Naylor, Paula Danziger, E. L. Konigsburg, Gary Paulsen, and many others. Paulsen and Naylor brought out books with predictable patterns, often repeated before (but still good): Paulsen's *The Haymeadow* (Delacorte) follows a fourteen-year-old's season watching his family's sheep in a remote area; as is often the case with Paulsen, the book is suitable for both middle grades and young adults. Naylor's *All But Alice* (Atheneum) portrays a young girl's response to peer pressure; like previous Alice books, this one is lightweight but enjoyable. From an African-American perspective, similar problems surface in *Koya DeLaney and the Good Girl Blues* (Scholastic), by Eloise Greenfield – a less formulaic tale than Naylor's. Danziger's book *Not for a Million Gazillion Dollars* (Delacorte) also picked up a hero, Matthew, from an earlier book. Joanna Hurwitz tells a neat and satisfying story in *Ali Baba Bernstein Lost and Found* (Morrow), and Eve Bunting's *Coffin on a Case* (HarperCollins) will please young mystery lovers.

Somewhat more demanding were three short novels from well-established storytellers. E. L. Konigsburg returned to the Manhattan of her Newbery-winning *From the Mixed-up Files of Mrs. Basil E. Frankweiler* in *Amy Elizabeth Explores Bloomingdale's* (Atheneum), doing for that famous store what she had previously done for the Metropolitan Museum. Nina Bawden explored some hidden horrors of childhood in *Humbug* (Clarion), a story of an awkward child victimized by a dreadful young hostess.

And in *Missing May* (Orchard) Cynthia Rylant revisited the rural West Virginia of several earlier books to trace the progress of a young girl's grief at losing beloved, elderly Aunt May, the closest thing to a mentor she has known. The figures of Cletus, a noncomformist classmate, and Ob, May's broken-hearted widower, who makes ingenious and beautiful "whirligigs," are well drawn.

Adventure and social responsibility combine in several fine books for the middle years. In *Devil's Bridge* (Macmillan) Cynthia de Felice again evokes a rural setting and believable suspense as she did in her popular novel *Weasel.* The new book, however, is more serious and examines death directly and well. Robert Westall's *Stormsearch* (Farrar, Straus and Giroux), a British import, shows the impact of a chance discovery on a whole family; a model ship leads to new understanding of family history. With an African setting *Rescue!,* by David Kelleher (Dial), pits two children's desire to save chimpanzees from experimentation against their realization that they can provide no alternative for the animals.

Friendship between misfits, a perennial theme, produced two of the best books for this age group. *Words of Stone* (Greenwillow), the eighteenth book from Kevin Henkes, far surpasses his earlier work in its examination of two lonely children. Blaze Werla, who lives with his father and grandmother, begins seeing strange messages spelled out in stones on a hillside; through these he meets the overweight and eccentric Joselle Stark, who has been dumped on her grandmother by an irresponsible mother. Needing friendship desperately, the two are unskilled in normal human relationships and have major (but believable) problems. The two children in *Underrunners* (Viking), by the prolific New Zealand author Margaret Mahy, also come from damaged families: Tris lives with his well-meaning but distant father, and Winola is in the Featherstonehaugh Children's Home. In a convincing metaphor the "underrunners" turn out to be hidden tunnels and trenches lacing the countryside.

The Young Adult field was dominated by longtime professionals and by high-quality imports. Walter Dean Myers's *Somewhere in the Darkness* (Scholastic) traces a boy's journey from New York to rural Arkansas with a father who is a prison escapee and, it turns out, terminally ill. And Cynthia Voigt's *David and Jonathan* (Scholastic) examines a friendship strained by the intrusion of a Holocaust survivor who comes to live with one of the boys. Both *Somewhere in the Darkness* and *David and Jonathan* revolve around reinterpreting the past, and a surprising number of other young adult titles

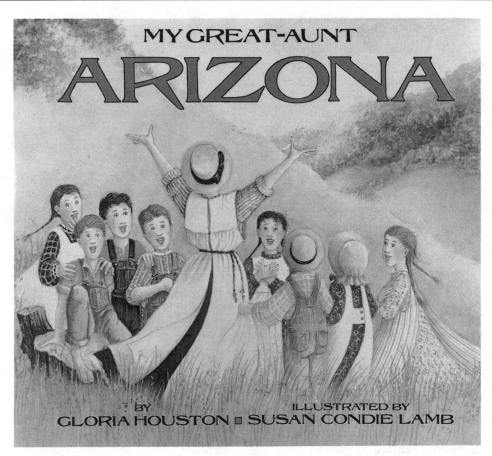

Dust jacket for the book Gloria Huston based on experiences she had while growing up in Appalachia

shared this focus. Several titles were set in the more distant past, such as the Colliers's tale of the Industrial Revolution, *The Clock* (Delacorte), and a tale of sixteenth-century Mexico, *The Diving Bell* (Scholastic), by Todd Strasser, who usually writes about contemporary teen culture. A relative newcomer to young adult publishing, Lensey Namioka, brought out her third novel, *The Coming of the Bear* (HarperCollins). This provocative book depicts a clash of cultures in early Japan, between the ethnic Japanese and the Ainu.

Though many fine young adult books concerned the past, most were firmly set in the eternal here-and-now that usually characterizes fiction for this age group. Several fine books dealt with accomplishment and success in very different ways. Robert Lipsyte continued his distinguished career with *The Chemo Kid* (HarperCollins), which combines a realistic approach to surviving cancer with a fable-like theme about physical strength and a happy ending. Francesca Lia Block once again skewered the unreal world of Los Angeles in her third book, *Cherokee Bat and the Goat Guys* (HarperCollins), in which

Cherokee, Witch Baby, Raphael, and Angel Juan form a rock group, are corrupted by their success, and have to be rescued by the benevolent Coyote. (In another California story, Ron Koertge's *The Harmony Arms* from Little, Brown, the L.A. scene is equally surreal but more amusing.) And, in a stunning debut, Joan Bauer won the Delacorte Prize for a first young adult novel with *Squashed* (Delacorte), the story of overweight Ellie Morgan, who is obsessed by the desire to grow the biggest pumpkin in Iowa.

Love, sex, and violence, the staples of young adult plots, characterized two thoughtful books with strong characters in well-realized settings. Joyce Sweeney, introduced to readers when she took the first annual Delacorte Prize some years ago, contrasts fourteen-year-old Deidre's crush on a much older musician with her cousin's physically abusive relationship in *Piano Man* (Delacorte), set in a convincingly sweltering Florida. Rural Virginia in the 1950s is the setting for Ruth White's sensitive novel *Weeping Willow* (Farrar, Straus and Giroux), a story of a young girl growing up in a poor household with a sexually abusive stepfather. Despite its subject matter, the book, which follows Tiny through all four years of high school, escapes being either didactic or depressing.

Two offerings from established young adult writers took the form of fables. Abandoning the complexities of *After the First Death* and some later experiments in theme and genre, Robert Cormier returns to the stark confrontation between good and evil he first explored in *The Chocolate War* (1974), in the brief *Tunes for Bears to Dance To* (Delacorte). Cormier presents once again a teenager influenced to do wrong and unable to resist. Though readers may find the horrible grocer, Mr. Hairston, somewhat improbable in his apparent lack of any kind of motivation, what happens to Henry and his friendship with old Mr. Levine is frightening and sure to provoke discussion. Cynthia Voigt's *Orfe* (Atheneum) presents another kind of fable: an adaptation of the Orpheus myth in which the characters are powerless to resist their fate. In a reverse twist Orfe, the irresistible singer, is female, and Yuri is her husband, carried back to an underworld of drugs by the inhabitants of "the house" where addicts live.

One of the foremost fantasy series for young adults concludes in Lawrence Yep's *Dragon War* (HarperCollins), the fourth of his books based on Chinese mythology. This volume tells of the Dragon princess Shimmer's quest to recover a magic cauldron from the evil Boneless King; her helpers are a monkey (drawn, like Shimmer, from Chinese tradition) and two young humans.

Imports, mostly from Great Britain, were of high quality. Foremost among these was Peter Dickinson's Whitbread Award winner, *AK* (Delacorte), depicting a young man in the imaginary African country of Nogala; the title refers to the hero Paul Nagomi's best friend, his gun. As always, Dickinson writes smoothly, and the pace is fast, so that only at the end does the reader notice how disturbing this tale of war and corruption really is. Two alternate endings are provided, one hopeful and one not; both seem equally probable. Berlie Doherty's *Dear Nobody* (Orchard) won the Carnegie Medal. Though it concerns teenage pregnancy, the book is in no way typical of the usual variations on the plot. When Helen is unable to go through with an abortion, both teenagers are forced to come to terms with their own families (which they really learn about for the first time). The title comes from a series of letters which Helen writes to her unborn baby, whom she calls "Nobody" because she wishes

it did not exist. In another, more straightforward coming-of-age story, Michelle Magorian's *Not a Swan* (HarperCollins) shows a seventeen-year-old girl reaching maturity under pressure during World War II; Magorian's sensitive writing and the psychological complexity of her characters make up for the extensive use of coincidence in the plot line. Vivien Alcock dissects the effects of white-collar crime on a family in *A Kind of Thief* (Delacorte), in which the children of an embezzler are parceled out to grudging relatives when their father goes to prison and their young stepmother returns to Italy.

In *Grace* (Farrar, Straus and Giroux), the story of a young woman whose daring rescue of shipwrecked passengers in 1838 captivated a whole country, Jill Paton Walsh goes back in history beyond her usual World War II setting to examine a short and tragic life. Despised by the people of her own region, Grace died young of consumption.

It is not only characters in books who die, and the world of children's books lost some of its best friends in 1992. Isaac Asimov, whose "adult" science fiction was read avidly by several generations of young readers, also turned out a large number of books especially for them. Particularly in the 1950s, when the cold war rivalry with his native Soviet Union crested, Asimov sought to make science and exploration appealing with his Lucky Starr series as well as with many informational books about the solar system and science generally. (Being Asimov, he insisted on adding updated prefaces to the Lucky Starr books when they were reissued; the science was no longer accurate.) Later, he collaborated with his second wife, Janet, in the Norby series of robot books for younger children.

The British children's writer Mary Norton, creator of the miniature world of the Borrowers, leaves no successors in her particular subject area; less well known perhaps is her fantasy *Bedknobs and Broomsticks* (1971), which became a popular Disney movie starring Angela Lansbury. Walt Morey, author of *Gentle Ben* (1965, also made into a Disney movie), died early in the year. The author-illustrator James Marshall, to whom Maurice Sendak dedicated his work for *I Saw Esau,* died in October. He was best known for his hippopotamus couple, George and Martha. Children's book illustration also lost Oscar de Mejo, whose alphabet *Oscar de Mejo's ABC* (HarperCollins) was one of the *New York Times Book Review*'s ten best-illustrated books of 1992.

The Year in Literary Theory

Barry Faulk and Michael Thurston
University of Illinois at Urbana-Champaign

In 1992 literary theory continued to be marked by the scrutiny of practices that have been traditionally neglected in standard histories: marginal literacies, subcultures, excluded identities. Literary theorists continued to reach outside the academy in the hope of establishing links with marginal groups, casting these groups as their real constituency. This assertion suggests that the year in literary theory was indeed a "politicized" year, if by the word is meant the desire to speak to communities largely ignored by previous academic study. There are less charitable ways to read this desire, and the media at large is full of them: Roger Kimball's attack in the 31 December 1992 *Wall Street Journal* on session topics at the Modern Language Association (MLA) speaks of contemporary academic life beset by "every radical trend" and typically using literature to "castigate Western society for being racist, sexist, imperialistic, etc." However, the encouragement of politically engaged scholarship has left its mark on the most important theoretical endeavors of this past year; much of this work necessitates a reexamination of the Arnoldian "function of criticism."

In the article mentioned above, Kimball notes that at the MLA "the real action, and crowds, were at panels devoted to 'Cultural Studies,'" even generously defining the term for the uninitiated to consist of "radical political sermonizing." The year 1992 saw the publication and reception of *Cultural Studies: Now and in the Future* (Routledge), a mammoth anthology generated out of the conference of the same title held at the University of Illinois at Urbana-Champaign in April 1990. A more helpful definition of Cultural Studies than the one Kimball offers would point to the Centre for Contemporary Studies at the University of Birmingham (England) and the early work of British critics Raymond Williams and Richard Hoggart. Cultural Studies came from the impulse to find links between the divergent scholarly work of scholars who shared a common commitment to the political Left. This political resolve led to scholarship that was in many ways dedicated to the culture that these scholars believed they left behind when they entered the university. Richard Hoggart put Leavisite reading practices to elegiac use in *The Uses of Literacy* (1959), his loving evocation of a working-class culture largely untouched by mass media. Sometimes this scholarly work was an attempt to think through specific impasses in Labour party politics or among the New Left during the 1960s; crises of this nature usually determined how Continental theory was taken up by the Centre's leaders, such as Stuart Hall. Cultural studies work also analyzed Great Britain's political turn to the right and the triumph of Margaret Thatcher's England, as evidenced by Hall's *The Hard Road to Renewal* (1988).

Part of the current success of Cultural Studies in the American academy is no doubt due to the fact that other work prepared the way for a book such as *Cultural Studies:* the increasing citation of work from the Centre for Cultural Studies at Birmingham (including the work of Williams, Hoggart, and Hall), as well as groundbreaking works such as Janice Radway's *Reading the Romance* (1984) and Dick Hebdige's *Subcultures* (1988), have familiarized American scholarly communities with the methods and concerns of British Cultural Studies. The publication of *Reading into Cultural Studies* (Routledge), edited by Martin Barker and Ann Beezer, subjects texts important in the formation of Cultural Studies – such as Tony Bennett's *Bond and Beyond* (1987) and Tania Modleski's *Loving with a Vengeance* (1988) – to a reconsideration of their methodology and research strategies.

The proliferation of cultural criticism in the academy has already provoked the ire of more-traditional humanists, especially those who represent the academy in public-sector journalism. The assimilation of Cultural Studies among American academics no doubt is seen by some as part of "the Crisis in English Studies" detailed in Walter Jackson Bate's earlier attack in *Harvard Magazine* on the politically charged topics conspicuous at MLA sessions in 1982. For these reasons the work in *Cultural Studies* is symptomatic in many ways of the shape of contemporary literary theory. The massive tome includes work by scholars, many of whom were initially concerned with textual study and literary theory: however, both the conference and the book bring together intellectuals from various sites, among them the Australian public sector, sociologists and media scholars working in British academia, and American AIDS activists. However, this diversity is precisely the point and reflects the work and breadth of outlook that has come to influence more traditionally "literary" study. Certainly it is emblematic in its concern with the political consequences of academic study, the micropolitics of literature, and a perhaps final deemphasis on exclusively formalist study of media or literary texts.

Physically, the book is a gargantuan hybrid – eight hundred pages, forty articles – and studies of William Shakespeare (Peter Stallybrass) jostle against readings of the politics of 1968 (Kobena Mercer) and of *Star Trek* fanzines and *Hustler* (Constance Penley). Edited by Lawrence Grossberg, Cary Nelson, and Paula Treichler, *Cultural Studies* includes work by activists as well as academics, and Jan Zita Grover's essay "AIDs, Keywords, and Cultural Work" is among the book's strongest and most provocative. While covering such disparate subject matters as real-estate advertisements in Australia, New Age culture, crime fiction, and Trekkies, the common strain running through the book is an intense focus on social institutions, including the academy, and their social effects. The theoretical bases of the disparate work vary, though common commitments to Italian theorist Antonio Gramsci and to recent post-Marxist theorists such as Ernesto Laclau and Chantal Mouffe seem common to most of the scholars involved. The work of Meaghan Morris, Catherine Hall, Donna Harraway, Radway, Grover, and several others is marked by the important influence of feminism, while essays by Lati Mani and Homi Bhabha bring the concerns of postcolonial theory to the forefront. It is a book that refuses easy assimilation and may be off-putting, with its intense theory-speak, to a broad range of academics. The problems that surfaced when the presenters at the "Cultural Studies" conference engaged in discussion, recorded in the question/answer sessions included in the volume, return to questions that haunt literary study. They constantly return to the relation between popular culture and the institutions of literary study, between the student/client that scholars serve and other con-

stituencies. As oppositional politics increasingly affects academic work, there is a growing desire to take up the Cultural Studies imperative to read diverse cultural phenomena relationally; in other words, to examine how literature works in conjunction with other forces in the culture, such as attitudes toward race, gender, or national identity.

However, while *Cultural Studies* includes many scholars, including Stuart Hall, openly concerned about the ready assimilation of Cultural Studies by American academics (to become overly "academic" is still considered the death knell of "politicization"), the year in literary theory indicates that this assimilation has largely occurred. The *South Atlantic Quarterly* is regularly devoted to what it labels "cultural criticism" (the Winter 1992 issue titled "Writing Cultural Criticism," for example); *Social Text*, issue 30, was concerned with reevaluating the legacy of Raymond Williams (Andrew Ross and Catherine Gallagher were among those who tried to rethink their relation to Williams's scholarly commitments). Recent work in critical pedagogy such as Henry A. Giroux's *Border Crossings* (Routledge) also indicates that a style of critical scholarly engagement with literary texts (and nonliterary texts, subsumed under the common rubric of "culture") has come to mark academic thinking. Cultural Studies has served to provoke academics to rethink the politics of the knowledge they produce, the services they perform, and the links between their work and a larger public. Unfortunately, this has not led to a reconsideration of the language that academics use when they talk about "popular" subjects or popular culture. The future of jargon, of lit-crit-speak, will no doubt come to the fore in 1993: the increasingly specialized, hermetic language in which cultural criticism has routinely come to be produced in the academy will have to be reevaluated if the desire to speak to larger constituencies (and to avoid being miscast by journalists who speak about the academy to a general public) remains viable.

Hall, in "Cultural Studies and its Theatrical Legacies," shows an awareness of the necessity for theoretically sophisticated work to speak in less clotted and jargon-laden sentences and address "theoretical" concerns to broader audiences. Addressing the marginality of Cultural Studies in "real world" struggles, he writes:

> AIDS is one of the questions which urgently brings before us our marginality as critical intellectuals in making real effects in the world. . . . Against the urgency of people dying in the streets, what in God's name is the point of cultural studies?. . . [But] How could we say that the question of AIDS is not also a question of who gets

Double title page for Jonathan Goldberg's study of links between Renaissance literature and contemporary sexuality

represented and who does not?. . . These are things cultural studies can address.

Kimball's coverage of the "blatantly politicized" MLA also speaks of the prominence of "exotic sexual subjects" among American academics. Yet the increasing prevalence of "Queer Theory" among literary critics (Columbia, Duke, and Rutgers Universities have all recently initiated series of critical books in queer theory) not only upsets neoconservatives such as Kimball but also many gay and lesbian scholars who are worried about being assimilated into academic work as usual. Michael Warner notes in *VLS* (June 1992) that the term *queer theory* has "outstripped anyone's sense of what exactly it means." The work of these scholars, and their inquiries into such disparate top-

ics as gender, the history of sexuality, and how the body is constructed and mediated textually, have indelibly marked the year in literary theory. Like Cultural Studies, queer theory has gained an academic vogue because its points of departure share a degree of theoretical sophistication and indicate new ways to consider problems that have beset critical theory over the last twenty years. Specifically, queer theory has engaged the legacy of Michel Foucault, exploring how language mediates and constructs meanings, involves political issues of servitude and freedom, and indicates the temporal limitations of what are assumed to be constants: the coherent body or the body. Eve Kosofsky Sedgwick's 1990 *Epistemology of the Closet* claims that her exploration moves "in accord with Foucault's demonstration – whose results I take to be axiomatic": that modernity has "placed what it calls sexuality in a more and more distinctively privileged relation to our most prized constructs of individual identity, truth and knowledge." Sedgwick's argument places what is often at the margins of official discourse, sexuality, at the center of our most significant concepts. The spectacle of queer theory's success in 1992 would not be so marked if these theorists did not make vital claims on questions that concern scholars in feminism and film theory. Sedgwick's claim indeed reads like another retelling of the rise of modernity: like Karl Marx's narrative of class struggle or Weber's story of the steady encroachment of instrumental rationality. Part of the ease with which queer theory has made its concerns central to literary theory at large is that its curriculum and agenda are not too far divorced from academic concerns. The strong claims that Judith Butler's *Gender Trouble* (1990) makes for the disruptive nature of lesbian identity come from her encounter with poststructuralist axioms which assert that "language is not an exterior medium or instrument into which I pour a self and from which I glean a reflection of that self " but "an open system of signs by which intelligibility is insistently created and contested." Butler's groundbreaking study, along with Sedgwick's work still considered a turning point in gay and lesbian literary study, relies on post-structuralist thinking to question the stable foundations of gender identity and praise a "literary" style – parody – for its ability to destabilize gender hierarchy.

Queer theory, like cultural studies, has similar desires to speak for others who are not located in an academic environment and to engage contemporary issues (such as AIDS) in polemical ways that suggest a new openness between scholarship and audiences outside the academy. Jonathan Goldberg's *Sodometries* (Stanford University Press) is a recent and noteworthy example of how sensitively the study of sexuality can be brought to bear on traditional literary paradigms and literary study. Goldberg's study, like much Cultural Studies work, attempts to make literary study more responsive to broader contexts. It opens by invoking both the Gulf War and *Bowers* v. *Hardwick,* a U.S. Supreme Court decision upholding a Georgia statute against sodomy. Following Foucault's suggestive comment in *The History of Sexuality* (1978) that "sodomy" is "that utterly confused category," Goldberg's work proceeds from the perceptual confusion as to whether sodomites are "persons" or judicial constructs created in relation to other cultural constraints. *Sodometries* opens with subjects common in

traditional literary study of Renaissance texts – the poetics of court life, Shakespeare's Prince Henry, Edmund Spenser's *Shepherdes Calendar* (1579) – but argues that the displaced fears about male-male relations in these texts have current consequences. Goldberg attempts the arduous task of linking modern sexualities with an analysis of how literary texts configured male-male relations before homosexuality was "invented." What is perhaps most provocative about Goldberg's study is the way it challenges the foundational work of such "New Historicist" scholars as Stephen Greenblatt, Leah Marcus, and Louis Montrose. Instead of opening out from a stylish anecdote of colonial oppression to find homologous structures of repression in the *Henry IV* plays as did Stephen Greenblatt's "Invisible Bullets" (originally published in *Glyph,* 8 [1981]), Goldberg's study moves from key moments in the formation of high canonical literature to moments of political import, specifically the colonization of America. He reverses the usual moves from context to text and finds similar homophobia in both, thereby unsettling the usual methodological practice of an already historically acute body of scholarship.

Kristina Straub's *Sexual Suspects* (Princeton University Press) also discusses how margins play a central role in the definition of cultural hierarchies. The "sexualized" actor and actress of eighteenth-century England in popular biography is examined in order to re-create how the "critical consciousness" was born. The search for the private sexualities of actresses in a diversity of pamphlets is scrutinized in order to gain an insight into the beginnings of "publicity" and the status of performers on display. At stake for Straub in these inquiries are such complex issues as sexuality, the psychology of spectatorship, and the discourse of aesthetics. The creation of "critical" discourse and the explicit dynamics of authentic "spectatorship" is explored in Thomas Hobbes, Joseph Addison and Sir Richard Steele; this construct is both elaborated and placed at risk in the presence of the "player." Defining the role of the actor is central in defining crucial boundaries between gender roles as well as the articulation of the detached, objective "spectator." Straub examines how the figure of the spectator haunts the construction of authoritative knowledge during the period. She locates a concern with the politics of spectatorship and the "power differential between the watcher and the watched" in Hobbes as well as contemporary film theorists who speculate how the "male gaze" structures both how stories are told and films are made.

Although extending into the 1960s, Mary Louise Pratt's complex *Imperial Eyes* (Routledge) suggests important connections between eighteenth-century travel writing, including sentimental travel literature, the scientific exploration of native cultures, and the work of classification and taxonomy performed by Comte Georges-Louis Leclerc de Buffon and Carolus Linneaus. Pratt's research in Andean history, the rhetorical fashioning of South America, and the specific dynamics of "creole self-fashioning" are especially noteworthy. Her study "emphasizes how subjects are constituted in and by their relations to each other. It treats the relations among colonizers and colonized, or travelers and 'travelees,' not in terms of separateness or apartheid, but in terms of copresence, interaction, interlocking understandings and practices."

In nineteenth-century studies Judith Walkowitz's landmark *City of Dreadful Delight* (University of Chicago Press) offers a masterful survey of how the city, its spaces and topics, circulated in late-Victorian England. *The City of Dreadful Delight* opens and closes with a consideration of the Jack the Ripper controversy and the way sexual violence was figured by various media. Walkowitz is concerned with how sexual danger was represented in late-Victorian London and how these dangers played a constitutive role in how the city itself was imagined. She is particularly concerned with how various media scandals, such as the "Maiden Tribute of Babylon" (a scandal concerning young prostitutes "sacrificed" to rapacious aristocrats) or the controversies over marriage vented in the correspondence page of the *Daily Telegraph*, literally circulated throughout the metropolis. Walkowitz studies these scandals for what they reveal about the dialogue such scandals opened, as well as about the opportunities and liabilities of London life. Such controversies, Walkowitz copiously argues, galvanized public participation to incite, in her words, "a wide panorama of social actors," including working-class women and men. In her words, "these campaigns facilitated middle class women's forceful entry into the world of publicity and politics." The wealth of evidence on which Walkowitz draws makes essential reading for any literary scholar interested in how public life and media scandal interlocked to create narrative styles that touched on a variety of audiences and literacies (including belles lettres, here represented by Olive Schreiner, George Bernard Shaw, Walter Besant, and Henry James).

Mary Jean Corbett's *Representing Femininity* (Oxford University Press) also examines how different discursive and social factors impinged on professional women (writers, actresses) and how these working women imagined and fashioned their iden-

tities in a variety of genres and registers. Corbett's study is sensitive to noting how suffragettes complicated the categories and expectations attributed to women's writing. Corbett's book is important for the texts it brings to scrutiny – not only the autobiographies of women writers but also actresses (including Ellen Terry and Irene Vanbrugh) and suffragettes (including Cicely Hamilton and Constance Lytton) – in order to analyze how middle-class women represented themselves.

Both Corbett and Walkowitz are critically aware of how literary forms are impinged on by social circumstances. Likewise, Joseph Bristow's recent essay, "*Dorian Gray* and Gross Indecency," included in his *Sexual Sameness: Textual Differences in Lesbian and Gay Writing* (Routledge) details how late-Victorian legislation impinged on Oscar Wilde's imagining of Dorian Gray. Bristow notes how Wilde's fiction was affected by the passage of the Criminal Law Amendment (1885) and shared the same elements as the Cleveland Street Affair (in which wealthy men were arrested in a homosexual brothel) as it was publicized: the corruption of youth and the danger of cross-class liaisons. Bristow sees *Dorian Gray* as a polemical text in these circumstances. Like Walkowitz, Bristow finds literature often involved in the elaboration of identities provoked by media scandals that shook late-Victorian London. In this context Bristow finds Wilde's *Dorian Gray* (1890) specifically "opposing the social undesirability of cross-class sexual relationships."

A specific trend in literary studies that is linked to those suggested in *Cultural Studies* moves specifically toward the analysis of literary institutions themselves as objects of study. Two books published in 1992 also exemplify this focus on the institutional formations behind the teaching and transmission of literature. A new book by Peter Bürger, *The Decline of Modernism* (Pennsylvania State University Press), outlines a history of artistic Modernism and the critical institutions that both enable and critique it. Bürger assiduously develops a theory to enhance understanding of Modernism and, simultaneously, its decline. A cultural theory "concerned with the social function of art or literature," Bürger begins, "must study the relationship between art or literature and rationalization." His history significantly works through the social mechanisms that turned art and religion into what Bürger labels "functional equivalents." He concludes:

The separation of this world and the other world is replaced by a corresponding separation of art and everyday life. On the basis of this opposition, the aesthetic form can be delivered from the obligation to serve certain purposes and be considered as something of independent value.... The quasi transcendent quality of works of art demands a reception which corresponds to religious contemplation.

However, this tale of rationalization is not left as the last word on how institutions necessarily function. Bürger goes on, in his second chapter, to work through Walter Benjamin's "redemptive critique," reading Benjamin through the filter of Jürgen Habermas. The "redemptive critique," Bürger argues, places emphasis on "the historical truth content of the objective cultural forms of the past." The result of such critique is that "the work has the status of material which is placed on the same level as other manifestations of reality." The work of the critic is to disrupt "the continuum of history," to prise from the historical narrative of progress "a piece of the past," and to redeem that piece "by applying it to the present." To Bürger, such a concern with tradition is not simply conservative; rather, the application of the past to the present, if properly achieved, is always a "radical" project. The "redemption" that occurs in the redemptive critique, then, is that mode dealing with the past that "contributes to the solution of the problems of the present." Bürger works through Benjamin toward an activist criticism, which takes as part of its object of analysis the institutions of criticism themselves. This theory informs his readings, later in the book, of modernist texts such as Wyndham Lewis's *Tarr* (1918), readings which go beyond the texts themselves to consider, as much of the theoretical work described here does, the institutions in which those texts are reproduced and reactivated in a society.

Two other books in 1992 exemplify this trend and its productive results. Michael Bérubé's *Marginal Forces/Cultural Centers: Tolson, Pynchon and the Politics of the Canon* (Cornell) focuses on the cases of two writers, Melvin Tolson and Thomas Pynchon, to examine the influence of such literary institutions as anthologies and libraries on the process of canon formation. Bérubé sets his project against the limitations of reader-response criticism, explaining his project as an active attempt to discuss how cultural products are remade by institutional interpretation:

What I have attempted is a way of reconstructing the passages between cultural products and their appropriations by cultural centers, a way of reading texts and their receptions against each other in an interplay that shuttles between textual representation and sociohistorical reception – reception that in turn takes the form of

critical (that is, cultural) representation (in journals, reviews, canons, and classrooms).

Bérubé's analysis of Tolson's very selective (and distorted) representation in anthologies of African-American poetry and of the role such critics as Karl Shapiro and Allen Tate played in the development of Tolson's reputation are especially illuminating and provocative.

Gerald Graff's *Beyond the Culture Wars: How Teaching Conflicts Can Revitalize American Education* (Norton) highlights the institution itself. Repeating the critique he made in *Professing Literature* (1987) of the current arrangement of English departments into "periods," which students are expected to "cover," Graff proposes a reorganization of educational institutions into "learning communities"; these would be interdisciplinary and would take as their curricular matter the issues at stake in the creation of curricula themselves. Such reorganization would take the work of institutional critics a step further, focusing attention on the roles of institutions in the constitution of subjects, providing students themselves with the opportunity to create knowledges instead of passively receiving them. Graff argues that "the most powerful and influential of recent theorists argue that literature is a scene of contradictions that cannot be submerged under any 'totalizing' ideology." His recommendations for "teaching the conflicts" over traditional methodologies and texts makes it clear that "literature," the set of institutional spaces and practices in which literary texts are situated and activated, can be an invigorating and productive discipline.

The "culture wars" also served as occasion for the gathering of recent essays by one of the most important theorists and commentators on African and African-American literature in 1992. Henry Louis Gates, Jr.'s *Loose Canons: Notes on the Culture Wars* (Oxford University Press) collects essays on topics ranging from the canon controversies of the last several years to the state of black literary studies in the British and American academy today. While Gates is perhaps best known for his theorizing of tradition in African-American literature, the subject of his *The Signifying Monkey* (1991), those essays in *Loose Canons* which were provoked most directly by the canon debates seem already dated, because the parameters of the debates they address have so rapidly changed. The most important work in the book can be found in the three essays which make up the book's second section, focusing attention on "The Profession."

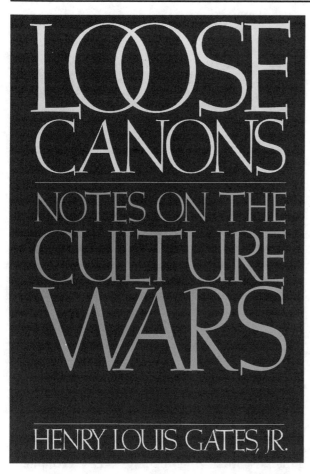

Dust jacket for Henry Louis Gates, Jr.'s collection of essays addressing recent controversies over inclusion of works by minority writers among the books traditionally studied in college classrooms

"'Tell Me Sir, . . . What Is Black Literature'" treats the institutionalization of black studies and traces the mutual importance of black-studies programs and the popularity and availability of the work of black women writers such as Toni Morrison, Alice Walker, and Gloria Naylor. Gates charts the relocation of emphasis in black studies from social anthropology to literary studies, a relocation partially enabled by the replacement of a predominantly male Black Aesthetic by the work of black women writers. His analysis leads to a final, hopeful consideration of the present state of African-American criticism. Gates concludes:

Black studies has functioned as a strategic site for autocritique within American studies itself. No longer, for example, are the concepts of "black" and "white" thought to be preconstituted; rather, they are mutually constitutive and socially produced. The theoretical work of feminist writers of African and African-American literature, moreover, has turned away from a naive-

ly additive notion of sexism and racism. Especially in this work, we have come to understand that critiques of "essentialism" are inadequate to explain the complex social dynamism of marginalized cultures.

Gates's collection holds forth the possibility that "Black Studies" will become an institutional site where scholarly work in American studies can be "institutionally" scrutinized and complicated in ways that reflect the real complexity of lived experience among "marginalized cultures."

Another collection of essays published in 1992 deserves attention. *Feminism and American Literary History* (Rutgers University Press) brings together a decade's work by an important scholar of American literary history, Nina Baym. Baym's work in recovering neglected work by women writers of the nineteenth century has been especially influential, and the book includes essays elaborating on the reasons behind her recovery work. Gathered under the heading "Writing New American Literary History," these essays include "Woman and the Republic: Emma Willard's Rhetoric of History" and "Sarah Hale, Political Writer," a consideration of the important editor of *Godey's Lady's Book*. The well-known essays "Melodramas of Beset Manhood" and "Putting Women in Their Place" demonstrate the sexism latent in traditional histories of American literature and in the work of canonical American male writers.

"Early Histories of American Literature," though, is Baym's most considered and thoroughly theorized examination of the cultural and political function of literary institutions. Reading the early histories of American literature and the promotional statements of contemporary publishers and educators, Baym's essay explores some of the material consequences of the teaching of American literature; she finds the institution of New England as the cultural center of American literature and the teaching of the works of New England writers in the common schools working "to reconcile [the poor] to genteel poverty by stressing the primacy of spiritual over material values."

Of other work focusing on gender and sexuality in American literature during 1992, Liz Yorke's essay, "Constructing a Lesbian Poetry for Survival: Broumas, Rukeyser, H. D., Rich, Lorde," which appears in *Sexual Sameness,* stands out. Pointing out the need for lesbian writers and critics to "be attentive to the silences, to identify, theorize, and explore . . . the gap between lesbian lives and those dominant discourses which problematically avoid, distort, suppress, or condemn the actualities of lesbian existence," Yorke goes on to read poems by five lesbian poets to determine the strategies by which they bring lesbian "libidinal differences, sexualities and cultural identities" disruptively into language. In her discussion Yorke moves easily between subtle close readings of the poetry and the theoretical arguments needed "to produce and develop a lesbian reading practice," which resists the New Critical tendency to read poems as self-contained artifacts and allows biographical consideration of the lives of the poets to bear on interpretations of their work. Biographical considerations, however, are subordinated to Yorke's linguistically oriented readings, which show quite effectively the strategies by which H. D. "makes use of the unsatisfactory heterosexual codes . . . in order to produce a lesbian encoding of her alternative story" or Rich metonymically overcomes division and "invokes the very physical presence . . . of her lover." In Lorde's acceptance of the need for violent action, Yorke finds "a radical challenge to the gender asymmetries characteristic of the white patriarchy, which would limit female participation in the culturally constructed forms of militarized power." All of the poets she considers, Yorke concludes, "subvert, contest, or displace conventional heterosexist poetic discourses."

If, in 1992, we can detect an increasing self-consciousness about the "institutions of criticism" and the consequences of theory beyond academic environs, this expanded awareness has not proved debilitating. In fact, a critical cognizance of whom literary theorists speak for and whom they have spoken for in the past has, so far, had significant positive effects. One obvious reward of "institutional criticism" is that it gives previously marginalized groups the language to address and articulate their own concerns. It may also be argued that the concern with the apparatus of institutional criticism has encouraged especially thoughtful and legitimate "historical" scholarship among literary theorists. The essays in the books by Baym and Gates, for example, exemplify the insights into historical processes that accompany the concern with how "literature" and "literary theory" have previously been taught and assimilated by academics and broader publics. Goldberg's witty rehearsal of how previous Shakespeare criticism has "desired" Prince Hal indicates that newer criticism has been able to proceed because of a clear insight into the ideological limits of previous scholarly work. It should also be noted that Goldberg's ingenious reading is heavily dependent on past "blind-

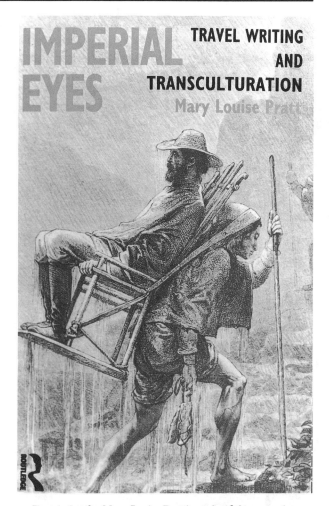

Dust jacket for Mary Louise Pratt's study of the connections between eighteenth-century travel writing and the sociological work carried out under imperialist regimes

ness" in order to secure his own "insight"; his relation to previous scholarly endeavor is neither derogatory nor reverent. It may not be too extravagant to hope that a scrutiny of old research practices can continue to be productive in this way: not as antiquarian exercise or dogmatic ideological critique but as preliminary work toward establishing new goals for academic work. Apprehension over theory's social function might help literary scholars to avoid, in the long haul, the charges of "specialization" and "mandarinism" so frequently leveled at theoretical work. Perhaps only an awareness of both the limits *and* the possibilities that the academy has offered intellectuals in the past can allow new, practical goals for literary scholarship to be articulated today.

The Year in Literary Biography

William Foltz
University of Hawaii

The year 1992 provided both embarrassments and riches in literary biography. There are biographies which are important because their subjects wrote great literature: James Thomson and Gerard Manley Hopkins in poetry, and Edgar Allan Poe, Nathaniel Hawthorne, and Anthony Trollope in prose. There are biographies which are important because their subjects were associated with those who wrote great literature: George Henry Lewes because of his association with George Eliot, and Olivia Clemens because of her marriage to Samuel Langhorne Clemens. Some biographies inflate the importance of their subjects, like those of Fanny Fern and Jean Rhys. Other biographies make no great claims for their subjects but provide the reader with an interesting and entertaining reading experience, such as those books on Margaret Mitchell, S. S. Van Dine (Willard Huntington Wright), Richard Harding Davis, Elizabeth Bishop, and Antonia White.

Thomson's *Seasons* was ably edited ten years ago. The editor, James Sambrook, has now become the poet's no-less-able biographer in *James Thomson (1700–1748): A Life* (Oxford), a work in which thorough scholarship has not prohibited felicities of style. Surely the temptation for a textual editor is to highlight the poems rather than the poet. But Sambrook has drawn a portrait of the poet and his friends. In many ways this is a study not just of Thomson but of literary and political friendships in the London of the second quarter of the eighteenth century. And among Thomson's friends was David Mallet, Samuel Johnson's despised Scot. Sambrook's retelling of Thomson's early friendship with Mallet starts in Edinburgh in the mid 1720s, and then moves on to London, where Mallet introduced him not only to aristocratic patrons such as George Dodington, later George, first Baron Lyttelton, to whom Thomson felt himself a captive bard, but even, after Thomson's initial success with *Winter,* to princely connections. All this is told with narrative ease. Perhaps too much of the contemporary idea of eighteenth-century London still comes

from Johnson; Sambrook presents the slightly earlier London: the book could use a map so the reader could locate and appreciate the author's topographical discoveries and a map of the suburbs, especially Richmond, the poet's lettered and indolent retreat. And too often it is Johnson, either in his *Lives of the Poets* (1781) or as reported by James Boswell, who prejudices readers even today in his reference to Thomson as a man of "gross sensuality and licentiousness of manners" (some of the eight portraits in this book support Johnson). It is to Sambrook's credit that his conclusion that Thomson had the "social qualities of a man's man" modifies rather than rejects Johnson's judgment.

An example of Sambrook's thoroughness is his examination of *Sophonisba.* Thomson sold the copyright of the play, along with that of *Spring,* but probably made almost three hundred pounds from the performances, one of which was at the command of the Prince of Wales, an event the biographer justly argues has momentous political and patronal significance for Thomson. Of the play itself Sambrook says "spare, chaste, and correct to a fault." And Sambrook is correct: readers interested in Carthage are better off with the *Aeneid* or Gustave Flaubert's *Salammbô* (1863). Sambrook recounts details of the play's cast, its reception, and its parody by Henry Fielding; there are several corrections to the received record. As for the cast, Sambrook found the burial place and pallbearers of Anne Oldfield, the actress whose delivery of many lines probably made the play. The famous anecdote in the *Life* of 1753, that, upon hearing "O Sophonisba! Sophonisba O!," some wit exclaimed, "Oh Jamey Thomson, Jamey Thomson Oh!," is an occurrence too good to be true because Fielding's notorious takeoff, "Oh *Huncamunca, Huncamunca,* oh" appears for the first time only in a later revision of *Tom Thumb* (1730). Thomson's reaction was Olympian – or Scottish – indifference: he never removed the line. This is thorough and detailed history. In fact the index anatomizes the poet into fifty topics of his life and over eighty regarding his poems and plays.

Perhaps autopsy prevents panorama. How did Thomson's *Seasons* become Joseph Haydn's in 1801? Is there a link between part 4 of *Liberty* (1735), with its praise of pre-Winckelmann hyperthyroid Hellenistic Greek sculptures, and Gotthold Lessing's 1766 *Laokoön*? Lessing, Sambrook points out, was Thomson's distinguished champion who had translated Sheil's *Life* and Thomson's *Agamemnon*. Sambrook rarely wanders beyond his subject's death in 1748, but within those confines his judgments are confident, his explanations sure. Readers will come to appreciate the complexities of ecclesiastical preferment, why "Miltonic" was a political adjective, and how one could be surveyor-general of customs for the Leeward Islands while remaining in Great Britain. The biographer's literary judgments are similar. Sambrook distinguishes between the fluid verse paragraph of John Milton and Thomson: Thomson's reader does "move slowly against a driving mingled hail of commas, semi-colons, dashes, and stops" in *Winter*. And finally, after Sambrook's dispassionate analysis of *Coriolanus,* we need not feel guilty for not having read it – yet. But read it we might, if only to oblige this clear and sane biographer.

One hundred years after Thomson began *Winter,* Gerard Manley Hopkins, another poet who tried to balance God with nature, was born, but not until recently was he happy in his biographers. Father Lahey's 1930 biography was fulsome; Father Pick's 1966 work was unbalanced (he argued priests have no business being poets – and Hopkins himself believed this for a while). Paddy Kitchen's *Gerard Manley Hopkins* twelve years later moved in the right direction: to the poet's interior, an interior well, but almost excessively, explored by Robert Martin's *A Very Private Life* (1991). The last two biographers had access to the previously censored journals and, in Martin's case, a full edition of the poems. And now, almost a half a century after Father Bischoff promised a full treatment of the poet, we finally have Norman White's *Hopkins: A Literary Biography* (Clarendon Press). There are three major concerns with which a biographer of Hopkins is faced: the Anglican's conversion, the poet's inspiration, and the man's sexuality. This most recent work examines all three.

In addition to the resources recently available to Kitchen and Martin, White has located and used further letters of Hopkins's Scottish friend A. W. M. Baillie. More important, White had access to the papers of Humphrey House. These papers include partial drafts for a biography and House's notes from his interviews. White's personal investigations led him to walk those parts of the British Isles Hopkins visited – and Hopkins walked as much as William Wordsworth – to interview a porter in Dublin, a retired scout in Oxford, and the landlord of the Three Crowns and even to prowl through the boxes of Benjamin Jowett's rather dull lecture notes at Balliol College. White's itineraries are rarely dull, though a map would be helpful: after all, the *Journals* have maps. Hopkins's (corrected) journal entries with his poems and letters join almost imperceptibly with White's investigations into county histories, interviews, and kitchen accounts to form a smooth narrative.

White has read everything which could bear on Hopkins including the poet's father's book on insurance, his uncle's on Chinese oracle bones, a study of Irish whiskey, and the 1873 and 1890 ordnance maps of the Isle of Man. The select bibliography runs to over 250 items. The book has copious extracts, printing possibly 20 percent of the early diaries and journals. This is not so with the poems: White often prints earlier versions to jolt the reader out of his familiarity.

What is White's concluding point? Well, if Hopkins actually said (as Father Lahey would have the reader believe), "I am so happy, I am so happy," as, like Prince Albert, he lay dying of bad drains and typhoid, he probably did not believe it. Probably the biographer's conclusion is that, "an overall and coherent pattern cannot be imposed on the works as a whole, nor on the life" as White insists on the first page of the preface to his almost five-hundred-page biography.

The biography has six parts: after thirty pages or so on Hopkins the boy (to age nineteen), White moves generally, by segments of five and six years, to Hopkins as student, Jesuit, poet, fortune's football, and finally stranger. As does Martin in his biography, White devotes many pages (130) to Hopkins's student years (1863–1868) at Oxford, years in which his intellectual triumphs ended in a crisis of sexual identity and religious faith.

It is difficult to recreate the shock felt by Hopkins's family when he converted, but White succeeds. In fact, judging from letters from as late as the 1950s, the family resented the matter being raked up by the official Jesuit biographer. Now that all the poet's immediate family is dead, White can explain how the conversion was seen as dishonest, un-English, and unmanly. If anything, White is too gentle; a more typical reaction was the almost pathological hatred found in the oft-reprinted *Secret*

History of the Oxford Movement (1897), by Walter Walsh. White's condemnation, not of Hopkins's conversion, but of his coldness to his family, is refreshingly correct: childish petulance, self-righteous protestation, and insensitive adolescent assertiveness all coalesced to make Hopkins a most intelligent prig. White argues that the poet's removal to Rome was gradual, a reaction based on his earlier religious training against Balliol's liberalism. Not every reader, however, will agree that Hopkins's apostasy also involved an inability to deal with his own "temperament," that, unable to resolve his indiscriminate sexual feeling, Hopkins entered the Roman Communion to crush it. That there was sexual tension is now clear from the full text of the journals and notebooks; what remains to be determined – if it can be – is the extent to which Hopkins's erotic admiration of the young Digby Mackworth Dolben also aided his conversion. Martin, who views Hopkins as a man in emotional turmoil who wrote poems, has argued for Dolben's primacy; White, who finds Hopkins a poet in emotional turmoil, argues for greater complexity.

Hopkins makes a new start (1868–1874) by becoming a Jesuit. From Roehampton outside of London for his novitiate, to Stonyhurst in cold Lancashire for his philosophate, to congenial holidays on the Isle of Man, Hopkins is shown undergoing the rigors of hieratic basic training. The details of what it was like in the mid nineteenth century to become a Jesuit are not pleasant reading; even a sympathetic reader today will find the regimen both masochistic and sadistic. But these uncomfortable details do help explain some of the almost hysterical journal entries. White leavens these disturbing pages by citing a novice from Dennis Meadow's 1953 *Obedient Men,* which asks if one wears a chain *outside* the trousers. It is understandable why Hopkins found the Isle of Man a relief.

Then came three important years ("1874–77, The Poet"). In these sixty compressed pages White examines the rebirth of Hopkins the poet, whose *Wreck of the Deutschland* mystified readers. A biographer of Hopkins is always tempted to go overboard on the poetry, and the most tempting poem with which to do so is *The Wreck of the Deutschland.* If the biographer can pass this dragon, Hopkins's first major poem, without falling into lengthy but biographically irrelevant disquisitions on Mariology and Christology, on prosody, on the height of the tall nun (with whom Hopkins has an affair in a Kingsley Amis novel – so famous has this poem become), and stick to the poem in relation to the poet, then the biography succeeds. White's biography has

done so. He does not ignore the poem; in fact his discussion ranges over eighteen pages but is not merely explication de texte. White links a discussion of Welsh poetics to Hopkins's excessive pastoral scruples about learning the language. And he shows that wreck poems (the *Hesperus* also sinks) were common in the nineteenth century, but to Hopkins's family, since his father was a marine insurer, a sea disaster was a godsend. White concludes that the poem looks forward more to the Dublin years than it reflects the Welsh and that the rejection of the poem by both his puzzled colleagues and unsympathetic superiors set up that barrier between Hopkins's central self and public image which the Dark Sonnets seem to document.

Assigning him to various parochial duties (Hopkins felt himself kicked around, hence part 5's title "Fortune's Football, 1877–1884"), his order eventually and effectively exiled him poetically, socially, and aesthetically to Dublin ("The Stranger"), where only death ended his "near madness and despair" in 1889.

And the poems of his exile are difficult. Granted that there is not a consistent reading of Hopkins's life, that the poet is not some round character in a carefully structured Jamesian novel, still a literary biographer must let a reader know to what extent a poem is autobiographical. If "Carrion Comfort" is an Ignatian exercise on the part of Hopkins, an "attempted self-diagnosis," who then is this "protagonist" who opens the sonnet on the next page of White's biography? This protagonist surfaces also in "I wake and feel the fell of dark" but becomes, two pages later in "Thou art indeed just, Lord," Hopkins the Tennysonian child with "no language but a cry." White wants the speaker of the poem to be three people at the same time: Hopkins, a Jesuit contemplating despair, and the Victorian intellectual undergoing his crisis of faith. But aside from occasionally mixing a persona with an author – assuming the two can, or even should, be separated – White's biography makes the reader knowledgeable about the times and more appreciative of the poet. What reader can ask for more?

If Hopkins is finally getting balanced attention, George Henry Lewes is finally getting attention. Lewes is usually both defined and remembered as George Eliot's other, the ape to her horse. This is unfair to both, and Rosemary Ashton only allows the novelist to begin her career two-thirds of the way through the thorough and entertaining *G. H. Lewes: A Life* (Oxford University Press). The reader who wishes to pursue Lewes only as Eliot's adjunct should reread, as Ashton recommends,

Gordon S. Haight's 1968 biography of Eliot along with his two-volume 1978 edition of the post-1854 Lewes letters. Ashton's argument of when the relationship began forces the reconsideration of the standard chronology of George Eliot. In fact, this biography puts Eliot in her place – and Lewes in his.

Consequently, the reader should not expect a series of trenchant comments on Eliot's *Felix Holt the Radical* (1866) but should admire Ashton's analysis of sixty-three articles, twelve books (including novels), and five plays. In this biography 1866 is remarkable for Lewes's articles on Auguste Comte and Benedict de Spinoza, his trip to Spain with Eliot, and his legitimate children's settling in Natal. Ashton is to be praised for her nine-page chronology, which allows the reader to summarize her material.

The range of Lewes's articles is extraordinary: from his early work on Arabian philosophy for an 1847 *Edinburgh Review* to his last, "On the Dread and Dislike of Science," in the *Fortnightly Review* of 1878, when he was sixty-one. And in between he followed up his 1856 "Sea-side Studies" by enclosing a manuscript called simply "Sketches of Clerical Life" from a friend. John Blackwood accepted both Lewes's remarks on sea anemones and George Eliot's first fiction for the same issue of his magazine.

One emphasis, then, of this biography, is the breadth of Lewes's interests and the extent of his participation in the liberal intellectual life of the mid nineteenth century. The other – and especially interesting if more confusing – emphasis is Lewes's interior life. Even with the pre-1854 letters Haight passed on to Ashton, the interior life of her subject is, as she immediately admits, difficult to reconstruct. Ten years, from 1846 to 1855, of Lewes's journal have been destroyed, no letters between Eliot and Lewes survive (even her journals before 1854 were destroyed at her death by Walter Cross, her husband of less than a year). And worse, there is only one letter from his wife Agnes, who bore him four legitimate children and four more (two of whom he legitimated) to Thornton Hunt. What letters are left, Ashton has read, despite the fact that they are deposited in thirty-six libraries.

Since most will read this because of George Eliot, most will read that part of Ashton's biography which chronicles the beginning of their relationship. Ashton argues that Eliot did not, like some blue-stocking Nora, slam the door when she left John Chapman's erotically crowded house one day in October of 1853 and then move in with Lewes by

noon. The beginning of their affair was earlier, less dramatic, but more discreet. In addition to Eliot's own letters, letters replete with ambiguous remarks about Herbert Spencer and Lewes, and the behavior of Eliot heroines and heroes, Ashton relies on a previously unexamined – and undated – letter of Lewes to F. O. Ward, a friend of his from his medical school days. Ashton found the letters stuck in a first edition of John Forster's *Life of Dickens* (1871–1874) sitting on a shelf at the Harry Ransom Humanities Research Center. Dating the letter by references to Charlotte Brontë's *Villette* (1852), Lewes's future articles on fish, and sexually charged expressions (nicely documented from the work of Eric Partridge), Ashton concludes that their intimacy began in March or April 1853, a good half year before she left Chapman's house in the Strand and over a year before they eloped to the toleration of Weimar and Berlin. That they remained devoted till they died is more important, Ashton agrees, than when they began their devotion. Yet, citing Virginia Woolf, she does "record the atoms as they fall"; Ashton's densely documented recordation and recreation convinces. And she does rein in her speculations about what they said when and to whom and about what. Some of the thirty-one illustrations are familiar, but those of Lewes, megalocephalic, and his oddly dignified wife still attract the eye. The genealogical chart would be more useful at the front of the book, especially since Ashton has discovered Lewes's own illegitimate birth. The footnotes could use running page numbers at the top.

But Lewes's life did not begin with becoming Eliot's lover and then business manager. His unconventionality started with his genes. Ashton is the first biographer to discover a father who deserted both a wife and a mistress; the latter was Lewes's mother. There are not, then, many documents about Lewes's early life on Jersey and perhaps at Boulogne; nor was Lewes forthcoming. Ashton has uncovered the little we know of his early life. Lewes comes into clearer sight in the 1830s, when he joined the radical circles around Leigh Hunt, mostly a group of Shelley sycophants. And given the irregularities of Percy Bysshe Shelley's life, a biography of whom Lewes planned, and the irregularities of Lewes's mother and father, perhaps we should expect that Lewes would not only join Hunt's son Thornton in starting a radical journal, the *Leader,* of which he was literary editor and Thornton political, but that Thornton would join Lewes's wife Agnes. Agnes bore him four bastards, the first only two weeks after the initial issue of the *Leader.* Thornton later challenged Lewes to a duel

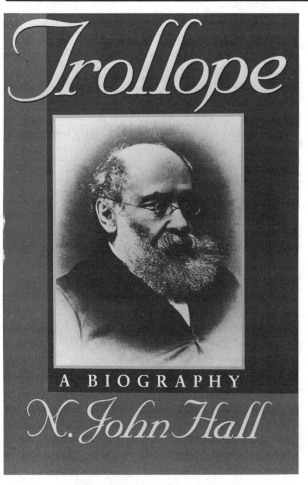

Dust jacket for N. John Hall's biography of the British novelist whose Chronicles of Barsetshire exemplify his belief that "a novel should give a picture of common life enlivened by humor and sweetened by pathos"

over child support. These people were not the young and the restless: they read books. And one, which Lewes reviewed, presents Thornton Hunt's sponging and parasitic father: we can find the father in Horace Skimpole of Charles Dickens's *Bleak House* (1852–1853); the son, Ashton demonstrates, is hidden in some of Lewes's articles.

By the time Chapman introduced him to Eliot in a bookstore in 1851 he was unhappy. But by this date Lewes had taught English in Berlin, where he met Ivan Turgenev; published on French drama in the *Westminster Review,* thanks to John Stuart Mill's good offices; discussed G. W. F. Hegel in the *British and Foreign Review* and George Sand in the *Foreign Quarterly Review*; and published a four-volume history of philosophy. He had written two novels and reviewed many others, especially *Jane Eyre* (1847) and *Bleak House;* his skepticism about Sir William Crookes' spontaneous combustion (for Lewes was scientific as well as literary) temporarily estranged

Dickens. Ashton has collected many of Lewes's articles in her earlier *Versatile Victorian: Selected Critical Writings of G. H. Lewes* (1991); in this biography she provides the reactions of other Victorians to him, and not simply the literary (Anthony Trollope, Thomas Carlyle, Alfred, Lord Tennyson), but the philosophical (Mill, Spencer) and scientific (Sir Richard Owen, T. H. Huxley): the list under "Friendships" in the generally inclusive index presents twenty-six names, most of whom he knew before he met Eliot. Ashton has restored the proper emphasis: Eliot, the managing editor of a journal, left with him; he, a central figure in London's intellectual life, did not leave with her. Despite ill-health and the demands her career made on him – he was able to ask nine thousand pounds for *Romola* (1863) – Lewes continued as a central figure and a more prosperous one. In 1865, the year before *Felix Holt* was published, fourteen years after he met Eliot and thirteen before his death, Trollope offered him, at six hundred pounds annually, the editorship of the new *Fortnightly Review.* The first issue had Walter Bagehot on the English Constitution, Sir John Herschel on atoms, the opening of Trollope's *The Belton Estate,* and Frederic Harrison – the only man to make Procopius dull – on trade unions. This perhaps is Lewes's contribution to nineteenth-century England: the contributors he could assemble.

Trollope, who, like Lewes, knew everyone, said of Lewes that his was "a peculiarly valuable literary life"; so was Trollope's, and so is N. John Hall's *Trollope: A Biography* (Oxford University Press). This year Trollope books have reached a climax. At the present rate we may have as many biographies of Trollope each decade as he wrote novels. Within the last twenty years there has been the gracefully informed, but amazingly ill-documented, *Anthony Trollope* (1971), by James Pope Hennessy, splendid on Ireland since the author's grandfather was probably the model for Phineas Finn; then, published in 1975 and recently reprinted, one of C. P. Snow's last works is an appreciation of the novelist with over one hundred related illustrations (this one has twenty-seven); Robert Super's *Trollope in the Post Office* (1981) was continued in his *Chronicler of Barset* (1988). Hall, the editor of the letters of Trollope, has wisely decided not to write his biography as a response to Super's year-by-year chronicle (but fortunately the running heads keep track of the years); he has opted to take a different approach or series of approaches. Henry James, half in fun, spoke of Trollope's novels as "baggy monsters"; what we have here is also baggy, and all the better for it since it reflects the subject's novels. For those readers who finished all his novels before the age of thirty, can there be too many biographies of a man who wrote nearly fifty novels? Of course not.

When it comes to the novels the reader would be ill advised to read only the three to four pages devoted to a particular work and not the remarks scattered on ten to twelve other pages. The three to four pages of focused attention generally consist of light but expert plot summary joined to a search for the originals of the characters and events. Benjamin Disraeli, Sir John Russell, William Gladstone, and John Bright all appear in the Palliser novels, as does disestablishment in Ireland and the Second Reform Bill. The equating of the real with the fictional began as soon as the novels appeared: there is not too much new here. We then get perhaps a page of succinct literary analysis; Hall finds Trollope more optimistic than many critics, for example, the four weddings at the end of *The Way We Live Now* (1875) are comedic resolution, not ironic overkill. And then, most usefully, Hall provides reception criticism. Here Hall has done his digging: not only does the material presented in Donald Arthur Smalley's *Critical Heritage* appear, but contemporary editorials in the (London) *Times* which bear upon the novels' thematic concerns. Equally valuable are Hall's remarks on specific novels, scattered through the biography. Readers who expect a literary biography to be an introduction to a paperback reprint, with all the material in one place, may find this work a bit wordy. If, however, they pursue the novel through the biography, a fuller understanding emerges. In the discussion of the two Phineas Finn novels (*Phineas Finn* [1867–1869] and *Phineas Redux* [1873–1874]) and *The Way We Live Now*, Hall informs the reader about lodgings in London; anti-Semitism; Trollope's electoral hopes; his similarity to characters in the novels (a rare equation); parallels to his nonfiction articles; what he was paid for each novel; how well the volume was illustrated; and its publishing history. Further, Hall shows how many early novels, even Trollope's first, anticipate the late novels both stylistically and thematically; he also reports where Trollope and some modern readers rank each particular work in the canon. The politicians portrayed fictionally in these novels surface sixteen times in the biography outside the discussion of novels in which they prominently figure – sometimes to dine with Trollope. One consequence of Hall's method is that the later novels into which the earlier ones lead generally get fuller discussion; but Hall has compensated for this. His discussions of early works such as *The Kelleys and the O'Kelleys* (1848) and *The Macdermots of Ballycloran*

(1847) receive almost as much treatment as the "famous" ones. If Hall has favorites, he hides them well.

But much remains hidden in this biography, and this is not necessarily Hall's fault. Though Trollope wrote many letters, they are fairly bland: it is as though he expected his colleagues in the post office to open them. We can go for over sixty pages in Hall's work without seeing the novelist's interior. In the middle of Trollope's career a son emigrates, a niece arrives, a brother marries the sister of Dickens's mistress, but we only have his less-than-revealing letters and public comments. Perhaps because Trollope wrote so much for the public – almost as many articles as novels (fifty), over twenty short stories, and edited journals – he had little time to record his interior life. Hall does locate the most autobiographical elements in the novels: Trollope's failed father in his earliest and most tragic novel, *The Macdermots*; the gaucherie of young men loose in London in *The Three Clerks* (1858) and of Johnny Eames in *The Small House at Allington,* (1862–1864); the tubercular deaths of his sisters in *The Bertrams* (1859) and *Marion Fay* (1882).

From the remarks of Trollope's friends, Hall demonstrates that Trollope shares his characters' public behavior: pigheaded like Dr. Whortle, an early riser like Will Belton, a tourist like George Bertram. The only character whose interior is like Trollope's is probably Dr. Thorne: decayed family, forced to a profession, temperamental, and a push-over when it comes to women. But rather than develop the analogies, Hall investigates copyright, compensation, and the number of editions. That is no doubt what Trollope would prefer, but a modern reader? Hall admits the correspondence between the narrator and author is especially difficult to find in Trollope's case because the novelist's "personality is so elusive." But cannot the works provide some clue? After all, the conflict between father and son has been marked and analyzed in John Stuart Mill's *Autobiography* (1873) and Matthew Arnold's poems; why not in Trollope's novels?

Hall's research is thorough and his use of detail is almost imperial in its lavishness. Before we get to the vicar of Bullhampton, we are treated to a brief literary biography of his original, Norman Mcleod: the Free Church mission attacked the Scotsman architecturally (they built a rival church next door) and the English vicar had to face a Methodist chapel. In addition we learn about Sabbatarianism in Scotland, what a Barony Church is, the problems of editing a journal such as *Good Words,* and the number of bastards born in

Strathbogie. This is a bit too rich. The closer Hall keeps to his subject and his work, the happier the biography. For example, the four accounts we get of Trollope's killing Mrs. Proudie come from contemporary memoirs and an investigation of the manuscript of *The Last Chronicle of Barset* (1866–1867) at Yale. That a biographer would comment on Trollope's letters and editorials in various journals is expected; fortunately Hall investigates the replies to Trollope's often strong opinion in four different periodicals.

Since Hall organizes his biography by place – Harrow, Ireland, and homes in London – maps would have helped. The index is excellent: someone who read the book compiled it. This is important for a novelist, half of whose novels contain a character's name in the title: Miss Mackenzie occurs almost two hundred pages before her eponymous novel. Part of the length of this biography is due to its very completeness: among the four hundred people Trollope ran into and which the index lists, some are bound to be obscure – even to specialists. This entails biographical disquisitions. But one would wish the work no shorter.

After Melchizedek the most famous resident of Salem was the correspondent of Trollope, Nathaniel Hawthorne, but unlike that Old Testament king and the English novelist, Hawthorne never reconciled himself to the present. And the burden of his past is what Edwin Haviland Miller explores in *Salem Is My Dwelling Place* (University of Iowa Press), the exterior past of a Puritan witch-burning generation, the interior past of a deprived childhood. Miller sees Ilbrahim, "The Gentle Boy" (the earliest and most popular story of Hawthorne's during his lifetime), as Hawthorne himself. The literary reading of this story convinces: the focus is on the unloved child, not on religious persecution in the late 1600s nor on motherhood; but Miller's link to Hawthorne's seafaring father who died abroad may cause some readers to pause. But the advantage of this biography lies in what makes us pause: Hawthorne, no less than Poe, demands a psychological biography. Miller has stripped the veil from Mr. Hooper and his creator to present us with men "hesitant, tremulous and often deeply depressed." This biography of displaced parricide, matricide, and fratricide is, as Miller quickly acknowledges, indebted to earlier psychological studies, especially that of Frederick C. Crews's *Sins of the Fathers* (1966). But while indebted, Miller is independent. And, unlike Crews, he has not repented. The child is father to the man throughout Hawthorne's life. Miller, admittedly conflating the last stories

("Grimshawe" and the two Septimus works) finds a final double self-portrait: the Hawthorne who was once Ilbrahim becomes at last Ilbrahim's vacillating and despairing father, Tobias. Has patriarchy replaced Original Sin? This biography may not be an easy read, but it is rarely a dull one.

Miller's earlier work, on Herman Melville and especially Walt Whitman, has prepared him for the problems faced by all Hawthorne biographers. In 1853, before they moved to London, Hawthorne burned all his wife Sophia's letters, letters that no doubt covered his courtship and engagement. In addition, his friends – and all of Hawthorne's friends were loyal – when he said he wanted no biography, obliged as much as they could. Not so his child Julian nor his sister-in-law. In addition, Sophia heavily excised her letters, leaving only parts of about one hundred letters from him. These remnants, when we add them to her surviving fifteen hundred letters and to her journals, can give us some insight – but often more insight into Sophia than Nathaniel. Oddly enough, Miller defends her excisions: she "acted out of love, a deep abiding love. . . . in her excision she was not flouting his will, she followed his example." For a biographer this is special pleading.

There are also the problems of earliest biographies: that of a son is unlikely to provide the truths we seek. The biography by Hawthorne's son Julian was written in the dark shadow of his father's fame and under the influence of Elizabeth Peabody, his mother's sister, a sister who had imagined – and with some cause – sixty years earlier that Hawthorne would marry her. The most remarkable new material which Miller uses to extend the earlier biographies is the unpublished Peabody family letters from the Berg Collection. These letters assist in our understanding Sophia and, consequently, Hawthorne.

This is particularly true of Hawthorne's courtship: both Peabody sisters were confused about Hawthorne's marital intentions, and perhaps even more so as Hawthorne was seeing, or infatuated with, Mary Sparks (née Silsbee). Miller is able to untangle Julian's account, which relied too heavily on the animus and memory of a woman fifty years later. By a judicious use of the (excised) letters, he establishes the confusion of a man torn between the "sophisticated eroticism" of a nineteen-year-old and the "spiritual eroticism" of a woman in her thirties. Miller, locating Silsbee in Zenobia of *The Blithedale Romance* (1852) and in Miriam Schaefer of *The Marble Faun* (1860), suggests that Hawthorne, in his inherited role of Puritan brutalizer, wreaks a secret revenge on Silsbee in these two works. This sort of argument is more convincing in Miller's treatment of "Young Goodman Brown," where there seems to be a clearer case for the overlap of Hawthorne with the protagonist's fear of sexuality.

Though all readers will agree that "Critics must be careful . . . not to impose their own simplifications upon Hawthorne's profound penetration into human depths," sometimes Miller's desire not to impose vitiates his rhetorical effectiveness in analyzing both the life and the works. Why is Richard Manning, Hawthorne's grandfather, only "apparently" benign? Did Hawthorne at times drink too much? Can a biographer be too well mannered? Can a critic fail to make up his mind? In "The Artist of the Beautiful," it does not help to be told that Owen's butterfly represents the soul and immortality and death and the winged phallus. As Miller points out, a Georgia O'Keeffe floral vulva does resemble Rappaccini's plant: this is illuminating in a discussion of "Rappaccini's Daughter." But then Rappaccini "may" intend Giovanni to be Beatrice's (also known as Margaret Fuller) incestuous brother, and her death "may" be the unconscious desire of both her father and her lover/brother. Baglioni "may" be deviant rather than paternal, and the French titles of Hawthorne's stories in the introduction to "Rappaccini's Daughter" "presumably" hide autobiographical intent: the concessive mode four times in two paragraphs is a bit much. And the discovery of three myths in "Alice Doane's Appeal" (Narcissus, Oedipus, and Abraham and Isaac) darkens rather than illuminates Hawthorne's psyche: we are not sure who has slept with or killed whom — and of which gender. Miller is better when his criticism is up front.

While this work has an interior focus, Miller does place Hawthorne within his literary tradition: the successor of Washington Irving, but not as distinctly American as Mark Twain or Melville. Six chapters provide a different angle on Brook Farm, Concord, and the Berkshires. The Peabody letters demonstrate that Carlyle was right about Margaret Fuller. Melville comes off sympathetic, his intuitive analysis of the man and his works remains faultlessly prescient. We also have a clearer view of Hawthorne in the flesh, not only from this volume's photographs but from the remarks of sixteen of Hawthorne's friends about his gait, his gestures, his frowns. Miller is good with the rural, Salem, Brook Farm, and Concord in the 1840s, and the urban, Florence and Rome in the late 1850s, but better with Pearl's forest and the hollows of early Boston.

If, as the jacket says, we have waited ten years for this biography, some time could have been spent to excise the chestnut ("time's winged chariot"), to dump the slang (Melville, completing *Moby-Dick* (1851), was "on a high much of the time"), to elevate the vulgar ("Crack-up," the title of an illuminating final chapter, hardly reflects the subject's psychic turmoil). Further, reference to the Centenary Edition by volume and page only is a bit severe. The 250-item bibliography is clearly complete, but not so the index. It is almost all titles and names: few places are listed, and no themes. There is no "politics, national," "incest, in family . . . in stories," or "transcendentalism." And even the names are not all there: an index that records "Apollo" twenty-one times should not neglect Sophia's use on page 259. But Miller has succeeded. He has avoided both "reductionist debunking" and "hagiography." If biography is "of necessity a fiction," this fiction observes consistency in plot and character.

The question associated with the title of the first chapter of Joyce Warren's *Fanny Fern: An Independent Woman* (Rutgers University Press) is "Who Is Fanny Fern?" Well, Hawthorne did not include her among the damned mob of scribbling women. In fact he praised her *Ruth Hall* (1855). She also wrote "The way to a man's heart is through his stomach." Fern is difficult to place: her writing's lack of sentimentality excludes her from the company of Susan Warner's *Wide, Wide World* (1851) or Maria Cummins's (1854) *Lamp Lighter,* the most recent members of the Other American Renaissance; Fern's heroine's refusal to acquire power by self-abnegation, by retreating into the parlor, distinguishes her from sentimental heroines. The same is true of Fern's life: heroine and novelist were both damned for their lack of filial obedience and femininity.

Despite the maddening lack of a bibliography, Warren's research appears to be extensive, utilizing such resources as the Beinecke Library at Harvard, the Massachusetts Historical Society, the Library of Congress, unpublished manuscripts at Smith College, interviews with a great-grandchild, twenty-four illustrations (but none of the horrid second husband), and copious selections from Fern's novels and columns; all these almost come together to portray Fanny Fern (1811–1872, born Sarah Payson Willis). Generally admitting that she is drawing extensive inferences from Fern's writings, Warren recreates her subject's first marriage from *Ruth Hall* and the second, to a "gross sensualist," from *Rose Clark* (1856). Fern's success with women readers of her time is probably due to her articulate suffering:

the poverty and isolation that followed her first husband's death in 1846, the indifference of her own family, especially her brother, the editor of the *Mirror* – all these are part of *Ruth Hall*. Equally interesting is the information of which we can be sure: that she went from fifty cents for her first article ("The Model Husband," 1851) to one hundred dollars per column of type in 1855, from widowed former seamstress to first female columnist (a mixture of Dorothea Dix and Miss Manners), and from publication in a small Boston paper to an international audience (by 1854, 180,000 copies of *Fern Leaves from Fanny's Portfolio* [1853] and *Little Ferns for Fanny's Little Friends* [1853] were sold in England and America). Her disastrous second marriage in 1849 was at her father's urging: Warren's inferences about her misery from *Rose Clark* are convincing. Her rise to stardom, her removal to New York, her columns for that city's *Ledger* from 1856 to two days before death, these Warren covers well – and from primary sources. Less satisfactory is her treatment of Fern's happy third marriage, when she was forty-four, to a man eleven years her junior, James Parton, who not only reviewed *Jane Eyre* (1847) and praised *Shirley* (1849), but succeeded Poe on the *Evening Mirror*. Here Warren must rely on the accounts of some who disapproved and extrapolate the virtues of Horace Gates, the good guy in *Ruth Hall*.

The chapter on Fern's most famous work, *Ruth Hall,* the work Hawthorne praised (he said it had "character and value") is disorganized; it also appeared earlier in *Style* (1988). Warren is forced to acknowledge that Fern's publishers, in the contract that Fern signed with Mason Brothers, promised to "use extraordinary exertions to promote the sale" of her novel, but she fails to establish the extent to which the novel's success was independent of the publisher's fulsome praise, the sort of hype found on this biography's book jacket. We are told "the novel succeeded because of intrinsic qualities which today still draw readers to *Ruth Hall*. The principal reason for the long-lasting appeal of Fern's novel was her ability to write outside the conventions of the time." True, it sold seventy thousand copies when it was published, but it then remained unreprinted for over three-quarters of a century, and when it was republished in 1986, it was by the publisher of this biography. Where then are these long-lasting appeals?

Ruth Hall, then, is not an obscure, but an unfamiliar novel. In the biography we should not have to read sections on the publisher and the critics before we get the plot summary. And even when we get it, we may be unsure of what happened unless we have paid very close attention to the preceding 120 pages in which Warren uses the novel to explicate the life. Ruth's husband dies, she then meets a variety of people from "minority groups and the uneducated classes," takes up the practice of journalism (Fern is able to pay off old scores in this roman à clef), enters "the competitive male world, and prevails in it," and ends up with not a new husband (Warren makes this very clear) but with ten thousand dollars in bank stock. There are subplots. There is also a fire.

Warren's critical remarks consist of a considered defense of the novel's short chapters and abrupt changes of tone, an unconvincing analysis of the novel's alleged radical stylistic departure from other popular nineteenth-century fiction (Warren cites a few words from the text to establish "terseness"), and too often a conflation of Fern, Ruth, and miscellaneous foreigners. An example of this critical approach reads:

> Fern realized that the hierarchical structure that she and other women had been conditioned to believe was fixed by God and Nature was, in fact, a construct, that is, a power system constructed by, and designed to preserve the power of, those in power.... Fern's novel can be read as a portrayal of the Derridaean dismantling of the first principle.

This is the fervor of a convert, not the judgment of a biographer. And this sort of polemic mars the value of her work – and the biography has merit. But the epilogue is particularly offensive: not because of any special critical slant, but simply because of otiose and flabby prose whose clichés ("escalating violence ... gory statistics") are balanced by etymological horrors ("phallogocentric"). But perhaps this reviewer is guilty of that hapax legomenon. Warren is much better, and this is the value of her biography, when she examines reception criticism and untangles literary feuds. Her explanation of Fern's feud with Whitman, to whom she first gave praise and then money, is most convincing: her list of six reasons why she liked him is slightly mechanical but perceptive. Chapter 17 offers gems from Fern's wisdom on literature, children, domesticity, and social reform. Her opinions are interesting and, Warren insists, correct.

Perhaps too often biography gives way to hagiography, as the interests of author and subject coincide. The worse Warren makes Fern's detractors appear, the better Fern looks. Her brother Nathaniel (whom Poe called an estimable man in his private relations) had a good feel for the literary market: his rejection of her first works may have been justified. Also, the better Warren makes Fern's friends look, the better Fern looks. Fern's friend and correspondent. Gen. Benjamin Butler is actually "Beast Butler," the military governor of occupied New Orleans who ordered his troops to treat the patriotic ladies of that city as whores – surely a clear case of the patriarchy Warren finds Fern condemning. This biography, nevertheless, is valuable.

More valuable, sometimes with the same cast, is Kenneth Silverman's *Edgar A. Poe: Mournful and Never-Ending Remembrance* (HarperCollins), a psychological study of the man and his works. More than Warren's life of Fanny Fern, this book presents us with the literary life of mid-nineteenth-century America, not simply New York and Boston, but Richmond, Baltimore, Washington, and Philadelphia. And see these cities' critics: Nathaniel Willis (Fern's brother who published "The Raven" and to whom Poe's aunt applied for details of Poe's last days); Evert Duyckinck, who helped Poe publish, but from whose "Young American" movement he kept aloof; and Horace Greeley, who lent him fifty dollars. Then there are those Poe disliked partially because he was a Southerner: Hawthorne, Alcott, Ralph Waldo Emerson, and the whole Concord and Cambridge crowd including Margaret Fuller, whose request that Poe return another's indiscreet letters led to a brawl (Poe lied about it, Silverman concludes). And of course, the infamous feud or even war with Henry Wadsworth Longfellow: Poe called him a metrically incompetent, morally tainted plagiarist: Silverman nicely summarizes this war in ten succinct pages. In addition to the well-known figures above, the biographer brings out the less familiar: William Gilmore Simms, whose novel Poe harshly criticized in 1835 but who tried to assist him ten years later; Charles Frederick Briggs, whose *Broadway Journal* published forty of Poe's tales and which Poe later and disastrously mismanaged; the publisher Rufus Wilmot Griswold, who bribed Poe successfully to puff his creations and who forty days after his own wife's death bribed the sexton to open her coffin, kissed her forehead, and fainted. Details such as these, though discovered fifty years ago, do flesh out the nineteenth-century cult of the dead: neither Poe nor Dante Gabriel Rossetti seem that bizarre.

The notes are difficult to use. References follow the first words of paragraphs from the text, which are reprinted in heavy type; but one page of notes can cover as many as ten pages of text. And since there are no footnotes in the text, it is difficult to decide what might be documented. Further, since there is no separate bibliography, the references in

Dust jacket for Kenneth Silverman's psychological biography of the American poet and fiction writer who invented the detective story

the notes, though not cryptic, are heavily abbreviated. It is a shame HarperCollins did not spend the money for a clearer documentation. But the notes are a disparate treasury of further suggestions. In a half page we begin with Arthur Hobson Quinn's *Life* of 1941 and Dwigney Thomas and David Kelly Jackson's *The Poe Log* for the balloon hoax in the *New York Sun,* move to "Notes on Flying" from the *Psychoanalytic Quarterly* of 1983, and wind up with a book of essays on Jacques Lacan, Jacques Derrida, and C. Auguste Dupin the detective, who, Silverman reminds us, first smoked a pipe.

This biography often uses psychological methods of interpretation for two reasons: Poe can disappear from recorded sight for over two years and a biographer has to talk of something, and Poe wrote Poe's strange short stories and poems. Silverman insists that his biography is "not an argument but a narrative," and further, that he is not out to prove any particular psychoanalytic theory. Though

Silverman reserves his heaviest psychological criticism of Poe's writings for the notes, this is not true of his consideration of events in Poe's life. A man who marries a thirteen-year-old – but only for *her* happiness, he claimed – and an author who buries people alive calls for analysis. At times it seems as though the biographer despairs of making sense of Poe. This is particularly true of the discussions of the murky romances with Fanny Osgood and Elizabeth Ellet. Silverman argues that the consequences of Poe's "moral primness and complex aversion" lead him "to depict women as far-off statues, fearful revenants, or pimply hags." Fortunately Silverman is more thorough when Poe comes to Sarah Helen Whitman, née Power: Poe recycled his Helen poems for her; she played with power in her poems to him. After two days he proposed to her in a cemetery. But the marriage between the transcendental – and rich – friend of Margaret Fuller and the poor Virginian roué was not made in the heavens of Whitman's astrological speculations. Silverman re-creates what Poe saw and sympathetically accounts for what he chose not to see. The reader realizes that Poe lived his fiction. The reader also comes to appreciate Silverman's analysis of Poe's poetry and fiction: the flat declarative sentences of the tales forecast modern films of violence; his child-bride's illness is the Red Death; no audience can be expected to digest the obscure equivalent of twenty sonnets (the complete "Al Aaraff"); Poe's gothic is not everyone's, and style can determine authorship in the Longfellow wars. Some of this is new, some is not, and some is overstated (Silverman presents Poe as the first writer in English to use poetic techniques in prose fiction), but Silverman has assembled the details of Poe's life and works in such a way that the psychological complexities of the man and his writings are the clearest we are likely to have them in this well-written literary biography.

Unlike G. H. Lewes, significant in his own right, Olivia ("Livy") Langdon Clemens might have remained as only a nice, rich girl from Elmira, New York, whose neighbors were Thomas K. Beecher, Julia Ward Beecher, and Harriet Beecher Stowe. But then she married Mark Twain, and now, ninety years after her death, we have her biography in Resa Willis's *Mark and Livy: The Love Story of Mark Twain and the Woman Who Almost Tamed Him* (Atheneum). Twain's family relations were treated lightly in 1960 by Caroline Harnsberger in her *Mark Twain, Family Man*, but this is the first study of Twain's wife. The two recent volumes of Twain's reedited letters from the years 1853 to 1868 (University of California Press) have also assisted Willis

though they end a year before his marriage. Her further use of the earlier but standard biography by Albert Bigelow Paine (1912) is judicious. Willis has mastered much new material: Livy's mother's diary, and especially Livy's letters to her mother (the letters are now at the University of California, Berkeley), and some of the Stowe family papers. Now that many of the facts are assembled, it is unlikely another study will be needed. Livy had no insides – though this is not the impression the biographer wished to give. A reader might hope that this biography would correct the impression that Livy was the censor of Twain, that – to exaggerate – had she not censored him, Huck Finn would speak with the verbal exuberance and perhaps about the same subjects found in Twain's *1601*. Oddly enough, it seems Twain censored Livy's reading.

And, to the charge that Livy censored, Willis argues neither for guilt or innocence – she just ignores the subject. This is good politics but bad biography. But she also ignores most literary matters in this serviceable biography of a sickly lady whose husband made poor financial decisions. Two generations ago Van Wyck Brooks insisted of Twain that "from the moment of his marriage his artistic integrity had been destroyed" – an obviously exaggerated claim based on a revisionist but straight reading of Twain's *Autobiography* (1924). Willis's reading of the *Autobiography* is not revisionist. In fact, Willis so scrupulously avoids accusing Livy of any malign literary influence that she is led to ignore what would interest any reader of Twain. In 1939 Livy's family house, set on its own block, was pulled down, exposing a tunnel which led to the Beechers' Park Church, a stop on the Underground Railroad. Livy's family was thoroughly abolitionist. Can this explain why Twain might have found her interesting? Twain quoted his wife to William Dean Howells in a published letter which Willis quotes but does not date: "I will give you a motto [said Livy to Twain], & it will be useful to you if you will adopt it: 'Consider every man colored till he is proven white.' " Could this be the ironic donee for *Puddin'head Wilson*? Not to this biographer. Of the 280 pages of narrative, perhaps forty-four mention Twain's writings; a mention being a reference to the circumstances under which he wrote: where, what sort of weather, perhaps what he was paid. After the *Autobiography,* referred to thirteen times, *Huckleberry Finn* and *The Prince and the Pauper* receive the most mention. This is not to say this biography is without human interest. It records Twain's excessive, even for the nineteenth century, grief; his daughter's musical career and marriage to Ossip

Gobrilowitsch; Gandhi guiding them through Hindu temples; a house-slippered but gaga novelist, once Livy's Sunday school teacher, asking strangers if they had read her book *Uncle Tom's Cabin.* But Livy herself is of little literary interest: she had a fine instinct for the cliché as her commonplace book witnesses. This, forgivable and understandable in adolescence – for who under twenty-five might not underline "A thing of beauty is a joy forever"? – is less charming in an adult.

Livy and the biography are best when Twain, having poured money into the infamous typewriter scheme, goes broke. He is one hundred thousand dollars in debt at the age of fifty. Though his salvation at the hands of a vice-president of Standard Oil has been told before, Willis uses unpublished letters to flesh out the emotional consequences of bankruptcy. In their moral heroism in paying off the creditors we are reminded of Walter Scott. Fortunately Twain lectured rather than wrote to pay his debts. Willis has written a useful book; Atheneum has taken pains with its production. But we lack an interior view of Clemens and his bride. Willis takes her title, second hand, from a Victorian sex manual: "in marrying, they have simply captured a wild animal . . . the taming of which is to be a life work of the woman"; her title promises a taming almost never seen.

In 1897 Rebecca Harding Davis remarked, in print, on Walt Whitman's being "coarse and vulgar by breeding" (she also detested Bronson Alcott). Ten years earlier Whitman, after being interviewed by her twenty-three-year-old son Richard, had admitted that "such tall, wholesome looking fellows are rare among American youngsters." Richard approved of his mother's judgment, calling it a "coup de grace"; he would probably have also approved of Whitman's praise. It is a mark of Arthur Lubow's thoroughness in *The Reporter Who Would Be King: A Biography of Richard Harding Davis* (Scribners) that he can join and document the relations between these three writers. Rebecca, whose "Life in the Iron Mills" (1861) is almost forgotten and whose advice (don't sell your talent) her son too often ignored, influenced, or, better, repressed her son for decades – along with her other children. Whitman's praise remains, though the adolescent and his prose have almost vanished one hundred years later. It is this vanished adolescent face, both of RHD – as he came to be called – and of America from 1864 to 1916 that Lubow recalls in this needed study. Davis survives today only as a simulacrum: Roland Headly in the comic strip *Doonesbury.*

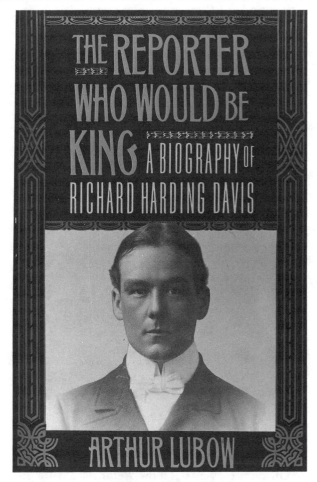

Dust jacket for Arthur Lubow's biography of the American writer who achieved fame as a war correspondent and invented the fictional debonair male counterpart to the turn-of-the-century Gibson girl

And what a face it was. Its jaw had its antetype in the prognathous fish of the Silurian and later Hapsburgs: its massive squareness matched those massive bosoms drawn by his friend Charles Dana Gibson. It is nicely reproduced along with three other line drawings and thirty-six photographs, all of which help define Davis's appearance. And appearance it is, Lubow argues: no one who looked that good could write that well. Hence, his journalism will survive, but not his fiction.

Gerald Langford's impressionistic *RHD Years* was fine when it came out in 1961, but the recent interest in turn-of-the-century America calls for re-evaluations of what have been seen as minor talents. Lubow's biography is an extraordinary improvement on earlier works: he has interviewed survivors, explored publishers' archives, checked the text of the letters at the University of Virginia, consulted those owned by Davis's grandson, and is the first to cite those of Davis's wife and mother-in-law. Lubow's task involved organizing the 350 men and gentlemen, women and ladies, presidents and kings whom Davis met over a fifty-year period. In fact, so dense is this writer's life that there should have been a yearly chronology some place in the biography: too often one must backtrack ten pages to discover what year is being discussed. The index needs improvement. Lubow's narrative line is clear and not loaded down with irrelevant details. Lubow writes well: "The fighting in Greece [the Greco-Turkish war of 1896–1897] was not only chivalrous, it was rare"; but sometimes too well: "His was the unexamined life."

The outline of Davis's active life can be read on the front pages of newspapers, from the Johnstown Flood, his first big story (and one for which he was not prepared: he ran out of white shirts), to the hypersartorial elegance of the Spanish-American War (the jacket photo looks like a parody of Abercrombie and Fitch). If there was a war in South Africa, Manchuria, Cuba, or Mexico he was there and probably comfortably so; if there was a pageant, he viewed it: he saw Victoria's Jubilee, and – more impressive because of clever bribery – he was one of fewer than ten Americans to see the coronation of Nicholas II. The coronation took five hours; William Randolph Hearst took two full pages to report it. On public events Lubow is thorough: for instance, he read eighteen stories in the New York *Evening Sun* to cover Davis's coverage of New York's first electrocution, in 1889.

Lubow's biography is especially rich in what had come to be called "period details," for example, that Davis, returning from Panama, introduced the avocado to Charles Delmonico – the rest is culinary history. But Lubow's details are not merely decorative, but important, for they are based on thorough archival digging. This is particularly true of what Davis made. In 1887, when Davis started, cub reporters made thirty dollars a week; seven years later Hearst paid him five hundred dollars to cover the 1895 Harvard-Princeton game: the edition sold out – but we do not learn who won. A year later Hearst paid him three thousand dollars a month to cover the war in Cuba; *Collier's* paid one thousand dollars a week for coverage of the Russo-Japanese War in 1904–1905; the *Tribune* paid the same for coverage of the Mexican troubles (Tampico) in 1914. And having written so much (his collected works came to twelve weighty volumes in 1916), Scribners not only paid him royalties of twenty thousand dollars for a six-volume edition of his

writings in 1905, but offered three thousand dollars for a series of articles; the total of forty thousand words was later published as a book with a 15 percent royalty. When it now takes us fifteen dollars to buy what cost RHD one, we must ask: does Wolf Blitzer do so well? and can he write? Lubow is excellent, then, not only on wars and casualties but press wars and compensation: he shows that the blockbuster and its publicity predate World War I. However, when a biographer remarks that writers tend to mortgage their futures to country estates, the reader should expect to learn what Davis paid for his 204-acre Crossroads Farm in the wilds of Westchester.

Lubow's biography works when his details support his narrative. The same is true of the useful excerpts Lubow presents from Davis's journalism: the last cigarette before the firing squad, Theodore Roosevelt's blue polka-dot handkerchief in the hot green tropics, the monotonous gray of the uniforms invading Brussels. The last account is still anthologized. Of all the chapters dealing with his journalism the account of the Spanish-American War is the best. It marks, Lubow insists, the high point of Davis's career as a journalist, for he found the hero America needed and help boost him to the presidency. Even though Theodore Roosevelt privately called Davis "an everlasting cad," both knew when they found symbiotic excellence, and both supported their mutual distortions of history. Lubow is thorough, balanced, and sardonic about Roosevelt, about Davis as his toadyish publicist, and about the War Department. A map would be further evidence for the reader that the Rough Riders did not go up San Juan Hill as much as they stumbled into the ambush of Las Guásimas.

But by 1919, less than a generation later, younger writers saw not the specific detail, but "shrapnel, chivalry, sauce mousseline" – unfairly, as Lubow points out. Lubow also points out – and perhaps Davis too often becomes an unwitting prophetic figure in this biography – that Davis was the first war correspondent to realize how the spread of electronic media (cables in the instance of the 1905 Russo-Japanese War) allows governments to manipulate the once-free reporters.

The biography is less successful with Davis's private life. There seem to be valid reasons. Davis's first wife enjoyed painting portraits of women; with her he shared dog breeding and billiards but not conjugal relations. She survived until 1955, and her companion still lives. Davis, like his sister Nora (a "dear friend" of his wife, Lubow hints), entered, apparently well aware, into marriages which excluded marital relations. His sister's ended in scandal: her husband had one day to leave England. Davis's ended in divorce. Lubow is unclear about much of this: surely he could have quoted from the newspaper accounts he footnotes. But perhaps there is another reason for the lack of clarity: Davis had no private life for he suffered from chivalrous neurasthenia, the cult of the male virgin.

Davis's fiction is like his private life: there is little interior. Disguises, cases of mistaken identity, chivalrous devotion, and insouciant boulevardiers appear again and again for thirty years. Lubow dismisses the novels but suggests some short stories deserve a second look. Worthy of a second look in this biography are Davis's encounters with Stephen Crane in Greece and Cuba and Jack London in Japan. And this is the importance of Davis and a biography of him: the peripheral view provides scale.

Most readers will have to search their memories twice for John Loughery's *Alias S. S. Van Dine* (Scribners). First one recalls what the dust jacket announces, "The Man who Created Philo Vance," and then one tries to place the real author. The front cover's inner flap tells us: Willard Huntington Wright (1887–1939); the back cover has a coupon for a free Philo Vance mystery. But the reader will get more than a freebie: Loughery's book covers the fight for modern art in pre–World War I America when Wright headed recon for the avant-garde; the change in sexual mores (Wright was a lecher and later a drug addict); the rise of the detective novel, a genre to which Wright added wit; and how to sell out to Hollywood. Wright's generation follows Richard Harding Davis's: they have so little in common that neither appears in the index of the other's biography.

Of course, Wright was not the only querulous intellectual before World War I – his colleagues on the *Smart Set* included H. L. Mencken and George Jean Nathan – but he was the most urbane and rude. Loughery begins with Wright's brief editorship of that magazine in 1913: he had arranged for the publication of one poem by William Butler Yeats, ten by Ezra Pound, and two stories by D. H. Lawrence. The poems made it into print, some readers thinking those of Pound were a joke played by the editor; the owner rejected Lawrence's "The Prussian Officer" and Robert Frost's "Death of the Hired Man" and then fired Wright for financial improprieties – Mencken agreed he had to go. Wright could spot winners even if he had had only two courses at Harvard: in one, Charles Townsend Copeland, the teacher of T. S. Eliot, John Dos Passos, and Walter Lippmann, gave him an "A"; he

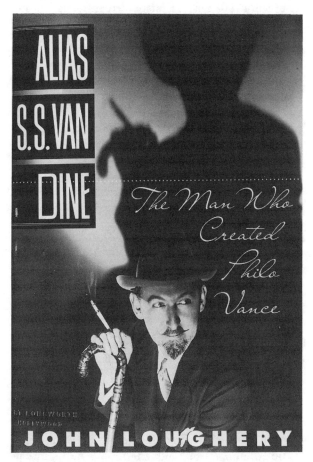

Dust jacket for John Loughery's biography of Willard Huntington Wright, who wrote as S. S. Van Dine

was dismissed from the other, and the college, for allegedly showing up in class with a glass of absinthe. His services to literature are sure, but the reader and Loughery both wonder if Wright were guided by shock value rather than a disinterested recognition of merit. Too often Wright wished to prove that sex could exist in literature.

The biographer is also art critic for the *Hudson Review,* and his expertise makes sense of a forgotten movement, Synchromism, best seen, Loughery argues, as an attitude toward painting rather than a doctrinaire school. Among the leaders of Synchromism was Wright's brother Stanton Macdonald-Wright, who survived as a professor and whose widow Loughery interviewed in Beverly Hills. And since Wright's brother was part of the prewar art world, the chapters devoted to the avant-garde picture a vanished world: the Armory Show, when cubists invaded the New World, is notorious; less memorable are the Orphists of Synchromism. The claims that Wright's *Modern Painting: Its Tendency and Meaning* (1915) foresaw even beyond the color-field art of the 1960s may be misplaced enthusiasm, but Wright's service to the art world is clear.

What this sympathetic biography also makes clear is that a man of letters could not survive in America. Today universities pick up the slack; in 1926 Warren G. Harding's normalcy paid little. So two-thirds through his life (at age thirty-seven) and two-thirds through this biography (page 170), Wright, as S. S. Van Dine, begins the first of nine splendid murder mysteries, one, *The "Canary" Murder Case* (1927), selling twenty thousand copies in one week and ranked by William Lyon Phelps as one of the ten best novels of 1927. Fame and the famous followed: lunch with Dorothy Parker, trysts with starlets, friendship with stars. There are fine pictures of both Basil Rathbone and William Powell as Philo Vance. But then came new people: Dorothy Sayers, the translator of Dante; Nero Wolfe, the stay-at-home raiser of orchids. An epicene Lord Peter, a philistine Archie, and finally Sam Spade (all "booze and erections") destroy his popularity. The final two chapters are sad. Everything runs backwards: Wright turns his failed screenplays into failing novels. His life is the reverse of the next novelist mentioned in this essay.

When Rabbi Simeon, in order to preserve the tradition of the Pentateuch's Mosaic authorship, insisted that Moses wrote of his death, but wept while he did so, one understands the rabbi's moral intent though one may probably dismiss his facts. When Carole Angier insists that in 1931 Jean Rhys in *After Leaving Mr Mackenzie* prophetically and "perfectly" describes the last months of her dying in the winter of 1977–1978, we realize that the elements between the conjunction in this biography's title, *Jean Rhys, Life and Work* (Little, Brown) overlap to the point of equation. This gives us over 650 pages of life documented by work, and the works are fiction. This would be fine if we have read lots of Rhys, but most of us know only *The Wide Sargasso Sea* (1966) — and that after having read Charlotte Brontë's *Jane Eyre* – and perhaps some of the stories republished by Norton ten years ago. So when Angier cites even those works by Rhys recently reprinted by Penguin, which also published Angier's short study of Rhys in 1985, some titles may not be familiar. And we certainly have not read material still in manuscript held by Rhys's literary executor which even the biographer has some doubts about.

The initial chapters of this biography proceed clearly: family and birth in Dominica, schooling in London, rejection from Beerbohm Tree's acting academy for her accent. But then the confusion and overlapping begin. Jean, chorus girl and part-time

worker in the sex industry ("*demi-monde*") of London, meets "the love of her life" at a supper party after the show, "just the way it was meant to happen." Angier's research is admirable: an interview in 1984 with Rhys's lover's surviving nephew, with the namesake of his cousin in 1984 (seventy-two years later), and with three others; obituaries in the Times, Edwardian play bills, a history of Hambros Bank, both *Burkes,* a manuscript at Tulsa, and a manuscript of *Recollections* sent by Rhys to Angier. The biographer has discovered much that is germane: Rhys's lover's name, Lancelot Grey Hugh Smith; his profession, broker; his emotional state, a failed engagement to a Hambro daughter. And there is much that is not: one brother was an admiral, another an admiral and a Knight of the British Empire and a commander of the guard at Queen Victoria's funeral, and thirty-five acres surrounded their family home. But then the works enter. Extrapolating from *Voyage in the Dark* (1934), *Good Morning, Midnight* (1939), *Triple Sec* (an unpublished novel-cum-diary), and the words of Rochester from *The Wide Sargasso Sea*, we learn that Lancelot was not a legman, but an elegant, distinguished, and polite gentleman who loved Rhys reluctantly and confusedly; she would play dress up: a little girl in a white frock, a lady in a black velvet dress, a woman in a tight blue dress. When Angier cites and paraphrases the above works, this reader is hard put to keep the equations going between people and characters: Julian, Lancelot, Jean, Walter, Suzy, Guy, Tony, Anna – all merge, alas. And then the trusting biographer enters:

> But I think he had accepted the code of chivalry . . . Lancelot was a dreamer, like Jean, and took seriously the ideals of service, charity, and the obligations of power. He could rescue and raise her, he could treat her like a child, a goddess and a slave.

The story of a forty-year-old stockbroker and a twenty-year-old chorus girl became what might be expected: not the languorous, if slightly soiled, fatal eroticism of Alfred, Lord Tennyson's *Lancelot and Elaine,* but a *Pretty Woman* with a realistic ending: he dumped her and went to New York. But Jean Rhys did not expect this, nor apparently did Angier.

Rhys continues dancing, has engagements during the War, meets the Dutchman John Lenglet: their child, kept near an open window in January, dies in the hospital. Was Rhys responsible? At crucial – because moral – points like this the biographer enters: "I think the death of her first child was one of the sorrows of her life; but most of her sorrows were part guilt, and so was this one." So it was manslaughter not infanticide: is this a biography or a brief ? The fifty pages on Ford Madox Ford (Beast to her Beauty) are not so much morally as sexually complex. Angier is faced with four people, three of whom are "novelists, fantasists, and sometimes plain liars" (Ford wrote *When the Wicked Man* [1931], Lenglet, "Sous les Verrons," and Rhys, *Postures* [1928]); the fourth, Stella Bowen, Ford's mistress, covered the same ground as the above novels in her angry autobiography *Drawn from Life* (1984).

It takes courage and organization to write a life of Rhys, especially as she goes through several husbands: her second, Leslie Tilden Smith, seems a quiet, dull sort hardly visible in her fiction. Yet it is during this marriage that Rhys begins to become what readers will see as a brick-throwing, legally incompetent, foul-mouthed drunk — yet still a genius, or, as the biographer explains, "her most primitive, most lawless, most repressed self," emerged. Much of her later life — after World War II — is the triumph of the "hidden savage below" over "the lady above" to the delight of court reporters, dismay of her friends, and fear of her neighbors.

Angier, in separate chapters, spends between thirty-five and fifty pages on each of Rhys's novels; if we count the incidental discussion of them, a good third of this volume is literary criticism. And her bibliography is impressive: more than two hundred articles and twenty-four books (half of which were published within the last ten years; Rhys is a timely subject). Angier sees *The Wide Sargasso Sea* as Rhys's triumph: only in this novel did Rhys achieve artistic control over her self-pity. This lack of control injured her earlier novels, Angier argues, for Rhys was the rejected child of *Voyage in the Dark*, the suffering Julia in *After Leaving Mr Mackenzie,* the hating Sasha and Marya of *Good Morning, Midnight,* the betrayed lover of *Postures*. But, unlike many critics, Angier sees no progress from male rejection to eventual compassion between men and women. Just as the biography mixes life and works, so art and life get mixed up. Angier does not like Rochester in or out of a novel, and as for Jane Eyre, she is "plain and not at all chic [unlike mad Antoinette and Jean Rhys], but she gets Rochester because she is better at handling men." Further, Brontë's Bertha burns down the house, unlike Rhys's Antoinette. This section bears rereading. Better, or at least less controversial, is her sensitive analysis of the novel's language and imagery.

When the novel came out in October 1966, so did Rhys after years of obscurity. The fifty pages devoted to the very writing of this complex novel

reveal the appalling emotional and physical privation Rhys suffered, and she was seventy at the time. No one, having read this chapter, will wish to rent a cottage in Devon. It was Rhys's luck — something Angier sees as a pattern — to have one or two sympathetic people in the village of Cheriton Fitzpaine, and of these few — for other families thought her mad — one, the vicar, became her editor and rescuer. The last decade of her life brought her fame, republication, prizes, travel, and, for the first time in forty years, money. But, as Angier says — and in italics — of this woman who lived for "pleasure and writing": *It had all come too late.*

Little, Brown are generous in publishing a 750-page biography which, though it deserves a commercial success, may not achieve it. This sounds like ingratitude, but they could have gone a bit further, perhaps one more signature. The notes are not concise but squished. The forty-six published stories are alphabetically abbreviated so that "I Used to Live Here Once" looks like a Thracian war cry, IUTLHO; "Rapunzel, Rapunzel" like an MTV special, Rap Rap. One could live with this — and even with no date of publication — if they were listed alphabetically and not in the order of their occurrence in the text. With names it is worse: seventy-five people are listed by initials in twenty-six lines of type and again by order of their occurrence in the text. The thoroughness of Angier's research is almost obviated by the awkwardness of her citations. Separating authorial and fictive intrusion from the narrative of this work is difficult, but what remains is much like a Rhys novel, a dark triumph.

Antonia White's *Frost in May* had a certain critical success when it appeared in 1931 as did Jean Rhys's *After Leaving Mr Mackenzie;* the same will be true of these *Diaries, 1926–1957* (Viking, Penguin). They cover White's interior life from the age of twenty-seven to age fifty-eight. And this is only the first volume; the second will go to her death in 1980. We see her interior to the point of our stultification. The republication of her 1931 best-seller along with the next three novels (all written twenty years later) has less to do with literary merit, I suspect, than with devotion and friendship. Her companion for her last two years was the publisher of Virago Press.

Hers was not the happiest of families, neither that of Antonia and her parents nor that of Antonia and her children by various fathers. It is her daughter Susan Glossop/Hopkinson Chitty who has edited forty notebooks, a million words, into two volumes of 125,000 words each. She has also provided us with 112 brief biographical sketches of people —

and two cats – who, we suppose, figure in the diary. Some entries are brief: of a Chelsea neighbor, Betty Gill, we learn she "used to do a dance dressed in muff " – that is it; nor do we find this dancing in the text. The editor tells on page 172 of a critic for the *Observer* who was "conducting an affair" with another *Observer* critic's wife "in the basement"; but on page 330, he "courted her secretly at night in the kitchen," and White served as chaperon. I think it does make a difference, if not in morality at least in comfort. And I know it makes a difference that the diaries, as edited by her daughter, contain no mention of this unobserved affair. And, since Dylan and Caitlin Thomas were staying at the same house, either above stairs or in another room, what did they think? The diary is silent. Actually, there are two other diaries mixed in with the forty notebooks, one on her analysis, the other, originally in French, on her erotic life. Both bore. White was right when she said sex is not indecent but most writing about it is.

So what is Chitty's editorial point? I am not sure. Do not, then, assume the biographical sketches are completed in the diary. The same is true of the index. What we learn about literary figures from the 1930s hardly approaches the anecdotal. Meetings with Djuna Barnes and Peggy Guggenheim must have been interesting, but not in these entries. The editor admits that these diaries "are not exclusively for the literary. Life keeps breaking in." What then do we have? The guilty torments inflicted by a fanatical inability to come to terms with sex, Roman Catholicism, and analysis. And of her struggles in the pew, on the couch, and in the bed, it is with the first that she shows the most insight. Some of the diaries reveal, others of them embarrass, and some do both. The reader further interested in White's life may wish to read the 1988 recollections of Susan Chitty's half-sister, *Nothing to Forgive; a Daughter's Life of Antonia White*.

If it takes three hours and forty minutes for a motion picture to realize a huge novel, we should not be surprised it took Darden Asbury Pyron almost a quarter of a million words to write *Southern Daughter: The Life of Margaret Mitchell* (Oxford University Press) and 1,237 footnotes to document his witty and comprehensive biography. The first writer to attempt turning *Gone With the Wind* into a film, Sidney Howard, despaired: the novel did everything "at least twice," he complained. He was fired, as were F. Scott Fitzgerald and Ben Hecht. This biography does everything at least once, and once is enough. But, like the movie, we would not want it any shorter. Pyron has written more than a life: he has recreated the moral climate of the 1930s

in the South and the quarter century that lead to that extraordinary decade. If *Gone With the Wind* "blotted out the stigma of Appomattox," one explicit aim of this biography is to rescue Mitchell and her novel from what Pyron sees as critical contempt, a contempt ironically arising from the same region: the South gave us the New Criticism, too. But with the rise of Pop and American Studies, Pyron's defense sounds a bit shrill.

Atlanta, like Los Angeles in the 1950s, is filling up with foreigners; one of Pyron's tasks is to show us the city Mitchell's family helped build after the Civil War but before Peachtree Center. He has succeeded not only because his family is southern, but because he has read everything Mitchell wrote: her journalism for the *Atlanta Journal,* hundreds of letters, tens of scrapbooks. This rarely consulted material is at Emory University, the University of Georgia, the Atlanta Historical Society, and the New York Public Library. He talked with survivors: her family and fellow debutantes are remarkably long lived. And, equally important, he read what she read. So we get both empirical precision, including streets, food, and hairnets, and suggestive analysis. Pyron's young Mitchell is a mixture, or, as one called her, "a babyfaced little vamp," with both a longing for male attention and a fear of sexuality. After a few years at Smith College she returned to Atlanta and boasted of a chaste stable of men between the ages of nineteen and thirty. A notorious debutante, the ushers at her first marriage were former suitors. That lasted ten months and forced her to work: her four years on the *Atlanta Journal* exposed her, Pyron argues, to the reality behind the magnolia. Her collection of books with curious engravings also fleshed out her knowledge. A second marriage, to John Marsh, was made in heaven: he was a lawyer, a copy editor, and a proofreader who let her alone to write, in secret, what one close friend called, half-kidding, the Great American Novel. The rest, as David Selznick would say, is history. In 1989 dollars *Gone With the Wind* has made $800 million.

The chapter on the film's gestation ("Hollywood Follies") and the next on its birth in Atlanta ("Pee Soup") show us two cities pursuing impossible beauty and impossible history. Mitchell reacted with horror and delight; so will the pleased readers of this biography. Blacks were superebonized, pillars multiplied like virulent bacilli, and Selznick's work schedule began with the burning of Atlanta. And though these chapters will interest the general reader, the following postwar chapters will terrify anyone who has signed a contract with a publisher.

The thirty-five photographs give us Mitchell, her family, stills from *Gone With the Wind* (now owned by another Atlantan, Ted Turner), and, amazingly, the very young Martin Luther King, Jr., at the Junior League's Charity Ball; he appears with the choir of the Ebenezer Baptist Church who, like him, are in slave costume.

If the documentation for *Southern Daughter* is thorough, that for Anne M. Wyatt-Brown's *Barbara Pym: A Critical Biography* (University of Missouri Press) looks equally impressive: 20 percent of the book is documentation, including a bibliography of almost two hundred items spread over thirty-three pages. But it is not equally impressive: there is simply not that much on Pym as Pym. What then does the bibliography offer us? A selection of psychological studies Wyatt-Brown consulted and then cited in this attenuated and fleshless biography. Can one imagine a Dickens biographer citing "Death and the Mid-Life Crisis"? It is as if he or she were to use Dickens as some sort of troubled paradigm. And this is how Wyatt-Brown treats Pym in what is too often a gerontological study of an Old Lady of Shalott's psyche. She is not the first to do this: the troubles began in 1977, when Philip Larkin decided Pym was neglected and said so in the *Times Literary Supplement*. The search for the etiolated feminine was on.

The new Pym is no longer the witty commentator whose novels displayed the quiet fools of postwar Britain with quiet sympathy. In fact, the new Pym seems not to have a birthday nor her biographer any pictures of her: like Max Beerbohm, Pym has the gift of perpetual old age. Wyatt-Brown maintains that Pym's change of style in her posthumous *An Unsuitable Attachment* (1982) reflects a psychic and chronological maturity, not a different aesthetic; Marcia's odd behavior in *Quartet in Autumn* (1977) "exposed the dangers of the gerontological theory of disengagement, which was first espoused in 1961." And, as a general rule, the sexual unhappiness of her characters can be traced to Pym's unhappy emotional life. Wyatt-Brown cites her diaries to establish this point, yet Pym ripped the pages dealing with her sexual initiation from the diaries. And though the biographer admits, later, "It is impossible to tell exactly how much sexual experience Pym actually had with any men," this does not prevent Wyatt-Brown from rather quickly equating the fictional with the real character.

Yet, despite our feeling of being trapped in Pym's psyche, Wyatt-Brown's biography offers us much. Her careful examination of early drafts, especially of *Some Tame Gazelle* (1950), her first novel, which was fifteen years in the writing, illustrates the

novelist's careful planning. The plot summaries are admirable, her sympathy balanced.

Lorrie Goldensohn, herself a poet and teaching at Vassar College, has given us a northerner who went South in her *Elizabeth Bishop: The Biography of a Poet* (Columbia University Press). It is a book about the poetry of a famous Vassar graduate but not a consistent biography; the dust jacket has it better: *A Biography*. Reticence must account for some of this. Jean Rhys and Bishop both died in 1979, but at eighty-nine and sixty-eight years of age. Of Bishop there are still emotional survivors. But reticence can not account for only three pages on her childhood. Better to see this as an admirable, sensitive study of literary friendships, from Marianne Moore to Robert Lowell, joined to a meditation about Bishop's emotional life, a life which the index chops into separate categories: eroticism, sexuality, lesbianism, inversion, intimate relations, and gender. Goldensohn claims that Bishop's poetry, with its resistance to self-display, derives from her position as a lesbian; this a tenable argument, but since Bishop was aware of her class (like Lowell, she had a trust fund), she may have had that class's reticence. (But Lowell never did, and perhaps that was his attraction for her.) In any event, what is best about this book is its often passionate literary criticism of individual poems and her redefinition of Robert Lowell's influence. Goldensohn convinces us that Lowell's practical and professional assistance has tended to obscure Bishop's poetic independence: we see the relationship from Bishop's side, not Lowell's.

There are curious and important gaps in this biography. Her longtime companion, Maria Carlota Costellat de Marcedo Soares, of whom we have a fine photograph, whom both Bishop and her biographer mercifully simply call Lota, and with whom Bishop lived until death and a Brazilian revolution intervened, appears piecemeal: we gather that they met in New York, (this much is clear from a 1953 letter to Lowell, which Goldensohn cites) but when and how? If Bishop had not seen her for "five of six years," why? From a section of her poems, *Cold Spring* (1955), Goldensohn selects four poems for extensive and convincing analysis: "Faustina, or Rock Roses," the famous "Invitation to Miss Marianne Moore," "The Shampoo," and "Over 2000 Illustrations. . . ." This section is dedicated to Dr. Anny Baumann; the biographer cites four letters to Dr. Baumann, generally fails to supply more than the year of their composition, and tells us that she was Bishop's "personal physician." That is it. Flipping through my text of Bishop's *Complete Poems*

(1969), I notice that, of seven dedicatees, this biography provides information about two. These people must have meant something to Elizabeth Bishop. But not, apparently, to her biographer.

And even in her literary friendships things are obscure. In one sense an author flatters readers by not explaining everything, but at times the reader is mystified. The reader is presented with parts of a letter from Robert Lowell in which – and to use the biographer's language – Lowell is trying to explain how his "amorous excitement" led him to wish "for more than loving friendship." Fine. But who are the [Richard] Eberhardt's in-laws, when was the poetry conference at Bard College, and what precisely was the explosion at Yaddo? No doubt we could recover this information from David Kalstone's *Becoming a Poet* (1989), which she cites copiously (fifteen times). But why should we?

The author offers a partial explanation for this disorganized biography but compelling critical study. On a whim, and just before she began writing a chronological examination of the texts, she flew to Brazil, where she discovered a cache of Bishop's papers. Among them was a 1940–1942(?) twenty-six-line love poem, "It is marvelous"; the poem is good (two non-gender specific lovers awake in an electrical storm, impassioned), but it forced Goldensohn to rearrange her material. So we begin with three Brazilian chapters before we get to Vassar, her meeting and debating with Marianne Moore, and finally Lowell. As we move from chapter to chapter we realize that, from Goldensohn's point of view, Bishop lived her life imagistically, not from year to year, but from metaphor to developing metaphor. The discovered poem becomes a "Key to All Mythologies."

At times Goldensohn must think her readers yahoos or Sen. Jesse Helms's enthusiastic constituents: I doubt all male readers of this book will "discount the power of loving relationships between women," or that the "monolingual North American" will ignore the importance of Brazil. Incidently, does Goldensohn include Canadians among the benighted monolinguists? Even if we grant the pressure of reorganization, it cannot explain why a title fell out from the endnotes, why people who appear with Bishop in undated photographs are not in the index, and why Columbia University Press did not catch certain infelicities of style. The author's "monocularities" obscure valuable criticism.

Rhys, Bishop, and Rolfe Humphries all died in 1979. Most readers will know of Humphries either as the mentor of Louise Bogan and Theodore Roethke or as the translator of Ovid's *Metamorphoses*

and Juvenal's *Satires,* not realizing or remembering he brought Bogan and Roethke together, translated Martial and Federico García Lorca, went bald young, and published nine books of poetry. This mix of information typifies the 125 (out of 1,500 from eight different libraries) letters Richard Gillman and Michael Paul Novak have ably edited and the University of Kansas Press ably printed in *Poets, Poetics, and Politics: America's Literary Community Viewed from the Letters of Rolfe Humphries, 1910–1969* (University of Kansas Press). Both the editors were younger friends and students of Humphries. Ruth Limmer's graceful twenty-five-page biographical essay, "In the American Grain," gives us the correct amount of background and events to make sense of the letters, verse, and translations. Twenty photographs chronicle him, his family, and his friends over a seventy-five-year period: we see him on the cover of *Babyhood* at eleven months and at Amherst College when he retired. For thirty-two years while he wrote poetry, reviewed and encouraged others, and translated thousands of lines of verse, he taught high school. And then the fools fired him, a folly which benefited Amherst for eight years.

Many of his thirty-seven correspondents must have been alternately stung and flattered by his letters: stung by his acerbic criticism, flattered that he would take so much time. His letters to Roethke and Bogan in the 1930s are a marvel, less polite than Hopkins's to Robert Bridges, but as incisive. We should regret that his book reviews are not reprinted – one poet called him a "literary terrorist." Humphries provides vivid judgments on over thirty of his contemporary poets. And the editors have prefaced each of the seven sections of the letters with lengthy excerpts from Humphries's own poetry, poetry that we should look at again. The temptation in a book of letters is to go for the big names: this book contains seventeen letters to Edmund Wilson, twenty-three to Roethke, twenty-nine to Bogan. The temptation should be indulged. Humphries had a sure instinct for spotting pretense and folly. He was not taken in by sentimental poetics: if, he wrote the *New Republic* in 1943, we should pardon Pound's treason for the sake of his poetry, why not pardon bad poets for the sake of their patriotism? Nor was he taken in by sentimental politics: he offered, for free, to write an introduction to the 1949 New Directions *Selected Poems of Ezra Pound* so convinced was he of the merits of the *Cantos* and *Personae*.

But other correspondents felt his personality. He was not a man who tolerated folly. To a president of Amherst, his alma mater, who, objecting to the alma mater's song, asked for alternative verses,

Humphries suggested "We will sing of many a victory / In English, Amstuds, Math — / Let the golden haze of college days / Make no one psychopath." Few of these letters are dull; none is of the cigar-ordering sort. And regardless of the degree of selectivity, a well-edited and -printed book of letters will always delight: the reader can become the biographer.

After thirty years most of what we know about Alistair MacLean comes from the hype of his book jackets. In some ways Jack Webster's *Alistair MacLean: A Life* (Chapmans) is a dust jacket writ big: short paragraphs, no documentation, unswerving enthusiasm. At a chapter's end we do not ponder what we have read, we go to the next chapter — and that is how we read the adventure stories, at least until the early seventies: *HMS Ulysses* (1956), *The Guns of Navarone* (1961), *Ice Station Zebra* (1963), and *Where Eagles Dare* (1967) were written between 1955 and 1969. After that there is a serious falling off which disappointed thousands. MacLean's last novel, *Santorini* (1986), published a year before his death — he was only sixty-four — suggested that the island of Thera might explode again, the Mediterranean empty, and tectonic plates buckle — and we really did not care, alas. Webster explains the fall succinctly and without being overly apologetic: an excess of drink and women, or alcoholism and divorce. There is little hype at this point in the biography, but much enthusiastic sympathy. We have a man given to excess but also to extraordinary generosity.

The son of a Scottish minister famous for his preaching will probably not tend to see the world in terms of gray. He will learn the power of the spoken word, hence his novels' dialogue transfers easily into films. And further, a black-and-white world of good guys and bad guys not only appeals to our tired imagination but sells. Perhaps also, Webster argues, the precipitate end of his first marriage (after a trip of three weeks his wife returned to their Swiss villa to discover a strange nightie belonging to a woman who "combed his hormones" — whatever that means — and a husband three weeks in love and seeking a divorce) was a reaction to the sexual repression associated with Calvinism's more somber forms. Or, in book jacket prose: "This was discovery time [the Swinging Sixties], when more than eight bells tolled [the title of his 1966 novel], the moment of carnal truth which he had long heard condemned from the Scottish pulpit — that moment when the gates of hell fling wide and lustful men descend into the pits of depravity. And now it had all happened to Alistair. . ." But perhaps, judging from the wedding picture, all this happened because he was forty-nine and balding, she thirty-five and zaftig.

His second wife predeceased him, and less than a week after MacLean's death the London tabloids printed her ghostly slanders; his first wife was happy to assist Webster with his researches as was one of their children.

Yet this biography is satisfactory. It is best at MacLean's professional career: the schoolteacher veteran who in 1954 turns his experiences of the Murmansk run into a £100,000 best-seller. There was a triumphant opening of *The Guns of Navarone* in 1961, a royal opening: the photograph of MacLean beholding the queen bears study. The movie, taking two years and $10 million to produce, was preceded by amazing publicity: one press release seems to have relocated the Black Sea. MacLean's ability to write movie scripts was recognized immediately by the American producer Elliot Kastner, a "working-class lad" from Harlem who, having apocopated a line from *Richard III,* continued the novelist's success in *Where Eagles Dare* (not perch). Webster's MacLean has that depth of character we find in the novels. A good read.

Dictionary of Literary Biography Yearbook Award for a Distinguished Literary Biography Published in 1992

Dust jacket for Norman White's biography of the nineteenth-century Jesuit poet who invented "sprung" rhythm, a violation of conventional poetic meter that had a profound influence on twentieth-century experimental poetry

Norman White's *Hopkins: A Literary Biography* (Oxford University Press) is the first thorough biography of Gerard Manley Hopkins, the most puzzling nineteenth-century English poet. White's exploration illuminates the puzzles. It may take a thousand pages of clear and graceful narration, but by the book's end we have, if not the clearest, then the best documented explanation of how Hopkins's religious and consequent social isolation can be linked to his linguistic and sexual oddities. And, equally important, how there is no link between the sexually unhappy adolescent who wrote bad imitations of Keats and the unhappy Jesuit who wrote superb sonnets.

White's success is, in part, dependent on full access to the complete private journals, the autopsy of those landscapes that drew Hopkins's hypersensitive eye, and being a master of the secondary material. But his greater success reflects the rare ability of sympathetic organization: sympathetic in his readings of the poems, organized in his balancing of life and times.

— William Foltz

Book Reviewing in America VI

George Garrett
University of Virginia

and

David R. Slavitt
University of Pennsylvania

The toss between Judith Krantz and Thomas Mann, punk and Proust, will no doubt continue to be argued.
—Terry Eagleton, *TLS,* 18 December 1992.

This is an industry that operates entirely in some ways on word of mouth, personal relations. I think most people are astonished by how small the publishing world is. If you spend any time at all in any aspect of it — editorial, as a writer, as a publicist, whatever — you very quickly get to know everybody in it. There's sort of one floating party, and you're at it once a week.
—Tom Mallon, literary editor of *GQ,* interviewed by Kristin van Ogtrop 29 September 1992.

The Year of the Woman, also the year of the Olympics, an election year which brought Bill Clinton to the Oval Office, a year of economic change, confusion, and recession, a year of wars and the rumors of war, a year of famine and various plagues, 1992 was likewise, in spite of everything else, a busy year in American publishing. People on the inside reported a slow year, a tough year at the marketplace. The hard facts and numbers will be along later. For now we have speculation and symbolism. For the latter, symbolic maybe of the year in commercial publishing, there is the photograph published in illustration of the American Booksellers Association convention during the last weekend of May in Anaheim, California (*Washington Post,* "Style," 26 May), showing a huge Magic Johnson hunkering down, crouching low to embrace fellow author Dr. Ruth Westheimer, both showing a wealth of teeth, grimacing in what might be taken for a grin. Or a personal anecdote. Myself driving west on Interstate 81 toward Tennessee from Virginia, pausing to use the facilities in a rest stop. In the stall I cannot ignore the usual dimwit and depressing graffiti, but something unusual catches my

eye, neatly printed across the door: "MADONNA'S NEW BOOK IS IN THE STORES." Is this a new form of advertising and publicity? Has the publisher of *Sex* (Warner) sent publicity and promotion people out on the road to capture the attention of prospective readers? Is no place safe, nothing sacred?

Business may have been bad, slow anyway; but the great crapshoot, betting big bucks on the future, continued. Terry McMillan earned an advance of $2.64 million on paperback rights of her novel *Waiting to Exhale* (Viking). Arthur Ashe accepted an advance of $1 million for a memoir tentatively titled *Days of Grace.* Meanwhile Mia Farrow, following a great deal of publicity about her broken relationship with Woody Allen, signed on with a generous Doubleday for $3 million to tell her story. Popular professionals took a turn at the trough: $35 million to Mary Higgins Clark from Simon and Schuster for a multiple book contract; Barbara Taylor Bradford took home $20 million from HarperCollins for her next three novels; HarperCollins also coughed up $10 million to Len Deighton for four books; Robert Harris was paid $1.8 million for the Harper Paperback edition of his novel *Fatherland* (Random House), a "what-if" book which has Germany win World War II and Hitler live to celebrate his seventy-fifth birthday. Geoffrey C. Ward and Ken Burns, creators of the Public Broadcasting System (PBS) documentary *The Civil War* received an advance of $3 million for a projected illustrated volume about the American West. Thomas Harris, who wrote the novel from which the hugely successful film, *Silence of the Lambs,* was adapted, was advanced $5 million for his next two novels. Following disappointing sales of his latest, *The Road to Omaha,* Robert Ludlum moved from Random House to Bantam for an undisclosed inducement.

Tom Clancy picked up $12 million for one book, courtesy of Putnam; and Knopf lured Dean Koontz into its stable with a three-book contract worth $18–20 million. Meantime, hoping to cash in here and now, Warner Books announced a promotion budget of $500,000, equal to that expended on *Scarlett*, for *The General's Daughter*, by Nelson DeMille. No less optimistic, Viking published a first printing of 1.5 million copies of Stephen King's *Dolores Claiborne*. Places to display and sell all these books: slow economy or not, Walden now has twelve hundred bookstores and is creating a chain of "super-bookstores," Basset Book Shops, of which fifty or more should be open by 1994. Some of the implications of the impact of the "superstores," characterized by a huge inventory of books for sale at substantial discounts in a large spacious environment, is evident in a *Publishers Weekly* (hereafter identified as *PW*) 23 November story of how a neighboring Basset cost one of Connecticut's outstanding independents, Barrett Bookstore of Stamford, 75 percent of its business in less than a year. Competitor Leonard Riggio, who owns 50 percent of Barnes & Noble (which in turn owns Doubleday and Scribner's bookstores), 791 B. Dalton stores, and 270 college bookstores (see "Barnes and Noble's Boss Has Big Growth Plans That Booksellers Fear," by Meg Cox, *Wall Street Journal*, 11 September), plans to open one hundred superstores. His empire was described as being in some financial difficulty because of the "contracting" of the once profitable mall stores. To be sure, risks in publishing remain serious. Some idea of those risks, together with some indication of the lack of care and attention to product by publishers, is indicated in a *PW* story of 2 March about how an examination of ten history textbooks, representing $20.3 million annually from the Texas Education Agency, turned up fifty-two hundred errors, including such boners of misinformation as the wrong date for Pearl Harbor and the assertion that Harry Truman dropped an atomic bomb to end the Korean War.

Seeking any effective way to reduce losses and minimize risks, publishers have moved in some mildly surprising directions. In "Book Publishers Turn to Product Tie-Ins" (*Wall Street Journal*, 5 August), Meg Cox points out how Janet Darley's *Tangled Vines* (Little, Brown) was published with a tie-in to Vichon Vineyard and James Michener's *Mexico* (Random House) is being promoted by and for Princess Cruises, together with other examples of discounts available on other products for book buyers. Cox writes: "What next? Companies paying to have their products plugged in novels, just like they do in the movies?" Earlier in the year, on 21 July, Joanne Lipman of the *Wall Street Journal* had caught many prominent publishers making outrageous claims that their books could be legitimately called "bestsellers." In "The Making of a Best Seller Is a Mighty Serious Business," Lipman summed up: "For crafty publishers, it's almost always possible to find some way to call a book a best seller." More evidence of the risks of publishing at all levels and the transitory nature of even the most extraordinary success is found in the sad fact that hugely successful author Alex Haley, who died in February at age seventy, was reported to have been more or less broke and $1.5 million in debt (*PW*, 12 October). In an effort to raise money the estate held an auction where Haley's manuscript for *Roots* sold for $71,500 and the typescript of *The Autobiography of Malcolm X*, with marginalia and emendations by both Haley and Malcolm X, was bought for $110,000. The framed citation for Haley's Pulitzer Prize earned $50,000 from the Hewett Family Foundation of San Francisco.

Another death which rocked the literary world was that of William Shawn, formerly long-time editor of the *New Yorker*, on 8 December. Writer Elizabeth Drew, honoring his memory in "The Civilized Editor" (*Washington Post*, 9 December), did not shy away from admitting his eccentricity: "His legendary eccentricities were all true. He wouldn't ride in an elevator alone, or travel over bridges or through tunnels. He never flew on an airplane. Obviously, this circumscribed his travel."

Ever since the announcement on 30 June, widely proclaimed to be "a publishing earthquake," that thirty-eight-year-old Tina Brown of *Vanity Fair* had been named to replace Robert Gottlieb as editor of the *New Yorker*, the publicity mills, not in any way discouraged by Brown, have been grinding out exceedingly fine news about that magazine. One of the best, among many, of the early reaction and background pieces was Mark Feeny's "Something's Got to Give: Cachet and Cash Clash" (*Boston Globe*, 5 July): "With its devotion to Volvo politics and Volkswagen graphics, the *New Yorker* was increasingly out of step with the greed and gloss of the Reagan '80s." The magazine had evidently been losing its owner, Advance Publications (chairman: S. I. Newhouse, Jr.), something like $10 million a year. Meantime *Vanity Fair*, owned by the same conglomerate, had been making a buck. Soon the accounts of arrivals and departures at both magazines filled the press. "Magazine Talent Is the Talk of the Town" headlined the *Wall Street Journal* on 4 August, letting the world know that Brown had already brought on board Martin Amis, William Styron, Richard Price, and Norman Mailer: "Other editors are watching the hiring spree with a mixture of defensiveness and dread." By 25 September Charles Trueheart could publish in the *Washington Post* a piece on the subject of "Tinafication," the coming of the first Brown-edited issue on 5 October. Trueheart quoted a nervous and insistently anonymous *New Yorker* writer – "She's happy to treat you like a star, but she doesn't want to treat you like an artist." When the issue appeared it drew prompt reviews and critiques from many places. (See Walter Goodman, "Paging Through a New Yorker," *New York Times,* 29 September.) Once that issue and the next were out and around, people noted that one item, "The Art of Sniping," concerned William Shawcross's biography of Rupert Murdoch, said to contain an unflattering portrait of Tina Brown's husband – Harold Evans. The book had been published in Britain but is not scheduled here until 1993 (by Simon and Schuster). The negative review of a book still unpublished in America, and the personal attack on Shawcross, at once drew a public and passionate (or passionately *staged*) reply from David Cornwell (John le Carré): "The issue of the *New Yorker* dated 12th October contains one of the ugliest pieces of partisan journalism that I have witnessed in a long life of writing . . ." Writing a joint article, "The Talk of the Town" (*Washington Post,* 15 October), David Streitfeld and Charles Trueheart reported to the waiting world that Brown's reaction was "gleeful." And so on. The publicity in magazines and papers has been unceasing and received a shot in the arm by the death of former editor Shawn in time to be mourned in the double Christmas–New Year issue.

Other items which aroused the attention of literary journalists during the year included lawsuits, charges of plagiarism, and the continuing involuntary servitude of Salman Rushdie. Plagiarism, the fact and the idea of it, seems to have been in the air of 1992. On the one hand playwright Henry Denker lost the copyright infringement suit he had brought against Alfred Uhry, charging that his *Driving Miss Daisy* was plagiarized from Denker's *Horowitz and Mrs. Washington.* On the other hand the charges by film director Barry Levenson and writer David Simon (*New York Times,* 3 June) that Warner Bros. plagiarized from Simon's *Homicide* (1991) for the new television series *Polish Hill* have not been settled. Meantime, two genre novels by Pauline Dunn were withdrawn from circulation by Zebra when it was discovered that they both borrowed a bit too freely from *Phantoms* (Putnam's, 1983), by Dean

Koontz. At year's end, in a new twist, the distinguished Schuyler Chapin was accused of lifting chunks and passages from his own work. "Can an author plagiarize himself and, if so, who sues whom?" asks Joseph McClellan (*Washington Post,* 30 December). Chapin's editor dismisses the whole thing – "He's not plagiarizing from anyone else and there's no law against plagiarizing yourself."

Serious literary legal matters also were addressed. In a case brought by writer Dan Moldea against the *New York Times* for a libel contained in a book review, the judge ruled against him, arguing that a book review is "unverifiable opinion." In a battle first joined in 1988, the family and estate of John Cheever and Academy Chicago, which had contracted to publish *The Uncollected Stories of John Cheever,* settled out of court, apparently to the distinct advantage of no one except lawyers. (See "Cheevers, Publisher End Fight," by David Streitfeld, *Washington Post,* 25 January.) Reading like something one would find in a genre novel, an unpublished novel, *Points of Origin,* by John Orr, was read by a jury and evidently played a part in the verdict of a criminal arson case in California. (See David Streitfeld, "Book Report," *Washington Post,* 23 August.) A lawsuit closely watched by the literati, matching Knopf editor and perennial public figure Gordon Lish against *Harper's Bazaar* magazine, came to its courtroom conclusion in early December. Lish sued *Harper's Bazaar* for copyright infringement for publishing an abbreviated version of his letter to prospective students in his private creative-writing class under the title "A Kind of Magnificence" (*Harpers,* December 1990). When Lish first brought the suit, Alice Turner, fiction editor for *Playboy,* was widely quoted as finding words for the general consensus – "I haven't met a single person who doesn't think this is lunacy on Gordon's part." Lunacy or not, the case went to court, and during the trial Lish was quoted as to the impact of the publication of his letter in the magazine (*New York Times,* 4 October): "It was as if my body had been spread open to those who held me in low esteem." In the 7 December issue of *PW* the finale of the show is briskly surmised: "Dismissing charges of libel and defamation, Judge Morris E. Lasker ruled that *Harpers* was in violation of the fair-use doctrine of the copyright act." Lish's attorney had the last word. "Lish is vindicated," he said.

By this time, going into the fourth year of hiding out and (more or less) lying low, Salman Rushdie may well have wished his problems were of the kind that could be settled in a civilized courtroom or even out in the open face-to-face. As it is,

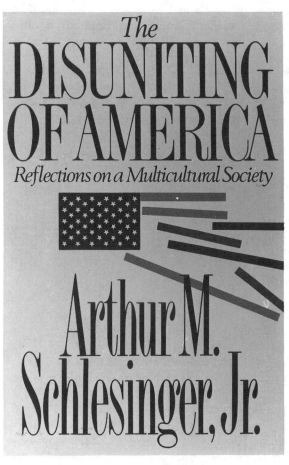

Dust jacket for Arthur M. Schlesinger, Jr.'s defense of traditional, liberal values

he has been, partly thanks to himself and his clever agents and some dedicated (if diminishing in number) friends, much in mind if mostly out of sight. A lengthy, end-of-the-year article by Philip Weiss in *Esquire* ("The Martyr," January 1993) presents a summary of the whole story, but we learn new information as well: how "Rushdie misses the pleasures of unregulated life"; how he watches hours of reruns of *Dynasty;* that, in addition to his trips to Washington, D.C., and Columbia University, he has visited Colorado, Norway, Finland, and Germany, thanks to elaborate and expensive security measures; that he is arrogant, indifferent to the needs and concerns of others, often unreliable, and hopelessly self-centered. Of his character his ex-wife, writer Marianne Wiggins, says: "He's not the bravest man in the world but will do anything to save his life." Perhaps more generously, Weiss writes: "The author is a provocateur, and like all provocateurs, he both seeks attention and he thinks he's being clever when he's being mean." He quotes British critic A. Alvarez saying that "Rushdie

wanted to be the most famous writer in the world, and now he is and it's not what he expected."

At a certain point, though, all publicity is beyond being labeled good or bad. Or so it seems to various observers of the contemporary scene. Writing for the *Boston Globe* ("Cashing in on Bad Publicity," 5 April), Matthew Gilbert describes "an increasingly sophisticated publicity mechanism, one in which almost any attention, positive or negative, is good." (I have not yet met a publishing publicist who would disagree with that judgment.) Gilbert cites Rushdie in his article, though he is willing to allow that his current notoriety is dearly bought. "While he has made money from the terrorist threats," Gilbert writes, "Rushdie finds little redemption in his windfall." Still, windfall or not, 1992 was not the best of years for Ahmed Salman Rushdie. The amount of the bounty for his murder was raised in June, and all expenses incurred were added as a fringe benefit to the prospective killer or killers dedicated to the "extermination of the cursed writer Rushdie." "We have to get sympathetic governments to threaten Iran with economic sanctions and being brought before the International Court of Justice in the Hague," Rushdie said. No such luck. Meantime, later in the year, the Iranian foundation which manages the reward money allotted for killing Rushdie reported it has been profitably invested and is growing steadily (*New York Times,* 12 November). Perhaps more wounding than that news was the publication in the *Paris Review* of an interview with Nobel Prize–winning Egyptian author Naguib Mahfouz in which Mahfouz stated, concerning the blasphemy of *The Satanic Verses,* "I found the insults in it unacceptable." He went on to criticize Rushdie in a more complex fashion. "If a writer comes to the conclusion that his society's laws or beliefs are no longer valid or even harmful, it is his duty to speak up. But he must be ready to pay the price for his outspokenness." Not all things went badly for Rushdie, however. In the spring the paperback of *The Satanic Verses* (Consortium) finally appeared. The identity of "Consortium" publishers, except for the fact that it has a corporate address in Dover, Delaware, is unknown. Rushdie's thoughts and feelings about *The Wizard of Oz* appeared in the *New Yorker* (11 May) in a personal essay – "Out of Kansas" – reaching a serious conclusion: "In the end, ceasing to be children, we all become magicians without magic, exposed conjurers, with only our simple humanity to get us through." An abridged version of the piece, "Reflections on Oz," was published in *Chicago Tribune Books,* 13 December. Rushdie wrote several book reviews and, most memorably, a touching memorial for British writer Angela Carter in which his rigid self-concern is all but overwhelmed by a genuine expression of grief for another human being ("Angela Carter, 1940–92; Good Wizard, a Very Dear Friend," *New York Times Book Review,* 8 March). A version of Rushdie's critique of Oz is now available in the British Film Institute's Film Classics series, distributed by the Indiana University Press; and the University of Nebraska Press is bringing out *The Rushdie Letters* (February 1993), a collection of public letters to Rushdie by "internationally renowned authors," together with his reply, "1,000 Days in a Balloon." Rushdie is reported to be hard at work on a new novel, *The Moor's Sigh,* scheduled for 1994 publication by Pantheon, Rushdie's new American publisher.

All is not well at America's bookstores. In "Literary Larceny" (*Los Angeles Times,* 11 October), Roy Rivenburg argues that book theft is now becoming a serious problem in the nation, with smaller shops losing from ten thousand to thirty thousand dollars a year to shoplifting. Earlier, on 23 August, David Streitfeld was among the first to point out, in "Runaway Bestsellers" (*Washington Post Book World),* that many of these ripped-off books were popular novels by black women, stolen to be resold at significant retail discounts. See also "Thieves Diminish Black Authors' Breakthrough," by Courtland Milloy (*Washington Post,* 7 October).

But not all the year's news of the publishing scene was downbeat and discouraging. On Tuesday, 22 September, hundreds of American writers, coast to coast, acting on the inspiration of novelist Frederick Busch and under the organization Save Our Strength, gave readings to benefit the homeless and raised many thousands of dollars thereby. Technology conferred benefits and changed things. For example, novelist Tama Janowitz was able to transform her latest novel, *The Male Cross-Dresser Support Group* (Crown), into a forty-second video version which was shown on MTV, saving readers and nonreaders alike hours of wasted time. And in Stockholm new technology and the dedication of craftsmen made possible the engraving of the Swedish commemorative postage stamp for Nobel Prize–winner Derek Walcott to be cut and in production in six days rather than the usual four to six weeks.

Of the doctrine and practice of Political Correctness (hereinafter PC), which busily inhabited the pages of many newspapers and magazines of all kinds all through 1991, it can be safely said PC is not dead, it is only sleeping. Or pretending to be asleep. Certain specialized publications such as the *Chronicle of Higher Education* and the *AWP Chronicle* continue to support the cause of PC with journalistic guerrilla action as well as classic fervor. The pages of the *Chronicle of Higher Education* became at once the recorder and broadcaster of the inexorable creeping progress of PC in American higher education. After the end of the year (6 January 1993), immediately following the annual pep rally of the MLA convention, the gloves were off. See "The Pursuit of Truth Is Inherently Disruptive and Anti-Authoritarian," by Betty Jean Craige:

> The critique of the traditional model of culture does indeed have political consequences. Laying bare patriarchal values in literature, for example, may alert students to patriarchal values in our laws and customs. Exposing the racial attitudes implicit in Western historians' accounts of the world may arouse criticism of American foreign policy. The pursuit of truth therefore becomes political action, dangerous to those content with the present order of things.

Which way to the Revolution? And, from the other side of the fence, the *Wall Street Journal* from time to time makes barnyard noises. See " 'Heterotexuality' and Other Literary Matters," 31 December, where Roger Kimball reports on the 1992 MLA convention: "Although academics love to castigate Western society for being racist, sexist, imperialistic, etc., they do not at all like being criticized themselves. Several panelists railed against the hostile, obtuse journalists who would unfairly criticize the MLA in days to come." Kimball does not mention the attempt by the MLA to deal with the press. Believing their problems derive more from public relations than ideology, the MLA announced in the *MLA Newsletter* (Winter 1992) a special workshop for members on Sunday, 22 December, "Smart Ways to Handle the Press": "Participants will learn how to talk to reporters, handle difficult interview tactics, and develop a proactive message strategy on issues that concern them." One strategy which came to fruition in 1992 has already been identified as a new version of an immemorial quarrel, exemplified, and dealt with on a limited basis, by James Atlas in *Battle of the Books: The Curriculum Debate in America* (Norton), which proves to be solid journalism and comes down strongly in favor of the need "to preserve and affirm the idea of basic literacy, of learning grounded in a core of knowledge." Arthur M. Schlesinger, Jr., who praised and supported the Atlas book, entered the fray himself, attacking from a liberal point of view "the new orthodoxy" of the PC people in *The Disuniting of America: Reflections on a*

The Critics Bear It Away

American Fiction and the Academy

Frederick Crews

Dust jacket for the collection of essays in which Frederick Crews attacks the excesses of contemporary literary criticism

Multicultural Society (Norton): "Our task is to combine due appreciation of the splendid diversity of the nation with due emphasis on the great unifying Western ideas of individual freedom, political democracy, and human rights." Coming from this impeccable source, Schlesinger's modest proposal drew blood on the left. A large book with a more limited focus but serious implications, widely reviewed and argued over, was David Lehman's *Signs of the Times: Deconstruction and the Fall of Paul de Man* (Poseidon), which not only detailed the multiple duplicities of Paul de Man, one of deconstruction's patron saints, but also offered close and skeptical critical readings and interrogation of previously untouchable stars of the PC movement such as Richard Rorty, Jacques Derrida, J. Hillis Miller, Jeffrey Mehlman, and so forth, and even a certain amount of intellectual comedy at the expense of the puffing and blowing, backing and filling, of people, such as Harold Bloom and Frank Lentricchia as they sought to distance themselves from the late de Man. No wonder Cynthia Ozick, in her book-jacket blurb,

called *Signs* "provocative, even a little daredevil." Donning masks of moderation and more or less sweet reasonableness, the PC people produced a basket of books designed, on the one hand, to be or seem to be cautionary advice to mostly unnamed extremists of their own persuasion while shrugging off their critics as, at best, ill informed and irrelevant. Among the works of positive-thinking apostles (or converts) to thoughtful moderation was Gerald Graff's *Beyond the Culture Wars* (Norton), which puts a new spin on things: "Given a faculty that is reasonably representative of the current diversity of academic culture, an integrated curriculum figures to be more theoretically, historically, and politically self-aware than a faculty that teaches in isolation." Translation: *Give peace a chance. On my terms. . . .* Prominent African-American critic and (currently) Harvard professor Henry Louis Gates, Jr., came forth from the well with *Loose Canons* (Oxford). His history of the background and his own arguments are based on the unquestioning acceptance of most of the primary PC premises. "While I may be taken to have argued for the retrieval of liberalism, however refashioned, as a viable, reformable agenda," he writes in summary and conclusion, "I distrust those – at the left, right, or center – who would erect an opposition between leftism and liberalism." Morris Dickstein's *Double Agent: The Critic and Society* (Oxford) has some intelligent and fair-minded historical evaluations of the century's prominent earlier generation of critics (R. P. Blackmur, Northrop Frye, F. W. Dupee, Edmund Wilson, Malcolm Cowley, and so forth) and pauses, very briefly, to honor at least the idea of the next generation critics who write for literary and general magazines ("I could list two dozen superb young critics still in their thirties and forties who write for such general magazines"), his heart goes out to his own list of "the respected if controversial figures in critical theory today": Derrida, Bloom, de Man, Geoffrey Hartman, Stanley Fish, Sandra Gilbert, Susan Gubar, Edward Said, Henry Louis Gates, Jr., Gerald Graff, and Jerome McGann. PC's starting lineup. More genuinely "moderate" by far and more critical of his own home team, even of himself in earlier intellectual positions, is Frederick Crews in *The Critics Bear It Away* (Random House). His book is composed primarily of essay reviews written for the *New York Review of Books,* following the recent developments of criticism and scholarship on some significant American writers, chiefly Nathaniel Hawthorne, Mark Twain, Ernest Hemingway, William Faulkner, Flannery O'Connor, and John Updike. He is better on the earlier authors; and though he is often boldly critical of the more obvious excesses of his critical and scholarly peers, he has little or no use for his conservative opposition ("cultural nostalgics"). Some of the opposition is playing rough, to be sure. Polemical, if generally useful studies abound, two of the better examples being Martin Anderson's *Impostors in the Temple* (Simon and Schuster) and Richard M. Huber's *How Professors Play the Cat Guarding the Cream* (George Mason University Press). Another strong, and well-argued, attack is *Academic Capitalism & Literary Value* (University of Georgia Press), by Harold Fromm. Fromm's position is clear at the outset: "Deconstruction, Marxism, feminism, black studies – even with all the valuable insights and techniques they have given us – operate in accordance with their own aggressive, sometimes covert, agendas, which often have a way of being much less pure than their practitioners are willing to let on." Distinctly moderate in this charged context are David Bromwich's *Politics By Other Means* (Yale University Press) and James Davison Hunter's *Culture Wars* (Basic Books). Bromwich is fed up with the japes and pasquinades of both the political Left and the Right – "The experiment of allowing politicians to educate us down to their level has been tried." Hunter's book is accurately described (on the jacket) by the distinguished Robert Coles: "An extraordinary intellectual achievement – a careful and considered analysis of the sources of the moral and cultural conflicts which continue to confront us in late twentieth century America."

More directly to the point at hand and perhaps the battleground of next year and after are anthologies which can be used in the classroom. Even though he has been closely involved with the American, indeed the international Left, Paul Berman is too good a journalist not to have gathered at least a representative presentation of the problems and issues in *Debating P.C.: The Controversy Over Political Correctness on College Campuses* (Laurel). The selections for the "debate" are lively and interesting; for instance, in the section on "Free Speech and Speech Codes" he presents (among others) Nat Hentoff, who is for free speech, versus the Stanley Fish of "There's No Such Thing as Free Speech and It's a Good Thing, Too." Richard Bolton's *Culture Wars* (New Press) is a collection of documents of all kinds, dealing with the controversies concerning the arts, especially the National Endowment for the Arts, during the past several years. That publishers plan to move into the area of anthologies concerned with "the culture wars" in the near future is evident in the report to me by Mark Edmundson (author of

Towards Reading Freud, 1990), my colleague at the University of Virginia, that he has been contacted by a major publisher to put together an anthology of heavy-hitters who will, it is hoped, dispose of the arguments of Dinesh D'Souza and other concerned conservatives. The book is *Wild Orchids and Trotsky* (Penguin, 1993).

Meanwhile the war goes on. On Sunday, 26 December, many newspapers picked up and published an interview by George W. Cornell of Associated Press with Rev. Avery Dulles, "internationally influential Roman Catholic theologian." Cornell's traditional lead paragraph says it all in brief: "America is caught in a 'culture war' that threatens the nation's political heritage, according to a leading Roman Catholic theologian, who terms it a 'major crisis of our day.'"

If at times it seems as if "the culture wars" are diverting the attention of literary journalists from their central duty, it is worth noting that traditional books of criticism, based on book reviewing in depth, continued to appear, here and there, during 1992. The University of Missouri Press published several collections of critical essays. John W. Aldridge's *Classics & Contemporaries* ranged forward from Henry James to work by Robert Coover and Donald Barthelme. Aldridge also published a somewhat more provocative gathering, *Talents and Technicians: Literary Chic and the New Assembly Line Fiction* (Scribners), which was reviewed in many places, including odd ones such as *Vanity Fair*. Monroe K. Spears brought out *Countries of the Mind* (University of Missouri Press), a gathering of thirty-one literary essay-reviews, dealing with various subjects from Michel Montaigne to T. S. Eliot and W. H. Auden, and Richard Wilbur and Howard Nemerov. Also from Missouri came a group of essays by veteran critic Robert B. Heilman on British and American novels – *The Workings of Fiction*. From Louisiana State University Press came a major contribution to the criticism of contemporary poetry – *Compulsory Figures: Essays on Recent American Poets,* by Pulitzer Prize–winning poet Henry Taylor. Taylor's book contains extended essays, all of which began as reviews, on the work of seventeen poets, some well and widely known, others likely to be better known thanks to Taylor's intelligent and sensitive attention.

Things are beginning to happen to the book sections and pages of many newspapers. Just when it seemed that, with a couple of exceptions, terminal shrinkage and a yawning indifference had set in, when not only publicists but also editors, finally even many authors, were openly asserting that, as far as book reviews are concerned, everything else except for the *New York Times,* the *Washington Post,* National Public Radio, and maybe *USA TODAY* is all but irrelevant to the brief, butterfly life history of a literary book – just then, within no more than the last year or so, there has been a turnaround. Book pages, even the shrunken ones, are suddenly alive again, even influential. Of course, book editors, themselves, down in the same old trenches and fighting for survival, may not have noticed the change or believed it if they noticed. But it is real enough to the engaged observer.

How has this come to pass? No one is certain, to be sure; but there are clearly apparent reasons and causes. The growing number of bookstores all across the country, the beleaguered independents as well as the conglomerate chains, has resulted in a need for regional and local publicity. Publishers have begun to learn how to market literary books as well as blockbusters. The major blockbusters are not generally "review driven." They are sold to the stores well in advance of their appearance, and they are sustained by various kinds of advertising. Literary books, with maybe no more than mid list prospects in a best-case scenario, can be sold and sustained by other means and for a longer period than was usual a few years ago. Once upon a time reserved for bestselling authors and public figures, one of the best of these ways and means is the "tour," large-scale (twenty to thirty towns and cities) or small (five to ten). Both chain stores and independents regularly support readings and signings of new "literary" books. These events bring customers into the stores, customers who browse and tend to buy books, even if not always the featured book of the occasion. Bookstores seem to like the idea and the results of it. Chapters ("A Literary Bookstore"), an independent bookstore in Washington, D.C., for example, advertised widely and presented nine reading-signings – John Haines, Pam Houston, Seamus Heaney and others, Nicholson Baker, George Packer, Gioia DeLiberto, Sandra Cisneros, and Robert Stone – during March 1992 alone. Publishers can profit from the closer relationship with the stores and from the cumulative "visibility" earned by their peripatetic authors. If the effects are gradual and the profits, if any, small, it is still cheaper than serious advertising. And it has been demonstrated that, always allowing for rare cases, conventional advertising is not likely to enhance the sale prospects of a literary book in the urgent short run. Increased visibility is earned, regionally and locally, by "news," by feature pieces and interviews in local papers, and also, though separately, by re-

views which can mean something directly to bookseller, author, and publisher. Paul Bogaards, Knopf's highly successful promotion director, is quoted by *Publishers Weekly* ("Beating the Drum for Books," 30 November) on the subject: "This kind of hands-on involvement of the bookstore is a major change in the publicity operation in recent years." Many academic institutions are actively involved, as well. With more than two hundred full-scale creative-writing programs at American colleges and universities and with almost every other institution of higher learning (and even many secondary schools, public and private) offering courses in creative writing, there are hundreds of poets and fiction writers and, increasingly, nonfiction writers also, firmly established and entrenched in academe. For many years, beginning mostly after World War II, there has been a constant kind of interchange of visits and readings among these writers. Now, more and more, booksellers, publishers, and working journalists take advantage of this network for their own purposes. Here are a few simple and altogether typical examples from my own community.

Author Frederick Buechner visited the University of Virginia under the auspices of the Department of Religious Studies. Buechner is an ordained Presbyterian minister as well as author of about thirty books of fiction and nonfiction. One evening he gave a lecture, "Art and Religion," to a large audience, and the next he read from his forthcoming novel, *Son of Laughter* (HarperCollins, 1993). At both events long lines waited for him to sign copies of his books, most bought at local bookstores. Both local papers produced feature articles about Buechner and his work, and the locally oriented *Observer Magazine* (9–15 April) published an interview which included a comment for the occasion by novelist John Irving, a former student of Buechner's: "I acknowledge most of all, how much I owe to the writing of my former teacher Frederick Buechner." Something of the same routine publicity treatment greeted William Styron in late October when he came to participate in the annual Virginia Festival of American Film. Styron used the occasion, the twenty-fifth anniversary of the 1967 publication of his novel *The Confessions of Nat Turner,* to defend himself against critics of the novel. This made some news, and the story appeared with a photograph of Styron in a panel discussion, sitting next to civil-rights activist Julian Bond. Simultaneously contributing editor Barbara Rich of the *Observer Magazine* (29 October–4 November) published an interview with Styron, one which included some advance attention to his current work-in-progress

— *The Ways of the Warrior*. In both cases the attention came well in advance of the arrival of books on the scene.

This same sort of thing, before and after publication, is happening all over the country all the time and involves both well- and little-known literary writers. Larger papers (*Chicago Tribune Books, Washington Post Book World, Los Angeles Times Book World, Boston Globe,* for example) regularly publish schedules of upcoming literary events, readings, and signings in their catchment areas. These are busy schedules. Some of these events will lead directly to feature stories. Frequent feature stories these days, most often found in parts of the paper other than exclusively on the book pages, are author profiles and interviews, usually concerned with touring writers of national importance. Thus, for example, the "People" section of the *Baltimore Sun* regularly presents a good-sized story, complete with color photograph, of a literary author. A typical feature story, and a good one of the kind, was "Edna O'Brien Finds Passion in Her Corner of the Earth," by Tim Warren, on 7 June. Inevitably these pieces make use of some of the conventional tropes of the celebrity-personality piece: "'Madness? I think highly charged, more than mad,' she says in her precise diction, the lilt of her native Ireland coming through despite having lived more than three decades in England. 'Nell doesn't go over into the abyss — whatever the word is — of madness.'" Richard Bausch and his new novel, *Violence* (Houghton Mifflin/Seymour Lawrence), easily found space on the front page of the *Washington Post* "Style" section ("The Author, Giving Rise to 'Violence,'" by Elizabeth Kastor, 2 March). A large, page-dominating black-and-white photo of Bausch (following custom of most newspapers the *Sun* presented Edna O'Brien in color) is followed by an interview-book review-critique-personality piece ("He is lying now nearly horizontal in a recliner, a ginger-hued man in the floppy clothes of someone who works at home"). This habit of journalism, apparently a rhetorical aside intended to establish immediacy and authenticity and to demonstrate that the reporter has actually laid eyes on the subject, appears almost everywhere. For example, this note from an otherwise serious piece, albeit a front-page lead story ("Novelist Updike Sees a Nation Frustrated By Its Own Dreams," by Dennis Farney) in the *Wall Street Journal* (16 September): "At 60, with his puckish grin and tousled forelock of silver hair, there remains something alert and boyish about the man. And something impish too." Or this traditional, if lively, lead for a piece in the *New York Times Maga-*

Dust jacket for David Lehman's investigation of Paul de Man's past and the ethics of deconstruction

zine (22 November) by Mira Stout on novelist Julian Barnes ("Chameleon Novelist"): "Late one afternoon, the novelist Julian Barnes and I meet at the busy Baker Street tube station in London to catch the 4:14 to Northwood. Buying his ticket, Barnes has the air of an undercover agent; anonymous and detached from the swarm." It may well be that the increasing use of writers as subjects for interviews and profiles results from the fact that the stars and celebrities of popular culture are more likely to be found on television talk shows or radio interviews.

In any case, for a complex of reasons, literary writers are more and more the subject of newspaper reporting both locally and nationally. And behind all of it stands the book review. Without a record of reviews it is highly unlikely that Barnes or Bausch or O'Brien would capture the interest of journalists. Thus, these days it can matter a good deal to a particular book at a particular time, what a local reviewer in Roanoke, Virginia; Portland, Maine; or Orlando, Florida, has to say.

To get a sense of the shape and direction of newspaper book reviewing this year in America I continued to look at the daily papers that I always read year round – the local papers wherever I find myself, the *Wall Street Journal,* the *Washington Post,* and the *New York Times.* All three of these papers offer outstanding daily book reviews. For the Sunday book pages, I expanded my horizons somewhat in 1992, limited mainly by accessibility, to include the *Washington Times,* the *Boston Globe,* the *Sun* from Baltimore, the *Philadelphia Inquirer,* the *Chicago Tribune,* and the *Los Angeles Times.* All of these, except for the *Globe,* which gradually drifts into town on Wednesday, were available on Sunday morning. Taken together with the *New York Times Book Review, Washington Post Book World,* the *New York Review of Books,* and a wide ranging sampling of magazines of all kinds, I was given the opportunity to study one aspect of the state of the American literary scene and how it works. Admittedly, accessibility favored the East and the notorious Eastern Literary Establishment, but at least the *Chicago Tribune* and the *Los Angeles Times* gave some clues as to how other cultural centers are thinking and feeling.

All of these papers routinely, under one heading or another, deal with popular genre types (mysteries, thrillers, fantasy, and science fiction, romances and historical fiction), mostly in short notices within the context of a chronicle review. Similarly, all of them call attention to a limited number of paperbacks, both reprints and originals. Audio books are now a subject of regular attention. Local and regional writers receive dutiful attention, to be sure – though it needs to be observed that each of these areas seems to have a considerable crew of writers who are of more than local interest and have more than local impact. The extent of the local attention is more a matter of "position" in the paper than anything else. All of these papers devote more attention to children's books than before. The rest of the available space (smallest in the *Sun* which, like many papers, is now reduced to a single page; most in the *New York Times Book Review,* often thirty pages or more) is devoted to reviewing literary trade books, both fiction and nonfiction. During this year it seemed to me that nonfiction occupied about two-thirds of the reviewing space. It was a year of many important biographies, memoirs, histories, and so forth, but in the absence of not-yet-available statistics, it is not clear that the preponderance of nonfiction-book reviews represents an accurate reflection of the 1992 pub-

lishing scene or is a reaction to reader interest or the concerns of the reviewing publications. My own interest and chief concern was American literary fiction; and, in general, looking at it as objectively as possible, I have to concede that these reviewing media managed, each in its own way, to review most of the "important" works of literary fiction published during the year. Although as a writer, myself, I would have preferred a better literary world, one in which more discovery and celebration of little-known or ignored talents were possible, in which the adventurous work of small presses and university presses was more appropriately considered, and allowing for the facts of life in the contemporary literary scene, I must admit, first, that faced with the constant necessity of prompt editorial choice (well in advance of publication) of which literary works are worthy of reviewing attention, I could not have done much better. Second, I would have to take note that all of these papers reviewed at least *some* books which came from outside of the conventional loop of commercial publishing. The sense of sameness, the fact that, for example, John Updike's *Memories of the Ford Administration* was given prompt and extensive coverage in all of these papers, is less the result of consensus or collusion among the reviewing media than a sense of responsibility to the limited audience for *any* literary books and a response to the efforts of publishers, by promotion and publicity, to express their own argument for the importance of a given book. Sometimes, even in the case of a distinguished writer such as Updike, the requisite jostle and hustle for attention can lead to odd, if not silly, moments. In "What It Comes Down To: A Timeout to Talk about Words" ("Tempo," *Chicago Tribune,* 29 November), we read about a meeting in fact if not of minds between Phil Jackson, coach of the Chicago Bulls, and John Updike, a conversation in which Coach Jackson cheerfully says: "The book of yours that was most meaningful to me was *Of the Farm.*" Of course Updike and his publisher (Knopf) are veterans of the game. Another approach, one which might be called the Salinger Strategy and one which has been effectively used by various literary authors in our age of publicity, is the image of indifference and reclusiveness. Profiting from this image, cultivated or natural, was novelist Cormac McCarthy, whose "breakthrough" book, *All the Pretty Horses* (Knopf), was reviewed everywhere and earned him a National Book Award. McCarthy has for years been widely publicized as a reclusive writer who avoids publicity (most recently in "Cormac McCarthy's Venomous Fiction," by Richard B. Woodward, *New York Times Magazine,* 19 April). True or not, McCarthy's asserted independence from the system (often asserted by his publisher) has produced a considerable amount of copy. His novel was promptly reviewed by all of these papers.

The case for new talent is more complex. During the year several hundred first novels were published, and some of them were widely reviewed in the newspapers. A *PW* article, "What Sells First Fiction" (16 November) argues that a favorable review in the *New York Times Book Review* can be crucial and adds the view of Susan Davis, owner of Chapter II bookstore in Charleston, South Carolina. Davis stresses that "reading copies are the best thing other than national publicity to generate sales for a first novel." Carolyn Anthony, in "Beating the Drum for Books" (*PW,* 30 November), dealt in some detail with the phenomenon of Donna Tartt and her first novel, *The Secret History* (Knopf), whose sales ballooned to an astonishing 225,000 copies as a result of massive and elegantly orchestrated publicity (advance articles and stories in *Mirabella, Vanity Fair, Vogue, Elle, M, Entertainment Weekly, Newsday,* an appearance on the *Today* show), together with readings and community coverage across the nation. There was no way the papers could avoid paying serious attention to *The Secret History* if only as an example of abundant hype.

But, all things considered, one cannot fault any of these papers for serious failure to cover the year's literary books. Some of them have gone beyond simply reporting and have created literary news by making their own awards. *Chicago Tribune Books* presents annual Nelson Algren Awards and Heartland Prizes. The *Los Angeles Times Book Review* gives the Robert Kirsch Award, the Art Seidenbaum Award for First Fiction, and awards in poetry, biography, science and technology, history, and fiction.

The *Chicago Tribune,* the *Los Angeles Times,* and the *Washington Post* have separate sections for books, albeit smaller than the *New York Times Book Review.* The *Boston Globe* locates its book reviews within the "Arts Etc." section; the *Philadelphia Inquirer* places its book pages under "View"; the *Baltimore Sun* page (usually only one) is found in "Perspective." For quality of writing, one of the best of the lot, the *Washington Times,* was, briefly, a separate section, then became a part of "Commentary," moving to "Arts" during 1992. Some of these papers feature regular reviewing by an editor or staff writer. Among the productive regulars are Carlin Romano of the *Inquirer,* Joseph Coates of *Tribune Books,* Richard Eder of the *Los Angeles Times,* Gail Caldwell of

Dust jacket for Monroe K. Spears's essays and reviews on subjects ranging from Michel Montaigne to Howard Nemorov

the *Boston Globe,* and Colin Walters of the *Washington Times.* Two other high-quality professional reviewers whose work I read with great interest when (during vacation) it was accessible were William Robertson of the *Miami Herald* and Nancy Pate of the *Orlando Sentinel.* Week after week these critics produce model book reviews of professional quality, setting a standard and a tone for their book pages. The overall quality and interest is maintained by the matching of reliable reviewers with interesting books. Here a paper like the *Sun* can come into the competition. Stuck on a page or two and, like many American papers, taking some reviews "off the wire," from other papers, the *Sun* nevertheless makes good use of a few regulars who produce outstanding reviews. Novelist Madison Smartt Bell (who also reviews for others of these papers) and poet and curator Stephen Margulies are two of these. Anne Whitehouse's reviews of the poetry of Mary Oliver and James Dickey and of *The Volcano Lover* (Farrar, Straus and Giroux), by Susan Sontag, among others, were a delightful discovery. Colin

Walters of the *Washington Times* has some noteworthy regulars – George Core of the *Sewanee Review*, Donna Rifkind formerly of the *New Criterion,* poet Henry Taylor to write about poetry, and, from time to time, heavy hitters from Walters's native England, people such as A. L. Rowse and Anthony Powell. David Slavitt, Kit Reed, and John Calvin Batchelor enhance the book pages of the *Philadelphia Inquirer,* which also found Nigerian novelist T. Obinkaram Echewa, author of *I Saw the Sky Catch Fire* (Dutton), teaching in the neighborhood and arranged for him appropriately to review fellow Nigerian Ben Okri's *The Famished Road* (Doubleday) and *Possessing the Secret of Joy* (Harcourt Brace Jovanovich), by Alice Walker.

Matchmaking books and reviewers is the principal adventure of the book editors of these papers. The *New York Times Book Review,* leader of the pack, has prestige to offer, power and glory to demonstrate, and the widest range of connections to call upon; but because it must set the standards, it bears a heavy, sometimes inhibiting weight of responsibility. Most often its matches of books and reviewers are precisely appropriate even if (sometimes) a little unusual in interesting ways, as, for example, Richard Bausch on *Black Water* (Dutton), by Joyce Carol Oates (10 May), or Robert Stone reviewing (13 December) Julian Barnes's *The Porcupine* (Knopf) or Leonard Michaels on *Magroll* (HarperCollins), by Alvaro Mutis (29 November). The other papers can take more chances with pairings, sometimes with surprising and gratifying results. From the year at *Washington Post Book World:* Ursula K. Le Guin reviewing *Ever After* (Knopf), by Graham Swift, 22 March; Shashi Tharour on *Memories of Rain* (Grove Weidenfeld), by Sunetra Gupta, 29 March; Joyce Carol Oates's review of *A Stained White Radiance* (Hyperion), by James Lee Burke, 5 April; Ellen Douglas, 21 June, reviewing *And Do Remember Me* (Doubleday), by Marita Golden; Denise Giardina's *The Unquiet Earth* (Norton), reviewed by John Howland, Jr., 19 April. *Chicago Tribune Books:* Updike's *Memories of the Ford Administration* (Knopf), by Nicholas van Hoffman, 1 November; Paul Skenazy's review of Richard Marius's *After the War* (Knopf), 14 June; Madison Smartt Bell's review of *The Unquiet Earth,* 10 May; Lawrence Norfolk's *Lempriere's Dictionary* (Harmony), reviewed by Paul West, 21 December. *Los Angeles Times Book Review: Through the Ivory Gate* (Pantheon), by Rita Dove, reviewed by Kelly Cherry, 22 November; Ron Carlson's review of *Flying In to Love* (Scribners), by D. M. Thomas, 15 November; Paul West reviewing *Almanac of the Dead* (Simon and Schuster), by Leslie Marmon Silko, 2

February. *Philadelphia Inquirer:* William T. Vollmann's review of *Regeneration* (Dutton), by Pat Barker, 19 April; Toni Morrison's *Jazz* (Knopf), reviewed by Don Belton, 26 April; Madison Smartt Bell's review of *Talents and Technicians* (Scribners), by John Aldridge, 19 April; Jim Holt reviewing *Brightness Falls* (Knopf), by Jay McInerney, 31 May; Maureen Howard's *Natural History* (Norton), reviewed by Kit Reed, 1 November. *Baltimore Sun:* Anne Whitehouse's review of *I Am the Clay* (Knopf), by Chaim Potok, 31 May; Madison Smartt Bell's review of *Sailor Song* (Viking), by Ken Kesey, 23 August. *Boston Globe:* Pinckney Benedict's review of *The Unquiet Earth,* by Giardina, 7 June; Aharon Appelfeld's *Katerina* (Random House), by Louis Begley.

Outside the limited loop of newspaper reviewing but nevertheless noteworthy examples of matching book with reviewer are Ward Just's "Bill Kennedy's Great Game," review of *Very Old Bones* (Viking), *GQ,* May 1992, and Marianne Wiggins's devastating critique of Edna O'Brien's *Time and Tide* (Farrar, Straus and Giroux) in the *Nation,* 13 July.

With everyone else making lists of notable writers and notable books of the year, I can find no good reason not to make my own list of favorite newspaper book reviews and reviewers in 1992. Like any other list, it is not fair. Truth is, the quality of book reviewing in the magazines and newspapers I read was very high. One might sometimes disagree with conclusions and judgments, but could not fault many for style and persuasiveness. Nevertheless a few writers and their articles and reviews seemed to me outstanding and worthy of special attention. To do this I have created two basic categories: first, Gold Stars for well-written, positive reviews; second, Tomahawk Chop for savagery in well-executed negative notices. People are forever claiming that there are not enough negative or cautionary book reviews. All in all, they seem to be wrong, at least as far as 1992 is concerned.

Gold-Star Reviewers

Madison Smartt Bell, review of *The Secret History* (Random House), by Donna Tartt, *Baltimore Sun,* 27 September. "Her tone is deep, rich and reflective, carrying a pleasant shade of Peter Taylor's voice, perhaps, or weaker hint of Henry James."

Irving Malin, review of *Maria's Girls* (Mysterious), by Jerome Charyn, *Forward,* 7 August. "Mr. Charyn's Isaac Seidel novels have the brilliant elliptical quality of the biblical commentators and of the mystics."

Gene Lyons, review of *Nothing But Blue Skies* (Houghton Mifflin), by Tom McGuane, *Entertainment Weekly,* 18 September. "Somewhat to the dismay of critics who once praised him as his generation's Hemingway, McGuane, 52, has devoted much of his literary career to a series of domestic tragicomedies set against a landscape that inspires his characters to awe even as it mocks their emotional ineptitude and isolation."

David Slavitt, review of *The Volcano Lover* (Farrar, Straus and Giroux), by Susan Sontag, *Chicago Tribune Books,* 9 August. "Imagine Hannah Arendt having a good time by doing an impersonation of Kathleen Windsor – 'The Volcano Lover' is that peculiar."

Kit Reed, review of *Turtle Moon* (Putnam's) by Alice Hoffman, *Philadelphia Inquirer,* 10 May. "He's [a dog named Arrow] right up there with Anne Tyler's Edward in *The Accidental Tourist* and Bodger in Graham Greene's *The Human Factor.*"

Thomas Disch, review of *Live From Golgotha* (Random House), by Gore Vidal, *The Nation,* 16 November. "Gore Vidal is our Pope of Fools, and in *Live From Golgotha* he has produced the most sustained and programmatically outrageous blasphemy to tweak the nose of official piety since Monty Python's *Life of Brian.*"

Robert Ward, review of *After the War* (Knopf), by Richard Marius, *New York Times Book Review,* 21 June. "This is a novel that fans of such a simple work as Larry McMurtry's 'Lonesome Dove' and Pat Conroy's 'Prince of Tides' should love."

Tomahawk Chops

James R. Alvin, review of *Time, Like An Ever-Rolling Stream* (St. Martin's Press), by Judith Moffett, *Philadelphia Inquirer.* "I suppose there are people who will enjoy Judith Moffett's sequel to her *The Ragged World.* However, they will have to be people who conceive of canning tomatoes as an act of 'deep reverence.'"

Kate Braverman, review of *Amazon* (HarperCollins), by Barbara G. Walker, *Los Angeles Times,* 13 September. "This book is entirely filled with sub-dimensional caricatures. It is a contrivance of unplausible plot developments and dialogue of the 'Me Tarzan, You Jane' variety."

Michiko Kakutani, review of *Flying In to Love* (Scribners), by D. M. Thomas, *New York Times,* 29 September. "He has turned the story of the President and his assassination into a sordid and willfully sensationalistic tale about an oversexed man and the people he turned on."

Alexander Theroux, review of *The Blindfold* (Poseidon), by Siri Hustvet, *Washington Post,* 10 September. "There is much self-examining vanity in her, so much cheese-paring rhetoric brought to bear on many inconsequential episodes, humorless contretemps after contretemps, with cryptic things being said – much college and Sensitive New Age rhetoric – but so little is ever resolved that you start to feel the flaws of the first novel (which this is)."

Donna Rifkind, review of *The Lost Father* (Knopf), by Mona Simpson, *Washington Post,* 4 February. "In all her voyages around the country and the globe she seems to have garnered nothing except frequent-flyer miles."

Donna Rifkind, review of *Jazz* (Knopf), by Toni Morrison, the *Washington Times,* 12 April. "In 'Jazz' Toni Morrison's considerable anger seems to have channeled all its energy away from story-telling and toward a scornful disregard for the reader."

Peter S. Prescott, review of *Bay of Arrows* (Holt), by Jay Parini, *New York Times Book Review,* 20 September. "Now for the next question that everyone's been avoiding. Can a politically correct novel be a good novel too? 'Bay of Arrows' makes a strong case for the negative."

John Calvin Batchelor, review of *West of Everything* (Oxford), by Jane Tompkins, *Chicago Tribune Books,* 5 April. "Bluntly Tompkins attacks the Western as sexist, racist, impertinent, anti-intellectual and probably sadomasochistic, slave-mongering and genocidal and possibly responsible for perverting the souls of every American to the point that the USA is a war-mongering superpower of white male anti-Christs."

Michael Mewshaw, review of *Beyond Center Court* (Morrow), by Tracy Austin with Christine Brennan, *Washington Post,* 31 July. "She describes one uplifting occasion when she addressed a convention of Pontiac executives. 'It was quite a day. I was on first, then came General Norman Schwarzkopf . . . followed by singer Lee Greenwood, who finished the evening with his song, Proud to Be an American. There was not a dry eye in the house!' Maybe you had to be there.' "

The title of the best all-around literary journalist clearly goes to a *Washington Post* writer – David Streitfeld. Streitfeld's regular column in *Washington Post Book World,* "Book Report," together with his features and interviews for the daily "Style" section in the *Post,* taken with his occasional chronicle reviews of genre books, demonstrates a sympathetic, but entirely unsentimental understanding of the literary scene from all angles. He knows publishing, and he monitors that world carefully. He understands writers, their charades and hustles as well as their legitimate joys and sorrows. In dealing with both the publishers and their writers, he is close to being fearless. If he has limitations they are those of youth; he is not yet secure enough to trust his sense of "discovery" of new or neglected talents outside of the usual hierarchy and network. His final piece in 1992, "The Wandering Jew" (*Washington Post,* 31 December) concerns the year of Salman Rushdie:

'The Satanic Verses,' whose alleged blasphemy is the cause of all the trouble, was finally published in this country in paperback nine months ago. Hardly anyone cared. The days when the book sold briskly as a way of giving the finger to the Ayatollahs are long gone.

Among the quarterlies and literary magazines the situation of book reviewing keeps changing slightly. Among the established quarterlies (the *Sewanee Review* celebrated its centennial in 1992. See Edmund Fuller, "A Literary Citadel Honored," *Wall Street Journal,* 25 November.) the *Virginia Quarterly Review,* the *Sewanee,* and the *Hudson Review* continue to offer a full range of critical essays and book reviews as well as new fiction and poetry. For example, the centennial issue of the *Sewanee Review* included critical essays by James Sloan Allen, Earl Rovit, J. R. Barbarese, Lewis P. Simpson, Robert B. Heilman, and Monroe Spears. In addition there were essay and chronicle reviews, dealing with about eighty books, written by M. E. Bradford, Edmund Fuller, Donald Hall, Pat C. Hoy II, Sam Pickering, Walter Sullivan, and others. "Current Books in Review" offered eleven shorter reviews of recent books. It needs to be added that, in terms of space for criticism and book reviewing, this issue is about average. Other periodicals showed a reduction in the amount of criticism and reviewing. The *Georgia Review* does less than it used to, though the quality of the pieces is high. It is a little early to pass judgment, but it seems that, under new editorial management, the *Southern Review* will publish a good deal less critical work than it did under Lewis P. Simpson. Dave Smith's Autumn 1992 issue is, predictably, filled with fiction and poetry by a variety of familiar and established names with minimal space left for reviews; but the reviews published are by very good writers – Fred Chappell, Richard Tillinghast, and Nathan A. Scott, Jr.; and the materials covered are timely and pertinent. Particularly worthy is Nathan Scott's judicious close look at *The Return of Nat Turner: History, Literature, & Cultural Pol-*

itics in Sixties America (University of Georgia Press), by Albert E. Stone.

If criticism is just holding its own or even losing ground in some of the literary magazines, it seems to be expanding its impact and influence in some other places. Particularly impressive is the *Review of Contemporary Fiction,* edited by John O'Brien and Steven Moore (who likewise edit the rapidly growing Dalkey Archive Press). Their emphasis remains chiefly "avant-garde literature," foreign and domestic, and without their attention over recent years many books would have received little, if any, notice. Now, in large part because of the attention and success garnered by the *Review,* "mainstream" publications are dealing with more experimental and adventurous works even as the *Review* pays a little more attention to more mainstream literary writing. The Summer 1992 issue of the *Review,* the "Jose Donoso/Jerome Charyn Number," is typical of one kind of regular issue, devoted mainly to the work of one or more established literary writers. This issue presents eighty-five pages on Chilean novelist Jose Donoso, twelve article-length pieces, including a checklist and an interview with the author; followed by a roughly equal section on the fiction of Brooklyn's Jerome Charyn. There is a full-length essay by the late Edoard Roditi – "The Fiction of Jane Bowles as a Form of Self-Exorcism." And finally there are some fifty fairly brief reviews of a wide variety of new books, ten of them written by the brilliant and prolific contributing editor Irving Malin. There are books by commercial publishers (Pantheon; Poseidon; Farrar, Straus and Giroux; Braziller; Bantam; Penguin; Random House; Dutton; Viking; Simon and Schuster) cheek by jowl with university press books (Columbia, Massachusetts, New Mexico, Wisconsin, Duke, Illinois, Nebraska, Texas) and books from old and new small presses (City Lights, Red Dust, Marlboro, Serpent's Tale, Black Sparrow, Shuffaloff, Story Line, Asylum Arts, Fiction Collective, Sun and Moon, Oasis, Arcade, Papier-Mache, Gnomon, Four Walls Eight Windows, Tundra). In short, though their chief subject matter is highly "literary," the editors of the *Review of Contemporary Fiction* manage to be authentically representative of the range and complexity of the American publishing scene. It becomes a little easier to conceive of the eighty thousand titles by nine hundred publishers produced in America during 1991. Of necessity the *Review* is also international in its orientation. The Fall 1992 issue, "New Italian Fiction," is built around excerpts from the work of fourteen contemporary Italian writers, introduced by guest editor Francesco Guardiani, and the usual fifty-odd pages of various reviews.

Also international and equally interested in a wide range and variety of literary culture is the huge (more than seven hundred pages) monthly magazine associated with the *Washington Times – The World & I.* This unusual magazine has been singled out for attention and praise in earlier volumes of the *DLB Yearbook,* and that praise deserves reiteration. Each issue has a section, "Book World," of roughly one hundred pages, consisting of a "Featured Book," including an excerpt, followed by several essays by various hands, "Commentary," followed by "Reviews," made up of ten or twelve essay reviews (of roughly twenty-five hundred words each) of new books. As if that were not enough, there are other sections which may or may not involve literary criticism: "The Arts," "Currents in Modern Thought," "Culture." The October 1992 issue of *The World & I* even manages to invade its own "Natural Science" section with a piece by critic Hugh Kenner, "Learning Not to Forget," which turns out to be a serious and extensive examination of the next generation of compact-disc technology. In that same issue the "Featured Book" is David James Duncan's *The Brothers K* (Doubleday). Among the works of fiction reviewed are Vyacheslav Pyetsukh's *The Enchanted Country* (Banner Magazine); *Ancestral Voices* (Viking), by Etienne van Heerden; *The Boy Without a Flag* (Milkwood), by Abraham Rodriguez, Jr.; Annie Dillard's *The Living* (HarperCollins); and, in "Listen to the Sisters!," by Charles R. Larson, an examination of new novels by black women writers – Terry McMillan, Toni Morrison, Marita Golden, Alice Walker, and Barbara Neely. Under "Currents in Modern Thought" there are five critics writing essays on "Looking for the Good: Ideals in American Literature," and, separately, "Words and Places: The Geography of Literature," by Larry Woiwode. The last proves to be a passionate attack on the Political Correctness of the Eastern Literary Establishment which, he concludes, "is truly nihilism gone Nazi."

Multiply the October 1992 issue by twelve and you have an idea of the book-reviewing scope of *The World & I.* I find that many editors, both of books and periodicals, are not as familiar with *The World & I* as they ought to be. Politics may have a lot to do with this. (To that extent Woiwode is right in his complaint.) Nevertheless *The World & I* is doing good service to our literature, as are two other conservative monthly magazines – *Chronicles* and the *New Criterion.* Under books editor Chilton Williamson, Jr., *Chronicles* has expanded both the variety and depth of its coverage. There are on average about a dozen essay-reviews for each issue. Similarly, the "Books" section of the *New Criterion* regularly publishes essay-reviews by an impressive list of conservative critics led by people such as Bruce Bawer, James Bowman, and James W. Tuttleton.

It may seem odd that most of the publications that feature full-length critical reviews, as distinguished from newspaper notices, are generally conservative in viewpoint unless it is that the whole idea of reviewing books, perhaps even the idea of the book, itself, is old-fashioned if not outmoded; but, in any case, the critical business of reviewing books continues in a variety of forms and places. And at least some serious readers are grateful that this is so.

As to the popular magazines. Among the somewhat beleaguered general-interest magazines the space allowed for book reviews has shrunk significantly. *Newsweek* and *Time* have now severely reduced their offerings. Under the much-reported new regime of Tina Brown at the *New Yorker,* books have become a back-of-the-book subcategory under the general rubric "The Critics." So far there has been one essay-review in each issue, somewhat shorter than in the earlier, more leisurely days and supplemented by a one-page "Books Briefly Noted" with five or six very short notices. It is too early to tell what will happen at the *New Yorker* except to acknowledge the impression that Ms. Brown does not seem likely to expand this kind of coverage. Ironically, just as some familiar places seem to be reducing their attention to books and literary matters some others are moving toward increasing concern. The fashion magazines, slick with coated paper, apt to be odoriferous with perfume samples, fat with flashy advertising of designer clothing and luxury products, seem to be finding more and more space for literary matters. Carol Houck Smith of Norton suggests that this development can be beneficial, particularly to those writers classified as "literary": "I think that this is the newest kind of literary repository. And I think it can give a literary writer some valuable exposure." Some of the books reviewed and writers featured in the fashion magazines during 1992 are, at first glance, surprising. Among literary writers in *Vogue,* for example: Nicholson Baker, Ellen Gilchrist, Fay Weldon, Anita Brookner, Francine Prose, Toni Morrison, David Lodge, William Kennedy, Richard Price, Jay McInerney, Alice Hoffman, Edna O'Brien, Terry McMillan, Susan Sontag, Elmore Leonard, Gloria Naylor, and John Updike. Some of the other magazines – *Elle, Mirabella, Vanity Fair, GQ,* and (sometimes) *Harper's*

Kristin van Ogtrop, book coordinator for Vogue

Bazaar – did almost as much, dealing with the same authors and many others. To understand this developing situation *DLB Yearbook* has asked Kristin van Ogtrop, book coordinator for *Vogue,* to write a short piece about the place of literary matters in the fashion magazines, a view from the inside. Ms. van Ogtrop has been with *Vogue* since 1990. Before that time she worked for Farrar, Straus and Giroux and as production office coordinator for Lear Levin Productions. She is a graduate of the University of Virginia and earned an M.A. in English at Columbia University.

SOME SURPRISES AND UNIVERSAL TRUTHS

Kristin van Ogtrop

It is a pretty fair assumption to say that most consumers do not buy American fashion magazines for their thought-provoking book reviews. That is why one sets out with the lowest expectations to look for books in these magazines. Surprises await –

some quite pleasant. Two magazines in particular, *Mirabella* and *GQ ,* have taken a brave step away from the pack of their competition, offering lots of book coverage with a broad range of reviewers, reviewees, and types of books. The remaining fashion "slicks" – *Vogue, Harper's Bazaar, Elle, Esquire,* and (stretching the definition of "fashion magazine") *Vanity Fair* – are a mixed bag. They all marched through 1992 like ducks on parade, intent (whether consciously or not) on repeating what the guy in front was doing. Occasionally each magazine would allow a peep of originality, but for the most part everyone was reviewing the same books as everyone else, and at the same time. No wonder that, to the untrained eye, they all look alike.

They look similar, in part, because none of the fashion magazines actually runs book "reviews." Most often, longer articles are devoted to author profiles to coincide with the publication of a book. These articles, while often written by well-known critics, are more straight publicity than review. Even the magazines which have pages of shorter reviews (*Vogue* – "Arts in Brief," *Mirabella* – "Short List," *GQ* – "Recommends") present these bylined mentions more as endorsements than critiques. Some criticism can squeak by, but the general feeling among editors is that, as there are so many books published each month, why waste precious pages tearing something down? There are some exceptions to this rule; criticizing something that is overloved and overhyped can make an editor feel original, *lawless.* But praise is generally the order of the month.

In the women's magazines, *Mirabella* continues to lead its competition in total book pages. With at least one long author profile/essay per month, as well as occasional "bookish" essays by established writers (such as Shirley Abbott's rereading of *Gone With the Wind* in April), *Mirabella* seems grounded in a historical literary perspective that is refreshing: in May, Sven Birkerts wrote a long piece to mark the publication of Ann Hulbert's *The Interior Castle: The Art and Life of Jean Stafford* (Knopf), and the August issue featured an adaptation from Carol Brightman's *Writing Dangerously* (Clarkson Potter), the biography of Mary McCarthy. Most books covered by *Mirabella* come from editors, agents, or writers themselves who already have a relationship with Amy Gross, the magazine's editor, or Pat Towers, the senior editor for books; these sources must consider pitching books five months in advance, to allow time for choosing the book, assigning a reviewer, and writing the piece. The books covered in *Mirabella* are fairly split between male and female authors, but this is not a conscious move on the part of the editors. *Mirabella* editors do make an effort to represent a range of interest in their book coverage – and to "discover" books their competition might not pick up – and use a "Short List" (mostly staff written) particularly for this purpose. One thing that is clear from 1992: *Mirabella* is very interested in excerpts; finding books to excerpt (or "adapt") is a much bigger priority (and greater challenge, since perhaps one in twenty excerpt possibilities even makes it to the desk of Gay Bryant, editor in chief) than finding new authors. In 1992 *Mirabella* ran excerpts or adaptations from Carol Matthau's *Among the Porcupines* (Random House), in May, Carol Brightman's *Writing Dangerously* (Potter), in August, and Eric Alterman's *Sound and Fury* (HarperCollins), in October.

Vogue, on the other hand, has decreased its number of excerpts over the years. "It's a lazy way to edit," says Michael Boodro, features editor. "I think a magazine should generate its own original material." Boodro has seen a slight decrease in book reviews in the magazine since the late 1980s, due mainly to a decrease in ad pages (the scourge of the early 1990s) – not because books have lost importance in the overall scheme. *Vogue* continued to present strong book coverage in 1992, with at least one long review per month, supplemented in five months with short, staff-written reviews in "Arts in Brief." On occasion *Vogue* will run a "round-up" or "trend"-type essay, such as April Bernard's July piece on sequelizing classics (*Wuthering Heights, Huckleberry Finn, Dr. Zhivago*) or Edward Jay Epstein's examination of four new books on the 1980s "robber barons." In book coverage there is as much attention paid to *who* is reviewing a book as to *which* book is being reviewed. Assigning a piece to a respected reviewer–A. N. Wilson, Jane Smiley, John Updike – signals to readers that *Vogue* takes its book coverage seriously. "I might care what John Updike thinks about Jane Doe's novel," Boodro insists, "but I probably won't care what Jane Doe thinks of Updike." Like *Mirabella, Vogue* does not consciously choose books written by women. Boodro asks, "Will it appeal to an intelligent sophisticated person of either sex?"

After *Mirabella* and *Vogue,* book coverage in the top women's fashion magazines has an erratic, slapdash feel. *Elle* showed some quirky originality in 1992: Stepen O'Shea's January essay on Canadian novelists (Alice Munro, Margaret Atwood, Audrey Thomas); Louise Farr's piece in March on women's attraction to books about sociopaths; and a Mark Dery article in May on "techno-feminist" writers. However, what *Elle* gains in breaking from the pack, angle-wise, it loses in its lack of big-name reviewers and its weak showing in fiction coverage, focusing instead on sociology and biography. Overall, it was slim pickings at *Elle* in 1992 – in one month, June, the magazine had no book coverage at all.

The late winter appointment of Liz Tilberis as editor in chief of *Harper's Bazaar* sent a ripple of fear and suspense through the halls of *Vogue, Mirabella,* and *Elle,* as editors held a collective breath and waited for Tilberis's much-touted first issue for September. Until that point, the *Harper's Bazaar* book coverage was a particularly weak element of the slim features pages in a moribund magazine. Tilberis – with Hearst Corporation president Claeys Bahrenburg looking over her shoulder – boosted ad sales and features pages both, changing the face of *Harper's Bazaar* at least for the present. There was no mention of books whatsoever in *Harper's Bazaar* in the months of January, March, April, and June. Business picked up in August with a Kaylie Jones piece on "highbrow and sinful" beach reading: the Yves Montand biography (Knopf), Josephine Hart's *Sin* (Knopf), and (for literary sunbathers) Susan Sontag's *Volcano Lover* (Farrar, Straus and Giroux). Tilberis cast a tentative line into the waters of book reviewing with one book piece in each of her first two issues: Brendan Lemon on Paul Auster and *Leviathan* (Viking) and a Mark Matonsek piece in October on the multitude of celebrity-penned children's books in bookstores today (Whoopi, Paulina – that crowd). However, the November issue blazed onto the newsstands with no fewer than three book-related pieces: Polly Samson on Antonia Fraser and *The Wives of Henry VIII* (Knopf), Lauren Hutton on William Burroughs and *The Cat Inside* (Viking), and Peggy Noonan on Edith Wharton and the dead novelist's puzzling present popularity.

The men's magazines are a funny lot, shattering expectations as they do. For those who still think that *Esquire* = literature, get over it. In 1992 *GQ* outpaced *Esquire* month after month in book reviews and author profiles (and fiction). While *Esquire* threw its reader the occasional book excerpt, *GQ* featured Mordecai Richler's bimonthly column, "Books and Things," as well as lengthy author profiles and "*GQ* Recommends," a small regular book review written by Tom Mallon, *GQ*'s literary editor. Although Mallon admits the book pages are probably read less than other sections of the magazine, *GQ*'s book coverage has increased in the past year. However, Mallon admits, "There is an evangelical quality to all of this coverage. . . . The nature of the coverage is to celebrate things, and to bring good things to people's attention." He is quick to add, "Which does not mean the magazine is at all Pollyannaish." Mallon allows that *GQ* attracts a male readership, but calls attention to his efforts to review and publish fiction by women (still not enough for this writer's taste). "I think a balance wouldn't be logical or desirable for this magazine," Mallon says, "but it would be wrong for the magazine to become a boy's club." *GQ* covers a wide variety of types of writers, from established literary sorts like Darryl Pinckney (March) and William Kennedy (May), to journalists like Joan Didion (May), to Interesting People You've Never Heard Of, like a female umpire named Pam Postema (June), to hard-boiled, gum-behind-the-ear sorts like James Ellroy (October). *GQ* is trying hard for that literary feel: to end every issue, a last page called Literary Fashion presents a fashion-oriented quote from the work of a major writer (with a big illustration).

Only one word can describe book coverage in *Esquire* in 1992: disappointing. Like *Elle, Esquire* made some stabs at originality in choices: a mention of *The Portable Beat Reader* (Viking), in January; Michael Wallis's *Pretty Boy: The Life and Times of Charles Arthur Floyd* (St. Martin's Press), in April; Tom Chiarella's *Foley's Luck* (Knopf), in September. But the *Esquire* book coverage goes slack in its manner of coverage: books appear most frequently in the short (and more often unbylined) "Man At His Best" section at the front of the magazine. *Esquire* did run several long excerpts in 1992, but of a quite predictable, macho/popular kind: from Richard Price's *Clockers* (Houghton Mifflin), in May; Jay McInerney's *Brightness Falls* (Knopf), in June; and Tom McGuane's *Nothing But Blue Skies* (Houghton Mifflin), in October. One solitary high point: a long September piece by Chip Brown on Ken Kesey. Women – authors and reviewers alike – fare far worse at *Esquire* than at *GQ*. On balance, the women's magazines are much more equality-minded about admitting the Other Sex than vice versa.

On 30 September the death knell tolled for *M*. The subscriber list was sold to *GQ*, and a few more editors were tossed out into what was already a bad job market. It is unlikely that readers will miss *M* for its high literariness; the book reviewing was dreadful (well, nonexistent) for most of the year. We cannot blame the editors: by the end *M* was a slim package indeed – one imagines anxious editors arm wrestling for page space. The essays of Daniel Max, however, deserve mention. In April he wrote an entertaining, original piece entitled "Late

Night with the Literati," about one night on the New York publishing party circuit; in September he provided a piece on what Washington is reading – long and informative, and another interesting idea. We can only hope to find more of Max (who covers books for *Variety*) elsewhere in the future.

Maybe Graydon Carter will give him a job. Conde Nast emperor Si Newhouse's unexpected sacking of Bob Gottlieb on 30 June and replacement by Tina Brown as editor in chief of the *New Yorker* kept the media buzzing for weeks. Brown's *Vanity Fair* was never a massive showcase for literary talent; under new editor in chief Graydon Carter, however, books seem to be slipping from their back-burner status and off the stove altogether. While *Vanity Fair* makes mention of the *largest* number of books among the magazines here discussed, it does so largely in the "Hot Type" page of what is now called "Vanities" (formerly "Fanfair"). And "Hot Type" is nothing more than a list, really, of thirteen or so books, many of which are reviewed more thoroughly in most other consumer magazines. From time to time in 1992 *Vanity Fair* devoted an entire "Fanfair" / "Vanities" page to an author with a new book; the May issue was the highlight in this sense, with Priscilla Rattazzi, Studs Terkel, and William Gibson and Dennis Ashbaugh all featured in "Fanfair." In the same month Michael Shnayerson wrote a long piece on Jay McInerney (more on his new marriage than his oeuvre), and Bob Colacello did his bit on Ivana (remember? – she became a novelist this year). However, these two articles are emblematic of the sort of long author profiles *Vanity Fair* publishes: the writer must be pretty, rich, or already famous, and it helps if he/she is all three. There are exceptions. The August issue featured a piece by Luke Jennings on English author James Hamilton-Patterson (and his new Random House novel, *The Great Deep*), and James Wolcott (lost, lamentably, to cover television at the *New Yorker*) managed four times this year to provide readers with essays on serious literary topics – written, as always, in his oddball style.

Finally, several Universal Truths about the way books are covered in fashion magazines. First: there is no room for "sleepers" or surprise best-sellers (Terry McMillan's *Waiting to Exhale,* which many of the magazines missed – or at least underestimated – is a perfect example). With a three-month lead time (at least), magazine editors must rely on agents, editors, and publicists to tell them what will be good. And so you have, in 1992, a phenomenon like Donna Tartt and *The Secret History* (Knopf). The word on Donna Tartt spread like the plague throughout the industry, infecting magazines and newspapers and television shows alike. The only magazines here studied that did not mention her are *Harper's Bazaar* and *GQ*; Tom Mallon of *GQ* describes the insular publishing world as "one floating party," and says, regarding cases like Tartt's, "You don't want to be taken in. You don't want to ride the curve of somebody." Which leads to the second Universal Truth, the catch-22 of magazine publishing: the tremendous tension between covering undiscovered talent, while at the same time not missing anything anyone else is doing. In the case of Donna Tartt, editors found a marriage of the two: an unknown writer, bursting onto the scene, whom *everyone* was covering. Too new to pass up, too hot to miss.

Such repetitive overkill can be prevented. Michael Boodro of *Vogue* feels publishers could make more of an effort to promote small books. Any book editor at any magazine would agree that publishers are completely indiscriminate in what they send out; sending the galley of a bodice-ripping romance or the autobiography of a professional wrestler to a magazine like *Vogue,* or *Mirabella,* or *any* of the women's magazines is a waste of time, money, paper, and hope.

And so one leaves the pages of the fashion magazines feeling satisfied that certain discerning readers could identify the work of Oscar de la Renta *and* Oscar Hijuelos. Most of the magazines could do more . . . but this reader is thankful when books make it in at all.

AN INTERVIEW WITH KRISTIN VAN OGTROP

George Garrett

GARRETT: Since, at last report, roughly four out of five readers of contemporary trade books, both fiction and nonfiction, are women (college-educated women and the majority forty and older), do the women's fashion magazines have this in mind, if only as a general responsibility to their own consumers? And, by the same token, does it seem to you that the publishers are aware of the power, *potential* power, anyway, of the fashion magazines to reach their consumers?

VAN OGTROP: The catch for us—and for our competitors, certainly – is that the average *Vogue* reader is the college-educated woman, many of them forty and older, although strictly speaking we're an early thirties magazine. So yes, we do

think about what our readers would like, although we do not dwell on the fact that the demographics of our readership and the book-buying segment of the population match up.

Now for the publishers – I definitely think they are aware of the power some of the fashion magazines have, book-wise. When I asked Paul Slovak, who is the director of publicity of Viking, if he felt that the reviews in fashion magazines were important to him, I got this silence, like – what do you mean? I get the feeling with literary writers – those who aren't going to make it to the best-seller list without lots of prodding – that publicists and editors are thrilled for any kind of publicity they can get. They know as well as we do that we're not going to print a blatantly bad review of *anything*. We're not out to ruffle feathers. Anyway, Paul Slovak told me this little story about how *Mirabella*'s excerpting of Blanche Cook's Eleanor Roosevelt biography was very instrumental in getting Cook on the *Today* show. Now, I don't have figures, but if that won't help sales, I don't know what will. I guess that's a sneaky, backdoor way of saying the fashion magazines help sales.

GARRETT: While it seems clear that the magazines furnish a good deal of news and information about the literary world, do you think they have any serious influence on sales of books or on general critical response and reputation?

VAN OGTROP: I think there is no question that serious coverage, even in the fashion magazines, will influence book sales; *particularly* because there is so much copycatting going on that certain authors – Gay Talese, Spalding Gray, Paul Auster and, obviously, Donna Tartt are good examples from 1992 – will get covered in just about all of the competitive men's and women's fashion magazines. A number of our readers read us *and* our competitors, every month. After a while I would just think people would feel almost forced to buy a certain book, after reading about it for the nth time.

I am surprised, in fact, how seriously fashion magazines reviews are taken sometimes. One personal example: I wrote a very short review of Gloria Naylor's *Bailey's Cafe* in the "Arts in Brief" section of *Vogue*'s September issue. Several weeks after the on-sale date of our issue, I got a call from a friend in Philadelphia who had noticed a quote from me in the *Bailey's Cafe* ad in the *New York Times*. I was astounded, to say the least: little nobody me, writing in *Vogue* of all places. I thought certainly Harcourt

Brace Jovanovich could do better than that for a writer like Gloria Naylor – which is not to say that I think my review was no good, but who am I? – but there it was again, the following Sunday in the book review. And the ad also used a quote from my friend Adele Sulcas at *Mirabella,* another relative nobody. Maybe this story just begs the question: what is more important, a glowing review or a prestigious reviewer? The answer probably depends on who you ask.

Now, to quickly answer the last part of your question: I don't think my little review in *Vogue* helped add to Gloria Naylor's reputation one iota. I do not think any reputations (literary, that is) are made in the fashion magazines.

GARRETT: You make it quite clear that the long lead time for literary journalism puts the magazines more or less at the mercy of agents, editors, publicists, all the hustlers and cheerleaders of the lit biz. It is quite clear, a good point, that under present conditions any kind of "discovery," outside of the boundaries of the Literary Establishment and separate from the ways and means of the publishing industry, is almost impossible. Can you see or imagine any efficient way to change that, to make a successful fashion magazine more of an independent power, a mover and shaker on the scene?

VAN OGTROP: Not really. Tom Mallon at *GQ* told me that he might consider devoting a small review to a paperback edition of a book he missed when it came out in hardcover. That's about the boldest step I've heard, frankly. The only way I could think of making a fashion magazine more in step with instant successes, or more able to *create* instant successes, is if there were such a thing as a *weekly* fashion magazine. When you're working with a magazine like the *New Yorker* or *Entertainment Weekly* you have a lot more flexibility, in a way. (I'm sure all of the weekly editors who work until 3 A.M. on closing nights would love to hear me say that.) But when you're dealing with a monthly and you've got to get things locked in so early for your advertisers, it's hard to wait till the last minute to assign your stories. I guess if I stayed up all night for seven nights in a row I might be able to think of a way to make the fashion magazines more in touch with movement, but nothing comes instantly to mind.

GARRETT: Sometimes, in the case of "literary" writers (and essentially that is what we are talking about here), the actual difference in sales between a "known" writer and an "unknown," at least

in hardcover, is negligible by any serious standard. It can make a real difference in paperback sales, for example, or maybe advances for future works and even for prizes and awards, if a given work by a writer is well or widely received in your pages. But it honestly does not look like you all make much difference, if any, in *sales.* Not like the prominent newspapers, for example. I wonder why. Got any guesses or ideas?

VAN OGTROP: Well, disregarding pretty much everything I've said so far, you can wonder how much our readers actually *read* our book coverage. Maybe we don't sell books because no one is reading the reviews. Now a lot of magazines, including most of Conde Nast, do these nifty little studies run by a man named Mark Clements; it's basically a mail-run thing where his company sends magazines to readers and asks them to rate each page: Very Interesting, Fairly Interesting, Somewhat Interesting, and so on. Each story (fashion shoot, book review, health column) is assigned percentages, degrees of interest if you will. The book pages rate just about as well (or as poorly) as everything else, and sometimes beat some of the more outre fashion spreads. Of course, they never rate as high as the fashion spreads can and sometimes do. (I have noticed that, at least in *Vogue,* reviews of books by women rate higher than reviews of books by men.)

But who knows? I was riding the subway this spring, watching a woman thumb through our April issue, our 100th anniversary issue, the one we'd all slaved and worried and driven each other to the brink of insanity over for months. I watched as this woman flipped quickly past each page of text and most fashion pages, and lingered lovingly over the ads. Who *knows* what readers are doing sometimes? Days like those you want to get a job in construction.

GARRETT: You mention, quite accurately, the personal element – the fact that an author's claim to attention is, in the context of fashion magazines, dependent on a number of personal variables which may or may not have anything much to do with the books. That makes sense in our world. But how about the books? Is one subject more important than another regardless of who the author is? Are there subjects (in and of themselves and never mind the quality of the works) which are understood to be of inherent interest to your readers? Are there taboo subjects? Are there ideas that might be defined as "unacceptable?"

VAN OGTROP: As far as fiction goes, there are no subjects that are taboo. There are certain subjects we're probably not as drawn to, and it's all very subjective, depending on what kind of person is choosing the books. You don't see a lot of novels in *Vogue* about suburban housewives, simply because we don't have any suburban housewives on staff. There are, however, a number of gay men at *Vogue,* and we may just have a disproportionate number of books about or by gay men, if anyone's checking. Personal taste is everything.

In nonfiction, I would say there are a number of taboo subjects. I had several women in my office a few weeks ago from HarperSan Francisco, which publishes a lot of wonderful and a few very strange books. They have a book coming up in the spring of 1993 on menstruation and the greatness of menstruation and how women ought to get in touch with their inner, essential, menstruating selves, and how PMS is a good thing, etc., etc. I thought to myself — "Women getting their periods. This will never sell at *Vogue*." It's too groovy and unshaven-leggy. There are also subjects we would never do not because they are taboo necessarily, but because they're being done on "Sally Jesse Raphael" and the "Maury Povich Show": bulimic sister of famous people, that sort of thing.

GARRETT: Following up on that. You mention, both obliquely and directly, the sense these magazines have of themselves as arbiters of taste and, indeed, as teachers as well. In a classical sense they intend to offer some instruction (in various ways) as well as delight. How does this work in books? That is, surely one part of it is to acquaint your readers, and give them some guidance, too, with the latest developments on the literary scene. But is there also the old pedagogical notion of working to change the readers' taste and values? Is there any sense of *advocacy* in the literary journalism of the fashion magazines? If so, what do they advocate?

VAN OGTROP: I don't think we are actively trying to change anyone's tastes. I do think we try to raise people's consciousnesses — to inform people of writers they may not know and to let them make their own decisions as far as whether they will like these new folks or not. I do think, in the kind of reviewers we hire and the type of books we cover, we are definitely aiming at the high end (educationally, financially) of our readership almost all of the time. We sometimes assume our readers have a whole literary frame of reference that I think few of them actually have. There's certainly a lot of cultural elitism flying around; I don't know if we maintain that to edify our readers or to satisfy ourselves. Books aside, I think our features do advocate open-mindedness and liberalism. You would never, for example, see an antiabortion article in *Vogue*. During one of our preelection features meetings, one of our senior editors accused another of wanting to vote for Bush. The accused editor cried, "I have never voted anything but Democratic in my entire life!" Among the group in that room, accusing someone of wanting to vote Republican was an insult of the highest order.

GARRETT: You are a writer, yourself, and are just now finishing up your first novel. Do you find it difficult to work as a journalist with books and the literary scene and to write your own fiction at the same time? Is there conflict and tension? Does your special knowledge of how things work condition the kind of writing you do?

VAN OGTROP: Actually I find it inspiring, mostly because I see some of the stuff that is getting published and think, "God, I can do that." I also feel like I am meeting a number of people in publishing who I would feel comfortable approaching with my own manuscript at some point. I have moments of frustration in which I'd much rather be a novelist than a person who spends lots of time thinking about other people's novels, but I absolutely love keeping on top of what's being published by whom. And while I think I'm getting a sense of what kind of book is pushed and what kind of book sells, this knowledge has no influence whatsoever on my own writing. I am completely impractical in that way.

GARRETT: A follow-up is this: when your book is finished and is published, do you have any notions about how to attract the attention of the fashion magazines? For instance, is there enough collegiality so that you can count on the chance of some attention and support? And, if you care to answer, how much would that kind of attention and support matter?

VAN OGTROP: Hmm — I don't have an easy answer for that one. I don't think I can count on support from my own magazine or any of the other fashion magazines — things just aren't that chummy. Maybe if I dropped out of magazines and *then* published a book; but while I'm in the thick of things, I feel like my own writing is somehow part of my "private life" and would remain separate from my professional world. I could very well see getting exposure in other magazines but not in fashion magazines; it would be sort of like being editor in chief or managing editor of a magazine and hiring your daughter to work as one of your editors. It's just a little too familiar and weird, even if your daughter is the smartest editor around. Of course I would love to have my own book reviewed in *Vogue* or any of our competitors, but that is more of a personal victory thing.

GARRETT: The future is precisely that which is *not* an extension of the present or imaginable in the terms of the present. Nevertheless (like the weather) everybody talks about it all the time. Considering at least the near and foreseeable future, how do you read the trends in the fashion magazines? Are we likely to see more and better and/or different literary coverage in the next few years? Or more of the same? And . . . what do you think the need is? That is, what changes and directions would you like to see take place?

VAN OGTROP: I'm not optimistic that we'll see any change in book coverage in the fashion magazines we've discussed here; sad as it is to admit, books are simply not a priority. If an editor in chief of a fashion magazine is given a limited page budget and asked to choose between a Steven Meisel photo spread of Linda Evangelista in Chanel and a review by Mr. Esteemed Critic on Ms. Literary Novelist (or even worse – and here I'm being a real cynic – Ms. Overweight, Bespectacled Literary Novelist), well, there's just no contest.

However, I'd like to see the system change a bit. This is a little like a teacher saying she wished all of her students would do their homework, but I wish fashion magazine editors took more time with books, period – not just relied on the handful of editors and publicists they know. Little writers *can* make big splashes, but only if editors are taking time to look at the hundreds of galleys they receive each year, and to actually give some of the more obscure ones a read. I can think of several instances this year when we've thought at *Vogue* (with the "Arts in Brief" section), "Oh, we've got too many male writers this month," or "We've got two nonfiction murder stories," and then we go sorting through the galleys, looking at writers we've never heard of. And it's not as difficult as panning for gold – the good stuff isn't so hard to find. That's where the "surprises" could come about; of course, the novelists and writers wouldn't find my proposal

surprising at all – the more idealistic among them probably think book editors do look at every galley – isn't that what they're paid for?

THE AMERICAN BOOK REVIEW: A SKETCH

David R. Slavitt

Finally, there is the case of the *American Book Review,* which sounds as if it were some kind of invalid, but that may be not too far off the mark. John Tytell, who is an executive editor (he shares these duties with Rochelle Ratner), describes its fourteen-year survival as "a continuing miracle." On the other hand, it is still going, and it manages to appear bimonthly with a circulation of some twelve thousand, which is roughly double that of, say, the *Georgia Review* (which, in turn, is double that of the *Sewanee Review*). The paper started as . . . a remark! Publisher Ronald Sukenick and Ishmael Reed were on their way back from a conference somewhere, and they were deploring the generally dismal state of American book reviewing, particularly in the *New York Times.* They agreed that a new publication was needed, one that would review serious books seriously, and pay more attention to the underappreciated books that university presses and the small presses bring out. As Sukenick remembers, each said to the other, "You do it," and that would have been the end of the story, except that Sukenick got a larger than usual income tax refund and handed it over to a bunch of pals, urging them to go ahead and try it – he was off to Europe on a Guggenheim. The paper was originally to be called the *Writers' Review* – which is still in the corporate papers somewhere. "When I got back from Europe, there was this paper," Sukenick recalls, "and I just got drawn into it."

In the time that has elapsed, its function has become more important, if only because the *Times* has gone the other way, cutting down on its "In Short" section from two pages a week to one in their Sunday book section, and entirely suspending book reviews in the Saturday edition of the daily *Times.* These outlets were what one university press sales manager called "our ghetto." An appearance in those parts of the paper was contemptible – and contemptuous – but it was better than nothing. (Having once had seventeen books in a row totally ignored by the *Times,* I was able to agree with the general import of this man's dour remarks.)

So, the *American Book Review* (*ABR*) took off – as a lark, if not exactly like a lark – and it had some foundation support for a time. It still gets houseroom and one partially salaried position, Donald Laing's managing editorship, from the University of Colorado at Boulder. All the others are unpaid volunteers, the two executive editors, and the five editors who work together, assigning and collectively passing on all the reviews: Russell Hoover, Larry McCaffery, Charles Russell, Barry Seiler, and Barry Wallenstein. For a time, many of the readers were getting copies free, for the paper was mailed for some years to every writer on the Poets and Writers list – but as their list kept getting larger, it became too expensive to continue this habit. (The rates for individual subscriptions are $24 for one year, $40 for two, and $150 lifetime – yours or its, whichever ends first.)

A recent issue I happen to have on hand has a focus on "Marginalized Sexuality," and there are seven tabloid-sized pages of reviews of such books as *Sexing the Cherry, The Child Garden,* and *The Two Mujeres* (all novels) as well as such Gay and Lesbian Studies texts as *How Do I Look? Queer Film and Video; Re-Belle et Infidèle: la traduction comme pratique de réécriture au féminin; The Intimate Wilderness: Lesbian Writers on Sexuality;* and *High Risk: An Anthology of Forbidden Writings.* There are books of such mainstream publishers as Norton, Dutton, HarperCollins, and the Atlantic Monthly Press, but the bias is clearly in favor of the university presses— Columbia, Harvard, Georgia, New Mexico, and Texas – and the small presses such as Greywolf, Curbstone, the Fiction Collective, or Timken Publishers, Incorporated. The traditional trade publishers do still, if only out of inadvertence, occasionally publish serious books that deserve notice. There are also a few ads for literary magazines and for books, as well as one house ad inviting inquiries from publishers and authors "for information about our surprisingly low ad rates."

The sad truth is that while the editorial parts of the *Times Book Review* have become less and less welcoming to any but the most predictable books, their advertising, which used to have an informational value, is more and more limited to those books for which commercial viability can be more or less confidently projected. In other words, what their reviews do not cover, their ads are also unlikely to feature, except in the case of some university press that has a long-term contract at lower rates and can list titles in what are fundamentally institutional announcements.

Some reviews are better than others, and indeed, some issues are better than others. But unlike the *New York Review of Books,* say, the *ABR* does not indulge in long social and political essays. It is a book review, and the assumption is that its readers want to know about books. On a cold but bright winter afternoon, in a Manhattan apartment from which one could look out at the sunlight glinting agreeably on the surface of the Hudson, Barry Wallenstein, who for the past six or seven years has been a member of that panel of nine editors who recruit reviewers and approve – or on occasion disapprove – their reviews, talked with me about what he conceived the mission of the paper to be. A kind of rueful elf, he said that the idea was "to fill the gap, which is growing more and more serious, since the *Times* and other journals review poetry rarely and books of small presses hardly at all. So we're covering literature that is otherwise neglected. And also we wanted to give creative writers a forum in which to review. All of our reviewers are, themselves, fiction writers and poets. We don't go to professional reviewers. Or academics. We thought it would be a lively way to present literature, by having the makers of the literature reviewing it."

AN INTERVIEW WITH BARRY WALLENSTEIN
David R. Slavitt

SLAVITT: How did you get involved with the paper?

WALLENSTEIN: I became involved when John Tytell asked me to become an editor. I'd already written for them, and they'd reviewed my poetry. Unfortunately, now that I'm an editor, they can't review me anymore, and that's one of the few places that would be likely to review me. It's closed off to me, but that's all right.

SLAVITT: Do you or do any of your colleagues have a sense of what kind of difference a review in *ABR* can make either to the sales and career of a book or to the career of its author?

WALLENSTEIN: It's very hard to generalize. I know I once gave a poet a very good review in *Choice* magazine, and he soon thereafter received an NEA grant, and he told me that that review had helped him in various ways. Of course, that review comes out early. It can help in sales, but more than that it can help in grant getting, or in getting teaching jobs. If I were to make a list of all the advantages that might flow from a good review, I'd put sales at the bottom of the list, although that might happen. I think it happens less with poetry. Poets sell their work themselves mostly, at readings and to a network of friends. But a good review is like a whole network of new friends. It also lets you quote something on the flap of your next book. There are all sorts of intangible if small rewards. In terms of the larger culture, they're very small rewards. And if you don't get any reviews . . . the process of writing a book of poems is very slow and very private, and the review is your one public accolade, unless you're a prize winner. A review is second to a prize, or maybe in some cases more important than a prize. But it is a prize, and in a world that gives so few rewards to literature, and fewer to poetry, a good review is a very important reward. Even if it doesn't translate into bucks or grants or anything else. It's very important. And the loneliness of the process of making the poems and even publishing the poems is a little bit ameliorated by the review.

SLAVITT: Would you describe the process by which a review, once it has been submitted, gets into the pile of manuscripts that you're going to print? And how do the books and the reviewers get chosen in the first place?

WALLENSTEIN: Once every few months, a list of books that have been sent in to *ABR* is circulated among the editors, and we farm the books out. We first call the managing editor, Don Laing, ask if this book has already been assigned, and say that, if not, we have a reviewer in mind. Sometimes an inquiry is sent to the reviewer to see if he or she is willing to do it, because we only pay fifty bucks for a review, although we were up against the wall with funding and for awhile had to suspend that. So it's not that easy to find reviewers.

SLAVITT: These are all ladies and gentlemen of leisure?

WALLENSTEIN: Or young writers who want to build up some credits. Or they are people who have been writing for us for years and, even if they could use the money, are still willing to sacrifice that for the kind of exposure they get in *ABR*. So the search for good reviewers is ongoing. And we have this list, although we're not bound by it. If I see a book that isn't on it, if a book wasn't sent to us, that doesn't mean we can't do it. I fill out a book-out form, so they'll know in Colorado who has which book. The reviewer has roughly six weeks to do it – because we don't want to do 1991 books in 1993, and it's difficult in a bimonthly to stay current. Between the time a review is

assigned, written, accepted, and published, easily a year can go by.

SLAVITT: The time pressure, I should think, has increased in recent years, as the shelf life of a new book – the time one can expect to be able actually to find it on the shelves of bookstores – has shrunk down from months to a matter of weeks. The book can be remaindered or pulped before the reviews come out.

WALLENSTEIN: I know, I know. Anyway, once the review comes in to Colorado, it's xeroxed and circulated among the two executive editors, the five editors, and Ron [Sukenick], the publisher. Each of us reads every review, and we have vote sheets, and we check off yes, no, or maybe, with comments. The comments can have to do with anything from copyediting to larger considerations – like, "I don't think we need this book. After all, it's Random House and has received a lot of attention." Or it can be too long. Or it can be a negative review that doesn't make a point – so what's the value of it? So we vote. We tend to accept most of the reviews that come to our attention because they've all been solicited. And there's a hesitation to reject a solicited piece. Unsolicited reviews come in, and they tend to get a more severe scrutiny – especially now, because we're working with a huge backlog of reviews. I don't remember how many yes votes are required. In my experience, I can remember only one or two reviews that I've solicited getting turned down. And there's grief in every case.

* * *

It is a slow and not altogether efficient process, but the paper is lively, diverse, sometimes a bit flaky, but almost always worth reading. When I asked Ronald Sukenick to suggest for me the directions in which he'd like to grow, he sighed and said that he'd like to go from bimonthly to monthly publication, but even before that, he'd want to get the circulation up to fifty or sixty thousand. The trouble is that such an undertaking requires the investment of dollars for direct mail and other advertising and publicity activities. And even though there is money now coming from the Lannan foundation and the NEA, many of the foundations from whom such monies might flow tend to view with suspicion an enterprise in which most of the work is done by volunteers, and that does not have a substantial, paid staff and a board of directors with bankers and captains of industry lending a certain *gravitas* and respectability to the outfit. "So, you see," he said, "it's another catch-22."

After Dinner Opera Company

Beth Flusser

It was summer of 1949, at Tanglewood, when Leonard Bernstein and Aaron Copland said to Richard Flusser, "you've got to do it. . . ." At the time there were no opera companies committed to producing American operas on a regular basis. That was what Flusser wanted to produce and that is why the After Dinner Opera Company (ADOCo) was born. Four decades later the mayor of New York City proclaimed 6 November 1989 to be "After Dinner Opera Company 40th Anniversary Day."

Virgil Thomson, composer and critic, attended the first performance in 1949 and later wrote, "Thanks for your contributions to opera here and now." With those words "here and now," Thomson acknowledged the unique aspects of the twentieth-century libretto and the librettists' efforts to develop and use the one-act form in order to abandon the old-fashioned demands of grand opera. In their effort to get away from the heroic and larger-than-life characters and story lines, the staples of seventeenth- through nineteenth-century opera, the twentieth-century librettists utilized short still lifes, fairy tales, abstractions, and hybrid works combining dance movement, chamber instrumental accompaniment, and partial narration. They found that American literature provided a rich supply of material for new operas. For forty-three years ADOCo has specialized in chamber operas, mostly by American composers and librettists featuring American professional performers and musicians. ADOCo became a participant in the exploration of American opera and, fittingly, in its first year presented an adaptation of Mark Twain's *The Celebrated Jumping Frog of Calaveras County,* with music by Lukas Foss; Ronald Jean's *Triple Sec,* with music by Marc Blitzstein; and Gertrude Stein's *In a Garden,* with music by Meyer Kupferman. In 1950 the *New York Times* recognized the significance of ADOCo's contribution by printing a six-column cartoon of ADOCo singers in a *Jumping Frog* performance.

ADOCo had its birth during that turbulent period following World War II when so many young men, having won the war, were determined to pursue unusual careers. Richard Stuart Flusser was such a young man. Always possessed of an ardent interest in music and opera, he felt that two conditions severely limited the opportunity for Americans to know and enjoy opera fully. The established companies tended to stick to the established repertoires, and "established repertoire" meant "no American opera." Furthermore, professional performances were presented in a limited number of cities. In 1949 Flusser set out to change things by founding ADOCo. His objective was to produce opera — mostly American and mostly contemporary — and to bring it to people all over the United States and Europe. To this end, ADOCo has toured from coast to coast in the United States and Canada and in many European cities, and Flusser continues today as ADOCo's artistic and stage director. ADOCo has opened new, important performing halls but has also played in cramped drawing-room-size quarters and in such expansive facilities as the vast open-air amphitheater of the Wollman Memorial in New York City's Central Park. ADOCo was the first Off-Broadway company to be invited to perform at an international music festival in Europe and the first American company to perform at the Edinburgh Festival in Scotland, in August 1956.

ADOCo has explored in depth the works of Gertrude Stein set to music by a variety of composers: Ned Rorem (*Three Sisters Who Are Not Sisters*), Meyer Kupferman (*In a Garden*), Vernon Martin (*Ladies Voices*), and Martin Kalmanoff (*Photograph*). Florence Wickham wrote the prologue and epilogue and Marvin Schwartz wrote the music in between for *Look and Long.* ADOCo performed the Kupferman work in Paris in 1956 for Alice B. Toklas.

Toklas wrote of the performance to Bernard Fay in *Staying on Alone* (1975):

A scene from the After Dinner Opera Company production of Gertrude Stein's In a Garden *at the Edinburgh Festival in 1956*

19 December 1956

One of the good things that happened was a performance of Gertrude's little play In a Garden made with some witty music into an opera. A little opera company from New York was asked to give it and two other one act operas at the Edinburgh Festival. They were so successful there that they conceived the idea of touring with them. They themselves – the scenery and costumes in a station wagon and performed in London-Copenhagen-finally Vienna and here. Gertrude would have loved it. The singing was good – very musicianly – and their appreciation and animation were contagious. I met them after the performance and then they came to see Gertrude's home.

Then the editors note:

In a Garden: The After Dinner Opera Company had presented Stein's In a Garden as set to music by Meyer Kupferman.

After performing *In a Garden* hundreds of times between 1949 and 1970, ADOCo devoted a whole program to Gertrude Stein, developing five Stein pieces under the umbrella title *When This You See,*

Remember Me. Peter Max created the poster. Three of the works, *In a Garden, Three Sisters Who Are Not Sisters,* and *Look and Long,* were from Stein's last writings, *The First Reader,* published posthumously in 1948. *Photograph* was from *Last Operas and Plays,* and *Ladies Voices* was from *Geography and Plays. Ladies Voices* was performed in connection with the Pennsylvania Opera Festival, where the ADOCo also performed two of Stein's larger works, *Mother of Us All* and *Four Saints in Three Acts,* with music by Virgil Thomson.

Thomson said Stein's writing "likes music." He added, "much of it, in fact lies closer to musical timing than to speech timings." All of the Stein works presented by ADOCo were set exactly as she wrote them. Thomson, as critic, said, "the most dependable device for holding attention is a 'theme' or story, the clean attachment for art patterns to such common bonds as sex and sentiment." Thomson, as composer, however, chose to set Gertrude Stein's texts, works which exemplified the abstract libretto. In order to hold an audience, to give it something to relate to in ADOCo's multimedia production, it seemed necessary to look deeply into Stein's writing

Beth Flusser (right) shaking hands with Alice B. Toklas in an apartment Toklas had shared with Gertrude Stein in the rue Christine, Paris, after a 1956 performance of Stein's In A Garden *(courtesy of Beth Flusser)*

and background. ADOCo completed extensive research with the help of Donald Gallup, curator of the Gertrude Stein Collection at Yale University library. In each of the five works, Stein is the central protagonist. The operas are often called charming; however, their meaning goes far deeper, which becomes evident when one looks into Stein's autobiographical writings.

The production's multimedia concept and execution allowed the performances to be seen and heard on several levels. The concept was the culmination of fourteen years of work and experimentation started in 1956 when ADOCo was invited to the Edinburgh Festival. (I had joined ADOCo in 1955 as stage manager and co–scenic designer with Peter Wingate.) Optimistically, we anticipated success there, which could lead to instant European bookings in a variety of theaters on the Continent, one-night stands in playing spaces which would range from historic opera houses to school gymnasiums with no stage. The solution was a *teatrino,* a structure made up of metal pipes which could be assembled to form a marionette theater for human

marionettes, our singers. On these metal posts and lintels were hung curtains, painted drops, and side-wing velours. The proscenium front curtain was a Wagner curtain which was opened by crew members on either side of what was in effect a giant toy theater. The effort to conceive and execute it was well worth the pain because ADOCo at Edinburgh was a triumph and the day after the opening performance at the Gartshore Hall (a performance space better than a gymnasium but not an eighteenth-century theater) booking offers arrived from Germany, Austria, France, Luxembourg, and Spain. We immediately accepted a four-week tour of the Amerika Haus circuit followed by weeks of performances in the other countries.

But Gertrude Stein's cubist writing style demanded more than facsimiles of locations, so in addition to places the screens were filled with additional information such as "ACT IV" in "ACT I." And then there was Stein's dialogue with herself. *Photograph* really required twin Steins, and the solution we hit upon was to have the soprano's performance on film so that she could walk, dance, sing,

A scene from the After Dinner Opera Company's first performance of Ring Lardner's adaptation of Carmen, *at the St. Regis Hotel in 1976 (photograph by Richard Flusser)*

and be the same height as her live twin counterpart. It made it possible for the "live" soprano to sing duets with "herself" on film. In the last twenty-two years many companies have produced *Photograph* with a live and filmed soprano. At times, some have borrowed our 1970 film.

Screens and projectors proved to be very important for our production of a very special version of *Carmen* with an American-language libretto by Ring Lardner. It was unpublished and unproduced, until ADOCo performed it at the St. Regis Hotel in New York City to launch the publication of *Pages*. That was the first of dozens of performances.

Ring Lardner, Jr., makes some wonderful observations in an introduction to his father's libretto-in-the-vernacular in *Pages*.

As readers familiar with the opera will observe, this is not just a case of Ring Lardner, humorist and master of American dialect, taking a classic and retelling it in New York vernacular of the 1920's, the way he did with traditional fairy stories like "Snow White" and "Cinderella." It is Ring Lardner, skilled musician and composer, working with music he loved and writing new words to

fit it according to principles evolved out of many years' experience as a singer and song-writer....

Characters and plot developments are carefully chosen to represent the nearest American equivalents to the Spanish ones. Clearly the idea behind it was to bring the music to the common man without the barriers of language and traditional opera staging....

The change from a military guardhouse in Seville to a police precinct in New York is an obvious one.... It was also quite logical to transform the toreador to the heavyweight boxing champion and the bull fighting arena to Madison Square Garden. Lillas Pastia's tavern becomes "a roadhouse on Long Island."

The multimedia production machinery we had developed by 1970 was just what we needed in 1976 to make Lardner's *Carmen* possible. Lardner switches act 1 of *Carmen* from Seville 1848 to New York City 1920, where the audience is taken on a whirlwind tour of sites dear to the hearts of New Yorkers: Child's Restaurant with the magical, mechanical pancake maker in the window, Schraffts, Ching Lun Fo, Brown's Chop House, Sherry's, the

St. Regis Hotel, the Automat, Manhattan speakeasies, the old Madison Square Garden, United Cigar Stores, and Bloom's Roadhouse on Long Island. Lardner, Jr.'s, comments:

> The most conspicuous change from the traditional plot is in the very ending, and I for one have no idea what effect my father had in mind. It looks as if Josephs (Don Jose) is about to kill Carmen as expected, using his policeman's gun instead of a knife. Then suddenly a completely new character appears, knocks out Josephs, the heavyweight champion, and the police captain, and goes off triumphantly with Carmen. He is identified with "Bill Fields' Shorty," who was a midget retainer of W. C. Fields'.... The distinctive feature of Ring Lardner's work as a whole is his use of common American speech ...

> My mammy's goofy, I'll admit;
> Her brains ain't what they were,
> But where would I of been if it
> Would not have been for her?

That is first-class Lardner.

The works of Seymour Barab, according to Central Opera Service surveys, are the most frequently performed works of any opera composer in America. ADOCo has performed twelve of his works since 1982, and by publication time of this article we will have added *Mating Habits of the Radical Chic,* based on A. R. Gurney's *The Problem,* in a world premiere at the National Arts Club in February 1993. Barab looks everywhere for suitable material from which to fashion his own librettos. He states that his relationship with ADOCo is "unique and most rewarding for a composer." He goes on to say that ADOCo is the most accessible company he has worked with. "Sadly," Barab says, "composers do not expect to have their works looked at and taken seriously, but Richard Flusser gives time and attention to new works. Most important, ADOCo gives multiple performances of works. Often starting with readings of the opera and progressing to fully staged productions, Flusser gives the composer the opportunity to make revisions at different stages along the way." Barab's personal favorite opera of his is *Father of the Child,* based on a section of *The Slaughter of 12 Hit Carols in a Pear Tree* by William Gibson, best known for his play *Two for the Seesaw* and his dramatization of *The Miracle Worker.* Gibson attended the world premiere of our ADOCo version at Lincoln Center's Bruno Walter Auditorium. He was very pleased. In fact, Barab says, every author he has spoken to has been very responsive and pleased at the prospect of having their words set to music; they immediately refer Barab to their agents, who have a hard time believing that American chamber opera is not a potential money font. Sadly, American chamber opera, even at its most successful, requires contributions and grants from foundations, businesses, government, and individuals to exist at all.

In 1992 Meet the Composer awarded ADOCo thirty thousand dollars, one of the largest commissioning grants for a new chamber opera. The opera will be entitled *Uliana Rooney* and will be based on the life of its own composer, Vivian Fine, who is setting to music the opera's libretto by Sonya Freedman. March 1994 is targeted as the month of the ADOCo world premiere.

American opera has successfully championed the one-act opera format in its chamber-size medium. In its effort to get away from the old-fashioned demands of the multiple-act grand opera form, American composers learned to explore American history, American literature, folktales, fairy tales, still lifes, news items, and story lines in which the chief protagonist, though no hero, could be an everyday, recognizable American. We are grateful to courageous composers and librettists for exploring and utilizing literary abstraction and asking us to "listen to the rain" and revel in the joys of ice cream. They give us librettos combining singing, chanting, spoken lines, and dance communication, and companies perform them despite the demands and rigors of multimedia production.

It has been a long time since December 1949 when our first friend Leonard Bernstein and our first mentor Aaron Copland indicated they were so satisfied and pleased with our attempts that they said in unison "you've got to do it." We have given thousands of performances, and we were the first American chamber opera company to be invited to perform at an international music festival in Europe. Many groups have turned to ADOCo for help and have successfully emulated us. Names of women composers and librettists do not even come to mind in grand opera, but they prominently appear in our repertoire.

ADOCo has presented the following: eighty chamber operas, seventy-seven by American composers including Seymour Barab, Marc Blitzstein, Lukas Foss, Ulysses Kay, Otto Leuning, Ned Rorem, Virgil Thomson, Frank Wigglesworth, and Alec Wilder; fifteen operas by women including Amy Beach, Susan Hulsman Bingham, Vivian Fine, Libby Larsen, Elizabeth Swados; operas by African-American and Asian composers including Michael Ching, Ulysses Kay, Carman Moore, William Grant Still, and Joyce Solomon.

In addition to Gertrude Stein and Ring Lardner, the breadth of literary figures whose works were set to music include Lucille Fletcher (Wallop), Edward Gorey, O. Henry, Langston Hughes, James Purdy, William Saroyan, James Thurber, and Mark Twain.

The following is a list of seventy-seven works by American composers performed by the After Dinner Opera Company.
(Title of opera, date of ADOCo first performance, composer [when composer is also the librettist (2) follows the composer's name], librettist).

Abigail Adams, 1988, Richard Owen (2);

Alice In Concert, 1989, Elizabeth Swados (2) based on *Alice in Wonderland* and *Through the Looking Glass* by Lewis Carroll;

Alice Meets the Mock Turtle, 1988, Susan Hulsman Bingham (2) based on *Alice in Wonderland* by Lewis Carroll;

Amor, 1984, John Mueter (2);

Apache Dance, 1982, Joseph Fennimore (2) based on the story *Don't Call Me by My Right Name* from *Color of Darkness* by James Purdy;

At Last I Found You, 1983, Seymour Barab (2) based on a story by Evelyn E. Smith;

The Big Black Box, 1984, Sam Morgenstern, Francis Steegmuller;

Blue Star, 1983, Judith Dvorkin (2);

Blues in the Subway, Alonzo Levister (2);

The Boor, 1949, Mark Bucci, Eugene Haun based on the play by Anton Chekhov;

The Boor, 1992, Ulysses Kay (2) based on the play by Anton Chekhov;

Buxom Joan, 1974, Raynor Taylor, realization by Conrad Strasser, Thomas Willett;

Cabildo, 1990, Amy Beach, Nan Stephens;

Carmen, 1976, George Bizet, Arr. Conrad Strasser, Ring Lardner based on Bizet's opera;

Elegies for the Fallen, 1988, Joyce Solomon, Rashidah Ismaili;

English Painter, 1984, Lee Hoiby based on a monologue by Ruth Draper;

Evangeline, 1985, Otto Luening (2) based on the poem by Henry Wadsworth Longfellow;

Eventide, 1983, James Fennimore (2) based on the story *Eventide* from *Color of Darkness* by James Purdy;

Fables For Our Time, 1984, Vernon Martin (2) based on *The Weaver and the Worm, The Rose and the Weed, The Lion Who Wanted to Zoom* by James Thurber;

Fair Means or Foul, 1983, Seymour Barab (2) based on a fairy tale;

Father of the Child, 1985, Seymour Barab (2) based on *Butterfingers Angel* from *The Slaughter of 12 Hit Carols in a Pear Tree* by William Gibson;

The Fisherman and his Wife, 1992, Susan Hulsman Bingham (2) based on a fairy tale;

Fit for a King, 1950, Martin Kalmanoff, Atra Baer;

Fortunes Favorites, 1982, Seymour Barab (2) based on *Baker's Dozen* by H. H. Monroe;

From the Diaries of Adam and Eve, 1984, Donald Grantham (2) based on the story by Mark Twain;

Garden of Live Flowers, 1988, Vivian Fine (2) based on *Alice in Wonderland* by Lewis Carroll;

The Gift of the Magi, 1987, Susan Hulsman Bingham (2) based on the story by O. Henry;

The Happy Hypocrite, 1991, Alonzo Levister (2) based on a story by Max Beerbohm;

Have You Heard, Do You Know, 1983, Louise Talma (2);

Housewives Cantata, 1990, Mira J. Spektor, June Siegel;

How Do You Do, Sir?, Christopher Pavlakis, Alfred Kreymborg;

Humpty Dumpty, 1988, Judith Dvorkin (2) based on *Alice in Wonderland* by Lewis Carroll;

Husbands, Wives and Lovers, 1993, Seymour Barab (2);

Implications of Melissa, 1984, Philip Carlsen (2);

Impossible Forest, 1962, Alec Wilder, Marshall Barrer;

In a Garden, 1949, Meyer Kupferman, Gertrude Stein;

The Incognitos, 1966, Nevitt Bartow, Philip Brownell;

Jewish Humor from Oy to Veh, 1990, Seymour Barab (2) based on folktales;

Jumping Frog of Calaveras County, 1950, Lukas Foss, Jean Karsavina based on *The Celebrated Jumping Frog of Calaveras County* by Mark Twain;

Ladies Voices, 1970, Vernon Martin, Gertrude Stein;

The Last Leaf, 1987, Susan Hulsman Bingham (2) based on a story by O. Henry;

Leo, 1986, Michael Ching, Fernando Fonseca;

Look and Long, 1970, Florence Wickham and Marvin Schwartz, Gertrude Stein;

Lord Byron, 1990, Virgil Thomson, Jack Larsen;

Mating Habits of the Radical Chic, 1993, Seymour Barab (2) based on *The Problem* by A. R. Gurney;

Midas, 1966, Relly Raffman, Albert Southwick;

A Moment of War, 1959, Richard Owen (2);

New World – What Columbus Did to the Indians, 1991, Leonard Lehrman, Joel Shatzky;

Opera, Opera, 1956, Martin Kalmanoff based on a play by William Saroyan;

Out the Window, 1985, Seymour Barab (2) based on *Par La Fenetre,* Georges Feydeau;

Passion in Principal's Office, 1987, Seymour Barab (2) based on a French farce by Georges Feydeau;

Perpetual, 1963, Ernest Kanitz, Ellen Terry;

Photograph, 1970, Martin Kalmanoff, Gertrude Stein;

Pietro's Petard, 1963, Hall Overton, Robert de Marie;

La Pizza Con Funghi, 1989, Seymour Barab (2) based on *Il Fornicazonie* by Michael Green;

Pot of Broth, 1961, Herbert Haufrecht (2) based on the story by William Butler Yeats;

Pot of Fat, 1956, Theodore Chanler, Hester Pickman based on a fairy tale;

Predators, 1985, Seymour Barab (2) based on *Beast of a Different Burden,* Faith Whitehill;

Requiem for a Rich Young Man, 1982, Norman Lockwood, Donald Sutherland;

The Ruined Maid, 1986, Seymour Barab (2) based on a poem by Thomas Hardy;

The Runaways, 1978, Louis Pisciotta, John Maglione;

The Silver Fox, 1985, Libby Larsen, John Olive;

Something New For the Zoo, 1984, Lee Hoiby, Dudley Huppler;

Sorry, Wrong Number, 1982, Jerome Moross, Lucille Fletcher (Wallop) based on the play;

Sweet Betsy from Pike, 1956, Mark Bucci based on a folk tale;

Tars from Tripoli, 1974, James Hewitt, reconstructed libretto, Beth Flusser;

The Telephone, 1953, Gian-Carlo Menotti (2);

Three Sisters Who Are Not Sisters, 1970, Ned Rorem, Gertrude Stein;

Triple Sec, 1950, Marc Blitzstein, Ronald Jeans;

Troubled Island, 1988, William Grant Still, Langston Hughes;

Waiting for the Barbarians, 1984, Vernon Martin (2) based on a poem by Constantine Cavafy;

War Scenes, 1987, Ned Rorem, Walt Whitman;

Who Am I? (or *Goosegirl*), 1988, Seymour Barab (2) based on a fairy tale;

The Whole World Kin, 1987, Susan Hulsman Bingham (2) based on a story by O. Henry;

Wild Gardens of the Loup Garou, 1985, Carman Moore (2) based on poems by Ishmael Reed and Colleen McElroy;

The Willowdale Handcar, 1986, Frank Wigglesworth, Edward Gorey.

A Symposium on *The Columbia History of the American Novel*

Paul Bauer
Marquette University

In his introduction to the new *Columbia History of the American Novel* (1992), a hefty and haphazard collection of essays by thirty-one different scholars spanning the distance between William Hill Brown, whose 1789 potboiler *The Power of Sympathy* is the first novel mentioned in the book, and Steven Millhauser, whose 1990 avant-garde novel *The Barnum Museum* is the last, general editor Emory Elliott goes to great lengths to identify the straw men whose existence ostensibly justifies the enterprise. They are, as the man said, the usual suspects: those benighted critics and scholars who "in a time not long ago" had had the temerity to believe, not just that they knew what a novel was, but that they "knew what 'American' meant." In their naiveté, he argues, this earlier generation of critics created criteria for literary greatness such as "the intricate but orderly structure, the details of characterization, the profundity of themes, the complexity of the imagery, symbolism, and allusions, and perhaps the power of the setting to evoke particular places, eras, or subtleties of human speech." But these "prescriptive judgements," it seems, though innocuous in themselves, masked a more sinister agenda of intolerance and exclusion in which white, Anglo-Saxon, Protestant, middle- and upper-class, heterosexual, male critics denied women and working-class and homosexual and minority writers access to the canon; by fostering standards of purely literary merit, critics denied innocent victims the status of Americans. In nine-hundred-odd pages the current volume aims – heroically, if one buys the rhetoric – to redress the grievances of these historically disenfranchised groups.

The agon described by Elliott, of course, represents less the reality of American literary history than a necessary fiction designed to satisfy the contemporary academic's apparently limitless craving for high moral purpose. Elliott surely knows that the generation of critics which he has in mind, in-

Dust jacket for the history highlighting the expanding canon of American literature

cluding giants such as F. O. Matthiessen, Alfred Kazin, Philip Rahv, Lionel Trilling, Richard Chase, R. W. B. Lewis, and Leslie Fiedler, makes a poor target for the self-righteous darts of the literary Lilliputians populating today's English departments; demonizing, even implicitly, a man such as Matthiessen, for instance, who committed suicide in

1950 rather than testify before the House Un-American Activities Committee, amounts to something of a scandal. Moreover, Elliott certainly should recognize that the poststructuralist view of history which informs his own volume theoretically precludes the kind of self-dramatizing narrative which would pit a noble present against a monolithically dismal past. As should be obvious from the near constant (and well-documented) fluctuations throughout this century in the reputations of writers such as Herman Melville and Henry James, the supposedly stable "canon" against which reformers would struggle has, in the by now cliché jargon of deconstruction, "always already" been contested. But historical veracity and theoretical consistency are clearly not the main goals of the volume, as is evident from Elliott's initial disclaimer, where he describes how the book "was not driven by a desire to be comprehensive," but by a desire to show "the ways that current critical perspectives provide fresh insights into the texts *and into the history of which novels were and remain a part*" [italics added]. What kinds of historical "insights" does he have in mind? The example he gives of Edgar Allan Poe's mythopoesis being "subtly connected to the public rhetoric that attempted to present slavery as a benevolent institution" makes it clear that the history to which his contributors will uniformly refer will be a melodrama of unmitigated oppression with the "American" of the book's title cast in the part of a cartoon villain.

Given this openly polemical program, the *Columbia History* thus demands to be read less as scholarship than as a document in the ongoing "culture wars," that is, as a political tract. Indeed, one of Elliott's associate editors refers to the selections in his part of the volume, with the kind of romantic hyperbole often found in recent academic writing, not as chapters or essays, but as "interventions" and "incursions." This is not to slight several stimulating and informative essays included in the book. The articles by Robert Levine on early-nineteenth-century reformist fiction, Bill Brown on early-twentieth-century popular novels, and Thomas Ferraro on ethnic writers deserve special mention, bridging as they do the gaps between writers who traditionally have been taught in college-level American-literature courses and deserving writers whose works have only recently been rediscovered or reevaluated by the professoriate. By aiming to teach more than they preach about authors such as Elizabeth Stoddard and Maria Child, Edgar Rice Burroughs and Zane Grey, and Abraham Cahan and Ole Rölvaag, these essays point toward what might

have been. But the volume as a whole still packages itself as a political statement, and that being the case, it seems most reasonable to ask what kind of politics it is that contemporary academic literary critics are offering us.

The answer may amaze readers who have not been following recent debates about the state of higher education in America. The volume's first essay sets the tone and the agenda. In "The Early American Novel," Jeffrey Rubin-Dorsky opens with a personal confession — it seems almost obligatory in the humanities circa 1993 to do so — that he too is "deeply troubled by the implications of extracting some notion of identity, some sense of representativeness, from a canonized literature written almost exclusively by white men." Without interrogating Rubin-Dorsky's rather mechanistic idea that the purpose of reading literature is to "extract" an identity, or the logical inference one might draw that women should only be interested in women's literature, blacks in African American literature, and so forth, what seems obvious from his statement is that the real purpose of his essay is not to trace the outlines of a new history of the early American novel (his canon of Susanna Rowson, Hannah Foster, Charles Brockden Brown, Hugh Henry Brackenridge, and James Fenimore Cooper is, in any event, thoroughly conventional), but to place *himself* on the politically correct side of the issue. In fact, he goes on to define the novel in such a way as to make a work's political correctness the sole criteria for determining its merit:

> I must add a note here about what I personally look for in American novels, that is, what makes novel reading a vital experience for me. In each new book I am interested in discovering what I call "cultural voice," the process or the means by which an author with a social conscience and a rich and liberating language, though usually speaking through a persona, presents us with a unified moral vision of America. "Voice" in this sense is the sound that results when fear is overcome so that truth can be asserted. It is the refusal to internalize, and thus be tamed by, the forces and agents of cultural repression. It is the cry of unsuppressed rage. . . .

For Rubin-Dorsky, any "unified moral vision of America" must clearly be a damning one, and it is thus not by accident that the book he goes on to describe as his "ideal American novel" is E. L. Doctorow's fictional treatment of the Rosenberg atomic spy case, *The Book of Daniel* (1971), a novel that simultaneously vilifies anticommunists of the Cold War era while glorifying campus radicals of the 1960s. When he turns to writers of early America, his nominal subject, he finds, however, a stark contrast with his hero:

> the novelists themselves were too conservative in their relation to the state, too ambivalent about the location of legitimate authority, and too uncertain about where their loyalties lay to have become genuine "cultural voices" and to have written powerful social critiques. Although they located the inequalities and incongruences in an American society that claimed to be egalitarian, and although they occasionally undermined cherished beliefs about reason and liberty as the girders of that society, these writers remained wedded to the rhetoric of the Revolution, and thus were still intent upon educating an American readership to be good citizens of the Republic.

So much for the young country Abraham Lincoln would call, despite all its manifest compromises, the "last, best hope of earth."

If the intrusion of such unalloyed anti-Americanism into a work of literary historiography seems surprising, consider Paul Lauter's essay on "American Proletarianism" in the novels of the 1930s. Lauter is the general editor of the *Heath Anthology of American Literature,* probably the one publication of the past few years that has affected most the way American literature gets taught in the modern university; his attitudes can thus be safely considered representative of the "interpretive community" now active on campuses. For Lauter, working-class novels of the Depression era should be addressed, "not as static subjects for antiquarian study" – yet another neat put-down of earlier generations of scholars – but as "important for contemporary debates over the relationship of art and politics *and about the very nature of what a socialist transformation of society might mean*" [italics added]. He often slips, in fact, into a baldly propagandistic mode of analysis, as when he notes that women's novels of the era dramatized "that putting into practice a collective ethos is central to fundamental social transformation"; or when he lauds the communist John Reed Clubs for providing the "institutional supports [that] are critical to the development of a culture rooted in working-class experience." The picture of America he assumes as a given is striking in its bleak extremism: his country is a "predatory society," its schools and businesses are "bourgeois institutions of acculturation and social control," its cities "urban jungles of capitalism." But the parallel picture of the Soviet Union is no less striking: "not only had the Soviet Union avoided the horrors of the Depression," he writes, "but the Communist Party and its allies took the lead at home in organizing the unemployed,

fighting for aid to the dispossessed, turning despair into militance." While he acknowledges the "intricacies of organizational infighting in the Soviet Union" – a nice way of referring to the purges and the Gulag – he submits the demurrer that these items "do not concern us here." It is astonishing stuff to read in the Yeltsin era.

Equally astonishing is the portrait of 1950s America, and the American middle class generally, that emerges in David Van Leer's essay "Society and Identity." Buying into what can only be called a naive and self-serving, popular-culture version of the era, Van Leer describes the post–World War II generation as "most notable for its isolationism, consumerism, conformity, apathy," as "repressive and anaesthetized – the generation of the Mouseketeers and 'Leave it to Beaver.'" This "idolatry of the normal," a "fanatical pursuit of conformity" resulting in "the institutionalized mediocrity of middle-class experience" – it is hard to overstate the exaggerations he indulges in – also characterized the era's academic community, "especially in its conception of literary value." "Truth," he writes, in a tone precisely registering the contemporary academic's contemptuous attitude toward critical predecessors, "was thought to be universal," and a critic such as Trilling is patronized for daring to locate literary excellence in "moral realism" and "stylistic and psychological richness." But the real tragedy of the era, according to Van Leer, lay in its intellectuals' rejection of a radical politics based on class consciousness in exchange for a "new conservatism" based on individual identity. Where previously "there had been strong support for various forms of socialism in America, and intellectualism and Marxism often went hand in hand," now intellectuals "tended to encourage individual self absorption over social involvement." Writers, such as Flannery O'Connor, with the audacity in their fictions to consider religion as a matter of personal import are thus derided for "an otherworldliness that unintentionally reinforced the status quo." J. D. Salinger, described as a popularizer of existentialism, thus suggests in his descent into silence "that the elevation of the individual over society did not lead to a constructive program for growth or change." Even the Beat writers Jack Kerouac and William Burroughs are now criticized for being "unable to overcome fully their white middle-class roots," while Norman Mailer is berated for having only belatedly understood "that although true political activism might arise in conjunction with individual rebellion, it could never result from it." Indeed, all of the writers Van Leer discusses are subjected to a kind of ideological screening process, show trials really, whereby those who fail to reject sufficiently the values of middle-class America, particularly its emphasis on individualism, are in effect read out of the party. Van Leer does not explain how he can castigate the 1950s generation for both conformity *and* individualism, or how one can fit Kerouac or Burroughs into a paradigm of "new conservatism," but consistency is not the issue. What is the issue is amply evidenced by the rhetoric, in which "middle class" becomes a synecdoche for everything evil in the world; the objective, once again, is for the critic to position *himself* at the correct end (read "extreme left") of the political spectrum, and it does not matter what he has to do to prove it. Thus one Chinese-American author, Lin Yutang, is attacked for writing an assimilationist novel, *Chinatown Family,* published in 1948, that "celebrated America as a land of economic opportunity," while another, C. Y. Lee, author of the 1957 novel *The Flower Drum Song,* is praised for the way his book's "apparent pro-Americanism was subtly undermined by . . . its use of generational conflict to characterize the cultural sacrifices attending assimilation." This is the type of ugliness that results when the sole criterion for judging novels becomes the degree to which they condemn the United States.

If the examples given so far of critical attitudes toward America, attitudes which can only be understood as a kind of ritual self-loathing, were isolated instances in the *Columbia History,* they could still perhaps be overlooked in return for the information the volume contains. Both Lauter and Van Leer, for instance, do good jobs of pointing the reader toward neglected works which are of undeniable interest to any cultural historian, regardless of ideological orientation, novels of the 1930s such as Edward Dahlberg's *Bottom Dogs* (1929) and Tess Slesinger's *The Unpossessed* (1934), novels of the 1950s such as Gwendolyn Brooks's *Maud Martha* (1953), Antonio Villarreal's *Pocho* (1959), Rona Jaffe's *The Best of Everything* (1958), and even Sloan Wilson's famous *The Man in the Gray Flannel Suit* (1959). I wish that Van Leer in particular would have at least mentioned other popular "middlebrow" writers such as James Gould Cozzens, John P. Marquand, and John O'Hara, whose works were massively important in the era he covers, if for no better reason than to define with more honesty the taste he criticizes so vehemently; that, however, is a relative quibble. For,

unfortunately, the political attitudes cited so far are decidedly *not* isolated instances, but so utterly typical of the volume that they appear to represent a kind of bizarre new orthodoxy.

Two examples must suffice. In his essay on "Postmodern Realism," for instance, José David Saldívar offers a vision of an America in which writers of color must "recover alternative histories in the unrecorded texts of history (songs, *cuentos,* and talk story) at the very moment when historical alternatives are in the process of being systematically expunged – CIA and FBI archives notwithstanding." He then goes on to applaud a new minimalism in fiction "that deals with the new underclass of silenced peoples in our cities of quartz (workers, women, and so-called ethnic minorities) who typically feel adrift, or who feel that their histories have been systematically erased by urban planners and Immigration and Naturalization Service death squads, or who feel 'controlled' by their access to controlled substances." Similarly, in an essay entitled "Colonialism, Imperialism and Imagined Homes," Ketu Katrak describes a world in which "alliances between colonialist and imperialist forces ensure a continuing imbalance of power and hegemonic control of 'third world' nations by covert colonizations in the guise of international aid agencies, as well as multinational capital, that transcend geographical boundaries and that make it increasingly difficult to hold any single entity accountable for perpetuating poverty"; a world in which "physical acts of conquest and aggression constitute only one aspect of colonial aspirations, [while] mental colonizations perpetuated in a colonizer's language, education and cultural values are often more devastating and resilient"; a world in which "United States domination is present in everyday realities of satellite communications bombarded into living rooms." The paranoia of these diatribes in light of the fact that despite such fantasies of oppression both have managed to gain tenure in prestigious American universities apparently does not occur to either Professor Saldívar or Professor Katrak. Nor does Saldívar seem at all sensitive to the fact that his constant references to the "whitemale" – his neologism – as the source of all societal evil might strike some grandsons of immigrants from Europe as explicitly racist. The reader does, however, wonder why the editors of the volume felt compelled to countenance such gratuitous insertions of personal hobbyhorses into articles which otherwise point suggestively toward works such as Arturo Islas's *The Rain God* (1984) or Bharati

Mukherjee's *Jasmine* (1989) which surely deserve more attention. The answer is obvious: the literature simply matters less than the politics. Thus (in a familiar pattern) an author such as Mukherjee is judged harshly, not because of any failings as a writer, but because she "overtly endorses the melting-pot concept and regards American society as the most welcoming of any in the world toward the 'other.'" Whether or not Mukherjee's sentiment about America is true, it is politically incorrect, and for that she must at least figuratively be punished.

What dynamic could motivate the kinds of ideological gymnastics and wholesale historical revisionism found in the *Columbia History?* What could drive its editors and authors alike to distort what might otherwise have been a useful and timely contribution to literary historiography into such a shrill manifesto of anti-Americanism? While surely some were compelled by sincere political commitment, the fundamental reason, one suspects, is economic. Simply put, academics in America, and particularly the young academics who dominate the volume in question, are rewarded when they can find a way to commodify themselves as victims, and to do that they require a convenient set of villains. Thus we are treated in an essay called "Constructing Gender" to the spectacle of Ed Cohen detailing the "unarticulate pain" of growing up gay in the "mutilating reality" of suburban, middle-class Maryland, how "from the age of thirteen on I had been plagued with an inflammatory bowel disease," and how he turned to books "in the hope of fitting my feelings into their plots." The books to which he turned are, again, tremendously interesting in themselves, including James Baldwin's *Giovanni's Room* (1956), Edmund White's *A Boy's Own Story* (1982), and Samuel Delany's science-fiction classic *Stars in My Pocket Like Grains of Sand* (1984), and well-meaning people would want to learn more about them. But the essay does not finally want to be about the books, nor does it want to appeal to sympathetic imaginations. Rather, it seems intended primarily as documentation of the writer's own status as a victim of a malevolent American society. As such it is of a piece with the balance of the book's essays. Paging through the *Columbia History,* in fact, the reader is constantly struck by the unavoidable conclusion that, if forms of discrimination such as racism, sexism, and homophobia did not exist in America, many of the writers would have to invent them.

Having criticized the book in relatively harsh terms, I would hasten to add by way of a conclusion that such criticisms do not imply that I think that

the opinions voiced in the new *Columbia History of the American Novel* should not be heard, or even that an activist, oppositional academy is not a good thing. Liberty loves extremisms. What does bother me, however, is that, for all the rhetoric of "inclusion" one hears in this book and on campuses in general, the intellectual community represented in the pages of the *Columbia History* is a community with remarkably little ideological diversity, with no right wing, and with precious little evidence of a true center; what passes here for inclusiveness, in other words, seems instead to offer a new and different set of exclusions. As much becomes clear in a smaller context when, at the end of the book, the editors present an appendix of authors' biographies. While their appendix quite properly "includes" American writers such as Denise Chavez, Maxine Hong Kingston, N. Scott Momaday, and Toshio Mori, it unaccountably "excludes" a writer of the stature of Sinclair Lewis. Lewis, the author of *Main Street* (1920), *Babbitt* (1922), *Arrowsmith* (1925), *Elmer Gantry* (1927), and *Dodsworth* (1929), a writer whose works gave American society in the 1920s a large measure of its cultural vocabulary, and not incidentally the country's first Nobel Prize winner, apparently does not fit the paradigm of the new historicism. Too white, too male, too middle class, and far too much of a political pragmatist, he finds no haven in the heartless world of contemporary literary criticism.

While the *Columbia History* may consciously or unconsciously censor contrary opinions, my idea in putting together this symposium was to seek out those who might disagree with me, if for no better reason than to test my own perceptions of the book as fatally flawed. The critics whose responses I solicited, Russell J. Reising of Marquette University and Ellen Weinauer of Indiana University, are both politically left of center. It is somewhat reassuring then that they too in the essays that follow find the book problematic, though obviously for different reasons.

AN ASSESSMENT

from Russell J. Reising

The essays collected in the first two sections of *The Columbia History of the American Novel* read the first century of novelistic production in the United States through a variety of reading codes recently emerging as central areas of inquiry in historicized literary studies. Abandoning the convention of a seamless, evolutionary narrative that would organize contributions in strictly linear, chronological fashion, editor Emory Elliott has chosen instead a historiographic theory that accounts for the emergence of novelistic writing in a series of microanalyses of a fractured and disparate field of discursive energies, a historiography informed by and more compatible with contemporary revisionist historiography along Foucauldian lines. Rather than organizing the *Columbia History* according to the chronological model that might include discussions of "The Novel Before 1800," "The Novel from 1800 to 1849," "The Novel from *The Scarlet Letter* to the Civil War," and so forth, and rather than having an author-driven narrative that might, according to a linear scheme, consider the works of Hannah Foster, Charles Brockden Brown, George Lippard, Edgar Allan Poe, Nathaniel Hawthorne, Herman Melville, Harriet Beecher Stowe, Louisa May Alcott, Elizabeth Drew Stoddard, and so forth, Elliott opts for considerations of "Autobiography and the Early Novel," "The Book Marketplace I," "Romance and Race," "Domesticity and Fiction," "Realism," "Fiction and Reform (I and II)," "Gender and Fiction," and so forth. This framework enables the *Columbia History,* in practice, to incorporate some of the "New Views" that the cryptic subtitle printed only on the volume's dust jacket promises. It is, however, an editorial decision at least partly responsible for the weakness of the *Columbia History* as a history.

This history of the American novel, according to Elliott's conception, is not a history at all, but an ensemble of both socio-ideological and traditional literary-historical points of dispersion in a massive discursive field. That these essays are arranged under the potentially incompatibly "traditional" headings of "Beginnings to the Mid-Nineteenth Century" and "The Late Nineteenth Century" in the first half of the collection (and similarly chronocentric headings in the second) would seem to neutralize the innovativeness of the microanalyses, if not to expose the incoherence of the volume's overall methodological assumptions. One need not adhere to a naive conception of historical development to recognize that the *Columbia History* takes away with one plan what it appears to offer with the other. In reality the essays collected here read like essays on various aspects of fiction writing in the United States that were extracted from the recent pages of journals, not like some newly imagined, yet unified analysis of American writing. They commonly overlap, as in the largely redundant discussions of

racial issues in "Fiction and Reform I" and "Romance and Race" (which is not in itself a problem), but they are also commonly oblivious to each other. For example, in "Fiction and Reform I" Robert S. Levine discusses "the enormous social impact of reform movements during the 1825–60 period," while, in "Fiction and Reform II" Phillip Brian Harper announces that "the second half of the nineteenth century in the United States was characterized by an enormous number of social reform movements," as though these movements were *new, surprising,* or *unpredictable,* and as though we had not already been initiated into the centrality of reform energies in fictional projects prior to the Civil War. Also, both discussions of fiction and reform fail to take the recent and highly educative work of David Reynolds into account, even though parts of *Faith in Fiction* (1981) and the entirety of *Beneath the American Renaissance* (1988) examine the reform discourses and agendas explicit in many popular and noncanonical works and, according to Reynolds's own problematic aesthetic assumptions, refined into veiled and more nuanced dramas by the "major" novelists of the time. Furthermore, while attempting to shed the label of naive historicism, the *Columbia History* nonetheless maintains a fairly strict chronological system, which itself calls attention to problems of the collection's vision. Why, for example, should "Nation, Region, and Empire" be a subheading specifically (perhaps solely) descriptive of late-nineteenth-century fiction? Had not Cooper and Melville toyed with those issues half a century earlier? Was not "Gender and Fiction" problematic for American fictionists well before the years of the historical slot that essay fills?

The problem may simply be one of inadequate research and negligent editing, but it most likely exposes a larger, structural problem inherent in the contradictory organizational divisions in the *Columbia History.* Are the rhetoric and logics which locate fiction so clearly within the discursive practices of social reform movements stylistically or ideologically demarcated by the Civil War? Are they continuous? Are they related at all? The volume loses the opportunity to mesh these related essays in a manner that could foreground their deeply related projects; it similarly fails to place its other inclusions in any meaningful dialogue with each other. At a time when Gerald Graff's injunction to "teach the debate" is gaining currency in literary studies as well as in pedagogical theory, these "new views" are anachronistically static and monologic. Rarely do the debates about any of these structural headings *or* the writers and texts under discussion emerge in any way at all. Granted, the volume's stress on diversity and on the reclamation of forgotten or marginalized writers is in line with contemporary revisionist literary historiography, but the diversity of American fictional projects lies unexamined, even within individual essays which might otherwise have made significant contributions by problematizing their own representations. I, for one, expected that the *Columbia History* would interrogate its own categories and strategies. However, the categories themselves are represented as univocal and natural.

So, while ostensibly foregrounding the socio-ideological pressures on and agendas of American fiction (and on the criticism collected in this edition), these essays and the collection as a whole continually elide or obscure their logics of inclusion and analysis. It *is* important (and a welcome contribution of this volume) that we understand, say, Harriet Beecher Stowe's work in as multivalent a fashion as the discussions of her work (her "novel-positions") under various rubrics suggest. The fragmentation and inconsistencies of the volume, however, certainly qualify its otherwise useful innovations. The collection fails when it demonstrates little, if any, awareness that the turf of "Domesticity and Fiction," "Fiction and the Science of Society," "Fiction and Reform," or "Gender and Fiction" (to name only a few) is highly contested and that little consensus exists regarding the internal pressures of these discursive practices. Is the *Columbia History* a "history" of "the American novel," or is it a minimally synthesized collection of various thematic approaches to localized moments in the practices of American fiction?

The individual contributions in the first two sections of the *Columbia History* are themselves an uneven mixture. What might the contributor of the section on "The Early American Novel," for example, mean when he declares that "there are no cultural voices in the 'early American novel'"? His four reasons for this putative absence merely rehearse the anachronistic line that bemoaned the lack of an "authentic American language," the lack of "cultural support of . . . creative efforts," the "parochial" and "didactic" cultural mandates for fiction writing, and, finally, Cooper's, Hawthorne's, James's, and Trilling's whipping boy of the "unsettled society" that results in no stable milieu within which fictionists can hone their craft. Surely, "new views" should be able to conceptualize "cultural voices" in more sophisticated and recent terms than these. Similarly, even if one believes that "the development of romance in the United States was linked

in unsettling ways to the business of race" (perhaps, *especially* if one believes such to be the case), why would the writer of "Romance and Race" focus almost exclusively on Poe's work, without arguing for Poe as representative, with only the vaguest references to *Narrative of A. Gordon Pym* (1837-1838), and with only passing references to Hawthorne, Melville, and Stowe? In the discussion of "Fiction and Reform I," furthermore, why are only *The Blithedale Romance* (1852) and *Uncle Tom's Cabin* (1852) discussed, and why is the fictional negotiation of reform energies represented as taking only obvious and explicit forms? Did American writers never embed reform issues or critiques in less contentious narratives and in more veiled discourses? On the other hand, the author of the section on "Nation, Region, and Empire" might have made her essay even stronger had she focused more deeply on several paradigmatic narratives rather than on brief summaries of works that touch in any way on the subject at hand. In what I find to be the least persuasive section, the author of "Gender and Fiction" asserts confidently and unproblematically that "as a group white women novelists were so successful that their work clearly threatened white men at the time," supporting this claim by commenting on Dreiser's concern with women protagonists and by arguing that the "exaggeratedly muscular novels of men such as Richard Harding Davis, Frank Norris, Winston Churchill, and Harold Bell Wright point at least in part to their anxiety not simply about virility in general but specifically about gender and the novel – who should be shaping it and what it should look like." Numerous gender concerns decisively shape novelistic output throughout American literary history, but just how the novelists mentioned are "exaggeratedly muscular" (or what that might mean), how anxiety about virility determines that muscularity, and why Dreiser's interest in women protagonists should be reduced to a symptom of his concern/fear about women novelists are never argued, clarified, or substantiated.

There are some gems of critical, historical, cultural, and theoretical work in this collection. Michael T. Gilmore's discussion of "The Book Marketplace I," Terence Martin's analysis of "The Romance," Robert Shulman's essay on "Realism," and Christine Bold's discussion of "Popular Forms I" are all excellent contributions to our understanding of the history of the American novel. They also represent some of the "New Views" the dust jacket promises. Unfortunately, they are the exceptions rather than the rule in this volume. Emory Elliott's innovative format for *The Columbia History of the American Novel* departs in important ways from the master narratives provided by traditional historiographical works and may well set a precedent for future attempts to retell the story of the emergence and development of American fiction. Like many innovations and like many projects of gargantuan proportions, however, this volume is, as Melville's Ishmael admits his leviathan, written narrative of *Moby-Dick* (1851) to be, "but a draught – nay, but the draught of a draught."

AN ASSESSMENT

from Ellen Weinauer

In her introduction to "The Early Twentieth Century" section of *The Columbia History of the American Novel,* Valerie Smith gives an account of literary production in this period which sums up the general approach to "literature" taken throughout the volume: "The chapters in this section," Smith writes, "remind us that culture and cultural production in the United States and around the world in the first half of the twentieth century were shaped by momentous political, technological, economic, and social developments." The authors of those chapters "all consider American novels in relation to the circumstances under which they are produced, circulated, and read." So too with the authors of most of the chapters in the *History*. In his general introduction to the volume, Emory Elliott notes that the "major aim of this 'literary history' . . . is to provide readers with lively and engaging discussions of the development of the novel in the Americas. Our emphasis, however, is upon the ways that current critical perspectives provide fresh insights into the texts and into the history of which the novels were and remain a part." By placing the term "literary history" in quotation marks, and by using the decisive "however" here, Elliott makes it clear that the *History* will not provide a traditional narrative of the development of a literary genre (with an emphasis on the *literary*); instead, it will attempt to challenge such a narrative by revealing the ways in which the development of this (and any) genre must be understood with reference to seemingly extraliterary "circumstances."

Although this is no longer, perhaps, a radical approach to literary concerns, the book will doubtless unsettle many in its tendency to privilege such "circumstances" and its refusal "to be comprehensive or to have chapters on single authors that would signal our assertions of who is 'major' and who is 'minor.'" While Elliott provides a loose definition of "the novel," he takes pains *not* to "provide criteria for distinguishing 'good' or even 'great' novels from 'poor' ones." The *History* wants to demonstrate that "Without diminishing any of the acclaim deserved by such writers as Melville, James, Twain, Faulkner, and Wharton for their many extraordinary works," we can acknowledge that "many works previously rejected . . . need rereading and reevaluation upon their own terms."

It is debatable, of course, whether we can actually have access to a text on its "own terms"; and the attempt to achieve that access can lead to an academic equivalent of "I'm OK, You're OK" – a denial that the academic profession does make distinctions and a refusal to take responsibility for them. Still, it is doubtless that our traditional approaches to literary history *have* elevated the few over the many and *have* often failed to acknowledge the ways in which both canonical and noncanonical writers are working in and out of a common – if differently experienced – cultural, political, economic, and social matrix. The *History* attempts to investigate that matrix, to look at works through the lens of history and, in doing so, to restore to view portions of "the rich literary heritage of the nation" which have in the past been "excluded from public appreciation."

As a student and a scholar of the nineteenth century, I find this approach useful and, at times, exhilarating. The nineteenth century is a period in which the differences between canonical (usually white male) and noncanonical (usually nonwhite and/or female) practitioners of the novel are deemed to be excessively pronounced. Even when the work of women and minority writers is brought into critical light, it is usually on specific (at times, apologetic) terms – terms very different from those with which we approach the canonical male writers. The work of culturally marginalized or politically oppressed groups is now studied, in other words, but it is not yet adequately integrated into a broad understanding of production (literary and otherwise) in the nineteenth century.

Many of the chapters in the *History* contribute to precisely this kind of understanding. In "Autobiography and the Early Novel," for example, Nellie McKay examines the ways in which African American and Native American "self-stories" (among others) blur the boundaries of "fact and fiction" that so vexed the novel in Republican America and thus contribute to its generic development. Michael T. Gilmore, in "The Book Marketplace I," examines "groupings" of novelists who "often seemed to occupy antipodal cultural spheres" – canonical men and "the domestic or sentimental women" – and shows that, despite their many differences, these "groups" are joined in having both "internalized but also set [themselves] against the social and economic universe" that existed at midcentury.

These are but two examples of the kinds of essays I find particularly intriguing in this volume: essays that allow us to move toward a more synthetic understanding of literary history, and that enhance our knowledge of the complex networks – economic, political, cultural – that join writers who and texts which seem to "occupy antipodal spheres." One key component in this developing knowledge, particularly for the nineteenth century, is the issue of race. While we have long recognized the significance of fictions that take up the slavery conflict explicitly (*Uncle Tom's Cabin*, "Benito Cereno" [1856]), we have been less able to recognize how texts can be more subtly inflected by the peculiar and perverse racial organization of antebellum (not to mention postbellum, or twentieth-century) America. It is precisely this kind of recognition for which Toni Morrison calls in her recent *Playing in the Dark: Whiteness and the Literary Imagination* (1992), and one which many of the authors in the *History* manifest. From an essay by Joan Dayan on "Romance and Race" – which treats, in particular, Poe's *Narrative of Arthur Gordon Pym* (1837–1838) – to an essay by Phillip Brian Harper ("Fiction and Reform II") which "trace[s] relations between [explicitly reformist] works and other less obviously 'political' works of the era," the *History* goes far in reminding us of the centrality of issues of race for all writers in "the Americas."

While I find much to commend in this volume, I must also admit to some reservations – reservations often rooted, ironically, in the very elements that allow the *History* to make its unique contribution. This text, for example, often performs its historical "excavations" at the expense of specifically generic considerations. While some essays do discuss the novel per se (its rise as a literary genre, its fragmentation in the twentieth century), the form itself is rarely the main issue. Students looking to understand the novel *as a genre* will not, I think, find what they are looking for. Other aspects of the methodology of the *History* leave me more troubled. Earlier, I commended the ways in which this volume performs necessary integrative functions. We should always be aware, however, that integration can cut both ways. Elliott writes that "we decided

not to 'ghettoize' the novels of minority writers in order to underscore the impact of minority cultures upon American culture as a whole and to problematize the boundary between 'major' and 'minor' literatures." While these are goals worth pursuing, to pursue them single-mindedly can lead us both to overlook the ways in which those marginalized literatures might well manifest significant lines of descent and to deny the implications of how those literatures have been classified in the past. In being sensitive to the problematic "class divisions" which have so skewed our literary canon and our understanding of literary history, the *History* may go too far the other way – thus preventing us from really understanding the effects of the class divisions we have been so prone to making.

Some of the same problems exist in the volume's treatment of the canon. Although the editors want to do away with some of our traditional canonical "boundaries," in fact many of those boundaries remain, exerting a subtle and implicit force throughout. The volume, for example, eschews biographical and single-author studies in favor of a thematic cultural approach – but then includes an appendix of author biographies that must necessarily be selective. We are alerted to the fact that while an author's name appears frequently in the index, this does not indicate "an editorial decision to pay special attention to particular writers over others," but rather "reflect[s] the degree to which a highly diverse group of critics turned to particular works as examples of the development of the novel as a genre and as a reflection of changes in American society." But, editorial decision notwithstanding, does not the predominance of an author's name indicate that distinctions are still being made on a critical level? And would we not do well, even as we try to break down those distinctions, to attend to the ways in which they have been and are being made? As Henry Louis Gates writes in a 1992 issue of *Profession,* "the sort of conversation and contestation that normally surround literary and cultural assessments, however contingent, can be a valuable part of literary pedagogy." Indeed, at this critical juncture in the life of the academy, such a conversation might well be the *most* valuable part of pedagogy. In forgoing this kind of discussion in favor of inclusion above all, the *History* remains blind to some of the very assessments embedded in its own pages and loses an opportunity to intervene truly in the ways we as a profession construct our literary histories and our relation to the world outside the academy.

Camden House: An Interview with James Hardin

Camden House was founded in Columbia, South Carolina, in 1979 by James Hardin and Gunther Holst, professors of German at the University of South Carolina, for the purpose of publishing works of high quality in the fields of English, American, German, and (quite recently) Scandinavian literature. Since that time Camden House has published nearly one hundred books, most of which are still in print. The main objective of Camden House publishing has been to publish books dealing with the history of literature and with literary criticism, and translation into English of significant literature from German and Germanic dialects. Recent important translations published by Camden House include the Swedish Romantic novel *The Queen's Diadem,* by Carl Jonas Love Almqvist; the best-selling novel *Dog Days* by the contemporary German writer Walter Kempowski; Rainer Maria Rilke's now-famous poem cycles *The Duino Elegies* and *Sonnets to Orpheus;* Erika Mitterer's prize-winning novel *All Our Games,* a story about the Holocaust as experienced by a young woman in Vienna; and *Pigeons and Moles,* a collection of the modern German writer Günter Eich's radio plays and poetry translated by the renowned English poet and translator Michael Hamburger.

All works published by Camden House are vetted and refereed by specialists in the fields concerned. All Camden House books are printed on acid-free paper, most hardback Smyth-sewn in library bindings.

Since the inception of Camden House, its books have been reviewed in over forty publications, including the *Times Literary Supplement, New York Times Book Review, Washington Post, Columbia* (S.C.) *State, Choice, German Quarterly, Journal of English & Germanic Philology, German Life and Letters, Arbitrium, Germanistik, Seventeenth Century News, Monatshefte, Colloquia Germanica, Daphnis, Goethe Yearbook,* and all the regional periodicals of the Modern Language Association. Camden House enjoys a reputation for quality, efficiency, and meticulousness with its primary constituencies: academics in the field of literature and research librarians. In 1991 Camden published twenty-two books; it published twenty-three more in 1992.

Hardin was interviewed in January 1993 in Columbia, S.C., by Matthew J. Bruccoli and James W. Hipp.

DLB: For openers, why would a full professor, who has a career as a teacher and a scholar, want to undertake all of the grief, aggravation, responsibility, and financial risk involved in running your own imprint.

HARDIN: Well, you've certainly enumerated the things that I have come to learn are present in running an imprint, running a small press.

DLB: Let's define that. How do you think of Camden House? As a small press? As an imprint?

HARDIN: I think of it as a small publishing house. The kind of manuscripts we try to acquire are those sought by university presses, though we are more specialized.

DLB: Without a university subvention.

HARDIN: Without the university subvention and with a different tax treatment – those two major differences – which means that not only do you pay taxes, but also, getting off on the business side, that you've got a very different bookkeeping system. So it is exactly as you say, a very tough undertaking because the person who undertakes this kind of operation has got to be interested not only in books, in my case literature and linguistics and the culture of Germany and Austria, but also has to be pretty well informed about the latest computer developments – which is one reason I have subscribed to four computer magazines – and about elementary accounting. One has to become something of an accountant. One has to deal with pervasive federal and state regulations and reporting that is very time consuming, as you well know. So it

James Hardin (photograph by Edward Scott)

doesn't leave as much time to devote to the acquisition of manuscripts as one would like.

DLB: You are publishing the same kinds of books for the most part as the university presses publish.

HARDIN: A bit more specialized, I think. Maybe 25 percent of our titles wouldn't be considered by most university presses because they are very specialized.

DLB: When you say specialized, you mean scholarly books appealing to an even smaller audience, a more specialized audience than most scholarly books? Is that what you mean?

HARDIN: That's correct.

DLB: You are competing against university presses which get free rent, free telephone, free electricity and heat, and some percentage of staff salaries paid by the university. You are competing with organizations that have this kind of financial advan-

tage. Are you (a) demented or (b) driven by some inexplicable compulsion to redress the wrongs of scholarship in your field?

HARDIN: Could be a combination of both of those. I think there is the dementia there, and the second point is certainly present too. Quite simply, there are few opportunities for decent and better-than-decent manuscripts in the field of Germanics to get into print in this country if they don't have the name Hitler or Napoleon or Jesus Christ in the title.

DLB: You left out Freud.

HARDIN: Freud, right. What we like to produce are well-made books that deal solidly with a closely defined, scholarly significant subject matter – in other words, monographs. Now occasionally we do try to put out books that deal with broader topics, such as our *Concise History of German Literature to 1900,* which is a book that fills a need and probably will sell well over the next few years, the kind of book a university press would be glad to publish. We've had other books like that, for example the very first volume in our series, Robert Cazden's *History of the German Book Trade in America to the Civil War,* which is a book that I think most university presses would love to get.

One area in which we do have a program, a philosophical program of sorts, is in the new series Literary Criticism in Perspective. Now while it is a truism that there are no longer absolutes in literary criticism, that no one has thought there are since the late nineteenth century, it has seemed to many of us that the most recent generation of literary critics has forgotten that. Their literary criticism, strongly informed as it is by deconstructionism, finds absolutes in absolutely nothing but tends to look down its doctrinaire nose at all other brands of literary criticism. I feel strongly that although the absolute truth is to be found nowhere in literary criticism and that, in fact, a well-made critical edition is the noblest scholarly task, there is more truth in some critical schools than in others. I lean for example toward historicism and a laying out of the philosophical background of the work in question as useful toward an understanding of the text. Biography is clearly important. The old New Criticism is of limited use outside the classroom. The books in the series therefore will tend to show, we think, which schools of literary criticism have been most fruitful in their analyses of literary works. They may do this implicitly or explicitly or, in some cases, not at all. But I suspect that over time the series will tend to show that good literary criticism did not begin with Derrida and Foucault or with semiotics – or for that matter with Freudian insights, Jungian prototypes, or Marxist dialectics. Quite the contrary.

DLB: What technological developments have made it possible for you to be running a small press on what, from anybody's viewpoint, is a pretty small scale?

HARDIN: The most important development for the small press was six or seven years ago, when I saw the first sheet roll out of a laser printer. The Times Roman looked beautiful to me. I said, "That's it. That's what I've been looking for for two years." A way to set type in-house. I talked up the idea of laser-printer–produced camera-ready copy with several university presses; in fact, I sent a query to thirty or thirty-five university presses asking would they accept copy like this? Was this not the way of the future? Maybe two or three said, "Yes, this may have promise." But most said, "The quality of this print is not acceptable at university

presses, and so on." What they didn't realize, of course, was that there were simple ways around the resolution problem, by producing oversized copy and reducing it to get higher resolution. And now, of course, with the new laser printers having resolution up to twelve hundred dots per inch, there is no real distinction between the old conventionally produced camera-ready copy and the new form on ordinary paper. So that was the main thing. Of course, before that, there was the personal computer and the standardization on the IBM personal computer standardization. So if you have a good printer who understands how to process such camera-ready copy, you can save lots of money over conventional typesetting. And the existence of a computer in virtually every academic's office also is an enormous help, since we can – and do – require that the book be prepared on computer so that we can work with the floppy disks or, even in some cases, with camera-ready copy. The problem we run into is that we lack the resources to do as good a job as we would like vetting and editing the texts.

DLB: When you say editing, what you really mean is line-editing?

HARDIN: Yes, and we're trying to do more and more of that. We cannot rely on the authors to edit their own texts. We do proof them. There again, technologically we're helped by spelling checkers, which are helpful but obviously don't take the place of a trained proofreader. A program called Grammatik® is an interesting example of a technological assist for the small publisher. In its reprogrammed form, more or less keyed to Strunk and White's *Elements of Style,* it helps us pick up clichés and other recurring phrases. It can go through a book of, say, 350 pages in fifteen or twenty minutes, assuming, of course, that the author has submitted the book on floppy disk. The program then marks the floppy with queries about questionable phrases and usually meaningless words, such as "numerous," "essentially," "basically," and "it goes without saying." Now, 90 percent of what the program marks is okay, but that remaining 10 percent is usually flawed and in need of revision. It is a first, primitive step toward getting the manuscript in better shape. I think too that the use of even such an elementary program raises the awareness of the authors that they must write precisely and clearly.

DLB: By raising the technological questions, you've opened the door to the ideas mentioned when we started: Is this the wave of the future? Is it going to be possible, because we've eliminated what you might call the "guild" aspects of book publishing and evolved past the idea of Leonard and Virginia Woolf in their basement with their manual presses, that this is what serious people are going to be doing in the future?

HARDIN: I think that the lines between so-called desktop publishing and other kinds of publishing have just about vanished. I just recently reviewed a book put out under the imprint of Pennsylvania State University Press and that was obviously printed on a laser printer. I think that in the humanities, certainly, authors will have to provide properly edited texts or formatted floppy disks that will eliminate a good deal of the typesetting cost if it's done properly. But for this method to work requires hiring some computer hackers, typically younger people, in university presses. That's a slot that I don't think many university presses have now.

DLB: Five years from now, ten years from now, how many scholars are there going to be doing what you're doing? Right now you're alone to my knowledge.

HARDIN: Actually, I don't know that small scholarly presses will arise in great numbers for the reasons you stated at the outset. It's so darn risky, and even now I worry about finances an awful lot, meeting the demands of paying the bills. I have put a lot of checks on the mantelpiece that I couldn't pay for awhile. I don't know that large numbers of people will want to get into it because it requires that you work every day of the week, long hours. I don't know how many people are crazy enough to want to do that.

DLB: Five hundred copies, three-hundred-page book. Or, let's do a monograph. A monograph, five hundred copies, what kind of up-front financial exposure does that involve, in round numbers?

HARDIN: Four thousand dollars before any kind of marketing costs are figured in.

DLB: Before you've paid for the catalogue. And mailing the catalogue.

HARDIN: That's right. And paid your employees, paid the FICA, and all that stuff.

DLB: The reason I asked the question was because many scholars who are interested in getting into some aspect of desktop publishing don't have a clue as to what kind of risks they are contemplating and I think it is necessary to include in this discussion of things to come, the wave of the future, the fact that even with the miracles of technology a cash gamble is still involved. Sometimes it comes back, and probably most of the time it doesn't come back.

HARDIN: Absolutely. And you've got to figure that the cost of the book which is, as you well know, maybe only 60 percent or 70 percent, in our case, of the real cost of doing business, and maybe less than that probably considering all the taxes, federal, state, and local. You've got a big financial problem there and to my thinking the only way to make a small academic press work is to put out a certain minimum number of books per year. If you can't do that, if you can't put out at least fifteen to twenty monographs per year, there's no way to break even unless you are subsidized by scholarly groups. And one must establish and follow a simple marketing plan. That's why we like to stick to a given format. We don't stray from that very much because if you do you can get into deep trouble – I don't think most small presses have the resources to recover. It's a big risk and you really don't know the full story until the end of the year. Then suddenly you're faced with taxes and other liabilities, such as royalties, that are difficult to predict.

In my experience publishing is a very tough business. But sometimes you get some very good surprises. We've been happy with sales of fiction translations from the German; they start slow but then move better than the monographs in general, and we've been very happy about that. There are two problems in this area: (1) there are very few people who are willing and able to translate well, and they must, of course, be paid, and (2) one has generally got to pay a substantial license fee to the German publisher, and so you are faced with a double disadvantage cost-wise. A third problem is that the great, presumably great writers, are already spoken for, like Günter Grass. But we've had a couple of successes just by sheer luck, for example, Kempowski's *Dog Days,* which is an excellent book.

There is one other thing that hasn't come up yet that I'd like to mention, and that is the role of Camden House as an intermediary in the field of German, as a link between the German and American cultures. We are not interested in doing the kind of book that is being published by most German academic presses. We have published one or

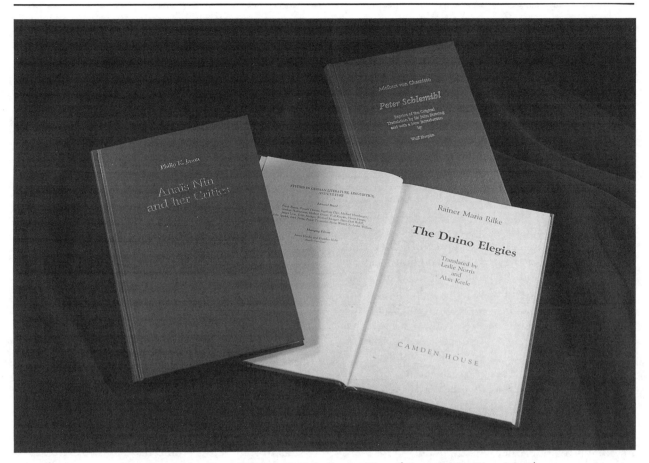

Three of the books to be published in 1993 by Camden House (photograph by Edward Scott)

two books written in German, but what we tell our authors is that we aim to print books understandable to the general reader – the *intelligent,* general reader. We like lucidity and directness. We subscribe, in short, to the principles of Jacques Barzun's *Simple and Direct.* We think the monograph ought to be simple and direct, to the extent possible. So, if we're different from any other publisher I think it would be chiefly in that area. We want to make German culture available to the intelligent reader of the English-speaking world.

DLB: How do the Germans feel about what you're doing?

HARDIN: We haven't had good sales in Germany actually. We were surprised by that. Maybe for the reasons I just gave you: most of our books are in English and they aim at the British and American public. Although I will say that the *Goethe Yearbook,* which we've published now for ten years, is international in scope as is the *Herder Yearbook,* of which the first volume came out just last year. And

some of our monographs, though they are in English, have a dual aim: to appeal to Germanists all over the world and to the reader interested in literature generally.

DLB: Apart from copyediting, how much rewriting do you have to do? That is, making stuff publishable and readable in a way that the author who knows the subject is incapable of writing?

HARDIN: We are unable to do a lot of rewriting because of financial and time restrictions. We try to avoid this problem by commissioning books to be written by scholars who have proven they can write well. If the author cannot write, we have to reject the manuscript.

DLB: What do you mean by commissioned?

HARDIN: We select a topic and then ask the author or editor to put out the book, as was the case with the *Concise History of German Literature.* It was commissioned five years ago, and it finally came out in 1992. And all our literary criticism books are commissioned. We find a good author on the topic, someone who writes well, and we provide the author specific guidelines for the book.

DLB: What is your best advice and your best warning to other professors who are contemplating becoming independent publishers?

HARDIN: Well, assuming that they really want to get into it, I think they should inform themselves by talking with people who have some experience with publishing to see what the problems are. If they then decide to proceed, they need to know that it's going to cost some money. Other than money, you risk your reputation. You don't want to start something and then not finish it. So once you start, you better be willing to go ahead. That's a risk because you may get into something you don't like, and then after four books you may wish you'd never entered into such a time-consuming activity. But you have committed yourself to your editors, authors, and to your college or university. I'd think twice and then twice again before plunging into scholarly publishing. Having gotten past all that, one ought to develop and stick to a plan. If one is going to do a monograph series, then I think it can be done if the publisher will maintain a close focus on a restricted subject area and try to achieve quality without getting bogged down in editorial detail. If one is going to do research books, the chief market is research libraries. Forget bookstores. Develop your mailing lists to libraries and professors. Do some direct mail, show the flag in scholarly periodicals. That would be my marketing plan.

DLB: You answered my question. I was getting ready to ask about the marketing and publicity, which, undoubtedly, sucks up the cost of larger publishers. You answered how you handle most of that. How successful is it? How would you like to improve, if you had the opportunity, on selling the books?

HARDIN: We never have figured out what is the most effective method. We have found that books we do advertise do better than books we don't, but we've never had time to be as scientific about it as we ought to. The direct mailings we've had showed us, for example, that a mailing to the Modern Language Association list of Germanists who were interested in literature is moderately effective. We've found that an ad in the *Times Literary Supplement* is moderately effective. We would like to try the *New York Review of Books,* but it's just too expensive.

We think our yearly catalogue is our best advertising. We print ten thousand copies of it and distribute five thousand in this country and five thousand in the rest of the world through our distributor, Boydell and Brewer.

DLB: What about fulfillment and distribution?

HARDIN: Fulfillment and distribution is done now in this country by the Johns Hopkins University Press consortium.

DLB: If this type of publishing were to become more common, do you think other types of consortiums to share costs would have to be developed to make it worthwhile, for people who aren't willing to spend all their waking hours doing this and their real job, or what they consider their real job?

HARDIN: We had a miniwarehouse at one time. We loaded the books there and rolled them down the ramps, and we then pulled them out to fill orders, and we wasted a lot of time doing that. But it was a good exercise in the practicalities of publishing. But, yes, I think they'd have to go to groups like Johns Hopkins, if they have a good enough product.

The Practice of Biography VII: An Interview with John Caldwell Guilds

Mary Ann Wimsatt
University of South Carolina

John Caldwell Guilds is currently Distinguished Professor of Humanities at the University of Arkansas in Fayetteville. Throughout his long career, he has filled the triple roles of teacher, scholar, and administrator. During the 1960s and early 1970s, he served the University of South Carolina as professor of English, head of the English department, and vice provost for liberal and cultural disciplines. From 1975 to 1979 he was dean of the College of Humanities and Fine Arts at the University of Houston; and from 1979 to 1988 he was dean of the J. William Fulbright College of Arts and Sciences at the University of Arkansas.

Despite heavy administrative responsibilities, Guilds has steadily produced scholarly studies of American and southern literature. He is the general editor of *The Centennial Edition of the Writings of William Gilmore Simms* (Columbia: University of South Carolina Press, 1969–1974); the editor of *Nineteenth-Century Southern Fiction* (New York: Merrill, 1970); the coeditor of *The Literature of South Carolina: A Tricentennial Anthology* (Columbia: University of South Carolina Press, 1971); the editor of *"Long Years of Neglect": The Work and Reputation of William Gilmore Simms* (Fayetteville: University of Arkansas Press, 1988); and the author of many articles on nineteenth-century authors.

Guilds's most recent book, *Simms: A Literary Life* (Fayetteville: University of Arkansas Press, 1992), is the first authoritative biography of the antebellum South's most prominent and influential man of letters – William Gilmore Simms, who produced more than seventy volumes depicting the settlement of America and the development of the antebellum South. A renowned author whose works were read and acclaimed throughout the country, Simms moved easily in literary circles both North and South, numbering Edgar Allan Poe, Herman Melville, James Fenimore Cooper, and Washington Irving among his friends. An acute cultural analyst

John Caldwell Guilds (photograph © 1991 University Relations, University of Arkansas)

who explored persistent elements in American society – expansionism, multiculturalism, violence, and flamboyant humor – Simms anticipates many strains in twentieth-century social inquiry.

WIMSATT: You're a native of South Carolina. Did your upbringing and undergraduate education in the state encourage you to enter academic life?

GUILDS: Well, I wouldn't have thought so at the time, but I now think they did in a general way.

193

My father had become president of Columbia College in Columbia, South Carolina, while he was still fairly young. He was also an English professor, and so people said I would naturally become an English professor. But I didn't decide to be one until after World War II.

I was a student at Wofford College during the war and was in my sophomore year when my ROTC unit was called up. I would have graduated in 1945. I was in the army for three years and was sent overseas. I saw action in Belgium and Holland and was wounded in Germany on 1 December 1944, right before the Battle of the Bulge. I started back to college the day after I left the army. I returned to Wofford and graduated from it.

WIMSATT: From Wofford you went on to Duke University, where you took your Ph.D. in 1954. How did your training at Duke lead you into the study of American literature and Simms?

GUILDS: Duke's English department in the 1950s was very strong – it had nationally known scholars, not only in American literature but also in British. In British there were Newman I. White, Paull Baum, and Allan Gilbert; in American, Jay B. Hubbell, Clarence Gohdes, and Arlin Turner.

Hubbell was the father of American literature, both the field and the journal. He and Norman Foerster had started the professional study of American literature in the 1920s. That was one reason he had been hired at Duke. For many years he and Foerster continued to lead the field; they even edited rival anthologies of American literature. And of course Hubbell was the founding editor in 1929 of the journal *American Literature,* which is still being published at Duke. Hubbell was a wonderful example for graduate students; he kept up with developments in scholarship and the profession. Not every scholar is a professional scholar, but he was, and the standard of work he inspired was high. His real strength in training graduate students was not in the classroom but as a research director – in other words, in a one-on-one situation. He always stressed the importance of extensive, accurate research.

I had courses with Hubbell and Gohdes simultaneously. Hubbell had known Gohdes at Southern Methodist University and had brought him to Duke. Arlin Turner came to Duke after I had nearly completed my course work. I managed to take a summer course with him; he also read my dissertation and served on my dissertation committee. At Duke at that time literary history was strongly emphasized, and so also was getting the facts right. Hubbell was a gold mine for students in American literature; he readily provided lists of topics needing work. Gohdes stressed the importance of accuracy and precision. He served as acting director of my dissertation–"Simms as a Magazine Editor, 1825–1845" – while Hubbell was in Jerusalem on a Fulbright. When I finished a draft of the piece, Gohdes said, "Didn't you have time to write a short dissertation?" So I trimmed it down. I ask my students the same question. I learned from Gohdes the value of compression.

WIMSATT: With *The South in American Literature* (1954), published after he had retired from Duke, Hubbell also started the professional study of southern writing. He had read widely in the work of many southern authors, and he particularly admired Simms. Did he encourage you to work on Simms?

GUILDS: Not directly at first, but when I grew interested in Simms he encouraged me vigorously. He knew a great deal about Simms; he was interested in Simms's writing and judged both the man and his work wisely and sympathetically. He and Vernon L. Parrington were pioneers in perceiving the value of Simms's work and stressing Simms's importance in American and southern cultural and literary history. You have to remember that even as late as the 1950s, Simms's reputation was still beclouded by William Peterfield Trent's unenlightened 1892 biography. Hubbell had studied under Trent at Columbia and understood Simms and the South better than Trent did. He knew there was serious work that needed to be done on Simms.

Charleston and South Carolina, of course, have gotten a bad rap in American history because of their role in starting the Civil War; and as a result the reputations of Simms and other South Carolina writers have suffered. Also, Trent and other scholars had insisted that living in Charleston had harmed Simms's writing. Hubbell was a good corrective to them because he pointed out the strengths of living in Charleston. He knew it had a vibrant intellectual life, lively discussion groups, and excellent private and public libraries – such as the Charleston Library Society – to which Simms had access.

But I didn't start out to work on Simms as a graduate student. I had written my master's thesis on Edgar Allan Poe under Hubbell, and he and I had planned that the thesis would be part of my dissertation. I went to colonial Williamsburg to use the

Nathaniel Beverley Tucker collection, looking for material on Poe, and found some letters by Simms there. This was before I knew Mrs. Oliphant – Mary Chevillette Simms Oliphant, Simms's granddaughter and the general editor of his letters. After I found the letters, Hubbell told me I needed to meet Mrs. Oliphant. He and she had corresponded and thought highly of each other.

WIMSATT: The making of a major biography is a story in itself. Did Hubbell encourage you to begin biographical work on Simms? What part did Mrs. Oliphant and Alexander Salley, the Simms collector, play?

GUILDS: Hubbell stressed in lectures and conferences that there was a crying need for a sound and thorough modern biography of Simms. But I didn't begin to think seriously about such a book until I went to the University of South Carolina in 1964 as head of the English department and saw the amount of Simms material available at the university – especially in the South Caroliniana Library, which is a treasure trove for scholars of antebellum culture. As for Salley, I don't think he really read Simms – he might have as a young man, but he was mainly interested in collecting Simms.

My interest in writing a biography of Simms grew while I served as the general editor of the centennial Simms textual edition in the 1960s and 1970s. I had started to suspect that the biographical study of Simms that C. Hugh Holman had begun would not in fact be finished, because Hugh had suffered a fate that has befallen other Simms scholars – he had become an administrator and had little time for research and writing. Also, Mrs. Oliphant supported my interest in writing a biography and aided me enormously. She gave me access to the restricted papers in her possession and also to those she had donated to the South Caroliniana Library.

WIMSATT: In what other ways did she help you?

GUILDS: Well, just knowing her was an experience in itself. She was a remarkable person in every way: intelligent, passionate, energetic, and a mine of information about Simms. She had edited the Simms *Letters* (1952–1982), and anyone who knows the enormous body of Simms's writing realizes that the six published volumes of his correspondence made the impossible task of writing a biography possible. Also, Mrs. Oliphant – or "Miss May," as her family and friends called her – had a tena-

Dust jacket for Guild's biography of the nineteenth-century southern writer

cious memory: she knew almost everything there was to know about Simms and his times. I talked with her extensively over a period of many years. Sometimes we would stay up until 2 A.M. or 3 A.M. in the morning talking about her grandfather. I didn't tape our early conversations, but I made notes on them, and then I began taping later ones. From talking with her I got a sense of Simms as a living presence. She'd been born after he died, and she'd known four of his children, and she remembered everything that had been said about him by any member of her family. So she made him come to life.

I think the two great advantages I had as Simms's biographer were the Simms *Letters,* totaling over two thousand letters in all, and Mrs. Oliphant. Mrs. Oliphant was a take-charge kind of person. She had some of Simms's characteristics, including enthusiasm, dedication, and commitment. She'd hung in there on the Simms letters during many long years; she was the moving force in getting them collected, annotated, and published. She had strong scholarly instincts even though she hadn't been trained as a scholar.

I have to say that she was lucky in her fellow editors of the *Letters,* Alfred Taylor Odell at Furman University and T. C. Duncan Eaves at the University of Arkansas. I believe Odell died near the time that the first volume of the letters went to press. Duncan Eaves was his successor. Duncan's scholarship was impeccable, and he was energetic, enthusiastic, and willing to work hard. Like Mrs. Oliphant, he was a native South Carolinian with a great interest in history and genealogy. The two complemented each other well.

Also Duncan, like Mrs. Oliphant, had an incredible memory, and he knew Simms's background thoroughly. I didn't realize what an invaluable resource Duncan was for training in biography until I went to the University of Arkansas in 1979. Duncan and Ben Kimpel at Arkansas had written a biography of Samuel Richardson and were then working on a book about Ezra Pound, which unfortunately they never completed. So Duncan knew something about writing biography.

Duncan, Jay Hubbell, and others were resources and inspirations for Simms scholars, but Mrs. Oliphant was the best resource of all. She was a charming lady who possessed the highest kind of southern etiquette, and she cared passionately about her grandfather. Like Simms, she had courage, spirit, and determination; and like him, she never allowed disability or illness to daunt her. As you know, she lived into her late nineties, and she was mentally alert to the end. The last time I saw her, I had brought part of the biography for her to read. Her opening question was, "Is it interesting?" She repeated the question many times, because she wanted people to know how interesting Simms is. I kept thinking about her remarks, and consequently I used oral history, including stories she had told me, to a greater extent than I might have done otherwise. Mrs. Oliphant knew that it wasn't easy for Simms to be well thought of in the twentieth century. She said the Civil War had ended Simms's reputation as surely as if someone had put a bullet through his heart. And she was right.

I've said the Simms *Letters* were also invaluable for the biography, and they were. Donald Davidson at Vanderbilt wrote a fine introduction to the *Letters.* It treated Simms and his culture knowledgeably and sympathetically. But it never became widely influential — it never seemed to change people's minds about Simms.

WIMSATT: It seems difficult to change people's minds about Simms, and that makes me wonder why James Fenimore Cooper's reputation hasn't suffered in the way Simms's has, despite the fact that Simms is in many respects the better writer. What things have helped preserve Cooper's reputation and harmed Simms's?

GUILDS: The scholar Perry Miller, who knew the literary history of New England well, wryly remarked, "New England took care of her own." The point is true of northern writers in general. They benefited from living in or near the big publishing centers, and of course they've benefited posthumously from the fact that after the Civil War the North rewrote American history, so to speak — deprecating, perhaps without entirely intending to do so, the South and especially Simms, because he was such an eloquent spokesman for antebellum southern culture. Cooper was a northerner and didn't write about slavery, and that helped him. Also, he masterminded the publication of his books, and he was lucky in his editors and publishers. Simms wasn't. In terms of professional authorship and publishing, Cooper was fortunate to live in the North. Simms considered moving there but didn't. If he had, his standing in the American literary canon might not have slipped.

It's worth pointing out here that, like Cooper, Simms was widely reprinted in Germany and England. In fact, a professor I know in Germany recently taught a seminar in Simms and Cooper. Also, there's a difference in the British and the American perception of Simms. The British focus on Simms the writer and aren't bothered, as we are, by the fact that he'd owned slaves.

WIMSATT: Are there other reasons why people have a negative attitude toward Simms?

GUILDS: The situation actually got started right after Simms died, when one of his best younger friends, Paul Hamilton Hayne, wrote article-length obituaries about him that in effect damned him with faint praise. I have hard feelings about Hayne because he pretended to be Simms's friend, but after Simms's death Hayne didn't say the kinds of things a friend should have said. He praised Simms as a man but didn't praise him enough as a writer. I think Hayne was jealous because Simms was a much better writer than he was and was better known and more productive. Hayne's work influenced Simms's nineteenth-century biographer William Peterfield Trent, and because there hasn't been a biography for a hundred years, until now, the Hayne-Trent view has held – despite the fact that Hubbell, Parrington, you, I, and others have assailed it.

Simms's oldest daughter, Augusta, didn't help matters either. She knew her father well and loved him, but I don't think she'd read his work. It was she who told Hayne and Trent that Charleston had failed to appreciate Simms; but according to Mrs. Oliphant, Augusta felt that *no one* appreciated Simms enough. So to have her say that Charleston didn't appreciate him really wasn't helping anything. But Hayne and Trent both bought her view. And American readers have bought *their* view.

So a bad press has been Simms's lot for more than a century. There is too much unenlightened detraction of Simms. And on the other hand, there have been people who could see no fault in him, and that hasn't helped things at all. Alexander Salley was one of those people. He may not have read much Simms, but he defended Simms and the southern way of life, and people, particularly in the North, didn't take him seriously. Unlike Salley, Donald Davidson was a literary critic, and a good one. He read widely in Simms, thought highly of Simms's works, and said so. But because Davidson was so unrestrainedly prosouthern in political issues, people both North and South thought he was waving the Confederate flag when he wrote about Simms.

And then there are the people who read only one or two things by Simms and stop. You need to read several works by Simms to begin to sense his talent. If you read him with any insight, you'll see that here is a writer of real power. He definitely belongs to the oral tradition in southern literature, as Davidson insisted. Simms himself said, "I write very much as I talk," and that's a good self-assessment.

WIMSATT: Why do scholars of American and southern literature need to know about Simms? What gives his work literary value?

GUILDS: Well, there are many things I could say, but I'll concentrate on just a few. As I've said, I know from my academic training and my experience in general that the South has been getting a bad rap in American history and literary history ever since the Civil War. Simms has suffered from this situation more than any other southern author. And he's been marginalized in ways that never happened to northern authors whose work is inferior in some respects to his – James Russell Lowell, Henry Wadsworth Longfel-

low, Cooper, and Irving. Americans today simply don't know about the enormous contributions Simms made to our national literature or to America's developing image of itself.

Let me put things this way. Alone among nineteenth-century American authors, Simms had a comprehensive vision of the development of America as a nation – a complex and varied land with enormous diversity in peoples and cultures. Also, he was the first – and I believe in the nineteenth century the only – American author with a vision of a unique, comprehensive American literature. He insisted that such a literature should draw on regional, racial, economic, and social diversity in order to create an amalgamated image of the new continent and the society developing on it. He described his vision of what a national literature should be in his correspondence with prominent and lesser-known literary and political figures of his day. He also discussed it in descriptive and polemical essays and expressed it through fiction, poetry, and drama.

As I say in the biography, "The time has come to acknowledge the magnitude of Simms's accomplishments as the only American author of the nineteenth century to envision, design, initiate, and consummate an epic portrayal of the development of our nation." In his writing, Simms sought to create a record of America's development – from the age of exploration in Florida and the Gulf South (in *The Lily and the Totem* [1850] and *Vasconcelos* [1853]) through the struggle for independence (in his popular romances of the Revolutionary War such as *The Partisan* [1835], *Woodcraft* [1854], *The Forayers* [1855], and *Eutaw* [1856]) up to his own time with the exploration, taming, and settlement of the frontier. In this last connection, it's important to note that he produced a series of novels set in various parts of the frontier South at several stages in its history. He showed the conflict between Indians and pioneers in the colonial era in *The Yemassee* (1835) and *The Cassique of Kiawah* (1859); described the nineteenth-century Georgia gold rush in *Guy Rivers* (1834); and portrayed the opening of the trans-Appalachian frontier in *Guy Rivers*, *Richard Hurdis* (1838), and *Border Beagles* (1840).

Of immense significance, too, is Simms's devotion to the task of helping other authors develop and promote American and southern literature. He gave unsparingly of his time, his energies, and often his money in various attempts at publishing journals that would provide a vehicle for young American authors – northern as well as southern. He was unique in the nineteenth century in both his vision

William Gilmore Simms

of a national literature with regional roots and his tenacity in pursuing the means to encourage and promote the creation and promulgation of such a literature.

As for your second question, about Simms's literary value, I'd say that he's a *much* better writer than he's generally thought to be. His gusto, sweep, and verve make all his writing memorable. And he excelled in inventing such living, vibrant characters as Captain Porgy in the Revolutionary War romances, Hell-Fire Dick in *The Forayers* and *Eutaw,* the mean-spirited Blodgits in the same books, and Aunt Betsey Moore in *The Cub of the Panther* (1869). He gave such figures levels of dialogue appropriate to their circumstances. Porgy speaks in elegant, allusive phrases suitable to his station as a gentlemanly plantation owner, whereas lower-class ruffians like

the Blodgits and Hell-Fire Dick use pungent dialect to get their points across. At one point in *The Forayers,* for instance, Hell-Fire Dick shouts: "Hello, in thar, Pete Blodgit! Up with you, my yaller chicken, and let's see ef you've got over the pip yit! Open to the sky-scrapers, and the bouncing wild cats; and hear'em scream to beat all nater! Whoo! Whoo! Whoo! Whoo!"

And let me stress, too, that Simms excelled in the tall tale. There are few finer American narratives in this genre than his late masterworks, *Paddy McGann,* "How Sharp Snaffles Got His Capital and Wife," and "Bald-Head Bill Baldy." The exuberance of these works, their inventiveness, the level of their comic fantasy, and their spicy, freewheeling language enable Simms to take rank alongside the best of the southern frontier humorists – Augustus Baldwin Longstreet and George Washington Harris.

In assessing Simms's achievement in literature, of course, we have to remind ourselves that nineteenth- and twentieth-century attitudes about what constitutes literary value differ widely. Read-ers in our century, influenced by James Joyce, William Faulkner, the New Critics and other writers, crave complex structure and intricate style. These things weren't so important to writers of Simms's time – and when I say this I mean to Herman Melville and Cooper as well as to Simms. Nor have they mattered greatly in our century to such writers as Thomas Wolfe, who, like Simms, had a natural gift for writing encyclopedic books in an enthusiastic manner. Like Wolfe, or for that matter Walt Whitman, Simms wrote with an exuberance and earthiness that transcended and often offended Romantic sensibility, particularly when he wrote, as he said, with his sleeves rolled up. If you want to see what I mean, read his story "Caloya," which treats the subject of attempted adultery so realistically that it shocked editors and readers of his time.

While we're on the subject of realism, I have a few further things to say. Our century, in the main, has valued realism above other elements in fiction. Simms in my view is the first true realist in American literature. He knew his subject matter intimately and portrayed it passionately, with amazing detail and objectivity. His depiction of the broad fabric of American society is amazingly astute and versatile. He portrays the plantation owner, the slave, and the freeman convincingly, just as he does the lives and tribulations of white settlers, Indians, and blacks. And he vividly renders the character and the foibles of the merchant and the carpetbagger, the dowager and the ingenue, the gold digger, the outlaw, and the pioneer. In the process he often treats topics considered taboo in the genteel salons of his day: sexual attraction, violence, organized crime, racial tension, even genocide. In *The Yemassee* he was, for example, the first American writer to deal directly and comprehensively with the genocide that white settlers practiced upon the Indian. He went further in *The Yemassee* than Cooper went in *The Last of the Mohicans* (1826).

WIMSATT: You worked on the biography for thirty years, in and around your administrative duties. Were there things you'd hoped to find and didn't? How did the book change or evolve over time?

GUILDS: Simms's father and uncle had immigrated to America from Ireland in the late eighteenth century, and not much is known about the Irish branch of the family. I spent some time in Ireland in the 1970s trying to track down Simms's Irish ancestors, with very little luck. I found a reference in Belfast to some Simmses who had come to America in the period I was looking for, the 1790s, but not much else. In 1986 I was working on the Simms biography in Cambridge, England. I went to Larne in Ireland and searched again for family information, but again found nothing. The name *Simms* is spelled many different ways in Ireland: Symmes, Semmes, Sims, and so forth. I found people interested in Simms and people wanting to claim kinship with him, but nothing definite.

As to how the biography changed or evolved, I'd put it this way: if I hadn't become an administrator I would have finished the book sooner. But it wouldn't be the book it is. It is written the way it had to be written, and it profited from its years of gestation. I didn't always have time to work on it, but even while I was doing other things I thought about Simms; and some of my ideas about him and his books changed as I went along. When I reread certain of his novels, for instance, I saw things in them I hadn't seen before. This of course affected what I did in the biography. After I stepped down as dean at Arkansas in 1988, I was finally able to devote full time to the book. And then I experienced what Simms said he did when he wrote. The writing just flowed.

WIMSATT: What holes or gaps remain in Simms research? In other words, what work remains to be done on him?

GUILDS: While I was writing the biography, I realized that somebody should write a book on Simms's relationships with his political and literary friends: James Henry Hammond and William Porcher Miles in South Carolina; James Lawson and Evert Duyckinck in New York; Edgar Allan Poe and Melville; others. I dealt with these relationships as fully as I could in the biography, but I couldn't cover everything about them.

Also, there's a great deal to be done on the ways in which Simms anticipates strains in later southern literature. The point I make in the biography that Simms is in many ways the father of southern literature needs to be fleshed out. A course could be offered, for example, on Simms and Robert Penn Warren. And the whole matter of Simms, Mark Twain, Faulkner, and Eudora Welty needs to

1A

Remarkable though it was, Simms's valor, without a
the well to write in commitment to literature, would have
contributed nothing to his status as a writer, however much it increased
his stature as man. ② His valiant efforts throughout 1866
"to resume [his] profession" generated no appreciable
momentum, but, mirabile dictu, late in 1867, despite in-
capitating illness, his creativity seemed to explode into
one of those marvelous surges that marked the earlier stages
of his career. During all this time he remained the
faithful and attentive father of six
motherless children, kept up a steady correspondence
with old friends, and new, and continued as
a recognized spokesman for his region's lost
cause and its hopes for the future. And, in
addition to what may be termed his major literary
efforts, no editorial task was too menial for his consideration if it promised even meagre compensation

And if his published works during the final four
years of his life fail to match those, for instance, of 1833-1836,
1838-1841, or 1853-1856, it is primarily because
his best writing in those terminal years never reached
book publication during his lifetime, either remaining
in manuscript or buried in periodicals. What makes
Simms's post-Civil War literary accomplishments
surprising is that no editorial
task was too menial for to poverty-stricken author if it promised even
meagre compensation.

USE
LATER

Page from the manuscript of Simms: A Literary Life

be explored. For too long it's been claimed that Simms and other antebellum authors were writing in one tradition, whereas postbellum and twentieth-century authors were writing in another; but this simply isn't true. Simms shares a broad interest in what scholars usually call "old southwestern humor" with Faulkner and Welty, for instance. And the raucous comedy in his books resembles that in Mark Twain.

There are other parallels between Simms and later southern authors. Simms's sense of place is as strong as Faulkner's and Welty's; and in treating race relations, he's aware, as Faulkner was, that social progress in the South is closely tied up with how whites and blacks get along. The racial attitudes of the tidewater plantation South affected the attitudes of people on the frontier or in the Gulf South. You see this in Simms's works set in this region of the South, like *Richard Hurdis* and *Border Beagles,* and you see it in Faulkner too – in such books set in the region as *Light in August* (1932).

WIMSATT: How is Simms relevant to the 1990s? Are efforts being made to get more of his books back into print?

GUILDS: I'll just say outright that a knowledge of Simms is absolutely essential to an informed understanding of American culture. Anyone who wants to know about the historical development of the country ought to know Simms's writing – and not just his fiction, but his historical works as well, such as *Views and Reviews* and *The Lily and the Totem.* Simms immersed himself in history in order to write these works, and nationally known historians – George Bancroft and others – recognized his ability as a historian and corresponded with him. I learned much of what I know about the development of American culture from studying Simms and the historical periods he wrote about.

Let me generalize a little further about Simms's importance for our era. The end of the twentieth century marks a stage of maturity in America's growth and offers a time for reflection upon and review of its past. The interest in family and racial roots, the fascination with the divisive war between the states – so effectively brought to mass attention through the recent Ken Burns television series on PBS – indicates a growing curiosity on the part of Americans about their past. And Simms's great knowledge of history and his vivid renditions of the colonial and antebellum eras make him a natural focus for contemporary interest in the past and how it's been depicted.

As for getting Simms back into print, the University of Arkansas Press, which published the biography, is bringing out a selected edition of Simms's fiction. I'm the general editor. The first four volumes will be *Guy Rivers, The Yemassee, Richard Hurdis,* and *Border Beagles.* These are novels about the contrast between the civilized and the frontier South in the colonial and antebellum eras. In them Simms concentrates on the diversity of early southern society. There's plenty of action in these books, and they have some fine comic passages. They're so colorful and varied that they'll appeal to just about anyone who reads them.

I've arranged with the Arkansas Press to bring out these volumes first because, unlike most other Simms scholars, I believe the frontier was his real element – and he depicted the actual frontier, not just a romanticized version of it. He made the frontier come alive in its strength and beauty; but unlike any other author of his day, including Cooper, he also made it come alive in its ugliness, its violence, its greed, its exploitation of man and nature. All the while he recognized its essential role in the development of the nation.

In fact, "William Gilmore Simms and the American Frontier" was the topic for the inaugural meeting of the Simms Society, held in Arkansas 15–17 April 1993. There were papers on his different depictions of the frontier, on his frontier humor, and on the contrast in his writing between the plantation and frontier South. Some of these papers will be published by the University of Arkansas Press in a volume devoted to the proceedings of the conference.

WIMSATT: What was the worst hardship you experienced while writing the biography, and how did you deal with it?

GUILDS: While I was working on the last sections of the biography, many traditions of scholarly inquiry began to shift, and I realized that the common body of knowledge about Simms that had existed since his death was no longer solidly in place. People had worked on Simms and his writing pretty steadily for, say, one hundred and fifty years; but around 1975 scholarship on him began to diminish, and it didn't pick back up again until the late 1980s. The last few years have seen the publication of several substantial books on Simms that advance important new ideas about him. So he's finally coming into his own.

This temporary lapse in Simms scholarship has a bad side, but it also has a good one. Readers coming to him now approach him with fresh eyes.

They may not be as familiar as we'd like with earlier scholarship, but they aren't affected by its biases either. They aren't encumbered by it as earlier scholars were, say, by Trent's views.

I get the sense from my own experience and from talking with people at professional meetings that a new cadre of students of southern history and literature is being trained, and Simms is important to these students. They read him and they like what they read. His reputation will continue to rise if professors teach his works in undergraduate and graduate classrooms and if they continue to publish books and articles about him.

Simms has recently been excluded from the canon because his opinions about southern social organization, which are fairly traditional, don't fit current notions of political correctness. The questioning of the canon now going on will benefit him. He's getting back in, and in a bigger way than he's been before. The canon isn't fixed any longer: it's fluid and flexible. Simms's vigorous depictions of America's struggles to come to terms with its racial, social, and cultural diversity appeal to canon revisionists.

WIMSATT: As you review your many years of work on the biography, what strikes you as your most memorable experience?

GUILDS: Something that happened to me not long before I finished the book. The ghost of Simms appeared to me in a vision. I was living at the time in Siegen, Germany, where my wife, Gertrud Bauer Pickar, was a visiting professor at the Universität Gemachtschulë. Early one morning, right before I woke up, I had a dream of Simms, or the ghost or spirit of Simms – it wasn't really a dream; it was a vision. He asked, "Why have I been forgotten?" Of course he hasn't been wholly forgotten, but until recently he hasn't been studied in the way he ought to be.

We've all heard of visionary experiences, but this was the first one that's ever happened to me. After talking it over with my wife, I decided to include it on a separate page of the book, right before the last chapter. Simms and his question inspired me. It was after the vision that my writing really started to flow. In the biography I make a real effort to right the wrongs that have been done to Simms, his writing, and his reputation. I keep remembering him and his query.

WIMSATT: In Simms's short story "Grayling," the ghost of a murdered man appears in a vision to a youth who then becomes his avenger. It sounds as if the spirit of Simms has affected you in a similar manner. You've become Simms's spokesman, and in a sense his avenger, because over many years you've immersed yourself in his life and writing, and now you've portrayed him fully and sympathetically in a major biography. Your book should intrigue people who don't know anything, or know only a little, about this remarkable antebellum author, and make them want to know more.

The Society for the History of Authorship, Reading and Publishing

Jonathan Rose
Drew University

Every field of scholarship has its moment of quickening. It arrives when the discipline is still relatively new, after its first researchers have opened up the territory. These pioneers must work alone, often unaware of each other's existence, trying as best they can to locate source material and solve methodological problems. Then, after a few decades, they discover each other and draw together. They organize conferences, journals, and professional societies; they collaborate on bibliographies and other reference works; and, drawing on a growing body of research, they find answers to questions that once seemed unanswerable.

Book history has now reached that milestone. The necessary groundwork – surveyed by Robert Darnton in *The Kiss of Lamourette* (1990) – has been done. Europeans have launched national book-history groups and, recently, the scholarly newsletter *In Octavo*. In the United States there are associations for specialists, such as the American Antiquarian Society, the Research Society for Victorian Periodicals (RSVP), and the American Printing History Association. What was lacking until recently was an international organization that brought together book historians working in all disciplines and in every national literature.

That deficiency was driven home when I was editing (with Patricia Anderson) two volumes for the Dictionary of Literary Biography: *DLB 106: British Literary Publishing Houses, 1820–1880* (1991) and *DLB 112: British Literary Publishing Houses, 1881–1965* (1991). The most difficult part of that project was the business of recruiting potential contributors. Clearly, they existed; but, lacking any central directory or newsletter for book historians, how could we locate them? Eventually we *did* find them (with help from RSVP and Britain's Book Trade History Group), and in the process we discovered something remarkable about book historians: they are scattered all over the disciplinary map. They teach in departments of history, literature, sociology, communications, journalism, library science, art, economics, classics, even anthropology. Many work outside the academy, as book trade professionals, librarians, archivists, journalists, book collectors, and museum curators.

If these specialists could be brought together in the same journal or conference room, the cross-fertilization would invigorate book history enormously. That is the rationale for organizing the Society for the History of Authorship, Reading and Publishing. SHARP is devoted to every aspect of book history: the social and economic history of authorship; the history of the book trade, including copyright, censorship, and underground publishing; the publishing histories of particular texts, authors, editors, imprints, and literary agents; the spread of literacy, book distribution, and library usage; canon formation and the politics of literary criticism; reception studies, reading practices, and reader response. SHARP aims to be a truly global network for scholars everywhere, in or outside the universities.

The first organizational meeting for SHARP was held 10 August 1991 at the University of California at Santa Cruz, as part of a Dickens Project conference on Victorian publishing. The response was very encouraging, and Drew University generously supplied seed money. Pending formal elections, a provisional government was set up, including Jonathan Rose (president), Simon Eliot (vice-president), Mickie Grover (treasurer), and Patrick Leary (secretary).

SHARP will hold its inaugural conference 9–11 June 1993 at the City University of New York Graduate Center. The program will include more than fifty papers presented by scholars from the United States, Canada, United Kingdom, Germany, Belgium, the former Czechoslovakia. Those papers will cover such topics as the iconography of the book, the transatlantic book trade, quantifying the history of reading, recent publishing history in central Europe, reprints and piracies, the invention of literary property, censorship, literary agents, the reconstruction of texts, the impact of popular culture on print culture, the politics of British publishing, book distribution and marketing in nineteenth- and twentieth-century America, the economics of book publishing, opportunities for female authorship, and the "reading revolution" in eighteenth-century Europe. Future conferences are tentatively planned for the Center for the Book at the Library of Congress (1994) and the University of Edinburgh (1995).

SHARP publishes a quarterly newsletter, *SHARP News,* a source of practical information on research, teaching, publications, and professional activities. It features calls for papers, conference reports, a list of recent publications on book history, authors' queries and research notes, short articles on teaching and collaborative research, and notes on archives and other research facilities.

In addition to its newsletter, SHARP has set up more-advanced machinery to establish lines of communication between book historians. Working out of Indiana University, Leary has launched SHARP-L, an electronic bulletin board. Anyone with access to an E-mail terminal can use this system to exchange information, queries, and research notes with hundreds of other scholars. To subscribe to SHARP-L, address an E-mail message to either LISTSERV@IUBVM (Bitnet) or, if outside the United States, LISTSERV@IUBVM.UCS.INDIANA.EDU (Internet); leave the "Subject:" header blank, and send the message SUBSCRIBE SHARP-L, followed by your first and last names. You can post a message by addressing it to either SHARP-L@IUBVM (Bitnet) or, outside the United States, SHARP-L@IUBVM.UCS.INDIANA.EDU (Internet). If you have questions about SHARP-L, you can contact Patrick Leary at PLEARY@IUBACS (Bitnet) or PLEARY@UCS.INDIANA.EDU (Internet), or write to him at the History Department, Indiana University, Bloomington, IN 47401.

As a newborn society, SHARP is still flexible and malleable. We have room for people with ideas and energy in our highly improvisational organization. Two projects currently in the early stages are a new book-history journal and a Reading Experience Database, the latter a collaborative venture between Britain's Open University and the Centre for the Book at the British Library.

By the end of 1992 SHARP had attracted three hundred members worldwide. Each member receives a subscription to *SHARP News* and a directory of SHARP members (the latter to be published in June 1993). For information contact Professor Jonathan Rose, History Department, Drew University, Madison, NJ, 07940, USA; or, in the United Kingdom, Dr. Simon Eliot, The Open University, 4 Portwall Lane, Bristol BS1 6ND, UK.

Ernest Hemingway's Toronto Journalism Revisited: With Three Previously Unrecorded Stories

Michael Reynolds
North Carolina State University

Seventy-seven years ago Ernest Hemingway (1899–1961) wrote his first piece of journalism for the Oak Park High School *Trapeze*. Over the remaining forty-six years of his life, he returned to journalism whenever he needed the money or the entrée its credentials provided, but he always insisted that his ephemeral newspaper work was not to be part of his professional bibliography. Despite Hemingway's several disclaimers, the importance of his news stories and features has been neither ignored nor underestimated by scholars. Written during Hemingway's literary apprenticeship when he was struggling to find his own voice, his early journalism is the best evidence of his transformation into the writer who wrote "Indian Camp" a few weeks after quitting his job on the *Toronto Star*. Because most of Hemingway's unpublished fiction from this period (1920–1923) was stolen, his literary biographers would have little evidence upon which to build their cases were it not for his journalism.

Since Hemingway's death in 1961 almost every feature, book review, and news story the author wrote has been found and reprinted, but research scholars have long known that they do not have everything. In 1992 William Burrill, following up on the research of William McGeary, listed twenty-five pieces that appeared in or were submitted to the *Toronto Star,* which reprinted thirteen of them in its 1 March 1992 Sunday issue. These discoveries bring Hemingway's total journalistic production between 1920 and 1923 to almost two hundred articles. Large claims resulted: "Hemingway's Toronto era will have to be rewritten," one sidebar claimed. To evaluate these new stories and the expectations they have raised, one needs a bit of background on Hemingway's brief relationship with the *Toronto Star*.

In the fall of 1918 Ernest Hemingway, recent graduate of Oak Park High School, signed on as a

Ernest Hemingway in Paris, 1924

cub reporter for the *Kansas City* (Missouri) *Star,* where he worked for seven months before leaving as a Red Cross ambulance driver bound for the Great War on the Italian front. In January 1920, still limping from his war wound and trading on his apprenticeship in Kansas City, Hemingway appeared at Greg Clark's *Toronto Star* desk looking for part-time work. J. Herbert Cranston, the editor, agreed to buy Hemingway's submissions on a piece-by-piece basis, as they suited the needs of the paper. This arrangement produced Hemingway features on dental schools, prizefights, free shaves, and trout fishing. Several of the newfound stories date from this period, including two stories on a new anesthesia and a comic invented account of a communist's arrival in Toronto during America's first Red Scare.

When Hemingway left Toronto in May 1920, his loose arrangement with the *Star* remained in place; over the next twenty months the paper regularly printed Hemingway features on Chicago gangsters, rum-running, and more trout fishing. From this period comes his rediscovered feature on Jack Dempsey – "The Superman Myth." In December 1921, when Hemingway and his new wife Hadley left Chicago for Paris, he traveled as a special correspondent to the *Star,* allowing him to submit features on a per-piece basis and occasionally to work for weekly wages and expenses while covering major European news events.

Between January 1921 and September 1923 the *Star* frequently printed Hemingway's submissions, which ranged from local color ("American Bohemians in Paris a Weird Lot"), to winter sports ("Try Bob-Sledding If You Want Thrills"), and the Great War ("A Veteran Visits Old Front, Wishes He Had Stayed Away"). Had such work been Hemingway's only journalism from his early Paris period, an important phase of his education would have been lacking. Fortunately for him and his latter-day readers, the *Star* sent Hemingway to cover four important political and military events: the Conference of Genoa (6–27 April 1922), the brief but intense Greco-Turkish war (29 September–21 October 1922), the Lausanne Peace Conference (21 November–15 December 1922), and the French military occupation of the German Ruhr (30 March–9 April 1923).

The immediate and long-range effects of these experiences have been well established by Hemingway's biographers and critics but bear repeating. These events began Hemingway's serious political education, giving him a privileged view of the postwar political leaders setting Europe's agenda: Jean-Louis Barthou, David Lloyd George, Benito Mussolini. While covering the stories, Hemingway developed his admiration for the insider, the experienced man who knows the language, food, and customs of the country. As a foreign correspondent, such expert knowledge was expected of him; when he had it, he used it; when he lacked firsthand experience, he pretended to it with such ease that read-

ers later believed him to have written nothing that was not autobiographical. This bilingual insider, adept at European travel and well remembered by bartenders and bullfighters, would become the trademark of his later fiction which was usually set in a foreign country.

Hemingway's short journalistic course in the sociopolitical aftermath of the Great War rubbed his Oak Park republicanism up against European socialism. The impact added to his sense of being a man without a political home, a man more opposed to fascism than socialism but distrustful of all government, an anarchist with a savings account. The experience also provided him with character types, themes, and images that would appear regularly in his fiction to the end of his life. His interest in the professional revolutionary (unpublished "New Slain Knight" and "The Revolutionist"), the gunrunner (unpublished section, *To Have and Have Not,* 1937), the saboteur (*For Whom the Bell Tolls,* 1940), and the paramilitarist (*Islands in the Stream,* 1970) begins during his *Toronto Star* days. Jake Barnes's journalism (*The Sun Also Rises,* 1926), the socialist subtext in *A Farewell to Arms* (1929), Harry's unwritten story of Constantinople in "Snows of Kilimanjaro," Colonel Cantwell's return to the site of his first wound (*Across the River and Into the Trees,* 1950), and the Paris streets of *A Moveable Feast* (1964) are firmly rooted in Hemingway's Toronto stories.

During that twenty-month period in Europe (1922–1923), Hemingway filed at least eighty-eight stories with the *Star,* all but a few of which were printed. Of the newly recovered twenty-five stories, only five are from Hemingway's European tour and only one of them, his unpublished interview with Georges Clemenceau, is a major piece. In September 1923 Hemingway returned to Toronto and the *Star* where he, for the first time since Kansas City, went to work as a staff reporter. Instantly unhappy with his new editor's management style, Hemingway quit after four months and returned to Europe to become the writer he believed himself to be. It is from Hemingway's second Toronto period that most of the twenty-five newfound articles date.

These articles, overlapping as they do with his already collected journalism, confirm patterns which became more obvious later in his career. Several of the stories are unexceptional, the sort a paper uses to add local color and fill empty space: "Talking Boy Actor Is A Toronto Lad," "Cars Slaying Toronto's Splendid Oak Trees," "Truth-Telling Ether A Secret," a Santa Claus fund appeal, and "Fifth Generation of Family Lives On Old Canadian Manor." Other additions supplement previously published Hemingway stories: two additional pieces on the Conference of Genoa; another estimate of the postwar condition of Germany; and two more pieces on Lloyd George's visit to the United States. The German story – "Two Revolutions Are Likely If Germany Suffers Collapse" (7 March 1923) – adds to the evidence of Hemingway's then growing interest in political revolutions, an interest for which there is ample evidence elsewhere. While increasing Hemingway's bibliography, none of these stories substantially changes the understanding of his development as a writer.

"The Superman Myth," Hemingway's previously uncollected 25 June 1921 feature on the approaching Jack Dempsey–Georges Carpentier heavyweight championship match, was the third in a series of prizefight stories he wrote for the *Star*. The first story (15 May 1920) focuses on the one hundred Toronto women who had come to the fights "ostensibly to see Georges Carpentier give a sparring exhibition." The second story – "Carpentier vs. Dempsey" (10 October 1920) – is written in the ring-wise voice of a veteran sportswriter by the barely twenty-one-year-old Hemingway. Belittling the champion Dempsey's supposed invincibility, which he calls "bunk and twaddle of the worst kind," Hemingway writes that Dempsey had fought only "bums and tramps, who were nothing but . . . set-ups for him." The European champion, Georges Carpentier, in contrast, had defeated a series of well-known and respected fighters. But Hemingway, by favoring the Frenchman, is favoring the man expected to lose, a character type who would become familiar in Hemingway's mature fiction. He also notes that Carpentier had "served through the war with honor," a reference to Dempsey, who had avoided the draft, written by a young man still defensive about having served as a Red Cross ambulance driver rather than as a soldier. The so-called Battle of the Century was an easy knockout for Dempsey.

Eight months later Hemingway's reprinted Dempsey story – "The Superman Myth" – ran on the editorial page of the *Star,* where it repeated much of the previous feature in more detail: Dempsey's championship was tainted; his opponents had been stumblebums; and insiders had known this for some time. His "Superman" piece is a gossipy, jaundiced view of the fight business, using judgmental adjectives and similes that rarely appear in Hemingway's mature fiction. The story speaks of "Willard's stupid, kindly face," of his "cow-like courage," of Dempsey "trembling like a scared school girl." "His nerves were gone," the reader is told, "and his face, according to ringsiders, was a ghastly green color." The objectivity which some think Hemingway learned at the *Star* is clearly a myth of its own, for most of his early newspaper work includes the journalist whose personal opinion is clearly part of the story.

The style of this article, written almost four years before "The Battler," is more interesting than its reworked content, for it provides a benchmark from which to measure change. Compare Willard's "stupid, kindly face" and "cow-like courage" with Hemingway's description of the fictional Ad Francis:

> In the firelight Nick saw that his face was misshapen. His nose was sunken, his eyes were slits, he had queer-shaped lips. Nick did not perceive all this at once, he only saw the man's face was queerly formed and mutilated. It was like putty in color. Dead looking in the firelight.

Here the writer, uninterested in passing judgments, gives the observed (Ad) and his observer (Nick) through objective eyes. Judgments are left to the reader. In his journalism Hemingway seldom removed himself from the story and even more seldom refrained from telling his reader how to respond. In his fiction Hemingway's touch is more subtle, his restraint a hallmark.

Twelve months after he wrote the Dempsey article, Hemingway, now in Paris, sent the *Star* "Talking With The Tiger," an interview with Georges Clemenceau which city editor John Bone refused to publish because of the old French politician's statement that Canada had not willingly done her part during the Great War. The thrust of this previously unpublished interview has been known for some time. But it was not known how little of the article was interview and how much of it was background, character description, narrative, and speculation. Like Hemingway's short stories written two years later, the "interview" opens in the middle of things: " 'That is the house of M. Clemenceau.' The chauffeur pointed." The following narrative gives the reader a clear, detailed view of the Clemenceau beach house, moves him up the drive and into the bedroom, where the skull of a tiger hangs above the window facing the sea. "It was bone white and polished and the two big teeth coming down represented the Clemenceau mustache. It looked exactly like the cartoons of the Old Tiger himself." (In his later fiction Hemingway would not need to tell what anything represented.) The narrative continues with the entrance and description of Clemenceau – bulky, brown tweeds, cap, face "brown as an Ojibway," white mustache. The remainder of the story includes the brief interview followed by a synopsis of the old man's varied career which began and continued as a political rebel. The interview itself is terse: Clemenceau refused to visit Canada on his American tour because he mistakenly thought Canada had refused to help France during the Great War.

When stripped of its prelude, setting, character sketch, and political background, the story is barely four column inches in which nothing happens. Eighteen months later Hemingway would write Gertrude Stein that he was working on a long fishing story – "Big Two-Hearted River" – in which nothing happened. For the reader of both stories, the observer is as important as what is being observed. In the *Star* piece Hemingway is present in the story, leading the reader through Clemenceau's house, examining books on the shelf, reacting to what he sees and hears. The closing paragraph has the old man staring out over the surf "curling along his beach" and "at the red sails of the fishing boats far out on the sea." " 'I was born near here,' " he tells Hemingway. " 'No. Not here. A little further up the coast.' " Just as Hemingway's short stories would soon avoid the "wow" ending, so does this interview which reveals much about the author's maturation during that apprentice year in France.

On 5 September 1923, when Hemingway and a now pregnant Hadley returned to Toronto and the *Star,* they found themselves in unpleasant circumstances. Instead of being featured as one of John Bone's favored reporters, Hemingway was working with a new editor, Hindmarsh, who generally disliked Bone's prima donnas and particularly disliked Hemingway. No sooner did Hemingway report for work than he was put on the night train to Kingston to cover the prison break of four convicts, including the bank robber Red Ryan. Hemingway filed three articles, none of which was printed with his by-line. "Escaped Convicts Still At Large" shows Hemingway writing against a deadline but still able to create an interesting narrative. From his sources he re-creates the prison break as if he had witnessed it: "The fat man carrying the long scantling leaned it against the wall and a slim kid, his prison cap pulled down over his eyes, swarmed up it to the top of the wall." As in more than one of his later fictions, Hemingway's characters, with the exception of Ryan, begin nameless: "a slim kid," "a big husky," "a little runt," "a thick set, ham-faced man."

In terms of Hemingway's later development, this article and its central character reappeared in

March 1926, when he was working on *The Sun Also Rises* revisions and wondering what to write about next. In his notebook, Hemingway wrote:

> I will write a picaresque novel for America. It will be about Red Ryan and his escape from Kinston pen. The flight – the hiding in the woods – the bank robbery in Toronto. . . . It will not be a story of a weak disappointed youth caught and sucked up by fate. It will be the story of a tough kid lucky for a long time and finally smashed by fate. . . . Crime is not a disease. Criminals are not diseased men. We are all criminals. The criminal is simply a more normal, better coordinated man. In the old days he was a professional fighter. In Spain he was a bull fighter. In America he is the bank robber. This does not include the dope heads who are the really diseased criminals.

On reviewing his notes, he told himself in parentheses, "This is horseshit." Although he never wrote the Red Ryan novel, his next fiction – the unpublished and unfinished "A New Slain Knight" – has a criminal breaking from custody and a central character who is a professional revolutionary with criminal tendencies. In *To Have and Have Not,* Hemingway portrays the fishing guide turned criminal in Harry Morgan, who is gut-shot while killing three Cuban bank robbers. Ad Francis, Colonel Cantwell, Santiago, Thomas Hudson, and Robert Jordan all live in secret societies where they are loners at heart. Red Ryan was not the only factor in Hemingway's developing identification with this character type, but Ryan's story did come at a crucial moment in the young writer's career.

The listing in the *Toronto Star* of the newfound Hemingway stories is confusing. Distinctions are not made between their appearances in the *Daily Star* and the *Weekly Star.* Dates are sometimes exact, sometimes vague, sometimes altogether missing. Where possible, approximate dating has been added in parentheses followed by a source. The source for the originally unpublished stories is nine Hemingway files in the *Star* archives.

Stories reprinted in the 1 March 1992 *Toronto Star:*

"Hemingway attacks Toronto's 'stay-home' mayor," undated and previously unpublished, probably early 1920;

"Truth-Telling Ether A Secret," a week after the "New Ether" story of 27 January 1920;

"Red Flag in Toronto," 14 February 1920;

"The Superman Myth," 25 June 1921;

"Genoa Scrubs Up For Peace Parley," 15 April 1922;

"Interpreters Make or Mar Speeches at Genoa's Parley," 15 April 1922;

"Before You Go On a Canoe Trip Learn Canoeing," 3 June 1922 (probably written much earlier);

"Talking With The Tiger," previously unpublished (interview took place 11 September 1922);

"Two Revolutions Are Likely If Germany Suffers Collapse," 7 March 1923;

"Escaped Kingston Convicts Still At Large," 10 September 1923;

"Fifth Generation of Family Lives On Old Canadian Manor," 20 October 1923;

"Cars Slaying Toronto's Splendid Oak Trees," (no month) 1923;

"She Sacrifices Herself That Children May Live," (no month) 1923.

Stories listed but not reprinted:

"New Ether To Credit of Toronto Surgeon," *Daily Star,* 27 January 1920;

"Offer Sir Donald Soviet Railroads," 10 September 1923;

"Convicts Set Fire To Stable At Pen And Made Escape," 11 September 1923;

"Convicts Break Away From Swamp Refuge," 12 September 1923;

British Coal feature, unpublished, dated 14 September 1923;

"An Absolute Lie, Says Dr. Banting, of Serum Report," 27 October 1923;

"Talking Boy Actor Is A Toronto Lad," (no month) 1923;

"Moscow Theatre Company Will Not Come To Toronto," (no month) 1923.

Other stories listed but undated:

"Who Is He?," profile of Mayor Swaddling, originally unpublished;

"Across from the post office," originally unpublished (c. 1922);

"On golf course with Lloyd George," originally unpublished (c. 8 October 1923);

"Lloyd George the Great Survivor," originally unpublished (c. 8–9 October 1923).

References:

Carlos Baker, *Ernest Hemingway: A Life Story* (New York: Scribners, 1968);

Charles A. Fenton, *The Apprenticeship of Ernest Hemingway* (New York: Farrar, Straus & Young, 1954);

Audre Hannenman, *Ernest Hemingway: A Comprehensive Bibliography, volume I & Supplement* (Princeton, N.J.: Princeton University Press, 1967, 1975);

Ernest Hemingway, *Dateline: Toronto,* edited by William White (New York: Scribners, 1985);

Michael Reynolds, *Hemingway: The American Homecoming* (Oxford: Blackwell, 1992);

Reynolds, *Hemingway: The Paris Years* (Oxford: Blackwell, 1986);

Robert O. Stevens, *Hemingway's Nonfiction* (Chapel Hill: University of North Carolina Press, 1968).

THE SUPERMAN MYTH

Jack Dempsey, a well-built, scowling, hard faced citizen of Utah, is regarded as a superman by several millions of people.

He has been pronounced the greatest fighter of all time, the hardest hitter, and the fastest heavyweight that ever climbed through the ropes. Many people fear for the safety of Georges Carpentier's life, when he shuts himself into the ring with this tremendous primitive force.

Most persons acquainted with things pugilistic believe that Jack Dempsey won the title of heavyweight champion of the world from Jess Willard at Toledo, Ohio, July 4th, 1919. The formal transfer of the crown did take place there – but Jess Willard lost the title in the Baltimore Hotel in Kansas City, Missouri.

Willard's stupid, kindly face, flushed by his efforts to make the best of the last few months before the strict enforcement of the 18th amendment, was one of the landmarks of the Baltimore. Jess Willard hated fighting and he was very fond of drinking. That doesn't make an ideal temperament for a fighter – but Willard never was a fighter at heart.

Picked by fate and Jack Curley, to be the man to defeat the renegade Johnson in a bout that had been in bad odor with every one acquainted with the back-stage workings of championship fighters, Willard became the champion. He defended his title once in a no decision fight against Frank Moran, a mediocre opponent, and then lapsed into more congenial pursuits.

On July 4th, 40 years old, heavy paunched, untrained and sodden and loggy with two years of steady drinking, he went forth with cow-like courage to fight Jack Dempsey for the championship of the world and $150,000 win, lose, or draw. In the first round the slim, sun-browned Dempsey slugged him to the canvas seven times. Willard looked dumbly and stupidly up at the tiger-like youth and staggered to his feet to earn his $150,000. At the end of the third round Dempsey was tired from smashing the big bulk and Willard seemed to be recuperating from the beating he had taken. Willard seemed the fresher of the two – Dempsey was hanging on to him and occasionally socking in a tired manner.

Willard's seconds tossed in a towel at the start of the fourth round. Jess believed he had given the fans a run for their admission – and he didn't need the championship anymore – he had $150,000.

That is the way Dempsey won the championship of the world. Since then he has fought twice. The first fight was with Billy Miske, a St. Paul light-heavyweight, and a close personal friend of Dempsey. Miske had been under a doctor's care for over a year and was unable to earn a living in the ring due to physical disability.

Dempsey gave Miske a crack at the "title" and incidentally a guarantee of $25,000 for his services. Miske, looking the sick man he was, made a few feeble leads at Dempsey. Dempsey hippodromed for a while and then abandoned friendship and speedily slugged Miske into unconsciousness – and the possession of $25,000.

Experts all over the country hailed the victory as a Dempsey superman triumph and only a few came out with the statement of Miske's true condition. In February the boxing fans refused to become wrought up over Dempsey's coming fight with Big Bill Brennan. It looked like another set-up. A few wagers were laid as to what round Dempsey would knock out the second-rate Chicago heavyweight.

Between the Miske and Brennan fights, however, Dempsey had been doing his training on Broadway, and his road work, some said, along the gay white way that has stopped more fighters than all the left hooks and right crosses in the world.

Dempsey entered the ring, the night of the Brennan fight, trembling like a scared school girl. His nerves were gone and his face, according to ringsiders, was a ghastly green color. No one could have recognized him as the brown-skinned, finely trained, young slugger who had cut down the ponderous Willard.

For twelve rounds Dempsey had all he could do to stay in the ring with the cumbersome, slow-moving, but awkwardly-hard hitting Brennan. In the twelfth round he knocked Brennan out with "the rabbit punch," a blow that is barred as a foul everywhere but in the United States.

Nearly every fight writer present said that if anyone but Brennan had been fighting Dempsey, the title would have changed hands. The superman myth seemed to be exploded. But now it is back again in full force.

"Throw out the Brennan fight," says Jack Kearns, Dempsey's manager, "don't pay any attention to it. It doesn't mean anything."

But why should it be "thrown out"? What has Dempsey done since that shows he is any more of a fighter than when he fought Brennan?

Jack Dempsey is not the man today that he was at Toledo. Two years of championship life coupled with whatever effects there might be from his wild years as a bum and tramp fighter have made a change in him. The public are rarely told of these things.

Before the Jeffries-Johnson fight, everyone in Jeffries' camp knew that it was a crime to allow him to enter the squared circles against the negro fighter. Jeffries was a wreck from high living. But who announced it before the fight?

Jim Corbett, who trained Jeffries, said the day before the bout: "It is an outrage to allow him to face Johnson." But what papers published the statement till after the battle?

Georges Carpentier has a chance on July 2nd that is the envy of half a dozen fighters.

Harry Greb, who knocked out Soldier Jones in Toronto early this spring, said the other day: "The Frenchman is lucky – any good fast man, who can hit, will take Jack Dempsey. I envy Carpentier his chance."

That is an inside opinion on the big fight.

Dempsey won in the 4th round.

* * *

TALKING WITH THE TIGER

Les Sables-D'Ollone, France. – "That is the house of M. Clemenceau." The chauffeur pointed.

The car turned into a road that ran straight down to the sea and we saw a low, white cottage set on a sandy headland. There was a barbed wire fence around the stakes jutting out of the sand, and on the sea-ward side a slim, white flagpole supported a great, red banner that waved and flapped in the wind.

Another car had turned into the road just ahead of us and we followed it through the gate in the barbed wire fence and stopped at the door of the cottage. A man of about forty-five got out of the car ahead of us and entered the cottage carrying a basket of groceries. His wife, in motoring clothes, followed him in. The Clemenceau cook in a white apron came out and took our cards.

The man who had carried in the groceries came out of the other end of the cottage and waved to us.

"Will you come and wait in my father's bedroom?" he said in French.

We walked ankle deep through the sand to the middle of the long cottage and Clemenceau's son waved us to enter the low doorway. "It will only be a minute," he explained, and was gone again.

The room was of plain boards. On one side was a wash stand with a basin and pitcher, on the other a writing desk. In back of the sofa where I sat was a comfortable bed. Over the bed was a bookcase. On the wall, the only ornaments were the mounted heads of antelope and buck Clemenceau had shot on his trip to India. Over the writing desk was a big crocodile's head with open jaws and silly-looking glass eyes. But the thing that caught and held your eye was a tiger skull that was nailed up over the window facing the sea. It was bone white and polished and the two big teeth coming down represented the Clemenceau mustache. It looked exactly like the cartoons of the Old Tiger himself.

I had gotten up to look at the titles of the books on the shelf above the writing desk and had only noted one, "The History of Buddhism" when we heard voices coming from the back of the cottage. Round the corner of the cottage, walking in the deep sand, came Clemenceau's son and Clemenceau himself walking with the son's wife, his arm through hers.

A bulky man, thickened by age, wearing a brown tweed suit, a funny, flat cap, his face as brown as an Ojibway, his white mustache drooping, his white eyebrows bushy, looking the tiger his pictures show him, his eyes twinkling as he talked to his plump daughter-in-law he came plodding through the sand. They stopped in front of the door.

"Au revoir papa!" The woman bent toward him to kiss him. Clemenceau put his arms around her and kissed her.

"Au revoir, my child. See you soon." They went on to their car and he came plodding into the room. His eyes smiled. They are the only things you can see while you are talking to him. They seem to get inside of your eyes somehow and fasten claws there. When he is talking all his brown, healthy, Chinese mandarin's face seems to have nothing to do with them. But his eyes smiled at us.

"Good day, gentlemen," he said in English. "It is a hard place to get to, isn't it? Come, we'll go to a better place to talk."

He motioned us to go out of the door ahead of him. I hesitated. "Go on. Go on." He put his hand on my back for me to go ahead.

In a sun room built onto the other end of the cottage and furnished with four big wicker chairs he stopped.

"Here we are," he said, smiling. "Now, which is Mr. Bird and which Mr. Hemingway? Good. It is a shame you have made such a long trip. I wired you last night not to come. I have not given interviews. But now you are here we can talk." His eyes twinkled. "Sit down, gentlemen."

We sat down and I looked at him closely. His face is remarkably like a Chinaman's. If the mustache, instead of being large and drooping, was cut in a narrow line, he would look exactly like a Mandarin. He was wearing a stand-up collar and a ready-tied, black bow tie and his gray-gloved hands rested in his lap. He speaks English jerkily, fluently, colloquially and with a French accent.

"I am glad Kipling said those things," he began in his concise, jerky manner. "They are true. But they are unfair. When the New York World cabled me to ask a reply to Kipling's statement, I said, 'no.' " The "no" chopped off and final as it used to be in the conferences of the big four at Versailles. "Then I went out and took a walk and thought 'yes, I will reply.'

"I have been thinking about going to the United States for the last three months and I thought, 'Here is a good chance to go and tell the Americans the truth.' " His eyes smiled.

Then I asked a question that waked the tiger in him, the tiger that always sleeps with one eye open and that when roused changes him from a very amiable and kind old gentleman to the wrecker of ministries, the man who is still the most dangerous political power in France.

"We are hoping you will come to Canada, sir," I said. At the word Canada his face went tiger. His eyes fastened into me and he leaned forward.

"I will not come to Canada." He jerked, emphasizing the not like an insult. "The Canadians rejected compulsory service and refused to help France."

"But," I said, "That was not Canada as a whole. The Canadian Army."

He had not listened to anything I had said. His face was still tiger.

"I know," he said, busy with his own thoughts. "I know. It was the influence of the Catholic priests. I know."

"But how about the rest of Canada. Not French Canada. Ontario. The Star invites you to come to Toronto."

"No, no, no," he jerked. "I can't do it. I can't do it. I can't mix things. I go to America only on a definite mission to explain the position of France to the people of the United States. I can't mix things. It is impossible to come to Toronto." He shook his head.

"Will you send a message to Canada?" I asked.

"What you have said about military service will not be very palatable. Besides it is not just to the rest of Canada."

"No," he jerked. The Clemenceau no is a quickly jerked, grunt. "No, no, I have nothing whatever to say to Canadians."

That ended that. The subject was closed. He smiled again and the talk was back on the friendly between you and me basis.

"Are you ever going to write your personal record and impressions of the war and the treaty as Lloyd George is doing now?" we asked.

"Never." Clemenceau said and smiled at both of us with his eyes. "I am not going back over things. If I tell the truth it will only make too much trouble, too many recriminations, raprochements [sic] – you understand? I am not going back over it."

He smiled off into his own thoughts again and then talked to us as though he were talking to himself. "I made the treaty – there is no use denying that. It doesn't work." He fastened his eyes into mine again. "I know why. But I'm not telling people why. It would only make worse enemies."

He stood up and we walked to the door. Clemenceau never looked out.

"It is nice here, eh?"

I looked out at the long line of white beach with a thin surf crisping on it and at the far off green hills. There was a smell of the sea and of rotted kelp. Clemenceau drew a deep breath.

"It's nice here," he said again, then pointed at the big, red banner on the flag pole. "That is the Japanese carp," he explained. "The symbol of virility. They hoist it whenever a male child is born. It is a gift from the wife of the Japanese ambassador."

While we were standing in front of the cottage, another motorcar came up the sand road and turned up the hill. Three men came trudging along through the sand. One of them looked like a florid-faced bookmaker. The other two were satellites and hung back. The bookmaker man, who began to look as though he might be a bartender as he came closer, I recognized.

"Ah, Tardieu," said Clemenceau.

Tardieu greeted us grudgingly.

"My, how many visitors I have," Clemenceau's eyes wrinkled. "What popularity."

All this in French. Tardieu, former French High Commissioner in the U.S., was in a huff. He is Clemenceau's Lieutenant and the Tiger, who is sharpening his claws, had evidently commanded his presence. Clemenceau was enjoying it thoroughly.

Tardieu – "I don't think much of the hospitality of your town. We got in at midnight and had to go to six hotels and none of them would let us in at that hour."

Clemenceau: "Ah. That is respectability."

Tardieu: "No. I told them I was a deputy."

Clemenceau: "Oh you should never have done that. We are not fond of parliamentarians in the Vendee."

Tardieu nursed his grouch and Clemenceau left him standing and walked with us to the gate. He was very charming. "Goodbye Mr. Bird. Goodbye Mr. Hemingway." He said, "perhaps I will see you in Paris in October." He was a very gracious and charming old man and he turned and waved to us and he plodded jerkily back through the sand to where Tardieu was waiting.

It was a 15 mile ride back to the fishing village of Les Sables-D'Ollone through a scrub-oak, sandy, plain where the houses are built close to the ground to avoid the wind and the farmers wage a losing fight against the blowing sand, manuring the ground with kelp hauled from the beach and building windbreaks to keep the encroaching sand out of their gardens. At Les Sables it rained, there was a typewriter and nothing to do until the next train 18 hours away. So I thought about Clemenceau. How did this Clemenceau differ from other men? How did he get to be the Tiger of France?

Because of his Asiatic face, many French scientists believe that he is a descendant of Attila's soldiers, some of whom settled in the Vendee after the Huns were routed in 451.

During the days of the second empire he was arrested and imprisoned for preaching republicanism.

He went to America in his youth and followed the Union army as a physician.

Later taught French in an American girls' school.

Married an American, Miss Mary Plummer.

In the storm of the Commune he returned to Paris and became Mayor of Montmartre, the active leader of the wild element that has given the Butte Montmartre its strange reputation. During the short time he was Mayor, two generals were shot by the Montmartre mob.

Charged into politicas and became known as "destroyer of ministries."

Became a newspaper editor and wrote several philosophical novels.

Attacked President Poincaire venomously within a month after Poincaire's election.

Drove Briand from office as Premier.

Was appointed Premier under Poincaire's presidency and saved France and perhaps the world.

He carries in his back the bullet fired by Cottin, an insane young radical after the Armistice. He made his first final retirement from public office in 1893 and is said to have destroyed 18 French ministries.

The last time he took office as Premier was when France was "bled white," when the fighting spirit of the troops were exhausted, after a serious mutiny had occurred, and when a peace was being negotiated that would have meant German domination of the world.

Immediately before he made himself Premier, women were parading the streets of Paris with banners reading, "Bring Back Our Soldiers." The French had failed in a ghastly offensive in the Champagne that had turned into a butchery. Morale could have been no lower.

Aristide Briand, the Premier, was said to have received secret offers of peace from Germany – and about to accept them. It looked as though France was done for.

Then came Clemenceau. He knew the Germans. In 1893, after the Casablanca incident he had said, "There will be no apology when Germany had demanded one. There was no apology. And there was to be no defeatist peace now."

Clemenceau came charging out of his retreat. He drove Briand and the others out of power, bucked up the French morale, and put the French into a state of mind where there was no longer any possibility of quitting.

Day after day Clemenceau visited the front, getting in touch with the soldiers. He made short, vigorous talks to the men and thousands of men have seen him under shell fire. Few people are aware how close he once came to being captured by the Germans. In 1918, he was still in a French village when the Germans entered in and had to be hidden away and later smuggled out by loyal French civilians.

Back of the lines, in Paris, at munition factories, in all centres the old tiger visited and became to the people the symbol of a France unconquerable. Then came the long strain of the Peace Conference and his serious wounding by an assassin. People said the old man was failing. His leathery skin was yellower than ever. The combinations of political groups that he had fought and defeated in his career formed a coalition and elected Deschanel for President of France, the position that belonged

to Clemenceau if any ever did. He retired from public life and went on a shooting trip to Africa and India.

He came back and went into retirement at his little place on the wild coast of the Vendee where I interviewed him. His health is back, he says he never felt better, and he is beginning to prepare, many people believe, for a political comeback. The Poincaire faction fear him more now than they ever did and they are shaking in their boots.

If Clemenceau's American tour is successful and a triumph, and the Poincaire group have no way out of giving it every aid, the Tiger may come sweeping back into power again. He says he knows why the Versailles treaty does not work. And he should. He made it. And that statement is a powerful weapon to wield on Poincaire who has proved that he cannot work the treaty.

It has been said of Clemenceau that France is his only remaining illusion. He is going to America now, alone, the only free man in Europe, to defend France. And if he decides that it is necessary for him, on his return, to become Premier in order to defend France better – he will be the next Premier.

Meantime, he stands and looks out at the surf curling along his beach, at his great red fish blowing in the wind at the top of the slim white pole, at the red sails of the fishing boats far out on the sea beating up from the coast of Spain toward the very pleasant land of France and he says – "it is a nice place – this. I was born near here, you know. No. Not here. A little further up the coast."

* * *

ESCAPED KINGSTON CONVICTS STILL AT LARGE

Special to The Star by a Staff Reporter.

Kingston Mills, Sept. 11. – The convicts have escaped northeast from McAdoo's Woods and Warden Ponsford is pursuing with guards in motor cars. It is believed the convicts are hiding near Collins Lake on the northwest of Kingston Mills.

Special to The Star by a Staff Reporter.

Kingston, Sept. 11. – With four of the five convicts who made a sensational escape from the penitentiary yesterday still at large this morning arrangements are being made to secure bloodhounds to assist in the search. Word was also received this morning from W. S. Hughson, inspector of penitentiaries, that a reward of $50 will be paid for the capture of each of the escaped convicts.

The four men still at large, and who are believed to be hiding in the bush and swamp between the Perth road and the Cataraqui river towards Kingston Mills, are:

Gordon Simpson, Toronto, serving ten years for robbery.

Arthur Brown, Toronto, serving ten years for highway robbery.

Patrick Ryan, alias Norman Slade, Hamilton, sentenced to 25 years and lashes for bank robbery.

Thomas Bryans, Montreal, serving ten years for manslaughter.

Edward McMullen, serving fourteen years for robbing a bank at Wyoming, Ontario, also escaped, but was recaptured three miles from the prison, weak with the loss of blood from a gunshot wound in the hand, received from a guard who fired on the party as they escaped.

Guards Out All Night

This morning the guards had been out all night. They were cold and hungry. Farmers were driving in to the town or working in the fields. There were no posses. Everyone in the countryside seemed content to leave the job of man-hunting to the professional man-hunters. The guards completely surrounded the entire woods and were especially thick along the east side to prevent the criminals from breaking across the main road and getting into the woods along the Rideau river. From there they might make their way north and be able to get food at the lumber camps. Everyone was cold and hungry, but there was news.

Last night about eleven o'clock on the narrow muddy road overgrown with underbrush that divides the seven hundred acres of bush into a north and south half, four guards and a scout on horseback were stationed. It was so dark the scout could not see his horse's head. But he heard the fence wires on the south side of the road creek. He shouted to the guards who were further down the road and then there was silence. The four men had their rifles ready.

Then in the dark there was a rush across the road. The guards fired into the dark at the sound and rushed forward. In the dark a man's voice said: "Are you hurt, shorty?" The guards shot again where the voice came from and one of them fired point blank as a man dashed by him toward the north side of the road. The men had crossed from the south tract of the woods to the northern half of the seven hundred acres. About fifteen rifle shots were fired in the dark. There is no blood and there are no bodies.

When the sun came up this morning the guards found a hammer and a heavy wrench that the men had dropped when they were fired on while crossing the road. These were taken from Thompson's car and had been taken as weapons when they fled into the woods. A few yards further up the road was a prisoner's cap, one of those gray-blue Sherlock Holmes shaped caps that all the prisoners wear.

I went over the ground where the shooting occurred with Warden Ponsford this morning. He had nothing to say for publication but is confident that all the men crossed into the northern tract during the night, although the guards say they think there were only three.

Warden Ponsford would not say whether the battery of R.C.H.A. at Kingston would be called out to put a tight cordon around the woods while the sixty prison guards, who all know the men by sight and are especially trained in this sort of work, advance in a tightening ring and beat the woods for the convicts. There will be an advance, probably of this kind, some time to-day.

Trace of Man Seen

About nine o'clock word was brought to the warden by one of the guards patroling the northern frontier of the woods that traces of one man had been found where he had climbed over a fence along the road that bounds the woods on the north. There was also an unconfirmed report that a farmer had seen one or two men crossing the road early this morning. If the men escape out of the north end of the woods it will be a long chase. There are several cheese factories a mile or so north of the present isolated territory, where it is believed the men will try and get food if they break through. They have had nothing since early yesterday morning.

It became known to-day that a long-term convict, who was stationed on duty in the stable which was set on fire by the five desperadoes to screen their bid for liberty, endeavored to foil the attempt of the five men to escape. When he tried to stop them in their desperate work, this convict was roughly handled, and when he persisted in his attempt to frustrate their plans, he was tied up with a rope inside the building, and had it not been for the quick work of another convict, who found him and released him, he would have been burned to death. It is understood that the action of this convict will be brought to the attention of the department of justice.

McMullen is regarded as the ringleader in the escape. He and Slade were regarded as two of the worst convicts in the prison and both have been closely guarded since they were brought to the penitentiary as it was feared they would plot a getaway. It is believed that the five men had been planning their method of escape for some time.

When back in the penitentiary McMullen stated that the plans for their escape had not worked out as they expected. He said that they figured that after they got over the prison walls they would be able to secure a high powered car from in front of the home of Mrs. H. W. Richardson, who lives close by the prison, and that they would be able to make a quick getaway. McMullen said that he understood that Mrs. Richardson was a millionaire and that he was sure that the car would be close at hand for their use. When they could not get a high powered car they were glad to take a Chevrolet car that was near but in this they were unable to make the speed they desired.

The capture of McMullen was due to the fact that he was weak from loss of blood from a shot he had received in the left hand from a revolver in the hands of Guard Allan, who chased the fleeing convicts in an automobile. When the convicts ran their car into a gateway, near Kemp's farm, about three miles from this city, and made for the woods close by, McMullen had to drop out of the flight and was found lying on the ground alongside a fence near the road about one hundred feet from the car. He was unarmed and as a result of his weakened condition he was not able to put up any fight. He declared to the guards who surrounded him that if he had not been shot they would never have taken him alive.

McMullen is now confined to the hospital at the penitentiary but it is stated that his condition is not regarded as at all serious. The shot from the revolver went through his index finger.

It was at ten o'clock yesterday morning that a great cloud of thick, yellow-white smoke began to pour from the barn just inside the east wall of the penitentiary. It was the thick dense smoke of a burning straw stack and as it rose it cut off the view of the guard standing with his rifle in the watchtower overlooking the burning barn.

Five men, in the grey prison clothes, ran out of the barn toward the twenty-foot, steep wall. One of them carried a long two-by-four in which spikes had been driven at intervals. The fat man carrying the long scantling leaned it against the wall and a slim kid, his prison cap pulled down over his eyes, swarmed up it to the top of the wall. He carried a

length of rope, which he fastened to the end of the scantling. He made the rope fast and then slid down the other side of the wall.

A big husky with a heavy undershot jaw followed him over. On his heels came a little runt who scrambled up the scantling like a monkey. He was followed by a thick set, ham-faced man who scrambled awkwardly over the wall.

Standing at the foot of the scantling, while they all went up was a thick, freckle-faced man whose prison cap could not hide his flaming head. It was "Red" Ryan. The others who had climbed over were Young Brown, Big Simpson, Runty Bryans and Wyoming McMullen.

The Guard Shoots

As "Red" Ryan started up the ladder, Matt Walsh, chief keeper of Portsmouth penitentiary, came running around the corner to see the burning barn. Walsh saw "Red" on the ladder and ran toward the scantling to try and jerk it down, shouting the alarm as he ran. "Red" saw him coming, realized that he was trapped, and came down the ladder. He had left a pitchfork leaning against the jail wall for just this emergency.

As Walsh reached the ladder "Red" reached for the pitchfork. Walsh tackled him and "Red" swung with all his might on Walsh's head with the pitchfork. Walsh went down and "Red" dropped the fork and went up the scantling and over the wall.

The men were strung out across the field outside the prison wall running for Mrs. Richardson's house where a car was standing. The guard in the tower was still cut off by the thick smoke. Allan Forsythe, the only other guard in sight, thought that he could stop them without shooting. He had dropped over the wall and was just behind the running men. He had never shot anyone and something held him back from beginning. He shouted at the men but they kept on going.

As they climbed into the little Chevrolet car belonging to "Shorty" Thompson, who was doing a painting job at Richardson's, Allan Forsythe commenced shooting. He couldn't tell what his shots did, but he was sure he had hit someone. The Chevrolet kept on going. Forsythe stopped a car that was passing and stepped out after the car careering wildly ahead up the road.

McMullen was at the wheel of the Chevrolet — that is, he was hunched over what was left of the wheel. One of Forsythe's shots had cut the wheel clean in two and smashed McMullen's left hand. He drove on with his right hand, hunched low, his face paling from the amount of blood he was losing. The other two big men were in the back of the car with "Young" Brown, the wild kid. On the front seat with McMullen sat "Runty" Bryans. One of Forsythe's bullets ripped through the back of the car and out the front above "Runty's" head. It would have hit a full sized man in the skull.

A Wild Chase

Back of the little car was strung out a wild chase. All sorts of cars had been commandeered in Kingston. As the little motor car went along the road from the penitentiary, through the streets of Kingston and north on the Inverary road, the cars behind kept gaining. Directly behind was the Ford commandeered by Forsythe, who kept on firing. The prisoners' car was going along a narrow strip of asphalt road with houses and cottages on either side. It looked as though any minute they might be overtaken. There was no cover on either side.

Then the road widened out into country stone road. The houses fell away. They crossed the two railway tracks of the Canadian Pacific and Canadian National, dipped down a long hill, past a quarry on the left, and were in farming and bush country. On the right they were passing a long stretch of thick, hardwood timber, the trees just going yellow and red in the fall. On the top of the hill they could see it stretched out for miles ahead. The men looking out behind could see that they had a lead of about two hundred and fifty yards on the nearest of the pursuing cars.

McMullen turned the car sharply to the left and ran it down the bank into a sunken field. The convicts ripped off the seats, grabbed the tool bags, the tire pump and jack, climbed the banks and cut across the Inverary road into the woods. As the last man was going into the woods Forsythe came up in his Ford. But his cartridges were gone.

There are seven hundred acres in the patch of woods the convicts are hiding in. It is bounded by roads on all sides and is surrounded by prison guards armed with rifles. Across the middle of the patch of woods runs a narrow, muddy road, overhung with trees.

McMullen Captured

Last night at about six-thirty, Warden Ponsford, who is in charge of the pursuit, found McMullen about forty yards from where the men entered the McAdoo's Woods. The warden, a kindly-looking grey-mustached man in a grey suit, felt hat and worried look in his eyes, was going over the route the men had taken into the woods when he saw a blue shirt lying under a low growing cedar. He thought it meant that one of the men was discarding his prison clothes and bent down to look. It was McMullen, white from loss of blood, lying under the little cedar, his shirt pulled over his head and his legs and shoes covered with grass.

Warden Ponsford pulled McMullen to his feet and called a patrol. Surrounded by twelve guards with rifles, McMullen was white and shaky. "I'm through," he said, "leave me alone." His hand was still bleeding.

One of the guards said: "Well, are you going to try and run, McMullen?" McMullen looked at the twelve rifle barrels: "What do you think I wanta do? Commit suicide?" They took him in a motor car back to the penitentiary over the same road he had driven in the morning. He was very quiet.

Stewart Patterson, one of Warden Ponsford's lieutenants in the man hunt, said the search parties must have passed McMullen twenty times as he lay there. The cover in the wood is so dense a man cannot make his way through it in places.

Matt Walsh, the head keeper, who was beaten up with a pitchfork by "Red" Ryan, is not seriously injured, although badly marked. He is commanding a detachment in the hunt. "I am leaving now to return to the woods where the men are believed to be cornered and where the closing in on them is due to start," he said to-day.

Gordon Simpson was serving a ten year term following his conviction in Hamilton, Toronto and Guelph for a series of robberies which he participated in, headed by the notorious Tommy Quinn, now serving ten years in Kingston, too, along with several others of the gang. Following his arrest after a large number of shop-breakings in Hamilton, Toronto, and throughout the province, Simpson was taken to Hamilton for trial, and on February 4, 1921, was sentenced to six years for shopbreaking and theft of cloth. Then he was brought to Toronto and sentenced on February 18, 1921, on five charges of shopbreaking and theft and received a five-year sentence on each charge, the sentences to run concurrently.

* * *

The William Charvat American Fiction Collection at the Ohio State University Libraries

Geoffrey D. Smith

Curator, William Charvat American Fiction Collection

Prior to his death on 5 June 1966, William Charvat, professor of American literature at Ohio State University, had been a guiding force in the development of the university libraries' American fiction collection, an endeavor that paralleled his own research in nineteenth-century American culture. Professor Charvat, the proleptic "new historian," studied the production of literary works, from manuscripts to finished, printed books, as creations dependent upon larger social, economic, and historical forces. In recognition of his contribution to the conceptual development of the American fiction collection at the Ohio State University Libraries, library officials, in 1966, designated rare American fiction titles as the William Charvat American Fiction Collection. Professor Matthew J. Bruccoli, Charvat's colleague and friend, coordinated efforts between the English department and the library to establish an acquisition fund to perpetuate development of American fiction holdings at Ohio State.

The newly designated Charvat Collection would build upon established holdings of American fiction at the university libraries. Of particular note, in July 1965, eleven months before Charvat's death, Hyman W. Kritzer, assistant director for public service at the university libraries, had expedited the block purchase of the Library Company of Philadelphia's American fiction holdings: all the fiction the company had acquired since 1880. The Charvat Collection fund had a strong base on which to build, and, though that original fund has long been exhausted, the support of the university libraries' administration and Friends of the Ohio State University Libraries has ensured the growth of the collection from one of interest for a local community to one of prominence for the national scholarly community.

Charvat, then, conceived and originated an American literary resource that certainly reflected

William Charvat

his own scholarly interests but, in turn, influenced his colleagues and generations of young scholars. Among Charvat's more notable scholarly publications are: *The Cost Books of Ticknor and Fields and Their Predecessors, 1832–1858,* coedited with Warren S. Tryon (New York: Bibliographical Society of America, 1949); *Literary Publishing in America, 1790–1850* (Philadelphia: University of Pennsylvania Press, 1959); and, posthumously, *The Profession of Authorship*

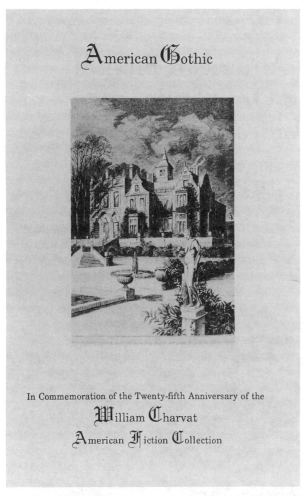

American Gothic

In Commemoration of the Twenty-fifth Anniversary of the

*William Charvat
American Fiction Collection*

Cover for the catalogue for the 1991 exhibition of books from the William Charvat American Fiction Collection at the Ohio State University Libraries

in America, 1800–1870: The Papers of William Charvat, edited by Matthew J. Bruccoli (Columbus: Ohio State University Press, 1968). In 1992 Columbia University Press reissued *The Profession of Authorship in America,* and the University of Massachusetts Press reissued *Literary Publishing in America,* reaffirming the enduring value of William Charvat's scholarship.

Since 1966 the William Charvat American Fiction Collection has become not only the richest book collection of the Ohio State University Libraries but also a preeminent literary and cultural resource for the national and international scholarly community. The criteria for inclusion of titles in the Charvat Collection are the same as defined by Lyle Wright in his bibliographies of American fiction, 1774–1900: first American printings of adult fiction by United States authors.

The Charvat Collection aims toward comprehensiveness in its acquisition of American fiction.

An enviable, but ultimately unattainable, goal, the Charvat Collection, nonetheless, has developed strong holdings of early American fiction (the later eighteenth century through 1875) and outstanding holdings for titles published from 1876 through 1900. Twentieth-century holdings of the Charvat Collection may be the strongest in the nation, rivaled only by the Library of Congress. For the first quarter of the twentieth century, approximately 10,500 of the estimated 14,000 titles published during that period, and which meet the criteria for inclusion, are preserved in the Charvat Collection.

The importance of the collection's twentieth-century holdings is attested to through the tangible support of external funding agencies. Acquisition and bibliographic support from the Strengthening Research Library Resources program of the Department of Education (1983–1985) and bibliographic support from the Research Resources Program of the National Endowment for the Humanities (1988–1992) will result in the *Bibliography of American Fiction, 1901–1925* (New York: Cambridge University Press, 1994), the logical successor to Wright's bibliographies of earlier American fiction. Though heavily reliant upon the holdings of the Charvat Collection, the *Bibliography of American Fiction* will record, as nearly as possible, all titles of American fiction published during the first quarter of the twentieth century. The completed work will also exist on a computer data base.

Patterned on its successful work with identifying and recording American fiction for the first quarter of the twentieth century, the Charvat Collection has begun a focused development and organization of its holdings for the period 1926–1950. With continued support from the National Endowment for the Humanities and commitment from the Cambridge University Press, publication of the *Bibliography of American Fiction, 1926–1950* is planned for the year 2000.

For later twentieth-century American fiction the Charvat Collection has built its holdings through selective purchase and donation. In 1986, however, the Charvat Collection began purchase of the vast majority of current American fiction through an approval plan with a national book distributor that supplies American fiction according to a specific selection profile, that is, the traditional Wright criteria. This approval plan will ensure that the Charvat Collection will retain its status into the next century as a major resource for the study of American literary and cultural history. The securing of contemporary works of American fiction in their original state (with dust jackets, for example) at the time of publication ensures that the books, stored in atmospherically controlled stacks, will retain their bibliographic integrity for scholarly use in the decades ahead.

Though the core of the Charvat Collection focuses on fiction that follows the Wright criteria, separate book collections exist in greater depth with holdings of successive printings, later editions, special and limited editions, and foreign editions. Among the author collections are the works of: Nathaniel Hawthorne, Jack London, Chester Himes, Jesse Stuart, and John Gardner. Discrete genre and publishers collections include: the science fiction paperback collection, the Grosset and Dunlap reprint collection, the nineteenth-century paperback collection, and the complete published works of the North Point Press.

Twentieth-century fiction titles are augmented by the manuscripts and papers of contemporary American authors, most notably Nelson Algren, William S. Burroughs, Frederick Busch, Raymond Carver, William Bradford Huie, James Purdy, Helen Hooven Santmyer, and William T. Vollman. Other manuscript collections include the archives of the Centenary Edition of the works of Nathaniel Hawthorne (most appropriately, since William Charvat was one of the founding editors of that distinguished editorial project) and the archives of *Conjunctions,* the journal of contemporary literature. The James Thurber Collection, the richest manuscript collection at Ohio State, is administratively distinct from the Charvat Collection but, nonetheless, is thematically related and housed with other American manuscript collections. Additionally, with respect to the manuscript collections, the Charvat Collection contains in-depth book collections of the authors' works.

The modern materials of the Charvat Collection complement the twentieth-century holdings of two other nationally recognized special collections at the Ohio State University Libraries: the Cartoon, Graphic, and Photographic Arts Research Library; and the Jerome Lawrence and Robert E. Lee The-atre Research Library. The Cartoon, Graphic, and Photographic Arts Research Library houses multimedia collections of primary-source materials representative of American culture. Cartoon art, film posters and stills, historic photographs, and magazine materials are held, in addition to more than ten thousand works of cartoon art. The papers of Milton Caniff, the Walt Kelly Collection, the Woody Gelman Collection of Winsor McCay cartoons, and the Will Eisner Collection are among the notable cartoon-art collections. The archives of the American Association of Editorial Cartoonists and the National Cartoonists Society are in the library. In addition to its historical documentation of Western theater, the Jerome Lawrence and Robert E. Lee Theatre Research Library's primary-source materials include the Lawrence and Lee Collection, the Twyla Tharp Collection, the Robert Eyen Collection, and the Robert Breen Collection. The assembly of twentieth-century materials from the Special Collections at Ohio State University makes for a unique research experience for the interdisciplinary scholar of the literary, visual, and performing arts.

The William Charvat American Fiction Collection has developed dramatically since its inception over a quarter of a century ago. Though the scope of the collection has expanded from its original criteria to include twentieth-century materials and manuscripts, it is hoped that the intentions of the staff, supporters, and users of the collection remain faithful to the intellectual spirit of William Charvat, a spirit so eloquently described by Professor Charvat's friend and peer, the distinguished scholar Howard Mumford Jones, in his conclusion to *Scholarship, Novelty, and Teaching* (1968):

> The best contribution of the scholar to education is to enrich scholarship, to continue it, to make it available to all those competent and ready to accept the philosophy that scholarship implies. Such seems to me still the proper goal and appropriate contribution of the scholar to this or any other time. If I understand him, correctly, this also William Charvat believed.

First International F. Scott Fitzgerald Conference

Jackson R. Bryer
University of Maryland

and

Alan Margolies
John Jay College, City University of New York

and

Ruth Prigozy
Hofstra University

The First International F. Scott Fitzgerald Conference, held 24–27 September 1992 at Hofstra University, Hempstead, New York, was sponsored by Hofstra and the F. Scott Fitzgerald Society. Ruth Prigozy chaired the conference; Jackson R. Bryer and Alan Margolies were cochairmen of the program. Scholarly papers were delivered by, among others, Scott Donaldson, Richard D. Lehan, Robert A. Martin, Bruce L. Grenberg, Jeffrey Meyers, and Bickford Sylvester. Two panel discussions, "Memories of Fitzgerald," featured reminiscences by Honoria Murphy Donnelly (daughter of Gerald and Sara Murphy), Fanny Myers Brennan, Ring Lardner, Jr., Budd Schulberg, Tony Buttitta, and Frances Ring. Other panels included discussion on such topics as "The Early Fitzgerald," "Fitzgerald's Foreign Reputation," "Fitzgerald and Long Island," "Fitzgerald's Short Stories," "Aspects of Biography," and "Gender Issues in Fitzgerald." Frances Ring's one-act play, based on the correspondence between Fitzgerald and his daughter, was presented as a staged reading, starring George Grizzard as Scott and Elizabeth Enck as Scottie, directed by Richard Mason.

Additional speakers included Charles Scribner III, Wendy W. Fairey (daughter of Sheilah Graham), George Garrett, and John Kuehl. Lloyd Hackl narrated a slide presentation dealing with early Saint Paul, Minnesota, "In His Own Town: F. Scott Fitzgerald"; James J. Martine led a session devoted to teaching Fitzgerald; and Judith

and Raymond Spinzia's slide show on the Long Island estates which served as partial models for houses in *The Great Gatsby* (1925) provided a preview of the guided bus tour closing the conference which visited three of those estates and included a drive past 6 Gateway Drive, Great Neck, where the Fitzgeralds lived in 1922 and 1923.

The conference attracted more than 250 attendees. They heard Schulberg, in his keynote address, recall with considerable emotion his memories of Fitzgerald in Hollywood as well as at Dartmouth during the disastrous weekend Schulberg and the novelist spent there in 1939 working on the movie *Winter Carnival*. Schulberg later participated in a "Memories" panel with Lardner, who also spoke of his recollections of Fitzgerald and read humorous correspondence between his father and Fitzgerald; with Buttitta, who remembered Fitzgerald in the 1930s in North Carolina; and with Ring, who drew on her experience as Fitzgerald's secretary in 1939 and 1940. Another "Memories" panel featured Donnelly and Brennan, who recalled and showed slides of the Fitzgeralds, the Murphys, Rudolph Valentino, Pablo Picasso, and others.

Charles Scribner III spoke and presided over a luncheon celebrating Fitzgerald's ninety-sixth birthday, complete with a birthday cake. His talk dealt with his family's association with the novelist, with his own first exposure to Fitzgerald's work as a student at Princeton, and with his scholarly interest as an art historian in such matters as the source of the dust jacket for *Gatsby*.

Charles Scribner III and Frances Kroll Ring (photograph courtesy of Hofstra University)

Wendy W. Fairey's talk drew from her recently published memoir, *One of the Family* (Norton), in evoking her mother's stories of her relationship with Fitzgerald and in commenting on how the shadow of that relationship affected Fairey's own life. George Garrett's after-dinner talk dealt with the powerful influences of Fitzgerald's life and art on his own life and those of other American writers; while John Kuehl, in his luncheon address, spoke of the contributions of early Fitzgerald scholars and of his own forty-year career studying and writing about Fitzgerald.

In order to hear from as many scholars as possible and also to promote discussion between presenters and the audience (as well as among the presenters), this conference included panels in which participants gave five-to-six minute abridged versions of longer papers. In one such panel, on "The Early Fitzgerald," chaired by Peter L. Hays, Heidi Kunz Bullock spoke of social typology in *This Side of Paradise* (1920), while Nancy P. VanArsdale emphasized Princeton as the setting in the same novel. *The Beautiful and Damned* (1922) served as the focus for three others on that panel: Jonathan Fegley talked about it as "Fitzgerald's prototypical novel"; Stephen Frye dealt with its "eucharistic element"; and Neila C. Seshachari interpreted it as "an anti-fairy tale." The absurdist characteristics of Fitzgerald's only play *The Vegetable* (1923) were the subject of Pamela Jean Monaco's presentation.

Two panels on *The Great Gatsby* concerned new vantages from which to view the novel. The first, on gender issues, included papers by Mark Andrew Clark and Frances Kerr which examined in some detail Nick Carraway's sexual character, and a third, by Scott S. Derrick, on the feminine elements – with particular attention to Edith Wharton's influence. These three papers elicited some of the most spirited discussion. The second *Gatsby*

Budd Schulberg (photograph by Alan Margolies)

panel focused on Daisy Buchanan's voice (Warren Bennett), on elements of mystery, detection, and crime in the novel (W. Russel Gray), on Gatsby's romantic personality (Barbara Malinowska and Lawrence Broer), on Gatsby and Horatio Alger (Greg Metcalf), on the failure of language for the novel's characters (Sheryl A. Mylan), and on its African-American presence (Gary Storhoff).

The panel, "The Later Fitzgerald," chaired by Milton R. Stern, featured H. R. Stoneback, who pointed out how the Phillipe stories drew from their author's knowledge of Ernest Hemingway and his work; Edward J. Gleason, who spoke of the autobiographical allusions in the *Esquire* stories; Barry Gross, who discussed Fitzgerald's treatment of Monroe Stahr as Jewish-American hero; Joyce Baumgartner Anderson, who discussed the pastoral elements of *Tender Is the Night* (1934); and Dana Brand, who concentrated on tourism as a metaphor for modernity in the same novel.

Victor A. Doyno chaired a panel, "Fitzgerald's Short Stories"; Mona Houghton examined the author's revisions of "Majesty"; Barbara Sylvester pointed out textual problems in "Babylon Revisited"; John Kuehl explicated "Outside the

Cabinet-Maker's"; and Bryant Mangum explained some of the problems he was encountering in preparing a reader's guide to Fitzgerald's short fiction.

During the panel on "Aspects of Biography," Tracy Simmons Bitonti examined Zelda and Scott as characters in Tennessee Williams's play *Clothes for a Summer Hotel* (1983) and in Michael McGuire's *The Scott Fitzgerald Play* (1988), as well as Fitzgerald's work as an important presence in A. R. Gurney's drama *The Golden Age* (1981). Two other speakers on that panel looked at Fitzgerald's associations with Maryland (Diane S. Isaacs) and with Minnesota (Dave Page). The final speaker on the biography panel, Andrew Reid Burke, speculated on how drinking influenced Fitzgerald's writing in a positive way.

Chaired by George Wickes, the panel on the relationship between Fitzgerald and other writers ranged from Dale A. Berryhill's discussion of parallels between J. D. Salinger's *Catcher in the Rye* (1951) and *This Side of Paradise* through J. O. Tate's talk about Fitzgerald's influence upon Raymond Chandler's fiction and Phyllis Doyle's comments on the influence of those in the American past who wrote about or followed the tenets of individual-

Tony Buttita, Frances Kroll Ring, Budd Schulberg, Honoria Murphy Donnelly, Cecilia Ross, Eleanor Lanahan, Ring Lardner, Jr., Fanny Myers Brennan, Wendy W. Fairey, and Alex Clark (photograph by Alan Margolies)

ism to three papers on the Fitzgerald-Hemingway association and two on links with Keats. Claudia Barnett pointed to the symbol of the night in Fitzgerald's and Hemingway's fictions; Edward J. Rielly noted Hemingway's fictional portrayals of Fitzgerald; and Donald Junkins read from a discarded section of Hemingway's *A Moveable Feast* (1964) dealing with Fitzgerald. Catherine Burroughs discussed the resemblance of *The Beautiful and Damned* to Keats's treatment of the ancient Greek Lamia myth. Scott Harshbarger described how Fitzgerald learned from Keats how to turn cultural inferiority into a grand theme illustrating the plight of the romantic.

In the panel, "Fitzgerald and Women," Cyndy Hendershot looked at the female characters in the fiction; Elizabeth Anne Beaulieu was concerned with Zelda Fitzgerald's *Save Me the Waltz* (1932); Bernice Kert compared Fitzgerald and Hemingway as lovers, husbands, and supporters of their wives' work; and Koula C. Hartnett, drawing on material in her book, *Zelda Fitzgerald and the Failure of the American Dream for Woman* (1991), discussed the relationship between Zelda and Scott.

The panel, "Themes and Motifs in Fitzgerald's Works," included studies of money and the stock market (James Ellis), violence (Gertrude K. Hamilton), metamorphosis (Vincent Kohler), and theatricality (John T. Irwin). The panel on "Fitzgerald and Film" presented Gautam Kundu's examination of the relationship of *This Side of Paradise* to film; Scott F. Stoddart's analysis of the 1974 film adaptation of *Gatsby;* Susan J. Scrivner's inquiry into the relationship between "Babylon Revisited" and its 1954 film adaptation, *The Last Time I Saw Paris;* and Ben Nyce's views on the 1976 film version of *The Last Tycoon* (1941).

The conference attracted foreign scholars, most of whom participated in the panel, "Fitzgerald's Foreign Reputation." Sadao Nagaoka reported on the advances in Fitzgerald studies in Japan, as well as the formation in May 1989 of the Fitzgerald Club in that country, Svetlana Voitiuk spoke about Fitzgerald's standing in Ukraine and in the former Soviet Union, mentioning available translations and recent scholarship. A paper by Li Tianfang (Xi'an, China) described the impact of Fitzgerald's work on her own creative writing, emphasizing in particular Fitzgerald's gift for observation. Udo J. Hebel assessed the novelist's reception in Germany, emphasizing translations, television, and film adaptations, English-as-foreign-language courses, and scholarship, and provided an annotated listing for distribution.

Eduardo Jorge Ribeiro (University of Porto, Portugal) dealt with Fitzgerald's work in the 1930s, and Amitava Banerjee (Kobe College, Japan) focused on *The Crack-Up* (1945).

Long Island and Fitzgerald was the subject of a panel that included papers by Joann P. Krieg on the ways in which Great Neck affected the Fitzgeralds, by Roger Wunderlich on the relationship between Long Island and *Gatsby,* and by Robert B. Sargent, whose slide presentation illustrated architecture on Long Island's Gold Coast.

Aside from these panels there were full-length papers. Richard A. Davison's discussion of "Babylon Revisited" focused on the story's autobiographical elements as well as other aspects of Fitzgerald's art. Scott Donaldson described the dynamics of the Fitzgerald-Hemingway relationship and compared their responses to being jilted when they were young. Edward Gillin noted Fitzgerald's interest in Mark Twain as well as influences. Bruce L. Grenberg looked at the "depths of Fitzgerald's imagination" that went into the writing of "The Crack-Up." Jack Hendriksen discussed *This Side of Paradise* as a bildungsroman. Richard D. Lehan analyzed the structural patterns of the narrative in *Gatsby*. Quentin E. Martin talked about "Winter Dreams," emphasizing how most critics have misunderstood

Judy Jones's role in the story. Robert A. Martin described Fitzgerald's characters as linked to American history and civilization. Jeffrey Meyers analyzed the hostility toward the English in Fitzgerald's writing. Bickford Sylvester compared and contrasted Hemingway and Fitzgerald as regional writers, the first from the Midwest, the second as "midwestern/southern hybrid." Michel Viel discussed the problems of translating *Gatsby* into French. Eleanor Lanahan and Cecilia Ross, Fitzgerald's granddaughters, and Alexander P. Clark, former curator of manuscripts at Princeton University Library, were in attendance.

A volume of selected papers from the 1992 conference is planned. Videotapes and audiotapes for most of the sessions are available from the Hofstra Cultural Center, Hempstead, N.Y., 11550. Information about the F. Scott Fitzgerald Society is available from Ruth Prigozy, Hofstra University.

The next F. Scott Fitzgerald Society conference will be held jointly with the Hemingway Society from 3–9 July 1994 in Paris. The celebration of Fitzgerald's one-hundredth birthday is planned for the society's 1996 international meeting, tentatively scheduled for September 1996 at Princeton, New Jersey.

Literary Research Archives VIII: The Henry E. Huntington Library

Sara S. Hodson
The Huntington Library

In 1994 the Huntington Library, Art Collections, and Botanical Gardens will celebrate seventy-five years as a center for scholarly research and the public display of its vast treasures. Since its founding in 1919 the Huntington has developed and expanded within its original areas of endeavor, and it now encompasses significant British art holdings housed in the Huntington Gallery (formerly Henry Huntington's home); a young but growing American art collection in the Virginia Steele Scott Gallery, constructed in 1984; examples of rare plants on more than two hundred acres of botanical gardens; a library exhibit hall featuring displays of rare printed books and manuscripts; and a research library whose collections number approximately seven hundred thousand printed rare and reference books and more than three million manuscripts. The diamond jubilee affords a perfect occasion on which to explore the literary collections of this multifaceted jewel among North America's private research libraries.

To understand the context and development of the Huntington as a center for literary research, it is useful to trace briefly the history of the institution and that of its founder, Henry Edwards Huntington. Born in Oneonta, New York, on 27 February 1850, he was the fourth of seven children of Solon and Harriet Saunders Huntington. Exhibiting aptitude and initiative in practical, rather than scholarly, pursuits, Henry left his hometown for New York City at the age of twenty to begin working for a large hardware firm, where the ambitious young man rose rapidly. Meanwhile his uncle, Collis P. Huntington, had left his partnership with Solon in 1849, spurred by the California gold rush to try his hand at a trading venture in the West. Collis's business efforts succeeded, he entered into a partnership with Mark Hopkins in Sacramento, and the Huntington and Hopkins hardware com-

Henry E. Huntington (photograph by Arnold Genthe; Henry E. Huntington Archives, by permission of the Henry E. Huntington Library and Art Gallery)

pany became one of the West's largest and most prosperous. By 1861 Collis began investing heavily in the development of an overland railroad, an enterprise which would also see the close involvement of his nephew.

Henry achieved much success with his uncle's various railroad enterprises, and in 1892 he took over the management of the Southern Pacific Railroad. Once in California, as his business travels took him the length of the state, Henry became convinced that the future of the state lay in southern California, especially Los Angeles. He visited James de Barth Shorb at San Marino, Shorb's ranch bordering Pasadena just outside Los Angeles, and he began to investigate the potential of electric railways for developing cities as well as the territory surrounding them. Following Collis's death in 1900, Henry transferred the majority of his attention and energies from the Southern Pacific to the design and implementation of an electric railway system. He purchased the Shorb ranch in 1902 and watched the Los Angeles region achieve tremendous growth, spurred in large measure by his own Pacific Electric Railway Company and other enterprises.

Shortly before 1910 Henry Huntington announced his intention to retire at age sixty in order to enjoy other pursuits, and this transition roughly coincided with the transfer of the Pacific Electric system to the Southern Pacific company in 1910. Huntington's retirement from most of his business interests meant that he could devote far more of his attention (and wealth) to collecting. (Now divorced, Huntington consolidated his family and fortune by marrying his uncle's widow, Arabella, in 1913.) With the 1910 completion of the home he had commissioned from the architects Myron Hunt and Elmer Grey for the San Marino ranch, Huntington was able to transfer to Southern California the growing collection of books, manuscripts, and paintings he had long been amassing in New York City. A decade later his books and manuscripts found their home in the library building constructed on the ranch in 1920.

Huntington entered into his most active collecting years with his customary and highly successful businessman's methods and zeal, as well as with the collector's love of rare texts and autographs. In 1908 he purchased an 1896 reference work, *Rare Books and Their Prices,* and annotated its margins with the names of key books and authors from the Gutenberg Bible through Thomas Hardy. That became the guide for the rest of his collecting career. At the same time he began to purchase in bulk, the first major bulk purchase being made at the 1908–1909 auction of the library of Henry W. Poor. His acquisitions from the Poor sale totaled more than sixteen hundred lots, or about one-quarter of the sale, consisting largely of a variety of beautifully printed and bound books, incunabula, and illuminated manuscripts.

Soon, however, Huntington began to focus his collecting on the history and literature of the English-speaking peoples, and the books and manu-

scripts he bought comprise a large and significant portion, even today, of the literary holdings of the Huntington Library. Following the Poor sale Huntington's next major acquisition inaugurated his practice of purchasing entire libraries, a method that guaranteed the rapid development of a large library whose small gaps he could fill in with judicious and informed single purchases. The first complete library Huntington bought was the E. Dwight Church collection of Americana and English literature, and its acquisition in 1911 caught the attention of the press and other collectors, who were perhaps stunned equally by this unprecedented act and by the $1 million purchase price. The Church library, though small in size, consisted almost entirely of gems: in addition to the extensive Americana materials (including the manuscript of Benjamin Franklin's autobiography and the 1640 *Bay Psalm Book,* the first book printed in the American colonies), there were eleven William Shakespeare folios and thirty-seven quartos, as well as rare early editions of the works of John Milton and Edmund Spenser.

Almost simultaneously with the Church sale Huntington became the main purchaser at the auction of the vast library of Robert Hoe. His most famous acquisition from this sale was lot 269, the Gutenberg Bible in two volumes, purchased for the then-astonishing figure of fifty thousand dollars. Among the other treasures he obtained from Hoe's library are *The Book of St. Albans* (1486), William Caxton's edition of John Gower's *Confessio Amantis* (1386–1390, revised 1393), other Caxton editions, manuscript books of hours, medieval manuscript Bibles, Shakespeare quartos, and rare editions of the works of Jonathan Swift, John Dryden, and Alexander Pope.

The public and other collectors had hardly regained their composure following Huntington's performance in the Church and Hoe sales when in 1912 he bought Beverly Chew's extensive library of early English poetry. While the Chew Collection spans the sixteenth through the eighteenth centuries, the great wealth of material falls in the seventeenth century. Copies of the four Shakespeare folios and rarities by Spenser and Milton complement the Church acquisitions, and rare editions of the works of many less famous writers include multiple titles by Richard Braithwaite, John Cleveland, Francis Quarles, Edmund Waller, and George Wither, with smaller numbers of works by Charles Cotton, Abraham Cowley, Richard Crashaw, George Daniel, John Denham, John Donne, John Dryden, George Herbert, Thomas Heywood, and Thomas

Miniature of Geoffrey Chaucer on a page from the Ellsmere Manuscript of The Canterbury Tales, *a transcription dating from 1400–1410 (EL 26C9 f.153ᵥ; by permission of the Henry E. Huntington Library and Art Gallery)*

May. For the eighteenth century, there are works by John Gay and Oliver Goldsmith, plus some seventy-two items by Pope, including eighteen varying copies of the *Dunciad* (1728) printed during Pope's lifetime.

While the acquisition of the Chew library had significantly increased the Huntington Library's printed holdings in literature, the manuscript collections gained much stature in 1913 when Huntington purchased John Quinn's collection of literary autographs. Numbering 121 items, the manuscripts include early drafts of works by nineteenth-century literary figures. There are two stories by Thomas Hardy, eight novels by George Gissing, four essays and reviews by George Bernard Shaw, and a group of twenty-one verse and prose manuscripts by George Meredith. Members of the Pre-Raphaelite Brotherhood and their associates are represented by fifteen Dante Gabriel Rossetti verse manuscripts bearing annotations in the hand of William Michael Rossetti, who sold them to Quinn; twenty-eight sonnets by Christina Rossetti; two dozen manuscripts by William Morris; and twenty items by Algernon Charles Swinburne.

The Huntington Library's already strong holdings in printed and manuscript literary material achieved much additional distinction with the acquisition of the libraries of Frederic Robert Halsey and William Keeney Bixby in 1915 and 1918. Halsey's twenty-thousand-volume collection contained rare printed items for almost every major English author through the time of Robert Louis Stevenson and for most major nineteenth-century American authors. Special strengths included many first editions of Percy Bysshe Shelley's works, such as *Original Poetry by Victor and Cazire* (1810), *Queen Mab* (1813), *Alastor* (1816), *Laon and Cythna* (1818), and *Adonais* (1821), as well as a particularly valuable group of seventy-five Charles Dickens editions. On the American side, Edgar Allan Poe can be singled out, represented not only by all early editions of his collected poem, but also by a copy of *The Broadway Journal,* annotated by Poe and his fiancée, to whom he presented the volume. The Poe material also included a copy of one of the rarest of all American literary editions, *Tamerlane* (1827).

The exceptionally rich Bixby collection of manuscripts forms the foundation of the Huntington's nineteenth-century literary holdings, much as the Church and Chew collections serve as the cornerstone for earlier literature. Distinguished literary manuscripts include Shelley's notebooks, John Ruskin's *Seven Lamps of Architecture* (1849) with a separate volume of his drawings, and items by

Dickens, Robert Burns, Rudyard Kipling, John Greenleaf Whittier, Henry David Thoreau, Bret Harte, and many others. Sizable series of autograph letters represent Samuel Taylor Coleridge, William Wordsworth, Mary Shelley, Charles Lamb, William Makepeace Thackeray, Dorothy Jordan, Ralph Waldo Emerson, Nathaniel Hawthorne, Samuel Langhorne Clemens, and more.

A different kind of library, and one of more varied content, came to San Marino in 1917, when Huntington purchased the entire Bridgewater House Library. Founded by Sir Thomas Egerton, lord keeper of the great seal under Queen Elizabeth and lord high chancellor under James I, the library includes important additions from his third wife, Alice, Countess of Derby, and from his descendants, especially Francis, first Earl of Ellesmere. While the collection contains great numbers of historical and political documents, there are many literary treasures to be found as well. Chief among those must be placed the Ellesmere Chaucer, the celebrated circa 1410 manuscript of the *Canterbury Tales* containing color drawings of the pilgrims. Among other medieval manuscripts is a volume, once owned by John Shirley, containing poems by John Lydgate, Thomas Hoccleve, and others.

The Bridgewater House Library holds particular riches from the Renaissance. Sir Thomas Egerton and his wife were both patrons of letters, so authors' presentation copies, dedications, and complimentary verses added many literary riches to the family library. There are Shakespeare folios and quartos, Christopher Marlowe quartos, and first editions of almost all the lesser works of Milton, along with either manuscript or printed works by authors such as George Chapman, Robert Codrington, Ralph Crane, Sir John Davies, Randulph Hutchins, John Marston, Thomas May, and Francis Thynne.

From the Tudor and Stuart periods are manuscripts, including poems on Inigo Jones by Ben Jonson, poems by Donne, Thomas Middleton's *Game at Chesse* (1624), Anthony Wingfield's *Pedantius,* and Roger Boyle, first Earl of Orrery's *King Henry the Vth* and *Mustapha*. A manuscript volume of John Marston's *Masque in Honour of Alice Countess of Derby* also contains tipped-in leaves that are "discovered" every few decades by a researcher who attributes their authorship to Shakespeare.

The period from the mid eighteenth through the early nineteenth centuries was richly represented in the Bridgewater House Library by the Larpent Collection of plays. John Larpent was appointed the inspector of plays from 1778 to 1824 and not only retained copies of all the plays submitted to him for licensing but also set out to acquire copies of most, if not all, of the plays submitted after the passage of the Licensing Act in 1737. The resulting collection of twenty-five hundred plays, most of them manuscripts in the hand of a copyist, with a few bearing autograph authorial revisions, forms a rich archive for the study of eighteenth- and nineteenth-century British drama.

The Larpent Collection forms a perfect complement to the Kemble-Devonshire Collection of plays and playbills, which had been acquired by Huntington in 1914. The initial collection was gathered by the noted English actor John Philip Kemble, who sold it in about 1820 to William Spencer Cavendish, sixth Duke of Devonshire. The duke greatly augmented the collection, and it more than doubled in size, finally numbering over seventy-five hundred plays and 111 volumes of playbills. An almost complete run of playbills covers performances at Drury Lane from 1750 to 1782 and Covent Garden from 1760 to 1831. Among the many treasures of the collection may be counted the original manuscript of John Bale's *Kynge Johan,* a sixteenth-century manuscript (and the earliest known manuscript) of the Chester mystery plays, and autograph manuscript plays by Marston, William Percy, and John Horne. The gems among the printed volumes include some fifty-seven Shakespeare quartos, among them a copy of the 1603 *Hamlet,* plus 1594 and 1607 editions of *The Taming of the Shrew.* In addition, the Kemble-Devonshire Collection holds more than 90 percent of the known English plays for the period 1600–1800.

These collections and libraries, together with the others acquired by Huntington during the years of his greatest collecting activity, from 1910 into the 1920s, comprise the foundation of the vast storehouse of treasures and research materials that make up the Huntington Library today. Following Huntington's death in 1927, and through the present time, the library staff has continued to build upon, augment, and judiciously extend the holdings within the founder's stated collecting area of British and American civilization. Throughout those years, led by just five chief librarians (George Watson Cole, Leslie Bliss, Robert O. Dougan, Daniel H. Woodward, and William A. Moffett), the library has followed a dual plan: first, building to the strengths of the collections by filling in gaps, and second, developing and shaping the collecting policies into flexible guidelines that allow for both chronological and topical expansion of the holdings while remaining within the overall collecting fields.

Where has this dual approach taken the literary collections since the Huntington's early days? Curators continue to fill gaps in the rare-book holdings through focused purchases while they also embrace suitable opportunities to acquire titles by authors underrepresented or not at all present in the book stacks. In addition, the Huntington's collections have advanced in step with the twentieth century, with the ongoing acquisition of modern first editions for authors who were not yet well known or perhaps even alive during Huntington's life.

Similarly, for the literary manuscripts there is great breadth in the authors represented, and, for many of those authors, the collections exhibit much depth. As with the printed materials, the library seeks to build to the existing strengths of the manuscripts while at the same time extending the collections into modern literature of the latter part of this century. The *Guide to Literary Manuscripts in the Huntington Library,* published in 1979, provides a list of the holdings up to that year.

Given the vast size and scope of the Huntington's holdings and the impossibility of adequately describing such an array, the remainder of this discussion will focus primarily on the manuscripts, with highlights of related portions of the rare-book collections, and will cover the eighteenth through the twentieth centuries.

The quality and depth of the Huntington's holdings in both printed and manuscript materials for the eighteenth century have long been recognized, and perhaps the most stunning of all are the manuscripts for Jonathan Swift and Robert Burns. For Swift, a total of twenty-six literary manuscripts includes such treasures as "Anglo Angli," "On Poetry," and "A Letter to a Young Lady upon Her Marriage." For detailed descriptions of the Swift holdings, see George P. Mayhew, *Rage or Raillery* (San Marino: Huntington Library, 1967).

The Burns manuscripts are rich in autograph verses, numbering thirty-six separate manuscripts plus thirteen more poems written in a 1787 edition of Burns's *Poems, Chiefly in the Scottish Dialect . . .* (The Geddes Burns). Among the verses are "Behold, my love, how green the groves . . . ," "The Humble Petition of Bruar Water to the Noble Duke of Athole," "On a Scotch Bard, gone to the West Indies," "No Churchman am I for to rail and to write . . . ," and "On Scaring Some Water-Fowl in Loch Turit."

A major eighteenth-century collection is the sixty-nine-hundred-piece archive of Elizabeth Robinson Montagu (1720–1800), socially prominent author and intellectual. To her literary salons came such figures as Hannah More, Mrs. Vesey, Lord

Lyttelton, Horace Walpole, Samuel Johnson, Edmund Burke, David Garrick, and Sir Joshua Reynolds. Among Mrs. Montagu's acquaintances was her sometime social rival, Hester Thrale Piozzi, whose diary called *Thraliana* (1913) is one of the most important of the Huntington's manuscripts. In its six volumes, Mrs. Thrale followed Samuel Johnson's advice to "get a little book, and write in it all the little Anecdotes." She recorded observations about Johnson himself, as well as James Boswell, Goldsmith, and others. Johnson is represented in the Huntington manuscript collections. Along with twenty-six letters, there are six literary pieces, including three pages of a diary and a satiric poem, "Long-expected one and twenty," containing humorous advice to Sir John Slade, the nephew and ward of Henry Thrale, upon coming of age.

In the years since Henry Huntington's collecting days, as the library itself came of age, much of its literary acquisitions program has focused on materials from the nineteenth and twentieth centuries. Building on Henry Huntington's interest in the major figures in English literature, the library has added much to the material he had already acquired. The manuscript collections are especially strong for Victorian and earlier nineteenth-century novelists. The latter include Charlotte Brontë, for whom there are over one hundred letters, most written to her close friend Ellen Nussey, as well as poems by Charlotte and her sisters, Anne and Emily.

For Charles Dickens there is a superb collection of close to one thousand letters, many written to his friend and personal secretary William Henry Wills. They are joined by sets of original illustrations for *Nicholas Nickleby* (1838–1839), *Barnaby Rudge* (1841), and *The Old Curiosity Shop* (1840–1841), all by Hablot Knight Browne ("Phiz").

William Makepeace Thackeray occupies an almost equally prominent niche in the library stacks. Among the prose and verse manuscripts there are fragments of *The History of Pendennis* (1848–1850), parts of *Roundabout Papers* (1860–1863), and more than one hundred letters. Of perhaps the greatest interest are roughly two hundred Thackeray drawings, including nine for *Vanity Fair* (1847–1848) and seventy-eight for *Notes of a Journey from Cornhill to Grand Cairo* (1846).

An 1878 George Eliot notebook records her thoughts on such subjects as the roles of authors and the responsibilities of their art. Compiled after the publication of her major works, the notebook reflects the mature views of a successful novelist. A

1989 purchase brought to the Huntington six letters written by the youthful author in her first literary role as an assistant editor for the *Westminster Review*.

Extensive Robert Louis Stevenson holdings include several volumes of journals and notebooks, the manuscripts for *The Beach at Falesa* (1893) and *Kidnapped* (1886), the original diary on which *The Silverado Squatters* (1883) was based, and various notes on Hawaii and the South Seas, as well as ninety-one letters.

Nineteenth-century English poets, particularly the Romantics, are generously represented in the Huntington's collections. The Shelley notebooks, previously mentioned as part of the 1918 Bixby acquisition, constitute an exceptionally valuable source for analysis of the poet's habits of composition and revision. Along with these three small volumes are several verse manuscripts and twenty-eight letters. The excellent George Gordon, Lord Byron, material features corrected proof sheets for *Childe Harold* (1817), *The Corsair* (1814), and more than three dozen pieces of correspondence and verse. For William Wordsworth, in addition to a handful of verse manuscripts, there are 174 letters. Among the dozen manuscript verses and 53 letters by Samuel Taylor Coleridge is his 291-page commonplace book, whose contents include "On the Divine Ideas."

Of the English poets of the latter part of the century, the holdings are particularly strong for Alfred, Lord Tennyson, and the Brownings. Tennyson's letters number forty-three, and no fewer than thirty-six autograph manuscripts include "Break, break, break," portions of "Maud" and of "Idylls of the King," and forty-nine stanzas from "In Memoriam." The strength of the Elizabeth Barrett Browning manuscripts lies in the several notebooks and commonplace books filled with notes, drafts of poems and essays, and Greek exercises and translations. Of particular interest is her essay "A Glimpse into My Own Life and Literary Character." Complementing this material are forty-nine letters and twenty-six verse manuscripts. For Robert Browning, autograph verses including "Christmas Eve and Easter Day" and "How We Brought the Good News from Ghent to Aix" accompany more than two hundred letters.

The writings of the prolific poet and associate of the Pre-Raphaelites Algernon Swinburne may be found in abundance among the Huntington's manuscripts. A total of sixty-five prose and verse manuscripts include essays on Shelley, William Blake, and Dante Gabriel Rossetti, as well as the poems

"Atalanta in Calydon" and "The Tragedy of the Duke of Gandia."

Manuscripts by Swinburne's friend Dante Gabriel Rossetti and by other Pre-Raphaelite poets and artists came to the Huntington in 1913 and 1918 as part of the Quinn and Bixby collections and have been augmented over the years to become a superb collection of drawings, correspondence, and literary manuscripts. There are many hundreds of letters written by and between the Rossettis, William Holman Hunt and his family, Ford Madox Brown, Sir Edward Coley Burne-Jones, Sir John Everett Millais and Euphemia Millais, Ruskin (almost eight hundred), William Morris and his secretary Sir Sydney Carlyle Cockerell, and others. There is also an unpublished manuscript volume prepared by Frances C. Deverell entitled "The P.R.B. & Walter Howell Deverell: Letters from Dante Gabriel Rossetti & Others . . . ," with an introduction by William Michael Rossetti.

Among the literary manuscripts are poems by Dante Gabriel and Christina Rossetti and forty-six pieces by Morris, including *The Earthly Paradise* (1868–1870) in seven volumes, a translation of *The Odyssey* (1887), and two drafts of *The Glittering Plain* (1890). The Pre-Raphaelite manuscripts are rich in drawings, ranging from Ruskin's formal illustrations to quick sketches in the margins of letters. Morris's literary pieces, for example contain many drawings and doodles, including trial sketches for border designs. Perhaps the most engaging drawings are Burne-Jones's delightful self-caricatures in letters to friends. For complete details of all the Pre-Raphaelite manuscript holdings, see Sara S. Hodson, "A Checklist of Pre-Raphaelite Manuscripts in the Huntington Library," *Pre-Raphaelites in Context* (San Marino: Huntington Library, 1992).

Turning to American literary manuscripts of the nineteenth century, the holdings are richest for the years 1850 to the turn of the century, although significant authors from the earlier period are represented. For the novelist James Fenimore Cooper, there are drafts of several novels and stories. The material by William Cullen Bryant is richer, with almost fifty letters and over forty manuscript poems, among them "To a Waterfowl" and "To a Cloud." Also present is a draft of "Thanatopsis," in the hand of the poet's father Peter Bryant, who submitted several of his son's poems to the *North American Review,* unwittingly managing to conflate "Thanatopsis" and another poem on death into one piece under the single title.

Among more than fifty letters and manuscripts by Washington Irving is a letter written in 1852 to Nathaniel Hawthorne, expressing appreciation for a volume (presumed to be either *The House of Seven Gables* [1851] or *A Wonder Book* [1852]) Hawthorne had sent to Irving. Nearing the end of his life and career when he wrote the letter, Irving offered praise and encouragement to the younger author, whose writings he characterized as "among the very best that have issued from the American press."

Much of Hawthorne's life and works can be documented in the stacks of the Huntington. Autograph manuscripts, such as a preliminary draft of "Dr. Grimshawe's Secret" and notes for that story and others, accompany more than 200 letters, including 165 to his wife Sophia (replete with her expurgations) and additional family correspondence. Other Hawthorne letters include an 1861 epistle to the publisher and editor James T. Fields, in which Hawthorne harks back to Fields's discovery in a bureau drawer of the manuscript of *The Scarlet Letter* (1850) and his subsequent publication of the novel. Hawthorne attributes his success to Fields, writing, ". . . my literary success, whatever it has been or may be, is the result of my connection with you. Somehow or other, you smote the rock of public sympathy on my behalf, and a stream gushed forth in sufficient quantity to quench my thirst, though not to drown me."

The recipient of these words of tribute was a partner in the Boston firm of Ticknor and Fields and also the editor of the *Atlantic Monthly.* In his two literary roles Fields, along with his wife Annie, occupied a central post in the publishing, cultural, and social circles of New England throughout much of the second half of the nineteenth century. Indeed, his influence extended beyond his own region to encompass authors in England as well. The James T. Fields Collection (acquired from descendants in 1922, with additions in 1934, 1978, and 1986) at the Huntington reflects his wide influence, for a perusal of a list of the authors represented in its almost six-thousand pieces yields virtually every major and minor literary figure in New England, as well as a generous array of more-distant writers. Authors near and far found Fields to be a wise and shrewd, but also a tactful and eminently fair, editor and publisher, and those in and around Boston became close friends and associates of both James and Annie Fields. Henry Wadsworth Longfellow grew especially close to Fields, and the warmth of their friendship and of their literary relationship is easily perceived in the 124 letters from Longfellow to Fields.

Oliver Wendell Holmes, Sr., eminent physician and author as well as a founder of the *Atlantic*

The general reading room at the Huntington Library (by permission of the Henry E. Huntington Library and Art Gallery)

Monthly, occupied a house close by that of the Fieldses and was a frequent visitor. Manuscripts of Holmes's essays and other writings for the *Atlantic* complement 136 warm and fatherly letters written to James and Annie Fields. A partial list of other New England authors who abundantly populate the Fields collection with literary manuscripts and correspondence includes Emerson, Edward Everett Hale, Julia Ward Howe, William Dean Howells and James Russell Lowell (both of whom edited the *Atlantic Monthly*), Henry James, Charles Eliot Norton, Harriet Beecher Stowe, Celia Thaxter, and Whittier.

English authors whom the Fieldses met while abroad range from Mary Russell Mitford to Edward Lear, whose whimsical, self-deprecating wit emerges in an illustrated letter to "Mr. and Mrs. Discobbolos" depicting him and his cat Foss disembarking at Boston Harbor. The ever-impoverished Lear never actually made it to America, but Dickens did come for a lecture tour planned in large part by

James Fields. The English novelist quickly advanced from literary icon to friend, and the thirty-two letters from Dickens attest to the warmth of the relationship.

As might be expected for a couple whose circle of friends embraced prominent authors on both sides of the Atlantic, the Fieldses amassed an extensive library of inscribed or signed first editions. This library of over eight hundred volumes came to the Huntington in 1979 as an important complement to the Fields manuscript material and includes titles by virtually all of the individuals represented in the archive.

While the Fields collection can be considered a cornerstone of the Huntington's nineteenth-century literary holdings, there are many additional manuscripts that were acquired either as individual items or as parts of other collections. One of the premiere manuscripts in the Huntington's collections is Thoreau's *Walden* (1854), present in seven varying autograph drafts plus corrected proofs. *Walden* joins

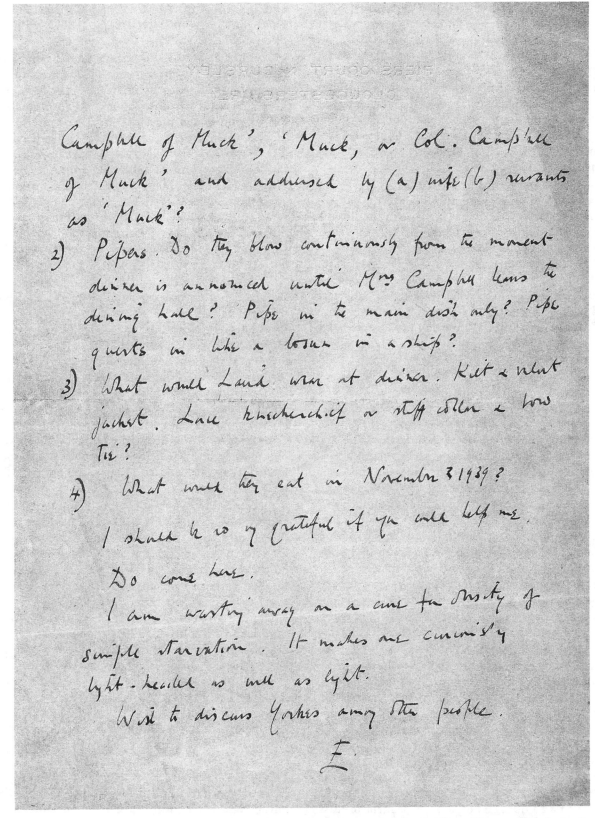

Campbell of Muck", 'Muck, or Col. Campbell of Muck' and addressed by (a) wife (b) servants as 'Muck'?

2) Pipers. Do they blow continuously from the moment dinner is announced until Mrs Campbell leaves the dining hall? Pipes in the main dish only? Pipe guests in like a bosun in a ship?

3) What would Laird wear at dinner. Kilt & velvet jacket. Lace handkerchief or stiff collar & bow Tie?

4) What would they eat in November 3 1939?

I should be so very grateful if you could help me.

Do come here.

I am wasting away on a cure for obesity of simple starvation. It makes one curiously light-headed as well as light.

Wish to discuss Yorkes among other people.

E.

Second page of a 22 August 1963 letter from Evelyn Waugh to John Patrick Balfour, third Baron Kinross, asking for details about Scottish battalion dinners that Waugh used in the Sword of Honor trilogy (Kinross Collection, by permission of the Henry E. Huntington Library and Art Gallery)

several dozen other Thoreau letters and manuscripts, including one complete and two partial drafts of *A Week on the Concord and Merrimack Rivers* (1849), an early draft of part 3 of *The Maine Woods* (1864), and 186 pages from his journal, to make the Huntington one of the principal centers for Thoreau research. This wealth of material grew even richer in 1991 with the arrival of a collection of correspondence for the Sewell family. Thoreau was a family friend, especially to Ellen Sewell, who declined his offer of marriage.

The literary treasures of the last century also extend to Poe. His autograph manuscript of "Annabel Lee" was a perennial favorite in the library exhibit hall, but scholars find more interesting such items as Poe's essay "About Critics and Criticism," an intriguing manuscript for its form, as well as its content, for it consists of small sheets of paper pasted end to end to make a roll 4 inches wide and 144 inches long. Other Poe pieces include a review of Eugene Sue's "The Wandering Jew," verses "To Mrs. M. L. S.," a series of twenty-five letters, and several portraits.

The career of Walt Whitman is represented by a varied group of manuscripts. The poet's voice is heard in some twenty verse manuscripts, including extracts from *Leaves of Grass,* and the essayist speaks in sixteen prose items. Among the latter are several pieces, such as the forty-plus pages of hospital notes, that relate to his experiences in the Civil War. Poet and essayist come together in Whitman's essay "Old Poets," written in 1890 for publication in the *North American Review*. The manuscript came to the Huntington in 1984 in the papers of Lloyd Stephens Bryce, who had been the editor of the *Review*. The Bryce Collection provides a bridge between east and west in nineteenth-century literary America, for also among its files is an autograph, much-corrected essay, "The Private History of the Jumping Frog Story," by Samuel Langhorne Clemens.

The Huntington possesses many manuscript items as well for Clemens's fellow western writers Ambrose Bierce and Bret Harte, but it is Clemens for whom the library's collections hold the greatest depth. The literary-manuscript pieces include the complete manuscript for *The Prince and the Pauper* (1882), chapter 7 of *A Tramp Abroad* (1880), and nine separate chapters and sections (portions in the hand of co-author Charles Dudley Warner) of *The Gilded Age* (1873). Of the extensive collection of signed first editions and other rare Clemens printed volumes, two stunning items (both acquired in 1989) are Clemens's own copy of *The Prince and the Pauper,* annotated by him for his public readings,

and his copy of *The Celebrated Jumping Frog of Calaveras County and Other Sketches* (1867), with the title story heavily revised by the author.

The Clemens letters constitute a particularly rich resource. No fewer than 105 letters (acquired from William Keeney Bixby in 1918) are written to Mary Mason Fairbanks, whom the youthful Clemens met on board the *Quaker City* en route to the Holy Land in 1867, a trip made famous in his book *The Innocents Abroad* (1869). Mrs. Fairbanks became his confidante, and he habitually addresses her as "Dear Mother" in his letters. This extraordinary correspondence affords an intimate look at the young author's life and early works, for he reveals his feelings for Olivia Langdon, the woman he would marry, and discusses many details about his current writing efforts.

Attaining a neat, and striking, parallel to the Clemens-Fairbanks correspondence, the Huntington received as a bequest in 1982 a collection of forty-four letters (with photographs) from Clemens to Frances Nunnally Winzer. The correspondence originates from another shipboard meeting, this one in 1907. Sailing to England to accept an honorary degree from Oxford University, Clemens, in the waning years of his life, met a young girl, Frances Nunnally, traveling with her mother. The two became friends, continued to correspond and to visit one another, and Clemens delivered the commencement address to Frances's high school graduating class.

Jack London occupies a place, not only at the center of California literature but also at the core of the Huntington's twentieth-century literary holdings for the state. The London Collection was acquired in several parts between 1925 and 1983 from London's widow Charmian and later from the Jack London Estate (now the Jack London Trust). Today the archive numbers more than thirty thousand manuscript drafts, letters, documents, photographs, and ephemeral items, making it by far the largest literary archive in the library. Over one thousand literary manuscripts encompass almost everything London wrote. A sampling of the many manuscripts and typescripts (nearly all bearing revisions) for his novels and other books includes *The Assassination Bureau, Ltd.* (1963), *Burning Daylight* (1910), *The Iron Heel* (1908), *John Barleycorn* (1913), *Martin Eden* (1909), *The Sea-Wolf* (1904, only a charred mass remaining, for the manuscript was burned in the San Francisco earthquake and fire of 1906), *Smoke Bellew* (1912), *South Sea Tales* (1911), *The Star-Rover* (1915), *The Valley of the Moon* (1912), and *White Fang* (1906). A June 1992 auction pur-

'If you want my opinion,' said Gwen Cellan-Davies, 'he's nothing but an old sham. I don't know how Rhiannon puts up with him, I really don't.'

Her husband was cutting the crusts off a ~~slice~~ *piece* of toast. 'Well, he seems to make a fair living out of what he ~~does~~. XThat makes him something considerably more than nothing but an old sham already, as far as I'm concerned. And there was ~~a~~ little ma- *the* tter of a CBE a couple of years ago. Of course - '

'Oh, successful enough indeed. Commercially. Financially. Selling Wales to the English and the Americans. Following the trail Dylan laid.'

'Which isn't such a bad - '

'On an altogether lower level of sensitivity and craftsmanship. No comparison in that way at all.'
'And a slightly lower level of consumption of alcohol.'

'As for that CBE, you get given one of those by going to London and hanging round the right people, ~~youxknowxthat~~ *don't be daft*. And ~~Rex~~ Reg ~~Griffiths~~ ~~Mannxxxxx~~ got one, only last year wasn't it so that'll show you how much they're worth. *A little pen-shifter like Reg .'*
'I ~~didn~~'t *had* heard ~~Rex~~ *Reg he* spent much time in London.'

'You know what I mean.'
a lot of things like that
Malcolm Cellan-Davies knew. He got up from the breakfast-table and went and refilled his teacup, adding a touch of skim milk and one of the new sweeteners that were supposed to leave no aftertaste. Back in his ~~chair~~ *seat* he placed between his left molars a *small* /prepared triangle of toast and ~~Mexican~~ ~~honey~~ *low-fat spread Mexican honey* and began crunching it gently but firmly. He had not bitten anything with his front teeth since losing a *top* middle one on a slice of ~~pork~~ ~~pie~~ *liver sausage* six years earlier, and the right-hand side of his mouth was a no-go area what with a hole in the lower jaw where stuff was always apt to lodge and a *disconcertingly* funny piece of gum *saw the* that seemed to have got detached from something and ~~just~~ waved/a-bout/ whenever it ~~had a~~ chance. His eyes slid off to the Western Mail and a report of the ~~Glamorgan-Kent~~ ~~match~~ *Neath-Llanelli game*

After lighting a cigarette Gwen went on in the same cheerful, almost vivacious style as before, 'Alun Weaver, CBE, is a old sham. At school with Dylan my eye. Oh, they were both at the Grammar right enough, but three years between them. He can't have known him. If he did, it means Dylan was taking an interest in boys three years younger, and I've heard a lot of things about him but that never. Muriel was telling

Page one from an early draft for Sir Kingsley Amis's The Old Devils *(AMS 82; by permission of the Henry E. Huntington Library and Art Gallery)*

chase brought a set of more than forty pages of notes for the novel *Adventure* (1911) to the Huntington, where it joins the autograph manuscript of the novel.

Among the manuscript short stories in the collection is "To Build a Fire," perhaps London's most famous story. The library has also acquired at auction in December 1991 an autograph letter dated 5 February 1902 from London to an editor for the magazine *Youth's Companion* (which first published "To Build a Fire") responding at length to the editor's questions about factual details in the story.

Extensive files of correspondence with book and magazine editors, publishing firms, agents, and filmmakers document London's full involvement in a wide range of literary enterprises, while letters from Eugene V. Debs, Alexander Irvine, and others deal with his socialist interests.

To complement the manuscripts and correspondence, the archive contains several thousand photographs, many the work of Jack or Charmian. Their eclectic camera work covers subjects from the London Ranch in California to scenes from Hawaii (most notably on Molokai) and Polynesia, to pictures from Jack's war-correspondent days in Korea (1902) and Mexico (1914). Rounding out the collections are London's information file and scrapbooks, along with a series of posters and broadsides.

The Jack London Library, which came to the Huntington in 1959, contains over five thousand volumes, many of them used by the author as source material for his writing. The wide range of subjects represented attests to London's lifelong hunger for knowledge. In particular, his interest in psychology and philosophy accounts for the presence of titles by William James, Otto Rank, Herbert Spencer, Friedrich Nietzsche, and Arthur Schopenhauer. One of the most important volumes is Carl Jung's *Psychology of the Unconscious* (1916), which London read just before his death, making more than three hundred notations in it.

With the London archive at the center of the Huntington's California literature holdings, the library has attracted several related satellite collections. Anna Strunsky Walling, whose papers came to the library in 1958–1962, had an affair with Jack London and cowrote with him *The Kempton-Wace Letters* (1903). The most significant material in this collection consists of 108 letters London wrote to Anna Strunsky during their literary collaboration — letters that, though overtly innocent, nevertheless clearly reveal the romantic attraction between the two.

With its long-held riches in English drama, including the Larpent and Kemble-Devonshire collections, the library now has complementary material for modern American (especially Californian) drama. There are archives for the screenwriters Zoë Akins, who won the Pulitzer Prize for her adaptation of Edith Wharton's "The Old Maid," and Sonya Levien, whose Oscar statuette, won for her *Interrupted Melody* (1955) script, lends a bit of glamour to the manuscript stacks. These two collections offer important and lively glimpses of the 1930s–1950s Hollywood film world and of the drama scenes in New York and Los Angeles. Further representation of drama in Los Angeles comes to the Huntington in the form of a collection of production files and well over six hundred scripts from the Mark Taper Forum theater in the city. One of the chief features of this annually growing archive is the presence of multiple, varying drafts of many of the plays. Along with a large collection of programs, scrapbooks, and other material from the Pasadena Playhouse, the Mark Taper Forum documents a significant part of the Los Angeles area's theater scene.

The two major twentieth-century American literary collections to come to the library within the last forty years were both purchased in 1975, and both have been augmented in the years following. The sixty-eight-hundred-piece Wallace Stevens archive includes the poet's literary manuscripts, among them a mostly complete run of his poems, plus four volumes of his journals, a notebook of early poems entitled "The Little June Book," and two commonplace notebooks with the titles "Poetic Exercises of 1948" and "Sur Plusieurs Beaux Sujets." Many literary and other major figures appear in the correspondence files, including Marianne Moore, Allen Tate, William Carlos Williams, Robert Frost, Jose Rodriguez Feo, Samuel French Morse, and Robert McAlmon. There are also family letters, especially to his wife Elsie, and letters between Stevens the insurance executive and his business colleagues. The archive is rounded out with several dozen photographs, his extensive files of genealogy correspondence, and his library of several hundred volumes. A 1989–1990 acquisition that complements the Stevens archive brought to the Huntington a collection of oral-history tapes and transcriptions created by Stevens scholar Peter Brazeau while interviewing Stevens's family, friends, and literary and business associates during the preparation of his oral-history biography of the poet.

The Conrad Aiken Collection numbers fifty-three hundred items. Among the literary manuscripts are his innovative autobiography *Ushant* (1952) and *The Clerk's Journal* (1971), an extended poem written in Aiken's youth but first published late in his life. Also in the archive is an early draft of Malcolm Lowry's *Ultramarine* (1933), with Aiken's autograph revisions. Although there is a rich cache of literary pieces, the real strength of the collection lies in the correspondence files. Included are scores of letters to and from Mary Hoover Aiken, Malcolm Cowley, John Davenport, Seymour Lawrence, Malcolm Lowry, Tate, and Louis Untermeyer. There are smaller runs of letters for a host of other literary figures, plus roughly two hundred photographs and Aiken's several-hundred-volume library. One of the finest of the series of letters, sixty-five (1914–1963) to Aiken, comes from T. S. Eliot. The early letters contain verses by Eliot, along with his comments about his own writings and about Aiken's.

While the 1970s saw the Huntington acquire heavily in modern American literature, in the 1980s the library entered more significantly into collecting twentieth-century British literature. Already in the collections were important manuscript holdings for James Joyce (including partial manuscripts of *Pomes Penyeach* [1927] and of the Penelope portion of *Ulysses* [1922]) and William Butler Yeats (over one hundred letters and his copy of the 1899 edition of *Poems,* extensively corrected for a new printing). New purchases in 1980 brought to the Huntington groups of letters by Bloomsbury group members and associates Vanessa Bell, her brother Thoby Stephen, husband Clive Bell, and son Julian Bell, all complementing a collection of letters by Leonard Woolf acquired in 1975.

A sizable acquisition in 1980 consists of the archive of John Patrick Balfour, third Baron Kinross. A writer and journalist and one of the Bright Young Things at Oxford in the 1930s, Kinross knew vast numbers of people and became a confidant to a good many of them. Thus, the extensive correspondence files constitute the strength of this collection. Of special interest are the letters from his fellow Oxford students, the writers Evelyn Waugh, Cyril Connolly, Christopher Sykes, and Sir John Betjeman.

Betjeman appears not only in the Kinross archive but also in a collection for the English novelist Sir Kingsley Amis, whose papers came to the Hunt-

ington in 1987, with further additions in 1992. At nearly four hundred items, the Amis collection is rich in drafts of his novels and stories, including the first draft of *Jake's Thing* (1978) and a synopsis, notebook, and several drafts of Amis's 1986 Booker Prize–winning novel, *The Old Devils*. In the correspondence files, a remarkable series of 114 lively, witty letters from Robert Conquest discusses personal and literary matters and offers up scores of bawdy limericks composed by Conquest and Amis.

The acquisition of the Kingsley Amis Collection extends the library's literary holdings to the present day, following the legacy begun with extraordinary vision by Henry Huntington nearly seventy-five years ago. The library staff faces a continuing challenge, as curators struggle to apply an often insufficient acquisitions budget to the ever-rising prices of the rare books and manuscripts market. Chief curator of rare books Alan Jutzi and chief curator of manuscripts Mary Robertson, assisted by specialist curators, confront new challenges in updating the collecting policy, for the Huntington must seek appropriate strategies to adapt to a changing and increasingly diverse society yet remain consistent with the original acquisitions focus. To meet these two challenges will be to exacerbate a third: the inevitable, and currently urgent, need for additional building space to house the burgeoning collections. President Robert A. Skotheim heads a developmental staff in a major endowment drive, whose success is crucial to the institution's ability to continue and expand its programs. Library Director William A. Moffett will guide the library as it seeks to increase its acquisitions resources, automate its cataloguing and other operations, and plan for expansion of the physical plant. Under the leadership of director of research Robert C. Ritchie, the Huntington awards research fellowships to more than seventy-five scholars per year. Among the sponsors of research awards is the W. M. Keck Foundation, which grants fellowships to young scholars. As the Huntington looks back on the history of its first seventy-five years, it also looks forward with anticipation to the next, knowing the library will undergo much change but confident that it will meet its many challenges and that it will remain faithful to its mission of collecting and making available literary and historical treasures.

The James Jones Society

George Hendrick
University of Illinois at Urbana-Champaign

The literary society devoted to the work of a single author provides a forum where individuals with varying interests in an author can join together to promote study and awareness and share information. Not exclusively academic, a society joins the scholar, the collector, and the fan in the appreciation of a writer's work. The James Jones Society is one of the newest of these groups and is representative of their makeup and goals.

The James Jones Society was organized on 16 November 1991 in Robinson, Illinois. Jones was born in Robinson in 1921 and lived there with his parents, Dr. and Mrs. Ramon Jones, until 1939, when he joined the U.S. Army. He was in Hawaii when World War II began, and he was wounded on Guadalcanal in 1943. He was returned to the United States to recuperate and was discharged from the army in 1944. He then moved into the Robinson home of Harry and Lowney Handy; Mrs. Handy was his teacher and sometime lover. He completed the still unpublished novel "They Shall Inherit the Laughter," but Maxwell Perkins at Scribners had doubts that this first novel was ready for publication. Jones proposed to Perkins an idea to write a novel about the peacetime army, and Perkins encouraged this new work. Jones began work in 1946 on what was to become *From Here to Eternity*. Finally completed in 1950 and published in 1951, the novel was a critical and financial success.

With some of the proceeds from his book royalties and the sale of film rights, Jones helped Lowney Handy found a writers' colony in nearby Marshall, Illinois. The purpose of the colony was "to develop and further creative writing in the United States, and in connection therewith to operate a home or colony to assist writers and authors. . . ." Lowney had her own inimitable way of teaching those who came to the colony. As John Bowers has written, Lowney was influenced by:

eclectic sources – from Far Eastern religious tracts, Tom Uzzell's *Narrative Techniques,* a smattering of modern fiction, the Bible, old wives tales, folk art, family

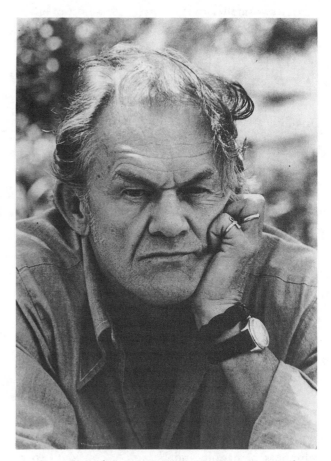

James Jones (photograph © 1985 by Nancy Crampton)

lore, and God knows what else. She churned up her sources and came out with her own peculiar philosophy about life and art. . . .We neophyte writers at the colony . . . copied word for word the prose of those masters in her favor (Hemingway, Fitzgerald, Dos Passos, and Tess Schlesinger) and we ate cottage cheese every day and were encouraged to hook ourselves up to enemas, something that had a curious Victorian twist to it.

Lowney's system of teaching was praised by some and called bizarre by others. By 1952 she had fifteen students, and over the years some flourished under her direction and began to publish, though none were to be as well known as Jones. Jones built an expensive home adjacent to the colony and took an active interest in the colony and its students in the years during which he was writing his much-maligned *Some Came Running* (1957).

Jones married Gloria Mosolino in 1957, broke his relationship with Lowney Handy, and departed from Marshall, never to return. From 1958 to 1974 Jones and his wife and children lived in Paris. All his life Jones continued his interest in young writers, giving them advice, reading their manuscripts, loaning them money, and writing to publishers in their behalf. The Joneses returned to the United States in 1974, and James died of congestive heart failure in 1977.

After leaving Illinois, Jones published *The Pistol* (1959), *The Thin Red Line* (1962), *Go to the Widow-Maker* (1967), *The Ice-Cream Headache and Other Stories* (1968), *The Merry Month of May* (1971), *A Touch of Danger* (1973), *Viet Journal* (1974), *WWII* (1975), and *Whistle* (1978).

During his lifetime some critics charged that Jones sold his literary talents for commercial success, that he had "a commonplace mind," "an antiquated approach to fiction," and a slovenly style. In recent times there has been renewed interest in Jones and his work. It began with Willie Morris's *James Jones: A Friendship* (1978) and continued with James R. Giles's *James Jones* (1981), which contains high critical praise for Jones's war trilogy, calling it "our most important fictional treatment of U.S. involvement in World War II." George Garrett's *James Jones* appeared in 1984 and was followed by Frank MacShane's *Into Eternity: The Life of James Jones* in 1985. The 1984 television documentary *James Jones: Reveille to Taps* was produced by J. Michael Lennon and Jeffrey Van Davis. George Hendrick edited *To Reach Eternity: The Letters of James Jones* in 1989; Thomas J. Wood and Meredith Keating's *James Jones in Illinois: A Guide to the Handy Writers' Colony Collection* also appeared that year. Giles and Lennon edited the important *James Jones Reader* in 1991.

Morris, Garrett, and others have pointed out the artistic virtues of Jones's critically maligned works such as *Some Came Running* and *Go to the Widow-Maker,* and the critical reassessment of Jones is certain to continue. Garrett's conclusion is likely to be repeated and expanded on in various ways by critics to come: "Boy and man, Jones never lost his energetic interest, his continual curiosity, the freshness of his vision. It was these qualities, coupled with the rigor of his integrity, which defined the character of his lifework."

Libraries now hold many of the important Jones manuscripts and papers. The major collections are at Yale University, Princeton University, and the University of Texas at Austin; the Handy Writers' Colony collection is at Sangamon State University, and the original manuscript of *From Here to Eternity* is at the University of Illinois at Urbana-Campaign.

In light of this scholarly and popular interest in Jones, a group decided to form a James Jones society, and several planning sessions were held in Robinson and on the campus of Sangamon State University in Springfield, Illinois. Two hundred of Jones's friends and admirers met in November of 1991 at Lincoln Trail College to celebrate the seventieth anniversary of his birth in Robinson and the fortieth anniversary of the publication of *From Here to Eternity*. Jones had been at Schofield Barracks, Hawaii, on 7 December 1941, so the fiftieth anniversary of the Japanese attack on Pearl Harbor was also commemorated. Later that day, at dinner, the group founded the James Jones Society, a mix of scholars, community people, and others who read James Jones or enjoy the films made from his novels.

The society holds annual meetings and publishes a newsletter about the life and work of Jones and the activities of the society. It plans to encourage critical and biographical studies of Jones and to award scholarships to students who are or will be participants in the creative-writing course at Lincoln Trail College. In addition the society will sponsor a major fellowship program for promising new writers of fiction. Current plans are to award the first scholarship and fellowship in 1993.

The James Jones Society has an eleven-member board of directors. Kaylie Jones, Jones's daughter and a novelist, is one of these directors and is particularly interested in the fellowship program. Gloria Jones, Jones's widow, and Jamie Jones, son of the writer, are ex officio members of the society. The president of the society for 1991–1992 was George Hendrick, professor of English at the University of Illinois at Urbana-Champaign. J. Michael Lennon, professor of English and vice-president for academic affairs at Wilkes University, was elected president in 1992. Membership dues are ten dollars annually; contributions to the society are tax deductible.

Inquiries about forthcoming activities of the society and information about joining the organization are available from Ms. Juanita Martin, treasurer of the James Jones Society, Lincoln Trail College, Route 3, Box 82A, Robinson, Illinois, 62454-9524.

Mark Twain on Perpetual Copyright: The House of Lords, London, 3 April 1900

On 3 April 1900, on one of the lecture trips he took to Great Britain during the last decades of his life, Samuel Langhorne Clemens testified before a select committee on copyright law of the British House of Lords. In this previously unrecorded testimony, discovered by William Cagle and his staff at the Lilly Library, Indiana University, Clemens set forth what he considered to be the final improvement copyright law needed "in order to become perfect." He was promoting perpetual copyright as opposed to the British copyright protection proposed to be limited to the life of the author and thirty years.

LORDS PRESENT:
Viscount Knutsford.
Lord Monkswell.
Lord Thring.
Lord Farrer.
Lord Avebury.

The LORD MONKSWELL in the Chair.

Mr. SAMUEL CLEMENS, is called in; and Examined, as follows:

LORD MONKSWELL: You are the author who writes under the name of Mark Twain?

MARK TWAIN: Yes.

LORD MONKSWELL: I understand you desire to make a statement to the Committee and then to take a discussion on your views as a whole?

MARK TWAIN: If you please.

LORD MONKSWELL: Will you do so, if you please?

MARK TWAIN: I think that the copyright laws of England and America are now so nearly what they ought to be that they need only one commercially trifling but morally gigantic amendment in order to become perfect; that emendation, I think, would be the removal of the 42 years' limit and the return to perpetual copyright. I have called this a commercially trivial change, and I will presently try to show that that is a just and rational estimate of it; but for the moment I wish to say a word upon the reasons advanced in justification of limited copyright. One of them I am persuaded is fallacious: it is the one which makes a distinction between an author's property and real estate, and pretends that the two are not created, produced or acquired in the same way, and that this warrants a differing treatment of the two by the law. It is my conviction that this is untrue, that the source whence they proceed is the same in both cases. By the usual phrasing a book is merely a "combination of ideas"; that that is but a nebulous thing upon which to base a property right, and that it is therefore just and fair that such a property right should not be permanent. And yet we know quite well that there is no property of any kind which is not the result of the application of some man's intellectual gifts; some man's labour of brain as well as of hand, some man's successful combination of ideas. The man who purchases a landed estate had to earn the money by the superiority of his intellect at the bar, in trade, in manufactures, in combining railway systems or other industry. His land is what a book is, the result of his brain work; a combination and exploiting of ideas. There is no difference between the two, they both stand for the same thing. He has acquired his land by the fruit of his brain, and the law concedes that it is his, that it is his property, not a mere temporary loan, and that he may transmit it to his posterity for ever, they to hold it and enjoy it unrebuked. All property, of whatsoever kind, all wealth, stands for the same thing, — some man's successful exercise of his intellectual forces. But the law breaks the rule in the case of a book. Why? The answer is, "For reasons of public policy." I frankly admit that that is quite sufficient answer if it can be shown that it is *sound* public policy, and confers a valuable benefit upon the nation, a benefit considerable enough to largely compensate for the hardship it puts upon the author and his heirs. It is my conviction that a copyright limit is not sound policy, and that it confers no large benefit upon anyone. It is believed by a great many people that when a copyright dies the law

Mark Twain surrounded by children on shipboard, circa 1905. The boy in the dresslike garment is Morley Kennerley, who later became a London publisher (Collection of the late Jean Kennerley).

gives the book to the public as a free gift. This is not so, it merely gives the author's profit in it to the public; the profit of the publishers remains theirs. That is another unfair discrimination. The 42 year limit *kills* a fairly popular book now and then, which could have had a longer life, but for the limit. Half-a-dozen publishers jump for the book at once; they glut the market for six weeks with ultra cheap editions; as a rule they all get their fingers burnt; that book sinks out of sight, and the public may have to go without it for 10 years. One cannot resurrect any but a very strong book after a trance like that. Out of every hundred tons of books sold, about 99 of them are "light literature." Then, to benefit the nation substantially, you would need to furnish it the 99 tons at as cheap a rate as possible; the other ton is not of consequence. My works are light literature — very light, many unthinking thinkers think they think. Now, in my experience, copyright, or the absence of it, does not affect my books here. The cheap edition very soon follows the high-priced

one, and the cheap price is just the same upon the books which lack English copyright as it is upon those which possess it. These books are closely packed with printed matter, and are sold at two shillings. The destruction of the copyright could hardly cheapen them more — certainly not enough to make the empire lose its sleep for joy over the windfall. I believe that book prices follow the natural laws of trade, and that the public demand determines the prices, not the publisher, and not parliamentary legislation. A publisher will make any honourable sacrifice that has money in it. He does not differ from the rest of this thoughtful human race; he works his intellect and combines his ideas in the interest of the landed estate, endowed with perpetual copyright, which he means to buy some day. If Shakespeare were restricted to a single publisher, to day, on perpetual copyright, you could have him in 25 styles, at 25 prices, just as at present; and if the public wanted him at sixpence, there would be enough of the public to make the sixpence profitable to the publisher, and that as yet unknown edition would appear. Permanent cheap editions of deathless books would be assured by perpetual copyright. I judge so from human nature and from a certain impressive object lesson which is in my mind. I believe there is only one book in the world which has been justly and fairly treated since Queen Anne's time. The English Bible is the only existing book, so far as I know, which possesses the fair and honourable grace of perpetual copyright. Has that deprived the public of marvellously cheap editions? You will grant that it has not. Now then as to the value to the nation of terminable copyright. Is it great enough to make it worth the trouble of Parliament to continue it? When the State sets the example of disregarding a commonly accepted moral law in the material interests of the public, it should make sure that the commercial advantage accruing to the people shall be great enough to richly compensate the injury done the nation's honour, the blunting of its sense of justice, should it not? It is my conviction that the State ought seldom to lower the standard of morals; that indeed it ought never to lower it except after deep and prayerful consideration of the possible results, and the full persuasion that the money gained will be worth more than the morals; and it is my thought that whenever the State lowers the standard and finds later that the dereliction is not paying a sufficient profit above cost, it would be merely plain business wisdom to cease from propagating that offence and seek another one. My plea for a return to perpetual copyright is merely this, that terminable copyright does not take pennies enough out of the pockets of an author's heirs to make the thing worth while. Practically there is no substantial advantage in it for anybody; if the State were going to take China, I should say, "That is an immense matter, and the financial grandeur of the seizure justifies it, — let the morals go, China will be better off than she was before, the general world will be advantaged, and there's plenty of morals left." But the taking of pennies is quite another thing; there is no dignity in it, and, what is perhaps of more consequence, there is no money in it. I believe that even the most general and cursory glance at the facts will indicate this. How many Britons are there whose books, issued in the present century, have outlived the 42 year limit? By what I conceive to be a rather liberal estimate, I place the number of 42 year immortals at 65. Shall we guess that out of the works of each of them 10 volumes lived the 42 years? It is a total of 650 limit surviving volumes in 100 years. Shall we allow each in its old age an annual sale of 1,000 copies? And shall we allow on an average a

royalty of 1*s*. 6*d*. on each volume? It is an annual total of about 10*l*. royalty upon each volume. Total per year to each of 65 families of orphans, 100*l*. Total annual income to the 65 families from the 650 volumes, 6,500*l*. There is not a professional man of repute in London who cannot earn the whole of it in a year. It is this trifling sum, and only this trifling sum, which by grace of limited copyright the richest nation in the earth annually takes out of the pockets of the children of the little handful of illustrious men who in the stretch of a century have done so great and acknowledged a share in building the British power, broadening the world's civilization, and spreading wide the glory of the English name. Is it matter for pride, is it matter for congratulation, that this ancient and mouldy wrong should be suffered to continue? Great Britain issues 5,000 new books per year. None of these, except 6 1/2 volumes, need the Committee's help. The others will never reach within a thousand miles of the 42 year limit. They are amply and even superfluously and extravagantly protected. The mighty bulk of them will be dead and gone inside of five years. A few of them will live fifteen, others will live ten; but if you average the life of the 5,000 books straight through, a copyright limit of six months would answer all their necessities. The Committee is in no way concerned about their salvation; no legislation could achieve it. The whole batch can be set aside as being perfectly safe under the existing law or any other, for that matter. The only real question, the only important question, the only high and worthy question, as it seems to me is, how to save the 6 1/2 volumes. So strictly is it narrowed down! In a century 650 volumes out of a total of 500,000 are produced which outlive the 42 years. It is an average of 6 1/2 volumes a year. Legislation can save them from harm. Perpetual copyright can save them from hurt and do them honour. There was never a time in history when a five year limit would not have amply protected 99 books out of every hundred published. Consequently there was never a time when a time limit of any kind was worth considering or establishing. In the present excellent condition of the copyright laws, I feel that there is but the one question of great and commanding importance left: What shall be done about the 6 1/2 books a year? Is it a small thing? It looks so, my Lords, but it is just what Parliaments have been worrying over for 200 years without suspecting it perhaps. If nothing at all is done about it no publisher need care, for in his case the matter of the half dozen books is of no consequence, his guild issues 5,000 new books a year, and that is where its profit lies, the 6 1/2 books are of no consequence, they cannot discoverably affect the guild's pocket. No one in the whole earth is interested in what may be done concerning the 6 1/2 volumes, except the widows and orphans of the men that write them. If Parliament should so amend the law as to say that every book shall have copyright from the day of its issue, without term or limit so long as the book is kept in print and on sale, and for two or three years after it has been allowed to get out of print by any accident (that lapse to extinguish its copyright), that amendment could affect the pocket of two-thirds of one whole author every year, and the pockets of a total of 65 authors and their heirs in a century. My Lords, I trust you will grant the crucial importance of the amendment suggested – the return to perpetual copyright, the abolition of the time limit, in the interest of the widows and orphans of the authors of the 6 1/2 books, and in the interest of the 65 writers who in a century do approximately as high service in cheering, instructing, and entertaining the nation, and in pushing its moral, commercial, and political advancement as do the Admirals and Generals who defend it, and whom the State justly rewards with titles and estates, which descend with the people's grateful approval and applause to their children. In America when slavery had existed two centuries, and a multitude equalling the population of the London of to-day, were subjects of the lash, with none to plead their cause but a handful of courageous and devoted but ineffectual agitators in the north, a woman wrote a book which roused the nation's sleeping humanity, and brought on that explosion which swept slavery out of existence, set those millions free, and purged clean the American name from the shamefullest reproach that can rest upon any land claiming a place in the world's civilizations. The authoress is dead, the copyright is dead, the children live, the book lives, and the profits go to the publishers.

LORD MONKSWELL: The Committee are much obliged to you; but when I had a conversation with you upon the subject you suggested that copyright if it was perpetual should be subject to some condition as to the price of the book, and its being kept in print. Do you still adhere to that condition?

MARK TWAIN: Only in this way: You remember what a difficulty we found in arranging that; I mean to avoid evasions. I thought it all over and I cannot think of any other way. What I suggested that day was that at the end of any limit you please,

you, the author, must provide an edition at one-eighth the ordinary price of the book as before, and he must keep it always where the public can get it at that price, one-eighth; and that whenever for one year he should allow that book to be out of print, that loses him his copyright; it is extinguished. That is what we spoke of; but you suggested yourself that it would be very difficult to determine that feature.

LORD MONKSWELL: But is there not another difficulty about it, namely, that for different kinds of books you would want a very different kind of proportion. If you had a second term of perpetual copyright subject to a condition of that kind, would it not be better to put it in the hands of some authority to settle what the price of the book should be, rather than to say that in every case it ought to be one-eighth?

MARK TWAIN: Yes, I think so. I think that would be much better.

LORD MONKSWELL: Then in what you said about the public you appear to think that the public are really hardly interested in this matter of perpetual copyright even in the case of the 6 1/2 good books that survive the century. But it occurs to me that in the case of Lord Tennyson's poems, the public is very much interested in them indeed. Some books would be published very much cheaper if there was no copyright?

MARK TWAIN: Yes, but not cheaper than they would be if there was perpetual copyright.

LORD MONKSWELL: Why not?

MARK TWAIN: For this reason; that if you have the whole trade in your own hand you can afford to make ventures, which you could not do if anybody can step in and take advantage of the venture you have made. I give this instance, among others, as one that occurs to me, at any rate. In 1873 I was in Edinburgh and Mr. Black showed me a little sixpenny Sir Walter Scott that he was issuing, and he said he was selling three quarters of a million of those in a year. I asked him how he could do it, publishing them at that price, and he said that it was because they were protected by notes made, perhaps, in Sir Walter's last years, and the copyright on those notes was still alive. But he said, when the copyright on those notes dies this whole thing is thrown over to the public, and without doubt no man can afford to publish at sixpence.

Brought from the Lords 8 August 1900.

R E P O R T

FROM THE

SELECT COMMITTEE OF THE HOUSE OF LORDS

ON THE

COPYRIGHT BILL [H.L.]

AND THE

COPYRIGHT (ARTISTIC) BILL [H.L.];

TOGETHER WITH THE

PROCEEDINGS OF THE COMMITTEE,

MINUTES OF EVIDENCE,

AND APPENDIX.

Session 1900.

Ordered, by The House of Commons, *to be Printed,*
8 August 1900.

LONDON:
PRINTED FOR HER MAJESTY'S STATIONERY OFFICE,
BY WYMAN AND SONS, LIMITED, FETTER LANE, E.C.

And to be purchased, either directly or through any Bookseller, from
EYRE AND SPOTTISWOODE, EAST HARDING STREET, FLEET STREET, E.C., **and**
32, ABINGDON STREET, WESTMINSTER, S.W.; or
JOHN MENZIES & CO., ROSE STREET, EDINBURGH, and
90, WEST NILE STREET, GLASGOW; or
HODGES, FIGGIS, & CO., LIMITED, 104, GRAFTON STREET, DUBLIN.

1900.

377.

Title page for the hearings of the committee in the House of Lords in which Mark Twain argued for
the restoration of perpetual copyright

LORD MONKSWELL: But at the same time in the case of a great poet like Lord Tennyson you do find, even where the copyright has a very long term still to run, that the editions published by the publishers are not cheap editions?

MARK TWAIN: I have a cheap edition, I do not know just how cheap it is, but the whole of it is there in one volume in small type, but clear and clean. I got it I do not know how many years ago, but it had everything in it, and I should not say it cost more than a shilling. I do not know how the thing can be cheaper than that.

LORD MONKSWELL: Then this Bill, as you know, does propose to lengthen the term a great deal; I suppose there would be very few widows and orphans of an original author (at all events, if he happened to live to be an old man) who would survive the copyright limit if we had a term of life and 30 years?

MARK TWAIN: Yes, I quite see that; and the other thing is mere sentiment, which has no business in business, I suppose; and the belief that I have that this rule is under the government of the common law – the ordinary law – that where a man has a business which is all his own, and he finds that there is a great big class that he has not got into his toils yet, he will find out some way to get it in – he will seek for it. You see when they publish these cheap editions how ephemeral they are. You can get this cheap edition when the copyright is dead for six months; you can get it for a year perhaps, and you will then hunt a long time, in some cases, before you can get that cheap edition again. It interrupts the whole thing; breaks into it.

VISCOUNT KNUTSFORD: I do not quite understand who is to decide when the cheap edition is wanted; you make it a condition for perpetual copyright that there should be a cheap edition published?

MARK TWAIN: Yes.

VISCOUNT KNUTSFORD: I put aside the question of price because I think you agree with Lord Monkswell that it would be impossible to fix a price and say it must be one-eighth; but what I want to know is, who is to decide when the cheap edition is wanted?

MARK TWAIN: It would not be decided when a cheap edition was wanted. As I had the matter in my mind, it was merely this: that if you take an ordinary book and propose to make this cheap edition, you can make it for next to nothing almost.

VISCOUNT KNUTSFORD: I do not think you see the point; I have not put my point clearly to you. I am not saying that you cannot make a cheap edition pay, quite the contrary; but you say that you are not to have perpetual copyright in a book which has come out, say, in three volumes, unless you are prepared to make a cheap edition; who is to decide when you are to make that cheap edition, or when such cheap edition is wanted?

MARK TWAIN: That comes under something that was not in the statement which I have made. That was a suggestion of a copyright limit; and whatever limit you place, 50 years, or 1,000 years, or 20 years, or anything you please, at the expiration of that limit, then, this cheap edition must come.

VISCOUNT KNUTSFORD: Then if I publish a book dealing with any period of English history, do you mean that, in order to secure perpetual copyright in it, I must at the end of some limit – say 10 years – which is to be fixed, I suppose, by Parliament?

MARK TWAIN: Certainly.

VISCOUNT KNUTSFORD: I must publish a cheap edition?

MARK TWAIN: Yes; and so long as you keep that cheap edition actually on sale where people could get to it, your copyright is preserved, and for one year afterwards.

VISCOUNT KNUTSFORD: Then it is to be for the Parliament of any country to decide what is the time within which you are to publish a cheap edition?

MARK TWAIN: I should say that one year or two years after the expiration of that time limit this edition must appear.

VISCOUNT KNUTSFORD: I do not suppose you will find two people agree about the time limit. Publishers would certainly very strongly disagree with authors. If the publisher would like it, as would be very probable, postponed, it might answer for the author (it depends upon the class of his book) to have a cheap edition very soon?

MARK TWAIN: The publisher might be interested in a very narrow limit; he might indeed. He is interested in perpetual copyright, because if he transacts his business properly he and his heirs get that book and go on publishing it.

VISCOUNT KNUTSFORD: Surely, considering the extraordinary difference in books, that whereas you may have a book that is very easily printed and very easily put out, you may have a book full of engravings that is very expensive, or a book like Herbert Spencer's books, that has only been evolved by great research and long consideration, do you put these books on the same footing?

MARK TWAIN: Precisely.

VISCOUNT KNUTSFORD: Parliament is to say that a cheap edition is in all cases to be published within ten years?

MARK TWAIN: Just the same. I should say that if Parliament chose to make some differences regarding books where illustrations were absolutely necessary, I should suppose that it could be done; but where the illustrations were not absolutely necessary I would not require that they should be put into that cheap edition.

VISCOUNT KNUTSFORD: I do not know about legislation in the United States, but I am sure you would never get legislation of that kind in this country or abroad. As you know, there is no country that has perpetual copyright. We are assimilating our law now to the laws of the continent, Germany and France, by making the term of copyright until death, and then a certain number of years afterwards?

MARK TWAIN: Yes.

VISCOUNT KNUTSFORD: You see a great many people, and many of the most eminent; have you ever planted out this doctrine of perpetual copyright on them and seen how it is taken?

MARK TWAIN: Oh, yes; now and then I have. Do you mean with publishers, or with whom?

VISCOUNT KNUTSFORD: I would say with many of the eminent people you have met, and also with legislators?

MARK TWAIN: I have never known anyone to object when he came to consider how small an affair it was; that it was no use to rob any man unless you can rob him largely, and make it respectable in that way.

VISCOUNT KNUTSFORD: We do not think that we rob any man if we give him life and 30 years afterwards?

MARK TWAIN: You give him his real estate for a longer time than that.

VISCOUNT KNUTSFORD: I think it is a question whether you do not rob him more by insisting on cheap editions within 10 years for certain books. Your difficulty is that you do not take into consideration the different classes of books?

MARK TWAIN: I will make this answer to that: that all books shall be exactly alike, and all shall be issued at one-eighth; and that when a man has written a book which he cannot afford, and the publisher cannot afford, to issue at one-eighth of the price because of the cost of the engravings and such things, that copyright dies, it dies there and then; and then you have done a far more just thing than you have if you take away everybody's copyright at the end of the limit.

VISCOUNT KNUTSFORD: It seems to me that you cannot possibly work a greater injustice upon the author of a book than to take away his copyright, because it does not pay for him to publish a cheap edition in a certain number of years?

MARK TWAIN: It might pay him exceedingly well.

VISCOUNT KNUTSFORD: You may think so, but he may not think so, and it may as a matter of fact not be so. How about a cheap edition of Herbert Spencer's works, for instance?

MARK TWAIN: A cheap edition of Herbert Spencer's works is perfectly easy to accomplish; they are not filled with engravings; it is the mere type of the matter which can be reproduced at one-eighth without any loss to anybody.

LORD MONKSWELL: Would you sell any of Herbert Spencer's works, would you sell enough; because there are only a certain number of persons who want to buy a work of that kind, and therefore the price must be considerable to enable the publisher to publish at a profit?

MARK TWAIN: Let us consider then two things: Herbert Spencer at the full price. How much does that pay in a year; does it pay 100*l.*? You do not want to put it any lower than that. If it pays 100*l.*, he has only to take that 100*l.* and turn it into a cheap edition, and if the people do not want the cheap edition, they need not take it; but if they want it they take it, and that cheap edition will pay both publisher and author, and pay them a nice profit too.

LORD MONKSWELL: But surely Herbert Spencer and the publisher together know their own business; and I should have thought if the publisher refuses during copyright, which is a considerable term, to publish a cheap edition of Herbert Spencer's works, it is because he supposes it would not pay?

MARK TWAIN: That is exactly why he does not do it. But the argument for a limited copyright has always been founded upon a fallacy, and that is that at the end of the limit the book is given as charity to the nation, which is not true. It is nothing but the author's share in it which is given as a charity to the public; the publisher's share in it remains just as good as before.

LORD MONKSWELL: But I thought that you rather agreed with me that it would be impossible to adopt the one-eighth, because for one reason it would be almost impossible for anyone to decide what the original unit was, the first, second, or third edition; and for another reason, that you must have different prices for different books. I will read you what Herbert Spencer said when he was examined by the Copyright Commission of which Lord Knutsford was a member. On the 6th of March 1878 he said "I have calculated what length of time it has taken to repay my losses" (he had previously told the Commission that he had published at a loss and was out of profit for a long time) "and find they were repaid in 1874; that is to say, in 24 years after I began I retrieved my position." It appears to me that this conditional copyright of yours would be absolutely of no use to Herbert Spencer, and that under your system of copyright he never would

have got back his losses, because you would only have given him 20 years in which to do so?

MARK TWAIN: You cannot make a law to save your lives, no Parliament ever existed that could make a law which did not inflict a hardship upon somebody. But this hardship would be inflicted on six men only in a century, and not on any more.

LORD MONKSWELL: Are not those exactly the six men whom we want to protect from hardship?

MARK TWAIN: The law may want to protect them from hardship, but the law cannot do it. In the case of Herbert Spencer you propose to destroy his copyright with a limit, and whether you make the limit long or short you are apt to hit somebody and cut somebody's legs from under him by that Act.

LORD MONKSWELL: My point is that you do manage to give Herbert Spencer some remuneration for his very important work, by giving him a long term of unconditional copyright. In point of fact for certain books a period of unconditional copyright is the only period during which the author derives any benefit?

MARK TWAIN: Then now I will say this, which I intended to say a little while ago when you told me what the limit is that you are proposing, and how you are proposing to extend it. That is qualified perpetuity itself. This copyright law would suit me entirely so far as I am personally concerned with this wider limit that you make, and certainly it should suit anybody that ever lived. I do not see how anybody could find any fault with it, and as I said awhile ago, it is merely an ornamental piece of sentimentality, my maintaining that copyright should be perpetual on the great grounds of right and justice. I do not require right and justice on those terms at all; there is not enough of it in the world to make it worth while; but I still do think that there is a sort of stateliness, when you are doing an unjust thing, in doing it for something that is large, that is compensating.

LORD MONKSWELL: My suggestion is that in such cases as Herbert Spencer's there is more right and justice in our unconditional copyright for life and 30 years than there is in your conditional copyright of, say, 20 years, and after that a copyright which would practically give him no benefit?

MARK TWAIN: I believe that myself. I did not know what the proposition before the Committee was at all. I might have asked, but I did not.

VISCOUNT KNUTSFORD: We are only adopting (perhaps too late) the limit that is given by other European nations, of life and so many years after?

MARK TWAIN: Yes, and that being an addition to those 42 years?

LORD FARRER: I should like to ask you as regards one question of fact with regard to the copyright in Sir Walter Scott's works; which you said in 1873 were republished in many volumes at 6*d.* owing to there being still a copyright in the notes. I believe (you will correct me if I am wrong) that the copyright has now run out?

MARK TWAIN: It must necessarily have run out; it could not have had more than a year to live when Mr. Black told me that.

LORD FARRER: Is it not true, as I have seen stated in many newspapers, that there were a larger amount of cheap editions of Scott sold last year than in any year, and that it is a constantly increasing property?

MARK TWAIN: That is quite likely the case; and what I was arriving at was this: that they had cheap editions and plenty of them before the copyright in the notes was dead, and that that is the best way to get those cheap editions and to put the thing on a fair basis between both publisher and author. I am persuaded you would have a cheap edition when they were still covered by the copyright.

LORD FARRER: Then so far as that goes, at any rate, the expiration of the copyright under the present law has not prevented the cheap editions, as I think you at one period thought it might, if a work like Sir Walter Scott is cheapened enormously after the expiration of the copyright?

MARK TWAIN: You must make a difference, you see. You are trying to do right as nearly as you can by everybody, and then you must not single out Sir Walter Scott, and must not single out Shakespeare; you must single out the weaker man who goes to the wall. You cannot kill Sir Walter Scott by taking away the copyright at all. No matter how many publishers publish Sir Walter Scott, they do not necessarily need to suffer any loss by it. If you take a person who is not so strong whose book could have lived a good while longer but for this onslaught which is made by the publisher when the copyright dies, you have destroyed his goods. You cannot kill Sir Walter, but you can kill *him.*

VISCOUNT KNUTSFORD: Forty years after his death?

MARK TWAIN: I am speaking for his children; I am not speaking for him. I have not a word for him; he cannot be affected under this present law.

LORD FARRER: On that answer I should like to ask, is there any other form of brain produce that becomes perpetual property?

MARK TWAIN: I do not know any form of property that is not a produce of the brain.

LORD FARRER: Take patents, for instance, as being the nearest brain production; you would not suggest that they should become perpetual, would you?

MARK TWAIN: I should not. If I were an inventor I might have looked largely into the thing, and might have found some reason for objecting; but not being an inventor, it occurs to me that there comes in a matter of sound public policy. I say that this is not sound public policy. But, whenever a thing is sound public policy, if it shears off a few heads, shear them off. But in an inventor's case, I think his time is rather limited; it is a little too short; it ought to be a little longer than that. There should be a discrimination made between an invention which will sharpen a lead pencil and an invention that will navigate the air, or something that is costly, and representing a great deal of money and large plant and everything. That is the only fault I find. With all ordinary inventions 17 years is long enough, I think; and it could make a very great difference to this world if patents were made perpetual.

LORD FARRER: The only other question I wish to ask as regards perpetuity, or anything like it, is whether you have considered in what way such property should be fixed at death, because apparently a very large amount of revenue is now raised by taxation of property, and is there no possible means of estimating that?

MARK TWAIN: No; I do not suppose there is. A publisher's books would show, and you would be able to tax him. I do not like to mention it where there are indiscreet people, but I was taxed by this Government some years ago. They found out how to tax me. There was not anything about taxing copyright and royalties in books, and I was so curious to know how it was that they taxed me after I had escaped so long that I wrote and had an explanation of it. I got all the documents from the Department here, and that which was the principal one showed that apparently nothing had been overlooked that was taxable except copyright in books. It was not mentioned in Schedule 3, No. 3, No. 16, and all the imaginable things in little printed paragraphs spread over this vast sheet of brown paper; and then I looked, being referred to Schedule D., to see what my literature was taxed under, and it was taxed as gas works, which is absolutely true. It hurt me, but still that was what they taxed me under. Now, if you can tax an author's copyright under gas works, you must not be troubled about what you are going to tax, and how you are going to get it hereafter.

LORD MONKSWELL: I do not know, but I think, in answer to Lord Farrer, the probability is that there is some means of valueing the copyright. When a man dies the value of the unexpired residue of his copyright is capitalised, and his heirs have to pay on that capital value, I should think?

MARK TWAIN: I should think so. You could not be any more exact perhaps in that than you could with an estate that was producing a certain rental; you could not say it would always produce that rental.

LORD FARRER: And you would value the perpetual copyright on the rental?

MARK TWAIN: Yes, upon what proceeds from it; in a given number of years you could average it.

LORD THRING: I understand that you do not very much object to this Copyright Bill, in which we give the term of life and 30 years?

MARK TWAIN: To that I have no objection.

LORD THRING: Except where one or two European countries go beyond us; but still you are satisfied with it?

MARK TWAIN: Entirely.

LORD THRING: I am not so much against your perpetuity; but your objection is a sentimental one?

MARK TWAIN: Yes.

LORD THRING: I think after what Lord Knutsford and Lord Monkswell have said, you must admit, I have not a shadow of doubt in my own mind that if you were to ask an English author whether he would rather have this Bill or have your perpetuity with no conditions attached to it, he would prefer the Bill, because there is nothing authors object to so much as the conditions, and I think rightly?

MARK TWAIN: Quite right.

LORD THRING: That is, I believe, what defeated the Canadians who wanted to have conditions?

MARK TWAIN: I only spoke of that one-eighth, that cheap edition, to Lord Monkswell in a conversation the other day. I dropped that clean out when I came to immediate perpetual copyright.

LORD THRING: Then I will ask you one question which I am afraid you will think rather impertinent. Have you brought your views before the United States authorities; because we should be delighted in England if you could carry a Bill like this in the United States?

MARK TWAIN: I have not, and I have not had anything to do with any copyright measures at all since years ago when we used to go down and persecute Congress in the interests of International Copyright in Mr. Cleveland's term, and we got it through. I went before the Senate with Mr. Lowell, who was Minister here, and we talked of it, and it was carried; it went into force about 1890 or 1891 and has remained in force ever since. But that is a long time ago, and I have had nothing to do with it since. If I were there I should just as soon go and try to accomplish it as not.

LORD THRING: You know as well as I do that the Chase Act is better than nothing, but presses rather heavily upon publishers?

MARK TWAIN: It is better than nothing, really a great deal better than nothing. I did not go down to Washington to advocate the Chase Act at all; I went down there to advocate General Hawley's Bill. General Hawley's Bill was based exactly as I should have liked to see the thing based, just on the matter of the simple justice and fairness of the thing. But talking with the friends of the Chase Bill they seemed to have a certain right on their side. They said, as to this publishing of European books, there is a great deal of capital in that business, it has been here a good while; it is a sort of vested interest, the law permitted it, and there was no reason why these people should not put this money into what was called illegitimate printing (which it was not) and publishing, and that you invade these people's business with your Hawley Bill and destroy it, and you give them no remuneration; you should respect their rights; their printers are involved, their book publishers are involved, their paper makers are involved, there are lots of interests here besides the interests of the author. And so finally it was made a compromise and the Chase Bill was put through. It is not the Bill I should have preferred.

LORD AVEBURY: Would it not meet your views and perhaps the objections which have been started by Lord Knutsford and the Chairman, if the condition as regards a cheap edition were to commence after the 30 years which is contemplated in this Bill?

MARK TWAIN: Yes.

LORD AVEBURY: It would then be a change which would give some authors an advantage, and would put no one at a disadvantage; because if they did not wish to issue a cheap edition, or could not do so economically, they would simply do nothing, and the copyright would cease?

MARK TWAIN: Now, as I understand it, you are proposing this at the end of 75 years from the birthday of the book.

LORD AVEBURY: No; what I am suggesting is this: This Bill, if I understand it correctly, gives copyright for the life of the author and 30 years afterwards?

MARK TWAIN: Yes.

LORD AVEBURY: You suggest in the interests of justice (and it seems to me there is very much force in your contention) that there is no reason

why copyright property should be treated differently from real estate; but then you propose to meet the difficulty that there might be in the way of obtaining books cheaply at all by the condition that there should be an obligation upon the owner of the copyright to issue a cheap edition?

MARK TWAIN: Yes.

LORD AVEBURY: Then my suggestion was that that duty on the part of the representatives of the author to issue a cheap edition should commence when the 30 years had expired, and in that way the children would be no worse off than at present?

MARK TWAIN: No.

LORD AVEBURY: And by issuing the cheap edition they would retain their property?

MARK TWAIN: Yes.

LORD AVEBURY: That, I think, would meet, would it not, your views?

MARK TWAIN: Entirely. The reason I mentioned the 75 years is that I am getting it in my head, whether it belongs there or not, that the 42 years' limit of to-day is extended by adding 30 years' to it. Is that it?

LORD MONKSWELL: No; it is life and 30 years. The former copyright was for a term of 42 years, or the life of the author and seven years from the time he died, whichever was the longest. Now we have only one term, and that is the life of the author and 30 years afterwards. That might by chance be shorter than 42 years?

MARK TWAIN: You have not any 42 years' term.

LORD MONKSWELL: We have no 42 years' term or the life of the author and seven years after, whichever is the longer. It might so happen that if a man died directly after he produced his work, the 30 years' limit would be shorter than the term originally given; but in most cases it would be longer?

MARK TWAIN: That limit is a troublesome thing for the injury it puts upon the public. Any copyright that is not perpetual puts an absolute damage upon the public, and you can see it in this way. You get your eyes fastened on half a dozen men who live, Shakespeare and the others, and you overlook the fact that there are 5,000 books printed every year, and you do not require anybody to print one of those books as a cheap edition. When a book by chance has lived its 42 years, as it is with us, you cannot compel anybody to publish a cheap edition, and a cheap edition is not published. In the case of the great majority of books it is not published because there does not happen to be a call for a cheap edition. There would not be a call for Mr. Darwin's books large enough to make it worth while to publish an exceedingly cheap edition. There are plenty of books where there would be a call of some consequence.

LORD AVEBURY: Is there not another reason which might be advanced in support of your views, viz.: that if the copyright remained vested in the family there would be someone who would have an interest, not merely a pecuniary interest, but also a moral interest in seeing that the books were republished if it could be done without a too heavy loss?

MARK TWAIN: Yes.

LORD AVEBURY: And might not that be also a reason why in the interests of authors it would be desirable that there should be property vested in some one person. It very often would not pay the publisher to issue a book if he was liable to find that another publisher was issuing the same book at the same time?

MARK TWAIN: No.

LORD AVEBURY: Whereas if the property of the book was vested in the family, they would know that there could be no competing edition at the same time, and therefore it might be their interest both pecuniarily, and also from the interest that they would naturally feel in their ancestor's book, to issue the book unless it was a book that would only be published at a dead loss?

MARK TWAIN: That is true. The publisher would know at the end of his time when the author would say "Now I must protect my copyright or lose it; within the year we must issue this very cheap edition. Do you want to go on with it and do it?" And the publisher would say "It will not pay me to do it"; and that would end that question. Why would it not pay him to do it. Merely because the previous editions were not paying. If they were pay-

ing he would naturally want to protect them and keep them alive; and if he should say "No, I do not want to do that," that should end that question. That author has lost his copyright; but it was not valuable, it was not worth keeping. No book is going to be allowed to die when it will pay to keep it alive.

LORD AVEBURY: Then just one other question. I think I understood you to say in reply to Lord Thring that you had no information as to what view the United States would be likely to take of such a suggestion as you have laid before the Committee?

MARK TWAIN: No, I should not be able to forecast that. We get so many of our laws from England, and certainly in the matter of copyright laws I think they have usually proceeded from England. I do not know that we have initiated any considerable detail in copyright law for its benefit, I do not think we have; we get them from England.

LORD AVEBURY: But you have not always followed our legislation in this matter?

MARK TWAIN: Sometimes we prefer to avoid that course and follow some other.

VISCOUNT KNUTSFORD: A little wobbling occasionally –

LORD THRING: I am afraid for 56 years, as I think one of your own writers says, we have been struggling for a Copyright Act in America, international copyright, and at last we have succeeded in obtaining only the Chase Act. As you know the Chase Act is encumbered by excessive restrictions?

MARK TWAIN: Yes, it is.

LORD THRING: Therefore I think I can answer that if your proposition were put at the present moment before the United States Congress it is perfectly certain they would not accept it?

MARK TWAIN: No, I should not say that.

VISCOUNT KNUTSFORD: They do not like sentimental proposals?

MARK TWAIN: No, of course they do not. I should not put it to them in a sentimental way, while I would be talking to them man to man. And that is the only way that we have ever accomplished anything in copyright law, by talking to the members individually; and that is what we did. I say "we," meaning myself. I talked to the Members of the Lower House individually. I got in on the floor of the House under some pretext which perhaps was not strictly virtuous, I do not know whether it was; I had no right on the floor of the House, but the Serjeant-at-Arms let me alone, and I did talk to Members individually, and was able to remove certain objections that were pretty well embedded in them; and when they got those out they were willing to vote for this Bill.

LORD THRING: But you have heard of the mechanical element in the argument, have you not?

MARK TWAIN: What is that?

LORD THRING: You have heard of the mechanical element in the argument on copyright?

MARK TWAIN: I have heard of that over there on the Chase Bill.

LORD THRING: Is it not the mechanical element that prevents the Chase Bill being enlarged in the way that you wish?

MARK TWAIN: Yes, it is, that is true. But you will see that if I were urging this project of perpetual copyright there, it could not affect the mechanical element in any way that I know of; it is only international copyright that can affect the mechanical element.

LORD AVEBURY: When you spoke of the one-eighth would you kindly explain to the Committee what was in your mind, the one-eighth of what?

MARK TWAIN: I meant only this. Take a volume of Mr. Darwin's book, for instance, and say this book's retail price is 8*s.* in this cloth binding; very good, the term has expired, and within one year the publisher must produce all the matter that is in that book, every word of it, in a volume for which you would have to pay only a shilling, and he will get a profit. The heirs of Mr. Darwin will receive a profit out of that shilling; the publisher will receive a profit out of that shilling, so that nobody has really lost. But if you say, "This is a philosophical work written by *me* on the subject of Spiders and Pitcher Plants and

such things," the publisher would say, "Let it go; we cannot publish it at any price and make it pay." That is a perfectly simple proposition, if a book does not pay you cannot continue either edition of it.

LORD MONKSWELL: But I thought you were willing to give up your one-eighth, because you saw a difficulty as to whether it should be one-eighth of the first or second or third edition; and moreover you saw a difficulty in there being different kinds of books, some having a large circulation and some a necessarily small one; and you were willing to propose that this condition of price should be determined by somebody for that purpose?

MARK TWAIN: Yes, it would be much better.

VISCOUNT KNUTSFORD: I never heard of the establishment of a body yet, that should determine this question of price?

MARK TWAIN: It was Lord Monkswell that mentioned it.

LORD THRING: I think Lord Avebury's suggestion of a patent would do. What you would like would be this: that at the expiration of say 30 years the heirs or executors, strictly speaking, might apply to the Privy Council to prolong the term on the same conditions that they now prolong patents. That would be the technical way of doing it. I do not say it would be of any value.

VISCOUNT KNUTSFORD: It seems to me it comes to this: that you have a feeling about the words perpetual copyright, and you say, yes, have perpetual copyright but saddle it with the condition that the copyright shall be lost unless you have a cheap edition in a certain number of years?

MARK TWAIN: Yes.

VISCOUNT KNUTSFORD: We do not object to your calling it perpetual copyright if you like, but our condition is that it ends at the death and 30 years after death?

MARK TWAIN: Yes, life and 30 years after death.

VISCOUNT KNUTSFORD: I have heard nothing to show me that the author does not gain more by our proposal and the author is the person we have to consider. We have of course to consider the public, but the author is the person we have mainly to consider.

MARK TWAIN: I am glad to hear you say that. It has never been said before.

VISCOUNT KNUTSFORD: And it seems to me that by your plan the author will suffer a great deal more than he does by ours?

MARK TWAIN: There is not a book, I think you cannot mention a book, that would not have what would be for that book a cheap edition if there could by any possibility be a call for it. The trouble with this law of ours in America is at the end of the copyright. The term of copyright is made ostensibly to procure a cheap edition for the public; but then there is nothing in the law which requires that cheap edition, and the cheap edition does not always appear, and it will not appear unless there is some protection for the ordinary book.

LORD MONKSWELL: Do you wish to say anything more to the Committee on this subject?

MARK TWAIN: I was only going to suggest that taking death and 30 years afterward, if a book has lived that long, there is no question but what it will pay to bring out a cheap edition if you are forced to do it; there is no doubt about it at all.

LORD MONKSWELL: I am not quite sure. Take the case of Herbert Spencer's works. I have little doubt that his works will live 30 years after he is dead, but only probably in the minds of a very small number of the public?

MARK TWAIN: Then you have only to say that to the publisher of that day, and he will say at once "Let the copyright go"; and the owner of the copyright will say the same. We do not propose to publish a cheap edition or any other kind at a loss.

VISCOUNT KNUTSFORD: Still it seems to me that you are blessing our Bill altogether?

MARK TWAIN: I am doing that, yes, I am applauding it; I am far from being inconvincible.

The Witness is directed to withdraw.

Ordered, – That this Committee be adjourned.

From *Report from the Select Committee of the House of Lords on the Copyright Bill [H. L.] and the Copyright (Artistic) Bill [H. L.]; Together with the Proceedings of the Committee, Minutes of Evidence, and Appendix,* Session 1900 (London: Printed for Her Majesty's Stationery Office by Wyman and Sons, 1900).

A Publisher's Archives: G. P. Putnam

Ezra Greenspan
University of South Carolina

Although literary historians in all periods have been engaged in unearthing new materials, the respect their work has received from the general population of literary scholars, not to mention from the general reader, has varied with changes in the critical climate. For a variety of reasons, the climate for that kind of work seems right now to be a favorable one, and it is likely to remain so through the rest of the decade. If that guess is right, those researchers who spend hours in obscure libraries or sealed-off special collections rooms investigating seemingly arcane matters in dusty books, indecipherable manuscripts, and yellowing newspapers may find that the published reports of their findings will prove useful and interesting to more people (and to more kinds of people) than has typically been the case. Still, there will be skeptics who will ask: what interest can anyone possibly take in the dry-as-dust archives of old publishers? And, as regards the specific subject of this article, they may wonder: what interest can anyone possibly take in the archives of an old-fashioned publisher, such as George Palmer Putnam (1814–1872), whose idea of a good book was Washington Irving's *A History of New York by Diedrich Knickerbocker* (1809) or Sir Walter Scott's historical novels?

The most direct answer is that publishers play a major role in the construction of literary culture – even of what recent generations mean by literary culture. While publishers (or their forerunners) may have been around for hundreds of years, their contribution to letters has become increasingly a primary one ever since the commercialization of culture, when they became centrally placed agents in the making of books. While this may have been true in American culture since the generation of Putnam, what has given a new academic interest to the phenomenon of publishing has been the emergent historicist interest in refiguring the terms and shape of American culture. That intellectual reorientation has brought new attention to the historicity of the book and generated intense discussions of a host of book-related issues, ranging from the composition

George Palmer Putnam

of the canon to that of the makers and consumers of letters. Operating in these terms, a younger generation of scholars has been led, if not always for the same reasons, to accept the realization of an earlier generation that publishing history may be more akin to cultural than to economic history.

Understood in this broadly historicist context, the activities of a publisher such as Putnam become more readily appreciable as a subject of considerable literary historical value and usefulness. Putnam was as involved as any other man of his time in many of the causes and movements that shaped the culture of nineteenth-century America. To explore

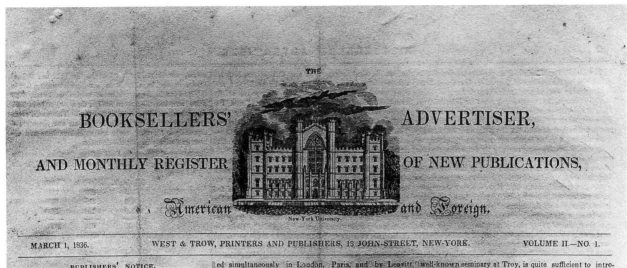

THE

BOOKSELLERS' ADVERTISER,

AND MONTHLY REGISTER OF NEW PUBLICATIONS,

American and Foreign.

New-York University.

MARCH 1, 1836.   WEST & TROW, PRINTERS AND PUBLISHERS, 13 JOHN-STREET, NEW-YORK.   VOLUME II.—NO. 1.

PUBLISHERS' NOTICE.

The publishers would state, that they have been induced to resume the publication of "The Booksellers' Advertiser," from the frequent inquiries that are made for it, and the many regrets that have been expressed by the Trade, here and in Europe, at its discontinuance.

It will be open to all the Trade, at 75 cents per square. Short notices of works, and quarterly lists of new publications, will be inserted gratuitously. The paper will be printed quarterly, and sent gratuitously to all the Trade, Colleges, and other Literary Institutions, Public Libraries, Literary Associations, &c. And all such institutions, (as may be desirous of seeing it regularly,) will please communicate their wishes to the publishers, postage paid.

The haste in which this number has been prepared, has prevented any matter of general interest.

The future numbers will also contain lists of new publications in Europe. The second number will be issued on the 1st of May.

March 1, 1836.

Communicated.

Duties on Books.—It seems to be very generally admitted by all parties that the tax on the importation of books, is much too heavy and restrictive—that it injures the cause of literature at large, without benefiting any body—Uncle Sam only excepted. And surely, now that the revenue of the old gentleman is so large that he don't know how to spend it, he should at least permit us to bring books into his territory, without such a commercial *ad gium*.

It is objected—the duty protects the American citizen—but in nineteen cases out of twenty we think this is not true. All foreign works of a popular character are reprinted here at any rate. It is not those of which foreign editions are imported: but those more extensive and important works—Theological, Classical, Scientific, &c. which are too heavy to bear reprinting, but are still called for constantly by our students, and clergy, and literary men.

Table of Duties on Books.

Books in the English language in boards or
sheets   -   -   -   26 cts. per lb.
"   in do. do. bound   -   -   30 cts.   "
"   "   Greek and Latin, 1-2 the above rates
"   "   Modern Languages of Europe   -   4 cts. per vol.
"   "   Hebrew and Oriental Languages   -   4 cts. per vol.
"   All printed prior to 1776   -   4 cts. per. vol.
                                                                        P.

New-York City Libraries.

"The Society Library" in Nassau-st., is conducted by a board of directors chosen annually by the Stockholders; price of shares, $40.

No. of vols. in the Library—25,000.

Founded—1754.

"The Mercantile Library Association" Clinton Hall:—composed principally of Clerks, who pay an annual fee of $2—which entitles them to the privilege of the Library and Reading Room, and also of introducing friends from other places. A course of twenty four literary and scientific lectures is given every winter, to the whole of which, members are admitted for the trifling fee of one dollar. No. of vols. in the Library—about 10,000.—: Founded   P.

Communicated.

Recollections of the Private Life of La Fayette — By M. Jules Cloquet.—A volume under this title has been publish-

* We saw some Bibles in his office the other day, on which he had the conscience to exact three dollars and three quarters each.

ed simultaneously in London, Paris, and by Leavitt, Lord, & Co. in this city. It is written by the distinguished surgeon who was the friend and medical adviser of the general, and abounds with characteristic anecdotes, interesting original letters, and other documents which were given to the writer by La Fayette himself. Unlike other biographies of that great and good man, this volume but slightly touches on his public career, which is, already familiar to every intelligent American—and indeed to every enlightened inhabitant of the globe:—it gives us, emphatically, a picture of *his private life;* exhibits him as a husband and affectionate in his domestic relations, than he was brave, noble and patriotic in his public services—services rendered in the purest spirit of philanthropy, not to his own and his "adopted country" only, but to mankind.   P.

Universal History in Perspective—Accompanied by an Atlas. By Emma Willard, author of a system of ... tington. We are indebted to the publisher for a copy of this work somewhat in advance of publication, and have examined it as far as we have had opportunity, with a great deal of interest. The study of history is, at least to us, one of the most fascinating as well as instructive, that can be pursued: and though it is often objected that outlines and "summaries" which briefly record that Henry VII. was succeeded by Henry VIII.—and that a battle happened on such a time, in such a place, &c.—that these details are dry and tedious to the pupil, and are seldom retained in the memory, yet it is certainly important that the leading features in the story of the past should be linked together in a systematic and comprehensive chain, so that the whole may be viewed in *perspective*—and the transactions of different ages and nations may be considered according to their relative importance. But Mrs. Willard's Perspective History, as she has very aptly termed it, is not dry or tedious. So far as we have looked over it, judgment and taste are apparent both in the selection and arrangement of the topics; the style is at once clear, comprehensive, and engaging. The plan of the Atlas is quite new, we believe, and gives additional interest and illustration to the subject. It contains—I. A Chronological Picture of Nations or Perspective Sketch of the Course of Empire. II. The Progressive Geography of the World, in a series of Maps—the first showing all those parts which were known 1921, B. C. the rest being enveloped in darkness. In the next one we see some increase of territory enlightened, and so on gradually, in the different maps, the state of the world at ten successive periods is brought before the eye at once.

The general chart strikes us at first as more elaborate, perhaps, but less clear and distinct than that of Lesage as re-modelled by Worcester and others—but either of them is admirably adapted to the purpose. Mrs. Willard's reputation as the author of the History of the Republic of America, and several other works, and as principal of the

well-known seminary at Troy, is quite sufficient to introduce to the public this new work; and once established in such good society, it will soon gain new friends by its intrinsic merits.   P.

Communicated.

Cheap Literature.—"Competition," they say, is the life of Business—and if the "enlightened public" receive benefit from novels at half price, they are most certainly under obligations to those enterprising rival publishers of Gotham and the "city of brotherly love", who, with the most disinterested and kind-hearted benevolence are giving away, for 50 pennies apiece, the productions of the notorious Bulwer—who deems misfortune the cause of error and its atonement:—of the renowned and gallant Capt Marryatt who sends his midshipman laughing to the mast head, and coolly gives the sharks a supper of supercargoes and bishops—and lovers: and of him too on whose fate has fallen the mantle of Scott."—Verily in this age of ballooming and railroading—printing by steam—when the machinery of book-making is such, that it is only necessary to put your rags in the mill and they come out Bibles—all ready printed—there is no telling what human invention will accomplish next. We like this go-ahead sort of spirit—and this "generous rivalry" for the good of mankind. How it originated in the present case we know not. The right of re-publishing foreign books is vested by custom, (for of course there is no law about it,) either in the one who receives the first copy, or he who "announces" it first—(which is not yet settled,) but this rule is sometimes excepted by courtesy in the case of a work by an author whose previous ones had been published by any house. For instance, Bulwer seems to be identified with Harper; Marryatt, with Carey and Hart. But the Rubicon was passed. Harper printed Stories of the Sea—Carey printed Rienzi—and so on. Only imagine, Messrs. Colburn & Bentley, that the same production you so modestly announce in three vols. post 8vo. 1l. 11s. 6d. ($7,00) is traded among the democrats, respectably printed and done up in cloth, for 2-3 sterling!

By the way, our *publishing trade* appears to be flourishing, if we may judge from the number or the sale of new publications. The wheels of business move on with spirit and precision. During the past year in spite of losses by fires, &c. mutual confidence between booksellers throughout the country has scarcely been ruffled or impaired in a single instance. The renowned literati of Cliff-st. who seem disposed to do *all* the publishing which is likely to *pay* (apropos, my *brothers*—No monopolies! *vide Eve. Post.*) announce that they shall issue two novels a month at 50 cents apiece. Take heed to your ways, ye who send Libraries by mail, or you'll be driven from the field by the steam presses of Cliff-street before you find out that even sixpenny numbers may be outdone in cheapness. O! that literature should thus be reduced into questions of shillings and pence!   P.

Front page of the March 1836 issue of the periodical Putnam wrote and edited in the years 1834 to 1837, during spare time from his job as a bookstore clerk (courtesy of the American Antiquarian Society)

LONDON BOOK AGENCY.

WILEY & PUTNAM,
WHOLESALE DEALERS IN
ENGLISH AND OTHER FOREIGN BOOKS,
No. 35 *Paternoster Row,* LONDON, *and No.* 161 *Broadway,* NEW-YORK.

THE Subscribers have established at No. 35 Paternoster Row, London, an Agency conducted by one of the house under the same firm as in New-York, for the purchase of choice ENGLISH, FRENCH, and GERMAN PUBLICATIONS, for Universities and Private Libraries ; and for the sale of American Books, Periodicals, and Copyrights.

Such an arrangement, it has been often suggested, would be very desirable for Authors and Publishers on this side, who wish either to effect sales of their own editions of original works suited to the English market, or to secure a London Copyright therefor : while to Literary Institutions, and Individuals about making additions to their libraries, it offers the following inducements, viz. :

I. All orders, either for the Trade or for Gentlemen wishing but a single Book, will be personally and carefully attended to by one of the firm, who is well acquainted with the British and Continental Book Market ; purchases are made of the Publishers, direct, without the usual commissions of a London Agent : and in many cases, rare and voluminous works are obtained, at the Library Auction Sales and otherwise, at prices much depreciated.

II. If funds to three-fourths the amount of any considerable order are furnished in advance, the commission charged for all purchases is but 10 per cent. on the original cost at the lowest wholesale prices ; and as our purchases are often made in quantities for the Trade, or in exchange for American Books, we can usually deliver English Books in New-York at prices as low, and sometimes much less, than those of the London Publishers.

III. Books for Incorporated Literary Institutions we engage to furnish *free of duty ;* and in most cases, they will be received in New-York within seventy days from the date of the order.

Having been favored with orders from the following Institutions, we have the pleasure of referring to their Directors, viz. :

Columbia College, New-York.
University of the City of New-York.
Mercantile Library Association, New-York.
Society Library and Athenæum, New-York.
Geneva College, Geneva, N.Y.
Military Academy, West Point, N.Y.
Michigan University and State Libraries, Detroit.
Dartmouth College, Hanover, N.H.
Yale College, New Haven, Conn.
Hartford Institute, Conn.

Connecticut Institute.
Athenæum, Salem, Mass.
Williams College, Mass.
United States' Naval Lyceum, Brooklyn.
United States' War Department, Washington.
University of Virginia.
University of Alabama.
University of Georgia.
University of Louisiana.

*** Orders for FRENCH & GERMAN Books executed on the same terms, and the Goods shipped direct from Havre or Hamburgh.

The MAGAZINES and PERIODICALS of every description forwarded by the Steamers, or by the Liverpool Packets, of the 1st of each Month, the day of Publication in London.

ENGLISH AND FOREIGN CATALOGUES FURNISHED.

Your orders are respectfully solicited, addressed as above, 161 Broadway, New-York ; or 35 Paternoster Row, London.

WILEY & PUTNAM.

Circular advertising the London Book Agency, which Putnam founded and ran during the late 1830s and 1840s (courtesy of the Harvard University Archives)

the archives documenting his life and career is to gain entrance into such fundamental issues as the way books were made authorially and commercially in the nineteenth century, the "value" they had in their society, the role nationalism played in the construction of American literary culture, the manner in which publishers' tastes influenced the selection and appearance of books published, and the precariousness of the situation in which authors and publishers found themselves in an era of volatile markets and no international copyright.

The real issue, then, is not the value of publishing archives but the condition in which they have survived – to the extent that they have survived at all. In only the rarest cases has the central archive – the mother lode – of a publishing house or publisher survived intact. Researchers in the field continually experience the frustration of needing to answer the large questions they seek to understand on the basis of limited remains. One reason why this is particularly true with regard to publishing archives can be explained most graphically by reference to the correspondence in 1852 between Spencer F. Baird, the assistant secretary of the Smithsonian Institution, and Putnam in which Baird inquired who was liable for losses incurred in the eventuality of a printing-office fire. Putnam referred that question to his friend John Trow, one of New York's most successful printers, before sending Baird his response. By the end of the Civil War, as matters turned out, Putnam, Trow, and Baird all would see their offices or facilities destroyed by fire. In fact, in the Smithsonian fire of 1865 that gutted the room of its secretary, the United States lost what was unquestionably one of its richest correspondence files, which no doubt included dozens of Putnam's letters as well as the letters of many other scholars, writers, editors, and publishers.

No less destructive of publisher archives has been the attitude of publishers themselves, who have seldom, as a generality, taken a historical perspective on their work and who have consequently placed little value on their papers and records. A major exception to this rule, ironically, was Putnam, the closest approximation his generation had to a genuine annalist. (J. C. Derby, the author of the much-cited *Fifty Years among Authors, Books and Publishers* [1884] was in Putnam's class neither as a publisher nor as a writer.) Putnam, in fact, seriously considered publishing a book of professional reminiscences in the early 1860s, despite the objections of James Fields and others, but never managed to assemble anything more substantial than the several brief series of reminiscent sketches he brought out during that decade in the publishers' trade journal *The American Publishers' Circular* and his own *Putnam's Monthly*. Despite his heightened sense of the historical significance of his profession and of its contribution to modern literary culture, Putnam had no more success than did his peers in preserving his records. The reasons are typical. Many of his office records went up in smoke in the 1850s. And many others, no doubt, were lost or misplaced during the frequent changes of address that Putnam, like virtually all publishers of his century, made in looking for more-spacious or better-situated quarters. And finally, again as happened with most publishers, those of Putnam's archives that did survive were safe only as long as his company remained in family hands. With the loss of family control over G. P. Putnam's Sons in 1930 came the final dispersal of most of what had until then remained together.

So what remains? For decades the answer was categorical: only widely scattered bits and pieces. That is the reason, presumably, why Putnam has received remarkably little serious scholarly or journalistic attention over the course of our century, despite his widely recognized stature as one of the foremost American publishers of the nineteenth century. While it is clear that many parts of the central Putnam archive that passed down from G. P. Putnam to his family have not survived, it is now known that one impressive part has. That is the part inherited (and probably mounted in folio albums) by his son and successor, George Haven Putnam, which the latter utilized in the composition of his impressive *Memoir of George Palmer Putnam* (1903). That collection of albums disappeared after George Haven Putnam's death in 1930, before mysteriously reappearing in 1991 and being auctioned at Swann Galleries. Purchased by Princeton University Library, where it complements the Holt and Scribner archives and solidifies Princeton's position as one of the most important depositories of publishing ar-

chives in this country, it gives the fullest access available to an appreciation of Putnam's career.

The collection consists of seven folio albums of correspondence – four of which are miscellaneous correspondence with Putnam; one, primarily of authorial proposals to Putnam; and two, of general correspondence with the publisher or editor of *Putnam's Monthly*. It runs virtually the full chronology of Putnam's mature career, from the late 1830s to the early 1870s, and covers the full spectrum of his varied activities – as London head of Wiley and Putnam; leader in the movement among American publishers for international copyright legislation; central figure in the professionalization of his occupation; friend to many American writers and artists and patron of native letters and painting; and correspondent of an impressive array of the leading writers, editors, and politicians of his time. It also includes a small quantity of copies of Putnam's outgoing letters, which are very revealing of his taste, personality, and views. While certainly one of the finest autograph collections of nineteenth-century Americana in existence (including letters by Nathaniel Hawthorne, Ralph Waldo Emerson, Herman Melville, Margaret Fuller, William Gilmore Simms, and James Fenimore Cooper), its chief value lies in the density of the information it provides of Putnam and, given Putnam's centrality in the institutionalization of the publishing industry in America and of its contribution to the national culture, in the detailed view it affords of the American literary scene during the mid-century era.

What that collection most conspicuously lacks, an intimate approach to the man, is in part compensated for by the miscellaneous collection of letters and memorabilia left to the Library of Congress by his son Herbert, who was a longtime librarian there and the longest-lived of the twelve Putnam children. That collection contains the bulk of the surviving Putnam family papers. Although only a small portion of the collection bears directly on G. P. Putnam, that surviving portion does allow the viewer to compile a close-up portrait of Putnam the man and publisher. It includes letters written by Putnam to his fiancée over a six-month period in 1840 and 1841; a scattering of his letters to his wife, mother, and children; a scattering of his wife's letters back home to Putnam's mother during their years in England and in later years to her children and others; and dozens of letters by the various Putnam children, although most of them postdate their father's death. The largest concentration of this correspondence covers what is otherwise one of the least accessible periods of Putnam's life, the years in the 1840s when he and his family lived in London, where he was running the first overseas office of an American publishing house. Unfortunately, most of the letters sent to the family in America were written by his wife, since the Putnams generally followed a male-female distinction between business and personal correspondence, and thus provide a mostly indirect view of Putnam's professional life. Still, they contain enough information to help document an exciting time in the growth of American publishing, as the historic imbalance in the Anglo-American literary cultural relationship was rapidly reaching a new point of equilibrium – due, in no small measure, to Putnam's efforts. The collection also contains interesting miscellaneous material, including the family genealogy, wills, and some legal papers.

Given the affiliation of the family and firm with New York City, one would naturally expect to find large amounts of Putnam material in its libraries, and that is precisely the case. In fact, one of the several richest depositories of Putnam material in this country is the New York Public Library (NYPL). It has, first of all, the correspondence with the New York Book Publishers' Association of many of America's leading authors, editors, and publishers relating to the lavish Crystal Palace dinner in honor of American authors hosted by the publishers' association in September 1855. Putnam, the secretary of the association and the organizer of the dinner, was farsighted enough to recognize the historic significance of the occasion and kept the letters, bound in two handsome volumes, in his own personal collection. The NYPL also has a small collection of miscellaneous correspondence to and from Putnam, some of it historically important. In addition, uncatalogued but equally valuable are the Putnam letters interspersed in two of the NYPL's most important manuscript holdings, the Duyckinck Papers and the Lenox Papers. Those letters to and from Evert Duyckinck, especially when read against the correspondence between the two men in the Putnam Archive at Princeton, yield one of the most detailed documentary looks at American literary professionalism in the 1840s on record. As to the papers of James Lenox, whose collection became a mainstay of the NYPL, its three-way correspondence among Putnam, Lenox, and Henry Stevens in 1846 and 1847 yields fascinating information concerning the formation of the Lenox collection and the process by which Stevens replaced Putnam as Lenox's chief European agent. It also contains the important letter in which Putnam offered Lenox the chance to buy the "Mazarin" copy

of the Gutenberg Bible, at the time about to be auctioned at Sotheby's in London. Although Putnam's agent placed the winning bid for the Bible, Lenox needed to be cajoled before agreeing to pay what he initially considered the extravagant bill for five hundred pounds, a decision which first brought the Gutenberg Bible into the United States.

Other concentrations of Putnam materials can be found at various university libraries. Cornell University has the single largest surviving file of Putnam letters to one individual, nearly one hundred dating from the late 1840s to the early 1870s to his longtime friend the author Bayard Taylor. This file is supplemented by another dozen or so letters from Putnam to Andrew Dickson White and James Morgan Hart, as well as numerous letters from George Haven Putnam to Taylor, White, and Hart. Altogether, they provide considerable biographical information about Putnam, as well as details about his day-to-day publishing operations. Columbia University has a fairly large Putnam collection, which arrived via the connection of George Haven Putnam, whose second wife had been dean of Barnard, with the university. It consists of considerable business correspondence, although most of it is that of the son rather than the father and relates to the affairs of the firm in the later nineteenth century when it was under Haven Putnam's control. The University of Virginia has a small Putnam collection within the general holdings of the Barrett Collection. Much of it consists of correspondence concerning G. P. Putnam's publication of *Homes of American Authors,* one of Putnam's pet publishing ideas of the early 1850s in tribute to the proliferation of American letters. The collection includes letters to Putnam from, among others, Cooper, Henry Wadsworth Longfellow, Irving, Simms, R. W. Griswold, J. P. Kennedy, C. M. Sedgwick, W. H. Prescott, R. H. Dana, and G. W. Curtis, as well as about a dozen and a half letters by Putnam. And scattered through the various libraries of Harvard University are several Putnam files and collections. At the Gray Herbarium is a rather full file of correspondence from 1844 until 1859 between Putnam and the Harvard botanist Asa Gray. In the university archives is interesting material relating to the service Putnam did Harvard College as a foreign-book agent in the 1840s. And in the Houghton Library are a variety of Putnam and Putnam-related collections, including a file of correspondence with Longfellow; a file of accounts and miscellaneous documents relating to Melville; much of the correspondence of Joshua Dix and Arthur T. Edwards, the successors to Putnam as publishers of *Putnam's*

Monthly; and correspondence with the firm of G. P. Putnam and Company in the cost books of Ticknor and Fields, as well as occasional allusions to the business affairs of Putnam or *Putnam's Monthly* in the correspondence of James Russell Lowell, G. W. Curtis, Charles F. Briggs, and others.

Taken together, these various archives provide only a very partial portrait of Putnam, his career, and his company. One is therefore forced back upon one's ingenuity to fill the gaps in and to make connections between known points of intersection. One good way of doing that is to go at a figure like Putnam indirectly – via the connections he had with people, places, institutions, and issues. For example, one can find references to Putnam and, occasionally, important information about him in the files of writers and editors close to him, such as G. W. Curtis (at Harvard and the NYPL) and Bayard Taylor (at the Huntington Library). Some of the only financial information about the way his firm handled its accounts, for example, can be found in the Melville Papers at Harvard, where many of the Wiley and Putnam accounts for *Typee,* carefully collected by Melville's lawyer-brother, Allan, eventually were deposited. Similarly, one can supplement the knowledge of Putnam's handling of *Putnam's Monthly* gained from reading through the Princeton archive by reading through the files of its first editor, Charles F. Briggs (at the Massachusetts Historical Society), or of its successor publishers, Dix and Edwards (at Harvard), and of Frederick Law Olmsted (at the Library of Congress). One can follow up on Putnam's important service to libraries around the country as a foreign-book agent by searching for – and sometimes finding – his letters from Europe in the archives of the nineteenth century's major college libraries. Then again, given the international dimensions of Putnam's career, an aggressive researcher may also choose to follow the trail of Putnam's connections with the various British and Continental publishers and authors with whom he had extensive dealings back to the institutions where their papers are located.

Alternatively, one can approach Putnam through the vast physical evidence he left behind. For one thing, Putnam was one of the most "literary" publishers of his generation (as his son would be of the next generation of publishers), who wrote and edited a considerable amount over the course of his mature life. Those sources provide substantial information about his life and activities, as do articles about him and his company in the newspapers and magazines of his own era. For another

thing, Putnam published hundreds of books and several leading periodicals during his career, which provide a considerable body of evidence regarding his tastes and views. For example, from the "Publishers' Notice" alone that he wrote for his firm's lavishly illustrated catalogue for the 1853 New York World's Fair, one can infer much of his publishing philosophy. Similarly, one can infer a great deal about his views concerning American letters, the arts, copyright, democracy, authorial professionalism, and other such matters simply by studying the lists of the books that he published, as well as by examining individual copies of those books – their contents, formats, bindings, prefaces, and advertisements.

All these collections and these methods of finding additional materials in uncatalogued sources will yield a considerable pool of information about Putnam and his times. But experienced researchers know both the exhilaration and the frustration of doing primary research, and the pursuit of a figure like Putnam offers just such mixed emotions. For all the hundreds of letters that can be found in archives, there are thousands of others that are no doubt lost and others that yet remain to be located. In London, Putnam typically stayed up long after midnight writing business letters back to clients in the United States – this, after a day in the office spent partially answering correspondence.

The experience of meeting the past as close as possible to its own terms was well, if archly, stated by Emily Dickinson in the opening lines of Poem 371:

A precious – mouldering pleasure – 'tis–
To meet an Antique Book–
In just the Dress his Century wore–
A privilege – I think–

His venerable Hand to take–
And warming in our own–
A passage back – or two – to make–
To Times when he – was young–[.]

Scholars today will no doubt differ over the meaning or constitution of the "mutual mind" of past and present, of which the poem speaks, and over the means of negotiating the "passage" between them. But those who wish to understand the past on its own terms can hardly do better than to begin their search by following the trail of evidence the past has left in the kinds of archives discussed here. The facsimiles on the following nine pages are examples of the materials in Putnam's papers.

Page from Putnam's 23 August 1843 letter to historian George Bancroft, reporting on recent developments in the campaign for the acceptance of American literature in Britain and on the Continent (courtesy of the Massachusetts Historical Society)

20 Clinton Place
Nov 29. 1845

My dear Putnam.

I have a world of things to write about. Pray Heaven some of them be not forgotten!

In the first place I have to acknowledge your generous confidence reposed in my schemes and thank you for the interest with which you receive my suggestions. I had long, whether from infant and boyish years having been passed in my father's bookstore, had an eye on the trade and written many schemes for them in the empty air when Mr Wiley applied to me for counsel — so the apple had not ripened in a day though it was ready for shaking. I had surveyed the ground pretty thoroughly — so that nothing new has been started in opposition which I had not for the most part *rejected*, having taken care to sweep a broad boundary line for the 'library' to include all that was good. When you see that the series includes the pick of Murrays, Moxons, Chapmans, Pickerings publications, works of different classes and others besides you will say that the "area of freedom" is sufficiently large. I only wish that this "area of freedom" like our political one had not a black spot in it. What slavery is to the one pillaged Copyright are to the other. Yet this is a great improvement on former dispensations. The mental rights of authors are religiously preserved not a word or letter being mutilated; good editions are printed; an unusual class of good books are brought into vogue and a common corrupt class driven out and more than

---

Page from the letter to Putnam in which New York author and editor Evert Duyckinck outlines his plans for the Library of Choice Reading, published by Wiley and Putnam (29 November 1845). The series, which eventually comprised nearly one hundred volumes, made inexpensive editions of the classics available to American readers (courtesy of Princeton University Library).

Page from the letter in which Putnam offered to sell to James Lenox of New York the first copy of the Gutenberg Bible brought into the United States (James Lenox Papers, Rare Books and Manuscripts Division, New York Public Library, Astor, Lenox and Tilden Foundations)

No. 82 Cliff St
Jan'y 30, 1847.

Dear Sir —

In reply to your favor received last evening, (but without date,) and as a reason why we shall publish "Lavengro," we beg to say —

That you have, without cause, reprinted two of our publications upon us.

There is still another reason, but as the above is deemed quite sufficient, it is unnecessary to give it at present, especially as we have reason to know that you have for some time been familiar

Geo. P. Putnam Esq.

Page from a letter to Harper and Brothers in which Putnam complains about their unauthorized publication of works by British authors with whom Putnam had book contracts. Such conduct made Putnam a staunch advocate for an international copyright law, which was not enacted until 1891 (courtesy of Princeton University Library).

Pittsfield Sep: 7th 1855

Dear Sir: I have been honored by an invitation to an Entertainment to be given by the N. Y. Book-Publishers' Association on the 27th Inst: —

If in my power I shall be most happy to be present at so attractive a festival.

Respectfully Yours

H. Melville

G. P. Putnam Esq.
Secretary

Herman Melville's acceptance of Putnam's invitation to the banquet held in the Crystal Palace at the 1855 World's Fair in New York honoring American authors (New York Book Publishers' Association Records, Rare Books and Manuscripts Division, New York Public Library, Astor, Lenox and Tilden Foundations)

Page from a draft of Putnam's will, dated 1866 (courtesy of the Library of Congress)

Julian Symons at Eighty

Ashley Brown
University of South Carolina

See also the Symons entry in *DLB 87: British Mystery and Thriller Writers Since 1940,* First Series.

BOOKS: *Confusions about X* (London: Fortune, 1938);

The Second Man (London: Routledge, 1943);

The Immaterial Murder Case (London: Gollancz, 1945; New York: Macmillan, 1957);

A Man Called Jones (London: Gollancz, 1947);

Bland Beginning (London: Gollancz, 1949; New York: Harper, 1949);

A. J. A. Symons: His Life and Speculations (London: Eyre & Spottiswoode, 1950);

The Thirty-First of February (London: Gollancz, 1950; New York: Harper, 1951);

Charles Dickens (London: Barker, 1951; New York: Roy, 1951);

Thomas Carlyle: The Life and Ideas of a Prophet (London: Gollancz, 1952; New York: Oxford University Press, 1952);

The Broken Penny (London: Gollancz, 1953; New York: Harper, 1953);

The Narrowing Circle (London: Gollancz, 1954; New York: Harper, 1955);

Horatio Bottomley: A Biography (London: Cresset, 1955);

The Paper Chase (London: Collins, 1956); republished as *Bogue's Fortune* (New York: Harper, 1957);

The Colour of Murder (London: Collins, 1957; New York: Harper, 1957);

The General Strike: A Historical Portrait (London: Cresset, 1957; Chester Springs, Pa.: Dufour, 1957);

The Gigantic Shadow (London: Collins, 1958); republished as *The Pipe Dream* (New York: Harper, 1959);

The Progress of a Crime (London: Collins, 1960; New York: Harper, 1960);

A Reasonable Doubt: Some Criminal Cases Re-examined (London: Cresset, 1960);

Julian Symons (photograph © Jerry Bauer)

The Thirties: A Dream Resolved (London: Cresset, 1960; Westport, Conn.: Greenwood, 1973; revised edition, London: Faber & Faber, 1975);

Murder! Murder! (London: Fontana, 1961);

The Detective Story in Britain (London: Longmans, Green, 1962; expanded, 1969);

The Killing of Francie Lake (London: Collins, 1962); republished as *The Plain Man* (New York: Harper & Row, 1962);

Buller's Campaign (London: Cresset, 1963);

The End of Solomon Grundy (London: Collins, 1964; New York: Harper & Row, 1964);

The Belting Inheritance (London: Collins, 1965; New York: Harper & Row, 1965);

England's Pride: The Story of the Gordon Relief Expedition (London: Hamilton, 1965);

Francis Quarles Investigates (London: Panther, 1965);

Critical Occasions (London: Hamilton, 1966);

Crime and Detection: An Illustrated History from 1840 (London: Studio Vista, 1966); republished as *A Pictorial History of Crime* (New York: Crown, 1966);

The Man Who Killed Himself (London: Collins, 1967; New York: Harper & Row, 1967);

The Man Whose Dreams Came True (London: Collins, 1968; New York: Harper & Row, 1968);

The Man Who Lost His Wife (London: Collins, 1970; New York: Harper & Row, 1970);

Bloody Murder: From the Detective Story to the Crime Novel (London: Faber & Faber, 1972); republished as *Mortal Consequences: A History from the Detective Story to the Crime Novel* (New York: Harper & Row, 1972); revised as *Bloody Murder* (Harmondsworth, U.K.: Penguin, 1974; revised again, 1985);

Notes from Another Country (London: London Magazine Editions, 1972);

The Players and the Game (London: Collins, 1972; New York: Harper & Row, 1972);

The Plot Against Roger Rider (London: Collins, 1973; New York: Harper & Row, 1973);

The Object of An Affair, and Other Poems (Edinburgh: Tragara, 1974);

A Three Pipe Problem (London: Collins, 1975; New York: Harper & Row, 1975);

Ellery Queen Presents Julian Symons' How to Trap a Crook and 12 Other Mysteries, edited, with an introduction, by Ellery Queen (Frederic Dannay and Manfred B. Lee) (New York: Davis, 1977);

The Blackheath Poisonings: A Victorian Murder Mystery (London: Collins, 1978; New York: Harper & Row, 1978);

The Tell-Tale Heart: The Life and Works of Edgar Allan Poe (London: Faber & Faber, 1978; New York: Harper & Row, 1978);

Conan Doyle: Portrait of an Artist (London: Whizzard, 1979; New York: Mysterious, 1988);

The Modern Crime Story (Edinburgh: Tragara, 1980);

Sweet Adelaide: A Victorian Puzzle Solved (London: Collins, 1980; New York: Harper & Row, 1980);

Critical Observations (London & Boston: Faber & Faber, 1981; New Haven, Conn.: Ticknor & Fields, 1981);

The Great Detectives: Seven Original Investigations (London: Orbis, 1981; New York: Abrams, 1981);

The Detling Murders (London: Macmillan, 1982); republished as *The Detling Secret* (New York: Viking, 1983; Harmondsworth, U.K. & New York: Penguin, 1984);

The Tigers of Subtopia, and Other Stories (London: Macmillan, 1982; New York: Viking, 1983);

The Name of Annabel Lee (London: Macmillan, 1983; New York: Viking, 1983);

1948 and 1984 (Edinburgh: Tragara, 1984);

The Criminal Comedy of the Contented Couple (London: Macmillan, 1985); republished as *A Criminal Comedy* (New York: Viking, 1986);

Dashiell Hammett (San Diego: Harcourt Brace Jovanovich, 1985);

Two Brothers (Edinburgh: Tragara, 1985);

Makers of the New: The Revolution in Literature, 1912–1939 (London: Deutsch, 1987; New York: Random House, 1987);

The Kentish Manor Murders (London: Macmillan, 1988; New York: Viking, 1988);

Death's Darkest Face (London: Macmillan, 1990; New York: Viking, 1990);

The Thirties and the Nineties (Manchester, U.K.: Carcanet, 1990);

Portraits of the Missing (London: Deutsch, 1991);

Something Like a Love Affair (London: Macmillan, 1992; New York: Mysterious Press, 1992).

Collections: *The Julian Symons Omnibus,* introduction by Symons (London: Collins, 1966);

The Julian Symons Omnibus (Harmondsworth, U.K.: Penguin, 1984).

OTHER: *An Anthology of War Poetry* (Harmondsworth, U.K. & New York: Penguin, 1942);

Between the Wars: Britain in Photographs (London: Batsford, 1972);

"Progress of a Crime Writer," in *The Mystery and Detection Annual,* edited by Donald K. Adams (Beverly Hills, Cal.: Adams, 1974), pp. 238–243;

Verdict of Thirteen: A Detective Club Anthology, edited by Symons (New York: Harper & Row, 1979);

Tom Adams, *Agatha Christie: The Art of Her Crimes,* commentary by Symons (New York: Everest House, 1981);

A. J. A. Symons to Wyndham Lewis, edited by Symons (Edinburgh: Tragara, 1982);

Wyndham Lewis, *The Essential Wyndham Lewis,* edited by Symons (London: Deutsch, 1989).

I met Julian Symons during the summer of 1962 after a brief correspondence about some editorial matters. As the coeditor of a volume of essays on Wallace Stevens, I had talked him into letting us reprint "A Short View of Wallace Stevens," which he had originally published in *Life and Letters Today* in 1940. This was in fact the first study of the poet's work to have appeared in England, and it had at least that historical importance. At the time when it came out, Stevens's poetry had yet to be published there; eventually, in 1953, T. S. Eliot would bring out *Selected Poems* through Faber and Faber. So for Julian to have written this at all, especially during wartime circumstances, was a mark of his critical acumen. But in 1962 he was somewhat reluctant to let us reprint it. His opinions had shifted somewhat, no doubt, and Stevens himself in 1940 had begun a glorious late period of creativity that lasted until his death in 1955. Anyone writing on him in 1962 would have had the advantage of surveying his entire life's work. Nevertheless, I prevailed upon Julian to let us have his essay, which is in print in *The Achievement of Wallace Stevens* (1962). It states a point of view about Stevens that is still worth taking up: "There is not one of Stevens' more important poems which does not have for its explicit or implied subject *the poet and his poetry,* rather than a consideration of man as a social animal." I suspect that this remark – a genuine prejudice, perhaps – is one with which Julian would agree in 1992. At any rate, in 1940 he was well ahead of most people in England in having read so many American writers. When I came to know him, I realized that he had developed an extensive transatlantic literary culture on his own without having yet been to America.

I had another reason for being interested in Julian in 1962. It seemed that he owned a portrait of himself painted by Wyndham Lewis. During the 1950s I had had a Lewis period in my literary development; I had collected and read most of Lewis's books and gone to the Tate Gallery to see the famous portraits of Ezra Pound and Edith Sitwell. My student Tom Carter, at Washington and Lee University, had edited a special Lewis number of *Shenandoah,* and in September 1953, with an advance copy of the magazine in hand, I had called on Lewis at Notting Hill Gate. In 1956, only a few months before Lewis's death, the Tate Gallery had mounted an important exhibition called "Wyndham Lewis and Vorticism." I did not attend, but I knew from the catalogue that it included Lewis's portrait of Julian. The portrait was begun in 1939; it was then stored while Lewis was in America and completed only in 1949, not long before he went blind and had to abandon painting.

So in 1962, when I was in London, I eagerly accepted an invitation to have Sunday lunch with Julian and his wife Kathleen in Blackheath. I had been on the edge of Blackheath before, but only after climbing the hill from Greenwich Park as the result of another literary pilgrimage. On that earlier occasion I had tried to follow the route of Joseph Conrad's wretched character Stevie (in *The Secret Agent*), who was sent to blow up the Greenwich Observatory. This time I went down to Blackheath by train, according to instructions from Julian, who is always very precise about railway schedules for his guests.

I emerged from the station wondering what he would look like – I had not yet encountered the Wyndham Lewis portrait. I did not see anyone at first, but then a tall commanding figure came striding across the Heath, and we seemed to recognize each other immediately. We went on to Shooters Hill Road, where I met the charming Kathleen and their neighbors Roy and Kate Fuller. Roy Fuller, who died in 1991, was one of the finest poets of his generation; he managed to combine his literary career with his profession as a solicitor for a building society. He had been one of Julian's closest friends for many years. I gathered that at one time Blackheath had been the residence of several other literary figures, including Kathleen Raine and Bonamy Dobrée. The Fullers continued to live there, but Julian and Kathleen before long would pull up stakes and move to the Romney Marsh in Kent. Julian's years in Blackheath proved to be very useful for him in the long run, however, because eventually this became the setting for his Victorian crime novel, *The Blackheath Poisonings* (1978), which in turn has been adapted into a successful television drama (1992). Blackheath was still rich in domestic architecture thirty years ago, and houses themselves have a large part in the action of the novel.

Julian was born in 1912 in Clapham, a large sprawling district south of the Thames. Its center is Clapham Common, which I know only from the photograph (taken early in the century) on the jacket of *Notes from Another Country,* a charming memoir that Julian published in 1972. (By then the Symonses had moved back to London, this time to Battersea, not far from Clapham.) *Notes* is a rather modest and episodic account of his early years; as he says, it is "a self-portrait mostly in terms of other people." He seems to have spent a lot of time playing cricket with his chums on the common. One might want to know more about his education, because he never attended one of the great public schools or ancient universities that have been the typical training grounds for British literati. Was he inspired by some schoolmaster? He decided to be a writer at an early stage of life, and in fact he had a model within his immediate family, his older brother A. J. A. Symons (1900–1941), the author of a remarkable biography called *The Quest for Corvo*

(1934). A J, as Julian always calls him, was in some respects a figure of the 1890s born into another age, a gourmet and a dandy as well as a serious writer whose main interest was biography. He never lived long enough to realize the full potential of his considerable talent, and indeed he sought social as well as a literary success in the London of the 1930s. Julian has honored him on several occasions: a full-length biography, originally published in 1950 and reprinted as an Oxford Paperback in 1986; a collection of A J's *Essays and Introductions* (his remaining shorter pieces) in 1969; and a very limited edition of some of A J's letters to Wyndham Lewis that Julian published in 1982.

This last item is interesting for what it led to. As Julian says in a brief commentary, A J and Lewis apparently had little in common as the basis for a literary friendship. A J, the younger man, was apt to consort with survivors of the 1890s such as Vyvyan Holland, while Lewis was a friend of Eliot and Ezra Pound, his colleagues in the avant-garde of 1914. But the relationship lasted until Lewis's departure for America in 1939. Julian met Lewis through A J during the early 1930s. Many years later, soon after Lewis's death in 1957, he wrote a memoir of their friendship, which seems to have existed somewhat independently of Lewis's relationship with A J. It was all the more remarkable, because Julian was thirty years younger and rather leftish, though decidedly independent, in his politics at a time when Lewis was considered a Fascist by many. (His unfortunate *Hitler* of 1931 did his reputation no good during the Marxist 1930s, even though he later disowned it.) But Julian has always been one of Lewis's best advocates, and his own practice as a writer of crime novels gives him a point of view that is especially useful in judging Lewis's fiction. As he has pointed out in essays and reviews, during the 1930s Lewis turned to the thriller as a serious fictional convention, and the result in at least one case, *The Revenge for Love* (1937), was one of his finest achievements in the novel.

Like many other novelists, Julian started out as a poet. During the 1930s he was friendly with Ruthven Todd and Gavin Ewart, later Roy Fuller, and he founded a little magazine called *Twentieth Century Verse,* which published these poets and others. They were very much aware of the slightly older generation of W. H. Auden, whom they admired, but they were certainly not imitators of the Audenesque manner. Julian managed to sustain his magazine from 1937 to 1939. Aside from the poems written by his friends, he published two unusual numbers, one in homage to Lewis, the other con-

Drawing of Symons by Wyndham Lewis, 1938 (courtesy of Julian Symons)

cerned entirely with American poetry. The latter number contained new poems by eighteen Americans ranging from Stevens and Allen Tate to the then barely known John Berryman and Delmore Schwartz. What of Julian's own poetry? He published steadily in those days, and his first two books were collections of verse: *Confusions About X* (1938) and *The Second Man* (1943). After that the *proseur* took over. His poems used to appear in Oscar Williams's anthologies of the 1940s, but otherwise they were not usually known in America. There was a late flowering of poetry in *The Object of An Affair* (1974), beautifully printed on a hand press in Edinburgh; that was the occasion on which Julian published the first part of a sonnet sequence called "Marmont Soliloquising," which one hopes will be continued when his muse descends again.

Julian turned to the crime novel somewhat by accident. According to his account of it in *Notes from Another Country,* his friend Ruthven Todd proposed a collaboration on a story that would be set against the background of the famous 1936 Surrealist Exhibition; in the course of the action "friends should be introduced, libelled, and either killed off or appear as particularly nasty suspects." Todd did not carry forward his own idea, so Julian wrote the novel by himself and put the typescript in a drawer, where it was discovered six years later by Kathleen, who suggested that he send it to a publisher. This was *The Immaterial Murder Case* (1945), which the author will not allow to be reprinted. Perhaps he mistrusts its comic element, although social satire is a strong and recurrent feature of his later novels. At any rate, the modest success of this first one gave him the courage to abandon the advertising agency where he was chief copywriter and take up literature as a profession.

There is an amusing counterpart to *The Immaterial Murder Case*. At the same time that Julian was secretly writing his novel, Dylan Thomas had the idea of writing a comic crime novel to be called *Murder of the King's Canary,* involving the choice of a new poet laureate. Thomas finally talked his friend John Davenport into a collaboration, and during the summer of 1940, while the Battle of Britain was raging, they actually finished it. As in the case of Julian's novel, it was closely based on living figures, so much so that it could not be published at the time. It finally came out in 1976. In the introduction to the Penguin edition, Constantine FitzGibbon (Dylan Thomas's biographer) suggests that Thomas had read Lewis's *The Apes of God* (1930), a satire on literary celebrities; and this may have set Thomas going. Julian certainly read *The Apes of God* when it was first published and caused such a controversy; whether elements of its style got into his novel, I'm unable to say. He is very strong on plot, and he faults his early book – "appallingly bad" – on that score. It was, after all, originally Todd's idea.

Once he got started as a crime novelist, Julian took the genre seriously. Eventually he became its historian in *Bloody Murder: From the Detective Story to the Crime Novel* (1972), now the standard account of the subject. His history is based on his reading of thousands of crime stories; it is the work of an acknowledged addict. As the subtitle suggests, Julian sees a kind of evolution in the genre from the classic "whodunit" of Edgar Allan Poe, Wilkie Collins, and Arthur Conan Doyle to the crime novel whose main interest is frequently the psychology of the murderer. There is an early version of this kind of novel in William Godwin's *Caleb Williams* (1794), and several great writers, including Fyodor Dostoyevski in *Crime and Punishment,* have used murder and subsequent guilt as the subject of fiction. But Julian restricts the crime novel to a carefully plotted fiction in which the psychology of the murderer or victim is the main element. Often there is no detective, and frequently the clues and mechanical devices that lead to the revelation of the case are of slight importance. The crime novel is thus different from the detective story in the Golden Age of the 1920s and 1930s, where the amateur detective himself – Lord Peter Wimsey or Hercule Poirot – is the central character. The detective's fame is carried from one book to another, whereas the reader seldom remembers the name of the victim or murderer. Occasionally there might be variation in the scheme, as in Agatha Christie's *The Murder of Roger Ackroyd* (1926), but essentially the whodunit is based on a predictable set of conventions.

Most of the memorable writers of the Golden Age were British, but during that period certain Americans of a new type emerged, notably Dashiell Hammett and the British-born California writer Raymond Chandler. Julian considers these writers important for their range of characterization and social commentary – usually an unsparing exposé of the urban scene. Hammett's *The Glass Key* came out in the same year as William Faulkner's *Sanctuary* (1931), and Julian thinks that it can easily stand the comparison:

> Constant re-reading of it offers fresh revelations of the way in which a crime writer with sufficient skill and tact can use violent events to comment by indirection on life, art, society, and at the same time compose a novel admirable in the carpentry of its structure and delicately intelligent in its suggestions of truths about human relationships. As a novel *The Glass Key* is remarkable, as a crime novel unique.

So *The Glass Key* – "the peak of the crime writer's art in the twentieth century" – stands as a model of its kind, and Julian's comment on it here is probably a credo for his own practice in this field. He certainly didn't stop his admiration for other writers with the Golden Age. He is thoroughly up to date in his enthusiasms – for instance, Patricia Highsmith, "the most important crime novelist at present in practice." As a top reviewer he has advanced more than one career, at least in England. As for *Bloody Murder* (entitled *Mortal Consequences* in the United States), it received the Edgar Allan Poe Award of the Mystery Writers of America in 1972 – one of the first of many honors bestowed on Julian by his fellow crime writers in several countries.

He expanded three short but important chapters of *Bloody Murder* in the direction of critical biography during the next decade or so. *The Tell-Tale Heart: The Life and Works of Edgar Allan Poe* (1978) is a full-scale account of the subject, based on extensive research that Julian found time for while he was a visiting professor at Amherst College. It separates the life of Poe from a direct examination of his work, and it might be considered the most sensible book on the subject for the general reader. "Sensible" is indeed the best term to use in describing Julian's critical procedures; he is surely descended from the tradition of British empiricism that is typical of critics from Samuel Johnson to Eliot, F. R. Leavis, and George Orwell (the latter a friend of Julian's during the 1940s). He is willing to accept novel approaches to literary works if they are genuinely illuminating. In the case of his Poe book, for instance, he takes Marie Bonaparte's Freudian interpretation of Poe's life seriously while he questions her reading of the stories. Likewise he considers but rejects Richard Wilbur's claim that Poe is essentially an allegorist like Herman Melville and Nathaniel Hawthorne. He followed the Poe book with short illustrated biographies of Arthur Conan Doyle (1979) and Hammett (1985) which allowed him to elaborate his accounts of these important figures in *Bloody Murder*.

Julian's own novels are so extensive that one can not possibly do justice to them in a short essay; there are twenty-seven to date, as of 1992. In *Bloody Murder* he quotes a passage from himself about his serious intentions in writing crime fiction:

> The thing that most absorbs me in our age is the violence behind respectable faces, the civil servant planning how to kill Jews more efficiently, the Judge speaking with passion about the need for capital punishment, the quiet obedient boy who kills for fun. . . . If you want to show the violence that lives behind the bland faces that most of us present to the world, what better vehicle can you have than the crime novel?

At this point in *Bloody Murder* he makes a brief reference to a few of his early novels — *not* to do so would be unscholarly in a history of the genre — and then he (or perhaps Faber and Faber) calls on Edmund Crispin (the late Bruce Montgomery, an outstanding crime novelist) to add an extended footnote, part of which I quote:

> First, Symons's earlier work, mostly using the framework of orthodox detective fiction, culminates (1954) in an outstandingly fine example of the genre, *The Narrowing Circle*. Secondly, a recurrent, highly agreeable factor in many of his stories — from *The Immaterial Murder Case* (1945) right up to *The Man Who Lost His Wife* (1970) — has been a mordantly effective sense of satire. Thirdly, his accomplishment has been much more varied than his own brief account of it implies; this can be seen at its fullest stretch in *The Man Who Killed Himself*

Dust jacket for Symons's book of eight loosely connected miniatures, in all of which he appears as a character

(1965), where psychological interest is underpinned by a dazzlingly clever plot.

Since Edmund Crispin's succinct comments could refer to only half of Julian's oeuvre, as of 1970, I shall briefly elaborate the third point that he makes. In 1967 Julian published *The Man Who Killed Himself,* one of his finest studies of "the violence behind respectable faces." It is the kind of book that Georges Simenon might have written, but it is set within a contemporary English milieu rich in social detail. Could the title have been suggested to Julian by "The Man Who Lost Himself," a critical piece that he published in 1957? That was an account of a famous Victorian mystery, the Tichborne case. The title surely was responsible for the titles of two novels that followed, *The Man Whose Dreams Came True* (1968) and *The Man Who Lost His Wife* (1970). By the time that he wrote the last of these, Julian was beginning to travel frequently to the Continent, and later novels move to exotic settings, Yugoslavia in this case. The title, *The Man Who. . . ,* has been perpetuated this year, 1992, in honor of Julian's eightieth birthday. For this occasion Macmillan, his publisher, commissioned thirteen famous crime writers (including Eric Ambler and P. D. James) to write short stories; the title of each begins with "The Man Who. . . ." Only Ambler fails to carry out *that* part of the scheme.

Another phase of Julian's work that had not started by 1970 was represented by *The Blackheath Poisonings* of 1978. This Victorian crime novel was followed by *Sweet Adelaide* (1980, based on an actual murder case of 1886 that is still a mystery) and *The Detling Murders* of 1982. These fictional excursions into the past came rather naturally to Julian, because he had often worked in the field of Victorian social history and biography; two of his early books are studies of Charles Dickens (1951) and Thomas Carlyle (1952). The most recent novels, beginning with *The Criminal Comedy of the Contented Couple* (1985), mark a return to the contemporary scene. One of them, *Death's Darkest Face* (1990), is based on a very ingenious time scheme that moves back and forth from the 1930s to the 1960s, and in the end Julian introduces himself into the case as an "armchair detective." This novel has its counterpart in his literary history called *The Thirties: A Dream Resolved* (1960), a valuable illustrated account of the period by one who had some part in it. Julian likes to think of himself as a man of the 1930s, that being the decade in which he came of age; he often looks back on it fondly. In 1990 he reprinted it with a long postscript, and at that time the book became *The Thirties and the Nineties,* in which one decade is set off against the other. (The illustrations are unfortunately missing from the new version.) Julian finds much that is dismaying in the artistic and literary fashions of the present decade, and he lets Wyndham Lewis have the last word, in describing (during the 1950s) the kind of figure who would dominate the artistic scene of the future: "The exhibitionist extremist promoter driving the whole bag of tricks into a nihilistic nothingness or zero."

Lewis has an important part in Julian's major critical work, *Makers of the New: The Revolution in Literature, 1912–1939,* which came out in 1987. This book goes over some of the same ground that Hugh Kenner covers in *The Pound Era* (1971); both writers have Lewis, James Joyce, Pound, and Eliot as their central figures – the "men of 1914," in Lewis's phrase. But *Makers of the New* has a somewhat different emphasis; it is partly based on the files of the little magazines – notably the *Egoist* and the *Little Review* – where much of the early important work of these writers first appeared. And Julian allows himself far more independence in judging them than Kenner does; he will not accept everything that Eliot and the others wrote as being of the highest importance. He carried the subject forward to a second generation of writers (Ernest Hemingway and Hart Crane among others) as modernism found its true home in the United States. But *Tarr* (1918), *Ulysses* (1922), *Hugh Selwyn Mauberley* (1920), and *The Waste Land* (1922) still represent for him the peak in Anglo-American literary culture of this century.

Julian's recent *Portraits of the Missing* (1991) is one of his most original and amusing achievements in fiction and social history. It consists of eight loosely connected miniatures, each of which could have been a novel. In a sense Julian himself is the principal character (at least the observer) even though each episode is based on a mostly fictional figure whom he could not quite fit into one of his novels. Numerous persons who one knows are "real," some of them still living, move in and out of the scene. The satiric element is stronger than ever. So here the author has devised a scheme (adapted from Max Beerbohm's *Seven Men* [1919]) that easily accommodates both history and fiction. This is a late work, a jeu d'esprit, by one who has survived much of the twentieth century with undiminished zest and intelligence. He is a model for what an independent man of letters can still be.

New Literary Periodicals: A Report for 1992

Richard R. Centing
Ohio State University

The following report on new literary periodicals, the sixth in a series of annual reports appearing in the *Dictionary of Literary Biography Yearbook,* documents scholarly journals, annuals, newsletters, and reviews launched in 1992, along with some 1990 and 1991 titles that were not covered last year. Any 1992 titles that are missed will be covered in *Yearbook: 1993.* These descriptions are not meant to be evaluative, although the importance of a few titles is stressed. By highlighting outstanding facets of each serial, our intention is to bring them to the attention of librarians and scholars for purposes of collection development and scholarly submission and to alert indexing services of the need for the inclusion of new titles in their core lists. Please contact the author with any comments on the report for 1992 or suggestions for inclusion in the 1993 report.

Before the survey of new periodicals begins, attention should be drawn to a major directory of English-language literary journals that should now be considered the first stop for information on the existing universe of publications. *The Fifth Directory of Periodicals Publishing Articles on American and English Language and Literature, Criticism and Theory, Film, American Studies, Poetry and Fiction* (Athens: Ohio University Press, 1992), compiled by Richard G. Barlow, is a classified directory that updates and expands *The Fourth Directory of Periodicals,* published in 1974 and compiled by Donna Gerstenberger and George Hendrick. The expanded *Fifth Directory* is organized into six general categories: (1) literature, (2) criticism and theory, (3) film, (4) language and linguistics, (5) american studies, and (6) poetry and fiction. A subject index allows access to single-author journals under the name of the author – for example, "Hughes, Langston" leads to the *Langston Hughes Review* (1982) – or by general subject – for example, "Humor" leads to *Studies in American Humor* (1974). The directory is selective, so that only two major titles are included on James Joyce, skipping the newsletters on Joyce that we have covered in the *DLB Yearbook.* The entries in the directory provide basic information such as address, scope, and styles of submission, much the same kind of information that can be found in the *MLA Directory of Periodicals,* whose last edition of 1990–1991 contains listings on the MLA Master List as of 23 February 1990.

American Periodicals: A Journal of Historical, Critical, and Bibliographical Commentary (Research Society for American Periodicals, University of North Texas, P.O. Box 5096, UNT Station, Denton, TX, 76203) is an annual that was first published in fall 1991. The editor is James T. F. Tanner, who also serves as treasurer for the Research Society for American Periodicals (RSAP), an organization interested in studies of American literary periodicals of the nineteenth century. Since summer 1990 the society has also published the *RSAP Newsletter.* The new journal is the scholarly outlet for researchers in American periodical history. The first annual contains eight long articles, seven book reviews, the constitution of the RSAP, and a bibliography of recent scholarship on American periodicals. Journals discussed in the articles include *The Crayon, Scribner's Monthly,* and *Five O'Clock.* Excellent illustrations drawn from nineteenth-century periodicals decorate and enhance the journal.

Art & Understanding (900 Central Avenue, Suite 177, Albany, NY, 12206) is a quarterly newsletter dedicated to publishing poetry, essays, diary entries, and short fiction concerning the AIDS crisis and its relationship to literature and the arts. The premiere issue, Fall 1991, includes original poetry by Tim Dlugos, a widely published poet who died of AIDS on 3 December 1990 at the age of forty; "The Care and Treatment of Pain," a poem in memory of Allen Barnett, by David Bergman, recipient of the 1984 Elliston poetry prize for *Cracking the Code* (Columbus: Ohio State University Press, 1985); and poems by Mark O'Donnell, Sam Ambler, Linda Boulette, and Pat Vivian. Janet Howey, a worker in an AIDS hospice, offers horrific descriptions of the ways of death from AIDS. Supported by the AIDS Council of Northeastern New York, *Art & Understanding* is edited by David Waggoner.

Cover for the first issue of the journal founded to continue the tradition of the New York Public Library research bulletins, the last of which was published in 1987

Winter 1992 is the date of the first number of *At Random* (Random House, 201 East 50th Street, New York, NY, 10022), a promotional magazine that includes excerpts from new books published by Random House and its associate imprints, Times Books and Villard. It is published a minimum of three times a year and distributed free of charge in bookstores. There are excerpts from Edward de Grazia's study of censorship, *Girls Lean Back Everywhere* (1992); Anita Brookner's novel, *A Closed Eye* (1991); and James A. Michener's memoir, *The World Is My Home* (1992), featuring his description of the running of the bulls at the annual San Fermin festival in Pamplona, Spain. Michener mentions Ernest Hemingway, and a photograph of a bare-chested Hemingway, taken by *Vogue* magazine in 1950 at the Finca Vigia, Cuba, illustrates the first cover of *At Random*. The Hemingway photograph is reprinted from *On the Edge: Images from 100 Years of Vogue* (1992). *At Random* also includes miscellaneous book news such as a list supplied by Salman

Rushdie of the books he is currently reading, a report that Marlon Brando is writing his autobiography, and photographic coverage of a party for Norman Mailer, who had just published *Harlot's Ghost* (1991). Some of the authors are also interviewed at the time their book is published. It is edited by Helen Morris and issued in print runs of fifty thousand.

The semiannual *Biblion* (New York Public Library, Publications Office, 8 West 40th Street, 3rd Floor, New York, NY, 10018) revives the NYPL tradition of bibliographic research bulletins that were published from 1897 to 1987. The new series begins with Fall 1992, promising articles "about the collections, services, and staff of the New York Public Library's Research and Branch Libraries, as well as original research based on the Library's resources." The editor, Anne Skillion, special assistant to the director, Paul Fasana, begins her first issue with talks given on the occasion of the Berg Collection's acquisition of the Vladimir Nabokov Archive. Other articles discuss translations of the Book of Common Prayer, Russian coronation albums, and the history of the Municipal Reference Library of the City of New York, 1913–1969. Anthony M. Warren, assistant librarian for resources in the Research Libraries, provides the first annual, selective bibliography of 1990 publications of which the NYPL is the subject, author, or publisher. For example, under "B" are listed the annual bibliographic guides published by G. K. Hall that document acquisitions by the NYPL in such areas as black studies, dance, and theater arts. The late Lola Szladits (1923–1990) is memorialized in a series of short tributes by such writers as Herbert Mitgang of the *New York Times;* she had served as curator of the Berg Collection of English and American Literature. The journal is handsomely produced and illustrated with such reproductions as a page from an Esperanto Book of Common Prayer.

Common Knowledge (Oxford University Press, 200 Madison Avenue, New York, NY, 10016) "publishes work in the arts, social sciences, cultural studies, and intellectual history." It is published three times a year and edited by Jeffrey M. Perl. The subjects of the articles cover a multitude of topics from Ludwig Wittgenstein to feminism, although many of the articles stress literary concerns. "Books, Canons, and the Nature of Dispute," by G. Thomas Tanselle, offers insights into the relationship of textual criticism, the canons of literature, and "so-called rare-book collections." Four letters from poet Philip Levine respond to the life and work of Henri Coulette. Richard E. Palmer, chair of the philosophy department at MacMurray College (Jacksonville, Illinois), translates "Toward a Philosophy of Style," by Manfred Frank, professor of philosophy at the University of Tübingen. A complex essay by Julia Kristeva is also translated. The journal concludes with a few book reviews. The editorial board boasts such names as Stanley Cavell, Hugh Kenner, Czeslaw Milosz, and Susan Sontag. The journal began publishing in 1992.

Sponsored by the International Society for Contemporary Legend Research, *Contemporary Legend* (Hisarlik Press, 4 Catisfield Road, Enfield Lock, Middlesex, England EN3 6BD) is an annual compilation of scholarly articles and bibliographies that was first issued in 1991. Legend is interpreted in its broadest sense as including "Sagen, dites, popular rumors, sayings and beliefs as well as narrative," recognizing that "no consensus exists as to the definition of contemporary legend." In contrast to exponents of electronic information, the journal feels that the permanence of a printed text is superior to a "computerized world of information overload." The complex interactions of popular culture and folklore are analyzed, along with stories about cattle mutilation and freeway violence. One article on AIDS-infected employees of fast-food franchises utilizes field journals of English students at Wayne State University. The editor, Paul Smith, is in the Department of Folklore, Memorial University of Newfoundland, Canada. His editorial board is affiliated worldwide.

Current Books Magazine (Washington Media Group, Inc., P.O. Box 34468, Bethesda, MD, 20827) is a bimonthly that first appeared in summer 1992. The editor, Edwin S. Grosvenor, calls it a "sampling of excerpts," which is one way to describe this magazine that presents around thirty selections from new books in each issue. The selections are reprinted in classified sections such as "Poetry," "Fiction," "Sport," and "Personalities." Three poets are represented in the first issue: Robert Creeley, Mona van Duyn, and Philip Levine. The fiction includes stories by Jane Smiley and Joyce Carol Oates. Cartoons are also included: two cartoons from Gary Larson's "Far Side" anthology *Wiener Dog Art* (1990) and a strip from G. B. Trudeau's "Doonesbury" collection *I'd Go With The Helmet, Ray* (1991). "Abraham Lincoln Up Close," by Gore Vidal, is adapted from his introduction to Lincoln's works in the Library of America edition. Former president Jimmy Carter contributes "The

Joy of Fishing" from the current Bantam Books edition of *An Outdoor Journal: Adventures and Reflections* (1988). Rushdie's essay "Is Nothing Sacred?" is taken from *Imaginary Homelands* (1991). The magazine was lauded in *USA TODAY* and other national media, possibly reflecting the fact that the editor/publisher is from the family that founded *National Geographic*.

Hellas: A Journal of Poetry and the Humanities (Aldine Press, Ltd., 304 South Tyson Avenue, Glenside, PA, 19038) is a semiannual, the first issue of which is dated Spring 1990. The editor is Gerald Harnett. The primary thrust of *Hellas* is the advancement of poetry and poetics through a unique combination of scholarly articles and original poetry that favors a return to meaning and meter as opposed to what it calls "meaninglessness and inelegantly ordinary diction." Its critical stance appears to counter the trends of critical theories such as deconstruction. One of the essays on "Poetic Innovation" is by William Baer, the editor of the journal of New Formalism, *The Formalist* (1990). Baer's essay approves William Butler Yeats's criticism of Ezra Pound's poetry as being too experimental, and it uses that ammunition to propound "metrical verse in formal stanzas." Each volume of *Hellas* totals over three hundred pages, and the range of subjects covered is enormous, advocating New Classicism but also fearful of Augustan poetry that "has the tone and feeling of moral essays rather than lyric poetry." Another article compares two poems by Horace and Maria Rainer Rilke about fountains and provides new translations of both poems. The pronunciation of Greek meter and intelligibility in music are two other examples of the wide-ranging essays. The original poetry is by established writers like Lewis Turco and younger students like Katherine Varnes. Poet Dana Gioia chimes in with a defense of form in verse and against "free-verse." *Hellas* was voted an honorable mention in the best new journal category for 1991 by the Conference of Editors of Learned Journals.

Irish Studies Review (Newton Park, Bath, Avon, England BA2 9BN) is a semiannual sponsored by the British Association for Irish Studies. Edited by Neil Sammells, Paul Hyland, and David Timms, the first issue is dated Spring 1992. The illustrated articles cover various subjects of interest, such as the revolutionary decade 1912–1922 and education in summer schools in Ireland. The bulk of the magazine, however, involves literary topics such as British television drama, the making of the *Great Book of Ireland,* the making of the *Field Day Anthology of Irish Writing,* and the work of Dermot Bolger, "one of

Ireland's hottest young writers" and founder of Raven Arts Press. New poetry by Tony Curtis, Anne Haverty, and Matthew Sweeney is also included. One essay is concerned with the distorted image of Ireland presented in films, and another is by Fay Weldon on contemporary Irish fiction. There are hardly any references to Joyce except to comment that "the young and penniless James Joyce nevertheless owned 105 ties." An insert in the *Irish Studies Review* is the first number of the British Association for Irish Studies *Newsletter,* dated Spring 1992, "offered as a companion pull out to the new BAIS journal." The first item in the *Newsletter* is an address by Mary Robinson, the president of Ireland, to the University of Liverpool's Institute of Irish Studies, 16 December 1991. Other Irish-studies programs across Ireland are also profiled in the *Newsletter.*

Reflecting the interests of the Poetics and Linguistics Association in stylistic analysis, *Language and Literature* (Longman Group UK Ltd., Longman House, Burnt Mill, Harlow, Essex, England CM20 2JE) is published three times a year and first appeared in 1992. The editor is Mick Short of the University of Lancaster. He is assisted by an international editorial board. One essay studies Hemingway's style in the vignette from *In Our Time* (1925) that begins "They shot the six cabinet ministers at half past six in the morning against the wall of a hospital." Two other essays address dialect in writing and pronouns in William Shakespeare's *As You Like It.* There are three book reviews.

The Literary Network News (Council of Literary Magazines and Presses, 154 Christopher Street, New York, NY, 10014) is an eight-page newsletter informing the literary community on issues pertaining to freedom of expression, with a special focus on the National Endowment for the Arts. The quarterly was first issued in September 1992. The network is a project that is jointly administered by Poets and Writers and the Council of Literary Magazines and Presses (CLMP). The newsletter contains short items on banned books, list of organizations that support free expression, and an interview with poet Donald Hall about the directions of the NEA. No editor is identified, although Lisa J. Cooley is listed as project coordinator.

Maledicta Monitor: Verbal Aggression Newsletter (Maledicta, P.O. Box 14123, Santa Rosa, CA, 95402) is a quarterly update to *Maledicta: The International Journal of Verbal Aggression,* which has been issued in various states of frequency since 1977. They are both edited by Reinhold Aman, a former professor of philology and medieval literature, and are devoted to documentation and scholarship of "bad words" (*maledicta* in Latin), verbal abuse, slang, nicknames, swear words, insults, racial jokes, and all forms of improper language. The newsletter tracks the sayings of television comics such as Johnny Carson, reprints information on slang from local newspapers, runs notices about new books in the field, and attempts to source the first appearance of new terms. Various race/gender/ethnic offensive words are presented without censorship and basically without analysis. The first issue of *Maledicta Monitor* was Fall 1990.

The first issue of *Monad: Essays on Science Fiction* (Pulphouse Publishing, Inc., Box 1227, Eugene, OR, 97440) is dated September 1990. The second issue is dated March 1992, and its frequency is correctly listed as irregular. The editor is Damon Knight (1645 Horn Lane, Eugene, OR, 97404), an American science-fiction writer and editor. His editorials call for essays that are "entertaining but not frivolous, serious but not dull." *Monad* seeks to avoid the academic approach. The first essay, "Children, Women, Men, and Dragons," is by Ursula K. Le Guin and is the text of a talk she gave at the Göteborg Book Fair in Sweden in 1989. A short contribution by Brian W. Aldiss, "I Dream Therefore I Become," reflects on Aldiss's need to express his dreams while still writing for a commercial audience. In "Academic Criticism of Science Fiction: What It Is, and What It Should Be," Gary Westfahl claims that academic criticism is driven by the demands of tenure and promotion. William F. Wu, an American writer of Chinese descent, discusses the use of such terms as "Oriental" and "Asian" in science fiction. The twelve essays in the first two issues are an excellent sampler of opinion from writers in the field.

Charles Raisch edits the irregular *New Mystery* (New Mystery Group, 175 Fifth Avenue, Suite 2001, New York, NY, 10010), whose first issue came out in 1991 dated July/August and whose second issue is merely called number two. It is a fanzine that publishes book reviews and original mystery fiction. Authors such as Shizuko Natsuke, Bill Crider, John Lutz, David Zeltserman, William Ruud, and Albert Ashforth appear in each heavily advertised issue. Fillers such as the addresses of mystery bookstores conclude its mysterious pages.

Popular Culture in Libraries (Haworth Press, Inc., 10 Alice Street, Binghamton, NY, 13904) is a quarterly that was first published in December 1992, although the cover bears the date 1993. It is edited by Frank Hoffmann, School of Library Science, Sam Houston State University. He is advised by a "Board of Consulting Editors" that includes academics from English, history, communications, music, African-American studies, and sociology. The types of materials to be covered in the journal include comic books, all kinds of fiction, the mass media, oral tradition, and mass movements such as woman suffrage. The journal will focus on describing collections in libraries and archives, in addition to reviewing new books in the field. The first issue contains articles relating to the famous Bowling Green State University Popular Culture Collection, whose Ray Bradbury Collection contains "more than 1,500 published works." Other articles provide original research on comic-strip theatricals (stage productions based on comic strips such as "Li'l Abner"), with a chart on turn-of-the-century versions such as "The Yellow Kid," "The Katzenjammer Kids," and "Little Nemo"; music from Africa; and the Washington Post Photo Research Center. The journal is very concerned about bringing the scholar into decisions concerning collection development in libraries.

Prosthesis (University of Western Ontario, Centre for the Study of Theory and Criticism, London, Ontario, N6A 3K7, Canada) is an annual journal of critical theory that is edited by graduate students and whose contributors are graduate students from the United States and Canada. It calls for submissions from a multitude of disciplines, including Marxian analysis, feminist studies, art history, and psychoanalysis. The subjects of the articles include a discourse analysis of Plato's *Dialogues,* a critique of the critical theory of Jürgen Habermas, a critique of the critical theory of Michel Foucault, the application of the structural semiotics of A. J. Greimas to Zen koans, the relationship of gender to art history, and subjectivity in feminist theory. Ban Wang, a Chinese Ph.D. candidate in comparative literature at UCLA who has translated into Chinese Emerson's essay "The American Scholar," offers "Symbol vs. Allegory: Reading Benjamin's Theory of Allegory through Hegel." The editors are Grant Stirling and Imre Szeman. The first annual, for 1992, concludes with three book reviews.

Sharp News (Society for the History of Authorship, Reading and Publishing, c/o Editor, Jonathan Rose, Drew University, Department of History, Madison, NJ, 07940) is a quarterly newsletter whose first issue is dated Winter 1991–1992. SHARP is a new scholarly organization devoted to all aspects of book history. Its inaugural conference was held in New York City 9–11 June 1992, jointly sponsored by the English and history departments of the City University of New York Graduate Center. The newsletter includes an introduction to the goals of the society and announcements about conferences of other societies interested in publishing

history, provides details on SHARP e-mail that is available on electronic networks, and lists new books and articles on the field (including French and German publications).

Textual Studies in Canada (University College of the Cariboo, Faculty of Arts, Kamloops, British Columbia, V2C 5N3 Canada) is an annual that was first issued in 1991. It is group-edited by Catherine Carlson and six others. Its goal is to provide a "collaborative and interdisciplinary forum in which researchers and teachers can address issues related to the study of texts within a Canadian context." Discourse analysis, popular culture, critical theory, feminism, reading theory, rhetoric, and composition are listed as "appropriate subjects." The first annual is over two hundred pages long and includes essays titled "Toward a Canadian Rhetoric," "The Grain of Sand in the Oyster: Competency Testing as a Catalyst for Attitude Change at the University," and "Meals and Manners: Women and Language in Upper Canada." A section called "The Postcard Project" reproduces postcard art sent to *TSC.* Original poetry is also included, such as "Over-Ripe Grain" by the well-known Canadian writer George Bowering. It concludes with four substantial book reviews.

Ralph Waldo Emerson (1803–1882) is the object of scrutiny in the semiannual *Emerson Society Papers* (c/o the Secretary, Wesley T. Mott, Ralph Waldo Emerson Society, Worcester Polytechnic Institute, Worcester, MA, 01609), an eight-page newsletter issued since spring 1990. It is edited by Douglas Emory Wilson, one of the editors of *The Collected Works of Ralph Waldo Emerson* (Harvard University Press). The newsletter publishes abstracts of papers given at Emerson conferences, memorializes deceased Emerson scholars, has news on forthcoming meetings, reviews new books, and has short articles such as "Emerson and Brook Farm," by Len Gougeon (University of Scranton). Emerson is also studied in *ESQ: A Journal of the American Renaissance* (formerly *Emerson Society Quarterly,* 1955–1968).

Emily Dickinson (1830–1886) is currently the subject of the major *Dickinson Studies* (formerly the *Emily Dickinson Bulletin,* 1968–1978) and the minor *Single Hound* (1989). They are now joined by the exemplary *Emily Dickinson Journal* (University Press of Colorado, P.O. Box 849, Niwot, CO, 80544), a semiannual edited by Suzanne Juhasz of the University of Colorado, Boulder. Sponsored by the Emily Dickinson International Society, its first issue of 1992 includes five essays on Dickinson's response to the singer Jenny Lind, her letters, her use of the gothic, her death poems, and her inclusion of the

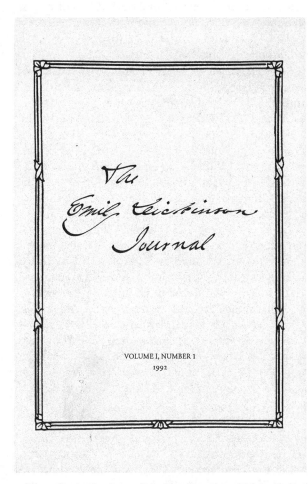

Cover for the first issue of the journal sponsored by the Emily Dickinson International Society

feminine in Christian discourse. There are two review essays covering new books on Dickinson.

Frank Wedekind (1864–1918), the German dramatist, poet, and short-story writer, is the subject of the annual *Frank Wedekind Yearbook* (Peter Lang, 62 West 45th Street, 4th Floor, New York, NY, 10036). The editors are Rolf Kieser, professor of German literature, City University of New York, and Reinhold Grimm, professor of comparative and German literatures, University of California, Riverside. Wedekind scholars offer nine essays on such topics as the Lulu plays, a comparison of Wedekind and Franz Kafka, and an analysis of the bibliographies on Wedekind. The first annual for 1991 contains an introduction by Grimm which claims there is a renaissance in Wedekind studies, for which the yearbook plans to be the English-language focal point.

The first issue of *Stephen Crane Studies* (Virginia Polytechnic Institute and State University, Department of English, Blacksburg, VA, 24061) appeared in spring 1992. The semiannual is edited by Paul

Sorrentino. Sponsored by the Stephen Crane Society, whose first meeting was in San Diego in 1990 at the American Literature Association Conference, the modest twenty-four page journal contains four articles on such subjects as the final charge in *The Red Badge of Courage* (1895) and postmodern critical approaches to Crane studies.

American poet Robert Frost (1874–1963) is the subject of the *Robert Frost Review* (Robert Frost Society, Winthrop College, Department of English, Rock Hill, SC, 29733), an annual which started in 1991. The editor, Frost scholar Earl J. Wilcox, used to edit the *Robert Frost Newsletter,* which appeared annually within the *South Carolina Review* in a special section on Frost. The new review is dedicated to "the dean of Robert Frost criticism," Laurence Perrine, who contributes an analysis of Frost's poem "The Telephone." Other essays study the texts of Frost's "November," his humor, the influence of William Wordsworth, and the influence of British poet Andrew Lang, particularly *Grass of Parnassus* (1888). Book reviews and news items complete the review.

Sinclair Lewis (1885–1951) is the subject of the *Sinclair Lewis Society Newsletter* (Illinois State University, English Department, Normal, IL, 61761). The Sinclair Lewis Society held its first meeting 30 May 1992 as part of the American Literature Association Conference in San Diego. The semiannual newsletter was first issued in fall 1992. Its six unnumbered pages include business information about the organization, notices on new books, and an article on teaching Sinclair Lewis. The editor, Sally E. Parry, is a professor at Illinois State University, where she teaches American literature, women's studies, and film. Her doctoral dissertation from Fordham University in 1986 is on Sinclair Lewis, and she has also published numerous papers on his work. The current newsletter is not related to the *Sinclair Lewis Newsletter* that was issued by Saint Cloud State University from 1969 to 1976.

E. E. Cummings (1894–1962), the American poet and novelist, is the dedicated focus of *Spring: The Journal of the E. E. Cummings Society* (c/o the editor, Norman Friedman, 33–54 164th Street, Flushing, NY, 11358), whose first annual volume came out late 1992. This new series replaces an earlier newsletter issued quarterly from April 1981 to June 1991. The editor, poet Norman Friedman, is a major scholar of Cummings's work. The annual includes articles on *The Enormous Room* (1922) and studies of the play *him* (1927), Cummings's relationship with *The Dial,* and a plea for an E. E. Cummings stamp during his centennial in 1994. An annotated bibliography of recent Cummings scholarship concludes the annual.

American novelist Vardis Fisher (1895–1968), known for historical novels such as *Children of God* (1939), which is about the rise of Mormonism, is the subject of the *Vardis Fisher Newsletter* (Dancing Badger Press, 1260 East Stratford Avenue, Salt Lake City, UT, 84106). The quarterly began in 1990 and is associated with the Vardis Fisher Society run by Mick McAllister. The newsletter is a modest effort with articles on such subjects as Fisher's novel *The Mothers: An American Saga of Courage* (1943). There is a book review of Tim Woodward's biography of Fisher, *Tiger on the Road* (1989). The only library location for the newsletter is the Stewart Library of Weber State University in Ogden, Utah, where an extensive Fisher collection is housed.

There have been two periodicals devoted to William Faulkner (1897–1962): the *Faulkner Journal* (University of Akron, Department of English, Akron, OH, 44325) and the *Faulkner Newsletter & Yoknapatawpha Review* (P.O. Box 248, Oxford, MS, 38655). The following two publications bring the total to four.

The semiannual *Faulkner Studies* (Yamaguchi Publishing House, 72 Tsukuda-cho, Ichijoji, Sakyoku, Kyoto, 606 Japan) began in 1992. The editors are Michel Gresset (University of Paris), Kenzaburo Ohashi (Tsurumi University), Kiyoyuki Ono (Chiba University), and Noel Polk (University of Southern Mississippi). The journal is already being indexed in the CD-ROM version of the *MLA International Bibliography*. The journal announces its desire to be "an international journal," so all the articles "will be published in English." The first issue features two articles on Faulkner's novel *Mosquitoes* (1927), and Haruko Ohmine's "The Umbilical Cord of Narrative in *Absalom, Absalom!*" It also includes a review essay of three books of Faulkner criticism. The second issue studies *A Fable* (1954), *As I Lay Dying* (1930), the two manuscripts of the introduction to *The Sound and the Fury* (1929), and the short story "Uncle Willy." Also, four books of Faulkner criticism are reviewed.

Teaching Faulkner (Southeast Missouri State University, Center for Faulkner Studies, One University Plaza, Cape Girardeau, MO, 63701) is a semiannual newsletter whose first number is dated Spring 1992. The editor is Robert W. Hamblin. The newsletter grew out of the "Teaching Faulkner" sessions that have been, since 1989, a part of an annual conference held at the University of Mississippi. The six-page newsletter has short pieces on teaching Faulkner in Amsterdam, a teacher/scholar project

on Faulkner's French reputation, and strategies for teaching *The Sound and the Fury*.

The semiannual, independent *Alea* (Gnosis Press, P.O. Box 42, Prince Street Station, New York, NY, 10012) was first issued in spring 1990. The original editor, Ethan Anton, has returned to his native Czechoslovakia, and the review is now coedited by Stephen Sartarelli and Thomas Epstein. It is devoid of book reviews, advertisements, and other fillers and publishes poetry, short stories, and essays. The title, *Alea,* means "chance" or "die" (dice) in Latin, and the editors hope to focus on the "hidden, divine aspect of chance and creation." Leading writers from around the world are the contributors, and many pieces are presented in translation from Russian, French, Spanish, and Italian. An excerpt from a novel-in-progress by John Hawkes is included, along with poetry by Mario Luzi, Leonard Schwartz, Edwin Honig, and Nina Kossman. Essays of high intelligence, such as "Innate Totems," by Allen S. Weiss, author of *The Aesthetics of Excess* (1989), discuss surrealism and André Breton. The Romanian-French author E. M. Cioran is interviewed. The journal is illustrated with artwork.

Array is an independent published three times a year (c/o publisher/editor Bess A. Holloway, 3400 22nd Street, Boulder, CO, 80304); the first issue is dated Spring/Summer 1992 and includes six poems, three fiction pieces, and four essays. The contributors are all educated residents of Colorado except Lauren D. Holloway of Ranchos de Taos, New Mexico, "a high school student who writes, paints and participates in musical productions locally." Holloway's essay "Life in New Mexico" notes that "the church bells ring frequently, reminding those attending local bars that there is still a God and there is still a community, and there certainly is still a Spanish Catholic Church." Margaret Volpe Posnick, a professional dancer with a "strong interest in the writing arts," wonders – in her poem "Dual Illusions" – about "dancers who write."

The first issue of *Black Bough* (P.O. Box 465, Somerville, NJ, 08876) is copyright 1992. The poetry journal is devoted to haiku and the related forms of tanka, senryu, and *haibun*. The first issue has sixty-five poems. The editors are Kevin Walker and Charles Easter. It has no stated frequency.

The Bridge: A Journal of Fiction & Poetry (14050 Vernon Street, Oak Park, MI, 48237) is an independent semiannual whose first number was dated Fall 1990. The editor, Jack Zucker, is a widely published poet and poetry activist in Michigan. Established poets such as Alberta Turner, Harriet Zinnes, Ruth Whitman, and X. J. Kennedy are published, along with lesser-known talents such as Lawrence Pike, Yvonne Hardenbrook, and Hank Malone. A good Detroit-area poet, Henrietta Epstein, offers "Memories of Normandy Street, Detroit," in which she describes the boys she loved as those who "studied Latin and never fought in the right wars." Epstein's poem "Lists" asks for her name to be removed from various lists if one cannot hear her voice "as you set your clock at midnight." The fiction writers have substantial credentials: Steven Tudor, Judith McCombs, John Pesta, and Evelyn Shefner. The book reviews treat interesting subjects such as Donald Hall's long poem, *The One Day* (1988).

Looking like an underground newspaper, the *Cleveland Review* (P.O. Box 181093, Cleveland Heights, OH, 44118) is published and edited by Geoffrey Singer. The contents are mainly poetry, presented in a variety of typefaces and illustrated with numerous photographs and drawings. Announced as a quarterly, the first number came out in fall 1991, while the second number is dated Winter/Spring 1992. Some of the authors are Todd Kalinski, Michelle Perez, Ben Gulyas, Ansel Weese, Amy L. Young, Bill Shields, and Georgiana Eckles.

Sarah Randolph, the editor of the annual *Cosmos* (Cosmos Press, P.O. Box 1456, Provincetown, MA, 02657), is a poet and weekly columnist for the *Provincetown Paper*. The first *Cosmos* is dated Summer 1992 and contains ten poems, a couple of very short prose pieces, and illustrative drawings. The Cosmos Press also publishes books, and some of its authors, such as Candice Reffe, are represented in *Cosmos*.

June 1992 saw the first appearance of the monthly *Dallas Review* (P.O. Box 852757, Mesquite, TX, 75185). It publishes poetry, stories, and light essays. The nationwide roster of contributors does include writers from Greater Dallas. The editor is Bob McCranie. One poet, identified as R. Yurman from San Francisco, reacts to paintings of breasts in his or her poem "Gallery Opening." Sharon Warycka, a former nurse, reacts in the story "Keepsakes" to the belongings of the dead. Other contributors include Mary Diesel and Mary Armstrong.

The Four Directions: American Indian Literary Quarterly (Snowbird Publishing Company, P.O. Box 729, Tellico Plains, TN, 37385) was first available early in 1992. The editor is Joanna Meyer, a Cherokee/Navajo who is a registered nurse specializing in trauma and acute critical care. The quarterly features original poetry, short stories, artwork, and essays by American Indians. Burning Bear (Chickamauga Cherokee/Creek), Little Rock Reed (Lakota), and John Reuther (Lakota) are among the contributors. Book reviews are included, such as

Cover for the first issue of a quarterly devoted mainly to short fiction

a long response by Mary Lockwood, an Inupiaq writer, to Gary Snyder's *The Practice of the Wild* (1990). Social issues, such as the impact of AIDS on the American Indian, are also covered.

The ambitiously produced and promoted *Glimmer Train Stories* (Glimmer Train Press, Inc., 812 SW Washington Street, Suite 1205, Portland, OR, 97205) is an independent quarterly mainly devoted to short fiction. It also includes general articles and interviews. Edited by two sisters, Susan Burnmeister and Linda Davis, the periodical pays "$300 for first publication and anthology rights." As its publicity says, it is "Printed on acid-free, recycled stock and packed in a tall paperback format." On newsstands, it appears as a brightly illustrated harbinger of delightful reading. With its ISSN, bar code on the cover, trademarked logo, witty asides, and unexpected graphics, *Glimmer Train* seduces the reader into sampling its contents. Each story is preceded by another packaging surprise: a biographical statement by each author along with a charming childhood photograph of the author. One of the short stories, "The Reunion Joke," is by David Huddle, the Robert Frost Professor of American Literature at the University of Vermont since 1971. His childhood photograph shows him in band uniform, and his biographical statement includes important credits in fiction, nonfiction, and poetry. Another author, Elizabeth Inness-Brown, published in the *New Yorker,* while Amy Selwyn, who works at the *New York Times,* appears in print for the first time. The first three issues (Winter, Spring, and Summer 1992) include interviews with Siobhan Dowd, from the American chapter of PEN International; Vana O'Brien, an actress from Portland, starring in the West Coast premiere of Peter Shaffer's *Lettice and Lovage;* Gerard Byrne, an Irish painter; Maina Wa Kinyatti, an exile from Kenya; and Dennis Clemmens, a Portland watercolor artist. *Glimmer Train Stories* is the most professional of all the literary reviews launched in 1992.

Named after the county in which it is situated, *Habersham Review* (Piedmont College, Demorest, GA, 30535) is a prestige vehicle created to enhance the image of a small (enrollment 588), private, Congregational church–related liberal-arts college that has embarked on an ambitious expansion program. The coeditors, David L. Greene and Lisa Hodgens, clearly introduce the semiannual in their introduction, "At the Beginning," which announces their intention to "feature work by Southern writers and writing centered on the South." Both newcomers and established writers contribute short stories and poetry. As each issue plans to feature an interview with a prominent southern writer, the first issue, Autumn 1991, interviews the novelist Terry Kay and publishes his short story, "Death in a Small Town." The advisory board includes one of America's finest editors, Stanley W. Lindberg, editor of the *Georgia Review.*

Harvard Review (Harvard University, Poetry Room, Cambridge, MA, 02138) released its premier issue in spring 1992. Slated to appear three times a year, each issue runs over two hundred pages. The editor, Stratis Haviaras, a native of Greece, curates the Poetry Room. The focus of the review is on original poetry, although it includes a sizable selection of fiction, essays, letters to the editor, and book reviews. A section called "Columns" includes short pieces on such topics as the culture wars, postmodernism, the theft of manuscripts from the Harvard Library, communicating with students at lunch, and the social function of the theater. The list of contrib-

uting poets is studded with names from the current pantheon: A. R. Ammons, John Ashbery, Seamus Heaney, and Charles Simic, along with lesser lights. Numerous translations of established figures such as Arthur Rimbaud and George Seferis are also included. The fiction includes translations of the short fiction of Ivan Mandy, a prominent Hungarian fiction writer. The signed reviews cover new poetry, criticism, biographies, film, Judaic songbooks, letters of famous authors, and reference tools on spoken-word cassettes: the whole gamut of the humanities. The *Harvard Review* is a busy international literary café, worthy of the prestigious name it carries.

The annual *Heartlands Today* (Firelands College, Writing Center, Huron, OH, 44839) is an anthology of essays, poetry, fiction, and photography that seeks "a living portrait of what it means to live in the Midwest today." Coedited by Nancy Dunham and Larry Smith, it first appeared in 1991. The majority of the contributors are from Ohio, Michigan, Wisconsin, and nearby states. A few contributors, such as Gary Snyder, are from outside the Midwest. A poem called "Detroit Was the City" is by Gary Pacernick, a professor at Wright State University, where he edits the poetry magazine *Images.* A writer from Texas, Carolyn Banks, contributed the essay "Growing Up Polish in Pittsburgh." Some book reviews are also included.

An epigraph from Jack Kerouac, "love's multitudinous boneyard of decay," decorates the title page of *Holdout* (Back Bay Station, Boston, MA, 02117), an independent semiannual published and edited by Glenn Stout. Proclaiming it has "no sense of political correctness," the first issue, Spring 1991, offers poems and short fiction from Boston-based writers such as George Fifield, a video artist and graphic designer, and Luke Salisbury, who teaches at Bunker Hill Community College.

The first semiannual issue of *Left Bank* (Blue Heron Publishing, Inc., 24450 NW Hansen Road, Hillsboro, OR, 97124) appeared in winter 1991 and the second issue in summer 1992. The best writers from the Pacific Northwest (including British Columbia) are showcased in this handsome review, which features essays, interviews, poetry, stories, and artwork. The editorial statement says that *Left Bank* authors "must have a strong connection to the Pacific Northwest." This regional qualification does not seem a limitation when names such as Ursula K. Le Guin, William Stafford, Ken Kesey, Wallace Stegner, and Barry Lopez are in the table of contents. Each issue of *Left Bank* has a theme, with the first on "Writing and Fishing," the second on "Extinction," and the third on "Sex/Family/Tribe." The third number reprints cartoons by Matt Groening and photographs of German street youth by Marsha Burns. The interview with Tess Gallagher in the second number was conducted in "the house she and Raymond Carver built as a writing retreat and romantic hideaway." Gallagher reacts strongly against the attention-getting article by Dana Gioia, "Can Poetry Matter?" (*Atlantic Monthly,* May 1991). Gallagher claims there is a wider audience for poetry than Gioia will admit. The editor of this intelligent review is Linny Stovall.

Long News: In the Short Century (P.O. Box 150–455, Brooklyn, NY, 11215) is a carefully crafted semiannual compilation of poetry, visual art, and stories which was first issued in 1991. Avant-garde in spirit and open to experimental forms and bizarre manipulations of images, the demanding lines require very close reading. The adventurous Clark Coolidge appears along with erotic photographs from performance artist Carolee Schneemann. Novelist Lewis Warsh here submits two poems. The editor of *Long News,* Barbara Henning, includes a surreal piece called "My Body, I Want." She is the author of the chapbook *Smoking in the Twilight Bar* (United Artists, 1988).

Maverick in the Chaparral (Route 2, P.O. Box 4915, Eagle Pass, TX, 78852) is an independent semiannual literary review publishing poems and very short stories. The publisher/editor is Carol Cullar, who also produced the blockprint cover art. Over thirty contributors from the Southwest (including California) are included, along with some from New York and Maine, with backgrounds as librarians, playwrights, and academic teachers. The first issue is dated April 1992. "Does the poem remain a central / aspect of your life?" asks Bayla Winters's "Like Sweet Respiration."

Meantime (420 Clinton Avenue, Apartment 5C, Brooklyn, NY, 11238) is an independent semiannual that began in fall 1992. It is devoted to stories and poems and is illustrated with photographs. The editor is William A. Eno, whose biographical statement says he is a "handyman." The contributors are called freelance writers, students, and massage therapists. The following is a complete poem, "Humpty Dumpty," by Sinclair Rankin: "Sometimes / I can't even bother to / clear the crap / off my bed." Rankin is also identified as a handyman.

Spring 1992 is the date of the first issue of the independent semiannual *Misnomer: The Matchhead of Reality* (P.O. Box 1395, Prestonsburg, KY, 41653). It is edited by Eric Cash and Jeff Weddle. The majority of the stapled sixty pages is devoted to poetry,

with the prolific Lyn Lifshin featured in the Fall 1992 issue. There are a few very short prose pieces. Small-press readers will recognize contributors such as Arthur Winfield Knight and A. D. Winans (both based in California), but many of the contributors are uncredentialed beginners. The last page features an advertisement for *Sure: The Charles Bukowski Newsletter* (surveyed in the *Yearbook: 1991*), and Bukowski is announced as the featured poet for the Spring 1993 issue of *Misnomer.*

The semiannual *New Poetry Journal* (Barbara Goodell, 82 East Maynard Avenue, Apt. A, Columbus, OH, 43202) was first published December 1991. Its thirty-nine pages contain thirty-six poems, including five by Barbara Goodell, the editor and publisher, who "is 56 years old and has been writing poetry for three years." Her own chapbook, *My Poetry* (1991), is available from the above address. Other authors in the journal are Michele Blumberg, Richard Bittner, Paula Amann, and Rae Beno. The styles and themes are simplistic and sentimental.

North Coast Review (Poetry Harbor, 1028 East 6th Street, Duluth, MN, 55805) was first published November 1992. It comes out three times a year and mainly publishes Minnesota poets such as Judy Lindberg, Oddio Nib, Greta Gaard, Francine Sterle, and Bud Backen. Five poems are included by Margaret Chilton, the 1968 winner of the Edna St. Vincent Millay Award. The publisher, Poetry Harbor, also sponsors radio broadcasts, writing workshops, poetry readings, and distributes *We Are All Living With Aids: A Rural Experience,* a 1992 chapbook of AIDS-responsive poetry. No one is listed as editor.

The semiannual *Northeast Arts* (Boston Arts Organization, Inc., J.F.K. Station, P.O. Box 6061, Boston, MA, 02114) began in 1992. African-American poet Leigh Donaldson is the editor. It contains poetry, very short fiction, and light essays on such subjects as the acceptance of jazz. One poem, "Ramada Inn," is by Otto Laske, a composer of computer music. One story, "The Oak & the Olive," is by novelist Sebastian Lockwood. A fine prose poem, "Ideals" by Thomas Wiloch, examines the interaction of a millionaire and a poor man.

The Olentangy River flows through Columbus, Ohio, near Ohio State University. The *Olentangy Review* (Moonkind Press, P.O. Box 02431, Columbus, OH, 43202) publishes poetry, short stories, and artwork. This independent semiannual is edited by the married team of Darryl Price and Melissa J. Price. The contributors are mostly from central Ohio and include Steve Abbott, an adjunct faculty of Columbus State Community College; and Elizabeth Ann James, "an eco-feminist" and "free-lance writer." A short story by Damian Kapral, "Dos Gatos en Caracas," is his first publication. The first two issues are dated Spring 1992 and Autumn 1992/Winter 1993. The Moonkind Press also issues chapbooks by the Prices.

The semiannual *One Meadway* (211 West 92nd Street, number 47, New York, NY, 10025) is published "under the auspices of Sarah Lawrence College." The first issue is dated Spring 1991. The founding editors are Dani Shapiro and Julie Shigekuni. The literary review publishes fiction, poetry, and nonfiction. There is no editorial introduction, no statement of purpose or plans, nor any explanation of its relationship to Sarah Lawrence College. The contributors have an active list of credits, and some, such as Stephen Dobyns, have an extensive vita. The entire nonfiction section consists of an interview with short-story writer Stuart Dybek, a professor at Western Michigan University, and an essay by Dobyns, "Writing the Reader's Life," about the importance of structure ("structure is strategy imposed upon time"). *One Meadway* also contains twenty-six poems and seven short stories.

The attractive *Open City* (Suite 14A, 118 Riverside Drive, New York, NY, 10024), published and edited by Thomas Beller and Daniel Pinchbeck, is an independent literary journal of fiction, poetry, nonfiction, and artwork. The first issue appeared in 1991 with no indication of frequency. A Grove Press author, Diane Williams, opens the journal with six very short stories. Her style is simple, although the nuances of the tales are elusive and complex. Other contributors are free-lance writers in New York City and artists connected with galleries such as Sonnabend. One writer is "at work on her first novel," and one is "writing a literary biography of Jim Thompson." The title of the journal refers to the Roberto Rossellini film of the same name and to the connotations of the word *open,* "the sense of possibility, the receptivity to the outsider." Hubert Selby, author of *Last Exit to Brooklyn* (1964), contributes "La Vie en Rose," a prose tribute to Edith Piaf that contains numerous references to jazz performers by nicknames such as "Bessie," "Prez," "Bird," and "Lady Day."

The *Oxford American* (115 1/2 South Lamar, Oxford, MS, 38655), a general-interest literary magazine, is edited by Marc Smirnoff. The quarterly first appeared in spring 1992. The roster of contributors is truly impressive, and contributions include poetry from John Updike, Charles Bukowski, X. J. Kennedy, and Fred Chappell; fiction by Barry Hannah; commentary by William F. Buckley, Jr., and Richard Ford; and essays by Louis D. Rubin, Jr., and Lewis Nordan. Writer

John Grisham, who lives in Oxford, Mississippi, reacts to the shadow of William Faulkner. An excellent interview, "Pauline Kael: The Critic Wore Cowboy Boots," elicits her opinion of movies based on Faulkner. And he is discussed again in a review of *Phil Stone of Oxford: A Vicarious Life* (University of Georgia Press, 1991). Also included are numerous advertisements from book publishers.

Promoted as "a magazine for creative fiction, poetry, & nonfiction," the *Pittsburgh Quarterly* (PQ, 36 Haberman Avenue, Pittsburgh, PA, 15211) is edited and published four times a year by Frank Correnti. The first issue is dated Winter 1991. Many of the pages are devoted to poetry, with contributions by regulars of the literary-magazine scene such as Laurel Speer, Arthur Winfield Knight, and D. Steven Conkle, along with poets from the Pittsburgh region. The interviews are an important feature, as with Sue Powers's interview with Greek-American Konstantinos Lardas, author of *Mourning Songs of Greek Women* (Garland, 1992). The widely published graphic artist John Sokol offers portraits of Pablo Neruda and William Burroughs. The portraits are drawn using words of the writers as the graphic line. Each issue has one or two short stories.

Raizirr (Urbanus Press, P.O. Box 192561, San Francisco, CA, 94119) is published and edited by Cameron Bamberger and Peter Drizhal. The first issue of this independent annual appeared in 1991. A variety of familiar names of the literary underground have contributed, such as A. D. Winans, Arthur Winfield Knight, and Lyn Lifshin. There are a few black-and-white illustrations, including reproductions of passport photos and artwork. The bulk of the journal is poetry along with a few very short prose pieces. Bohemian in spirit, with countercultural themes that reflect the attitudes of the Beat Generation, *Raizirr* is an irreverent mixture of street language and rhetorical lunacy.

The semiannual *Salamander* (c/o the Editor, Jennifer Barber, 48 Ackers Avenue, Brookline, MA, 02146) publishes poetry, short fiction, and short essays. The first issue is dated Fall 1992. It features established writers such as Maine poet Ira Sadoff, and newcomers such as novelist Susan Monsky, author of *Midnight Suppers* (Houghton Mifflin, 1983). Native Ohioan Sabra Loomis, author of the poetry collection *Rosetree* (Alice James Books, 1989), offers "Delia" and "The Music Cabinet" in *Salamander.* The poems by Barbara Helfgott Hyett are from *The Double Reckoning of Christopher Columbus* (University of Illinois Press, 1992).

The inaugural *Snail's Pace Review* (Snail's Pace Press, Inc., RR no. 2, P.O. Box 363, Brownell

Road, Cambridge, NY, 12816) is dated Spring 1991. The independent semiannual is edited by Ken Denberg and Darby Penney. It is devoted entirely to poetry. The contributors are an international crowd ranging from librarians to fiction writers, such as A. J. Wright, Jennifer Willoughby, Floyd Skloot, Halina Poswiatowska, Mordecai Marcus, Susan Ludvigson, and Harry Humes. Fred Chappell's "The Small Goodbye" says we must "wake in the morning convinced of having seen Brazil / And with no memory of ever having been there." Lee Upton's "Cuckoo Clock" says "The bird tells the hour, promptly / in three calls, without regret."

Pound's poem "Tenzone" (1913) takes its title from the Provençal literary term meaning a dialogue or debate in verse. "I beg you my friendly critics," Pound exclaims, "Do not set about to procure me an audience." *Tenzone* (Stone Cold Publishing, P.O. Box 236, Boston, MA, 02258) takes its title from the poem by Pound and reprints it as the first contribution to this bimonthly poetry journal. Looking for the "overlooked," the first issue of January/February 1993 (released December 1992) offers twenty-three poems by Dianne Holcomb, John Grey, Ernest A. Wight, Jr., B. Z. Niditch, Alvah K. Howe, Nita Penford, Joyce Wilson, Maureen Ryberg, and Robert S. Pease. The editor is Paul Cordeiro.

During autumn 1991 the first issue of *Three-Lobed Burning Eye* (Skankin' Dead Press, 150 Kreischer-Darrow, Bowling Green State University, Bowling Green, OH, 43403) appeared, illustrated with a demon's face with a pencil between its teeth. Inside more-alternative graphics surround the poetry and fiction. The contributors include poet Gay Brewer, on Raymond Chandler and David Mamet, whose poem "Down Where It's Cool" ends with the line: "creeping as on a thousand legs." Bob Gates, a professor in the English department at Syracuse University, contributed the very short story "Memoirs of the New Civilization," which takes place in a "postmodern deconstructed anti-humanistic" world where ex-presidents play horseshoes and tell dirty jokes. Stuart Friebert, director of the Creative Writing Program at Oberlin College, contributes two poems: "The Next One to Fall" and "The Grizzly Bear and the Chicken Flip." Other contributors are students or recent graduates of various institutions across the United States. *Three-Lobed Burning Eye* is published three times a year and is edited by Andrew Fuller and Matthew Duncan.

TO: A Journal of Poetry, Prose and the Visual Arts (P.O. Box 121, Narberth, PA, 19072) is a semiannual review that was first issued in summer 1992. It is edited by Seth Frechie and Andrew Mossin. The

journal's title is borrowed from the Objectivists' TO Press of the 1930s, and the editors will favor "work that intersects and renegotiates the modernisms of Stein, Williams, Duchamp, Stieglitz, *et al.*" Renowned San Francisco photographer Jock Sturges provides a portfolio of photographs of nudes that includes full frontal nudity of children. A. D. Coleman, photography critic for the *New York Observer,* contributes an essay on the FBI investigation of Sturges. The poetry includes John Ashbery's "The Departed Lustre" ("one is grateful for the patterns"), six poems by Raymond Federman, translations from the Italian, and work by Rachel Blau Du Plessis and Charles Bernstein. A short story by Stephen Dixon, "Moon," is from his recent collection *Long Made Short* (1992). The journal concludes with a "Documents and Reviews" section that includes an essay on Gertrude Stein's 1923 word portrait, "If I Told Him: A Completed Portrait of Picasso," along with six signed book reviews of mainstream and small presses.

Tomorrow: Speculative Fiction (Pulphouse Publishing, Inc., P.O. Box 1227, Eugene, OR, 97440) is a bimonthly devoted to original short stories and novelettes in the science fiction/horror/fantasy genre. The editor is Algis Budrys, who submits the only essay to the magazine, "Writing: Part One," in which he posits seven principles for the short story, concluding that "what most readers want most of the time is story, and that is what we are going to teach you." New talents are published in *Tomorrow* along with professionals such as Gene Wolfe. The first issue, released in fall 1992, is dated January 1993.

Charles E. Combs, director of theater, Plymouth State College, is the editor of the annual *New England Theatre Journal* (New England Theatre Conference, 50 Exchange Street, Waltham, MA, 02154), whose first issue appeared in 1990. J. Ellen Gainor, a professor of theater at Cornell University, studies female characters in George Bernard Shaw; Stuart E. Baker, a professor of theater at Florida State University, examines the theatrical images in William Shakespeare's *Taming of the Shrew;* and an article on managing ensemble theater in academe is by Thomas Leff, a free-lance director and designer. Other articles discuss German theater during 1919–1933 and exercises for actors. The New England connection is not dominant, although the journal calls for papers on New England theater.

The spring 1992 debut of the semiannual *TheatreForum* (University of California – San Diego, Department of Theatre, 9500 Gilman Drive, La Jolla, CA, 92093) enhances the coverage of contemporary theater tenfold. The editor, Theodore Shank, says his "chief aim is to document, discuss, and disseminate theatreworks which are innovative and provocative." International in scope, the heavily illustrated journal "embraces all aspects of live theatre performance including dance theatre, music theatre, performance art, mime, and forms yet to be devised." Playscripts on the cutting edge receive original publication in *TheatreForum,* with the first two issues publishing four new works: Mac Wellman's *7 Blowjobs;* the Maly Drama Theatre of Russia's *Gaudeamus;* Neil Bartlett and Nicolas Bloomfield's *A Judgement in Stone;* and José Rivera's *Marisol.* Interviews are also a continuing focus, including discussions with Athol Fugard, choreographer Wim Vandekeybus, and director Tina Landau. There are numerous articles on such subjects as the economics of Polish theater and Ariane Mnouchkine's reworking of the Greek classics in *Les Atrides.* NADA Théâtre, SOON 3, and GWAR are examples of groups covered in this avant-garde proselytizer.

The original series of *Modern Poetry in Translation,* which was founded by Ted Hughes and Daniel Weissbort, ran for forty-four issues from 1966 to winter 1981–1982. The new series of the revived title, *Modern Poetry in Translation* (King's College London, Department of French, Strand, London, England WC2R 2LS), began in summer 1992 as a semiannual. Daniel Weissbort (University of Iowa) is now the sole editor. The first number runs over two hundred pages and includes special features on "the major French poet of his generation," Yves Bonnefoy. This section includes a translation into French by Bonnefoy of a poem by John Donne. Other parts of *MPT* include translations into English of poems by Pier Paolo Pasolini and Paul Celan. The translations include brief introductory remarks by the translator. Four German poets are translated by Michael Hamburger. Michael Hulse contributed an essay on "German Poetry in Recent English Translation."

Stuart Gillespie of the Department of English, University of Glasgow, is the editor of the annual *Translation and Literature* (Edinburgh University Press, 22 George Square, Edinburgh, Scotland), which first appeared in 1992. The advisory board includes people such as Umberto Eco, Frank Kermode, and George Steiner. The first part of the scholarly journal includes four articles on English translations of Vladimir Mayakovsky, Samuel Beckett's translations of his own work, George

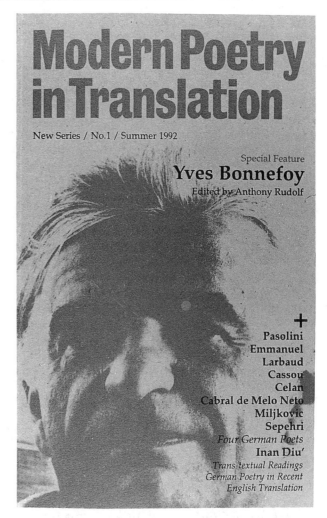

Cover for the first issue of the new series of the journal founded in 1966 by Ted Hughes and Daniel Weissbort

Chapman's translation of Homer's *Iliad* (1611), and a look at translation theory, which was established by the Romans (not by Plato, who "was committed to an epistemology in which truth was received directly from the gods"); the fifth article is "A Checklist of Restoration English Translations and Adaptations of Classical Greek and Latin Poetry, 1660–1700." The "Translators' Forum" has two articles on Virgil's *Aeneid* and dramatists of the Spanish Golden Age by the translators of these works. Other sections include actual translations of French poetry and a discussion of a Middle Dutch translation of the *Roman de la Rose* made around 1280. Over twenty book reviews cover new translations of Rilke, Kimon Friar, and Luis de Camões.

Isaac Asimov

(2 January 1920 – 6 April 1992)

William F. Touponce
Indiana University – Purdue University, at Indianapolis

SELECTED BOOKS: *Pebble in the Sky* (Garden City, N.Y.: Doubleday, 1950; London: Transworld [Corgi], 1958);

I, Robot (New York: Gnome Press, 1950; London: Grayson & Grayson, 1952);

The Stars, Like Dust (Garden City, N.Y.: Doubleday, 1951; Saint Albans, U.K.: Panther, 1958);

Foundation (New York: Gnome Press, 1951; London: Weidenfeld & Nicolson, 1953);

David Starr: Space Ranger, as Paul French (Garden City, N.Y.: Doubleday, 1952; London: World's Work, 1953);

Foundation and Empire (New York: Gnome Press, 1952; Saint Albans, U.K.: Panther, 1962);

The Currents of Space (Garden City, N.Y.: Doubleday, 1952; London: Boardman, 1955);

Second Foundation (New York: Gnome Press, 1953; London: Brown, Watson, 1958);

Lucky Starr and the Pirates of the Asteroids, as French (Garden City, N.Y.: Doubleday, 1953; London: World's Work, 1953);

The Caves of Steel (Garden City, N.Y.: Doubleday, 1954; London: Boardman, 1954);

Lucky Starr and the Oceans of Venus, as French (Garden City, N.Y.: Doubleday, 1954; London: G. Prior, 1979);

The Martian Way and Other Stories (Garden City, N.Y.: Doubleday, 1955; London: Dobson, 1964);

The End of Eternity (Garden City, N.Y.: Doubleday, 1955; London: Hamilton, 1959);

Lucky Starr and the Big Sun of Mercury, as French (Garden City, N.Y.: Doubleday, 1956; London: G. Prior, 1979);

The Naked Sun (Garden City, N.Y.: Doubleday, 1957; London: M. Joseph, 1958);

Lucky Starr and the Moons of Jupiter, as French (Garden City, N.Y.: Doubleday, 1957; London: G. Prior, 1979);

Earth is Room Enough (Garden City, N.Y.: Doubleday, 1957; London: Hamilton, 1960);

Isaac Asimov (photograph © 1986 by Layle Silbert)

Lucky Starr and the Rings of Saturn, as French (Garden City, N.Y.: Doubleday, 1958; London: George Prior, 1979);

The Death Dealers (New York: Avon, 1958); republished as *A Whiff of Death* (New York: Walker, 1968);

Nine Tomorrows: Tales of the Near Future (Garden City, N.Y.: Doubleday, 1959; London: Dobson, 1963);

The Intelligent Man's Guide to Science, 2 volumes (New York: Basic, 1960);

The Rest of the Robots (Garden City, N.Y.: Doubleday, 1964; London: Dobson, 1967);

Fantastic Voyage (Boston:: Houghton Mifflin, 1966; London: Dobson, 1966);

Through a Glass, Clearly (London: New English Library, 1967);

Asimov's Mysteries (Garden City, N.Y.: Doubleday, 1968; London: Rapp & Whiting, 1968);

Nightfall and Other Stories (Garden City, N.Y.: Doubleday, 1969); republished as *Nightfall One and Nightfall Two* (Saint Albans, U.K.: Panther, 1971);

The Gods Themselves (Garden City, N.Y.: Doubleday, 1972; London: Gollancz, 1972);

The Early Asimov (Garden City, N.Y.: Doubleday, 1972; London: Gollancz, 1973);

Today and Tomorrow and. . . . (Garden City, N.Y.: Doubleday, 1973); republished as *Towards Tomorrow* (London: Hodder & Stoughton, 1977);

Tales of the Black Widowers (Garden City, N.Y.: Doubleday, 1974);

Buy Jupiter and Other Stories (Garden City, N.Y.: Doubleday, 1975; London: Gollancz, 1976);

Murder at the ABA (Garden City, N.Y.: Doubleday, 1976);

The Bicentennial Man and Other Stories (Garden City, N.Y.: Doubleday, 1976; London: Gollancz, 1977);

In Memory Yet Green: The Autobiography of Isaac Asimov, 1920–1954 (Garden City, N.Y.: Doubleday, 1979);

In Joy Still Felt: The Autobiography of Isaac Asimov, 1954–1978 (Garden City, N.Y.: Doubleday, 1980);

Asimov on Science Fiction (Garden City, N.Y.: Doubleday, 1981);

Foundation's Edge (Garden City, N.Y.: Doubleday, 1982);

The Robots of Dawn (Garden City, N.Y.: Doubleday, 1983);

The Winds of Change and Other Stories (Garden City, N.Y.: Doubleday, 1983);

Robots and Empire (Garden City, N.Y.: Doubleday, 1985);

Foundation and Earth (Garden City, N.Y.: Doubleday, 1986);

Robot Dreams (New York: Berkley, 1986);

The Alternate Asimovs (Garden City, N.Y.: Doubleday, 1986);

The Best Science Fiction of Isaac Asimov (Garden City, N.Y.: Doubleday, 1986);

Fantastic Voyage II: Destination Brain (Garden City, N.Y.: Doubleday, 1987);

Prelude to Foundation (Garden City, N.Y.: Doubleday, 1988);

Asimov's Galaxy: Reflections on Science Fiction (Garden City, N.Y.: Doubleday, 1989);

Nemesis (Garden City, N.Y.: Doubleday, 1989).

OTHER: *The Hugo Winners,* edited, with commentary, by Asimov (Garden City, N.Y.: Doubleday, 1962);

Before the Golden Age: A Science Fiction Anthology of the 1930's, edited, with commentary, by Asimov (Garden City, N.Y.: Doubleday, 1974);

Isaac's Universe, Volume One: The Diplomacy Guild, edited by Martin H. Greenberg, with an introduction by Asimov (New York: Avon, 1990);

Isaac's Universe, Volume Two: Phases in Chaos, edited by Greenberg, with an introduction by Asimov (New York: Avon, 1991).

Because Isaac Asimov published nearly five hundred books during his lifetime, most of them in the field of science popularization, the above list of fictional works represents only a fraction of his output. Nonetheless, science fiction holds a central place in that output, for it is as a science-fiction writer that he primarily wished to be remembered. As such, Asimov wrote some of the most influential books and stories in the field. During the 1940s and 1950s, his relationship with John W. Campbell, Jr., the editor of *Astounding Science Fiction,* popularized some of the most widely used conventions in science fiction, particularly the notion of robots engineered by human reason to follow the Three Laws of Robotics, and the science-fiction mystery story.

For many readers of science fiction Asimov became the consummate Golden Age science-fiction writer whose stories and novels displayed an optimistically clear faith in the powers of reason to solve humanity's problems. But Asimov did not simply embody the norms of Campbellian science fiction. Asimov's relationship with Campbell, while admiring, was fraught with ideological differences. In the robot stories that Asimov sold to Campbell, Asimov did not mind making human beings superior to robots, but he had qualms about Campbell's racism and invented the all-human Galactic Empire — another important convention of Golden Age science fiction — for his Foundation stories in order to avoid having humans of the Aryan type win out over intelligent alien species, which was the kind of story Campbell wanted to publish. In fact, it was only in the last two years of his life that, relatively free of Campbellian influences, Asimov finally designed (though he did not write) another imaginative universe in which there were five intelligent alien species, widely different in nature, besides mankind (see the two volumes of *Isaac's Universe* [1990, 1991]).

Because of his relationship with Campbell, and the length limitations of magazine publication during the Golden Age, most of Asimov's output as a science-fiction writer expressed itself in the form of short stories or novellas later collected for book publication. Until recently these works were organized in two separate series based on two separate invented sciences – robotics (the robot novels) and psychohistory (the Foundation novels) – with the Galactic Empire novels falling in between. But in 1982, citing pressures from his publishers and fans, as well as his own need to rationalize his fictional universe into a coherent vision, Asimov began writing both sequels and "prequels" to his two series, linking them together into a vast fifteen-novel epic of the future of humanity.

At the very least, these circumstances give rise to two important and equally valid ways of discussing Asimov's fictional achievements: according to the circumstances of their publication in the context of Asimov's life (the order of discussion in this entry), or according to the internal chronology of the books themselves and their importance in terms of future history, not publication date. Asimov himself suggested that the latter approach might be the more coherent one in terms of narrative understanding (see his Preface to *Prelude to Foundation* [1988]). It was such a narratological approach that I adopted for my 1991 study of Asimov. Clearly some books, such as *The End of Eternity* (1955), which was never very important in Asimov's canon previously, are now more important because they lay down narrative ground rules for later books – in this case the entire timeline of Asimov's unified vision. What is more, Asimov answered critics of his earlier works in the process of writing these later novels. Inevitably, then, and in one form or another, future critical readings of Asimov will have to take into account the internal narrative development that these works effect on the whole extent of the Asimovian universe and consider how they critically recast the role of earlier works.

Isaac Asimov was born to middle-class Jewish parents on 2 January 1920 in Petrovichi, Russia, then part of the Smolensk district of the Soviet Union. In 1923 the Asimovs (now including Asimov's sister Manya) immigrated to the United

States, settling in the New York City borough of Brooklyn, where the family owned and operated a series of candy stores and where Asimov spent his formative years. Asimov's father was a stern, authoritarian man who loved to tell stories and parables in Yiddish designed to improve the young Asimov's mind (Asimov could speak and understand both Yiddish and English with equal fluency, though not Russian). Asimov's mother had a more earthy character and even enjoyed off-color jokes that Isaac would never have dared tell to his father, but she did not follow the same philosophy of child rearing. She was an extremely ill-tempered woman who often administered corporal punishment. Whenever Isaac performed as less than a prodigy at school, she lectured him severely, making use of the extensive Yiddish vocabulary of derogatory terms.

In effect, Asimov went to segregated public schools throughout his childhood, since the student body was always heavily Jewish. After ordinary school was over, he attended Hebrew school. But he never really mastered the Hebrew language and at home he was brought up with no religious training. Although Asimov's father had loaded him down with Talmudic aphorisms about how to conduct himself properly, the elder Asimov was not Orthodox. When Isaac reached thirteen, he was not bar mitzvahed. As a result, Isaac Asimov never had to break or struggle with a Russian-Jewish religious past in order to become a writer in America. He seems to have been an atheist and freethinker from the start.

Any free time Asimov had after school, however, was spent helping his father in the candy store, which severely limited his social life and conditioned him to a rigid work schedule. His father's imputations about laziness leading to a bad end seem to have shaped Asimov's character permanently. More than anything else, Asimov declared in his autobiography, it was the memory of his father that made him so prolific: "I am forever and always in the candy store, and the work must be done."

On the subject of literary influences, Asimov's early experiences in the candy store also proved fateful. The candy store sold magazines, including pulp magazines: the detective stories, the Westerns, and most importantly for Asimov, the science-fiction magazines. In 1929 he began reading science-fiction magazines such as *Amazing Stories* and *Science Wonder Stories*. Because the latter had science in its title, young Asimov was able to persuade his father that it would make suitable reading matter. Once his father had given in, the other magazines were

Robert Heinlein, L. Sprague de Camp, and Asimov at the U.S. Navy Yard in Philadelphia, 1944

soon to follow, and Asimov eventually became a fan, writing letters that were published in *Astounding Stories.*

In 1930 Asimov entered junior high school, where he began to retell stories from the science-fiction magazines to his classmates. A year later he attempted his first fiction writing by imitating boys' series books. At about the same time he got his first adult library card and became an assiduous librarygoer. The insular life of the candy store drove him further and further into the world of literature as a means of escape. His early book reading was primarily in nineteenth-century British fiction: "I became a spiritual Englishman and a conscious Anglophile." This fact helps to explain why Asimovian character dialogue — even in futuristic settings — is studded with British phrases. Perhaps it is also part of this felt spiritual Englishness which led Asimov to lay claim to certain eccentricities conventionally associated with the British Romantics — love of cemeteries for instance — and later in his life to sport a pair of voluminous Victorian sideburns.

As for most serious twentieth-century fiction, Asimov found that it was quite beyond him. He never discovered twentieth-century realism or fan-

tastic literature — never read Ernest Hemingway or F. Scott Fitzgerald or James Joyce or Franz Kafka — but he did discover an abiding love for history and historical fiction. Of all the twentieth-century writers who interested him, he reread primarily Agatha Christie and P. G. Wodehouse. Thus it is not accidental that besides science fiction, mystery and humor (including some humorous fantasy) were in fact the only other genres in which he chose to write (see *Asimov's Mysteries* [1968] and any of the humor books in which he cultivated his public image as a sensuous dirty old man).

At Boys High School of Brooklyn in 1934 he published his first nonprofessional story, "Little Brothers" — a humorous essay after the style of Robert Benchley — in the school's literary semiannual. The next year he entered Seth Low Junior College, an undergraduate college of Columbia University. For the first time he tried to write science fiction. What emerged was an epic story about a catastrophe that destroyed photosynthesis on Earth, a story which has not survived. The fan letters that he wrote to *Astounding Stories,* however, do survive. They made Asimov a member of an organization known as First Fandom, whose membership consists of those who had been active fans of science fiction prior to 1938. Surprisingly, Asimov was never very active in science-fiction fandom, although he did briefly join the Futurians where he met Frederik Pohl, who was later to operate as a sometime literary agent for Asimov, shortly to become a professional writer at nineteen.

In 1936 he transferred to the main campus of Columbia University, where he switched his major from biology to chemistry. Because of an aversion to dissection, he began to doubt whether he wanted to go to medical school as his parents wished. During the next two years his growing interest in historical fiction intensified his interest in history itself. He read H. G. Wells's *Outline of History* (1920) and Edward Gibbon's *Decline and Fall of the Roman Empire* (1776). Throughout this period he continued to read magazine science fiction avidly and wrote more letters to *Astounding*. In June 1938 he finished his first piece of fiction ever completed with a view toward publication. A story entitled "Cosmic Corkscrew," it dealt with a concept of time as a helical structure. He delivered the story personally to John W. Campbell, Jr., the editor of *Astounding,* who impressed Asimov immensely. Campbell rejected the story, and eventually it was lost, but Asimov had begun a professional relationship with a man who was to be a greater influence on him than anyone but his father.

From mid 1938 on, Asimov began to write more and more stories, submitting them to various science-fiction pulp magazines, but always hoping to break into Campbell's *Astounding,* which had the most prestige. His first published story, "Marooned off Vesta," appeared in the March 1939 issue of *Amazing Stories,* a magazine that Hugo Gernsback had founded. Among Asimov's other early stories was "Strange Playfellow" (later retitled "Robbie"), which concerned a sympathetic and noble robot that served as nursemaid for a little girl. The first of his positronic robot stories, it was eventually published in 1940 in *Super Science Stories.* Although Campbell had rejected "Strange Playfellow," he did accept another story, "Trends." As an editor, Campbell was looking for stories that involved specifically described scientific extrapolation, and "Trends," about the social resistance to space flight, took shape as a story very much in Campbell's mold. After eight consecutive rejections and revisions, he finally accepted it for publication (it is now collected in *The Early Asimov* [1972]). Asimov regarded this story as his first significant publication.

The summer of 1939 was one of doubt and uncertainty for Asimov. He had graduated from Co-

lumbia and obtained his bachelor of science degree in chemistry but had not been accepted into medical school. What was more, Columbia initially seemed unwilling to take him for graduate work in chemistry. But by agreeing to double up on required courses in his first year of graduate study, he convinced the admissions board that he was seriously interested in chemistry. That summer Asimov attended the First World Science Fiction Convention in New York, where he met many luminaries in the science-fiction field – illustrators, writers, and editors – and gave a brief speech.

For the next eleven years of his literary career, Asimov wrote nothing but magazine science fiction, most of it under Campbell's guidance. In December 1940 he met with Campbell and worked out the Three Laws of Robotics, which governed the production of all the later robot stories and novels. The Laws were already implicit in the workings of the early robot stories, but Campbell apparently was the one who first stated them explicitly. At any rate, Asimov was tired of the typical robot story, in which the robot turned against its maker. He wanted robots that were engineered to be safe, just as other human-made tools were.

The Three Laws of Robotics are now stated at the outset of Asimov's short-story cycle, *I, Robot* (1950): (1) A robot may not injure a human being or, through inaction, allow a human being to come to harm; (2) A robot must obey the orders given it by human beings except where such orders would conflict with the First Law; and (3) A robot must protect its own existence as long as such protection does not conflict with the First or Second Law. These laws are supposedly quoted from a textbook, the *Handbook of Robotics* (56th edition, 2058 A.D.). By quoting his Laws of Robotics (in Asimov, the term *robot* includes computers) at the outset of his story, Asimov gives the impression that we are already operating within the confines of an established science. Therefore the Laws function, in a fictional context, as a verbal representation of the paradigm of a "new" science, robotics. Of course they are not meant to be strict scientific definitions of the sort a real scientific paradigm would generate. Asimov assumed those meanings to be specified by cybernetics, the mathematical psychology of thinking machines, and by the fictional technological marvel that is the positronic brain – a "spongy globe of platinum-iridium" about the size of a human brain, but one in which "brain paths" are "marked out" (and are therefore open to scientific observation and manipulation) by the production and manipulation of positrons. Positrons were discovered in cosmic rays in 1932, but their existence had been theorized earlier. By incorporating knowledge of them in his robot stories, Asimov included actual science in the stories' shared background.

Asimov did not systematically present the scientific concepts underlying the new science. Instead, he worked out the inherent verbal and situational ambiguities in the Three Laws, which provided him with the conflicts and uncertainties required for new stories. As Asimov points out in his introduction to *The Rest of the Robots* (1964), to his great relief, "it always seemed possible to think up a new angle out of the sixty-one words of the Three Laws." Nonetheless, the Three Laws do function as a kind of scientific paradigm. As Thomas Kuhn points out in *The Structure of Scientific Revolutions* (second edition, 1970), the paradigm that provides the basis for a new tradition of scientific research never completely resolves all of its problems. In fact, resolving these puzzles and problems becomes the primary activity of scientists working within the paradigm. For Kuhn, as for Asimov, paradigms are constitutive elements of science, and the object of normal science is to solve a puzzle or problem whose very existence is assumed to confirm the validity of the paradigm.

Normal science (that is, robotics) is, then, an enterprise that aims to refine, extend, and articulate a paradigm already in existence. According to Kuhn, one of the most important foci for research in normal science is empirical work (which may include the "instrumentation" of a theory in the field-testing of scientific equipment) undertaken "to articulate the paradigm theory, resolving some of its residual ambiguities and permitting the solution of problems to which it had previously only drawn attention." Hence the fact that most of Asimov's robot stories take the narrative form of a puzzle or problem is not just a formal issue. With these stories, Asimov was trying to represent a period of normal science in which robotics has already been established. Furthermore, he sought to involve the reader in the intellectual pleasures of ingenious puzzle solving that occurs within a new scientific paradigm.

For example, "Runaround" (*Astounding,* March 1942), the story in which the Three Laws of Robotics are first explicitly formulated and in which the word *robotics* first occurs (the *Oxford English Dictionary,* in its Supplement, credits Asimov with inventing the word, which now denotes a real science), concerns the instrumentation of a new type of robot, SPD-13 (Speedy), designed to work in the mines of Mercury. Checking the workings of the ex-

perimental robots in this and in other stories are a pair of wisecracking engineers named Powell and Donovan. Their solving of puzzles and problems presented by the basic design of the robot brain represents for the reader the endeavors of normal science.

As the story opens the robot has been sent out to retrieve some selenium for the team's photocell banks, which will soon fail without it, allowing the full force of the sun to enter the mining station. However, Speedy has not returned. Powell and Donovan search for the robot and eventually find it circling a pool of selenium, seemingly drunk (showing Asimov's English influences, the robots sings snatches from the comic operas of Gilbert and Sullivan). Through a combination of observation and deduction based on the Three Laws of Robotics, the team arrives at the truth: Speedy is stuck in an equilibrium between the potentials of laws two and three. The team infers the presence of a volatile iron carbonyl, given off by volcanic action, that threatens to corrode Speedy's positronic circuits. That is, Speedy has responded to an order by human beings to retrieve the selenium (law two) but has sought to avoid a danger to himself at the site (law three). The solution is finally found when Powell decides to get outside of both laws by appealing to the transcendent First Law of Robotics. By exposing himself to the sun, he puts himself in a life-threatening situation, and Speedy snaps out of his confusion to rescue him.

In addition to being one of Asimov's most cognition-oriented robot stories, "Runaround" (now collected in *I, Robot*), is a classic story of normal science, for the paradigm makes possible both the problem and its expected solution. The paradigm itself is never questioned or put at serious risk (as is the science of psychohistory in the Foundation novels). Although Powell risks his life, he does so with every confidence that Speedy will behave in accordance with the Three Laws, unless of course Speedy's circuits are too damaged for him to respond.

The end product of a "peculiar symbiotic relation" with Campbell, the robot stories became Asimov's first true mark on the field of science fiction. But it was another story, "Nightfall," also written in close association with Campbell, that made him a major figure. Many people within science-fiction fandom consider "Nightfall" to be the best science-fiction story ever written. It is frequently anthologized and is the only story of Asimov's to be made into a feature-length movie (he did not script *Fantastic Voyage,* but only wrote the novelization). In

Cover of the special Isaac Asimov issue of the Magazine of Fantasy & Science Fiction, *October 1966*

1990 Asimov published a novel-length version of the story, co-authored with Robert Silverberg. But as a matter of fact, near the end of the story, which explores the reactions of human beings on a planet where the night sky appears once in a thousand years, Campbell inserted a concluding paragraph of his own without consulting Asimov. Asimov believed that this final paragraph seriously flawed the story. And since the story is still published with the Campbell ending, Asimov himself never considered it to be among his best stories. But after it he never wrote another science-fiction story that remained unpublished, so it did constitute a milestone in his career. Certainly, after the publication of "Nightfall" in the September 1941 issue of *Astounding* (which featured a front-cover illustration of the story), Asimov was accepted as a major figure in the field, at the age of twenty-one.

The next big step in the development of Asimov's career was the Foundation series. As previously mentioned, Asimov leaned toward the production of more robot stories for Campbell because of an ideological quirk of Campbell's that bordered on overt racism. Campbell wanted white Europeans to win out over extraterrestrials in the stories he published. In Asimov's view, this was an unfortunate reflection of the ongoing historical situation in which the Nazis were slaughtering the Jews in Europe. Being a Jew, Asimov was not intent on boosting the Aryan myth. He was fixed in his intention to prevent Campbell from foisting upon him his notions of the superiority and inferiority of races. In August 1941 Asimov developed the idea of writing a future-historical epic about the fall of a Galactic Empire, suggested to him in part by Gibbon's *Decline and Fall*. Although Asimov was thinking about a novelette, Campbell wanted an open-ended series of stories, all fitting into a particular future history involving the fall of the First Galactic Empire, an interregnum, and the rise of the Second Galactic Empire. For Asimov the surest way to resist Campbell in the context of a Galactic Empire was to write about an all-human Galaxy, a concept that had apparently not been used up to that time. At any rate Asimov is often given credit for establishing this convention (it appears later in Frank Herbert's Dune series, for example, to which Asimov's Foundation series is often compared).

Asimov worked on the series until 1950, eventually publishing eight separate stories that were later shaped into three novels that subsequently became the Foundation Trilogy. At least one of the stories, "Dead Hand" (*Astounding,* April 1945), was influenced by Arnold Toynbee's *A Study of History* (1934–1961), which tells of recurring cycles in the historical process and seems to reflect historical determinism. But the Foundation Trilogy novels are most famous for their postulation of an extraordinary science of history, psychohistory – "the prediction of future trends in history through mathematical analysis" – that would reduce the interregnum years of barbarism from thirty thousand years to one thousand by means of the Seldon Plan, named after the scientist-mathematician who invented psychohistory. Just as Asimov had earlier predicted the use of assembly-line robotics and narrated the theory of the positronic brain with his robot stories (which he continued to produce during the 1940s), he now narrated scientific theory and cognition in another, more sweeping, historical context.

Some critics have tried to identify psychohistory with Marxism, but it is clear from the later Foundation novels (beginning with *Foundation's Edge* in 1982) that Asimov never intended his invented science to be based on historical determinism. It is the robot stories which follow the rules of an established paradigm of science which is never seriously questioned. But the Foundation stories on the other hand actually narrate the quest for the foundation of a science. Although psychohistory has many parallels with what Kuhn calls periods of "extraordinary science," when scientists are confronted with striking anomalies which force them to recast or discard paradigms, it tends to follow a more Popperian model of how science proceeds. For Karl Popper the criterion of the scientific status of a theory is its falsifiability, refutability, or testability. The method of science, then, is criticism (that is, attempted falsification); Popper called his philosophy of science "critical rationalism." Similarly Asimov remarks in an essay on the nature of science fiction, "A Literature of Ideas" (collected in *Today and Tomorrow* [1973]), that "the uniqueness of science comes in this: the scientific method offers a way of determining the False. Science is the only proven gateway to proven error."

Psychohistory, if by that we mean the notion of science as a steady accumulation of positive knowledge (Kuhn's normal science, robotics), is never allowed to become a foundation for the series. As early as the first novel of the classic trilogy, when we find out that the project of the Encyclopedia Galactica – which was supposed to compile and preserve all of human knowledge during the interregnum – was only a ruse, we are led to question the notion of science being founded on anything other than a perpetual quest to prove itself wrong. By the time of the mutant Mule (a dangerous anomaly not predicted by the new science) in the second and third novels it is clearly stated that psychohistory as the foundation of the Seldon Plan is not an absolute – it is "neither complete nor correct" but the best that could be done at the time. Although psychohistory has clearly stated verbal laws like robotics, among them the conditions that the population be large enough for mathematical study and that it not know about the machinations of the Seldon Plan (a requirement that creates many hierarchies of knowledge and not a little paranoia in the series), it is described as an "evolving mechanism." Absolutes, great final generalities of thought, are here rejected by Asimov as signs of decaying culture. The later novels in the series, especially *Foundation and Earth* (1986), proceed by uncovering the hidden assumptions underlying the laws of psychohistory, in effect laying bare the unthought premises from which the stories of the classic Foundation series were generated. The

Seldon Plan is finally revealed as only the "second best" plan for the salvation of mankind.

At any rate, and largely because of the two invented sciences of robotics and psychohistory embodied in two separate series, by 1947 Asimov had become a science-fiction writer of the first rank. But his personal life had changed considerably by that time. He had earned his M.A. in chemistry in 1941, but because of the war he had to suspend his studies to be a junior research chemist at the U.S. Navy Yard in Philadelphia, where L. Sprague de Camp and Robert Heinlein (whom Asimov accepted as the best science-fiction writer in the field) also worked. Working in the Navy Yard was a permanent break with the candy store (after nearly sixteen years of working in the latter), as well as his first real separation from his parents. He even stopped reading science-fiction magazines for the first time in thirteen years. During this period he also met and married his first wife, Gertrude Blugerman. The couple promptly set up housekeeping in Philadelphia.

Asimov was not drafted until after the victory over Japan. His military service was uneventful, except for a personal turning point that he experienced during his stay in Hawaii, which he records in his autobiography. After reflecting on an incident in which he tried to educate some of his fellow soldiers about the workings of the atom bomb, Asimov realized that his insistence on displaying his intelligence and learning to others wearied them and made people dislike him. This insight inspired a shift in his attitude toward others that enabled him to transform himself from a "generally disliked know-it-all" to a generally liked "genial nonpusher," as he was to describe himself in his later years.

In 1946 Asimov returned to his studies at Columbia, where he finished his Ph.D. in 1948. A year later he was hired as an instructor in biochemistry at the Boston University School of Medicine. He accepted the job largely because he felt insecure about his writing career. At the time, he could not see himself making a living as a science-fiction writer. One has to bear it in mind that the more lucrative market for science-fiction novels, as opposed to magazine science fiction, did not really begin to open up until the 1950s. In fact, Doubleday did publish Asimov's first science-fiction novel, *Pebble in the Sky*, in 1950. It is set some fifty thousand years in the future, in the Foundation universe, before the Empire's decline (which is chronicled in the Foundation series). Earth is now a planet despised as an outcast, despised by the rest of the Galaxy because of its radioactivity. Earth plans to exact revenge on the Empire by spreading a disease called Common Fever, which is harmless to Earthmen but fatal to Outsiders. In short, Earth plans to wage biological warfare. Most of the novel concerns various attempts to stop Earth's zealots from carrying out their plan of exacting payment from the Empire for the antitoxin.

Although this novel was a decent first effort which did make some money for him, Asimov could not help wondering if he might be a one-editor writer; as he had always discussed his stories with Campbell, he could not help thinking that much of their success was due to Campbell. So in the early 1950s, tired of the Foundation/robot rut and alienated by Campbell's increasing enthusiasm for pseudoscience (dianetics, psionic powers), Asimov decided to reach out to other editors in the field, especially to Horace Gold, editor of *Galaxy*. In 1952 Gold wanted a robot novel from Asimov and suggested a murder mystery in which a detective solves the crime with a robot partner. Gold wanted one condition of story to be that, if the detective did not solve the crime, he would be replaced by the robot. When Asimov wrote *The Caves of Steel* (which Gold serialized in *Galaxy* in 1953), he tried to resist the idea of robots replacing human beings, but the threat is still implicitly there.

With the publication of *The Caves of Steel* in book form (1954), Asimov reached, in his own estimation, the peak of his direct and spare writing style. He records in his autobiography that he was enormously pleased with the book, regarding it as an almost perfect fusion of two genres, mystery and science fiction. The balance of critical opinion on the book tends to agree with Asimov. Yet by 1954 Asimov had also reached a certain limit in his writing because it was confined to the specialized worlds of science fiction and biochemistry (he had co-authored a textbook on the subject in 1952). He thought that he could perhaps do better than *I, Robot* or the Foundation series, but not much better. Critical opinion on the novels that he published during this period – *The Stars, Like Dust* (1951), *The Currents of Space* (1952), and the Lucky Starr juveniles – tends to bear Asimov out on this evaluation as well. Although *The End of Eternity* (1955) is regarded as one of the best "ludic" or cognitively playful time-travel stories, and is now the linchpin of his entire narrative universe, Asimov was left unsatisfied. How could he move out of his specialized world and reach a larger and more remunerative audience?

The answer lay in nonfiction writing, and particularly in science popularization. In 1957 the Soviet Union launched Sputnik I, revealing what was perceived as a large gap between the United States and Russia in terms of science education. From this point onward, it was chiefly science popularization that interested Asimov. Never again was science fiction to form the main portion of his output. But in 1958 Asimov began a monthly science column for *The Magazine of Fantasy and Science Fiction* that continued up until his death. Many collections of his science essays have originated from this column, itself within the field of science fiction. In fact he was awarded a special Hugo Award in 1963 for his science articles.

So the break with science fiction was neither sudden nor entirely complete. True, during the 1960s and 1970s about 80 percent of his output was nonfiction, including the book which led to his recognition as a major figure in the field of science writing: *The Intelligent Man's Guide to Science* (1960), which was nominated for a National Book Award and has been printed in four editions (it is now called *Asimov's New Guide to Science*). Nonetheless, during this period he also managed to publish well over a hundred stories, collected in such books as *Nine Tomorrows* (1959) and *The Rest of the Robots* (1964). And in 1972, he published what many critics consider to be his best independent novel, *The Gods Themselves*. Not tied in to the Foundation or robot universes, the central scientific problem in the book involves an exchange of energy between two parallel universes, an exchange initiated by aliens because they are losing the energy they need to survive. For the first time in his career, Asimov created sympathetic and believable aliens whose use of energy in their reproductive cycle is tied to a scientific problem. The book won him both a Hugo and a Nebula Award.

At the same time he was garnering many of science fiction's top awards and was frequently a guest at conventions, his personal life was stable and relatively calm. In 1951, at about the same time that he was working on his biochemistry textbook, a son, David, was born. Four years later came a daughter, Robyn. Asimov seems to have been a doting – although, because of his prolific output, timebound – father. Even his divorce in 1973 was without much rancor (in his autobiography, Asimov dutifully records his infidelities). He soon afterward married Janet Jeppson, a psychiatrist, whom he had met at a science-fiction convention, and settled in Manhattan. There he pursued his free-lance career until the time of his death, lending his name to many publishing projects and enterprises within the science-fiction field, including in 1976 *Isaac Asimov's Science Fiction Magazine,* for which he wrote a regular editorial column that expressed his views on the nature of science fiction.

In 1977, however, Asimov was hospitalized after a heart attack. The attack left him plagued with angina pectoris, which worsened rapidly until 1983, when he underwent a triple coronary bypass operation. After that he was forced to keep his weight down in order to muster the strength he needed to finish the various publishing projects to which he was committed. Asimov returned to the world of the science-fiction novel in 1982 with *Foundation's Edge,* a novel-length sequel to the classic Foundation series, which had been left open-ended (at Campbell's insistence) over thirty years previously. Part of the book was featured in a special issue of *Isaac Asimov's Science Fiction Magazine* (December 1982), with commentaries by Arthur C. Clarke, Larry Niven, Frederik Pohl, Harlan Ellison, and others. Unquestionably it was the science-fiction publishing event of the year. The novel was on the *New York Times* best-seller list for twenty-five weeks and won a Hugo Award. Asimov followed up this success with *The Robots of Dawn* the following year.

As previously mentioned, the robot novels and the Foundation series were not originally related to each other. Indeed, no robots existed in the Galactic Empire, which was set thousands of years in the future (the robot novels are set in Earth's twenty-first century). But in *Foundation's Edge,* Asimov makes a point of referring to events in his non-Foundation novels (such as *The End of Eternity*), indicating how they might fit into the Foundation universe; he also mentions robots for the first time. In creating the narrative world of *The Robots of Dawn,* however, Asimov embarked on a course that would change his entire imaginative universe. That is, Asimov began to link the science of robotics with the science of psychohistory, which dominates the Foundation novels. In *Robots and Empire* (1985), telepathic robots themselves create the basis for psychohistory when they formulate a broader version of the First Law, the Zeroth Law, which states that "a robot must not injure humanity or, through inaction, allow humanity to come to harm." In effect, robotics becomes the "foundation" for psychohistory. *Foundation and Earth* (1986) works at the far end of the Asimovian universe, when Earth, the robots, and their true intentions are finally (re)discovered. And *Prelude to Foundation* (1988) works the middle ground between the two series (or more exactly, it could be called a "prequel" to the Foundation series). Asimov's 379th book, and the last he published in the series before his death (another book, *Forward the Foundation,* is scheduled to be published by Doubleday in spring 1993), it tells the story of Hari Seldon's development of psychohis-

tory with the help of the robot R. Daneel Olivaw (the robot partner of Elijah Baley in the early robot novels), who has survived incognito through the long centuries of mankind's Galactic Empire.

Few critical assessments of Asimov exist in which the whole extent of his imaginative universe is considered. Although Asimov proclaimed that his style had not changed in the intervening years, the later novels, at well over three hundred pages each, are in fact more complex in terms of narrative structure and theme. *Foundation and Earth,* for example, reads like an equation in three unknowns: the location and fate of the Earth, why the protagonist Trevize chooses Galaxia – a kind of living sentient galaxy – as the path of mankind's salvation, and what has happened to the robots are all interrelated mysteries in the narrative. It shows Asimov's skill as a storyteller that he never allows this complex narrative weave to degenerate into chaos or the many secrets it contains to interfere unduly with our rational comprehension of it. Also, his characters, or at least the main ones, seem more individualized. Asimov even stresses that Trevize's mind has "gaps" of understanding in it and that he is capable of doing unforeseen and surprising things. Asimov never arrived at a world as richly detailed as Frank Herbert's Dune series, to which Asimov's world is often compared; nevertheless, the complex narrative continuities of the later novels are evidence of Asimov's evolution as a writer.

Asimov had never been too concerned with developing convincing characters, as is well known. Even Susan Calvin, chief robopsychologist for United States Robots – a character who analyzes and interprets robot behavior (she appears in about a dozen stories), and a character touted by Asimov as one of his most well rounded – is little more than a stereotype: the frigid woman scientist who gives up family for career. Furthermore, in essays such "The Little Tin God of Characterization," published in the science-fiction magazine which bears his name (*Asimov's,* May 1985) he openly acknowledged his lack of interest in literary matters yet defended his mode of writing. Asimov argued that he was not interested in style, characterization, or poetic metaphor, but in ideas. Asimov always considered science fiction a branch of literature that existed for the purpose of presenting scientific ideas.

Thus it is not surprising that the tributes paid to him in the *New York Times* on his death were not from the reigning lords of literary criticism (Asimov openly detested literary critics anyway) but from scientists, people like artificial-intelligence pioneer

Cover of the first issue of Isaac Asimov's Science
Fiction Magazine

Marvin Minsky, who said that after "Runaround"
appeared in the March 1942 issue of *Astounding,* "I
never stopped thinking how minds might work," or
Joseph F. Engelberger, a leader in industrial robotics. Considered as a whole, Asimov's imaginative
universe has contributed much to the speculative
wealth of science fiction. His stories and novels
present us with the adventures of two invented sciences: robotics, a normal science, and psychohistory, an extraordinary one. The former follows the
rules of a paradigm, the Three Laws of Robotics,
that is broadened and deepened but never seriously
questioned. The latter follows a more Popperian
model in the sense that during the course of the
novels it is "risked" in a series of crises of the
Seldon Plan, which is finally found inadequate.
Because of this spirit of critical rationalism in
his works, which creates narratives that develop
through the testing and questioning of the assumptions on which they are founded, Asimov's universe
is therefore a superior one in terms of the qualities

characteristic of science fiction as a literature of
ideas.

Bibliographies:

Isaac Asimov, "My Hundred Books," in *Opus 100*
(Boston: Houghton Mifflin, 1969), 313–318;

Marjorie Miller, *Isaac Asimov: A Checklist of Works
Published in the United States, March 1939–May
1972* (Kent, Ohio: Kent State University
Press, 1972);

David M. Cox and Gary R. Libby, "A Bibliography
of Isaac Asimov's Major Science Fiction
Works Through 1976," in *Isaac Asimov,* Joseph
D. Olander and Martin H. Greenberg, eds.
(New York: Taplinger, 1977), pp. 217–233;

Asimov, "My Second Hundred Books," in *Opus 200*
(New York: Houghton Mifflin, 1979), pp.
325–329;

Asimov, "My Third Hundred Books," in *Opus 300*
(New York: Houghton Mifflin, 1984), pp.
373–377;

Stephen H. Goldman, "Isaac Asimov," in *Bibliography of American Fiction: 1919–1988* (New York:
Facts-On-File, 1991), pp. 59–68.

References:

Jean Fiedler and Jim Mele, *Isaac Asimov* (New York:
Ungar, 1982);

Neil Goble, *Asimov Analyzed* (Baltimore: Mirage
Press, 1972);

John L. Grigsby, "Asimov's 'Foundation' Trilogy
and Herbert's 'Dune' Trilogy: A Vision Reversed," *Science Fiction Studies,* 8, no. 24 (July
1981): 149–155;

James Gunn, *Isaac Asimov: The Foundations of Science
Fiction* (New York: Oxford University Press,
1982);

Donald M. Hassler, *Isaac Asimov* (Mercer Island,
Wash.: Starmont House, 1991);

Damon Knight, "Asimov and Empire," in his *In
Search of Wonder,* revised and enlarged edition
(Chicago: Advent, 1967), pp. 90-94;

Joseph D. Olander and Martin H. Greenberg, eds.,
Isaac Asimov (New York: Taplinger, 1977);

Joseph F. Patrouch, *The Science Fiction of Isaac Asimov*
(Garden City, N.Y.: Doubleday, 1974);

William F. Touponce, *Isaac Asimov,* (Boston: G. K.
Hall, 1991);

Donald A. Wollheim, "The Decline and Fall of the
Galactic Empire," in *The Universe Makers* (New
York: Harper & Row, 1971), pp. 37–42.

Papers:
Since 1964, Asimov's materials, including manuscripts (both first drafts and final copies), book editions, magazine reprints of stories, correspondence, and fan mail have been held by the Boston University Library, Boston, Massachusetts.

A TRIBUTE

from Poul Anderson

Enough other people will have paid tribute to Isaac Asimov the writer – the creator of first-rate, often groundbreaking fiction, the lucid and lively explainer of the real world in works whose subjects ranged over the whole of space and time and human knowledge. Let me offer a few words about Isaac Asimov the man.

We were not intimately acquainted, if only because of geography, but we met from time to time over the years, and those were always happy occasions for me. Now and then we swapped letters. His usually sparkled with the wit that he kept so much in play personally. In quieter fashion, they also showed the kindliness he gave to just about everybody, and the deeply concerned spirit that underlay the ebullience. Although we disagreed now and then, even in print, on matters of the utmost public importance, he never wavered in his commitment to everyone's right of free speech nor in his courtesy, and such disagreements never damaged a friendship if he could help it. We shall not look upon his like again.

A TRIBUTE

from Harlan Ellison

Everything he stood for, everything he tried to teach us, prevents me from eulogizing him by way of suggesting He Has Gone to a Better Place. I'd really like to; but he won't permit it.

In the 1984 collection of his science essays from this very magazine, *'X' Stands for Unknown,* Isaac wrote: "There seems to be a vague notion that something omniscient and omnipotent *must* exist. If it can be shown that scientists are not all-knowing and all-powerful, then that must be the proof that something else that *is* omniscient and omnipotent *does* exist. In other words: Since scientists can't synthesize sucrose, God exists.

"Well, God may exist; I won't argue the point here – "

And a year earlier, in *The Roving Mind,* he began an essay on "faith" titled "Don't You Believe?" like this:

"One of the curses of being a well-known science-fiction writer is that unsophisticated people assume you to be soft in the head. They come to you for refuge from a hard and skeptical world.

"Don't you believe in flying saucers, they ask me? Don't you believe in telepathy? – in ancient astronauts? – in the Bermuda triangle? – in life after death?

"No, I reply. No, no, no, no, and again no."

How dare I, then, dishonor all that he was about, publicly and privately, in print and in person, for fifty-four years, by suggesting that at last Isaac will be able to get first-hand answers to the questions that drove him crazy throughout most of his life, from [Charles] Darwin and [Wilhelm] Roentgen and [Albert] Einstein and Galileo and [Michael] Faraday and [Nikola] Tesla . . . just sitting around, shooting the breeze with the guys, as Archimedes mixes the drinks.

As it was for all of us who needed a question answered, who called Isaac at all hours of the day or night, who drowned him in requests for answers to conundra, so it will now be for Isaac, chasing down Cervantes and Willy Shakespeare and Jesus, buttonholing them for the answers to the maybe six or seven things in the universe he didn't know. Such little fantasies might make it easier to live with his death, but it would only be balm for those of us who listened to Isaac for decades but reverted to superstition when the bullets whistled past our ears.

Gone is gone, and with the passing of Isaac, who loved us deeply enough to chivy us toward smartness with a relentless passion, the universe has shrunk more than a little. He is gone and, as I write these words less than twelve hours later, there is no more crying left in me. Those of us here at the Magazine so dear to his heart, the Magazine that contained his cleverness and sensibleness and wisdom for 399 installments (not to mention all the stories), well, we've known he wouldn't be with us much longer for many months; and we've had time to wring ourselves out. And yet there is no end to the sense of helplessness and loss.

Isaac was as much a part of this journal through the years as paper and ink; and though gone, he remains with us. As he remains with the uncounted thousands of young people who read his essays and stories and went into careers of scientific inquiry, who understood the physical universe because he made it graspable, who became better able to handle their lives because he refused to allow them to accept dogma and bigotry and mendacity in place of common sense and logic.

For all of you who will mourn him in your own way, the most I have to offer (having been chosen to say goodbye to Isaac in this special venue that he called home for so long) is this one last anecdote of how he viewed himself and his imminent passage:

Janet was with him at the end, of course, and his daughter, Robyn. Janet told me, the day before he died, that toward the end Isaac had trouble speaking, could only manage a word or two from time to time. He would say *I love you* to Janet, and he would smile. But every once in a while he would murmur, "I want . . ." and never finish the sentence. "I want . . ."

And Janet would try to perceive what he needed, and she would say, "A drink of water?" or "Something to eat?" And Isaac would look dismayed, annoyed, chagrined that he couldn't put the sentence together; and after a moment he would let it slide, and forget he had spoken. Until the time came on the Sunday before he went back into the hospital for the last visit, when he managed to say, very clearly . . .

"I want . . . I want . . . Isaac Asimov."

And Janet told him he *was* Isaac Asimov, that he had *always* been Isaac Asimov. But he looked troubled. That wasn't what he meant. Then Janet remembered that Isaac had told her, some time ago, before he began to slip into abstraction and silence, that if there ever came a time when he didn't know who he was, if there came a time when his mind was not sharp, that he wanted to be let to go to sleep quietly, that extraordinary measures should not be taken.

And Janet understood that he was saying that he wanted to *be* Isaac Asimov again.

Then, in that final week before 2:30 A.M. New York time on Monday, April 6th, he was holding Janet's hand, and he looked up at her and said, very clearly, the last he would ever say, "I *am* Isaac Asimov."

Yes, he was. Yes, indeed, he was.

©1992 by the Kilimanjaro Corporation

A TRIBUTE

from Harlan Ellison

What day is it, only two days since he died? I've lost all track of time. Even knowing, for months, it didn't help. Even talking and crying with Janet and Marty the day before he went, it didn't help. I find it hurts and hurts, thinking of a world and a life without him in it. He was always there

whenever I called to ask a stupid question, to tell him a new joke, to see if he and Janet were up for Chinese when I was coming into the City. Like everyone else, I loved him so; and there is no end to the hurting. I wrote a piece for *F&SF,* and all the papers that called for a remark, and the phone calls from here and overseas. It just doesn't stop squeezing my heart. So what more is there to say? That great, dear man is gone. He said he'd never live longer than his father, Judah, had lived. 1896–1969. And we all hit him with rubber chickens, telling him he had the curse of a Russian Soul, that because he knew the answers to everything, that he would live forever, and bury all the rest of us. But he did, he knew the answers to everything, even when he'd go, and sure enough he even out-thought us on that one.

So what more is there to say? Here's a little one, that in and of itself doesn't mean much, except that it was so absolutely *Isaac,* it might give you a chuckle:

Back in 1978 Ben Bova and I sued Paramount and ABC-TV and a couple of smoothyguts thugs for copyright infringement, for stealing a tv project called "Brillo," based on a story Ben and I had done. And part of their defense was the cockeyed assertion that Ben and I couldn't sue them for picking *our* pockets because *we* had taken the idea for "Brillo" from Isaac's *Caves of Steel.*

So Isaac was subpoenaed to give a deposition by the deep-pockets attorneys for the studio; and I flew to New York to be there when Isaac gave his deposition: the New York Hilton, 10:10 A.M., October 1st, 1979. It rained that day.

He walked into the hotel room where I was waiting with my attorney, Henry W. Holmes, Jr., and the attorney representing the firm of Rosenfeld Meyer & Susman, Esqs., a guy named Robert H. Rotstein, Esq., and he shook off his umbrella, and he shucked out of his raincoat, and he hugged me long and hard, and Robert H. Rotstein, Esq. went several shades of pale.

For the next six hours – with but a short lunch break – this Rotstein, Esq. questioned Isaac. I have a copy of the transcript taken by the Certified Shorthand Reporter/Notary Public who took the deposition for use at the trial, and in a moment I'll quote directly from it. But it was an amazing performance.

Clearly, Rotstein, Esq. only had the vaguest idea of the man he was chivying, only the barest notion of the size of the intellect he was trying to confound. Isaac ran him in ever-decreasing circles, always answering fully and without hesitation, perceiving in advance where some convoluted and prolix query was going, and responding at one point to the query "Do you think Mr. Ellison and Mr. Bova misappropriated CAVES OF STEEL?" that he and I and Ben had been friends for almost thirty years (at that time), and that I wasn't the sort of pal who would steal from a pal, and even if I *were* that kind of rat, I wasn't stupid enough to steal one of the most famous stories ever published in the genre, and even if Ben and I *were* that stupid, that he didn't give a damn, because we were friends and if we'd needed to borrow from *Caves of Steel* it was all right with him, and he concluded with this:

"Despite everything I have heard today, and despite the fact that I'm even sensitive to the *appearance* of that sort of thing, I know absolutely that Harlan took no liberties with THE CAVES OF STEEL, and he is still my friend, and if I may say so, I don't believe he's the kind of person who would take undue liberties in the first place and if he were tempted to, it wouldn't be with a friend, and it wouldn't be with a book such as this."

Well, that took care of *that*.

Every time they tried at trial to introduce the concept of "borrowing" from Isaac, either my attorney or the judge would wave Isaac's deposition under their noses, and they would retreat, mumbling.

But that isn't the anecdote. Nor is the anecdote that Isaac was the sort of man who would give up a full day of his life to sit in a close, overheated, uncomfortable little hotel room to be deposed (which he hated a *lot*), just to help a friend. No, the anecdote that might give you a chuckle is this:

Right at the git-go, 10:10 A.M., after the unwary Rotstein, Esq., had asked Isaac to state his name and address, here is the verbatim record of Q&A:

Q: Dr. Asimov, would you state your current occupation?

A: I'm a writer.

Q: How long have you been writing professionally?

A: Forty years. That's not approximate. That's exact.

Q: Exact? Don't you overstate? I recall from your bio data that you published your first story, called "Marooned off Vesta," sometime in the latter part of 1938.

A: It was sold on October 31, 1938; it was published, that's the magazine it was *in*, reached the newsstands on March 19, 1939. It was the March 19, 1939 issue of *Amazing Stories*. Exact is a precise word, Mr. Rotstein.

Are your chuckling? Yeah, well, terrific. That's about all we've got left, two days later. A few chuckles, a great many memories, all that love with no place left to send it, and the incalculable, profound, lifelong effect he had on millions of people. But it doesn't quell in even the smallest degree the hurt and loss that remains.

©1992 by the Kilimanjaro Corporation

A TRIBUTE

from Frederick Pohl

Isaac Asimov was almost my oldest friend, since the days more than half a century ago when we were both struggling teenage would-be writers desperate to make our first sales. Isaac was a brilliant, energetic and wise human being; his death has left a great void in my life, and in the world.

A TRIBUTE

from Norman Spinrad

Author of some five-hundred books, only a relative handful of which were science fiction, expert on almost anything, and surely the greatest popularizer of science of all time, Isaac Asimov is still nevertheless still best known to the world as a science-fiction writer. Why? Perhaps because science fiction was his first and most enduring literary love, the work closest to his heart, somehow the center of everything he did. Surely Isaac himself would have wanted it that way.

A TRIBUTE

from Kurt Vonnegut

Isaac was President of the American Humanist Association. I spoke at a memorial service in his honor at a meeting of the Association in Portland, Oregon, in May of 1992. I said, "Isaac is in heaven now." The audience rolled in the aisles. That was about the funniest thing I could have said to a bunch of humanists. Isaac would have thought so, too.

Richard Yates

(2 February 1926 – 7 November 1992)

Ronald Baughman
University of South Carolina

See also the Yates entries in *DLB 2: American Novelists Since World War II* and *Yearbook: 1981.*

BOOKS: *Revolutionary Road* (Boston & Toronto: Atlantic/Little, Brown, 1961);
Eleven Kinds of Loneliness (Boston & Toronto: Atlantic/Little, Brown, 1962);
A Special Providence (New York: Knopf, 1969);
Disturbing the Peace (New York: Seymour Lawrence/Delacorte, 1975);
The Easter Parade (New York: Seymour Lawrence/Delacorte, 1976);
A Good School (New York: Seymour Lawrence/Delacorte, 1978);
Liars in Love (New York: Seymour Lawrence/Delacorte, 1981);
Young Hearts Crying (New York: Seymour Lawrence/Delacorte, 1984);
William Styron's Lie Down in Darkness: A Screenplay (Watertown, Mass.: Ploughshares, 1985);
Cold Spring Harbor (New York: Seymour Lawrence/Delacorte, 1986).

OTHER: *Stories for the Sixties,* edited, with an introduction, by Yates (New York: Bantam, 1963).

Richard Yates died on 7 November 1992 at the Birmingham, Alabama, Veterans Administration Hospital of complications from minor surgery following a ten-year struggle with emphysema. A memorial service was held 16 December 1992 at the Century Club in New York City during which novelist Kurt Vonnegut and Yates's publisher Seymour Lawrence presented eulogies. Among those who provided reminiscences of the author or read passages from his works were William Styron, André Dubus, Dan Wakefield, Robert Stone, and Vonnegut. Throughout his career Yates was praised and admired by other writers for his mastery of style and his unflinching grasp of the struggles of post–World War II middle-class Americans to lead fulfilling lives.

Richaed Yates (photograph © Jill Krementz)

Yates's art clearly draws upon events from his own life. Born in Yonkers, New York, on 2 February 1926, he was the son of a businessman father, Vincent M. Yates, and an artistic mother, Ruth Maurer Yates. As Yates's autobiographical protagonist states in *The Good School* (1978), his parents were "divorced as long as I can remember," and divorce figures prominently in the author's vision of the American myth of family life. Yates grew up in Manhattan, Scarsdale, and Cold Spring Harbor,

New York. He graduated from Avon Old Farms School, an undistinguished prep school in Avon, Connecticut, and the "good school" model for his later novel. From 1944 to 1946 he served as an infantry private, an experience that he dramatized in *A Special Providence* (1969). After the war he worked as a United Press International rewrite man in New York City from 1947 to 1949, and then from 1949 to 1950 he wrote publicity copy for Remington Rand in New York City, a job similar to Frank Wheeler's in *Revolutionary Road* (1961). After a two-year stay in Europe, during which he wrote fiction – one of Frank Wheeler's dreams – Yates worked as a free-lance writer from 1953 to 1959. Beginning in 1959 he accepted positions as writer in residence at various American universities, including the New School for Social Research, Columbia University, the University of Iowa Writers' Workshop, the University of Wichita, Boston University, the University of Southern California, Harvard Extension, and, finally, the University of Alabama at Tuscaloosa. In addition to filling these teaching positions, Yates served as a speechwriter for Attorney General Robert F. Kennedy in 1963. Also, in the early 1960s he worked in Hollywood as a scriptwriter, principally on a screenplay of William Styron's novel *Lie Down in Darkness* (1951). Although the movie was never produced, the script was published in 1985. All of these jobs served to sustain Yates while he focused on his writing. His 1948 marriage to Sheila Bryant, with whom he had two daughters, Monica and Sharon, ended in divorce in 1960; his 1968 marriage to Martha Speers, with whom he had a third daughter, Gina, ended in divorce in 1975.

Yates's literary heritage extended from Gustave Flaubert to F. Scott Fitzgerald, a lineage that emphasizes the artistry of realistic fiction. It was Fitzgerald, in fact, who inspired Yates to take seriously his writing career. As he stated in response to a 1979 *New York Times Book Review* survey:

> No single book made me decide to be a writer; that decision came as a consequence of boyhood and had little to do with books at all. But it was F. Scott Fitzgerald's *The Great Gatsby,* which I read for the first time at 22, that persuaded me to quit fooling around and get to work. The purity of that novel, the grace and the swiftly gathering power of it, showed me what a high, fine thing writing could be – and suggested too, as if in whispers, how much it might cost.

Yates's fiction achieved the level of "a high, fine thing" that earned him praise from such writers as Tennessee Williams, Vonnegut, and Styron and such reviewers as Jonathan Penner, James Atlas,

and DeWitt Henry. Penner stated in a 1978 *New Republic* review of *The Good School* that

> Yates's creative instincts owe much to tradition, little to fashion. In an age embarrassed by story telling, half-persuaded by chic critics that fiction should repel innocent belief, he tells stories that we believe. In a time when experiment with language is more highly valued than skill with it, he experiments no more than fish do with swimming. . . . But what chiefly makes Yates so rewarding to read . . . is what might best be called, in an old-fashioned word, his justness. None of his characters is more or less than human. With tenderness and irony as mutual correctives, he makes a compassionate advocate, but one who painfully admits justice in the fates – often disastrous – that his people earn for themselves. Emotion is kept honest.

Penner correctly identified two elements in Yates's fiction that have a direct bearing on his artistic achievement and may help explain why some readers are devoted to Yates and why some shy away from him. First, Yates dedicated himself to perfecting his skills as a realist: he created believable plots, fully developed characters, and recognizable settings, and he developed comprehensive themes through a clear, exact, but unobtrusive style. Yet four years after the publication of Yates's first and best-known novel, *Revolutionary Road,* the postmodern innovator John Hawkes declared in a *Wisconsin Studies in Contemporary Literature* interview that "the true enemies of the novel [are] plot, character, setting, and theme." Hawkes asserted that traditional realistic features of the novel should be diminished in favor of complex, allusive language, imaginative or even surreal vision, and innovative structure. This philosophical clash between realistic modern and nonrealistic postmodern writers placed Yates out of fashion with the new direction in American writing, as such writers as Hawkes, John Barth, Donald Barthelme, and Thomas Pynchon drew increasing critical attention.

Penner also emphasized Yates's insistence on emotional honesty, a coming-to-terms with the void that exists in the lives of his characters. For some readers Yates at times seemed almost obsessively attracted to this darkness – a characteristic that no doubt reduced his popular appeal. He focused on characters who try valiantly to make something of their lives but who are unable to overcome their own personal limitations or circumstances to achieve satisfactory lives. Yates did not withdraw from looking into the frailty of his characters' dreams. Yet, he tempered this darkness with a humor that ranges from mockery of the pompous to irony concerning the

In Memoriam

RICHARD YATES

1926 - 1992

December 16, 1992
The Century Club
New York City

Memorial Service

Eulogist	KURT VONNEGUT	
Reminiscences	ANDRÉ DUBUS (read by KURT VONNEGUT)	
	LOREE RACKSTRAW (read by KURT VONNEGUT)	
	CAROLYN GAISER	
Readers	WILLIAM STYRON	*Revolutionary Road*
	FRANK CONROY	*Revolutionary Road*
	E. BARRETT	
	PRETTYMAN, JR.	*Disturbing the Peace*
	DAVID MILCH	*The Easter Parade*
	DAN WAKEFIELD	*Young Hearts Crying*
	ROBERT STONE	"Jody Rolled the Bones"
		from *Eleven Kinds of*
		Loneliness
	KURT VONNEGUT	*A Good School*
Interlude	"For All We Know"	Art Blakey *Blusiana*
		Triangle
Reminiscences	SUSAN BRAUDY	
	RICHARD PRICE	
	RICHARD LEVINE	
Eulogist	SEYMOUR LAWRENCE (read by NICK LAWRENCE)	

*Donations may be sent to the New York Lung Association in the name
of Richard Yates or to the University of Iowa Richard Yates Fund.*

*Cover and list of speakers from the program for a memorial service held in Yate's honor at the Century Club, 16 December 1992 (courtesy of
Seymour Lawrence)*

overzealous to an amused but compassionate vision of the inevitable victim.

Through his poignant portraits of characters from childhood to adulthood to old age, Yates demythologizes the national dream of success and happiness in post–World War II America. Even as children his characters sense the disparity between the myth of what their life is supposed to be and the reality of what it is. Consequently, they fabricate an inner narrative, a personal mythology, as a means of facing the void at the center of their lives. The private inner journey from childhood to adulthood to old age is often a series of expectations that normally leads to disappointment and downfall. Yates's main figures are usually adults whose childhoods have been damaged, frequently as a result of growing up with divorced parents. Such childhoods create in these characters early realizations that they are outsiders; they harbor secret regrets about their immediate cir-

cumstances but construct hopeful visions about how their adult lives will be ultimately improved. Their expectations for adult happiness often depend on dreams of artistic achievement that will elevate them above others who lead apparently ordinary lives and who now disparage the dreamers.

April Wheeler in *Revolutionary Road,* for example, voices her childhood longings when she explains her personal history to Shep Campbell, a neighborhood friend who secretly loves April:

I still had this idea that there was a whole world of marvelous golden people somewhere, as far ahead of me as the seniors at Rye when I was in the sixth grade; people who knew everything instinctively, who made their lives work out the way they wanted without even trying. . . . Sort of heroic super-people, all of them beautiful and witty and calm and kind, and I always imagined that when I did find them I'd suddenly know that I belonged among them, that I was one of them, that I'd been meant to be one of them all along, and everything in the meantime had been a mistake. . . . I'd be like the ugly duckling among the swans.

But once she exposes her secret myth to another, April perceives the absurdity of her dream; she understands that she will never become one of the golden people, that they probably do not exist – at least for her; and she thus moves inexorably toward her own darkness with the death of her dream.

Yet other of Yates's main characters pursue their own variations on the quest to be among the golden people. Salesman John Wilder in *Disturbing the Peace* (1975) attempts to win fame and happiness from the shards of his life, after his lover, Pamela Hendricks, convinces him that his life's story – his unhappy marriage, his alcoholism, his brief confinement in a psychiatric ward – contains elements of great literature that he should present in a movie script or a play. Filled with grandiose visions, Wilder leaves his wife and son for Pamela and Hollywood. After reading Wilder's script, a professional Hollywood writer calls it – and Wilder's life – banal and cliché-ridden and declares that it can be transformed into real art only if Wilder's autobiographical protagonist meets with complete destruction: "He is a 'dark' character. . . . He systematically destroys everything that's still bright and promising in his life . . . and he sinks into a depression so deep as to be irrevocable. . . . The seeds of self-destruction are there in the man from the start." As a director/producer defines and passes sentence on the protagonist's life – "I say let him go crazy. Wipe him out" – Wilder listens in horror, realizing that he is foreseeing his own fate. Though he struggles against his downfall, Wilder ends his days locked behind the steel doors of a psychiatric ward in a disturbingly undisturbed passivity. That Wilder's life and spiritual death are seen by people more talented than he as "some cockamamie, two-for-a-nickel *Weltschmerz*" cliché emphasizes Yates's difficult theme that people who aspire to better lives must almost inevitably confront the darkness at the heart of their existence.

Even those who aim for lower, safer goals cannot escape the realization of despair in their lives. Yates's great skill as a writer is particularly evident when he provides in a single paragraph or a brief scene a summarizing moment in a character's life. This technique is illustrated in a paragraph from *Revolutionary Road* in which Mrs. Helen Givings, the Wheelers' neighbor and real estate agent, sits on the edge of her bed after a harrowing day and cries:

She cried because she'd had such high, high hopes about the Wheelers tonight and now she was terribly, terribly, terribly disappointed. She cried because she was fifty-six years old and her feet were ugly and swollen and horrible; she cried because none of the girls had liked her at school and none of the boys had liked her later; she cried because Howard Givings was the only man who'd ever asked her to marry him, and because she'd done it, and because her only child was insane.

Helen, like so many of Yates's characters, has actually asked for and received very little from life. Her "high, high hopes" have been, in fact, little more than to convince people to like her. Yet, like the more ambitious April Wheeler and John Wilder, she meets with disappointment and is forced to confront the terror implicit in so-called ordinary life.

Although Yates's vision in his fiction is disturbingly dark, his artistry elevates his characters' struggles into unique but universal expressions of individual heroism. He translates the American Dream into ordinary human terms – the dream of the restless housewife waiting to be welcomed into a circle of golden people, the dream of the unhappy salesman longing to express himself as a writer, the dream of the unloved mother hoping merely to be liked. Richard Yates's fiction affirms that in even the most ordinary life the struggle to gain a degree of joy, to counter encroaching despair, or to hold onto a moment of hope requires extraordinary valor. Yates's vision in his fiction has proved honest, just, profound, and undeniably real. As Randall Jarrell wrote of another figure who embodied the mythology of post–World War II America: "The world won't be the same without [him], / Or else it will be."

Interviews:

DeWitt Henry and Geoffrey Clark, "An Interview with Richard Yates," *Ploughshares*, 1, no. 3 (1972): 65–78;

"The Books That Made Writers," *New York Times Book Review*, 25 November 1979, pp. 7, 80, 82, 84;

Lee Grove, "Tales of Love, Talk of Lies," *Boston Magazine*, 73 (December 1981): 61–62, 64, 90, 92, 94, 96, 98, 100, 102.

References:

James Atlas, "A Sure Narrative Voice," *Atlantic Monthly*, 248 (November 1981): 84–85;

Fred Chappell, "Fred Chappell on Richard Yates's *Revolutionary Road*," in *Rediscoveries*, edited by David Madden (New York: Crown, 1971), pp. 245–255;

George Cuomo, "Richard Yates: The Art of Craft," *Denver Quarterly,* 19 (Spring 1985): 127–132;

John Enck, "John Hawkes: An Interview," *Wisconsin Studies in Contemporary Literature,* 6 (Summer 1965): 141–155;

DeWitt Henry, *"Disturbing the Peace," Ploughshares,* 3, no. 1 (1976): 159–165;

Jerome Klinkowitz, "Richard Yates: The Wedding of Language and Incident," in his *The New American Novel of Manners: The Fiction of Richard Yates, Dan Wakefield, and Thomas McGuane* (Athens: University of Georgia Press, 1986), pp. 14–59;

Joyce Carol Oates, "Dreams Without Substance," *Nation,* 209 (10 November 1969): 512–513;

Jonathan Penner, "The Novelists," *The New Republic,* 179 (4 November 1978): 42–45;

Theodore Solartoff, "The Wages of Maturity," in his *The Red Hot Vacuum and Other Pieces on the Writing of the Sixties* (New York: Atheneum, 1970), pp. 44–49.

A TRIBUTE

from Seymour Lawrence

Richard Yates and I "discovered" each other in 1952, when I was a young editor of the *Atlantic Monthly.* I recommended publication of his story "Jody Rolled the Bones," which later won first prize as the most notable *Atlantic "First"* of the year. We were both twenty-seven at the time, and we learned to our pleasure and surprise that we were born in the same month in the same year. We were fellow Aquarians, for whatever that's worth.

We became drinking pals, and we were entwined for life as author and publisher. In the early 1950s, at one of our boozy dinners at the Harvard Club in New York City, I urged Dick to write a novel. Five years later, after several false starts, he delivered the final manuscript of what would become a contemporary classic, *Revolutionary Road.* Years later, in a letter regarding another novel he was writing at the time, Yates remarked:

> I want it to be the way *Revolutionary Road* was when you bought it in 1960 – every sentence right, every comma and semi-colon in place.

Richard Yates was a consummate craftsman obsessed with perfecting his craft; Flaubert was his god. During the course of his natural life I published everything he wrote – except for one novel, *A Special Providence,* which he later tried to disown – six novels and two collections of short stories.

Dick drank too much and smoked too much. He was accident-prone and led an itinerant life, but as a writer he was all in place. Toward the end he was working as hard as he could, under great physical handicap, on a novel about the Kennedy years. He had emphysema and couldn't breathe without an oxygen tank. I called him about a week before he died, and he gasped over the phone: "Sam, I'm dying. I can't work any more. I can't do anything." I think of Dick fighting for air in a semidetached bungalow in Tuscaloosa. And it just breaks my heart. What a brave guy. What an American hero.

Literary Awards and Honors Announced in 1992

ACADEMY OF AMERICAN POETS AWARDS

LAMONT POETRY SELECTION
Kathryn Stripling Byer, *Wildwood Flower* (Louisiana State University Press).

WALT WHITMAN AWARD
Greg Glazner, *From the Iron Chair* (Norton).

AMERICAN ACADEMY AND INSTITUTE OF ARTS AND LETTERS AWARDS

ACADEMY-INSTITUTE AWARDS IN LITERATURE
Alice Adams, John Crowley, Richard Foreman, Vicki Hearne, Ruth Prawer Jhabvala, Tim O'Brien, Simon Schama, August Wilson

AWARD OF MERIT FOR POETRY
Charles Wright

WITTER BYNNER PRIZE FOR POETRY
George Bradley

E. M. FORSTER AWARD IN LITERATURE
Timothy Mo

GOLD MEDAL FOR DRAMA
Sam Shepard

SUE KAUFMAN PRIZE FOR FIRST FICTION
Alex Ullmann, *Afghanistan* (Ticknor & Fields).

RICHARD AND HILDA ROSENTHAL FOUNDATION AWARD IN LITERATURE
Douglas Hobbie, *Boomfell* (Holt).

JEAN STEIN AWARD FOR POETRY
James Applewhite

TRAVELING FELLOWSHIP IN LITERATURE
Lorrie Moore

HAROLD D. VURSELL MEMORIAL AWARD IN LITERATURE
Angus Fletcher

MORTON DAUWEN ZABEL AWARD IN POETRY
Jorie Graham

BANCROFT PRIZES

William Cronon, *Nature's Metropolis: Chicago and the Great West* (Norton).

Charles Royster, *The Destructive War: William Tecumseh Sherman, Stonewall Jackson, and the Americans* (Knopf).

JAMES TAIT BLACK MEMORIAL PRIZE

Iain Sinclair, *Downriver (Or, The Vessels of Wrath): A Narrative in Twelve Tales* (Paladin).

REBEKAH JOHNSON BOBBITT NATIONAL PRIZE FOR POETRY

Louise Glück, Mark Strand.

BOOKER PRIZE

Michael Ondaatje, *The English Patient* (Bloomsbury).

Barry Unsworth, *Sacred Hunger* (Hamish Hamilton).

BOOKER RUSSIAN NOVEL PRIZE

Mark Kharitonov, *Lines of Fate, or Milashevich's Trunk*

BRITTINGHAM AWARD FOR POETRY

Tony Hoagland, *Sweet Ruin* (University of Wisconsin Press).

JOHN BURROUGHS AWARD FOR NATURE WRITING

Kenneth S. Norris, *Dolphin Days: The Life and Times of the Spinner Dolphin* (Norton).

RANDOLPH CALDECOTT MEDAL

David Wiesner, *Tuesday* (Clarion Books).

CARNEGIE MEDAL

Berlie Doherty, *Dear Nobody* (Orchard).

CERVANTES PRIZE

Dulce María Loynaz.

COMMONWEALTH WRITERS PRIZE

BEST BOOK
Rohinton Mistry, *Such a Long Journey* (Faber & Faber).

BEST FIRST BOOK
Robert Antoni, *Divina Trace* (Robin Clark).

ANTONIO FELTRINELLI INTERNATIONAL POETRY PRIZE

John Ashbery

GOLDEN KITE AWARDS

FICTION
Jean Thesman, *The Raincatchers* (Houghton Mifflin).

NONFICTION
Russell Freedman, *The Wright Brothers: How They Invented The Airplane* (Holiday House).

PICTURE-ILLUSTRATION
Barbara M. Joosse, *Mama, Do You Love Me?*, illustrated by Barbara Lavallee (Chronicle).

GOVERNOR GENERAL'S LITERARY AWARDS

DRAMA
John Mighton, *Possible Worlds* and *A Short History of Night*.

FICTION (ENGLISH)
Michael Ondaatje, *The English Patient* (Bloomsbury).

FICTION (FRENCH)
Anne Hébert, *L'enfant chargé de songes* (Seuil).

POETRY (ENGLISH)
Lorna Crozier, *Inventing the Hawk* (McClelland & Stewart).

POETRY (FRENCH)
Gilles Cyr, *Androméde attendra* (L'Hexagone).

DRUE HEINZ LITERATURE PRIZE

Jane McCafferty, *Director of the World ! Other Stories* (University of Pittsburgh Press).

HUGO AWARDS

NOVEL
Lois McMaster Bujold, *Barrayar* (Baen).

NOVELLA
Nancy Kress, *Beggars in Spain* (William Morrow).

NOVELLETTE
Isaac Asimov, "Gold"

SHORT STORY
Geoffrey Landis, "A Walk in the Sun"

INGERSOLL PRIZES

T. S. ELIOT AWARD FOR CREATIVE WRITING
Muriel Spark.

RICHARD M. WEAVER AWARD FOR SCHOLARLY LETTERS
Walter Burkett.

INTERNATIONAL ASSOCIATION OF CRIME WRITERS AWARD

NORTH AMERICAN HAMMETT PRIZE
Elmore Leonard, *Maximum Bob* (Delacorte).

IRISH TIMES/AER LINGUS INTERNATIONAL FICTION PRIZE

Norman Rush, *Mating* (Knopf).

LANNAN LITERARY AWARDS

FELLOWSHIP FOR FICTION
Frank Chin.

FELLOWSHIPS FOR POETRY
Thomas Centolella, Killarney Clary, Suzanne Gardiner, Susan Mitchell, Luis J. Rodriguez.

FICTION
Gilbert Sorrentino.

NONFICTION
Noam Chomsky.

POETRY
A. R. Ammons.

RUTH LILLY POETRY PRIZE

John Ashbery.

LOS ANGELES TIMES BOOK PRIZES

FICTION
Art Spiegelman, *Maus: A Survivors Tale II: And Here My Troubles Began* (Pantheon).

ROBERT KIRSCH AWARD
Diane Johnson.

POETRY
Adrienne Rich, *An Atlas of the Difficult World* (Norton).

ART SEIDENBAUM AWARD FOR FIRST FICTION
Darryl Pinckney

MACARTHUR FELLOWSHIPS IN THE ARTS AND HISTORY

Robert Blackburn, Stanley Cavell, Amy Clampitt, Irving Feldman, Barbara Fields, Ann Ellis Hanson, Norman Manea, Paule Marshall, Amalia Mesa-Bains, Joanna Scott, Twyla Tharp, Laurel T. Ulrich.

EDWARD MACDOWELL MEDAL

Richard Wilbur.

LENORE MARSHALL/*NATION* PRIZE FOR POETRY

Adrienne Rich, *An Atlas of a Difficult World: Poems 1988–1991* (Norton).

SHIVA NAIPAUL AWARD

Gleb Shestakov.

NATIONAL BOOK AWARDS

FICTION

Cormac McCarthy, *All the Pretty Horses* (Knopf).

NATIONAL BOOK FOUNDATION MEDAL FOR DISTINGUISHED CONTRIBUTION TO AMERICAN LETTERS

James Laughlin

NONFICTION

Paul Monette, *Becoming a Man: Half a Life Story* (Harcourt Brace Jovanovich).

POETRY

Mary Oliver, *New and Selected Poems* (Beacon Press).

NATIONAL BOOK CRITICS CIRCLE AWARDS

BIOGRAPHY/AUTOBIOGRAPHY

Philip Roth, *Patrimony: A True Story* (Simon & Schuster).

CRITICISM

Lawrence L. Langer, *Holocaust Testimonies: The Ruins of Memory* (Yale University Press).

FICTION

Jane Smiley, *A Thousand Acres* (Knopf).

GENERAL NONFICTION

Susan Faludi, *Backlash: The Undeclared War Against American Women* (Knopf).

POETRY

Albert Goldbarth, *Heaven and Earth: A Cosmology* (University of Georgia Press).

NATIONAL JEWISH BOOK AWARDS

MAURICE AMADO FOUNDATION AWARD FOR SEPHARDIC STUDIES

Ross Brann, *The Compunctious Poet: Cultural Ambiguity and Hebrew Poetry in Muslim Spain* (Johns Hopkins University Press).

ARETE FOUNDATION AWARD FOR FICTION

Nathan Shaham, *The Rosendorf Quartet,* translated by Dalya Bilu (Grove Weidenfeld).

NONA BALAKIAN CITATION FOR EXCELLENCE IN REVIEWING

George Scialabba.

GERRARD AND ELLA BERMAN AWARD FOR JEWISH HISTORY

Marion A. Kaplan, *The Making of the Jewish Middle Class — Women, Family, and Identity in Imperial Germany* (Oxford University Press).

SANDRA BRAND AND ARIK WEINTRAUB AWARD FOR AUTOBIOGRAPHY AND MEMOIR

Henry Morgenthau III, *Mostly Morgenthaus: A Family History* (Ticknor ! Fields).

JEWISH THOUGHT

Yosef Hayim Yerushalmi, *Freud's Moses: Judaism Terminable and Interminable* (Yale University Press).

LEON JOLSON AWARD FOR BOOKS ON THE HOLOCAUST

Dalia Ofer, *Escaping the Holocaust: Illegal Immigration to the Land of Israel, 1939–1944* (Oxford University Press).

MORRIS J. AND BETTY KAPLUN AWARD FOR BOOKS ON ISRAEL

Itamar Rabinovich, *The Road Not Taken: Early Arab/Israeli Negotiations* (Oxford University Press).

SARAH H. AND JULIUS KUSHNER MEMORIAL AWARD FOR SCHOLARSHIP

Steven D. Fraade, *From Tradition to Commentary: Torah and Its Interpretation in the Midrash Sifre to Deuteronomy* (State University of New York Press).

RONALD LAUDER FOUNDATION AWARD FOR BOOKS ON CONTEMPORARY JEWISH LIFE

Lynn Davidman, *Tradition in a Rootless World: Women Turn to Orthodox Judaism* (University of California Press).

ONCE UPON A TIME BOOKSTORE AWARD FOR CHILDREN'S LITERATURE

Uri Orlev, *The Man From the Other Side,* translated by Hillel Halkin (Houghton Mifflin).

MARCIA AND LOUIS POSNER AWARD FOR CHILDREN'S PICTURE BOOK

Michelle Edwards, *Chicken Man* (Lothrop).

VISUAL ARTS

Painting a Place in America: Jewish Artists in New York 1900–1945, edited by Norman L. Kleeblatt and Susan Chevlowe (Jewish Museum/Indiana University Press).

NEBULA AWARDS

NOVEL

Michael Swanwick, *Stations of the Tide* (Century).

SHORT STORY

Alan Bennert, "Ma Qui."

NEW YORK DRAMA CRITICS CIRCLE AWARDS

BEST NEW AMERICAN PLAY

August Wilson, *Two Trains Running.*

BEST NEW PLAY

Brian Friel, *Dancing at Lughnasa.*

JOHN T. NEWBERY MEDAL

Phyllis Reynolds Naylor, *Shiloh* (Atheneum).

NOBEL PRIZE FOR LITERATURE

Derek Walcott.

OBIE AWARDS

Donald Margulies, *Sight Unseen.*

Robbie McCauley, *Sally's Rape.*

Paula Vogel, *The Baltimore Waltz.*

LAURENCE OLIVIER AWARD FOR BEST PLAY OF THE YEAR (LONDON)

Ariel Dorfman, *Death and the Maiden.*

PEN AMERICAN CENTER AWARDS

PEN/FAULKNER AWARD

Don DeLillo, *Mao II* (Viking).

PEN/HEMINGWAY FOUNDATION AWARD

Mark Richard, *The Ice at the Bottom of the World* (Vintage).

EDGAR ALLAN POE AWARDS

FIRST NOVEL

Peter Blauner, *Slow Motion Riot* (William Morrow).

GRAND MASTER

Elmore Leonard.

NOVEL

Lawrence Block, *Dance at the Slaughterhouse* (William Morrow).

POET LAUREATE OF THE UNITED STATES

Mona Van Duyn.

PRIX FÉMINA

Anne-Marie Garat, *Aden* (Seuil).

PRIX GONCOURT

Patrick Chamoiseau, *Texaco* (Gallimard).

PRIX MÉDICIS

Michel Rio, *Tlacuilo* (Seuil).

PRIX RENAUDOT

François Weyergans, *La Démence du Boxeur* (B. Grasset).

PULITZER PRIZES

DRAMA
Robert Schenkkan, *The Kentucky Cycle.*

FICTION
Jane Smiley, *A Thousand Acres* (Knopf).

POETRY
James Tate, *Selected Poems* (Wesleyan University Press).

SPECIAL AWARD
Art Spiegelman, *Maus* (Pantheon).

REA AWARD FOR THE SHORT STORY

Eudora Welty.

NICHOLAS ROERICH PRIZE

Amy Uyematsu, *30 Miles from J-town* (Story Line Press).

TEXAS INSTITUTE OF LETTERS LITERARY AWARDS

BOOK PUBLISHERS OF TEXAS AWARD FOR BEST BOOK FOR CHILDREN OR YOUNG ADULTS
Charlotte Baker Montgomery, *The Trail North* (Eakin Press).

BRAZOS BOOKSTORE AWARD FOR BEST SHORT STORY
Lee Merrill Byrd, "Major Six Pockets," in *Blue Mesa Review*

CARR P. COLLINS AWARD
FOR NONFICTION
Max Oelschlaeger, *The Idea of Wilderness* (Yale University Press).

FRIENDS OF THE DALLAS PUBLIC LIBRARY AWARD TO CONTRIBUTION FOR KNOWLEDGE
Robert S. Weddle, *The French Thorn* (Texas A&M University Press).

JESSE JONES AWARD FOR FICTION
Sarah Bird, *The Mommy Club* (Doubleday).

NATALIE ORNISH AWARD FOR POETRY
Andrew Hudgins, *The Never-Ending* (Houghton Mifflin).

PAISANO FELLOWS
Sigman Byrd, Sarah Glasscock.

LON TINKLE AWARD
Margaret Cousins.

WHITBREAD LITERARY AWARDS

BIOGRAPHY AND BOOK OF THE YEAR
John Richardson, *A Life of Picasso* (Cape).

CHILDREN'S NOVEL
Diana Hendry, *Harvey Angell* (Julia MacRae).

FIRST NOVEL
Gordon Burn, *Alma* (Secker ! Warburg).

NOVEL
Jane Gardam, *The Queen of the Tambourine* (Sinclair-Stevenson).

POETRY
Michael Longley, *Gorse Fires* (Secker ! Warburg).

JOHN WHITING AWARD

Rod Wooden, *Your Home in the West* (Methuen).

WHITING AWARDS

Roger Fanning, Eva Hoffman, R. S. Jones, Suzan Lori-Parks, J. S. Marcus, Jane Mead, Katha Pollitt, Keith Reddin, José Rivera, Damien Wilkins.

YALE YOUNGER POET

Nicholas Samaras, *Hands of the Saddlemaker* (Yale University Press).

Checklist: Contributions to Literary History and Biography

This checklist is a selection of new books on various aspects and periods of literary and cultural history, including biographies, memoirs, and correspondence of literary people and their associates.

Alldritt, Keith. *Churchill the Writer: His Life as a Man of Letters.* London: Hutchinson, 1992.

Bailey, Richard W. *Images of English: A Cultural History of the Language.* London: Cambridge University Press, 1992.

Barille, Elisabeth. *Anais Nin: Naked Under the Mask.* Translated by Elfreda Powell. London: Lime Tree, 1992.

Beauvoir, Simone de. *Letters to Sartre.* Translated and edited by Quinton Hoare. New York: Arcade, 1992.

Brightman, Carol. *Writing Dangerously: Mary McCarthy and Her World.* New York: Clarkson Potter, 1992.

Brooke, Rupert, and Noel Oliver. *Song of Love: The Letters of Rupert Brooke and Noel Oliver, 1909–1915.* Edited by Pippa Harris. New York: Crown, 1992.

Carey, John. *The Intellectuals and the Masses: Pride and Prejudice Among the Literary Intelligensia, 1880–1939.* London: Faber & Faber, 1992.

Carver, Raymond. *No Heroics, Please: Uncollected Writings.* Edited by William L. Stull. New York: Vintage, 1992.

Clay, John. *John Masters: A Regimented Life.* London: M. Joseph, 1992.

A Concise History of German Literature to 1900. Edited by Kim Vivian. Columbia, S.C.: Camden House, 1991.

Costello, Peter. *James Joyce: The Years of Growth, 1882–1915.* London: Kyle Cathie, 1992.

Crews, Frederick. *The Critics Bear It Away: American Fiction and the Academy.* New York: Random House, 1992.

Crosland, Margaret. *Simone de Beauvoir.* London: Heinemann, 1992.

David, Linda. *Children's Books Published by William Darton and His Sons.* With a historical calendar by Lawrence Darton. Bloomington, Ind.: Lilly Library, 1992.

Davison, Peter. *The Book Encompassed: Studies in Twentieth-Century Bibliography.* New York: Cambridge University Press, 1992.

Diliberto, Gioia. *Hadley.* London: Bloomsbury, 1992.

Donaldson, Scott, in collaboration with R. H. Winnick. *Archibald MacLeish: An American Life.* Boston: Houghton Mifflin, 1992.

Fender, Stephen. *Sea Changes: British Emigration and American Literature*. London: Cambridge University Press, 1992.

Fine, Richard. *James M. Cain and the American Authors' Authority*. Austin: University of Texas Press, 1992.

Garrett, George. *My Silk Purse and Yours: The Publishing Scene and American Literary Art*. Columbia: University of Missouri Press, 1992.

Garrett. *Whistling in the Dark: True Stories and Other Fables*. New York: Harcourt Brace Jovanovich, 1992.

Guilds, John Caldwell. *Simms: A Literary Life*. Fayetteville: University of Arkansas Press, 1992.

Hall, N. John. *Trollope: A Biography*. Oxford: Clarendon Press, 1991.

Hammond, J. R. *H. G. Wells and Rebecca West*. London: Harvester, 1991.

Hibberd, Dominick. *Wilfred Owen: The Last Year (1917–1918)*. London: Constable, 1992.

Humphries, Rolfe. *Poets, Poetics, and Politics: America's Literary Community Viewed from the Letters of Rolfe Humphries, 1910–1969*. Edited by Richard Gillman and Michael Paul Novak. Lawrence: University of Kansas Press, 1992.

Larkin, Philip. *The Selected Letters of Philip Larkin*. Edited by Anthony Thwaite. London: Faber & Faber, 1992.

Loughery, John. *Alias S.S. Van Dine: The Man Who Created Philo Vance*. New York: Scribners, 1992.

Lubow, Arthur. *The Reporter Who Would Be King: A Biography of Richard Harding Davis*. New York: Scribners, 1992.

Marnham, Patrick. *The Man Who Wasn't Maigret: A Portrait of Georges Simenon*. London: Bloomsbury, 1992.

McBride, Joseph. *Frank Capra: The Catastrophe of Success*. New York: Simon & Schuster, 1992.

McGilligan, Patrick. *George Cukor: A Double Life*. New York: St. Martin's Press, 1992.

Millgate, Michael. *Testamentary Acts: Browning, Tennyson, James, Hardy*. Oxford: Clarendon Press, 1992.

Moorehead, Catherine. *Bertrand Russell – A Life*. London: Sinclair Stevenson, 1992.

Nin, Anaïs, and Henry Miller. *A Literate Passion: Letters of Anais Nin and Henry Miller, 1932–1953*. Edited by Günther Stuhlmann. London: Allison & Busby, 1992.

O'Brien, Conor Cruise. *The Great Melody: A Thematic Biography of Edmund Burke*. Chicago: University of Chicago Press, 1992.

Paulson, Ronald. *Hogarth, Volume I: The 'Modern Moral Subject': 1697–1732*. London: Lutterworth, 1992.

Phelps, Barry. *P. G. Wodehouse: Man and Myth*. London: Constable, 1992.

Phillips, Catherine. *Robert Bridges*. London: Oxford University Press, 1992.

Phillips, Robert L., Jr. *Shelby Foote: Novelist and Historian*. Jackson: University Press of Mississippi, 1992.

Rosenberg, Deena. *Fascinating Rhythm: The Collaboration of George and Ira Gershwin*. London: Lime Tree, 1992.

Russell, Bertrand. *The Selected Letters of Bertrand Russell, Vol. I: 1884–1914*. Edited by Nicholas Griffin. London: Allen Lane, 1992.

Sackville-West, Vita, and Harold Nicholson. *Vita and Harold: The Letters of Vita Sackville West and Harold Nicholson*. Edited by Nigel Nicholson. London: Weidenfeld & Nicolson, 1992.

Seymour, Miranda. *Ottoline Morrell: Life on the Grand Scale*. London: Hodder & Stoughton, 1992.

Shillingsburg, Peter. *Pegasus in Harness: Victorian Publishing and W. M. Thackerey*. Charlottesville: University Press of Virginia, 1992.

Silverman, Kenneth. *Edgar A. Poe: Mournful and Neverending Remembrance*. New York: HarperCollins, 1991.

Skidelsky, Robert. *John Maynard Keynes, Vol. II: The Economist as Saviour*. London: Macmillan, 1992.

Stannard, Martin. *Evelyn Waugh: No Abiding City, 1939–1966*. London: Dent, 1992.

Taylor, William R. *In Pursuit of Gotham: Culture and Commerce in New York*. New York: Oxford University Press, 1992.

These United States: Portraits of America from the 1920s. Edited by Daniel H. Borus. Ithaca, N.Y.: Cornell University Press, 1992.

Vilain, Jean-Francois, and Philip R. Bishop. *Thomas R. Mosher and the Art of the Book*. Philadelphia: F. A. Davis, 1992.

Warren, Joyce W. *Fanny Fern: An Independent Woman*. New Brunswick, N.J.: Rutgers University Press, 1992.

West, W. J. *The Strange Rise of Semi-Literate England: The Dissolution of the Libraries*. London: Duckworth, 1992.

White, Anna McBride, and A. Norman Jeffares. *Always Your Friend: The Gonne-Yeats Letters, 1893–1938*. London: Hutchinson, 1992.

White, Antonia. *Antonia White: Diaries, 1926–1957*. Edited by Susan Chitty. New York: Viking, 1992.

White, Norman. *Hopkins: A Literary Biography*. New York: Oxford University Press, 1992.

Willis, Resa. *Mark and Livy: The Love Story of Mark Twain and the Woman Who Almost Tamed Him*. New York: Atheneum, 1992.

Zinnemann, Fred. *A Life in the Movies: An Autobiography*. New York: Scribners, 1992.

Necrology

Joachim Jean Aberbach – 24 May 1992
Stella Adler – 21 December 1992
Manolis Andronicus – 30 March 1992
Alfred Joseph Antoon, Jr. – 22 January 1992
William A. Arrowsmith – 20 February 1992
John Ashmead – 7 February 1992
Mary Wells Ashworth – 12 September 1992
Isaac Asimov – 6 April 1992
Anthony Astrachan – 10 February 1992
Nahman Avigad – 28 January 1992
Charles Andrew Barber – 4 July 1992
Walter Lanier "Red" Barber – 22 October 1992
Margaret Barker – 3 April 1992
Clarence Barnes – 2 February 1992
William Barrett – 8 September 1992
Dale R. Bauer – 5 August 1992
John Beaufort – 16 September 1992
Reid Beddow – 19 February 1992
Laslo Benedek – 11 March 1992
Jeane F. Bernkopf – 10 February 1992
Louis Biancolli – 13 June 1992
Mary Childs Black – 28 February 1992
Walter Blair – 29 June 1992
Rafe Blasi – 2 August 1992
Allan Bloom – 7 October 1992
Eugene Boe – 1 March 1992
Dwight L. Bolinger – 23 February 1992
Valentino Bompiani – 23 February 1992
Adele Bowers – 29 December 1992
Kay Boyle – 27 December 1992
John Bratby – 20 July 1992
Sidney D. Braun – 8 July 1992
Carl Bridenbaugh – 6 January 1992
James Brooks – 9 March 1992
Richard Brooks – 11 March 1992
James O. Brown – 1 September 1992
Alice I. Bryan – 30 October 1992
Leonard Burkat – 23 August 1992
Richard Burns – 31 August 1992
John Cage – 12 August 1992
Maris Cakers – 21 March 1992
Llewellyn L. Callaway, Jr. – 10 August 1992
Angela Carter – 16 February 1992
Wilfred Cartey – 21 March 1992
Herman Cherry – 10 April 1992
Robert Collins Christopher – 14 June 1992
Barbara Kauder Cohen – 29 November 1992

William Cole – 23 October 1992
Laurie E. Colwin – 24 October 1992
Frederick Combs – 19 September 1992
Ralph Cooper – 4 August 1992
William H. Cowles – 18 April 1992
L. S. Crenshaw – 27 March 1992
Joseph Toy Curtiss – 11 October 1992
Rae Dalven – 30 July 1992
Ray Danton – 11 February 1992
William Darrid – 11 July 1992
Elizabeth David – 22 May 1992
Donald Davis – 28 March 1992
Helen Deutsch – 15 March 1992
Martin Dibner – 11 January 1992
Monica Dickens – 25 December 1992
Pietro di Donato – 19 January 1992
Melvin Dixon – 26 October 1992
John Donovan – 29 April 1992
Carlyle Douglas – 10 August 1992
William Douglas-Home – 28 September 1992
Elsie Driggs – 12 July 1992
Donald Dryfoos – 3 September 1992
Philip Dunne – 2 June 1992
Jack Dunphy – 26 April 1992
Henry Ephron – 6 September 1992
David S. Epstein – 7 July 1992
Jaqueline Eubanks – 19 November 1992
Frederick Exley – 17 June 1992
M. F. K. Fisher – 22 June 1992
Carol Fitzgerald – 22 December 1992
Siegel Hall Fleisher – 28 November 1992
Thomas Fleming, Jr. – 2 March 1992
Ephim Fogel – 12 June 1992
Lillian Vallish Foote – 5 August 1992
Joseph Friedman – 15 September 1992
John E. Frost – 23 July 1992
William M. Gaines – 3 June 1992
Thomas Gallagher – 19 December 1992
Joan Hickcox Garrett-Goodyear – 23 April 1992
Theodor Herzl Gaster – 3 February 1992
George L. George – 31 December 1992
C. Virgil Gheorghiu – 22 June 1992
Lewis Gillenson – 4 September 1992
Len Giovannitti – 27 March 1992
Milton H. Gladstone – 21 February 1992
Howard H. Goodkin – 27 October 1992
Martin Goodman – 6 June 1992

Harry Gottlieb – 4 July 1992

Roberta Grossman – 13 March 1992

Don Gussow – 26 February 1992

Musa McKim Guston – 30 March 1992

Alex Haley – 10 February 1992

Desmond Winter Hall – 28 October 1992

Richard W. Hall – 29 October 1992

Jean Hamburger – 1 February 1992

Mitzi Berger Hamovitch – 31 December 1992

Gerald Hanley – 7 September 1992

Jerome S. Hardy – 31 December 1992

Robert L. Harkay – 19 November 1992

Mark Hawkins – 7 October 1992

S. I. Hayakawa – 27 February 1992

Friedrich A. von Hayek – 23 March 1992

Timothy S. Healy – 30 December 1992

Robert L. Hess – 12 January 1992

Eugene B. Horowitz – 10 January 1992

John Leslie Hotson – 16 November 1992

Robert W. Hovda – 5 February 1992

Wilbur S. Howell – 20 April 1992

Harry Louis Humes – 10 September 1992

Edward Hymoff – 9 July 1992

Peter Jenkins – 27 May 1992

Ellen H. Johnson – 23 March 1992

Dorothy R. Jones – 14 August 1992

Charles O. Kates – 6 September 1992

Edwin Kenney, Jr. – 8 December 1992

Etheridge Knight – 3 March 1991

Philip Kolb – 6 November 1992

Brett Elliot Langstaff – 27 October 1992

Bill Laughton – 9 January 1992

Lawrence Shubert Lawrence, Jr. – 18 July 1992

Heinrich M. Ledig-Rowohlt – 27 February 1992

Hellmut Lehmann-Haupt – 11 March 1992

Max Lerner – 5 June 1992

Oscar Lewis – 11 July 1992

Fritz Lieber, Jr. – 5 September 1992

Vaino Linna – 21 April 1992

Alan R. Liss – 20 August 1992

Audre Lorde – 17 November 1992

Leueen MacGrath – 27 March 1992

Ben Maddow – 9 October 1992

Walter Butler Mahoney, Jr. – 31 October 1992

Ralph Manheim – 26 September 1992

James Marshall – 13 October 1992

Robert A. Martinez – 3 April 1992

Samuel Marx – 2 March 1992

Wendell Mayes – 28 March 1992

Laurence J. McGinley – 15 August 1992

Scott W. McPherson – 7 November 1992

Eve Merriam – 11 April 1992

Gladys Merrifield – 25 September 1992

Michael Merritt – 3 August 1992

William F. Michelfelder – 13 December 1992

Caroline Miller – 12 July 1992

Walt Morey – 12 January 1992

Robert Morley – 3 June 1992

Robert Nigro – 5 August 1992

Mary Norton – 29 August 1992

Edgar J. Olsen – 25 July 1992

Evelyn Tennyson Openhym – 13 January 1992

Harry M. Orlinsky – 21 March 1992

Ronnie Paris – 4 February 1992

Thomas F. Parkinson – 14 January 1992

Paul G. Pavel – 14 July 1992

Robert Peak – 31 July 1992

Robert Dean Pharr – 1 April 1992

John Piper – 29 June 1992

Harrison G. Platt, Jr. – 17 September 1992

Jean Poiret – 14 March 1992

Francesca Primus – 27 January 1992

Kennett L. Rawson – 10 July 1992

Joe Richards – 19 January 1992

Hal Roach – 2 November 1992

J. Albert Robbins – 4 March 1992

Meade Roberts – 10 February 1992

Durant Waite Robertson, Jr. – 26 July 1992

Anne Johnstone Robinson – 16 October 1992

Dorothy Rodgers – 17 August 1992

Edouard Roditi – 10 May 1992

Barbara Rollock – 20 December 1992

Luis Rosales – 24 October 1992

David Rosenthal – 30 October 1992

Bruce Ruddick – 4 December 1992

Robert W. Russell – 11 February 1992

Kirk Scharfenberg – 27 July 1992

William Howard Schuman – 15 February 1992

Alvin Schwartz – 14 March 1992

Eric Sevareid – 9 July 1992

Charles H. Shattuck – 21 September 1992

William Shawn – 8 December 1992

Joseph Shuster – 30 July 1992

Sewell Sillman – 4 April 1992

Marshall Sklare – 1 March 1992

Cyril Stanley Smith – 25 August 1992

Ruth Southard Sohn – 28 August 1992

Barbara Miller Solomon – 20 August 1992

Eleanor P. Spencer – 17 November 1992

Philip M. Stern – 1 June 1992

Holly Stevens – 4 March 1992

Sterling A. Stoudemire – 26 May 1992

Floyd H. Stovall – 18 November 1991

John Sturges – 18 August 1992

Burt Supree – 1 May 1992

W. A. Swanberg – 17 September 1992

Glendon Swarthout – 23 September 1992

Albert Tavares – 28 July 1992

Paul Taylor – 17 September 1992
Rouben Ter-Arutunian – 17 October 1992
Isaiah Tishby – 15 March 1992
Lawrence W. Towner – 12 June 1992
Yoshiko Uchida – 21 June 1992
Alex Ullman – 6 November 1992
Ruth Marguerite Vande Kieft – 27 October 1992
Graham Voaden – 7 April 1992

Samuel S. Walker – circa 29 May 1992
Edward Warburg – 21 September 1992
Martin Williams – 13 April 1992
Ted Willis – 22 December 1992
Fanny Kemble Wister – 27 April 1992
Richard Yates – 7 November 1992
Avot Yeshurun – 22 February 1992

Contributors

Paul Bauer ....*Marquette University*
Ronald Baughman...*University of South Carolina*
Ashley Brown..*University of South Carolina*
Jackson R. Bryer ....*University of Maryland*
Richard R. Centing...*Ohio State University*
Barry Faulk.................................*University of Illinois at Urbana-Champaign*
Beth Flusser ....*New York, New York*
William Foltz...*University of Hawaii*
Edward Halsey Foster ....*Stevens Institute of Technology*
George Garrett...*University of Virginia*
Ezra Greenspan...*University of South Carolina*
George Hendrick ....*University of Illinois at Urbana-Champaign*
Sara S. Hodson ....*The Huntington Library*
Caroline Hunt ....*College of Charleston*
Howard Kissel...*New York Daily News*
Robert McPhillips...*Iona College*
Alan Margolies.............................*John Jay College, City University of New York*
Blanche Marvin ....*London Theatre Reviews*
Ruth Prigozy ....*Hofstra University*
Russell J. Reising ....*Marquette University*
Michael Reynolds ....*North Carolina State University*
Jonathan Rose ....*Drew University*
David R. Slavitt ....*University of Pennsylvania*
Geoffrey D. Smith ....*Ohio State University*
Michael Thurston.........................*University of Illinois at Urbana-Champaign*
William F. Touponce...................*Indiana University – Purdue University, at Indianapolis*
Kristin van Ogtrop ....*Vogue*
Ellen Weinauer ....*Indiana University*
Mary Ann Wimsatt...*University of South Carolina*

Cumulative Index

Dictionary of Literary Biography, Volumes 1-127
Dictionary of Literary Biography Yearbook, 1980-1992
Dictionary of Literary Biography Documentary Series, Volumes 1-10

Cumulative Index

DLB before number: *Dictionary of Literary Biography*, Volumes 1-127
Y before number: *Dictionary of Literary Biography Yearbook*, 1980-1992
DS before number: *Dictionary of Literary Biography Documentary Series*, Volumes 1-10

A

E

Cumulative Index

H

Cumulative Index

K

L

M

N

O

Q

R

S

T

U

V

W

Y

Z

ISBN 0-8103-5543-4

YEARBOOK

8965

(Continued from front endsheets)

Documentary Series

Yearbooks

LIBRARY
St. Michael's College Prep H.S.
19292 El Toro Rd., Silverado, CA 92676